T0332496

Modeling and Reasoning with Bayesian Networks

This book provides a thorough introduction to the formal foundations and practical applications of Bayesian networks. It provides an extensive discussion of techniques for building Bayesian networks that model real-world situations, including techniques for synthesizing models from design, learning models from data, and debugging models using sensitivity analysis. It also treats exact and approximate inference algorithms at both theoretical and practical levels. The treatment of exact algorithms covers the main inference paradigms based on elimination and conditioning and includes advanced methods for compiling Bayesian networks, time-space tradeoffs, and exploiting local structure of massively connected networks. The treatment of approximate algorithms covers the main inference paradigms based on sampling and optimization and includes influential algorithms such as importance sampling, MCMC, and belief propagation.

The author assumes very little background on the covered subjects, supplying in-depth discussions for theoretically inclined readers and enough practical details to provide an algorithmic cookbook for the system developer.

Adnan Darwiche is a Professor and Chairman of the Computer Science Department at UCLA. He is also the Editor-in-Chief for the *Journal of Artificial Intelligence Research* (JAIR) and a AAAI Fellow.

To Jinan, Layla, Sarah, Sikna, and Youssef.

Modeling and Reasoning with Bayesian Networks

Adnan Darwiche

University of California, Los Angeles

CAMBRIDGE
UNIVERSITY PRESS

CAMBRIDGE UNIVERSITY PRESS
Cambridge, New York, Melbourne, Madrid, Cape Town, Singapore,
São Paulo, Delhi, Dubai, Tokyo, Mexico City

Cambridge University Press
32 Avenue of the Americas, New York, NY 10013-2473, USA

www.cambridge.org
Information on this title: www.cambridge.org/9780521884389

First published 2009
Reprinted 2009, 2010 (twice)

A catalog record for this publication is available from the British Library.

Library of Congress Cataloging in Publication Data

Darwiche, Adnan, 1966–
Modeling and reasoning with Bayesian networks / Adnan Darwiche.
p. cm.
ISBN 978-0-521-88438-9 (hardback)
1. Bayesian statistical decision theory – Graphic methods.   2. Inference.   3. Probabilities.   4. Modeling.
I. Title.
QA279.5.D37   2009
519.5'42–dc22   2008044605

ISBN 978-0-521-88438-9 Hardback

Contents

Preface

Bayesian networks have received a lot of attention over the last few decades from both scientists and engineers, and across a number of fields, including artificial intelligence (AI), statistics, cognitive science, and philosophy.

Perhaps the largest impact that Bayesian networks have had is on the field of AI, where they were first introduced by Judea Pearl in the midst of a crisis that the field was undergoing in the late 1970s and early 1980s. This crisis was triggered by the surprising realization that a theory of plausible reasoning cannot be based solely on classical logic [McCarthy, 1977], as was strongly believed within the field for at least two decades [McCarthy, 1959]. This discovery has triggered a large number of responses by AI researchers, leading, for example, to the development of a new class of symbolic logics known as non-monotonic logics (e.g., [McCarthy, 1980; Reiter, 1980; McDermott and Doyle, 1980]). Pearl's introduction of Bayesian networks, which is best documented in his book [Pearl, 1988], was actually part of his larger response to these challenges, in which he advocated the use of probability theory as a basis for plausible reasoning and developed Bayesian networks as a practical tool for representing and computing probabilistic beliefs.

From a historical perspective, the earliest traces of using graphical representations of probabilistic information can be found in statistical physics [Gibbs, 1902] and genetics [Wright, 1921]. However, the current formulations of these representations are of a more recent origin and have been contributed by scientists from many fields. In statistics, for example, these representations are studied within the broad class of graphical models, which include Bayesian networks in addition to other representations such as Markov networks and chain graphs [Whittaker, 1990; Edwards, 2000; Lauritzen, 1996; Cowell et al., 1999]. However, the semantics of these models are distinct enough to justify independent treatments. This is why we decided to focus this book on Bayesian networks instead of covering them in the broader context of graphical models, as is done by others [Whittaker, 1990; Edwards, 2000; Lauritzen, 1996; Cowell et al., 1999]. Our coverage is therefore more consistent with the treatments in [Jensen and Nielsen, 2007; Neapolitan, 2004], which are also focused on Bayesian networks.

Even though we approach the subject of Bayesian networks from an AI perspective, we do not delve into the customary philosophical debates that have traditionally surrounded many works on AI. The only exception to this is in the introductory chapter, in which we find it necessary to lay out the subject matter of this book in the context of some historical AI developments. However, in the remaining chapters we proceed with the assumption that the questions being treated are already justified and simply focus on developing the representational and computational techniques needed for addressing them. In doing so, we have taken a great comfort in presenting some of the very classical techniques in ways that may seem unorthodox to the expert. We are driven here by a strong desire to provide the most intuitive explanations, even at the expense of breaking away from norms. We have also made a special effort to appease the scientist, by our emphasis on justification, and the engineer, through our attention to practical considerations.

There are a number of fashionable and useful topics that we did not cover in this book, which are mentioned in the introductory chapter. Some of these topics were omitted because their in-depth treatment would have significantly increased the length of the book, whereas others were omitted because we believe they conceptually belong somewhere else. In a sense, this book is not meant to be encyclopedic in its coverage of Bayesian networks; rather it is meant to be a focused, thorough treatment of some of the core concepts on modeling and reasoning within this framework.

Acknowledgments

In writing this book, I have benefited a great deal form a large number of individuals who provided help at levels that are too numerous to explicate here. I wish to thank first and foremost members of the automated reasoning group at UCLA for producing quite a bit of the material that is covered in this book, and for their engagement in the writing and proofreading of many of its chapters. In particular, I would like to thank David Allen, Keith Cascio, Hei Chan, Mark Chavira, Arthur Choi, Taylor Curtis, Jinbo Huang, James Park, Knot Pipatsrisawat, and Yuliya Zabiyaka. Arthur Choi deserves special credit for writing the appendices and most of Chapter 14, for suggesting a number of interesting exercises, and for his dedicated involvement in the last stages of finishing the book. I am also indebted to members of the cognitive systems laboratory at UCLA – Blai Bonet, Ilya Shipster, and Jin Tian – who have thoroughly read and commented on earlier drafts of the book. A number of the students who took the corresponding graduate class at UCLA have also come to the rescue whenever called. I would like to especially thank Alex Dow for writing parts of Chapter 9. Moreover, Jason Aten, Omer Bar-or, Susan Chebotariov, David Chen, Hicham Elmongui, Matt Hayes, Anand Panangadan, Victor Shih, Jae-il Shin, Sam Talaie, and Mike Zaloznyy have all provided detailed feedback on numerous occasions.

I would also like to thank my colleagues who have contributed immensely to this work through either valuable discussions, comments on earlier drafts, or strongly believing in this project and how it was conducted. In this regard, I am indebted to Russ Almond, Bozhena Bidyuk, Hans Bodlaender, Gregory Cooper, Rina Dechter, Marek Druzdzel, David Heckerman, Eric Horvitz, Linda van der Gaag, Hector Geffner, Vibhav Gogate, Russ Greiner, Omid Madani, Ole Mengshoel, Judea Pearl, David Poole, Wojtek Przytula, Silja Renooij, Stuart Russell, Prakash Shenoy, Hector Palacios Verdes, and Changhe Yuan.

Finally, I wish to thank my wife, Jinan, and my daughters, Sarah and Layla, for providing a warm and stimulating environment in which I could conduct my work. This book would not have seen the light without their constant encouragement and support.

1

Introduction

Automated reasoning has been receiving much interest from a number of fields, including philosophy, cognitive science, and computer science. In this chapter, we consider the particular interest of computer science in automated reasoning over the last few decades, and then focus our attention on probabilistic reasoning using Bayesian networks, which is the main subject of this book.

1.1 Automated reasoning

The interest in automated reasoning within computer science dates back to the very early days of artificial intelligence (AI), when much work had been initiated for developing computer programs for solving problems that require a high degree of intelligence. Indeed, an influential proposal for building automated reasoning systems was extended by John McCarthy shortly after the term "artificial intelligence" was coined [McCarthy, 1959]. This proposal, sketched in Figure 1.1, calls for a system with two components: a knowledge base, which encodes what we know about the world, and a reasoner (inference engine), which acts on the knowledge base to answer queries of interest. For example, the knowledge base may encode what we know about the theory of sets in mathematics, and the reasoner may be used to prove various theorems about this domain.

McCarthy's proposal was actually more specific than what is suggested by Figure 1.1, as he called for expressing the knowledge base using statements in a suitable logic, and for using logical deduction in realizing the reasoning engine; see Figure 1.2. McCarthy's proposal can then be viewed as having two distinct and orthogonal elements. The first is the separation between the knowledge base (what we know) and the reasoner (how we think). The knowledge base can be domain-specific, changing from one application to another, while the reasoner is quite general and fixed, allowing one to use it across different application areas. This aspect of the proposal became the basis for a class of reasoning systems known as *knowledge-based* or *model-based systems*, which have dominated the area of automated reasoning since then. The second element of McCarthy's early proposal is the specific commitment to logic as the language for expressing what we know about the world, and his commitment to logical deduction in realizing the reasoning process. This commitment, which was later revised by McCarthy, is orthogonal to the idea of separating the knowledge base from the reasoner. The latter idea remains meaningful and powerful even in the context of other forms of reasoning including probabilistic reasoning, to which this book is dedicated. We will indeed subscribe to this knowledge-based approach for reasoning, except that our knowledge bases will be Bayesian networks and our reasoning engine will be based on the laws of probability theory.

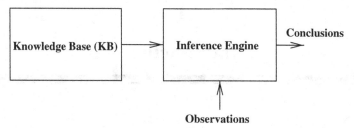

Figure 1.1: A reasoning system in which the knowledge base is separated from the reasoning process. The knowledge base is often called a "model," giving rise to the term "model-based reasoning."

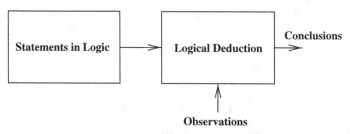

Figure 1.2: A reasoning system based on logic.

1.1.1 The limits of deduction

McCarthy's proposal generated much excitement and received much interest throughout the history of AI, due mostly to its modularity and mathematical elegance. Yet, as the approach was being applied to more application areas, a key difficulty was unveiled, calling for some alternative proposals. In particular, it was observed that although deductive logic is a natural framework for representing and reasoning about facts, it was not capable of dealing with assumptions that tend to be prevalent in commonsense reasoning.

To better explain this difference between facts and assumptions, consider the following statement:

If a bird is normal, it will fly.

Most people will believe that a bird would fly if they see one. However, this belief cannot be logically deduced from this fact, unless we further assume that the bird we just saw is normal. Most people will indeed make this assumption – even if they cannot confirm it – as long as they do not have evidence to the contrary. Hence, the belief in a flying bird is the result of a logical deduction applied to a mixture of facts and assumptions. For example, if it turns out that the bird, say, has a broken wing, the normality assumption will be retracted, leading us to also retract the belief in a flying bird.

This ability to dynamically assert and retract assumptions – depending on what is currently known – is quite typical in commonsense reasoning yet is outside the realm of deductive logic, as we shall see in Chapter 2. In fact, deductive logic is *monotonic* in the sense that once we deduce something from a knowledge base (the bird flies), we can never invalidate the deduction by acquiring more knowledge (the bird has a broken wing). The formal statement of monotonicity is as follows:

If Δ logically implies α, then Δ and Γ will also logically imply α.

Just think of a proof for α that is derived from a set of premises Δ. We can never invalidate this proof by including the additional premises Γ. Hence, no deductive logic is capable of producing the reasoning process described earlier with regard to flying birds.

We should stress here that the flying bird example is one instance of a more general phenomenon that underlies much of what goes on in commonsense reasoning. Consider for example the following statements:

My car is still parked where I left it this morning.
If I turn the key of my car, the engine will turn on.
If I start driving now, I will get home in thirty minutes.

None of these statements is factual, as each is qualified by a set of assumptions. Yet we tend to make these assumptions, use them to derive certain conclusions (e.g., I will arrive home in thirty minutes if I head out of the office now), and then use these conclusions to justify some of our decisions (I will head home now). Moreover, we stand ready to retract any of these assumptions if we observe something to the contrary (e.g., a major accident on the road home).

1.1.2 Assumptions to the rescue

The previous problem, which is known as the *qualification problem* in AI [McCarthy, 1977], was stated formally by McCarthy in the late 1970s, some twenty years after his initial proposal from 1958. The dilemma was simply this: If we write "Birds fly," then deductive logic would be able to infer the expected conclusion when it sees a bird. However, it would fall into an inconsistency if it encounters a bird that cannot fly. On the other hand, if we write "If a bird is normal, it flies," deductive logic will not be able to reach the expected conclusion upon seeing a bird, as it would not know whether the bird is normal or not – contrary to what most humans will do. The failure of deductive logic in treating this problem effectively led to a flurry of activities in AI, all focused on producing new formalisms aimed at counteracting this failure.

McCarthy's observations about the qualification problem were accompanied by another influential proposal, which called for equipping logic with an ability to jump into certain conclusions [McCarthy, 1977]. This proposal had the effect of installing the notion of assumption into the heart of logical formalisms, giving rise to a new generation of logics, *non-monotonic logics*, which are equipped with mechanisms for managing assumptions (i.e., allowing them to be dynamically asserted and retracted depending on what else is known). However, it is critical to note that what is needed here is not simply a mechanism for managing assumptions but also a criterion for deciding on which assumptions to assert and retract, and when. The initial criterion used by many non-monotonic logics was based on the notion of logical consistency, which calls for asserting as many assumptions as possible, as long as they do not lead to a logical inconsistency. This promising idea proved insufficient, however. To illustrate the underlying difficulties here, let us consider the following statements:

A typical Quaker is a pacifist.
A typical Republican is not a pacifist.

If we were told that Nixon is a Quaker, we could then conclude that he is a pacifist (by assuming he is a typical Quaker). On the other hand, if we were told that Nixon is a Republican, we could conclude that he is not a pacifist (by assuming he is a typical Republican). But what if we were told that Nixon is both a Quaker and a Republican? The two assumptions would then clash with each other, and a decision would have to be made on which assumption to preserve (if either). What this example illustrates is that assumptions can compete against each other. In fact, resolving conflicts among assumptions turned out to be one of the difficult problems that any assumption-based formalism must address to capture commonsense reasoning satisfactorily.

To illustrate this last point, consider a student, Drew, who just finished the final exam for his physics class. Given his performance on this and previous tests, Drew came to the belief that he would receive an A in the class. A few days later, he logs into the university system only to find out that he has received a B instead. This clash between Drew's prior belief and the new information leads him to think as follows:

> Let me first check that I am looking at the grade of my physics class instead of some other class. Hmm! It is indeed physics. Is it possible the professor made a mistake in entering the grade? I don't think so . . . I have taken a few classes with him, and he has proven to be quite careful and thorough. Well, perhaps he did not grade my Question 3, as I wrote the answer on the back of the page in the middle of a big mess. I think I will need to check with him on this . . . I just hope I did not miss Question 4; it was somewhat difficult and I am not too sure about my answer there. Let me check with Jack on this, as he knows the material quite well. Ah! Jack seems to have gotten the same answer I got. I think it is Question 3 after all . . . I'd better see the professor soon to make sure he graded this one.

One striking aspect of this example is the multiplicity of assumptions involved in forming Drew's initial belief in having received an A grade (i.e., Question 3 was graded, Question 4 was solved correctly, the professor did not make a clerical error, and so on). The example also brings out important notions that were used by Drew in resolving conflicts among assumptions. This includes the strength of an assumption, which can be based on previous experiences (e.g., I have taken a few classes with this professor). It also includes the notion of evidence, which may be brought to bear on the validity of these assumptions (i.e., let me check with Jack).

Having reached this stage of our discussion on the subtleties of commonsense reasoning, one could drive it further in one of two directions. We can continue to elaborate on non-monotonic logics and how they may go about resolving conflicts among assumptions. This will also probably lead us into the related subject of *belief revision*, which aims at regulating this conflict-resolution process through a set of rationality postulates [Gärdenfors, 1988]. However, as these subjects are outside the scope of this book, we will turn in a different direction that underlies the formalism we plan to pursue in the upcoming chapters. In a nutshell, this new direction can be viewed as postulating the existence of a more fundamental notion, called a degree of belief, which, according to some treatments, can alleviate the need for assumptions altogether and, according to others, can be used as a basis for deciding which assumptions to make in the first place.

1.2 Degrees of belief

A *degree of belief* is a number that one assigns to a proposition in lieu of having to declare it as a fact (as in deductive logic) or an assumption (as in non-monotonic logic). For example, instead of assuming that a bird is normal unless observed otherwise – which leads us to tenuously believe that it also flies – we assign a degree of belief to the bird's normality, say, 99%, and then use this to derive a corresponding degree of belief in the bird's flying ability.

A number of different proposals have been extended in the literature for interpreting degrees of belief including, for example, the notion of possibility on which fuzzy logic is based. This book is committed to interpreting degrees of belief as probabilities and, therefore, to manipulating them according to the laws of probability. Such an interpretation is widely accepted today and underlies many of the recent developments in automated reasoning. We will briefly allude to some of the classical arguments supporting this interpretation later but will otherwise defer the vigorous justification to cited references [Pearl, 1988; Jaynes, 2003].

While assumptions address the monotonicity problem by being assertible and retractible, degrees of belief address this problem by being revisable either upward or downward, depending on what else is known. For example, we may initially believe that a bird is normal with probability 99%, only to revise this to, say, 20% after learning that its wing is suffering from some wound. The dynamics that govern degrees of belief will be discussed at length in Chapter 3, which is dedicated to probability calculus, our formal framework for manipulating degrees of belief.

One can argue that assigning a degree of belief is a more committing undertaking than making an assumption. This is due to the fine granularity of degrees of beliefs, which allows them to encode more information than can be encoded by a binary assumption. One can also argue to the contrary that working with degrees of belief is far less committing as they do not imply any particular truth of the underlying propositions, even if tenuous. This is indeed true, and this is one of the key reasons why working with degrees of belief tends to protect against many pitfalls that may trap one when working with assumptions; see Pearl [1988], Section 2.3, for some relevant discussion on this matter.

1.2.1 Deciding after believing

Forming beliefs is the first step in making decisions. In an assumption-based framework, decisions tend to follow naturally from the set of assumptions made. However, when working with degrees of belief, the situation is a bit more complex since decisions will have to be made without assuming any particular state of affairs. Suppose for example that we are trying to capture a bird that is worth $40.00 and can use one of two methods, depending on whether it is a flying bird or not. The assumption-based method will have no difficulty making a decision in this case, as it will simply choose the method based on the assumptions made. However, when using degrees of belief, the situation can be a bit more involved as it generally calls for invoking *decision theory*, whose purpose is to convert degrees of beliefs into definite decisions [Howard and Matheson, 1984; Howard, 1990]. Decision theory needs to bring in some additional information before it can make the conversion, including the cost of various decisions and the rewards or penalties associated with their outcomes. Suppose for example that the first method is guaranteed to capture a bird, whether flying or not, and costs $30.00, while the second method costs $10.00 and is guaranteed to capture a non-flying bird but may capture a flying bird with a 25% probability. One must clearly factor all of this information before one can make the right decision in this case, which is precisely the role of decision theory. This theory is therefore an essential complement to the theory of probabilistic reasoning discussed in this book.

Yet we have decided to omit the discussion of decision theory here to keep the book focused on the modeling and reasoning components (see Pearl [1988], Jensen and Nielsen [2007] for a complementary coverage of decision theory).

1.2.2 What do the probabilities mean?

A final point we wish to address in this section concerns the classical controversy of whether probabilities should be interpreted as objective frequencies or as subjective degrees of belief. Our use of the term "degrees of belief" thus far may suggest a commitment, to the subjective approach, but this is not necessarily the case. In fact, none of the developments in this book really depend on any particular commitment, as both interpretations are governed by the same laws of probability. We will indeed discuss examples in Chapter 5 where all of the used probabilities are degrees of belief reflecting the state of knowledge of a particular individual and not corresponding to anything that can be measured by a physical experiment. We will also discuss examples in which all of the used probabilities correspond to physical quantities that can be not only measured but possibly controlled as well. This includes applications from system analysis and diagnostics, where probabilities correspond to the failure rates of system components, and examples from channel coding, where the probabilities correspond to channel noise.

1.3 Probabilistic reasoning

Probability theory has been around for centuries. However, its utilization in automated reasoning at the scale and rate within AI has never before been attempted. This has created some key computational challenges for probabilistic reasoning systems, which had to be confronted by AI researchers for the first time. Adding to these challenges is the competition that probabilistic methods had initially received from symbolic methods that were dominating the field of AI at the time. It is indeed the responses to these challenges over the last few decades that have led to much of the material discussed in this book. One therefore gains more perspective and insights into the utility and significance of the covered topics once one is exposed to some of these motivating challenges.

1.3.1 Initial reactions

AI researchers proposed the use of numeric degrees of belief well before the monotonicity problem of classical logic was unveiled or its consequences absorbed. Yet such proposals were initially shunned based on cognitive, pragmatic, and computational considerations. On the cognitive side, questions were raised regarding the extent to which humans use such degrees of belief in their own reasoning. This was quite an appealing counterargument at the time, as the field of AI was still at a stage of its development where the resemblance of formalism to human cognition was very highly valued, if not necessary. On the pragmatic side, questions were raised regarding the availability of degrees of beliefs (where do the numbers come from?). This came at a time when the development of knowledge bases was mainly achieved through knowledge elicitation sessions conducted with domain experts who, reportedly, were not comfortable committing to such degrees – the field of statistical machine learning had yet to be influential enough then. The robustness of probabilistic reasoning systems was heavily questioned as well (what happens if I change this .90 to .95?). The issue here was not only whether probabilistic reasoning was robust enough against such perturbations but, in situations where it was shown to be robust, questions were raised about the unnecessary level of detail demanded by specifying probabilities.

On the computational side, a key issue was raised regarding the scale of applications that probabilistic reasoning systems can handle, at a time when applications involving dozens if not hundreds of variables were being sought. Such doubts were grounded in the prevalent perception that joint probability distributions, which are exponentially sized in the number of used variables, will have to be represented explicitly by probabilistic reasoning systems. This would be clearly prohibitive on both representational and computational grounds for most applications of interest. For example, a medical diagnosis application may require hundreds of variables to represent background information about patients, in addition to the list of diseases and symptoms about which one may need to reason.

1.3.2 A second chance

The discovery of the qualification problem, and the associated monotonicity problem of deductive logic, gave numerical methods a second chance in AI, as these problems created a vacancy for a new formalism of commonsense reasoning during the 1980s. One of the key proponents of probabilistic reasoning at the time was Judea Pearl, who seized upon this opportunity to further the cause of probabilistic reasoning systems within AI. Pearl had to confront challenges on two key fronts in this pursuit. On the one hand, he had to argue for the use of numbers within a community that was heavily entrenched in symbolic formalism. On the other hand, he had to develop a representational and computational machinery that could compete with symbolic systems that were in commercial use at the time.

On the first front, Pearl observed that many problems requiring special machinery in logical settings, such as non-monotonicity, simply do not surface in the probabilistic approach. For example, it is perfectly common in probability calculus to see beliefs going up and down in response to new evidence, thus exhibiting a non-monotonic behavior – that is, we often find $Pr(A) > Pr(A|B)$ indicating that our belief in A would go down when we observe B. Based on this and similar observations, Pearl engaged in a sequence of papers that provided probabilistic accounts for most of the paradoxes that were entangling symbolic formalisms at the time; see Pearl [1988], Chapter 10, for a good summary. Most of the primitive cognitive and pragmatic arguments (e.g., people do not reason with numbers; where do the numbers come from?) were left unanswered then. However, enough desirable properties of probabilistic reasoning were revealed to overwhelm and silence these criticisms. The culminations of Pearl's efforts at the time were reported in his influential book, *Probabilistic Reasoning in Intelligent Systems: Networks of Plausible Inference* [Pearl, 1988]. The book contained the first comprehensive documentation of the case for probabilistic reasoning, delivered in the context of contemporary questions raised by AI research. This part of the book was concerned with the foundational aspects of plausible reasoning, setting clear the principles by which it ought to be governed – probability theory, that is. The book also contained the first comprehensive coverage of Bayesian networks, which were Pearl's response to the representational and computational challenges that arise in realizing probabilistic reasoning systems. On the representational side, the Bayesian network was shown to compactly represent exponentially sized probability distributions, addressing one of the classical criticisms against probabilistic reasoning systems. On the computational side, Pearl developed the polytree algorithm [Pearl, 1986b], which was the first general-purpose inference algorithm for networks that contain no

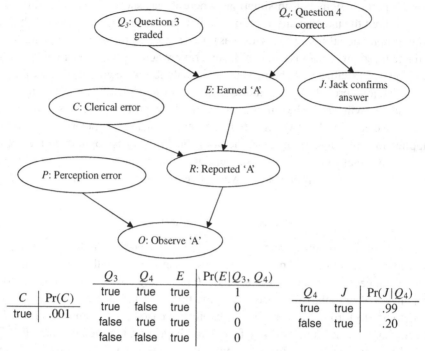

The table shown with the figure:

C	Pr(C)
true	.001

Q_3	Q_4	E	$Pr(E \mid Q_3, Q_4)$
true	true	true	1
true	false	true	0
false	true	true	0
false	false	true	0

Q_4	J	$Pr(J \mid Q_4)$
true	true	.99
false	true	.20

Figure 1.3: The structure of a Bayesian network, in which each variable can be either true or false. To fully specify the network, one needs to provide a probability distribution for each variable, conditioned on every state of its parents. The figure shows these conditional distributions for three variables in the network.

directed loops.[1] This was followed by the influential jointree algorithm [Lauritzen and Spiegelhalter, 1988], which could handle arbitrary network structures, albeit inefficiently for some structures. These developments provided enough grounds to set the stage for a new wave of automated reasoning systems based on the framework of Bayesian networks (e.g., [Andreassen et al., 1987]).

1.4 Bayesian networks

A *Bayesian network* is a representational device that is meant to organize one's knowledge about a particular situation into a coherent whole. The syntax and semantics of Bayesian networks will be covered in Chapter 4. Here we restrict ourselves to an informal exposition that is sufficient to further outline the subjects covered in this book.

Figure 1.3 depicts an example Bayesian network, which captures the information corresponding to the student scenario discussed earlier in this chapter. This network has two components, one qualitative and another quantitative. The qualitative part corresponds to the directed acyclic graph (DAG) depicted in the figure, which is also known as the

---

[1] According to Pearl, this algorithm was motivated by the work of Rumelhart [1976] on reading comprehension, which provided compelling evidence that text comprehension must be a distributed process that combines both top-down and bottom-up inferences. This dual mode of inference, so characteristic of Bayesian analysis, did not match the capabilities of the ruling paradigms for uncertainty management in the 1970s. This led Pearl to develop the polytree algorithm [Pearl, 1986b], which appeared first in Pearl [1982] with a restriction to trees, and then in Kim and Pearl [1983] for polytrees.

structure of the Bayesian network. This structure captures two important parts of one's knowledge. First, its variables represent the primitive propositions that we deem relevant to our domain. Second, its edges convey information about the dependencies between these variables. The formal interpretation of these edges will be given in Chapter 4 in terms of probabilistic independence. For now and for most practical applications, it is best to think of these edges as signifying direct causal influences. For example, the edge extending from variable E to variable R signifies a direct causal influence between earning an A grade and reporting the grade. Note that variables Q_3 and Q_4 also have a causal influence on variable R yet this influence is not direct, as it is mediated by variable E. We stress again that Bayesian networks can be given an interpretation that is completely independent of the notion of causation, as in Chapter 4, yet thinking about causation will tend to be a very valuable guide in constructing the intended Bayesian network [Pearl, 2000; Glymour and Cooper, 1999].

To completely specify a Bayesian network, one must also annotate its structure with probabilities that quantify the relationships between variables and their parents (direct causes). We will not delve into this specification procedure here but suffice it to say it is a localized process. For example, the probabilities corresponding to variable E in Figure 1.3 will only reference this variable and its direct causes Q_3 and Q_4. Moreover, the probabilities corresponding to variable C will only reference this variable, as it does not have any causes. This is one of the key representational aspects of a Bayesian network: we are never required to specify a quantitative relationship between two variables unless they are connected by an edge. Probabilities that quantify the relationship between a variable and its indirect causes (or its indirect effects) will be computed automatically by inference algorithms, which we discuss in Section 1.4.2.

As a representational tool, the Bayesian network is quite attractive for three reasons. First, it is a consistent and complete representation as it is guaranteed to define a unique probability distribution over the network variables. Hence by building a Bayesian network, one is specifying a probability for every proposition that can be expressed using these network variables. Second, the Bayesian network is modular in the sense that its consistency and completeness are ensured using localized tests that apply only to variables and their direct causes. Third, the Bayesian network is a compact representation as it allows one to specify an exponentially sized probability distribution using a polynomial number of probabilities (assuming the number of direct causes remains small).

We will next provide an outline of the remaining book chapters, which can be divided into two components corresponding to modeling and reasoning with Bayesian networks.

1.4.1 Modeling with Bayesian networks

One can identify three main methods for constructing Bayesian networks when trying to model a particular situation. These methods are covered in four chapters of the book, which are outlined next.

According to the first method, which is largely subjective, one reflects on their own knowledge or the knowledge of others and then captures it into a Bayesian network (as we have done in Figure 1.3). According to the second method, one automatically synthesizes the Bayesian network from some other type of formal knowledge. For example, in many applications that involve system analysis, such as reliability and diagnosis, one can synthesize a Bayesian network automatically from formal system designs. Chapter 5 will be concerned with these two modeling methods, which are sometimes known as the *knowledge representation (KR) approach* for constructing Bayesian networks. Our exposure here will be guided by a number of application areas in which we state problems and show how to solve them by first building a Bayesian network and then posing queries with respect to the constructed network. Some of the application areas we discuss include system diagnostics, reliability analysis, channel coding, and genetic linkage analysis.

Constructing Bayesian networks according to the KR approach can benefit greatly from sensitivity analysis, which is covered partly in Chapter 5 and more extensively in Chapter 16. Here we provide techniques for checking the robustness of conclusions drawn from Bayesian networks against perturbations in the local probabilities that annotate them. We also provide techniques for automatically revising these local probabilities to satisfy some global constraints that are imposed by the opinions of experts or derived from the formal specifications of the tasks under consideration.

The third method for constructing Bayesian networks is based on learning them from data, such as medical records or student admissions data. Here either the structure, the probabilities, or both can be learned from the given data set. Since learning is an inductive process, one needs a principle of induction to guide the construction process according to this *machine learning (ML) approach*. We discuss two such principles in this book, leading to what are known as the maximum likelihood and Bayesian approaches to learning. The maximum likelihood approach, which is discussed in Chapter 17, favors Bayesian networks that maximize the probability of observing the given data set. The Bayesian approach, which is discussed in Chapter 18, uses the likelihood principle in addition to some prior information that encodes preferences on Bayesian networks.[2]

Networks constructed by the KR approach tend to have a different nature than those constructed by the ML approach. For example, these former networks tend to be much larger in size and, as such, place harsher computational demands on reasoning algorithms. Moreover, these networks tend to have a significant amount of determinism (i.e., probabilities that are equal to 0 or 1), allowing them to benefit from computational techniques that may be irrelevant to networks constructed by the ML approach.

1.4.2 Reasoning with Bayesian networks

Let us now return to Figure 1.1, which depicts the architecture of a knowledge-based reasoning system. In the previous section, we introduced those chapters that are concerned with constructing Bayesian networks (i.e., the knowledge bases or models). The remaining chapters of this book are concerned with constructing the reasoning engine, whose purpose is to answer queries with respect to these networks. We will first clarify what is meant by reasoning (or inference) and then lay out the topics covered by the reasoning chapters.

We have already mentioned that a Bayesian network assigns a unique probability to each proposition that can be expressed using the network variables. However, the network itself only explicates some of these probabilities. For example, according to Figure 1.3 the probability of a clerical error when entering the grade is .001. Moreover, the probability

---

[2] It is critical to observe here that the term "Bayesian network" does not necessarily imply a commitment to the Bayesian approach for learning networks. This term was coined by Judea Pearl [Pearl, 1985] to emphasize three aspects: the often subjective nature of the information used in constructing these networks; the reliance on Bayes's conditioning when reasoning with Bayesian networks; and the ability to perform causal as well as evidential reasoning on these networks, which is a distinction underscored by Thomas Bayes [Bayes, 1963].

that Jack obtains the same answer on Question 4 is .99, assuming that the question was answered correctly by Drew. However, consider the following probabilities:

- $Pr(E = true)$: The probability that Drew earned an A grade.
- $Pr(Q_3 = true | E = false)$: The probability that Question 3 was graded, given that Drew did not earn an A grade.
- $Pr(Q_4 = true | E = true)$: The probability that Jack obtained the same answer as Drew on Question 4, given that Drew earned an A grade.

None of these probabilities would be part of the fully specified Bayesian network. Yet as we show in Chapter 4, the network is guaranteed to imply a unique value for each one of these probabilities. It is indeed the purpose of reasoning/inference algorithms to deduce these values from the information given by the Bayesian network, that is, its structure and the associated local probabilities.

Even for a small example like the one given in Figure 1.3, it may not be that trivial for an expert on probabilistic reasoning to infer the values of the probabilities given previously. In principle, all one needs is a complete and correct reading of the probabilistic information encoded by the Bayesian network followed by a repeated application of enough laws of probability theory. However, the number of possible applications of these laws may be prohibitive, even for examples of the scale given here. The goal of reasoning/inference algorithms is therefore to relieve the user from undertaking this probabilistic reasoning process on their own, handing it instead to an automated process that is guaranteed to terminate while trying to use the least amount of computational resources (i.e., time and space). It is critical to stress here that automating the reasoning process is not only meant to be a convenience for the user. For the type of applications considered in this book, especially in Chapter 5, automated reasoning may be the only feasible method for solving the corresponding problems. For example, we will be encountering applications that, in their full scale, may involve thousands of variables. For these types of networks, one must appeal to automated reasoning algorithms to obtain the necessary answers. More so, one must appeal to very efficient algorithms if one is operating under constrained time and space resources – as is usually the case.

We cover two main classes of inference algorithms in this book, exact algorithms and approximate algorithms. *Exact algorithms* are guaranteed to return correct answers and tend to be more demanding computationally. On the other hand, *approximate algorithms* relax the insistence on exact answers for the sake of easing computational demands.

Exact inference

Much emphasis was placed on exact inference in the 1980s and the early 1990s, leading to two classes of algorithms based on the concepts of elimination and conditioning. Elimination algorithms are covered in Chapters 6 and 7, while conditioning algorithms are covered in Chapter 8. The complexity of these algorithms is exponential in the network *treewidth*, which is a graph-theoretic parameter that measures the resemblance of a graph to a tree structure (e.g., trees have a treewidth ≤ 1). We dedicate Chapter 9 to treewidth and some corresponding graphical manipulations, given the influential role they play in dictating the performance of exact inference algorithms.

Advanced inference algorithms

The inference algorithms covered in Chapters 6 through 8 are called *structure-based*, as their complexity is sensitive only to the network structure. In particular, these algorithms will consume the same computational resources when applied to two networks that share the same structure (i.e., have the same treewidth), regardless of what probabilities are used to annotate them. It has long been observed that inference algorithms can be made more efficient if they also exploit the structure exhibited by network probabilities, which is known as *local structure*. Yet algorithms for exploiting local structure have only matured in the last few years. We provide an extensive coverage of these algorithms in Chapters 10, 11, 12, and 13. The techniques discussed in these chapters have allowed exact inference on some networks whose treewidth is quite large. Interestingly enough, networks constructed by the KR approach tend to be most amenable to these techniques.

Approximate inference

Around the mid-1990s, a strong belief started forming in the inference community that the performance of exact algorithms must be exponential in treewidth – this is before local structure was being exploited effectively. At about the same time, methods for automatically constructing Bayesian networks started maturing to the point of yielding networks whose treewidth is too large to be handled by exact algorithms. This has led to a surge of interest in approximate inference algorithms, which are generally independent of treewidth. Today, approximate inference algorithms are the only choice for networks that have a large treewidth yet lack sufficient local structure. We cover approximation techniques in two chapters. In Chapter 14, we discuss algorithms that are based on reducing the inference problem to a constrained optimization problem, leading to the influential class of belief propagation algorithms. In Chapter 15, we discuss algorithms that are based on stochastic sampling, leading to approximations that can be made arbitrarily accurate as more time is allowed for use by the algorithm.

1.5 What is not covered in this book

As we discussed previously, decision theory has been left out to keep this book focused on the modeling and reasoning components. We also restrict our discussion to discrete Bayesian networks in which every variable has a finite number of values. One exception is in Chapter 3, where we discuss continuous variables representing sensor readings – these are commonly used in practice and are useful in analyzing the notion of uncertain evidence. Another exception is in Chapter 18, where we discuss continuous variables whose values represent model parameters – these are necessary for the treatment of Bayesian learning. We do not discuss undirected models, such as Markov networks and chain graphs, as we believe they belong more to a book that treats the broader subject of graphical models (e.g., [Whittaker, 1990; Lauritzen, 1996; Cowell et al., 1999; Edwards, 2000]). We have also left out the discussion of high-level specifications of probabilistic models based on relational and first-order languages. Covering this topic is rather tempting given our emphasis on modeling yet it cannot be treated satisfactorily without significantly increasing the length of this book. We also do not treat causality from a Bayesian network perspective as this topic has matured enough to merit its own dedicated treatment [Pearl, 2000; Glymour and Cooper, 1999].

2

Propositional Logic

We introduce propositional logic in this chapter as a tool for representing and reasoning about events.

2.1 Introduction

The notion of an event is central to both logical and probabilistic reasoning. In the former, we are interested in reasoning about the truth of events (facts), while in the latter we are interested in reasoning about their probabilities (degrees of belief). In either case, one needs a language for expressing events before one can write statements that declare their truth or specify their probabilities. Propositional logic, which is also known as Boolean logic or Boolean algebra, provides such a language.

We start in Section 2.2 by discussing the syntax of propositional sentences, which we use for expressing events. We then follow in Section 2.3 by discussing the semantics of propositional logic, where we define properties of propositional sentences, such as consistency and validity, and relationships among them, such as implication, equivalence, and mutual exclusiveness. The semantics of propositional logic are used in Section 2.4 to formally expose its limitations in supporting plausible reasoning. This also provides a good starting point for Chapter 3, where we show how degrees of belief can deal with these limitations.

In Section 2.5, we discuss variables whose values go beyond the traditional true and false values of propositional logic. This is critical for our treatment of probabilistic reasoning in Chapter 3, which relies on the use of multivalued variables. We discuss in Section 2.6 the notation we adopt for denoting variable instantiations, which are the most fundamental type of events we deal with. In Section 2.7, we provide a treatment of logical forms, which are syntactic restrictions that one imposes on propositional sentences; these include disjunctive normal form (DNF), conjunctive normal form (CNF), and negation normal form (NNF). A discussion of these forms is necessary for some of the advanced inference algorithms we discuss in later chapters.

2.2 Syntax of propositional sentences

Consider a situation that involves an alarm meant for detecting burglaries, and suppose the alarm may also be triggered by an earthquake. Consider now the event of having either a burglary or an earthquake. One can express this event using the following propositional sentence:

$$\text{Burglary} \lor \text{Earthquake}.$$

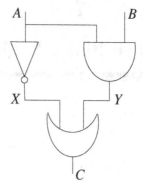

Figure 2.1: A digital circuit.

Here Burglary and Earthquake are called *propositional variables* and $\vee$ represents logical disjunction (or). Propositional logic can be used to express more complex statements, such as:

$$\text{Burglary} \vee \text{Earthquake} \implies \text{Alarm}, \tag{2.1}$$

where $\implies$ represents logical implication. According to this sentence, a burglary or an earthquake is guaranteed to trigger the alarm. Consider also the sentence:

$$\neg\text{Burglary} \wedge \neg\text{Earthquake} \implies \neg\text{Alarm}, \tag{2.2}$$

where $\neg$ represents logical negation (not) and $\wedge$ represents logical conjunction (and). According to this sentence, if there is no burglary and there is no earthquake, the alarm will not trigger.

More generally, propositional sentences are formed using a set of propositional variables, $P_1, \ldots, P_n$. These variables – which are also called *Boolean variables* or *binary variables* – assume one of two values, typically indicated by true and false. Our previous example was based on three propositional variables, Burglary, Earthquake, and Alarm.

The simplest sentence one can write in propositional logic has the form P_i. It is called an *atomic sentence* and is interpreted as saying that variable P_i takes on the value true. More generally, propositional sentences are formed as follows:

- Every propositional variable P_i is a sentence.
- If α and β are sentences, then $\neg\alpha$, $\alpha \wedge \beta$, and $\alpha \vee \beta$ are also sentences.

The symbols $\neg$, $\wedge$, and $\vee$ are called *logical connectives* and they stand for negation, conjunction, and disjunction, respectively. Other connectives can also be introduced, such as implication $\implies$ and equivalence $\iff$, but these can be defined in terms of the three primitive connectives given here. In particular, the sentence $\alpha \implies \beta$ is shorthand for $\neg\alpha \vee \beta$. Similarly, the sentence $\alpha \iff \beta$ is shorthand for $(\alpha \implies \beta) \wedge (\beta \implies \alpha)$.[1] A propositional *knowledge base* is a set of propositional sentences $\alpha_1, \alpha_2, \ldots, \alpha_n$, that is interpreted as a conjunction $\alpha_1 \wedge \alpha_2 \wedge \ldots \wedge \alpha_n$.

Consider now the digital circuit in Figure 2.1, which has two inputs and one output. Suppose that we want to write a propositional knowledge base that captures our knowledge about the behavior of this circuit. The very first step to consider is that of choosing the

---

[1] We follow the standard convention of giving the negation operator $\neg$ first precedence, followed by the conjunction operator $\wedge$ and then the disjunction operator $\vee$. The operators $\implies$ and $\iff$ have the least (and equal) precedence.

set of propositional variables. A common choice here is to use one propositional variable for each wire in the circuit, leading to the following variables: $A, B, C, X,$ and Y. The intention is that when a variable is true, the corresponding wire is considered high, and when the variable is false, the corresponding wire is low. This leads to the following knowledge base:

$$\Delta = \begin{cases} A & \implies & \neg X \\ \neg A & \implies & X \\ A \wedge B & \implies & Y \\ \neg(A \wedge B) & \implies & \neg Y \\ X \vee Y & \implies & C \\ \neg(X \vee Y) & \implies & \neg C. \end{cases}$$

2.3 Semantics of propositional sentences

Propositional logic provides a formal framework for defining properties of sentences, such as consistency and validity, and relationships among them, such as implication, equivalence, and mutual exclusiveness. For example, the sentence in (2.1) logically implies the following sentence:

$$\text{Burglary} \implies \text{Alarm.}$$

Maybe less obviously, the sentence in (2.2) also implies the following:

$$\text{Alarm} \wedge \neg\text{Burglary} \implies \text{Earthquake.}$$

These properties and relationships are easy to figure out for simple sentences. For example, most people would agree that:

- $A \wedge \neg A$ is inconsistent (will never hold).
- $A \vee \neg A$ is valid (always holds).
- A and $(A \implies B)$ imply B.
- $A \vee B$ is equivalent to $B \vee A$.

Yet it may not be as obvious that $A \implies B$ and $\neg B \implies \neg A$ are equivalent, or that $(A \implies B) \wedge (A \implies \neg B)$ implies $\neg A$. For this reason, one needs formal definitions of logical properties and relationships. As we show in the following section, defining these notions is relatively straightforward once the notion of a world is defined.

2.3.1 Worlds, models, and events

A *world* is a particular state of affairs in which the value of each propositional variable is known. Consider again the example discussed previously that involves three propositional variables, Burglary, Earthquake, and Alarm. We have eight worlds in this case, which are shown in Table 2.1. Formally, a world ω is a function that maps each propositional variable P_i into a value $\omega(P_i) \in \{\text{true, false}\}$. For this reason, a world is often called a *truth assignment*, a *variable assignment*, or a *variable instantiation*.

The notion of a world allows one to decide the truth of sentences without ambiguity. For example, Burglary is true at world ω_1 of Table 2.1 since the world assigns the value true to variable Burglary. Moreover, $\neg$Burglary is true at world ω_3 since the world assigns false to Burglary, and Burglary $\vee$ Earthquake is true at world ω_4 since it assigns true to

Table 2.1: A set of worlds, also known as truth assignments, variable assignments, or variable instantiations.

world	Earthquake	Burglary	Alarm
ω_1	true	true	true
ω_2	true	true	false
ω_3	true	false	true
ω_4	true	false	false
ω_5	false	true	true
ω_6	false	true	false
ω_7	false	false	true
ω_8	false	false	false

Earthquake. We will use the notation $\omega \models \alpha$ to mean that sentence α is true at world ω. We will also say in this case that world ω satisfies (or entails) sentence α.

The set of worlds that satisfy a sentence α is called the *models* of α and is denoted by

$$Mods(\alpha) \stackrel{def}{=} \{\omega : \ \omega \models \alpha\}.$$

Hence, every sentence α can be viewed as representing a set of worlds $Mods(\alpha)$, which is called the *event* denoted by α. We will use the terms "sentence" and "event" interchangeably.

Using the definition of satisfaction ($\models$), it is not difficult to prove the following properties:

- $Mods(\alpha \wedge \beta) = Mods(\alpha) \cap Mods(\beta)$.
- $Mods(\alpha \vee \beta) = Mods(\alpha) \cup Mods(\beta)$.
- $Mods(\neg\alpha) = \overline{Mods(\alpha)}$.

The following are some example sentences and their truth at worlds in Table 2.1:

- Earthquake is true at worlds $\omega_1, \ldots, \omega_4$:

$$Mods(\text{Earthquake}) = \{\omega_1, \ldots, \omega_4\}.$$

- $\neg$Earthquake is true at worlds $\omega_5, \ldots, \omega_8$:

$$Mods(\neg\text{Earthquake}) = \overline{Mods(\text{Earthquake})}.$$

- $\neg$Burglary is true at worlds $\omega_3, \omega_4, \omega_7, \omega_8$.
- Alarm is true at worlds $\omega_1, \omega_3, \omega_5, \omega_7$.
- $\neg$(Earthquake $\vee$ Burglary) is true at worlds ω_7, ω_8:

$$Mods(\neg(\text{Earthquake} \vee \text{Burglary})) = \overline{Mods(\text{Earthquake}) \cup Mods(\text{Burglary})}.$$

- $\neg$(Earthquake $\vee$ Burglary) $\vee$ Alarm is true at worlds $\omega_1, \omega_3, \omega_5, \omega_7, \omega_8$.
- (Earthquake $\vee$ Burglary) $\Longrightarrow$ Alarm is true at worlds $\omega_1, \omega_3, \omega_5, \omega_7, \omega_8$.
- $\neg$Burglary $\wedge$ Burglary is not true at any world.

2.3.2 Logical properties

We are now ready to define the most central logical property of sentences: consistency. Specifically, we say that sentence α is *consistent* if and only if there is at least one world ω at which α is true, $Mods(\alpha) \neq \emptyset$. Otherwise, the sentence α is *inconsistent*, $Mods(\alpha) = \emptyset$. It is also common to use the terms satisfiable/unsatisfiable instead of consistent/inconsistent, respectively. The property of satisfiability is quite important since many other logical notions can be reduced to satisfiability. The symbol false is often used to denote a sentence that is unsatisfiable. We have also used false to denote one of the values that propositional variables can assume. The symbol false is therefore overloaded in propositional logic.

We now turn to another logical property: validity. Specifically, we say that sentence α is *valid* if and only if it is true at every world, $Mods(\alpha) = \Omega$, where Ω is the set of all worlds. If a sentence α is not valid, $Mods(\alpha) \neq \Omega$, one can identify a world ω at which α is false. The symbol true is often used to denote a sentence that is valid.[2] Moreover, it is common to write $\models \alpha$ when the sentence α is valid.

2.3.3 Logical relationships

A logical property applies to a single sentence, while a logical relationship applies to two or more sentences. We now define a few logical relationships among propositional sentences:

- Sentences α and β are *equivalent* iff they are true at the same set of worlds: $Mods(\alpha) = Mods(\beta)$ (i.e., they denote the same event).
- Sentences α and β are *mutually exclusive* iff they are never true at the same world: $Mods(\alpha) \cap Mods(\beta) = \emptyset$.[3]
- Sentences α and β are *exhaustive* iff each world satisfies at least one of the sentences: $Mods(\alpha) \cup Mods(\beta) = \Omega$.[4]
- Sentence α *implies* sentence β iff β is true whenever α is true: $Mods(\alpha) \subseteq Mods(\beta)$.

We have previously used the symbol $\models$ to denote the satisfiability relationship between a world and a sentence. Specifically, we wrote $\omega \models \alpha$ to indicate that world ω satisfies sentence α. This symbol is also used to indicate implication between sentences, where we write $\alpha \models \beta$ to say that sentence α implies sentence β. We also say in this case that α entails β.

2.3.4 Equivalences and reductions

We now consider some equivalences between propositional sentences that can be quite useful when working with propositional logic. The equivalences are given in Table 2.2 and are actually between *schemas*, which are templates that can generate a large number of specific sentences. For example, $\alpha \implies \beta$ is a schema and generates instances such as $\neg A \implies (B \vee \neg C)$, where α is replaced by $\neg A$ and β is replaced by $(B \vee \neg C)$.

---

[2] Again, we are overloading the symbol true since it also denotes one of the values that a propositional variable can assume.

[3] This can be generalized to an arbitrary number of sentences as follows: Sentences $\alpha_1, \ldots, \alpha_n$ are mutually exclusive iff $Mods(\alpha_i) \cap Mods(\alpha_j) = \emptyset$ for $i \neq j$.

[4] This can be generalized to an arbitrary number of sentences as follows: Sentences $\alpha_1, \ldots, \alpha_n$ are exhaustive iff $Mods(\alpha_1) \cup \ldots \cup Mods(\alpha_n) = \Omega$.

Table 2.2: Some equivalences among sentence schemas.

Schema	Equivalent Schema	Name
$\neg$true	false	
$\neg$false	true	
false $\wedge\ \beta$	false	
$\alpha \wedge$ true	α	
false $\vee\ \beta$	β	
$\alpha \vee$ true	true	
$\neg\neg\alpha$	α	double negation
$\neg(\alpha \wedge \beta)$	$\neg\alpha \vee \neg\beta$	de Morgan
$\neg(\alpha \vee \beta)$	$\neg\alpha \wedge \neg\beta$	de Morgan
$\alpha \vee (\beta \wedge \gamma)$	$(\alpha \vee \beta) \wedge (\alpha \vee \gamma)$	distribution
$\alpha \wedge (\beta \vee \gamma)$	$(\alpha \wedge \beta) \vee (\alpha \wedge \gamma)$	distribution
$\alpha \implies \beta$	$\neg\beta \implies \neg\alpha$	contraposition
$\alpha \implies \beta$	$\neg\alpha \vee \beta$	definition of $\implies$
$\alpha \iff \beta$	$(\alpha \implies \beta) \wedge (\beta \implies \alpha)$	definition of $\iff$

Table 2.3: Some reductions between logical relationships and logical properties.

Relationship	Property
α implies β	$\alpha \wedge \neg\beta$ is unsatisfiable
α implies β	$\alpha \implies \beta$ is valid
α and β are equivalent	$\alpha \iff \beta$ is valid
α and β are mutually exclusive	$\alpha \wedge \beta$ is unsatisfiable
α and β are exhaustive	$\alpha \vee \beta$ is valid

Table 2.4: Possible worlds according to the sentence (Earthquake $\vee$ Burglary) $\implies$ Alarm.

world	Earthquake	Burglary	Alarm	Possible?
ω_1	true	true	true	yes
ω_2	true	true	false	no
ω_3	true	false	true	yes
ω_4	true	false	false	no
ω_5	false	true	true	yes
ω_6	false	true	false	no
ω_7	false	false	true	yes
ω_8	false	false	false	yes

One can also state a number of reductions between logical properties and relationships, some of which are shown in Table 2.3. Specifically, this table shows how the relationships of implication, equivalence, mutual exclusiveness, and exhaustiveness can all be defined in terms of satisfiability and validity.

2.4 The monotonicity of logical reasoning

Consider the earthquake-burglary-alarm example that we introduced previously, which has the eight worlds depicted in Table 2.4. Suppose now that someone communicates to us the following sentence:

$$\alpha:\quad (\text{Earthquake} \vee \text{Burglary}) \implies \text{Alarm}.$$

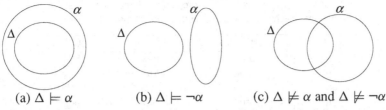

(a) $\Delta \models \alpha$ (b) $\Delta \models \neg\alpha$ (c) $\Delta \not\models \alpha$ and $\Delta \not\models \neg\alpha$

Figure 2.2: Possible relationships between a knowledge base Δ and sentence α.

By accepting α, we are considering some of these eight worlds as impossible. In particular, any world that does not satisfy the sentence α is ruled out. Therefore, our state of belief can now be characterized by the set of worlds,

$$Mods(\alpha) = \{\omega_1, \omega_3, \omega_5, \omega_7, \omega_8\}.$$

This is depicted in Table 2.4, which rules out any world outside $Mods(\alpha)$.

Suppose now that we also learn

$$\beta : \quad \text{Earthquake} \implies \text{Burglary},$$

for which $Mods(\beta) = \{\omega_1, \omega_2, \omega_5, \omega_6, \omega_7, \omega_8\}$. Our state of belief is now characterized by the following worlds:

$$Mods(\alpha \wedge \beta) = Mods(\alpha) \cap Mods(\beta) = \{\omega_1, \omega_5, \omega_7, \omega_8\}.$$

Hence, learning the new information β had the effect of ruling out world ω_3 in addition to those worlds ruled out by α.

Note that if α implies some sentence γ, then $Mods(\alpha) \subseteq Mods(\gamma)$ by definition of implication. Since $Mods(\alpha \wedge \beta) \subseteq Mods(\alpha)$, we must also have $Mods(\alpha \wedge \beta) \subseteq Mods(\gamma)$ and, hence, $\alpha \wedge \beta$ must also imply γ. This is precisely the property of *monotonicity* in propositional logic as it shows that the belief in γ cannot be given up as a result of learning some new information β. In other words, if α implies γ, then $\alpha \wedge \beta$ will imply γ as well.

Note that a propositional knowledge base Δ can stand in only one of three possible relationships with a sentence α:

- Δ implies α (α is believed).
- Δ implies the negation of α ($\neg\alpha$ is believed).
- Δ neither implies α nor implies its negation.

This classification of sentences, which can be visualized by examining Figure 2.2, is a consequence of the binary classification imposed by the knowledge base Δ on worlds, that is, a world is either possible or impossible depending on whether it satisfies or contradicts Δ. In Chapter 3, we will see that degrees of belief can be used to impose a more refined classification on worlds, leading to a more refined classification of sentences. This will be the basis for a framework that allows one to represent and reason about uncertain beliefs.

2.5 Multivalued variables

Propositional variables are binary as they assume one of two values, true or false. However, these values are implicit in the syntax of propositional logic, as we write X to mean

Table 2.5: A set of worlds over propositional and multivalued variables. Each world is also called a variable instantiation.

world	Earthquake	Burglary	Alarm
ω_1	true	true	high
ω_2	true	true	low
ω_3	true	true	off
ω_4	true	false	high
ω_5	true	false	low
ω_6	true	false	off
ω_7	false	true	high
ω_8	false	true	low
ω_9	false	true	off
ω_{10}	false	false	high
ω_{11}	false	false	low
ω_{12}	false	false	off

X = true and $\neg X$ to mean X = false. One can generalize propositional logic to allow for multivalued variables. For example, suppose that we have an alarm that triggers either high or low. We may then decide to treat Alarm as a variable with three values, low, high, and off. With multivalued variables, one would need to explicate the values assigned to variables instead of keeping them implicit. Hence, we may write Burglary $\implies$ Alarm = high. Note here that we kept the value of the propositional variable Burglary implicit but we could explicate it as well, writing Burglary = true $\implies$ Alarm = high.

Sentences in the generalized propositional logic can be formed according to the following rules:

- Every propositional variable is a sentence.
- $V = v$ is a sentence, where V is a variable and v is one of its values.
- If α and β are sentences, then $\neg\alpha$, $\alpha \wedge \beta$, and $\alpha \vee \beta$ are also sentences.

The semantics of the generalized logic can be given in a fashion similar to standard propositional logic, given that we extend the notion of a world to be an assignment of values to variables (propositional and multivalued). Table 2.5 depicts a set of worlds for our running example, assuming that Alarm is a multivalued variable.

The notion of truth at a world can be defined similar to propositional logic. For example, the sentence $\neg$Earthquake $\wedge$ $\neg$Burglary $\implies$ Alarm = off is satisfied by worlds $\omega_1, \ldots,$ ω_9, ω_{12}; hence, only worlds ω_{10} and ω_{11} are ruled out by this sentence. The definition of logical properties, such as consistency and validity, and logical relationships, such as implication and equivalence, can all be developed as in standard propositional logic.

2.6 Variable instantiations and related notations

One of the central notions we will appeal to throughout this book is the *variable instantiation*. In particular, an instantiation of variables, say, A, B, C is a propositional sentence of the form $(A = a) \wedge (B = b) \wedge (C = c)$, where a, b, and c are values of variables A, B, C, respectively. Given the extent to which variable instantiations will be used, we will adopt a simpler notation for denoting them. In particular, we will use a, b, c instead of $(A = a) \wedge (B = b) \wedge (C = c)$. More generally, we will replace the conjoin operator ($\wedge$) by a comma (,) and write α, β instead of $\alpha \wedge \beta$. We will also find it useful to introduce a *trivial instantiation*, an instantiation of an empty set of variables. The trivial instantiation corresponds to a valid sentence and will be denoted by $\top$.

We will consistently denote variables by upper-case letters (A), their values by lower-case letters (a), and their cardinalities (number of values) by $|A|$. Moreover, sets of variables will be denoted by bold-face upper-case letters (**A**), their instantiations by bold-face lower-case letters (**a**), and their number of instantiations by $\mathbf{A}^{\#}$. Suppose now that **X** and **Y** are two sets of variables and let **x** and **y** be their corresponding instantiations. Statements such as ¬**x**, **x** ∨ **y**, and **x** $\implies$ **y** are therefore legitimate sentences in propositional logic.

For a propositional variable A with values true and false, we may use a to denote A=true and $\bar{a}$ to denote A=false. Therefore, A, A=true, and a are all equivalent sentences. Similarly, ¬A, A=false, and $\bar{a}$ are all equivalent sentences.

Finally, we will use **x** ∼ **y** to mean that instantiations **x** and **y** are compatible, that is, they agree on the values of all their common variables. For example, instantiations $a, b, \bar{c}$ and $b, \bar{c}, \bar{d}$ are compatible. On the other hand, instantiations $a, b, \bar{c}$ and $b, c, \bar{d}$ are not compatible as they disagree on the value of variable C.

2.7 Logical forms

Propositional logic will provide the basis for probability calculus in Chapter 3. It will also be used extensively in Chapter 11, where we discuss the complexity of probabilistic inference, and in Chapters 12 and 13, where we discuss advanced inference algorithms. Our use of propositional logic in Chapters 11 to 13 will rely on certain syntactic forms and some corresponding operations that we discuss in this section. One may therefore skip this section until these chapters are approached.

A propositional *literal* is either a propositional variable X, called a *positive literal*, or the negation of a propositional variable ¬X, called a *negative literal*. A *clause* is a disjunction of literals, such as ¬A ∨ B ∨ ¬C.[5] A propositional sentence is in *conjunctive normal form* (CNF) if it is a conjunction of clauses, such as:

$$(\neg A \vee B \vee \neg C) \wedge (A \vee \neg B) \wedge (C \vee \neg D).$$

A *unit clause* is a clause that contains a single literal. The following CNF contains two unit clauses:

$$(\neg A \vee B \vee \neg C) \wedge (\neg B) \wedge (C \vee \neg D) \wedge (D).$$

A *term* is a conjunction of literals, such as $A \wedge \neg B \wedge C$.[6] A propositional sentence is in *disjunctive normal form* (DNF) if it is a disjunction of terms, such as:

$$(A \wedge \neg B \wedge C) \vee (\neg A \wedge B) \vee (\neg C \wedge D).$$

Propositional sentences can also be represented using circuits, as shown in Figure 2.3. This circuit has a number of inputs that are labeled with literals (i.e., variables or their

---

[5] A clause is usually written as an implication. For example, the clause ¬A ∨ B ∨ ¬C can be written in any of the following equivalent forms: $A \wedge \neg B \implies \neg C$, $A \wedge C \implies B$, or ¬$B \wedge C \implies \neg A$.

[6] A term corresponds to a variable instantiation, as defined previously.

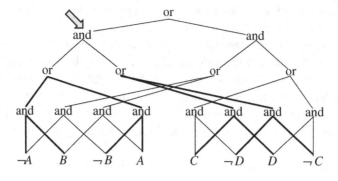

(a) Decomposability

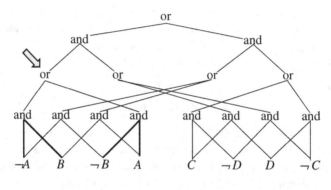

(b) Determinism

Figure 2.3: A circuit representation of a propositional sentence. The circuit inputs are labeled with literals $\neg A, B, \ldots$, and its nodes are restricted to conjunctions (and-gates) and disjunctions (or-gates).

negations).[7] Moreover, it has only two types of nodes that represent conjunctions (and-gates) or disjunctions (or-gates). Under these restrictions, a circuit is said to be in *negation normal form* (NNF). An NNF circuit can satisfy one or more of the following properties.

Decomposability. We will say that an NNF circuit is *decomposable* if each of its and-nodes satisfies the following property: For each pair of children C_1 and C_2 of the and-node, the sentences represented by C_1 and C_2 cannot share variables. Figure 2.3(a) highlights two children of an and-node and the sentences they represent. The child on the left represents the sentence $(\neg A \wedge B) \vee (A \wedge \neg B)$, and the one on the right represents $(C \wedge D) \vee (\neg C \wedge \neg D)$. The two sentences do not share any variables and, hence, the and-node is decomposable.

Determinism. We will say that an NNF circuit is *deterministic* if each of its or-nodes satisfies the following property: For each pair of children C_1 and C_2 of the or-node, the sentences represented by C_1 and C_2 must be mutually exclusive. Figure 2.3(b) highlights two children of an or-node. The child on the left represents the sentence $\neg A \wedge B$, and the one on the right represents $A \wedge \neg B$. The two sentences are mutually exclusive and, hence, the or-node is deterministic.

Smoothness. We will say that an NNF circuit is *smooth* if each of its or-nodes satisfies the following property: For each pair of children C_1 and C_2 of the or-node,

---

[7] Inputs can also be labeled with the constants true/false.

the sentences represented by C_1 and C_2 must mention the same set of variables. Figure 2.3(b) highlights two children of an or-node that represent the sentences $\neg A \wedge B$ and $A \wedge \neg B$. The two sentences mention the same set of variables and, hence, the or-node is smooth.

The NNF circuit in Figure 2.3 is decomposable, deterministic, and smooth since all its and-nodes are decomposable and all its or-nodes are deterministic and smooth.

2.7.1 Conditioning a propositional sentence

Conditioning a propositional sentence Δ on variable X, denoted $\Delta|X$, is a process of replacing every occurrence of variable X by true. Similarly, $\Delta|\neg X$ results from replacing every occurrence of variable X by false. For example, if

$$\Delta = (\neg A \vee B \vee \neg C) \wedge (A \vee \neg B) \wedge (C \vee \neg D),$$

then

$$\Delta|A = (\neg\text{true} \vee B \vee \neg C) \wedge (\text{true} \vee \neg B) \wedge (C \vee \neg D).$$

Simplifying and using the equivalences in Table 2.2, we get

$$\Delta|A = (B \vee \neg C) \wedge (C \vee \neg D).$$

In general, conditioning a CNF Δ on X and simplifying has the effect of removing every clause that contains the positive literal X from the CNF and removing the negative literal $\neg X$ from all other clauses. Similarly, when we condition on $\neg X$, we remove every clause that contains $\neg X$ from the CNF and remove the positive literal X from all other clauses. For example,

$$\Delta|\neg A = (\neg\text{false} \vee B \vee \neg C) \wedge (\text{false} \vee \neg B) \wedge (C \vee \neg D)$$
$$= (\neg B) \wedge (C \vee \neg D).$$

2.7.2 Unit resolution

Unit resolution is a process by which a CNF is simplified by iteratively applying the following. If the CNF contains a *unit clause* X, every other occurrence of X is replaced by true and the CNF is simplified. Similarly, if the CNF contains a unit clause $\neg X$, every other occurrence of X is replaced by false and the CNF is simplified. Consider the following CNF:

$$(\neg A \vee B \vee \neg C) \wedge (\neg B) \wedge (C \vee \neg D) \wedge (D).$$

If we replace the other occurrences of B by false and the other occurrences of D by true, we get

$$(\neg A \vee \text{false} \vee \neg C) \wedge (\neg B) \wedge (C \vee \neg\text{true}) \wedge (D).$$

Simplifying, we get

$$(\neg A \vee \neg C) \wedge (\neg B) \wedge (C) \wedge (D).$$

We now have another unit clause C. Replacing the other occurrences of C by true and simplifying, we now get

$$(\neg A) \wedge (\neg B) \wedge (C) \wedge (D).$$

Unit resolution can be viewed as an inference rule as it allowed us to infer $\neg A$ and C in this example. It is known that unit resolution can be applied to a CNF in time linear in the CNF size.

2.7.3 Converting propositional sentences to CNF

One can convert any propositional sentence into a CNF through a systematic three-step process:

1. Remove all logical connectives except for conjunction, disjunction, and negation. For example, $\alpha \implies \beta$ should be transformed into $\neg \alpha \vee \beta$, and similarly for other connectives.

2. Push negations inside the sentence until they only appear next to propositional variables. This is done by repeated application of the following transformations:

   Step 1: $\neg\neg\alpha$ is transformed into α.
   Step 2: $\neg(\alpha \vee \beta)$ is transformed into $\neg\alpha \wedge \neg\beta$.
   Step 3: $\neg(\alpha \wedge \beta)$ is transformed into $\neg\alpha \vee \neg\beta$.

3. Distribute disjunctions over conjunctions by repeated application of the following transformation: $\alpha \vee (\beta \wedge \gamma)$ is transformed to $(\alpha \vee \beta) \wedge (\alpha \vee \gamma)$.

For example, to convert the sentence $(A \vee B) \implies C$ into CNF, we go through the following steps:

   Step 1: $\neg(A \vee B) \vee C$.
   Step 2: $(\neg A \wedge \neg B) \vee C$.
   Step 3: $(\neg A \vee C) \wedge (\neg B \vee C)$.

For another example, converting $\neg(A \vee B \implies C)$ leads to the following steps:

   Step 1: $\neg(\neg(A \vee B) \vee C)$.
   Step 2: $(A \vee B) \wedge \neg C$.
   Step 3: $(A \vee B) \wedge \neg C$.

Although this conversion process is guaranteed to yield a CNF, the result can be quite large. Specifically, it is possible that the size of the given sentence is linear in the number of propositional variables yet the size of the resulting CNF is exponential in that number.

Bibliographic remarks

For introductory textbooks that cover propositional logic, see Genesereth and Nilsson [1987] and Russell and Norvig [2003]. For a discussion of logical forms, including NNF circuits, see Darwiche and Marquis [2002]. A state-of-the-art compiler for converting CNF to NNF circuits is discussed in Darwiche [2004] and is available for download at *http://reasoning.cs.ucla.edu/c2d/*.

2.8 Exercises

2.1. Show that the following sentences are consistent by identifying a world that satisfies each sentence:

(a) $(A \implies B) \wedge (A \implies \neg B)$.

(b) $(A \vee B) \implies (\neg A \wedge \neg B)$.

2.2. Which of the following sentences are valid? If a sentence is not valid, identify a world that does not satisfy the sentence.

(a) $(A \wedge (A \implies B)) \implies B$.

(b) $(A \wedge B) \vee (A \wedge \neg B)$.

(c) $(A \implies B) \implies (\neg B \implies \neg A)$.

2.3. Which of the following pairs of sentences are equivalent? If a pair of sentences is not equivalent, identify a world at which they disagree (one of them holds but the other does not).

(a) $A \implies B$ and $B \implies A$.

(b) $(A \implies B) \wedge (A \implies \neg B)$ and $\neg A$.

(c) $\neg A \implies \neg B$ and $(A \vee \neg B \vee C) \wedge (A \vee \neg B \vee \neg C)$.

2.4. For each of the following pairs of sentences, decide whether the first sentence implies the second. If the implication does not hold, identify a world at which the first sentence is true but the second is not.

(a) $(A \implies B) \wedge \neg B$ and A.

(b) $(A \vee \neg B) \wedge B$ and A.

(c) $(A \vee B) \wedge (A \vee \neg B)$ and A.

2.5. Which of the following pairs of sentences are mutually exclusive? Which are exhaustive? If a pair of sentences is not mutually exclusive, identify a world at which they both hold. If a pair of sentences is not exhaustive, identify a world at which neither holds.

(a) $A \vee B$ and $\neg A \vee \neg B$.

(b) $A \vee B$ and $\neg A \wedge \neg B$.

(c) A and $(\neg A \vee B) \wedge (\neg A \vee \neg B)$.

2.6. Prove that $\alpha \models \beta$ iff $\alpha \wedge \neg \beta$ is inconsistent. This is known as the *Refutation Theorem*.

2.7. Prove that $\alpha \models \beta$ iff $\alpha \implies \beta$ is valid. This is known as the *Deduction Theorem*.

2.8. Prove that if $\alpha \models \beta$, then $\alpha \wedge \beta$ is equivalent to α.

2.9. Prove that if $\alpha \models \beta$, then $\alpha \vee \beta$ is equivalent to β.

2.10. Convert the following sentences into CNF:

(a) $P \implies (Q \implies R)$.

(b) $\neg((P \implies Q) \wedge (R \implies S))$.

2.11. Let Γ be an NNF circuit that satisfies decomposability and determinism. Show how one can augment the circuit Γ with additional nodes so it also satisfies smoothness. What is the time and space complexity of your algorithm for ensuring smoothness?

2.12. Let Γ be an NNF circuit that satisfies decomposability, is equivalent to CNF Δ, and does not contain false. Suppose that every model of Δ sets the same number of variables to true (we say in this case that all models of Δ have the same *cardinality*). Show that circuit Γ must be smooth.

2.13. Let Γ be an NNF circuit that satisfies decomposability, determinism, and smoothness. Consider the following procedure for generating a subcircuit Γ_m of circuit Γ:

- Assign an integer to each node in circuit Γ as follows: An input node is assigned 0 if labeled with true or a positive literal, ∞ if labeled with false, and 1 if labeled with a negative literal. An or-node is assigned the minimum of integers assigned to its children, and an and-node is assigned the sum of integers assigned to its children.

- Obtain Γ_m from Γ by deleting every edge that extends from an or-node N to one of its children C, where N and C have different integers assigned to them.

Show that the models of Γ_m are the minimum-cardinality models of Γ, where the *cardinality* of a model is defined as the number of variables it sets to false.

3

Probability Calculus

We introduce probability calculus in this chapter as a tool for representing and reasoning with degrees of belief.

3.1 Introduction

We provide in this chapter a framework for representing and reasoning with uncertain beliefs. According to this framework, each event is assigned a degree of belief which is interpreted as a probability that quantifies the belief in that event. Our focus in this chapter is on the semantics of degrees of belief, where we discuss their properties and the methods for revising them in light of new evidence. Computational and practical considerations relating to degrees of belief are discussed at length in future chapters.

We start in Section 3.2 by introducing degrees of belief, their basic properties, and the way they can be used to quantify uncertainty. We discuss the updating of degrees of belief in Section 3.3, where we show how they can increase or decrease depending on the new evidence made available. We then turn to the notion of independence in Section 3.4, which will be fundamental when reasoning about uncertain beliefs. The properties of degrees of belief are studied further in Section 3.5, where we introduce some of the key laws for manipulating them. We finally treat the subject of soft evidence in Sections 3.6 and 3.7, where we provide some tools for updating degrees of belief in light of uncertain information.

3.2 Degrees of belief

We have seen in Chapter 2 that a propositional knowledge base Δ classifies sentences into one of three categories: sentences that are implied by Δ, sentences whose negations are implied by Δ, and all other sentences (see Figure 2.2). This coarse classification of sentences is a consequence of the binary classification imposed by the knowledge base Δ on worlds, that is, a world is either possible or impossible depending on whether it satisfies or contradicts Δ.

One can obtain a much finer classification of sentences through a finer classification of worlds. In particular, we can assign a *degree of belief* or *probability* in [0, 1] to each world ω and denote it by $\Pr(\omega)$. The belief in, or probability of, a sentence α can then be defined as

$$\Pr(\alpha) \overset{def}{=} \sum_{\omega \models \alpha} \Pr(\omega), \tag{3.1}$$

which is the sum of probabilities assigned to worlds at which α is true.

Consider now Table 3.1, which lists a set of worlds and their corresponding degrees of beliefs. Table 3.1 is known as a *state of belief* or a *joint probability distribution*. We will

27

Table 3.1: A state of belief, also known as a joint probability distribution.

world	Earthquake	Burglary	Alarm	Pr(.)
ω_1	true	true	true	.0190
ω_2	true	true	false	.0010
ω_3	true	false	true	.0560
ω_4	true	false	false	.0240
ω_5	false	true	true	.1620
ω_6	false	true	false	.0180
ω_7	false	false	true	.0072
ω_8	false	false	false	.7128

require that the degrees of belief assigned to all worlds add up to 1: $\sum_w \Pr(w) = 1$. This is a normalization convention that makes it possible to directly compare the degrees of belief held by different states. Based on Table 3.1, we then have the following beliefs:

$$\begin{aligned}
\Pr(\text{Earthquake}) &= \Pr(\omega_1) + \Pr(\omega_2) + \Pr(\omega_3) + \Pr(\omega_4) = .1 \\
\Pr(\text{Burglary}) &= .2 \\
\Pr(\neg\text{Burglary}) &= .8 \\
\Pr(\text{Alarm}) &= .2442
\end{aligned}$$

Note that the joint probability distribution is usually too large to allow a direct representation as given in Table 3.1. For example, if we have twenty variables and each has two values, the table will have $1, 048, 576$ entries, and if we have forty variables, the table will have $1, 099, 511, 627, 776$ entries. This difficulty will not be addressed in this chapter as the focus here is only on the semantics of degrees of belief. Chapter 4 will deal with these issues directly by proposing the Bayesian network as a tool for efficiently representing the joint probability distribution.

3.2.1 Properties of beliefs

We will now establish some properties of degrees of belief (henceforth, beliefs). First, a bound on the belief in any sentence:

$$0 \leq \Pr(\alpha) \leq 1 \qquad \text{for any sentence } \alpha. \tag{3.2}$$

This follows since every degree of belief must be in $[0, 1]$, leading to $0 \leq \Pr(\alpha)$, and since the beliefs assigned to all worlds must add up to 1, leading to $\Pr(\alpha) \leq 1$. The second property is a baseline for inconsistent sentences:

$$\Pr(\alpha) = 0 \qquad \text{when } \alpha \text{ is inconsistent.} \tag{3.3}$$

This follows since there are no worlds that satisfy an inconsistent sentence α. The third property is a baseline for valid sentences:

$$\Pr(\alpha) = 1 \qquad \text{when } \alpha \text{ is valid.} \tag{3.4}$$

This follows since a valid sentence α is satisfied by every world.

The following property allows one to compute the belief in a sentence given the belief in its negation:

$$\Pr(\alpha) + \Pr(\neg\alpha) = 1. \tag{3.5}$$

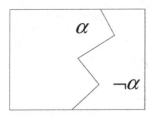

Figure 3.1: The worlds that satisfy α and those that satisfy $\neg\alpha$ form a partition of the set of all worlds.

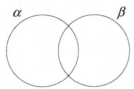

Figure 3.2: The worlds that satisfy $\alpha \vee \beta$ can be partitioned into three sets, those satisfying $\alpha \wedge \neg\beta$, $\neg\alpha \wedge \beta$, and $\alpha \wedge \beta$.

This follows because every world must either satisfy α or satisfy $\neg\alpha$ but cannot satisfy both (see Figure 3.1). Consider Table 3.1 for an example and let α : Burglary. We then have

$$\Pr(\text{Burglary}) = \Pr(\omega_1) + \Pr(\omega_2) + \Pr(\omega_5) + \Pr(\omega_6) = .2$$

$$\Pr(\neg\text{Burglary}) = \Pr(\omega_3) + \Pr(\omega_4) + \Pr(\omega_7) + \Pr(\omega_8) = .8$$

The next property allows us to compute the belief in a disjunction:

$$\Pr(\alpha \vee \beta) = \Pr(\alpha) + \Pr(\beta) - \Pr(\alpha \wedge \beta). \tag{3.6}$$

This identity is best seen by examining Figure 3.2. If we simply add $\Pr(\alpha)$ and $\Pr(\beta)$, we end up summing the beliefs in worlds that satisfy $\alpha \wedge \beta$ twice. Hence, by subtracting $\Pr(\alpha \wedge \beta)$ we end up accounting for the belief in every world that satisfies $\alpha \vee \beta$ only once.

Consider Table 3.1 for an example and let α : Earthquake and β : Burglary. We then have

$$\Pr(\text{Earthquake}) = \Pr(\omega_1) + \Pr(\omega_2) + \Pr(\omega_3) + \Pr(\omega_4) = .1$$

$$\Pr(\text{Burglary}) = \Pr(\omega_1) + \Pr(\omega_2) + \Pr(\omega_5) + \Pr(\omega_6) = .2$$

$$\Pr(\text{Earthquake} \wedge \text{Burglary}) = \Pr(\omega_1) + \Pr(\omega_2) = .02$$

$$\Pr(\text{Earthquake} \vee \text{Burglary}) = .1 + .2 - .02 = .28$$

The belief in a disjunction $\alpha \vee \beta$ can sometimes be computed directly from the belief in α and the belief in β:

$$\Pr(\alpha \vee \beta) = \Pr(\alpha) + \Pr(\beta) \quad \text{when } \alpha \text{ and } \beta \text{ are mutually exclusive.}$$

In this case, there is no world that satisfies both α and β. Hence, $\alpha \wedge \beta$ is inconsistent and $\Pr(\alpha \wedge \beta) = 0$.

3.2.2 Quantifying uncertainty

Consider the beliefs associated with variables in the previous example:

	Earthquake	Burglary	Alarm
true	.1	.2	.2442
false	.9	.8	.7558

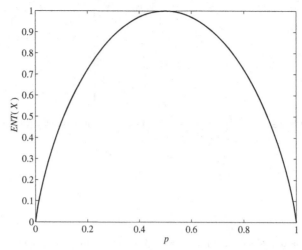

Figure 3.3: The entropy for a binary variable X with $\Pr(X) = p$.

Intuitively, these beliefs seem most certain about whether an earthquake has occurred and least certain about whether an alarm has triggered. One can formally quantify uncertainty about a variable X using the notion of *entropy:*

$$\mathrm{ENT}(X) \overset{def}{=} -\sum_{x} \Pr(x) \log_2 \Pr(x),$$

where $0 \log 0 = 0$ by convention. The following values are the entropies associated with the prior variables:

	Earthquake	Burglary	Alarm
true	.1	.2	.2442
false	.9	.8	.7558
ENT(.)	.469	.722	.802

Figure 3.3 plots the entropy for a binary variable X and varying values of $p = \Pr(X)$. Entropy is non-negative. When $p = 0$ or $p = 1$, the entropy of X is zero and at a minimum, indicating no uncertainty about the value of X. When $p = \frac{1}{2}$, we have $\Pr(X) = \Pr(\neg X)$ and the entropy is at a maximum, indicating complete uncertainty about the value of variable X (see Appendix B).

3.3 Updating beliefs

Consider again the state of belief in Table 3.1 and suppose that we now know that the alarm has triggered, Alarm = true. This piece of information is not compatible with the state of belief that ascribes a belief of .2442 to the Alarm being true. Therefore, we now need to update the state of belief to accommodate this new piece of information, which we will refer to as *evidence*. More generally, evidence will be represented by an arbitrary event, say, β and our goal is to update the state of belief $\Pr(.)$ into a new state of belief, which we will denote by $\Pr(.|\beta)$.

Given that β is known for sure, we expect the new state of belief $\Pr(.|\beta)$ to assign a belief of 1 to β: $\Pr(\beta|\beta) = 1$. This immediately implies that $\Pr(\neg\beta|\beta) = 0$ and, hence, every world ω that satisfies $\neg\beta$ must be assigned the belief 0:

$$\Pr(\omega|\beta) = 0 \quad \text{for all } \omega \models \neg\beta. \tag{3.7}$$

Table 3.2: A state of belief and the result of conditioning it on evidence Alarm.

world	Earthquake	Burglary	Alarm	Pr(.)	Pr(.|Alarm)
ω_1	true	true	true	.0190	.0190/.2442
ω_2	true	true	false	.0010	0
ω_3	true	false	true	.0560	.0560/.2442
ω_4	true	false	false	.0240	0
ω_5	false	true	true	.1620	.1620/.2442
ω_6	false	true	false	.0180	0
ω_7	false	false	true	.0072	.0072/.2442
ω_8	false	false	false	.7128	0

To completely define the new state of belief $\Pr(.|\beta)$, all we have to do then is define the new belief in every world ω that satisfies β. We already know that the sum of all such beliefs must be 1:

$$\sum_{\omega \models \beta} \Pr(\omega|\beta) = 1. \tag{3.8}$$

But this leaves us with many options for $\Pr(\omega|\beta)$ when world ω satisfies β. Since evidence β tells us nothing about worlds that satisfy β, it is then reasonable to perturb our beliefs in such worlds as little as possible. To this end, we will insist that worlds that have zero probability will continue to have zero probability:

$$\Pr(\omega|\beta) = 0 \quad \text{for all } \omega \text{ where } \Pr(\omega) = 0. \tag{3.9}$$

As for worlds that have a positive probability, we will insist that our relative beliefs in these worlds stay the same:

$$\frac{\Pr(\omega)}{\Pr(\omega')} = \frac{\Pr(\omega|\beta)}{\Pr(\omega'|\beta)} \quad \text{for all } \omega, \omega' \models \beta, \Pr(\omega) > 0, \Pr(\omega') > 0. \tag{3.10}$$

The constraints expressed by (3.8)–(3.10) leave us with only one option for the new beliefs in worlds that satisfy the evidence β:

$$\Pr(\omega|\beta) = \frac{\Pr(\omega)}{\Pr(\beta)} \quad \text{for all } \omega \models \beta.$$

That is, the new beliefs in such worlds are just the result of normalizing our old beliefs, with the normalization constant being our old belief in the evidence, $\Pr(\beta)$. Our new state of belief is now completely defined:

$$\Pr(\omega|\beta) \stackrel{def}{=} \begin{cases} 0, & \text{if } \omega \models \neg\beta \\ \dfrac{\Pr(\omega)}{\Pr(\beta)} & \text{if } \omega \models \beta. \end{cases} \tag{3.11}$$

The new state of belief $\Pr(.|\beta)$ is referred to as the result of *conditioning* the old state Pr on evidence β.

Consider now the state of belief in Table 3.1 and suppose that the evidence is Alarm = true. The result of conditioning this state of belief on this evidence is given in Table 3.2. Let us now examine some of the changes in beliefs that are induced by this new evidence. First, our belief in Burglary increases:

$$\Pr(\text{Burglary}) \quad = \quad .2$$
$$\Pr(\text{Burglary}|\text{Alarm}) \quad \approx \quad .741 \uparrow$$

and so does our belief in Earthquake:

$$Pr(\text{Earthquake}) \quad = \quad .1$$
$$Pr(\text{Earthquake}|\text{Alarm}) \quad \approx \quad .307 \uparrow$$

One can derive a simple closed form for the updated belief in an arbitrary sentence α given evidence β without having to explicitly compute the belief $Pr(\omega|\beta)$ for every world ω. The derivation is as follows:

$$Pr(\alpha|\beta)$$
$$= \sum_{\omega \models \alpha} Pr(\omega|\beta) \quad \text{by (3.1)}$$
$$= \sum_{\omega \models \alpha,\, \omega \models \beta} Pr(\omega|\beta) + \sum_{\omega \models \alpha,\, \omega \models \neg\beta} Pr(\omega|\beta) \quad \text{since } \omega \text{ satisfies } \beta \text{ or } \neg\beta \text{ but not both}$$
$$= \sum_{\omega \models \alpha,\, \omega \models \beta} Pr(\omega|\beta) \quad \text{by (3.11)}$$
$$= \sum_{\omega \models \alpha \wedge \beta} Pr(\omega|\beta) \quad \text{by properties of } \models$$
$$= \sum_{\omega \models \alpha \wedge \beta} Pr(\omega)/Pr(\beta) \quad \text{by (3.11)}$$
$$= \frac{1}{Pr(\beta)} \sum_{\omega \models \alpha \wedge \beta} Pr(\omega)$$
$$= \frac{Pr(\alpha \wedge \beta)}{Pr(\beta)} \quad \text{by (3.1).}$$

The closed form,

$$Pr(\alpha|\beta) = \frac{Pr(\alpha \wedge \beta)}{Pr(\beta)}, \tag{3.12}$$

is known as *Bayes conditioning*. Note that the updated state of belief $Pr(.|\beta)$ is defined only when $Pr(\beta) \neq 0$. We will usually avoid stating this condition explicitly in the future but it should be implicitly assumed.

To summarize, Bayes conditioning follows from the following commitments:

1. Worlds that contradict the evidence β will have zero probability.
2. Worlds that have zero probability continue to have zero probability.
3. Worlds that are consistent with evidence β and have positive probability will maintain their relative beliefs.

Let us now use Bayes conditioning to further examine some of the belief dynamics in our previous example. In particular, here is how some beliefs would change upon accepting the evidence Earthquake:

$$Pr(\text{Burglary}) \quad = \quad .2$$
$$Pr(\text{Burglary}|\text{Earthquake}) \quad = \quad .2$$

$$Pr(\text{Alarm}) \quad = \quad .2442$$
$$Pr(\text{Alarm}|\text{Earthquake}) \quad \approx \quad .75 \uparrow$$

That is, the belief in Burglary is not changed but the belief in Alarm increases. Here are some more belief changes as a reaction to the evidence Burglary:

$$
\begin{aligned}
\text{Pr(Alarm)} &= .2442 \\
\text{Pr(Alarm}|\text{Burglary)} &\approx .905 \uparrow \\[6pt]
\text{Pr(Earthquake)} &= .1 \\
\text{Pr(Earthquake}|\text{Burglary)} &= .1
\end{aligned}
$$

The belief in Alarm increases in this case but the belief in Earthquake stays the same.

The belief dynamics presented here are a property of the state of belief in Table 3.1 and may not hold for other states of beliefs. For example, one can conceive of a reasonable state of belief in which information about Earthquake would change the belief about Burglary and vice versa. One of the central questions in building automated reasoning systems is that of synthesizing states of beliefs that are *faithful*, that is, those that correspond to the beliefs held by some human expert. The Bayesian network, which we introduce in the following chapter, can be viewed as a modeling tool for synthesizing faithful states of beliefs.

Let us look at one more example of belief change. We know that the belief in Burglary increases when accepting the evidence Alarm. The question, however, is how would such a belief further change upon obtaining more evidence? Here is what happens when we get a confirmation that an Earthquake took place:

$$
\begin{aligned}
\text{Pr(Burglary}|\text{Alarm)} &\approx .741 \\
\text{Pr(Burglary}|\text{Alarm} \wedge \text{Earthquake)} &\approx .253 \downarrow
\end{aligned}
$$

That is, our belief in a Burglary decreases in this case as we now have an explanation of Alarm. On the other hand, if we get a confirmation that there was no Earthquake, our belief in Burglary increases even further:

$$
\begin{aligned}
\text{Pr(Burglary}|\text{Alarm)} &\approx .741 \\
\text{Pr(Burglary}|\text{Alarm} \wedge \neg\text{Earthquake)} &\approx .957 \uparrow
\end{aligned}
$$

as this new evidence further establishes burglary as the explanation for the triggered alarm.

Some of the belief dynamics we have observed in the previous examples are not accidental but are guaranteed by the method used to construct the state of belief in Table 3.1. More details on these guarantees are given in Chapter 4 when we introduce Bayesian networks.

One can define the *conditional entropy* of a variable X given another variable Y to quantify the average uncertainty about the value of X after observing the value of Y:

$$
\text{ENT}(X|Y) \overset{def}{=} \sum_{y} \text{Pr}(y)\text{ENT}(X|y),
$$

where

$$
\text{ENT}(X|y) \overset{def}{=} -\sum_{x} \text{Pr}(x|y) \log_2 \text{Pr}(x|y).
$$

One can show that the entropy never increases after conditioning:

$$
\text{ENT}(X|Y) \le \text{ENT}(X),
$$

that is, on average, observing the value of Y reduces our uncertainty about X. However, for a particular value y we may have $\text{ENT}(X|y) > \text{ENT}(X)$. The following are some entropies for the variable Burglary in our previous example:

	Burglary	Burglary|Alarm=true	Burglary|Alarm=false
true	.2	.741	.025
false	.8	.259	.975
ENT(.)	.722	.825	.169

The prior entropy for this variable is $\text{ENT}(\text{Burglary}) = .722$. Its entropy is .825 after observing Alarm=true (increased uncertainty), and .169 after observing Alarm=false (decreased uncertainty). The conditional entropy of variable Burglary given variable Alarm is then

$$\text{ENT}(\text{Burglary}|\text{Alarm}) = \text{ENT}(\text{Burglary}|\text{Alarm}=\text{true})\text{Pr}(\text{Alarm}=\text{true})$$
$$+ \text{ENT}(\text{Burglary}|\text{Alarm}=\text{false})\text{Pr}(\text{Alarm}=\text{false})$$
$$= .329,$$

indicating a decrease in the uncertainty about variable Burglary.

3.4 Independence

According to the state of belief in Table 3.1, the evidence Burglary does not change the belief in Earthquake:

$$\text{Pr}(\text{Earthquake}) \quad = \quad .1$$
$$\text{Pr}(\text{Earthquake}|\text{Burglary}) \quad = \quad .1$$

Hence, we say in this case that the state of belief Pr finds the Earthquake event independent of the Burglary event. More generally, we say that Pr finds event α *independent* of event β iff

$$\text{Pr}(\alpha|\beta) = \text{Pr}(\alpha) \quad \text{or } \text{Pr}(\beta) = 0. \tag{3.13}$$

Note that the state of belief in Table 3.1 also finds Burglary independent of Earthquake:

$$\text{Pr}(\text{Burglary}) \quad = \quad .2$$
$$\text{Pr}(\text{Burglary}|\text{Earthquake}) \quad = \quad .2$$

It is indeed a general property that Pr must find event α independent of event β if it also finds β independent of α. Independence satisfies other interesting properties that we explore in later chapters.

Independence provides a general condition under which the belief in a conjunction $\alpha \wedge \beta$ can be expressed in terms of the belief in α and that in β. Specifically, Pr finds α independent of β iff

$$\text{Pr}(\alpha \wedge \beta) = \text{Pr}(\alpha)\text{Pr}(\beta). \tag{3.14}$$

This equation is sometimes taken as the definition of independence, whereas (3.13) is viewed as a consequence. We use (3.14) when we want to stress the symmetry between α and β in the definition of independence.

It is important here to stress the difference between independence and logical disjointness (mutual exclusiveness), as it is common to mix up these two notions. Recall that

Table 3.3: A state of belief.

world	Temp	Sensor1	Sensor2	Pr(.)
ω_1	normal	normal	normal	.576
ω_2	normal	normal	extreme	.144
ω_3	normal	extreme	normal	.064
ω_4	normal	extreme	extreme	.016
ω_5	extreme	normal	normal	.008
ω_6	extreme	normal	extreme	.032
ω_7	extreme	extreme	normal	.032
ω_8	extreme	extreme	extreme	.128

two events α and β are logically disjoint (mutually exclusive) iff they do not share any models: $Mods(\alpha) \cap Mods(\beta) = \emptyset$, that is, they cannot hold together at the same world. On the other hand, events α and β are independent iff $\Pr(\alpha \wedge \beta) = \Pr(\alpha)\Pr(\beta)$. Note that disjointness is an objective property of events, while independence is a property of beliefs. Hence, two individuals with different beliefs may disagree on whether two events are independent but they cannot disagree on their logical disjointness.[1]

3.4.1 Conditional independence

Independence is a dynamic notion. One may find two events independent at some point but then find them dependent after obtaining some evidence. For example, we have seen how the state of belief in Table 3.1 finds Burglary independent of Earthquake. However, this state of belief finds these events dependent on each other after accepting the evidence Alarm:

$$\Pr(\text{Burglary}|\text{Alarm}) \quad\quad \approx \ .741$$
$$\Pr(\text{Burglary}|\text{Alarm} \wedge \text{Earthquake}) \ \approx \ .253$$

That is, Earthquake changes the belief in Burglary in the presence of Alarm. Intuitively, this is to be expected since Earthquake and Burglary are competing explanations for Alarm, so confirming one of these explanations tends to reduce our belief in the second explanation.

Consider the state of belief in Table 3.3 for another example. Here we have three variables. First, we have the variable Temp, which represents the state of temperature as being either normal or extreme. We also have two sensors, Sensor1 and Sensor2, which can detect these two states of temperature. The sensors are noisy and have different reliabilities. According to this state of belief, we have the following initial beliefs:

$$\Pr(\text{Temp} = \text{normal}) = .80$$
$$\Pr(\text{Sensor1} = \text{normal}) = .76$$
$$\Pr(\text{Sensor2} = \text{normal}) = .68$$

Suppose that we check the first sensor and it is reading normal. Our belief in the second sensor reading normal would then increase as expected:

$$\Pr(\text{Sensor2} = \text{normal}|\text{Sensor1} = \text{normal}) \approx .768 \uparrow$$

---

[1] It is possible however for one state of belief to assign a zero probability to the event $\alpha \wedge \beta$ even though α and β are not mutually exclusive on a logical basis.

Hence, our beliefs in these sensor readings are initially dependent. However, these beliefs will become independent if we observe that the temperature is normal:

$$\text{Pr(Sensor2} = \text{normal}|\text{Temp} = \text{normal}) = .80$$

$$\text{Pr(Sensor2} = \text{normal}|\text{Temp} = \text{normal, Sensor1} = \text{normal}) = .80$$

Therefore, even though the sensor readings were initially dependent they become independent once we know the state of temperature.

In general, independent events may become dependent given new evidence and, similarly, dependent events may become independent given new evidence. This calls for the following more general definition of independence. We say that state of belief Pr finds event α *conditionally independent* of event β given event γ iff

$$\Pr(\alpha|\beta \wedge \gamma) = \Pr(\alpha|\gamma) \quad \text{or } \Pr(\beta \wedge \gamma) = 0. \tag{3.15}$$

That is, in the presence of evidence γ the additional evidence β will not change the belief in α. Conditional independence is also symmetric: α is conditionally independent of β given γ iff β is conditionally independent of α given γ. This is best seen from the following equation, which is equivalent to (3.15):

$$\Pr(\alpha \wedge \beta|\gamma) = \Pr(\alpha|\gamma)\Pr(\beta|\gamma) \quad \text{or } \Pr(\gamma) = 0. \tag{3.16}$$

Equation (3.16) is sometimes used as the definition of conditional independence between α and β given γ. We use (3.16) when we want to emphasize the symmetry of independence.

3.4.2 Variable independence

We will find it useful to talk about independence between sets of variables. In particular, let **X**, **Y**, and **Z** be three disjoint sets of variables. We will say that a state of belief Pr finds **X** independent of **Y** given **Z**, denoted $I_{\Pr}(\mathbf{X}, \mathbf{Z}, \mathbf{Y})$, to mean that Pr finds **x** independent of **y** given **z** for all instantiations **x**, **y**, and **z**.

Suppose for example that $\mathbf{X} = \{A, B\}$, $\mathbf{Y} = \{C\}$, and $\mathbf{Z} = \{D, E\}$, where $A, B, C, D,$ and E are all propositional variables. The statement $I_{\Pr}(\mathbf{X}, \mathbf{Z}, \mathbf{Y})$ is then a compact notation for a number of statements about independence:

$$A \wedge B \text{ is independent of } C \text{ given } D \wedge E.$$

$$A \wedge \neg B \text{ is independent of } C \text{ given } D \wedge E.$$

$$\vdots$$

$$\neg A \wedge \neg B \text{ is independent of } \neg C \text{ given } \neg D \wedge \neg E.$$

That is, $I_{\Pr}(\mathbf{X}, \mathbf{Z}, \mathbf{Y})$ is a compact notation for $4 \times 2 \times 4 = 32$ independence statements of this form.

3.4.3 Mutual information

The notion of independence is a special case of a more general notion known as *mutual information*, which quantifies the impact of observing one variable on the uncertainty in another:

$$\text{MI}(X; Y) \stackrel{\text{def}}{=} \sum_{x,y} \Pr(x, y) \log_2 \frac{\Pr(x, y)}{\Pr(x)\Pr(y)}.$$

Mutual information is non-negative and equal to zero if and only if variables X and Y are independent. More generally, mutual information measures the extent to which observing one variable will reduce the uncertainty in another:

$$MI(X; Y) = ENT(X) - ENT(X|Y)$$
$$= ENT(Y) - ENT(Y|X).$$

Conditional mutual information can also be defined as follows:

$$MI(X; Y|Z) \stackrel{def}{=} \sum_{x,y,z} Pr(x, y, z) \log_2 \frac{Pr(x, y|z)}{Pr(x|z)Pr(y|z)},$$

leading to

$$MI(X; Y|Z) = ENT(X|Z) - ENT(X|Y, Z)$$
$$= ENT(Y|Z) - ENT(Y|X, Z).$$

Entropy and mutual information can be extended to sets of variables in the obvious way. For example, entropy can be generalized to a set of variables $\mathbf{X}$ as follows:

$$ENT(\mathbf{X}) = - \sum_{\mathbf{x}} Pr(\mathbf{x}) \log_2 Pr(\mathbf{x}).$$

3.5 Further properties of beliefs

We will discuss in this section more properties of beliefs that are commonly used. We start with the *chain rule:*

$$Pr(\alpha_1 \wedge \alpha_2 \wedge \ldots \wedge \alpha_n) = Pr(\alpha_1|\alpha_2 \wedge \ldots \wedge \alpha_n)Pr(\alpha_2|\alpha_3 \wedge \ldots \wedge \alpha_n) \ldots Pr(\alpha_n).$$

This rule follows from a repeated application of Bayes conditioning (3.11). We will find a major use of the chain rule when discussing Bayesian networks in Chapter 4.

The next important property of beliefs is *case analysis,* also known as the *law of total probability:*

$$Pr(\alpha) = \sum_{i=1}^{n} Pr(\alpha \wedge \beta_i), \tag{3.17}$$

where the events $\beta_1, \ldots, \beta_n$ are mutually exclusive and exhaustive.[2] Case analysis holds because the models of $\alpha \wedge \beta_1, \ldots, \alpha \wedge \beta_n$ form a partition of the models of α. Intuitively, case analysis says that we can compute the belief in event α by adding up our beliefs in a number of mutually exclusive cases, $\alpha \wedge \beta_1, \ldots, \alpha \wedge \beta_n$, that cover the conditions under which α holds.

Another version of case analysis is

$$Pr(\alpha) = \sum_{i=1}^{n} Pr(\alpha|\beta_i)Pr(\beta_i), \tag{3.18}$$

where the events $\beta_1, \ldots, \beta_n$ are mutually exclusive and exhaustive. This version is obtained from the first by applying Bayes conditioning. It calls for considering a number of mutually exclusive and exhaustive cases, $\beta_1, \ldots, \beta_n$, computing our belief in α under

---

[2] That is, $Mods(\beta_j) \cap Mods(\beta_k) = \emptyset$ for $j \neq k$ and $\bigcup_{i=1}^{n} Mods(\beta_i) = \Omega$, where Ω is the set of all worlds.

each of these cases, $\Pr(\alpha|\beta_i)$, and then summing these beliefs after applying the weight of each case, $\Pr(\beta_i)$.

Two simple and useful forms of case analysis are

$$\Pr(\alpha) = \Pr(\alpha \wedge \beta) + \Pr(\alpha \wedge \neg\beta)$$
$$\Pr(\alpha) = \Pr(\alpha|\beta)\Pr(\beta) + \Pr(\alpha|\neg\beta)\Pr(\neg\beta).$$

These equations hold because β and $\neg\beta$ are mutually exclusive and exhaustive. The main value of case analysis is that in many situations, computing our beliefs in the cases is easier than computing our beliefs in α. We see many examples of this phenomena in later chapters.

The last property of beliefs we consider is known as *Bayes rule* or *Bayes theorem:*

$$\Pr(\alpha|\beta) = \frac{\Pr(\beta|\alpha)\Pr(\alpha)}{\Pr(\beta)}. \tag{3.19}$$

The classical usage of this rule is when event α is perceived to be a cause of event β – for example, α is a disease and β is a symptom – and our goal is to assess our belief in the cause given the effect. The belief in an effect given its cause, $\Pr(\beta|\alpha)$, is usually more readily available than the belief in a cause given one of its effects, $\Pr(\alpha|\beta)$. Bayes theorem allows us to compute the latter from the former.

To consider an example of Bayes rule, suppose that we have a patient who was just tested for a particular disease and the test came out positive. We know that one in every thousand people has this disease. We also know that the test is not reliable: it has a false positive rate of 2% and a false negative rate of 5%. Our goal is then to assess our belief in the patient having the disease given that the test came out positive. If we let the propositional variable D stand for "the patient has the disease" and the propositional variable T stand for "the test came out positive," our goal is then to compute $\Pr(D|T)$.

From the given information, we know that

$$\Pr(D) = \frac{1}{1,000}$$

since one in every thousand has the disease – this is our prior belief in the patient having the disease before we run any tests. Since the false positive rate of the test is 2%, we know that

$$\Pr(T|\neg D) = \frac{2}{100}$$

and by (3.5),

$$\Pr(\neg T|\neg D) = \frac{98}{100}.$$

Similarly, since the false negative rate of the test is 5%, we know that

$$\Pr(\neg T|D) = \frac{5}{100}$$

and

$$\Pr(T|D) = \frac{95}{100}.$$

Using Bayes rule, we now have

$$Pr(D|T) = \frac{\dfrac{95}{100} \times \dfrac{1}{1,000}}{Pr(T)}.$$

The belief in the test coming out positive for an individual, $Pr(T)$, is not readily available but can be computed using case analysis:

$$Pr(T) = Pr(T|D)Pr(D) + Pr(T|\neg D)Pr(\neg D)$$

$$= \frac{95}{100} \times \frac{1}{1,000} + \frac{2}{100} \times \frac{999}{1,000} = \frac{2,093}{100,000},$$

which leads to

$$Pr(D|T) = \frac{95}{2,093} \approx 4.5\%.$$

Another way to solve this problem is to construct the state of belief completely and then use it to answer queries. This is feasible in this case because we have only two events of interest, T and D, leading to only four worlds:

world	D	T	
ω_1	true	true	has disease, test positive
ω_2	true	false	has disease, test negative
ω_3	false	true	has no disease, test positive
ω_4	false	false	has no disease, test negative

If we obtain the belief in each one of these worlds, we can then compute the belief in any sentence mechanically using (3.1) and (3.12). To compute the beliefs in these worlds, we use the chain rule:

$$Pr(\omega_1) = Pr(T \wedge D) = Pr(T|D)Pr(D)$$

$$Pr(\omega_2) = Pr(\neg T \wedge D) = Pr(\neg T|D)Pr(D)$$

$$Pr(\omega_3) = Pr(T \wedge \neg D) = Pr(T|\neg D)Pr(\neg D)$$

$$Pr(\omega_4) = Pr(\neg T \wedge \neg D) = Pr(\neg T|\neg D)Pr(\neg D).$$

All of these quantities are available directly from the problem statement, leading to the following state of belief:

world	D	T	$Pr(.)$			
ω_1	true	true	$95/100$	$\times$	$1/1,000$	$= .00095$
ω_2	true	false	$5/100$	$\times$	$1/1,000$	$= .00005$
ω_3	false	true	$2/100$	$\times$	$999/1,000$	$= .01998$
ω_4	false	false	$98/100$	$\times$	$999/1,000$	$= .97902$

3.6 Soft evidence

There are two types of evidence that one may encounter: hard evidence and soft evidence. *Hard evidence* is information to the effect that some event has occurred, which is also the type of evidence we have considered previously. *Soft evidence,* on the other hand, is not conclusive: we may get an unreliable testimony that event β occurred, which may increase our belief in β but not to the point where we would consider it certain. For example, our neighbor who is known to have a hearing problem may call to tell us they heard the alarm trigger in our home. Such a call may not be used to categorically confirm the event Alarm but can still increase our belief in Alarm to some new level.

One of the key issues relating to soft evidence is how to specify its strength. There are two main methods for this, which we discuss next.

3.6.1 The "all things considered" method

One method for specifying soft evidence on event β is by stating the new belief in β after the evidence has been accommodated. For example, we would say "after receiving my neighbor's call, my belief in the alarm triggering stands now at .85." Formally, we are specifying soft evidence as a constraint $\Pr'(\beta) = q$, where $\Pr'$ denotes the new state of belief after accommodating the evidence and β is the event to which the evidence pertains. This is sometimes known as the "all things considered" method since the new belief in β depends not only on the strength of evidence but also on our initial beliefs that existed before the evidence was obtained. That is, the statement $\Pr'(\beta) = q$ is not a statement about the strength of evidence per se but about the result of its integration with our initial beliefs.

Given this method of specifying evidence, computing the new state of belief $\Pr'$ can be done along the same principles we used for Bayes conditioning. In particular, suppose that we obtain some soft evidence on event β that leads us to change our belief in β to q. Since this evidence imposes the constraint $\Pr'(\beta) = q$, it will also impose the additional constraint $\Pr'(\neg\beta) = 1 - q$. Therefore, we know that we must change the beliefs in worlds that satisfy β so these beliefs add up to q. We also know that we must change the beliefs in worlds that satisfy $\neg\beta$ so they add up to $1 - q$. Again, if we insist on preserving the relative beliefs in worlds that satisfy β and also on preserving the relative beliefs in worlds that satisfy $\neg\beta$, we find ourselves committed to the following definition of $\Pr'$:

$$\Pr'(\omega) \stackrel{def}{=} \begin{cases} \dfrac{q}{\Pr(\beta)}\Pr(\omega), & \text{if } \omega \models \beta \\[2ex] \dfrac{1-q}{\Pr(\neg\beta)}\Pr(\omega), & \text{if } \omega \models \neg\beta. \end{cases} \tag{3.20}$$

That is, we effectively have to scale our beliefs in the worlds satisfying β using the constant $q/\Pr(\beta)$ and similarly for the worlds satisfying $\neg\beta$. All we are doing here is normalizing the beliefs in worlds that satisfy β and similarly for the worlds that satisfy $\neg\beta$ so they add up to the desired quantities q and $1 - q$, respectively.

There is also a useful closed form for the definition in (3.20), which can be derived similarly to (3.12):

$$\Pr'(\alpha) = q\Pr(\alpha|\beta) + (1 - q)\Pr(\alpha|\neg\beta), \tag{3.21}$$

where $\Pr'$ is the new state of belief after accommodating the soft evidence $\Pr'(\beta) = q$. This method of updating a state of belief in the face of soft evidence is known as *Jeffrey's rule*. Note that Bayes conditioning is a special case of Jeffrey's rule when $q = 1$, which is to be expected as they were both derived using the same principle.

Jeffrey's rule has a simple generalization to the case where the evidence concerns a set of mutually exclusive and exhaustive events, $\beta_1, \ldots, \beta_n$, with the new beliefs in these events being $q_1, \ldots, q_n$, respectively. This soft evidence can be accommodated using the following generalization of Jeffrey's rule:

$$\Pr'(\alpha) = \sum_{i=1}^{n} q_i \Pr(\alpha | \beta_i). \tag{3.22}$$

Consider the following example, due to Jeffrey. Assume that we are given a piece of cloth C where its color can be one of green (c_g), blue (c_b), or violet (c_v). We want to know whether the next day the cloth will be sold (s) or not sold ($\bar{s}$). Our original state of belief is as follows:

worlds	S	C	Pr(.)
ω_1	s	c_g	.12
ω_2	$\bar{s}$	c_g	.18
ω_3	s	c_b	.12
ω_4	$\bar{s}$	c_b	.18
ω_5	s	c_v	.32
ω_6	$\bar{s}$	c_v	.08

Therefore, our original belief in the cloth being sold is $\Pr(s) = .56$. Moreover, our original beliefs in the colors c_g, c_b, and c_v are .3, .3, and .4, respectively. Assume that we now inspect the cloth by candlelight and we conclude that our new beliefs in these colors should be .7, .25, and .05, respectively. If we apply Jeffrey's rule as given by (3.22), we get

$$\Pr'(s) = .7 \left(\frac{.12}{.3} \right) + .25 \left(\frac{.12}{.3} \right) + .05 \left(\frac{.32}{.4} \right) = .42$$

The full new state of belief according to Jeffrey's rule is

worlds	S	C	Pr'(.)
ω_1	s	c_g	$.28 = .12 \times .7/.3$
ω_2	$\bar{s}$	c_g	$.42 = .18 \times .7/.3$
ω_3	s	c_b	$.10 = .12 \times .25/.3$
ω_4	$\bar{s}$	c_b	$.15 = .18 \times .25/.3$
ω_5	s	c_v	$.04 = .32 \times .05/.4$
ω_6	$\bar{s}$	c_v	$.01 = .08 \times .05/.4$

Note how the new belief in each world is simply a scaled version of the old belief with three different scaling constants corresponding to the three events on which the soft evidence bears.

3.6.2 The "nothing else considered" method

The second method for specifying soft evidence on event β is based on declaring the strength of this evidence independently of currently held beliefs. In particular, let us define the *odds* of event β as follows:

$$O(\beta) \stackrel{def}{=} \frac{\Pr(\beta)}{\Pr(\neg \beta)}. \tag{3.23}$$

That is, an odds of 1 indicates that we believe β and $\neg \beta$ equally, while an odds of 10 indicates that we believe β ten times more than we believe $\neg \beta$.

Given the notion of odds, we can specify soft evidence on event β by declaring the relative change it induces on the odds of β, that is, by specifying the ratio

$$k = \frac{O'(\beta)}{O(\beta)},$$

where $O'(\beta)$ is the odds of β after accommodating the evidence, $\Pr'(\beta)/\Pr'(\neg\beta)$. The ratio k is known as the *Bayes factor*. Hence, a Bayes factor of 1 indicates neutral evidence and a Bayes factor of 2 indicates evidence on β that is strong enough to double the odds of β. As the Bayes factor tends to infinity, the soft evidence tends toward hard evidence confirming β. As the factor tends to zero, the soft evidence tends toward hard evidence refuting β. This method of specifying evidence is sometimes known as the "nothing else considered" method as it is a statement about the strength of evidence without any reference to the initial state of belief. This is shown formally in Section 3.6.4, where we show that a Bayes factor can be compatible with any initial state of belief.[3]

Suppose that we obtain soft evidence on β whose strength is given by a Bayes factor of k, and our goal is to compute the new state of belief $\Pr'$ that results from accommodating this evidence. If we are able to translate this evidence into a form that is accepted by Jeffrey's rule, then we can use that rule to compute $\Pr'$. This turns out to be possible, as we describe next. First, from the constraint $k = O'(\beta)/O(\beta)$ we get

$$\Pr'(\beta) = \frac{k\Pr(\beta)}{k\Pr(\beta) + \Pr(\neg\beta)}. \tag{3.24}$$

Hence, we can view this as a problem of updating the initial state of belief $\Pr$ using Jeffrey's rule and the soft evidence given previously. That is, what we have done is translate a "nothing else considered" specification of soft evidence – a constraint on $O'(\beta)/O(\beta)$ – into an "all things considered" specification – a constraint on $\Pr'(\beta)$. Computing $\Pr'$ using Jeffrey's rule as given by (3.21), and taking $\Pr'(\beta) = q$ as given by (3.24), we get

$$\Pr'(\alpha) = \frac{k\Pr(\alpha \wedge \beta) + \Pr(\alpha \wedge \neg\beta)}{k\Pr(\beta) + \Pr(\neg\beta)}, \tag{3.25}$$

where $\Pr'$ is the new state of belief after accommodating soft evidence on event β using a Bayes factor of k.

Consider the following example, which concerns the alarm of our house and the potential of a burglary. The initial state of belief is given by:

world	Alarm	Burglary	Pr(.)
ω_1	true	true	.000095
ω_2	true	false	.009999
ω_3	false	true	.000005
ω_4	false	false	.989901

One day, we receive a call from our neighbor saying that they may have heard the alarm of our house going off. Since our neighbor suffers from a hearing problem, we conclude that our neighbor's testimony increases the odds of the alarm going off by a factor of 4: $O'(\text{Alarm})/O(\text{Alarm}) = 4$. Our goal now is to compute our new belief in a burglary taking

---

[3] This is not true if we use ratios of probabilities instead of ratios of odds. For example, if we state that $\Pr'(\alpha)/\Pr(\alpha) = 2$, it must follow that $\Pr(\alpha) \leq 1/2$ since $\Pr'(\alpha) \leq 1$. Hence, the constraint $\Pr'(\alpha)/\Pr(\alpha) = 2$ is not compatible with every state of belief $\Pr$.

place, $\text{Pr}'(\text{Burglary})$. Using (3.25) with α : Burglary, β : Alarm and $k = 4$, we get

$$\text{Pr}'(\text{Burglary}) = \frac{4(.000095) + .000005}{4(.010094) + .989906} \approx 3.74 \times 10^{-4}.$$

3.6.3 More on specifying soft evidence

The difference between (3.21) and (3.25) is only in the way soft evidence is specified. In particular, (3.21) expects the evidence to be specified in terms of the final belief assigned to event β, $\text{Pr}'(\beta) = q$. On the other hand, (3.25) expects the evidence to be specified in terms of the relative effect it has on the odds of event β, $O'(\beta)/O(\beta) = k$.

To shed more light on the difference between the two methods of specifying soft evidence, consider a murder with three suspects: David, Dick, and Jane. Suppose that we have an investigator, Rich, with the following state of belief:

world	Killer	Pr(.)
ω_1	david	2/3
ω_2	dick	1/6
ω_3	jane	1/6

According to Rich, the odds of David being the killer is 2 since

$$O(\text{Killer} = \text{david}) = \frac{\text{Pr}(\text{Killer} = \text{david})}{\text{Pr}(\neg(\text{Killer} = \text{david}))} = 2.$$

Suppose that some new evidence turns up against David. Rich examines the evidence and makes the following statement: "This evidence triples the odds of David being the killer." Formally, we have soft evidence with the following strength (Bayes factor):

$$\frac{O'(\text{Killer} = \text{david})}{O(\text{Killer} = \text{david})} = 3.$$

Using (3.24), the new belief in David being the killer is

$$\text{Pr}'(\text{Killer} = \text{david}) = \frac{3 \times 2/3}{3 \times 2/3 + 1/3} = \frac{6}{7} \approx 86\%.$$

Hence, Rich could have specified the evidence in two ways by saying, "This evidence triples the odds of David being the killer" or "Accepting this evidence leads me to have an 86% belief that David is the killer." The first statement can be used with (3.25) to compute further beliefs of Rich; for example, his belief in Dick being the killer. The second statement can also be used for this purpose but with (3.21).

However, the difference between the two statements is that the first can be used by some other investigator to update their beliefs based on the new evidence, while the second statement cannot be used as such. Suppose that Jon is another investigator with the following state of belief, which is different from that held by Rich:

world	Killer	Pr(.)
ω_1	david	1/2
ω_2	dick	1/4
ω_3	jane	1/4

If Jon were to accept Rich's assessment that the evidence triples the odds of David being the killer, then using (3.24) Jon would now believe that:

$$\text{Pr}'(\text{Killer}=\text{david}) = \frac{3 \times 1/2}{3 \times 1/2 + 1/2} = \frac{3}{4} = 75\%.$$

Hence, the same evidence that raised Rich's belief from $\approx 67\%$ to $\approx 86\%$ also raised Jon's belief from 50% to 75%.

The second statement of Rich, "Accepting this evidence leads me to have about 86% belief that David is the killer," is not as meaningful to Jon as it cannot reveal the strength of evidence independently of Rich's initial beliefs (which we assume are not accessible to Jon). Hence, Jon cannot use this statement to update his own beliefs.

3.6.4 Soft evidence as a noisy sensor

One of the most concrete interpretations of soft evidence is in terms of noisy sensors. Not only is this interpretation useful in practice but it also helps shed more light on the strength of soft evidence as quantified by a Bayes factor.

The noisy sensor interpretation is as follows. Suppose that we have some soft evidence that bears on an event β. We can emulate the effect of this soft evidence using a noisy sensor S having two states, with the strength of soft evidence captured by the false positive and negative rates of the sensor:

- The false positive rate of the sensor, f_p, is the belief that the sensor would give a positive reading even though the event β did not occur, $\text{Pr}(S|\neg\beta)$.
- The false negative rate of the sensor, f_n, is the belief that the sensor would give a negative reading even though the event β did occur, $\text{Pr}(\neg S|\beta)$.

Suppose now that we have a sensor with these specifications and suppose that it reads positive. We want to know the new odds of β given this positive sensor reading. We have

$$
\begin{aligned}
O'(\beta) &= \frac{\text{Pr}'(\beta)}{\text{Pr}'(\neg\beta)} \\
&= \frac{\text{Pr}(\beta|S)}{\text{Pr}(\neg\beta|S)} \quad \text{emulating soft evidence by a positive sensor reading} \\
&= \frac{\text{Pr}(S|\beta)\text{Pr}(\beta)}{\text{Pr}(S|\neg\beta)\text{Pr}(\neg\beta)} \quad \text{by Bayes Theorem} \\
&= \frac{1-f_n}{f_p}\frac{\text{Pr}(\beta)}{\text{Pr}(\neg\beta)} \\
&= \frac{1-f_n}{f_p}O(\beta).
\end{aligned}
$$

This basically proves that the relative change in the odds of β, the Bayes factor $O'(\beta)/O(\beta)$, is indeed a function of only the false positive and negative rates of the sensor and is independent of the initial beliefs. More specifically, it shows that soft evidence with a Bayes factor of k^+ can be emulated by a positive sensor reading if the false positive and negative rates of the sensor satisfy

$$k^+ = \frac{1-f_n}{f_p}.$$

Interestingly, this equation shows that the specific false positive and negative rates are not as important as the above ratio. For example, a positive reading from any of the following sensors will have the same impact on beliefs:

- Sensor 1: $f_p = 10\%$ and $f_n = 5\%$
- Sensor 2: $f_p = 8\%$ and $f_n = 24\%$
- Sensor 3: $f_p = 5\%$ and $f_n = 52.5\%$.

This is because a positive reading from any of these sensors will increase the odds of a corresponding event by a factor of $k^+ = 9.5$.

Note that a negative sensor reading will not necessarily have the same impact for the different sensors. To see why, consider the Bayes factor corresponding to a negative reading using a similar derivation to what we have previously:

$$
\begin{aligned}
O'(\beta) &= \frac{\Pr'(\beta)}{\Pr'(\neg\beta)} \\
&= \frac{\Pr(\beta|\neg S)}{\Pr(\neg\beta|\neg S)} \quad \text{emulating soft evidence by a negative sensor reading} \\
&= \frac{\Pr(\neg S|\beta)\Pr(\beta)}{\Pr(\neg S|\neg\beta)\Pr(\neg\beta)} \quad \text{by Bayes Theorem} \\
&= \frac{f_n}{1-f_p}\frac{\Pr(\beta)}{\Pr(\neg\beta)} \\
&= \frac{f_n}{1-f_p}O(\beta).
\end{aligned}
$$

Therefore, a negative sensor reading corresponds to soft evidence with a Bayes factor of

$$
k^- = \frac{f_n}{1-f_p}.
$$

Even though all of the sensors have the same k^+, they have different k^- values. In particular, $k^- \approx .056$ for Sensor 1, $k^- \approx .261$ for Sensor 2, and $k^- \approx .553$ for Sensor 3. That is, although all negative sensor readings will decrease the odds of the corresponding hypothesis, they do so to different extents. In particular, a negative reading from Sensor 1 is stronger than one from Sensor 2, which in turn is stronger than one from Sensor 3.

Finally, note that as long as

$$
f_p + f_n < 1, \tag{3.26}
$$

then $k^+ > 1$ and $k^- < 1$. This means that a positive sensor reading is guaranteed to increase the odds of the corresponding event and a negative sensor reading is guaranteed to decrease those odds. The condition in (3.26) is satisfied when the false positive and false negative rates are less than 50% each, which is not unreasonable to assume for a sensor model. The condition however can also be satisfied even if one of the rates is $\geq 50\%$.

To conclude, we note that soft evidence on a hypothesis β can be specified using two main methods. The first specifies the final belief in β after accommodating the evidence and the second specifies the relative change in the odds of β due to accommodating the evidence. This relative change in odds is called the Bayes factor and can be thought of as providing a strength of evidence that can be interpreted independently of a given state of belief. Moreover, the accommodation of soft evidence by a Bayes factor can be emulated by a sensor reading. In particular, for any Bayes factor we can choose the false positive and negative rates of the sensor so its reading will have exactly the same effect on beliefs as that of the soft evidence. This emulation of soft evidence by hard evidence on an auxiliary variable is also known as the method of *virtual evidence.*

3.7 Continuous variables as soft evidence

We are mostly concerned with discrete variables in this book, that is, variables that take values from a finite, and typically small, set. The use of continuous variables can be essential in certain application areas but requires techniques that are generally outside the scope of this book. However, one of the most common applications of continuous variables can be accounted for using the notion of soft evidence, allowing one to address these applications while staying within the framework of discrete variables.

Consider for example a situation where one sends a bit (0 or 1) across a noisy channel that is then received at the channel output as a number in the interval $(-\infty, +\infty)$. Suppose further that our goal is to compute the probability of having sent a 0 given that we have observed the value, say, $-.1$ at the channel output. Generally, one would need two variables to model this problem: a discrete variable I (with two values 0 and 1) to represent the channel input and a continuous variable O to represent the channel output, with the goal of computing $\Pr(I=0|O=-.1)$. As we demonstrate in this section, one can avoid the continuous variable O as we can simply emulate hard evidence on this variable using soft evidence on the discrete variable I. Before we explain this common and practical technique, we need to provide some background on probability distributions over continuous variables.

3.7.1 Distribution and density functions

Suppose we have a continuous variable Y with values y in the interval $(-\infty, +\infty)$. The probability that Y will take any particular value y is usually zero, so we typically talk about the probability that Y will take a value $\leq y$. This is given by a *cumulative distribution function* (CDF) $F(y)$, where

$$F(y) = \Pr(Y \leq y).$$

A number of interesting CDFs do not have known closed forms but can be induced from *probability density functions* (PDF) $f(t)$ as follows:

$$F(y) = \int_{-\infty}^{y} f(t)dt.$$

For the function F to correspond to a CDF, we need the PDF to satisfy the conditions $f(t) \geq 0$ and $\int_{-\infty}^{+\infty} f(t)dt = 1$.

One of the most important density functions is the *Gaussian*, which is also known as the *Normal*:

$$f(t) = \frac{1}{\sqrt{2\pi\sigma^2}}e^{-(t-\mu)^2/2\sigma^2}.$$

Here μ is called the *mean* and σ is called the *standard deviation*. When $\mu = 0$ and $\sigma^2 = 1$, the density function is known as the *standard Normal*. It is known that if a variable Y has a

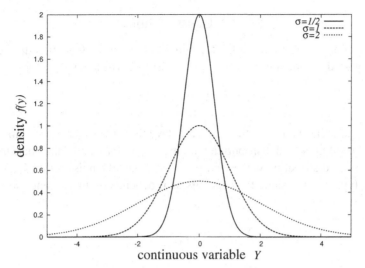

Figure 3.4: Three Gaussian density functions with mean $\mu = 0$ and standard deviations $\sigma = 1/2, \sigma = 1$, and $\sigma = 2$.

Normal density with mean μ and standard deviation σ, then the variable $Z = (Y - \mu)/\sigma$ will have a standard Normal density.

Figure 3.4 depicts a few Gaussian density functions with mean $\mu = 0$. Intuitively, the smaller the standard deviation the more concentrated the values around the mean. Hence, a smaller standard deviation implies less variation in the observed values of variable Y.

3.7.2 The Bayes factor of a continuous observation

Suppose that we have a binary variable X with values $\{x, \bar{x}\}$ and a continuous variable Y with values $y \in (-\infty, \infty)$. We next show that the conditional probability $\Pr(x|y)$ can be computed by asserting soft evidence on variable X whose strength is derived from the density functions $f(y|x)$ and $f(y|\bar{x})$. That is, we show that the hard evidence implied by observing the value of a continuous variable can always be emulated by soft evidence whose strength is derived from the density function of that continuous variable. This will then preempt the need for representing continuous variables explicitly in an otherwise discrete model.

We first observe that (see Exercise 3.26)

$$\frac{\Pr(x|y)/\Pr(\bar{x}|y)}{\Pr(x)/\Pr(\bar{x})} = \frac{f(y|x)}{f(y|\bar{x})}. \tag{3.27}$$

If we let Pr be the distribution before we observe the value y and let Pr$'$ be the new distribution after observing the value, we get

$$\frac{\Pr'(x)/\Pr'(\bar{x})}{\Pr(x)/\Pr(\bar{x})} = \frac{O'(x)}{O(x)} = \frac{f(y|x)}{f(y|\bar{x})}. \tag{3.28}$$

Therefore, we can emulate the hard evidence $Y = y$ using soft evidence on x with a Bayes factor of $f(y|x)/f(y|\bar{x})$.

3.7.3 Gaussian noise

To provide a concrete example of this technique, consider the Gaussian distribution that is commonly used to model noisy observations. The Gaussian density is given by

$$f(t) = \frac{1}{\sqrt{2\pi\sigma^2}} e^{-(t-\mu)^2/2\sigma^2},$$

where μ is the mean and σ is the standard deviation. Considering our noisy channel example, we use a Gaussian distribution with mean $\mu = 0$ to model the noise for bit 0 and another Gaussian distribution with mean $\mu = 1$ to model the noise for bit 1. The standard deviation is typically the same for both bits as it depends on the channel noise. That is, we now have

$$f(y|X=0) = \frac{1}{\sqrt{2\pi\sigma^2}} e^{-(y-0)^2/2\sigma^2}$$

$$f(y|X=1) = \frac{1}{\sqrt{2\pi\sigma^2}} e^{-(y-1)^2/2\sigma^2}.$$

A reading y of the continuous variable can now be viewed as soft evidence on $X = 0$ with a Bayes factor determined by (3.28):

$$k = \frac{O'(X=0)}{O(X=0)} = \frac{f(y|X=0)}{f(y|X=1)}$$

$$= \frac{\sqrt{2\pi\sigma^2}\, e^{-(y-0)^2/2\sigma^2}}{\sqrt{2\pi\sigma^2}\, e^{-(y-1)^2/2\sigma^2}}$$

$$= e^{(1-2y)/2\sigma^2}.$$

Equivalently, we can interpret this reading as soft evidence on $X = 1$ with a Bayes factor of $1/e^{(1-2y)/2\sigma^2}$.

To provide a feel for this Bayes factor, we list some of its values for different readings y and standard deviation σ:

σ	$-1/2$	$-1/4$	0	1/4	1/2	3/4	1	5/4	6/4
1/3	8,103.1	854.1	90.0	9.5	1.0	.1	.01	.001	.0001
1/2	54.6	2.1	7.4	2.7	1.0	.4	.14	.05	.02
1	2.7	2.1	1.6	1.3	1.0	.8	.6	.5	.4

(column header y spans the reading columns)

In summary, we have presented a technique in this section that allows one to condition beliefs on the values of continuous variables without the need to represent these variables explicitly. In particular, we have shown that the hard evidence implied by observing the value of a continuous variable can always be emulated by soft evidence whose strength is derived from the density function of that continuous variable.

Bibliographic remarks

For introductory texts on probability theory, see Bertsekas and Tsitsiklis [2002] and DeGroot [2002]. For a discussion on plausible reasoning using probabilities, see Jaynes [2003] and Pearl [1988]. An in-depth treatment of probabilistic independence is given in Pearl [1988]. Concepts from information theory, including entropy and mutual information, are discussed in Cover and Thomas [1991]. A historical discussion of the Gaussian distribution is given in Jaynes [2003]. Our treatment of soft evidence is based on Chan and Darwiche [2005b]. The Bayes factor was introduced in Good [1950, 1983] and Jeffrey's rule was introduced in Jeffrey [1965]. Emulating the "nothing else considered" method using a noisy sensor is based on the method of "virtual evidence" in Pearl [1988]. The terms "all things considered" and "nothing else considered" were introduced in Goldszmidt and Pearl [1996].

3.8 Exercises

3.1. Consider the following joint distribution.

world	A	B	C	Pr(.)
ω_1	true	true	true	.075
ω_2	true	true	false	.050
ω_3	true	false	true	.225
ω_4	true	false	false	.150
ω_5	false	true	true	.025
ω_6	false	true	false	.100
ω_7	false	false	true	.075
ω_8	false	false	false	.300

(a) What is $\Pr(A=\text{true})$? $\Pr(B=\text{true})$? $\Pr(C=\text{true})$?

(b) Update the distribution by conditioning on the event $C=\text{true}$, that is, construct the conditional distribution $\Pr(.|C=\text{true})$.

(c) What is $\Pr(A=\text{true}|C=\text{true})$? $\Pr(B=\text{true}|C=\text{true})$?

(d) Is the event $A=\text{true}$ independent of the event $C=\text{true}$? Is $B=\text{true}$ independent of $C=\text{true}$?

3.2. Consider again the joint distribution Pr from Exercise 3.1.

(a) What is $\Pr(A=\text{true} \vee B=\text{true})$?

(b) Update the distribution by conditioning on the event $A=\text{true} \vee B=\text{true}$, that is, construct the conditional distribution $\Pr(.|A=\text{true} \vee B=\text{true})$.

(c) What is $\Pr(A=\text{true}|A=\text{true} \vee B=\text{true})$? $\Pr(B=\text{true}|A=\text{true} \vee B=\text{true})$?

(d) Determine if the event $B=\text{true}$ is conditionally independent of $C=\text{true}$ given the event $A=\text{true} \vee B=\text{true}$?

3.3. Suppose that we tossed two unbiased coins C_1 and C_2.

(a) Given that the first coin landed heads, $C_1=h$, what is the probability that the second coin landed tails, $\Pr(C_2=t|C_1=h)$?

(b) Given that at least one of the coins landed heads, $C_1=h \vee C_2=h$, what is the probability that both coins landed heads, $\Pr(C_1=h \wedge C_2=h|C_1=h \vee C_2=h)$?

3.4. Suppose that 24% of a population are smokers and that 5% of the population have cancer. Suppose further that 86% of the population with cancer are also smokers. What is the probability that a smoker will also have cancer?

3.5. Consider again the population from Exercise 3.4. What is the relative change in the odds that a member of the population has cancer upon learning that they are also a smoker?

3.6. Consider a family with two children, ages four and nine:

(a) What is the probability that the older child is a boy?

(b) What is the probability that the older child is a boy given that the younger child is a boy?

(c) What is the probability that the older child is a boy given that at least one of the children is a boy?

(d) What is the probability that both children are boys given that at least one of them is a boy?

Define your variables and the corresponding joint probability distribution. Moreover, for each of these questions define α and β for which $\Pr(\alpha|\beta)$ is the answer.

3.7. Prove Equation 3.19.

3.8. Suppose that we have a patient who was just tested for a particular disease and the test came out positive. We know that one in every thousand people has this disease. We also know that the test is not reliable: it has a false positive rate of 2% and a false negative rate of 5%. We have seen previously that the probability of having the disease is $\approx 4.5\%$ given a positive test result. Suppose that the test is repeated n times and all tests come out positive. What is the smallest n for which the belief in the disease is greater than 95%, assuming the errors of various tests are independent? Justify your answer.

3.9. Consider the following distribution over three variables:

world	A	B	C	Pr(.)
ω_1	true	true	true	.27
ω_2	true	true	false	.18
ω_3	true	false	true	.03
ω_4	true	false	false	.02
ω_5	false	true	true	.02
ω_6	false	true	false	.03
ω_7	false	false	true	.18
ω_8	false	false	false	.27

For each pair of variables, state whether they are independent. State also whether they are independent given the third variable. Justify your answers.

3.10. Show the following:

(a) If $\alpha \models \beta$ and $\Pr(\beta) = 0$, then $\Pr(\alpha) = 0$.

(b) $\Pr(\alpha \wedge \beta) \leq \Pr(\alpha) \leq \Pr(\alpha \vee \beta)$.

(c) If $\alpha \models \beta$, then $\Pr(\alpha) \leq \Pr(\beta)$.

(d) If $\alpha \models \beta \models \gamma$, then $\Pr(\alpha|\beta) \geq \Pr(\alpha|\gamma)$.

3.11. Let α and β be two propositional sentences over disjoint variables $\mathbf{X}$ and $\mathbf{Y}$, respectively. Show that α and β are independent, that is, $\Pr(\alpha \wedge \beta) = \Pr(\alpha)\Pr(\beta)$ if variables $\mathbf{X}$ and $\mathbf{Y}$ are independent, that is, $\Pr(\mathbf{x}, \mathbf{y}) = \Pr(\mathbf{x})\Pr(\mathbf{y})$ for all instantiations $\mathbf{x}$ and $\mathbf{y}$.

3.12. Consider a propositional sentence α that is represented by an NNF circuit that satisfies the properties of decomposability and determinism. Suppose the circuit inputs are over variables $X_1, \ldots, X_n$ and that each variable X_i is independent of every other set of variables that does not contain X_i. Show that if given the probability distribution $\Pr(x_i)$ for each variable X_i, the probability of α can be computed in time linear in the size of the NNF circuit.

3.13. (After Pearl) We have three urns labeled 1, 2, and 3. The urns contain, respectively, three white and three black balls, four white and two black balls, and one white and two black balls. An experiment consists of selecting an urn at random then drawing a ball from it.

(a) Define the set of worlds that correspond to the various outcomes of this experiment. Assume you have two variables U with values $1, 2$, and 3 and C with values black and white.

(b) Define the joint probability distribution over the set of possible worlds identified in (a).

(c) Find the probability of drawing a black ball.

(d) Find the conditional probability that urn 2 was selected given that a black ball was drawn.

(e) Find the probability of selecting urn 1 or a white ball.

3.14. Suppose we are presented with two urns labeled 1 and 2 and we want to distribute k white balls and k black balls between these urns. In particular, say that we want to pick an n and

m where we place n white balls and m black balls into urn 1 and the remaining $k - n$ white balls and $k - m$ black balls into urn 2. Once we distribute the balls to urns, say that we play a game where we pick an urn at random and draw a ball from it.

(a) What is the probability that we draw a white ball for a given n and m?

Suppose now that we want to choose n and m so that we maximize the probability that we draw a white ball. Clearly, if both urns have an equal number of white and black balls (i.e., $n = m$), then the probability that we draw a white ball is $\frac{1}{2}$.

(b) Suppose that $k = 3$. Can we choose an n and m so that we increase the probability of drawing a white ball to $\frac{7}{10}$?

(c) Can we design a strategy for choosing n and m so that as k tends to infinity, the probability of drawing a white ball tends to $\frac{3}{4}$?

3.15. Prove the equivalence between the two definitions of conditional independence given by Equations 3.15 and 3.16.

3.16. Let X and Y be two binary variables. Show that X and Y are independent if and only if $\Pr(x, y)\Pr(\bar{x}, \bar{y}) = \Pr(x, \bar{y})\Pr(\bar{x}, y)$.

3.17. Show that $\Pr(\alpha) = O(\alpha)/(1 + O(\alpha))$.

3.18. Show that $O(\alpha|\beta)/O(\alpha) = \Pr(\beta|\alpha)/\Pr(\beta|\neg\alpha)$. *Note:* $\Pr(\beta|\alpha)/\Pr(\beta|\neg\alpha)$ is called the *likelihood ratio.*

3.19. Show that events α and β are independent if and only if $O(\alpha|\beta) = O(\alpha|\neg\beta)$.

3.20. Let α and β be two events such that $\Pr(\alpha) \neq 0$ and $\Pr(\beta) \neq 1$. Suppose that $\Pr(\alpha \implies \beta) = 1$. Show that:

(a) Knowing $\neg\alpha$ will decrease the probability of β.

(b) Knowing β will increase the probability of α.

3.21. Consider Section 3.6.3 and the investigator Rich with his state of belief regarding murder suspects:

world	Killer	$\Pr(.)$
ω_1	david	2/3
ω_2	dick	1/6
ω_3	jane	1/6

Suppose now that Rich receives some new evidence that triples his odds of the killer being male. What is the new belief of Rich that David is the killer? What would this belief be if after accommodating the evidence, Rich's belief in the killer being male is 93.75%?

3.22. Consider a distribution $\Pr$ over variables $\mathbf{X} \cup \{S\}$. Let U be a variable in $\mathbf{X}$ and suppose that S is independent of $\mathbf{X} \setminus \{U\}$ given U. For a given value s of variable S, suppose that $\Pr(s|u) = \eta\, f(u)$ for all values u, where f is some function and $\eta > 0$ is a constant. Show that $\Pr(\mathbf{x}|s)$ does not depend on the constant η. That is, $\Pr(\mathbf{x}|s)$ is the same for any value of $\eta > 0$ such that $0 \leq \eta\, f(u) \leq 1$.

3.23. Prove Equation 3.21.

3.24. Prove Equations 3.24 and 3.25.

3.25. Suppose we transmit a bit across a noisy channel but for bit 0 we send a signal -1 and for bit 1 we send a signal $+1$. Suppose again that Gaussian noise is added to the reading y from the noisy channel, with densities

$$f(y|X=0) = \frac{1}{\sqrt{2\pi\sigma^2}} e^{-(y+1)^2/2\sigma^2}$$

$$f(y|X=1) = \frac{1}{\sqrt{2\pi\sigma^2}} e^{-(y-1)^2/2\sigma^2}.$$

(a) Show that if we treat the reading y of a continuous variable Y as soft evidence on $X = 0$, the corresponding Bayes factor is

$$k = e^{-2y/\sigma^2}.$$

(b) Give the corresponding Bayes factors for the following readings y and standard deviations σ:

   (i) $y = +\frac{1}{2}$ and $\sigma = \frac{1}{4}$

   (ii) $y = -\frac{1}{2}$ and $\sigma = \frac{1}{4}$

   (iii) $y = -\frac{3}{2}$ and $\sigma = \frac{4}{5}$

   (iv) $y = +\frac{1}{4}$ and $\sigma = \frac{4}{5}$

   (v) $y = -1$ and $\sigma = 2$

(c) What reading y would result in neutral evidence regardless of the standard deviation? What reading y would result in a Bayes factor of 2 given a standard deviation $\sigma = 0.2$?

3.26. Prove Equation 3.27. Hint: Show first that $\Pr(x|y)/\Pr(x) = f(y|x)/f(y)$, where $f(y)$ is the PDF for variable Y.

3.27. Suppose we have a sensor that bears on event β and has a false positive rate f_p and a false negative rate f_n. Suppose further that we want a positive reading of this sensor to increase the odds of β by a factor of $k > 1$ and a negative reading to decrease the odds of β by the same factor k. Prove that these conditions imply that $f_p = f_n = 1/(k+1)$.

4

Bayesian Networks

We introduce Bayesian networks in this chapter as a modeling tool for compactly specifying joint probability distributions.

4.1 Introduction

We have seen in Chapter 3 that joint probability distributions can be used to model uncertain beliefs and change them in the face of hard and soft evidence. We have also seen that the size of a joint probability distribution is exponential in the number of variables of interest, which introduces both modeling and computational difficulties. Even if these difficulties are addressed, one still needs to ensure that the synthesized distribution matches the beliefs held about a given situation. For example, if we are building a distribution that captures the beliefs of a medical expert, we may need to ensure some correspondence between the independencies held by the distribution and those believed by the expert. This may not be easy to enforce if the distribution is constructed by listing all possible worlds and assessing the belief in each world directly.

The *Bayesian network* is a graphical modeling tool for specifying probability distributions that, in principle, can address all of these difficulties. The Bayesian network relies on the basic insight that independence forms a significant aspect of beliefs and that it can be elicited relatively easily using the language of graphs. We start our discussion in Section 4.2 by exploring this key insight, and use our developments in Section 4.3 to provide a formal definition of the syntax and semantics of Bayesian networks. Section 4.4 is dedicated to studying the properties of probabilistic independence, and Section 4.5 is dedicated to a graphical test that allows one to efficiently read the independencies encoded by a Bayesian network. Some additional properties of Bayesian networks are discussed in Section 4.6, which unveil some of their expressive powers and representational limitations.

4.2 Capturing independence graphically

Consider the *directed acyclic graph* (DAG) in Figure 4.1, where nodes represent propositional variables. To ground our discussion, assume for now that edges in this graph represent "direct causal influences" among these variables. For example, the alarm triggering (A) is a direct cause of receiving a call from a neighbor (C).

Given this causal structure, one would expect the dynamics of belief change to satisfy some properties. For example, we would expect our belief in C to be influenced by evidence on R. If we get a radio report that an earthquake took place in our neighborhood, our belief in the alarm triggering would probably increase, which would also increase our belief in receiving a call from our neighbor. However, we would not change this belief if we knew for sure that the alarm did not trigger. That is, we would find C independent of R given $\neg A$ in the context of this causal structure.

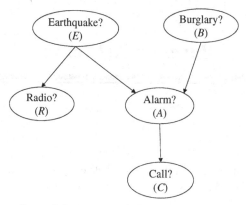

Figure 4.1: A directed acyclic graph that captures independence among five propositional variables.

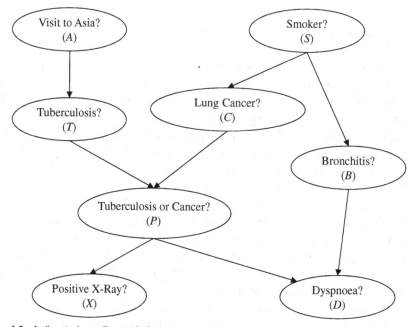

Figure 4.2: A directed acyclic graph that captures independence among eight propositional variables.

For another example, consider the causal structure in Figure 4.2, which captures some of the common causal perceptions in a limited medical domain. Here we would clearly find a visit to Asia relevant to our belief in the x-ray test coming out positive but we would find the visit irrelevant if we know for sure that the patient does not have tuberculosis. That is, X is dependent on A but is independent of A given $\neg T$.

The previous examples of independence are all implied by a formal interpretation of each DAG as a set of conditional independence statements. To phrase this interpretation formally, we need the following notation. Given a variable V in a DAG G:

- Parents(V) are the parents of V in DAG G, that is, the set of variables N with an edge from N to V. For example, the parents of variable A in Figure 4.1 are E and B.

- Descendants(V) are the descendants of V in DAG G, that is, the set of variables N with a directed path from V to N (we also say that V is an ancestor of N in this case). For example, the descendants of variable B in Figure 4.1 are A and C.

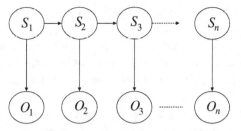

Figure 4.3: A directed acyclic graph known as a hidden Markov model.

- Non_Descendants(V) are all variables in DAG G other than V, Parents(V), and Descendants(V). We will call these variables the nondescendants of V in DAG G. For example, the nondescendants of variable B in Figure 4.1 are E and R.

Given this notation, we will then formally interpret each DAG G as a compact representation of the following independence statements:

$$I(V, \text{Parents}(V), \text{Non\_Descendants}(V)) \quad \text{for all variables } V \text{ in DAG } G. \quad (4.1)$$

That is, every variable is conditionally independent of its nondescendants given its parents. We will refer to the independence statements declared by (4.1) as the *Markovian assumptions* of DAG G and denote them by Markov(G).

If we view the DAG as a causal structure, then Parents(V) denotes the *direct causes* of V and Descendants(V) denotes the *effects* of V. The statement in (4.1) will then read: Given the direct causes of a variable, our beliefs in that variable will no longer be influenced by any other variable except possibly by its effects.

Let us now consider some concrete examples of the independence statements represented by a DAG. The following are all the statements represented by the DAG in Figure 4.1:

$$I(C, A, \{B, E, R\})$$
$$I(R, E, \{A, B, C\})$$
$$I(A, \{B, E\}, R)$$
$$I(B, \emptyset, \{E, R\})$$
$$I(E, \emptyset, B)$$

Note that variables B and E have no parents, hence, they are marginally independent of their nondescendants.

For another example, consider the DAG in Figure 4.3, which is quite common in many applications and is known as a *hidden Markov model* (HMM). In this DAG, variables $S_1, S_2, \ldots, S_n$ represent the state of a dynamic system at time points $1, 2, \ldots, n$, respectively. Moreover, the variables $O_1, O_2, \ldots, O_n$ represent sensors that measure the system state at the corresponding time points. Usually, one has some information about the sensor readings and is interested in computing beliefs in the system state at different time points. The independence statement declared by this DAG for state variables S_i is

$$I(S_t, \{S_{t-1}\}, \{S_1, \ldots, S_{t-2}, O_1, \ldots, O_{t-1}\}).$$

That is, once we know the state of the system at the previous time point, $t - 1$, our belief in the present system state, at time t, is no longer influenced by any other information about the past.

Note that the formal interpretation of a DAG as a set of conditional independence statements makes no reference to the notion of causality, even though we used causality to motivate this interpretation. If one constructs the DAG based on causal perceptions, then one would tend to agree with the independencies declared by the DAG. However, it is perfectly possible to have a DAG that does not match our causal perceptions yet we agree with the independencies declared by the DAG. Consider for example the DAG in Figure 4.1 which matches common causal perceptions. Consider now the alternative DAG in Figure 4.13 on Page 70, which does not match these perceptions. As we shall see later, every independence that is declared (or implied) by the second DAG is also declared (or implied) by the first. Hence, if we accept the first DAG, then we must also accept the second.

We next discuss the process of parameterizing a DAG, which involves quantifying the dependencies between nodes and their parents. This process is much easier to accomplish by an expert if the DAG corresponds to causal perceptions.

4.3 Parameterizing the independence structure

Suppose now that our goal is to construct a probability distribution Pr that captures our state of belief regarding the domain given in Figure 4.1. The first step is to construct a DAG G while ensuring that the independence statements declared by G are consistent with our beliefs about the underlying domain. The DAG G is then a partial specification of our state of belief Pr. Specifically, by constructing G we are saying that the distribution Pr must satisfy the independence assumptions of Markov(G). This clearly constrains the possible choices for the distribution Pr but does not uniquely define it. As it turns out, we can augment the DAG G by a set of conditional probabilities that together with Markov(G) are guaranteed to define the distribution Pr uniquely.

The additional set of conditional probabilities that we need are as follows: For every variable X in the DAG G and its parents $\mathbf{U}$, we need to provide the probability $\Pr(x|\mathbf{u})$ for every value x of variable X and every instantiation $\mathbf{u}$ of parents $\mathbf{U}$. For example, for the DAG in Figure 4.1 we need to provide the following conditional probabilities:

$$\Pr(c|a), \quad \Pr(r|e), \quad \Pr(a|b, e), \quad \Pr(e), \quad \Pr(b),$$

where a, b, c, e, and r are values of variables A, B, C, E, and R. Here is an example of the conditional probabilities required for variable C:

A	C	$\Pr(c|a)$
true	true	.80
true	false	.20
false	true	.001
false	false	.999

This table is known as a *conditional probability table* (CPT) for variable C. Note that we must have

$$\Pr(c|a) + \Pr(\bar{c}|a) = 1 \text{ and } \Pr(c|\bar{a}) + \Pr(\bar{c}|\bar{a}) = 1.$$

Hence, two of the probabilities in this CPT are redundant and can be inferred from the other two. It turns out that we only need ten independent probabilities to completely specify the CPTs for the DAG in Figure 4.1.

We are now ready to provide the formal definition of a Bayesian network.

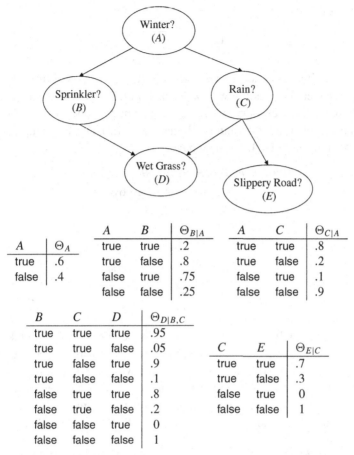

Figure 4.4: A Bayesian network over five propositional variables.

Definition 4.1. A *Bayesian network* for variables **Z** is a pair (G, Θ), where:

- G is a directed acyclic graph over variables **Z**, called the network *structure*.
- Θ is a set of CPTs, one for each variable in **Z**, called the network *parametrization*.

We will use $\Theta_{X|\mathbf{U}}$ to denote the CPT for variable X and its parents **U**, and refer to the set $X\mathbf{U}$ as a network *family*. We will also use $\theta_{x|\mathbf{u}}$ to denote the value assigned by CPT $\Theta_{X|\mathbf{U}}$ to the conditional probability $\Pr(x|\mathbf{u})$ and call $\theta_{x|\mathbf{u}}$ a network *parameter*. Note that we must have $\sum_x \theta_{x|\mathbf{u}} = 1$ for every parent instantiation **u**.   ∎

Figure 4.4 depicts a Bayesian network over five variables, $\mathbf{Z} = \{A, B, C, D, E\}$.

An instantiation of all network variables will be called a *network instantiation*. Moreover, a network parameter $\theta_{x|\mathbf{u}}$ is said to be compatible with a network instantiation **z** when the instantiations $x\mathbf{u}$ and **z** are compatible (i.e., they agree on the values they assign to their common variables). We will write $\theta_{x|\mathbf{u}} \sim \mathbf{z}$ in this case. In the Bayesian network of Figure 4.4, $\theta_a, \theta_{b|a}, \theta_{\bar{c}|a}, \theta_{d|b,\bar{c}}$, and $\theta_{\bar{e}|\bar{c}}$ are all the network parameters compatible with network instantiation $a, b, \bar{c}, d, \bar{e}$.

We later prove that the independence constraints imposed by a network structure and the numeric constraints imposed by its parametrization are satisfied by one and only one probability distribution Pr. Moreover, we show that the distribution is given by the following equation:

$$\Pr(\mathbf{z}) \stackrel{def}{=} \prod_{\theta_{x|\mathbf{u}} \sim \mathbf{z}} \theta_{x|\mathbf{u}}. \tag{4.2}$$

That is, the probability assigned to a network instantiation $\mathbf{z}$ is simply the product of all network parameters compatible with $\mathbf{z}$. Equation (4.2) is known as the *chain rule* for Bayesian networks. A Bayesian network will then be understood as an implicit representation of a unique probability distribution Pr given by (4.2). For an example, consider the Bayesian network in Figure 4.4. We then have

$$\Pr(a, b, \bar{c}, d, \bar{e}) = \theta_a \ \theta_{b|a} \ \theta_{\bar{c}|a} \ \theta_{d|b,\bar{c}} \ \theta_{\bar{e}|\bar{c}}$$
$$= (.6)(.2)(.2)(.9)(1)$$
$$= .0216$$

Moreover,

$$\Pr(\bar{a}, \bar{b}, \bar{c}, \bar{d}, \bar{e}) = \theta_{\bar{a}} \ \theta_{\bar{b}|\bar{a}} \ \theta_{\bar{c}|\bar{a}} \ \theta_{\bar{d}|\bar{b},\bar{c}} \ \theta_{\bar{e}|\bar{c}}$$
$$= (.4)(.25)(.9)(1)(1)$$
$$= .09$$

Note that the size of CPT $\Theta_{X|\mathbf{U}}$ is exponential in the number of parents $\mathbf{U}$. In general, if every variable can take up to d values and has at most k parents, the size of any CPT is bounded by $O(d^{k+1})$. Moreover, if we have n network variables, the total number of Bayesian network parameters is bounded by $O(n \cdot d^{k+1})$. This number is quite reasonable as long as the number of parents per variable is relatively small. We discuss in future chapters techniques for efficiently representing the CPT $\Theta_{X|\mathbf{U}}$ even when the number of parents $\mathbf{U}$ is large.

Consider the HMM in Figure 4.3 as an example, and suppose that each state variable S_i has m values and similarly for sensor variables O_i. The CPT for any state variable S_i, $i > 1$, contains m^2 parameters, which are usually known as *transition probabilities*. Similarly, the CPT for any sensor variable O_i has m^2 parameters, which are usually known as *emission* or *sensor probabilities*. The CPT for the first state variable S_1 only has m parameters. In fact, in an HMM the CPTs for state variables S_i, $i > 1$, are all identical, and the CPTs for all sensor variables O_i are also all identical.[1]

4.4 Properties of probabilistic independence

The distribution Pr specified by a Bayesian network (G, Θ) is guaranteed to satisfy every independence assumption in Markov(G) (see Exercise 4.5). Specifically, we must have

$$I_{\Pr}(X, \text{Parents}(X), \text{Non\_Descendants}(X))$$

for every variable X in the network. However, these are not the only independencies satisfied by the distribution Pr. For example, the distribution induced by the Bayesian network in Figure 4.4 finds D and E independent given A and C yet this independence is not part of Markov(G).

This independence and additional ones follow from the ones in Markov(G) using a set of properties for probabilistic independence, known as the *graphoid axioms,* which include symmetry, decomposition, weak union, and contraction. We introduce these axioms in this

---

[1] The HMM is said to be homogeneous in this case.

section and explore some of their applications. We then provide a graphical criterion in Section 4.5 called d-separation, which allows us to infer the implications of these axioms by operating efficiently on the structure of a Bayesian network.

Before we introduce the graphoid axioms, we first recall the definition of $I_{\Pr}(\mathbf{X}, \mathbf{Z}, \mathbf{Y})$, that is, distribution Pr finds variables $\mathbf{X}$ independent of variables $\mathbf{Y}$ given variables $\mathbf{Z}$:

$$\Pr(\mathbf{x}|\mathbf{z}, \mathbf{y}) = \Pr(\mathbf{x}|\mathbf{z}) \quad \text{or } \Pr(\mathbf{y}, \mathbf{z}) = 0,$$

for all instantiations $\mathbf{x}, \mathbf{y}, \mathbf{z}$ of variables $\mathbf{X}, \mathbf{Y}, \mathbf{Z}$, respectively.

Symmetry

The first and simplest property of probabilistic independence we consider is *symmetry:*

$$I_{\Pr}(\mathbf{X}, \mathbf{Z}, \mathbf{Y}) \text{ if and only if } I_{\Pr}(\mathbf{Y}, \mathbf{Z}, \mathbf{X}). \tag{4.3}$$

According to this property, if learning $\mathbf{y}$ does not influence our belief in $\mathbf{x}$, then learning $\mathbf{x}$ does not influence our belief in $\mathbf{y}$. Consider now the DAG G in Figure 4.1 and suppose that Pr is the probability distribution induced by the corresponding Bayesian network. From the independencies declared by Markov(G), we know that $I_{\Pr}(A, \{B, E\}, R)$. Using symmetry, we can then conclude that $I_{\Pr}(R, \{B, E\}, A)$, which is not part of the independencies declared by Markov(G).

Decomposition

The second property of probabilistic independence that we consider is *decomposition:*

$$I_{\Pr}(\mathbf{X}, \mathbf{Z}, \mathbf{Y} \cup \mathbf{W}) \text{ only if } I_{\Pr}(\mathbf{X}, \mathbf{Z}, \mathbf{Y}) \text{ and } I_{\Pr}(\mathbf{X}, \mathbf{Z}, \mathbf{W}). \tag{4.4}$$

This property says that if learning $\mathbf{yw}$ does not influence our belief in $\mathbf{x}$, then learning $\mathbf{y}$ alone, or learning $\mathbf{w}$ alone, will not influence our belief in $\mathbf{x}$. That is, if some information is irrelevant, then any part of it is also irrelevant. Note that the opposite of decomposition, called *composition*,

$$I_{\Pr}(\mathbf{X}, \mathbf{Z}, \mathbf{Y}) \text{ and } I_{\Pr}(\mathbf{X}, \mathbf{Z}, \mathbf{W}) \text{ only if } I_{\Pr}(\mathbf{X}, \mathbf{Z}, \mathbf{Y} \cup \mathbf{W}), \tag{4.5}$$

does not hold in general. Two pieces of information may each be irrelevant on their own yet their combination may be relevant.

One important application of decomposition is as follows. Consider the DAG G in Figure 4.2 and let us examine what the Markov(G) independencies say about variable B:

$$I(B, S, \{A, C, P, T, X\}).$$

If we use decomposition, we also conclude $I(B, S, C)$: Once we know whether the person is a smoker, our belief in developing bronchitis is no longer influenced by information about developing cancer. This independence is then guaranteed to hold in any probability distribution that is induced by a parametrization of DAG G. Yet this independence is not part of the independencies declared by Markov(G). More generally, decomposition allows us to state the following:

$$I_{\Pr}(X, \text{Parents}(X), \mathbf{W}) \quad \text{for every } \mathbf{W} \subseteq \text{Non\_Descendants}(X), \tag{4.6}$$

that is, every variable X is conditionally independent of any subset of its nondescendants given its parents. This is then a strengthening of the independence statements declared by Markov(G), which is a special case when $\mathbf{W}$ contains all nondescendants of X.

Another important application of decomposition is that it allows us to prove the chain rule for Bayesian networks given in (4.2). Let us first carry the proof in the context of DAG G in Figure 4.1, where our goal is to compute the probability of instantiation r, c, a, e, b. By the chain rule of probability calculus (see Chapter 3), we have

$$\Pr(r, c, a, e, b) = \Pr(r|c, a, e, b)\Pr(c|a, e, b)\Pr(a|e, b)\Pr(e|b)\Pr(b).$$

By the independencies given in (4.6), we immediately have

$$\Pr(r|c, a, e, b) = \Pr(r|e)$$
$$\Pr(c|a, e, b) = \Pr(c|a)$$
$$\Pr(e|b) = \Pr(e).$$

Hence, we have

$$\Pr(r, c, a, e, b) = \Pr(r|e)\Pr(c|a)\Pr(a|e, b)\Pr(e)\Pr(b)$$
$$= \theta_{r|e}\, \theta_{c|a}\, \theta_{a|e,b}\, \theta_e\, \theta_b,$$

which is the result given by (4.2).

This proof generalizes to any Bayesian network (G, Θ) over variables $\mathbf{Z}$ as long as we apply the chain rule to a variable instantiation $\mathbf{z}$ in which the parents $\mathbf{U}$ of each variable X appear after X in the instantiation $\mathbf{z}$. This ordering constraint ensures two things. First, for every term $\Pr(x|\alpha)$ that results from applying the chain rule to $\Pr(\mathbf{z})$ some instantiation $\mathbf{u}$ of parents $\mathbf{U}$ is guaranteed to be in α. Second, the only other variables appearing in α, beyond parents $\mathbf{U}$, must be nondescendants of X. Hence, the term $\Pr(x|\alpha)$ must equal the network parameter $\theta_{x|\mathbf{u}}$ by the independencies in (4.6).

For another example, consider again the DAG in Figure 4.1 and the following variable ordering c, a, r, b, e. We then have

$$\Pr(c, a, r, b, e) = \Pr(c|a, r, b, e)\Pr(a|r, b, e)\Pr(r|b, e)\Pr(b|e)\Pr(e).$$

By the independencies given in (4.6), we immediately have

$$\Pr(c|a, r, b, e) = \Pr(c|a)$$
$$\Pr(a|r, b, e) = \Pr(a|b, e)$$
$$\Pr(r|b, e) = \Pr(r|e)$$
$$\Pr(b|e) = \Pr(b).$$

Hence,

$$\Pr(c, a, r, b, e) = \Pr(c|a)\Pr(a|b, e)\Pr(r|e)\Pr(b)\Pr(e)$$
$$= \theta_{c|a}\, \theta_{a|b,e}\, \theta_{r|e}\, \theta_b\, \theta_e,$$

which is again the result given by (4.2).

Consider now the DAG in Figure 4.3 and let us apply the previous proof to the instantiation $o_n, \ldots, o_1, s_n, \ldots, s_1$, which satisfies the mentioned ordering property. The chain rule gives

$$\Pr(o_n, \ldots, o_1, s_n, \ldots, s_1)$$
$$= \Pr(o_n|o_{n-1} \ldots, o_1, s_n, \ldots, s_1) \ldots \Pr(o_1|s_n, \ldots, s_1)\Pr(s_n|s_{n-1} \ldots, s_1) \ldots \Pr(s_1).$$

We can simplify these terms using the independencies in (4.6), leading to

$$\Pr(o_n, \ldots, o_1, s_n, \ldots, s_1) = \Pr(o_n|s_n) \ldots \Pr(o_1|s_1)\Pr(s_n|s_{n-1}) \ldots \Pr(s_1)$$
$$= \theta_{o_n|s_n} \ldots \theta_{o_1|s_1} \theta_{s_n|s_{n-1}} \ldots \theta_{s_1}.$$

Hence, we are again able to express $\Pr(o_n, \ldots, o_1, s_n, \ldots, s_1)$ as a product of network parameters.

We have shown that if a distribution Pr satisfies the independencies in Markov(G) and if $\Pr(x|\mathbf{u}) = \theta_{x|\mathbf{u}}$, then the distribution must be given by (4.2). Exercise (4.5) asks for a proof of the other direction: If a distribution is given by (4.2), then it must satisfy the independencies in Markov(G) and we must have $\Pr(x|\mathbf{u}) = \theta_{x|\mathbf{u}}$. Hence, the distribution given by (4.2) is the only distribution that satisfies the qualitative constraints given by Markov(G) and the numeric constraints given by network parameters.

Weak union

The next property of probabilistic independence we consider is called *weak union:*

$$I_{\Pr}(\mathbf{X}, \mathbf{Z}, \mathbf{Y} \cup \mathbf{W}) \text{ only if } I_{\Pr}(\mathbf{X}, \mathbf{Z} \cup \mathbf{Y}, \mathbf{W}). \tag{4.7}$$

This property says that if the information **yw** is not relevant to our belief in **x**, then the partial information **y** will not make the rest of the information, **w**, relevant.

One application of weak union is as follows. Consider the DAG G in Figure 4.1 and let Pr be a probability distribution generated by some Bayesian network (G, Θ). The independence $I(C, A, \{B, E, R\})$ is part of Markov(G) and, hence, is satisfied by distribution Pr. Using weak union, we can then conclude $I_{\Pr}(C, \{A, E, B\}, R)$, which is not part of the independencies declared by Markov(G). More generally, we have the following:

$$I_{\Pr}(X, \text{Parents}(X) \cup \mathbf{W}, \text{Non\_Descendants}(X) \setminus \mathbf{W}), \tag{4.8}$$

for any $\mathbf{W} \subseteq \text{Non\_Descendants}(X)$. That is, each variable X in DAG G is independent of any of its nondescendants given its parents and the remaining nondescendants. This can be viewed as a strengthening of the independencies declared by Markov(G), which fall as a special case when the set **W** is empty.

Contraction

The fourth property of probabilistic independence we consider is called *contraction:*

$$I_{\Pr}(\mathbf{X}, \mathbf{Z}, \mathbf{Y}) \text{ and } I_{\Pr}(\mathbf{X}, \mathbf{Z} \cup \mathbf{Y}, \mathbf{W}) \text{ only if } I_{\Pr}(\mathbf{X}, \mathbf{Z}, \mathbf{Y} \cup \mathbf{W}). \tag{4.9}$$

This property says that if after learning the irrelevant information **y** the information **w** is found to be irrelevant to our belief in **x**, then the combined information **yw** must have been irrelevant from the beginning. It is instructive to compare contraction with composition in (4.5) as one can view contraction as a weaker version of composition. Recall that composition does not hold for probability distributions.

Consider now the DAG in Figure 4.3 and let us see how contraction can help in proving $I_{\Pr}(\{S_3, S_4\}, S_2, S_1)$. That is, once we know the state of the system at time 2, information about the system state at time 1 is not relevant to the state of the system at times 3 and 4. Note that Pr is any probability distribution that results from parameterizing DAG G. Note also that the previous independence is not part of Markov(G).

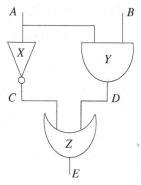

Figure 4.5: A digital circuit.

By (4.6), we have

$$I_{Pr}(S_3, S_2, S_1) \tag{4.10}$$

$$I_{Pr}(S_4, S_3, \{S_1, S_2\}). \tag{4.11}$$

By weak union and (4.11), we also have

$$I_{Pr}(S_4, \{S_2, S_3\}, S_1). \tag{4.12}$$

Applying contraction (and symmetry) to (4.10) and (4.12), we get our result:

$$I_{Pr}(\{S_4, S_3\}, S_2, S_1).$$

Intersection

The final axiom we consider is called *intersection* and holds only for the class of strictly positive probability distributions, that is, distributions that assign a nonzero probability to every consistent event. A strictly positive distribution is then unable to capture logical constraints; for example, it cannot represent the behavior of inverter X in Figure 4.5 as it will have to assign the probability zero to the event $A =$ true, $C =$ true.

The following is the property of intersection:

$$I_{Pr}(\mathbf{X}, \mathbf{Z} \cup \mathbf{W}, \mathbf{Y}) \text{ and } I_{Pr}(\mathbf{X}, \mathbf{Z} \cup \mathbf{Y}, \mathbf{W}) \text{ only if } I_{Pr}(\mathbf{X}, \mathbf{Z}, \mathbf{Y} \cup \mathbf{W}), \tag{4.13}$$

when Pr is a strictly positive distribution.[2] This property says that if information $\mathbf{w}$ is irrelevant given $\mathbf{y}$ and information $\mathbf{y}$ is irrelevant given $\mathbf{w}$, then the combined information $\mathbf{yw}$ is irrelevant to start with. This is not true in general. Consider the circuit in Figure 4.5 and assume that all components are functioning normally. If we know the input A of inverter X, its output C becomes irrelevant to our belief in the circuit output E. Similarly, if we know the output C of inverter X, its input A becomes irrelevant to this belief. Yet variables A and C are not irrelevant to our belief in the circuit output E. As it turns out, the intersection property is only contradicted in the presence of logical constraints and, hence, it holds for strictly positive distributions.

The four properties of symmetry, decomposition, weak union, and contraction, combined with a property called *triviality*, are known as the *graphoid axioms*. Triviality simply states that $I_{Pr}(\mathbf{X}, \mathbf{Z}, \emptyset)$. With the property of intersection, the set is known as the *positive*

---

[2] Note that if we replace $I_{Pr}(\mathbf{X}, \mathbf{Z} \cup \mathbf{W}, \mathbf{Y})$ with $I_{Pr}(\mathbf{X}, \mathbf{Z}, \mathbf{Y})$, we get contraction.

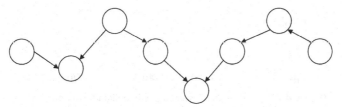

Figure 4.6: A path with six valves. From left to right, the type of valves are convergent, divergent, sequential, convergent, sequential, and sequential.

graphoid axioms.[3] It is interesting to note that the properties of decomposition, weak union, and contraction can be summarized tersely in one statement:

$$I_{\text{Pr}}(\mathbf{X}, \mathbf{Z}, \mathbf{Y} \cup \mathbf{W}) \text{ if and only if } I_{\text{Pr}}(\mathbf{X}, \mathbf{Z}, \mathbf{Y}) \text{ and } I_{\text{Pr}}(\mathbf{X}, \mathbf{Z} \cup \mathbf{Y}, \mathbf{W}). \quad (4.14)$$

Proving the positive graphoid axioms is left to Exercise 4.9.

4.5 A graphical test of independence

Suppose that Pr is a distribution induced by a Bayesian network (G, Θ). We have seen earlier that the distribution Pr satisfies independencies that go beyond what is declared by Markov(G). In particular, we have seen how one can use the graphoid axioms to derive new independencies that are implied by those in Markov(G). However, deriving these additional independencies may not be trivial. The good news is that the inferential power of the graphoid axioms can be tersely captured using a graphical test known as *d-separation*, which allows one to mechanically and efficiently derive the independencies implied by these axioms. Our goal in this section is to introduce the d-separation test, show how it can be used for this purpose, and discuss some of its formal properties.

The intuition behind the d-separation test is as follows. Let $\mathbf{X}$, $\mathbf{Y}$, and $\mathbf{Z}$ be three disjoint sets of variables. To test whether $\mathbf{X}$ and $\mathbf{Y}$ are d-separated by $\mathbf{Z}$ in DAG G, written $\text{dsep}_G(\mathbf{X}, \mathbf{Z}, \mathbf{Y})$, we need to consider every path between a node in $\mathbf{X}$ and a node in $\mathbf{Y}$ and then ensure that the path is blocked by $\mathbf{Z}$. Hence, the definition of d-separation relies on the notion of blocking a path by a set of variables $\mathbf{Z}$, which we will define next. First, we note that $\text{dsep}_G(\mathbf{X}, \mathbf{Z}, \mathbf{Y})$ implies $I_{\text{Pr}}(\mathbf{X}, \mathbf{Z}, \mathbf{Y})$ for every probability distribution Pr induced by G. This guarantee, together with the efficiency of the test, is what makes d-separation such an important notion.

Consider the path given in Figure 4.6 (note that a path does not have to be directed). The best way to understand the notion of blocking is to view the path as a pipe and to view each variable W on the path as a valve. A valve W is either open or closed, depending on some conditions that we state later. If at least one of the valves on the path is closed, then the whole path is blocked, otherwise the path is said to be not blocked. Therefore, the notion of blocking is formally defined once we define the conditions under which a valve is considered open or closed.

As it turns out, there are three types of valves and we need to consider each of them separately before we can state the conditions under which they are considered closed. Specifically, the type of a valve is determined by its relationship to its neighbors on the path as shown in Figure 4.7:

---

[3] The terms *semi-graphoid* and *graphoid* are sometimes used instead of graphoid and positive graphoid, respectively.

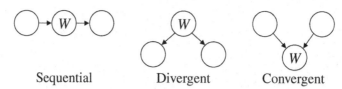

Figure 4.7: Three types of valves used in defining d-separation.

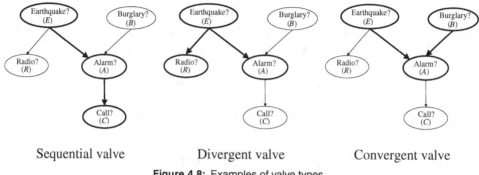

Figure 4.8: Examples of valve types.

- A *sequential valve* ($\rightarrow W \rightarrow$) arises when W is a parent of one of its neighbors and a child of the other.

- A *divergent valve* ($\leftarrow W \rightarrow$) arises when W is a parent of both neighbors.

- A *convergent valve* ($\rightarrow W \leftarrow$) arises when W is a child of both neighbors.

The path in Figure 4.6 has six valves. From left to right, the type of valves are convergent, divergent, sequential, convergent, sequential, and sequential.

To obtain more intuition on these types of valves, it is best to interpret the given DAG as a causal structure. Consider Figure 4.8, which provides concrete examples of the three types of valves in the context of a causal structure. We can then attach the following interpretations to valve types:

- A sequential valve $N_1 \rightarrow W \rightarrow N_2$ declares variable W as an intermediary between a cause N_1 and its effect N_2. An example of this type is $E \rightarrow A \rightarrow C$ in Figure 4.8.

- A divergent valve $N_1 \leftarrow W \rightarrow N_2$ declares variable W as a common cause of two effects N_1 and N_2. An example of this type is $R \leftarrow E \rightarrow A$ in Figure 4.8.

- A convergent valve $N_1 \rightarrow W \leftarrow N_2$ declares variable W as a common effect of two causes N_1 and N_2. An example of this type is $E \rightarrow A \leftarrow B$ in Figure 4.8.

Given this causal interpretation of valve types, we can now better motivate the conditions under which valves are considered closed given a set of variables **Z**:

- A sequential valve ($\rightarrow W \rightarrow$) is closed iff variable W appears in **Z**.
  For example, the sequential valve $E \rightarrow A \rightarrow C$ in Figure 4.8 is closed iff we know the value of variable A, otherwise an earthquake E may change our belief in getting a call C.

- A divergent valve ($\leftarrow W \rightarrow$) is closed iff variable W appears in **Z**.
  For example, the divergent valve $R \leftarrow E \rightarrow A$ in Figure 4.8 is closed iff we know the value of variable E, otherwise a radio report on an earthquake may change our belief in the alarm triggering.

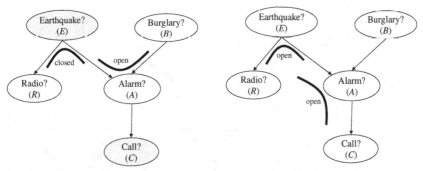

Figure 4.9: On the left, R and B are d-separated by E, C. On the right, R and C are not d-separated.

- A convergent valve ($\rightarrow W \leftarrow$) is closed iff neither variable W nor any of its descendants appears in $\mathbf{Z}$.
  For example, the convergent valve $E \rightarrow A \leftarrow B$ in Figure 4.8 is closed iff neither the value of variable A nor the value of C are known, otherwise, a burglary may change our belief in an earthquake.

We are now ready to provide a formal definition of d-separation.

Definition 4.2. Let $\mathbf{X}$, $\mathbf{Y}$, and $\mathbf{Z}$ be disjoint sets of nodes in a DAG G. We will say that $\mathbf{X}$ and $\mathbf{Y}$ are *d-separated* by $\mathbf{Z}$, written $\text{dsep}_G(\mathbf{X}, \mathbf{Z}, \mathbf{Y})$, iff every path between a node in $\mathbf{X}$ and a node in $\mathbf{Y}$ is blocked by $\mathbf{Z}$ where a path is blocked by $\mathbf{Z}$ iff at least one valve on the path is closed given $\mathbf{Z}$. ∎

Note that according to this definition, a path with no valves (i.e., $X \rightarrow Y$) is never blocked.

Let us now consider some examples of d-separation before we discuss its formal properties. Our first example is with respect to Figure 4.9. Considering the DAG G on the left of this figure, R and B are d-separated by E and C: $\text{dsep}_G(R, \{E, C\}, B)$. There is only one path connecting R and B in this DAG and it has two valves: $R \leftarrow E \rightarrow A$ and $E \rightarrow A \leftarrow B$. The first valve is closed given E and C and the second valve is open given E and C. But the closure of only one valve is sufficient to block the path, therefore establishing d-separation. For another example, consider the DAG G on the right of Figure 4.9 in which R and C are not d-separated: $\text{dsep}_G(R, \emptyset, C)$ does not hold. Again, there is only one path in this DAG between R and C and it contains two valves, $R \leftarrow E \rightarrow A$ and $E \rightarrow A \rightarrow C$, which are both open. Hence, the path is not blocked and d-separation does not hold.

Consider now the DAG G in Figure 4.10 where our goal here is to test whether B and C are d-separated by S: $\text{dsep}_G(B, S, C)$. There are two paths between B and C in this DAG. The first path has only one valve, $C \leftarrow S \rightarrow B$, which is closed given S and, hence, the path is blocked. The second path has two valves, $C \rightarrow P \rightarrow D$ and $P \rightarrow D \leftarrow B$, where the second valve is closed given S and, hence, the path is blocked. Since both paths are blocked by S, we then have that C and B are d-separated by S.

For a final example of d-separation, let us consider the DAG in Figure 4.11 and try to show that $I_{\text{Pr}}(S_1, S_2, \{S_3, S_4\})$ for any probability distribution Pr that is induced by the DAG. We first note that any path between S_1 and $\{S_3, S_4\}$ must have the valve $S_1 \rightarrow S_2 \rightarrow S_3$ on it, which is closed given S_2. Hence, every path from S_1 to $\{S_3, S_4\}$ is blocked by S_2 and we have $\text{dsep}_G(S_1, S_2, \{S_3, S_4\})$, which leads to $I_{\text{Pr}}(S_1, S_2, \{S_3, S_4\})$. This example shows how d-separation provides a systematic graphical criterion for deriving independencies, which can replace the application of the graphoid axioms as we did on Page 61. The d-separation test can be implemented quite efficiently, as we show later.

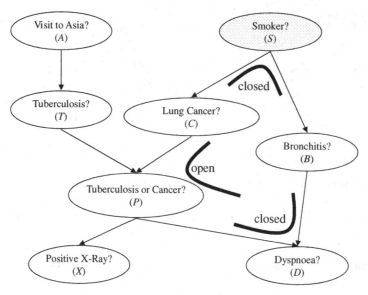

Figure 4.10: C and B are d-separated given S.

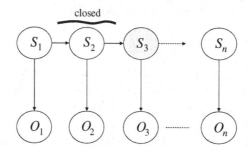

Figure 4.11: S_1 is d-separated from $S_3, \ldots, S_n$ by S_2.

4.5.1 Complexity of d-separation

The definition of d-separation, $\mathrm{dsep}_G(\mathbf{X}, \mathbf{Z}, \mathbf{Y})$, calls for considering all paths connecting a node in $\mathbf{X}$ with a node in $\mathbf{Y}$. The number of such paths can be exponential yet one can implement the test without having to enumerate these paths explicitly, as we show next.

Theorem 4.1. *Testing whether* $\mathbf{X}$ *and* $\mathbf{Y}$ *are d-separated by* $\mathbf{Z}$ *in DAG G is equivalent to testing whether* $\mathbf{X}$ *and* $\mathbf{Y}$ *are disconnected in a new DAG G', which is obtained by pruning DAG G as follows:*

- *We delete any leaf node W from DAG G as long as W does not belong to* $\mathbf{X} \cup \mathbf{Y} \cup \mathbf{Z}$. *This process is repeated until no more nodes can be deleted.*
- *We delete all edges outgoing from nodes in* $\mathbf{Z}$. ∎

Figure 4.12 depicts two examples of this pruning procedure. Note that the connectivity test on DAG G' ignores edge directions. Given Theorem 4.1, d-separation can be decided in time and space that are linear in the size of DAG G (see Exercise 4.7).

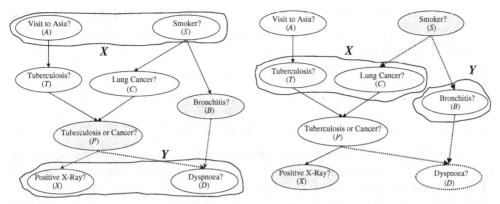

Figure 4.12: On the left, a pruned DAG for testing whether $\mathbf{X} = \{A, S\}$ is d-separated from $\mathbf{Y} = \{D, X\}$ by $\mathbf{Z} = \{B, P\}$. On the right, a pruned DAG for testing whether $\mathbf{X} = \{T, C\}$ is d-separated from $\mathbf{Y} = \{B\}$ by $\mathbf{Z} = \{S, X\}$. Both tests are positive. Pruned nodes and edges are dotted. Nodes in $\mathbf{Z}$ are shaded.

4.5.2 Soundness and completeness of d-separation

The d-separation test is *sound* in the following sense.

Theorem 4.2. *If* Pr *is a probability distribution induced by a Bayesian network* (G, Θ), *then*

$$\mathrm{dsep}_G(\mathbf{X}, \mathbf{Z}, \mathbf{Y}) \text{ only if } I_{\mathrm{Pr}}(\mathbf{X}, \mathbf{Z}, \mathbf{Y}). \qquad \blacksquare$$

Hence, we can safely use the d-separation test to derive independence statements about probability distributions induced by Bayesian networks. The proof of soundness is constructive, showing that every independence claimed by d-separation can indeed be derived using the graphoid axioms. Hence, the application of d-separation can be viewed as a graphical application of these axioms.

Another relevant question is whether d-separation is *complete*, that is, whether it is capable of inferring every possible independence statement that holds in the induced distribution Pr. As it turns out, the answer is no. For a counterexample, consider a Bayesian network with three binary variables, $X \rightarrow Y \rightarrow Z$. In this network, Z is not d-separated from X. However, it is possible for Z to be independent of X in a probability distribution that is induced by this network. Suppose, for example, that the CPT for variable Y is chosen so that $\theta_{y|x} = \theta_{y|\bar{x}}$. In this case, the induced distribution will find Y independent of X even though there is an edge between them (since $\Pr(y) = \Pr(y|x) = \Pr(y|\bar{x})$ and $\Pr(\bar{y}) = \Pr(\bar{y}|x) = \Pr(\bar{y}|\bar{x})$ in this case). The distribution will also find Z independent of X even though the path connecting them is not blocked.

Hence, by choosing the parametrization carefully we are able to establish an independence in the induced distribution that d-separation cannot detect. Of course, this is not too surprising since d-separation has no access to the chosen parametrization. We can then say the following. Let Pr be a distribution induced by a Bayesian network (G, Θ):

- If $\mathbf{X}$ and $\mathbf{Y}$ are d-separated by $\mathbf{Z}$, then $\mathbf{X}$ and $\mathbf{Y}$ are independent given $\mathbf{Z}$ for any parametrization Θ.

- If $\mathbf{X}$ and $\mathbf{Y}$ are not d-separated by $\mathbf{Z}$, then whether $\mathbf{X}$ and $\mathbf{Y}$ are dependent given $\mathbf{Z}$ depends on the specific parametrization Θ.

Can we always parameterize a DAG G in such a way to ensure the completeness of d-separation? The answer is yes. That is, d-separation satisfies the following weaker notion of completeness.

Theorem 4.3. *For every DAG G, there is a parametrization Θ such that*

$$I_{Pr}(\mathbf{X}, \mathbf{Z}, \mathbf{Y}) \text{ if and only if } dsep_G(\mathbf{X}, \mathbf{Z}, \mathbf{Y}),$$

where Pr *is the probability distribution induced by Bayesian network* (G, Θ). ∎

This weaker notion of completeness implies that one cannot improve on the d-separation test. That is, there is no other graphical test that can derive more independencies from Markov(G) than those derived by d-separation.

4.5.3 Further properties of d-separation

We have seen that conditional independence satisfies some properties, such as the graphoids axioms, but does not satisfy others, such as composition given in (4.5).

Suppose that $\mathbf{X}$ and $\mathbf{Y}$ are d-separated by $\mathbf{Z}$, dsep($\mathbf{X}, \mathbf{Z}, \mathbf{Y}$), which means that every path between $\mathbf{X}$ and $\mathbf{Y}$ is blocked by $\mathbf{Z}$. Suppose further that $\mathbf{X}$ and $\mathbf{W}$ are d-separated by $\mathbf{Z}$, dsep($\mathbf{X}, \mathbf{Z}, \mathbf{W}$), which means that every path between $\mathbf{X}$ and $\mathbf{W}$ is blocked by $\mathbf{Z}$. It then immediately follows that every path between $\mathbf{X}$ and $\mathbf{Y} \cup \mathbf{W}$ is also blocked by $\mathbf{Z}$. Hence, $\mathbf{X}$ and $\mathbf{Y} \cup \mathbf{W}$ are d-separated by $\mathbf{Z}$ and we have dsep($\mathbf{X}, \mathbf{Z}, \mathbf{Y} \cup \mathbf{W}$). We just proved that composition holds for d-separation:

$$dsep(\mathbf{X}, \mathbf{Z}, \mathbf{Y}) \text{ and } dsep(\mathbf{X}, \mathbf{Z}, \mathbf{W}) \text{ only if } dsep(\mathbf{X}, \mathbf{Z}, \mathbf{Y} \cup \mathbf{W}).$$

Since composition does not hold for probability distributions, this means the following. If we have a distribution that satisfies $I_{Pr}(\mathbf{X}, \mathbf{Z}, \mathbf{Y})$ and $I_{Pr}(\mathbf{X}, \mathbf{Z}, \mathbf{W})$ but not $I_{Pr}(\mathbf{X}, \mathbf{Z}, \mathbf{Y} \cup \mathbf{W})$, there could not exist a DAG G that induces Pr and at the same time satisfies dsep$_G(\mathbf{X}, \mathbf{Z}, \mathbf{Y})$ and dsep$_G(\mathbf{X}, \mathbf{Z}, \mathbf{W})$.

The d-separation test satisfies additional properties beyond composition that do not hold for arbitrary distributions. For example, it satisfies intersection:

$$dsep(\mathbf{X}, \mathbf{Z} \cup \mathbf{W}, \mathbf{Y}) \text{ and } dsep(\mathbf{X}, \mathbf{Z} \cup \mathbf{Y}, \mathbf{W}) \text{ only if } dsep(\mathbf{X}, \mathbf{Z}, \mathbf{Y} \cup \mathbf{W}).$$

It also satisfies *chordality:*

$$dsep(X, \{Z, W\}, Y) \text{ and } dsep(W, \{X, Y\}, Z) \text{ only if } dsep(X, Z, Y) \text{ or } dsep(X, W, Y).$$

4.6 More on DAGs and independence

We define in this section a few notions that are quite useful in describing the relationship between the independence statements declared by a DAG and those declared by a probability distribution. We use these notions to state a number of results, including some on the expressive power of DAGs as a language for capturing independence statements.

Let G be a DAG and Pr be a probability distribution over the same set of variables. We will say that G is an *independence map* (I-MAP) of Pr iff

$$dsep_G(\mathbf{X}, \mathbf{Z}, \mathbf{Y}) \text{ only if } I_{Pr}(\mathbf{X}, \mathbf{Z}, \mathbf{Y}),$$

that is, if every independence declared by d-separation on G holds in the distribution Pr. An I-MAP G is *minimal* if G ceases to be an I-MAP when we delete any edge from G.

By the semantics of Bayesian networks, if Pr is induced by a Bayesian network (G, Θ), then G must be an I-MAP of Pr, although it may not be minimal (see Exercise 4.5).

We will also say that G is a *dependency map* (D-MAP) of Pr iff

$$I_{\text{Pr}}(\mathbf{X}, \mathbf{Z}, \mathbf{Y}) \text{ only if } \text{dsep}_G(\mathbf{X}, \mathbf{Z}, \mathbf{Y}).$$

That is, the lack of d-separation in G implies a dependence in Pr, which follows from the contraposition of the above condition. Again, we have seen previously that if Pr is a distribution induced by a Bayesian network (G, Θ), then G is not necessarily a D-MAP of Pr. However, we mentioned that G can be made a D-MAP of Pr if we choose the parametrization Θ carefully.

If DAG G is both an I-MAP and a D-MAP of distribution Pr, then G is called a *perfect map* (P-MAP) of Pr. Given these notions, our goal in this section is to answer two basic questions. First, is there always a P-MAP for any distribution Pr? Second, given a distribution Pr, how can we construct a minimal I-MAP of Pr? Both questions have practical significance and are discussed next.

4.6.1 Perfect MAPs

If we are trying to construct a probability distribution Pr using a Bayesian network (G, Θ), then we want DAG G to be a P-MAP of the induced distribution to make all the independencies of Pr accessible to the d-separation test. However, there are probability distributions Pr for which there are no P-MAPs. Suppose for example that we have four variables, X_1, X_2, Y_1, Y_2, and a distribution Pr that only satisfies the following independencies:

$$\begin{aligned}
& I_{\text{Pr}}(X_1, \{Y_1, Y_2\}, X_2) \\
& I_{\text{Pr}}(X_2, \{Y_1, Y_2\}, X_1) \\
& I_{\text{Pr}}(Y_1, \{X_1, X_2\}, Y_2) \\
& I_{\text{Pr}}(Y_2, \{X_1, X_2\}, Y_1).
\end{aligned} \tag{4.15}$$

It turns out there is no DAG that is a P-MAP of Pr in this case.

This result should not come as a surprise since the independencies captured by DAGs satisfy properties – such as intersection, composition, and chordality – that are not satisfied by arbitrary probability distributions. In fact, the non existence of a P-MAP for the previous distribution Pr follows immediately from the fact that Pr violates the chordality property. In particular, the distribution satisfies $I(X_1, \{Y_1, Y_2\}, X_2)$ and $I(Y_1, \{X_1, X_2\}, Y_2)$. Therefore, if we have a DAG that captures these two independencies, it must then satisfy either $I(X_1, Y_1, X_2)$ or $I(X_1, Y_2, X_2)$ by chordality. Since neither of these are satisfied by Pr, there exists no DAG that is a P-MAP of Pr.

4.6.2 Independence MAPs

We now consider another key question relating to I-MAPs. Given a distribution Pr, how can we construct a DAG G that is guaranteed to be a minimal I-MAP of Pr? The significance of this question stems from the fact that minimal I-MAPs tend to exhibit more independence, therefore requiring fewer parameters and leading to more compact Bayesian networks (G, Θ) for distribution Pr.

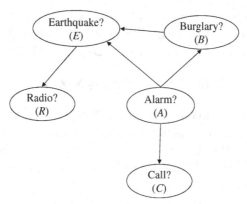

Figure 4.13: An I-MAP.

The following is a simple procedure for constructing a minimal I-MAP of a distribution Pr given an ordering $X_1, \ldots, X_n$ of the variables in Pr. We start with an empty DAG G (no edges) and then consider the variables X_i one by one for $i = 1, \ldots, n$. For each variable X_i, we identify a minimal subset $\mathbf{P}$ of the variables in $X_1, \ldots, X_{i-1}$ such that $I_{\mathrm{Pr}}(X_i, \mathbf{P}, \{X_1, \ldots, X_{i-1}\} \setminus \mathbf{P})$ and then make $\mathbf{P}$ the parents of X_i in DAG G. The resulting DAG is then guaranteed to be a minimal I-MAP of Pr.

For an example of this procedure, consider the DAG G in Figure 4.1 and suppose that it is a P-MAP of some distribution Pr. This supposition allows us to reduce the independence test required by the procedure on distribution Pr, $I_{\mathrm{Pr}}(X_i, \mathbf{P}, \{X_1, \ldots, X_{i-1}\} \setminus \mathbf{P})$, into an equivalent d-separation test on DAG G, $\mathrm{dsep}_G(X_i, \mathbf{P}, \{X_1, \ldots, X_{i-1}\} \setminus \mathbf{P})$. Our goal then is to construct a minimal I-MAP G' for Pr using the previous procedure and order A, B, C, E, R. The resulting DAG G' is shown in Figure 4.13. This DAG was constructed according to the following details:

- Variable A was added with $\mathbf{P} = \emptyset$.
- Variable B was added with $\mathbf{P} = A$, since $\mathrm{dsep}_G(B, A, \emptyset)$ holds and $\mathrm{dsep}_G(B, \emptyset, A)$ does not.
- Variable C was added with $\mathbf{P} = A$, since $\mathrm{dsep}_G(C, A, B)$ holds and $\mathrm{dsep}_G(C, \emptyset, \{A, B\})$ does not.
- Variable E was added with $\mathbf{P} = A, B$ since this is the smallest subset of A, B, C such that $\mathrm{dsep}_G(E, \mathbf{P}, \{A, B, C\} \setminus \mathbf{P})$ holds.
- Variable R was added with $\mathbf{P} = E$ since this is the smallest subset of A, B, C, E such that $\mathrm{dsep}_G(R, \mathbf{P}, \{A, B, C, E\} \setminus \mathbf{P})$ holds.

The resulting DAG G' is guaranteed to be a minimal I-MAP of the distribution Pr. That is, whenever $\mathbf{X}$ and $\mathbf{Y}$ are d-separated by $\mathbf{Z}$ in G', we must have the same for DAG G and, equivalently, that $\mathbf{X}$ and $\mathbf{Y}$ are independent given $\mathbf{Z}$ in Pr. Moreover, this ceases to hold if we delete any of the five edges in G'. For example, if we delete the edge $E \leftarrow B$, we will have $\mathrm{dsep}_{G'}(E, A, B)$ yet $\mathrm{dsep}_G(E, A, B)$ does not hold in this case. Note that the constructed DAG G' is incompatible with common perceptions of causal relationships in this domain – see the edge $A \rightarrow B$ for an example – yet it is sound from an independence viewpoint. That is, a person who accepts the DAG in Figure 4.1 cannot disagree with any of the independencies implied by Figure 4.13.

The minimal I-MAP of a distribution is not unique as we may get different results depending on the variable ordering with which we start. Even when using the same variable ordering, it is possible to arrive at different minimal I-MAPs. This is possible since we may have multiple minimal subsets $\mathbf{P}$ of $\{X_1, \ldots, X_{i-1}\}$ for which $I_{\text{Pr}}(X_i, \mathbf{P}, \{X_1, \ldots, X_{i-1}\} \setminus \mathbf{P})$ holds. As it turns out, this can only happen if the probability distribution Pr represents some logical constraints. Hence, we can ensure the uniqueness of a minimal I-MAP for a given variable ordering if we restrict ourselves to strictly positive distributions (see Exercise 4.17).

4.6.3 Blankets and boundaries

A final important notion we shall discuss is the *Markov blanket:*

> **Definition 4.3.** Let Pr be a distribution over variables $\mathbf{X}$. A *Markov blanket* for a variable $X \in \mathbf{X}$ is a set of variables $\mathbf{B} \subseteq \mathbf{X}$ such that $X \notin \mathbf{B}$ and $I_{\text{Pr}}(X, \mathbf{B}, \mathbf{X} \setminus (\mathbf{B} \cup \{X\}))$. ∎

That is, a Markov blanket for X is a set of variables that, when known, will render every other variable irrelevant to X. A Markov blanket $\mathbf{B}$ is *minimal* iff no strict subset of $\mathbf{B}$ is also a Markov blanket. A minimal Markov blanket is known as a *Markov boundary.* Again, it turns out that the Markov boundary for a variable is not unique unless the distribution is strictly positive.

Corollary 1. *If* Pr *is a distribution induced by DAG G, then a Markov blanket for variable X with respect to distribution* Pr *can be constructed using its parents, children, and spouses in DAG G. Here variable Y is a spouse of X if the two variables have a common child in DAG G.* ∎

This result holds because X is guaranteed to be d-separated from all other nodes given its parents, children, and spouses. To show this, suppose that we delete all edges leaving the parents, children, and spouses of X. Node X will then be disconnected from all nodes in the given DAG except for its children. Hence, by Theorem 4.1 X is guaranteed to be d-separated from all other nodes given its parents, children, and spouses. For an example, consider node C in Figure 4.2 and the set $\mathbf{B} = \{S, P, T\}$ constituting its parents, children, and spouses. If we delete the edges leaving nodes in $\mathbf{B}$, we find that node C is disconnected from all other nodes except its child P. Similarly, in Figure 4.3 the set $\{S_{t-1}, S_{t+1}, O_t\}$ forms a Markov blanket for every variable S_t where $t > 1$.

Bibliographic remarks

The term "Bayesian network" was coined by Judea Pearl [Pearl, 1985] to emphasize three aspects: the often subjective nature of the information used to construct them; the reliance on Bayes's conditioning when performing inference; and the ability to support both causal and evidential reasoning, a distinction underscored by Thomas Bayes [Bayes, 1963]. Bayesian networks are called *probabilistic networks* in Cowell et al. [1999] and *DAG models* in Edwards [2000], Lauritzen [1996], and Wasserman [2004]. Nevertheless, "Bayesian networks" remains to be one of the most common terms for denoting these networks in the AI literature [Pearl, 1988; Jensen and Nielsen, 2007; Neapolitan, 2004], although other terms, such as *belief networks* and *causal networks*, are also frequently used.

The graphoid axioms were identified initially in Dawid [1979] and Spohn [1980], and then rediscovered by Pearl and Paz [1986; 1987], who introduced the term "graphoids," noticing their connection to separation in graphs, and who also conjectured their completeness as a characterization of probabilistic independence. The conjecture was later falsified

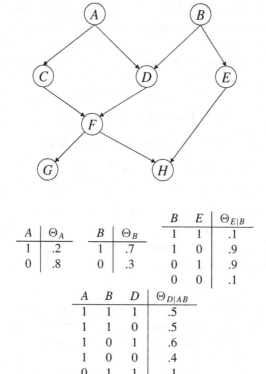

					B	E	$\Theta_{E\mid B}$
					1	1	.1
A	Θ_A		B	Θ_B	1	0	.9
1	.2		1	.7	0	1	.9
0	.8		0	.3	0	0	.1

A	B	D	$\Theta_{D\mid AB}$
1	1	1	.5
1	1	0	.5
1	0	1	.6
1	0	0	.4
0	1	1	.1
0	1	0	.9
0	0	1	.8
0	0	0	.2

Figure 4.14: A Bayesian network with some of its CPTs.

by Studeny [1990]. The d-separation test was first proposed by Pearl [1986b] and its soundness based on the graphoid axioms was shown in Verma [1986]; see also Verma and Pearl [1990a;b]. The algorithm for constructing minimal I-MAPs is discussed in Verma and Pearl [1990a]. An in-depth treatment of probabilistic and graphical independence is given in Pearl [1988].

4.7 Exercises

4.1. Consider the DAG in Figure 4.14:

(a) List the Markovian assumptions asserted by the DAG.

(b) Express $\Pr(a, b, c, d, e, f, g, h)$ in terms of network parameters.

(c) Compute $\Pr(A = 0, B = 0)$ and $\Pr(E = 1 \mid A = 1)$. Justify your answers.

(d) True or false? Why?

- $\mathrm{dsep}(A, BH, E)$
- $\mathrm{dsep}(G, D, E)$
- $\mathrm{dsep}(AB, F, GH)$

4.2. Consider the DAG G in Figure 4.15. Determine if any of $\mathrm{dsep}_G(A_i, \emptyset, B_i)$, $\mathrm{dsep}_G(A_i, \emptyset, C_i)$, or $\mathrm{dsep}_G(B_i, \emptyset, C_i)$ hold for $i = 1, 2, 3$.

4.3. Show that every root variable X in a DAG G is d-separated from every other root variable Y.

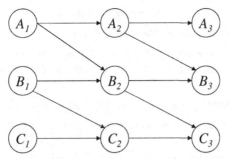

Figure 4.15: A directed acyclic graph.

4.4. Consider a Bayesian network over variables $\mathbf{X}$, S that induces a distribution Pr. Suppose that S is a leaf node in the network that has a single parent $U \in \mathbf{X}$. For a given value s of variable S, show that $\Pr(\mathbf{x}|s)$ does not change if we change the CPT of variable S as follows:

$$\theta'_{s|u} = \eta \, \theta_{s|u}$$

for all u and some constant $\eta > 0$.

4.5. Consider the distribution Pr defined by Equation 4.2 and DAG G. Show the following:

(a) $\sum_{\mathbf{z}} \Pr(\mathbf{z}) = 1$.

(b) Pr satisfies the independencies in $\mathrm{Markov}(G)$.

(c) $\Pr(x|\mathbf{u}) = \theta_{x|\mathbf{u}}$ for every value x of variable X and every instantiation $\mathbf{u}$ of its parents $\mathbf{U}$.

4.6. Use the graphoid axioms to prove $\mathrm{dsep}_G(S_1, S_2, \{S_3, \ldots, S_n\})$ in the DAG G of Figure 4.11. Assume that you are given the Markovian assumptions for DAG G.

4.7. Show that $\mathrm{dsep}_G(\mathbf{X}, \mathbf{Z}, \mathbf{Y})$ can be decided in time and space that are linear in the size of DAG G based on Theorem 4.1.

4.8. Show that the graphoid axioms imply the chain rule:

$$I(\mathbf{X}, \mathbf{Y}, \mathbf{Z}) \text{ and } I(\mathbf{X} \cup \mathbf{Y}, \mathbf{Z}, \mathbf{W}) \text{ only if } I(\mathbf{X}, \mathbf{Y}, \mathbf{W}).$$

4.9. Prove that the graphoid axioms hold for probability distributions, and that the intersection axiom holds for strictly positive distributions.

4.10. Provide a probability distribution over three variables X, Y, and Z that violates the composition axiom. That is, show that $I_{\Pr}(Z, \emptyset, X)$ and $I_{\Pr}(Z, \emptyset, Y)$ but not $I_{\Pr}(Z, \emptyset, XY)$. Hint: Assume that X and Y are inputs to a noisy gate and Z is its output.

4.11. Provide a probability distribution over three variables X, Y, and Z that violates the intersection axiom. That is, show that $I_{\Pr}(X, Z, Y)$ and $I_{\Pr}(X, Y, Z)$ but not $I_{\Pr}(X, \emptyset, YZ)$.

4.12. Construct two distinct DAGs over variables A, B, C, and D. Each DAG must have exactly four edges and the DAGs must agree on d-separation.

4.13. Prove that d-separation satisfies the properties of intersection and chordality.

4.14. Consider the DAG G in Figure 4.4. Suppose that this DAG is a P-MAP of some distribution Pr. Construct a minimal I-MAP G' for Pr using each of the following variable orders:

(a) A, D, B, C, E

(b) A, B, C, D, E

(c) E, D, C, B, A

4.15. Identify a DAG that is a D-MAP for all distributions Pr over variables $\mathbf{X}$. Similarly, identify another DAG that is an I-MAP for all distributions Pr over variable $\mathbf{X}$.

4.16. Consider the DAG G in Figure 4.15. Suppose that this DAG is a P-MAP of a distribution Pr.

(a) What is the Markov boundary for the variable C_2?

(b) Is the Markov boundary of A_1 a Markov blanket of B_3?

(c) Which variable has the smallest Markov boundary?

4.17. Prove that for strictly positive distributions, if $\mathbf{B}_1$ and $\mathbf{B}_2$ are Markov blankets for some variable X, then $\mathbf{B}_1 \cap \mathbf{B}_2$ is also a Markov blanket for X. Hint: Appeal to the intersection axiom.

4.18. (After Pearl) Consider the following independence statements: $I(A, \emptyset, B)$ and $I(AB, C, D)$.

(a) Find all independence statements that follow from these two statements using the positive graphoid axioms.

(b) Construct minimal I-MAPs of the statements in (a) (original and derived) using the following variable orders:

- A, B, C, D
- D, C, B, A
- A, D, B, C

4.19. Assume that the algorithm in Section 4.6.2 is correct as far as producing an I-MAP G for the given distribution Pr. Prove that G must also be a minimal I-MAP.

4.20. Suppose that G is a DAG and let $\mathbf{W}$ be a set of nodes in G with deterministic CPTs (i.e., their parameters are either 0 or 1). Propose a modification to the d-separation test that can take advantage of nodes $\mathbf{W}$ and that will be stronger than d-separation (i.e., discover independencies that d-separation cannot discover).

4.21. Let Pr be a probability distribution over variables $\mathbf{X}$ and let $\mathbf{B}$ be a Markov blanket for variable X. Show the correctness of the following procedure for finding a Markov boundary for X.

- Let $\mathbf{R}$ be $\mathbf{X} \setminus (\{X\} \cup \mathbf{B})$.
- Repeat until every variable in $\mathbf{B}$ has been examined or $\mathbf{B}$ is empty:
  1. Pick a variable Y in $\mathbf{B}$.
  2. Test whether $I_{\Pr}(X, \mathbf{B} \setminus \{Y\}, \mathbf{R} \cup \{Y\})$.
  3. If the test succeeds, remove Y from $\mathbf{B}$, add it to $\mathbf{R}$, and go to Step 1.
- Declare $\mathbf{B}$ a Markov boundary for X and exit.

Hint: Appeal to the weak union axiom.

4.22. Show that every probability distribution Pr over variables $X_1, \ldots, X_n$ can be induced by some Bayesian network (G, Θ) over variables $X_1, \ldots, X_n$. In particular, show how (G, Θ) can be constructed from Pr.

4.23. Let G be a DAG and let G' by an undirected graph generated from G as follows:

1. For every node in G, every pair of its parents are connected by an undirected edge.
2. Every directed edge in G is converted into an undirected edge.

For every variable X, let $\mathbf{B}_X$ be its neighbors in G' and $\mathbf{Z}_X$ be all variables excluding X and $\mathbf{B}_X$. Show that X and $\mathbf{Z}_X$ are d-separated by $\mathbf{B}_X$ in DAG G.

4.24. Let G be a DAG and let $\mathbf{X}, \mathbf{Y}$, and $\mathbf{Z}$ be three disjoint sets of nodes in G. Let G' be an undirected graph constructed from G according to the following steps:

1. Every node is removed from G unless it is in $\mathbf{X} \cup \mathbf{Y} \cup \mathbf{Z}$ or one of its descendants is in $\mathbf{X} \cup \mathbf{Y} \cup \mathbf{Z}$.
2. For every node in G, every pair of its parents are connected by an undirected edge.
3. Every directed edge in G is converted into an undirected edge.

Show that $\mathrm{dsep}_G(\mathbf{X}, \mathbf{Z}, \mathbf{Y})$ if and only if $\mathbf{X}$ and $\mathbf{Y}$ are separated by $\mathbf{Z}$ in G' (i.e., every path between $\mathbf{X}$ and $\mathbf{Y}$ in G' must pass through $\mathbf{Z}$).

4.25. Let X and Y be two nodes in a DAG G that are not connected by an edge. Let $\mathbf{Z}$ be a set of nodes defined as follows: $Z \in \mathbf{Z}$ if and only if $Z \notin \{X, Y\}$ and Z is an ancestor of X or an ancestor of Y. Show that $\mathrm{dsep}_G(X, \mathbf{Z}, Y)$.

4.8 Proofs

PROOF OF THEOREM 4.1. Suppose that $\mathbf{X}$ and $\mathbf{Y}$ are d-separated by $\mathbf{Z}$ in G. Every path α between $\mathbf{X}$ and $\mathbf{Y}$ must then be blocked by $\mathbf{Z}$. We show that path α will not appear in G' (one of its nodes or edges will be pruned) and, hence, $\mathbf{X}$ and $\mathbf{Y}$ cannot be connected in G'.

We first note that α must have at least one internal node. Moreover, we must have one of the following cases:

1. For some sequential valve $\rightarrow W \rightarrow$ or divergent valve $\leftarrow W \rightarrow$ on path α, variable W belongs to $\mathbf{Z}$. In this case, the outgoing edges of W will be pruned and not exist in G'. Hence, the path α cannot be part of G'.

2. For all sequential and divergent valves $\rightarrow W \rightarrow$ and $\leftarrow W \rightarrow$ on path α, variable W is not in $\mathbf{Z}$. We must then have some convergent valve $\rightarrow W \leftarrow$ on α where neither W nor one of its descendants are in $\mathbf{Z}$. Moreover, for at least one of these valves $\rightarrow W \leftarrow$, no descendant of W can belong to $\mathbf{X} \cup \mathbf{Y}$.[4] Hence, W will be pruned and not appear in G'. The path α will then not be part of G'.

Suppose now that $\mathbf{X}$ and $\mathbf{Y}$ are not d-separated by $\mathbf{Z}$ in G. There must exist a path α between $\mathbf{X}$ and $\mathbf{Y}$ in G that is not blocked by $\mathbf{Z}$. We now show that path α will appear in G' (none of its nodes or edges will be pruned). Hence, $\mathbf{X}$ and $\mathbf{Y}$ must be connected in G'.

If path α has no internal nodes, the result follows immediately; otherwise, no node of path α will be pruned for the following reason. If the node is part of a convergent valve $\rightarrow W \leftarrow$, then W or one of its descendants must be in $\mathbf{Z}$ and, hence, cannot be pruned. If the node is part of a sequential or divergent valve, $\rightarrow W \rightarrow$ or $\leftarrow W \rightarrow$, then moving away from W in the direction of an outgoing edge will either:

1. Lead us to $\mathbf{X}$ or to $\mathbf{Y}$ in a directed path, which means that W has a descendant in $\mathbf{X} \cup \mathbf{Y}$ and will therefore not be pruned.

2. Lead us to a convergent valve $\rightarrow W' \leftarrow$, which must be either in $\mathbf{Z}$ or has a descendant in $\mathbf{Z}$. Hence, node W will have a descendant in $\mathbf{Z}$ and cannot be pruned.

No edge on the path α will be pruned for the following reason. For the edge to be pruned, it must be outgoing from a node W in $\mathbf{Z}$, which must then be part of a sequential or divergent valve on path α. But this is impossible since all sequential and divergent valves on α are unblocked. ■

PROOF OF THEOREM 4.2. The proof of this theorem is given in Verma [1986]; see also Verma and Pearl [1990a;b]. ■

PROOF OF THEOREM 4.3. The proof of this theorem is given in Geiger and Pearl [1988a]; see also Geiger and Pearl [1988b]. ■

---

[4] Consider a valve $(\rightarrow W \leftarrow)$ on the path α: $\mathbf{X} \gamma \rightarrow W \leftarrow \beta \mathbf{Y}$. Suppose that W has a descendant in, say, $\mathbf{Y}$. We then have a path from $\mathbf{X}$ through γ and W and then directed to $\mathbf{Y}$ that has at least one less convergent valve than α. By repeating the same argument on this new path, we must either encounter a convergent valve that has no descendant in $\mathbf{X} \cup \mathbf{Y}$ or establish a path between $\mathbf{X}$ and $\mathbf{Y}$ that does not have a convergent valve (the path would then be unblocked, which is a contradiction).

5

Building Bayesian Networks

We address in this chapter a number of problems that arise in real-world applications, showing how each can be solved by modeling and reasoning with Bayesian networks.

5.1 Introduction

We consider a number of real-world applications in this chapter drawn from the domains of diagnosis, reliability, genetics, channel coding, and commonsense reasoning. For each one of these applications, we state a specific reasoning problem that can be addressed by posing a formal query with respect to a corresponding Bayesian network. We discuss the process of constructing the required network and then identify the specific queries that need to be applied.

There are at least four general types of queries that can be posed with respect to a Bayesian network. Which type of query to use in a specific situation is not always trivial and some of the queries are guaranteed to be equivalent under certain conditions. We define these query types formally in Section 5.2 and then discuss them and their relationships in more detail when we go over the various applications in Section 5.3.

The construction of a Bayesian network involves three major steps. First, we must decide on the set of relevant variables and their possible values. Next, we must build the network structure by connecting the variables into a DAG. Finally, we must define the CPT for each network variable. The last step is the quantitative part of this construction process and can be the most involved in certain situations. Two of the key issues that arise here are the potentially large size of CPTs and the significance of the specific numbers used to populate them. We present techniques for dealing with the first issue in Section 5.4 and for dealing with the second issue in Section 5.5.

5.2 Reasoning with Bayesian networks

To ground the discussion of this section in concrete examples, we find it useful to make reference to a software tool for modeling and reasoning with Bayesian networks. A screenshot of one such tool, Samlam,[1] is depicted in Figure 5.1. This figure shows a Bayesian network, known as "Asia," that will be used as a running example throughout this section.[2]

5.2.1 Probability of evidence

One of the simplest queries with respect to a Bayesian network is to ask for the probability of some variable instantiation $\mathbf{e}$, $\Pr(\mathbf{e})$. For example, in the Asia network we may be

---

[1] Samlam is available at *http://reasoning.cs.ucla.edu/samiam/*.

[2] This network is available with the Samlam distribution.

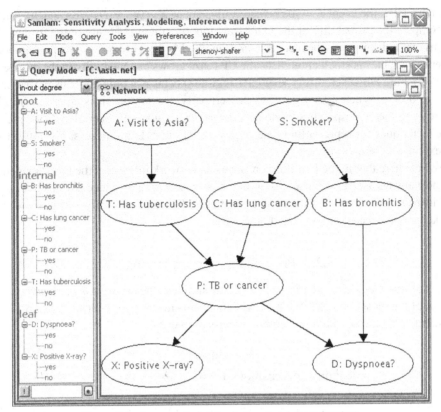

Figure 5.1: A screenshot of the Asia network from Samlam.

interested in knowing the probability that the patient has a positive x-ray but no dyspnoea, $\Pr(X = \text{yes}, D = \text{no})$. This can be computed easily by tools such as **Samlam**, leading to a probability of about 3.96%. The variables $\mathbf{E} = \{X, D\}$ are called *evidence variables* in this case and the query $\Pr(\mathbf{e})$ is known as a *probability-of-evidence* query, although it refers to a very specific type of evidence corresponding to the instantiation of some variables.

There are other types of evidence beyond variable instantiations. In fact, any propositional sentence can be used to specify evidence. For example, we may want to know the probability that the patient has either a positive x-ray or dyspnoea, $X = \text{yes} \vee D = \text{yes}$. Bayesian network tools do not usually provide direct support for computing the probability of arbitrary pieces of evidence but such probabilities can be computed indirectly using the following technique.

We can add an auxiliary node E to the network, declare nodes X and D as the parents of E, and then adopt the following CPT for E:[3]

X	D	E	$\Pr(e\|x, d)$
yes	yes	yes	1
yes	no	yes	1
no	yes	yes	1
no	no	yes	0

---

[3] We have omitted redundant rows from the given CPT.

Given this CPT, the event $E = \text{yes}$ is then equivalent to $X = \text{yes} \lor D = \text{yes}$ and, hence, we can compute the probability of the latter by computing the probability of the former.

This method, known as the *auxiliary-node method,* is practical only when the number of evidence variables is small enough, as the CPT size grows exponentially in the number of these variables. However, this type of CPT is quite special as it only contains probabilities equal to 0 or 1. When a CPT satisfies this property, we say that it is *deterministic.* We also refer to the corresponding node as a *deterministic node.* In Section 5.4, we present some techniques for representing deterministic CPTs that do not necessarily suffer from this exponential growth in size.

We note here that in the literature on Bayesian network inference, the term "evidence" is almost always used to mean an instantiation of some variables. Since any arbitrary piece of evidence can be modeled using an instantiation (of some auxiliary variable), we will also keep to this usage unless stated otherwise.

5.2.2 Prior and posterior marginals

If probability-of-evidence queries are one of the simplest, then *posterior-marginal queries* are one of the most common. We first explain what is meant by the terms "posterior" and "marginal" and then explain this common class of queries.

Marginals

Given a joint probability distribution $\Pr(x_1, \ldots, x_n)$, the *marginal distribution* $\Pr(x_1, \ldots, x_m)$, $m \leq n$, is defined as follows:

$$\Pr(x_1, \ldots, x_m) = \sum_{x_{m+1}, \ldots, x_n} \Pr(x_1, \ldots, x_n).$$

That is, the marginal distribution can be viewed as a *projection* of the joint distribution on the smaller set of variables $X_1, \ldots, X_m$. In fact, most often the set of variables $X_1, \ldots, X_m$ is small enough to allow an explicit representation of the marginal distribution in tabular form (which is usually not feasible for the joint distribution).

When the marginal distribution is computed given some evidence $\mathbf{e}$,

$$\Pr(x_1, \ldots, x_m | \mathbf{e}) = \sum_{x_{m+1}, \ldots, x_n} \Pr(x_1, \ldots, x_n | \mathbf{e}),$$

it is known as a *posterior marginal.* This is to be contrasted with the marginal distribution given no evidence, which is known as a *prior marginal.*

Figure 5.2 depicts a screenshot where the prior marginals are shown for every variable in the network. Figure 5.3 depicts another screenshot of Samlam where posterior marginals are shown for every variable given that the patient has a positive x-ray but no dyspnoea, $\mathbf{e}: X = \text{yes}, D = \text{no}$. The small windows containing marginals in Figures 5.2 and 5.3 are known as *monitors* and are quite common in tools for reasoning with Bayesian networks. According to these monitors, we have the following prior and posterior marginals for lung cancer, C, respectively:

C	$\Pr(C)$
yes	5.50%
no	94.50%

C	$\Pr(C|\mathbf{e})$
yes	25.23%
no	74.77%

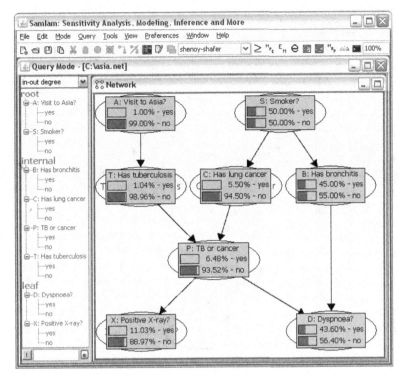

Figure 5.2: Prior marginals in the Asia network.

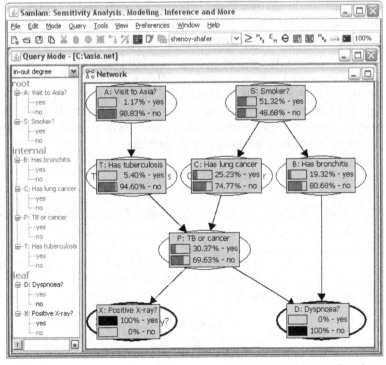

Figure 5.3: Posterior marginals in the Asia network given a positive x-ray and no dyspnoea.

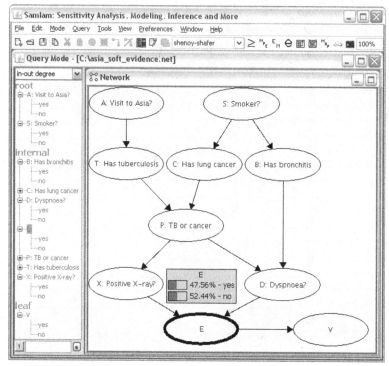

Figure 5.4: Representing soft evidence on variable E using auxiliary variable V.

Soft evidence

We have seen in Section 3.6.4 how soft evidence can be reduced to hard evidence on a noisy sensor. This approach can be easily adopted in the context of Bayesian networks by adding auxiliary nodes to represent such noisy sensors. Suppose for example that we receive soft evidence that doubles the odds of a positive x-ray or dyspnoea, $X =$ yes $\vee$ $D =$ yes. In the previous section, we showed that this disjunction can be represented explicitly in the network using the auxiliary variable E. We can also represent the soft evidence explicitly by adding another auxiliary variable V to represent the state of a noisy sensor, as shown in Figure 5.4. The strength of the soft evidence is then captured by the CPT of variable V, as discussed in Section 3.6.4. In particular, all we have to do is choose a CPT with a false positive rate f_p and a false negative rate f_n such that

$$\frac{1 - f_n}{f_p} = k^+,$$

where k^+ is the Bayes factor quantifying the strength of the soft evidence. That is, the CPT for E should satisfy

$$\frac{1 - \theta_{V=\text{no}|\,E=\text{yes}}}{\theta_{V=\text{yes}|\,E=\text{no}}} = \frac{\theta_{V=\text{yes}|\,E=\text{yes}}}{\theta_{V=\text{yes}|\,E=\text{no}}} = 2.$$

One choice for the CPT of variable V is[4]

E	V	$\theta_{v|e}$
yes	yes	.8
no	yes	.4

---

[4] Again, we are suppressing the redundant rows in this CPT.

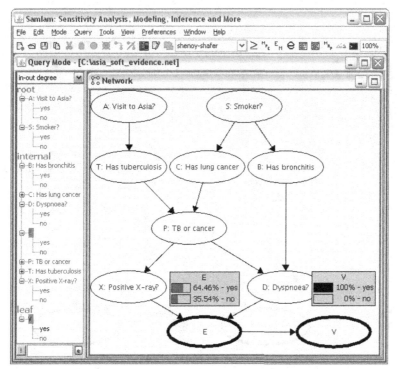

Figure 5.5: Asserting soft evidence on variable E by setting the value of auxiliary variable V.

We can then accommodate the soft evidence by setting the value of auxiliary variable V to yes, as shown in Figure 5.5. Note the prior and posterior marginals over variable E, which are shown in Figures 5.4 and 5.5, respectively:

E	$\Pr(E)$
yes	47.56%
no	52.44%

E	$\Pr(E\,|\,V=\text{yes})$
yes	64.46%
no	35.54%

The ratio of odds is then

$$\frac{O(E=\text{yes}\,|\,V=\text{yes})}{O(E=\text{yes})} = \frac{64.46/35.54}{47.56/52.44} \approx 2.$$

Hence, the hard evidence $V=\text{yes}$ leads to doubling the odds of $E=\text{yes}$, as expected.

As mentioned in Section 3.6.4, the method of emulating soft evidence by hard evidence on an auxiliary node is also known as the method of *virtual evidence*.

5.2.3 Most probable explanation (MPE)

We now turn to another class of queries with respect to Bayesian networks: computing the *most probable explanation* (MPE). The goal here is to identify the most probable instantiation of network variables given some evidence. Specifically, if $X_1, \dots, X_n$ are all the network variables and if **e** is the given evidence, the goal then is to identify an instantiation $x_1, \dots, x_n$ for which the probability $\Pr(x_1, \dots, x_n|\mathbf{e})$ is maximal. Such an instantiation $x_1, \dots, x_n$ will be called a *most probable explanation* given evidence **e**.

Consider Figure 5.6, which depicts a screenshot of Samlam after having computed the MPE given a patient with positive x-ray and dyspnoea. According to the result of this

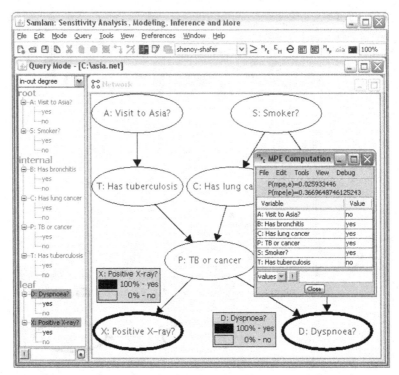

Figure 5.6: Computing the MPE given a positive x-ray and dyspnoea.

query, the MPE corresponds to a patient that made no visit to Asia, is a smoker, and has lung cancer and bronchitis but no tuberculosis.

It is important to note here that an MPE cannot be obtained directly from posterior marginals. That is, if $x_1, \ldots, x_n$ is an instantiation obtained by choosing each value x_i so as to maximize the probability $\Pr(x_i | \mathbf{e})$, then $x_1, \ldots, x_n$ is not necessarily an MPE. Consider the posterior marginals in Figure 5.3 as an example. If we choose for each variable the value with maximal probability, we get an explanation in which the patient is a smoker:

$$\alpha: \ A=\text{no}, \ S=\text{yes}, \ T=\text{no}, \ C=\text{no}, \ B=\text{no}, \ P=\text{no}, \ X=\text{yes}, \ D=\text{no}.$$

This instantiation has a probability of $\approx 20.03\%$ given the evidence $\mathbf{e}$: $X=\text{yes}$, $D=\text{no}$. However, the most probable explanation given by Figure 5.7 is one in which the patient is not a smoker:

$$\alpha: \ A=\text{no}, \ S=\text{no}, \ T=\text{no}, \ C=\text{no}, \ B=\text{no}, \ P=\text{no}, \ X=\text{yes}, \ D=\text{no}.$$

This instantiation has a probability of $\approx 38.57\%$ given evidence $\mathbf{e}$: $X=\text{yes}$, $D=\text{no}$.

5.2.4 Maximum a posteriori hypothesis (MAP)

The MPE query is a special case of a more general class of queries for finding the most probable instantiation of a subset of network variables. Specifically, suppose that the set of all network variables is $\mathbf{X}$ and let $\mathbf{M}$ be a subset of these variables. Given some evidence $\mathbf{e}$, our goal is then to find an instantiation $\mathbf{m}$ of variables $\mathbf{M}$ for which the probability $\Pr(\mathbf{m}|\mathbf{e})$ is maximal. Any instantiation $\mathbf{m}$ that satisfies the previous property is known as a *maximum a posteriori hypothesis* (MAP). Moreover, the variables in $\mathbf{M}$ are known as *MAP*

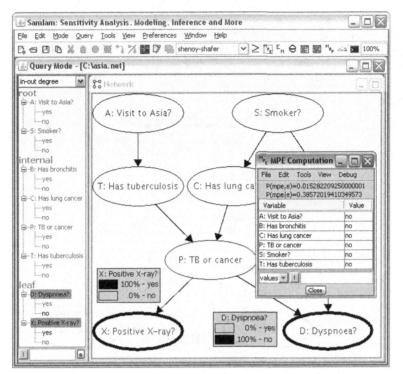

Figure 5.7: Computing the MPE given a positive x-ray and no dyspnoea.

variables. Clearly, MPE is a special case of MAP when the MAP variables include all network variables. One reason why a distinction is made between MAP and MPE is that MPE is much easier to compute algorithmically, an issue that we explain in Chapter 11.

Consider Figure 5.8 for an example of MAP. Here we have a patient with a positive x-ray and no dyspnoea, so the evidence is $X = $ yes, $D = $ no. The MAP variables are $\mathbf{M} = \{A, S\}$, so we want to know the most likely instantiation of these variables given the evidence. According to Figure 5.8, the instantiation

$$A = \text{no}, \ S = \text{yes}$$

is a MAP that happens to have a probability of $\approx 50.74\%$ given the evidence.

A common method for approximating MAP is to compute an MPE and then return the values it assigns to MAP variables. We say in this case that we are *projecting* the MPE on MAP variables. However, we stress that this is only an approximation scheme as it may return an instantiation of the MAP variables that is not maximally probable. Consider again the MPE example from Figure 5.7, which gives the following most probable instantiation:

$$A = \text{no}, \ S = \text{no}, \ T = \text{no}, \ C = \text{no}, \ B = \text{no}, \ P = \text{no}, \ X = \text{yes}, \ D = \text{no}$$

under evidence $X = $ yes, $D = $ no. Projecting this MPE on the variables $\mathbf{M} = \{A, S\}$, we get the instantiation

$$A = \text{no}, \ S = \text{no},$$

which has a probability $\approx 48.09\%$ given the evidence. This instantiation is clearly not a MAP as we found a more probable instantiation earlier, that is, $A = $ no, $S = $ yes with a probability of about 50.74%.

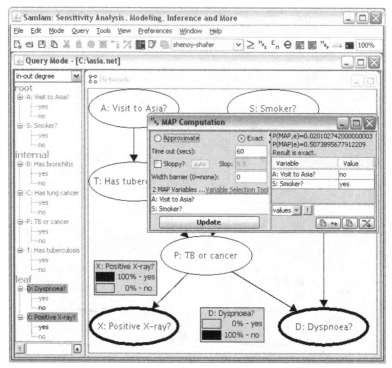

Figure 5.8: Computing the maximum a posteriori hypothesis (MAP) given a positive x-ray and no dyspnoea.

There is a relatively general class of situations in which the solution to a MAP query can be obtained immediately from an MPE solution by projecting it on the MAP variables. To formally define this class of situations, let **E** be the evidence variables, **M** be the MAP variables, and **Y** be all other network variables. The condition is that there is at most one instantiation **y** of variables **Y** that is compatible with any particular instantiations **m** and **e** of variables **M** and **E**, respectively. More formally, if $\Pr(\mathbf{m}, \mathbf{e}) > 0$, then $\Pr(\mathbf{m}, \mathbf{e}, \mathbf{y}) \neq 0$ for exactly one instantiation **y** (see Exercise 5.11). We later discuss two classes of applications where this condition can be satisfied: diagnosis of digital circuits and channel coding.

5.3 Modeling with Bayesian networks

We discuss in this section a number of reasoning problems that arise in real-world applications and show how each can be addressed by first modeling the problem using a Bayesian network and then posing one of the queries defined in the previous section.

Before we proceed with this modeling exercise, we need to state some general modeling principles that we adhere to in all our examples. Specifically, each Bayesian network will be constructed in three consecutive steps.

Step 1: Define the network variables and their values. We partition network variables into three types: query, evidence, and intermediary variables. A *query variable* is one that we need to ask questions about, such as compute its posterior marginal. An *evidence variable* is one about which we may need to assert evidence. Finally, an *intermediary variable* is neither query nor evidence and is meant to aid the modeling process by detailing the relationship between evidence and query variables. Query and evidence variables are usually immediately determined from the problem statement.[5] Intermediary variables are less obvious to determine and can depend on subtle modeling decisions. However, we will provide some specific rules for when intermediary variables are necessary and when they are not. Determining the values of variables may also not be that obvious and will be dealt with in the context of specific examples.

Step 2: Define the network structure (edges). In all of our examples, we are guided by a causal interpretation of network structure. Hence, the determination of this structure is reduced to answering the following question about each network variable X: What is the set of variables that we regard as the direct causes of X?

Step 3: Define the network CPTs. The difficulty and objectivity of this step varies considerably from one problem to another. We consider some problems where the CPTs are determined completely from the problem statement by objective considerations and others where the CPTs are a reflection of subjective beliefs. In Chapters 17 and 18, we also consider techniques for estimating CPTs from data.

5.3.1 Diagnosis I: Model from expert

The first modeling example we consider is from medical diagnostics. Consider the following commonplace medical information:

> The flu is an acute disease characterized by fever, body aches, and pains, and can be associated with chilling and a sore throat. The cold is a bodily disorder popularly associated with chilling and can cause a sore throat. Tonsillitis is inflammation of the tonsils that leads to a sore throat and can be associated with fever.

Our goal here is to develop a Bayesian network to capture this knowledge and use it to diagnose the condition of a patient suffering from some of the symptoms mentioned here.

Our first step is to identify network variables, which as we mentioned previously fall into three categories: query, evidence, and intermediary. To determine query variables, we need to identify those events about which we need to ask questions. In this case, we need to know whether the patient has a flu, a cold, or tonsillitis, which suggests three corresponding variables for this purpose; see Figure 5.9(a). To determine evidence variables, we need to identify those events about which we can collect information. These correspond to the different symptoms that a patient can exhibit: chilling, body ache and pain, sore throat, and fever, which again leads to four corresponding variables, as shown in Figure 5.9(a). The information given does not seem to suggest any intermediary variables, so we do not include any. The values of each of the identified variables can be simply one of two, true or false, although more refined information may suggest different degrees of body ache. Determining the network structure is relatively straightforward: There are no causes for the different conditions and the cause of each symptom is immediate from the given information.

---

[5] Note that the distinction between query, evidence, and intermediary variables is not a property of the Bayesian network but of the task at hand. Hence, one may redefine these three sets of variables accordingly if the task changes.

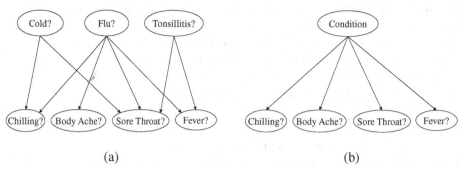

Figure 5.9: Two Bayesian network structures for medical diagnosis. The one on the right is known as a naive Bayes structure.

It is tempting to have a different network structure for this problem, which is shown in Figure 5.9(b). In this case, we decided to have one variable "Condition," which has multiple values: normal, cold, flu, and tonsillitis. This network is clearly simpler than the first one and is an instance of a very common structure known as *naive Bayes*. More generally, a naive Bayes structure has the following edges, $C \to A_1, \ldots, C \to A_m$, where C is called the *class variable* and $A_1, \ldots, A_m$ are called the *attributes*.

There is quite a bit of difference between the two structures in Figure 5.9 since the naive Bayes structure makes a key commitment known as the *single-fault* assumption. Specifically, it assumes that only one condition can exist in the patient at any time since the multiple values of the "Condition" variable are exclusive of each other. This single-fault assumption has implications that are inconsistent with the information given. For example, it implies that if the patient is known to have a cold, then fever and sore throat become independent since they are d-separated by the "Condition" variable. However, this does not hold in the structure of Figure 5.9(a) as a fever may increase our belief in tonsillitis, which could then increase our belief in a sore throat.

Here are some implications of this modeling inaccuracy. First, if the only evidence we have is body ache, we expect the probability of flu to increase in both networks. But this will also lead to dropping the probabilities of cold and tonsillitis in the naive Bayes structure yet these probabilities will remain the same in the other network since both cold and tonsillitis are d-separated from body ache. Second, if all we know is that the patient has no fever, then the belief in cold may increase in the naive Bayes structure, while it is guaranteed to remain the same in the other structure since cold is d-separated from fever.

We now turn to the specification of CPTs for the developed network structure. The main point here is that the CPTs for this network fall into one of two categories: the CPTs for the various conditions and those for the symptoms. Specifically, the CPT for a condition such as tonsillitis must provide the belief in developing tonsillitis by a person about whom we have no knowledge of any symptoms. The CPT for a symptom such as chilling must provide the belief in this symptom under the four possible conditions: no cold and no flu, cold and no flu, no cold and flu, or cold and flu. The probabilities needed for specifying these CPTs are usually obtained from a medical expert who supplies this information based on known medical statistics or subjective beliefs gained through practical experience (see also Section 5.4.1).

Another key method for specifying the CPTs of this and similar networks is by estimating them directly from medical records of previous patients. These records may appear as follows:

Case	Cold?	Flu?	Tonsillitis?	Chilling?	Bodyache?	Sorethroat?	Fever?
1	true	false	?	true	false	false	false
2	false	true	false	true	true	false	true
3	?	?	true	false	?	true	false
⋮	⋮	⋮	⋮	⋮	⋮	⋮	⋮

Each row in this table represents a medical case of a particular patient where "?" indicates the unavailability of corresponding data for that patient. Many of the tools for Bayesian network inference can take a table such as the one given and then generate a parametrization Θ of the given network structure that tries to maximize the probability of seeing the given cases. In particular, if each case is represented by event $\mathbf{d}_i$, then such tools will generate a parametrization Θ that leads to a probability distribution Pr that attempts to maximize the following quantity:

$$\prod_{i=1}^{N} \Pr(\mathbf{d}_i).$$

Each term $\Pr(\mathbf{d}_i)$ in this product represents the probability of seeing the case $\mathbf{d}_i$ and the product itself represents the probability of seeing all of the N cases (assuming that the cases are independent). Parameter estimation techniques are discussed at length in Chapters 17 and 18.

We close this section by noting that a diagnostic problem for a particular patient corresponds to a set of symptoms that represent the known evidence. The goal is then to compute the most probable combination of conditions given the evidence. This can be solved by posing a MAP query to the network with the MAP variables being cold, flu, and tonsillitis. If the evidence covers all of the four symptoms, the MAP query will then reduce to an MPE query.

5.3.2 Diagnosis II: Model from expert

We now consider another problem from medicine that will serve to illustrate some major issues that arise when constructing Bayesian networks:

A few weeks after inseminating a cow, we have three possible tests to confirm pregnancy. The first is a scanning test that has a false positive of 1% and a false negative of 10%. The second is a blood test that detects progesterone with a false positive of 10% and a false negative of 30%. The third test is a urine test that also detects progesterone with a false positive of 10% and a false negative of 20%. The probability of a detectable progesterone level is 90% given pregnancy and 1% given no pregnancy. The probability that insemination will impregnate a cow is 87%.

Our task here is to build a Bayesian network and use it to compute the probability of pregnancy given the results of some of these pregnancy tests.

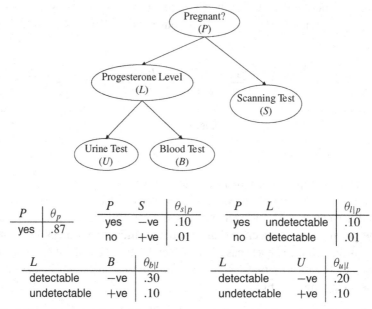

P	θ_p
yes	.87

P	S	$\theta_{s\|p}$
yes	−ve	.10
no	+ve	.01

P	L	$\theta_{l\|p}$
yes	undetectable	.10
no	detectable	.01

L	B	$\theta_{b\|l}$
detectable	−ve	.30
undetectable	+ve	.10

L	U	$\theta_{u\|l}$
detectable	−ve	.20
undetectable	+ve	.10

Figure 5.10: A Bayesian network for detecting pregnancy based on three tests. Redundant CPT rows have been omitted.

The information given here suggests the following variables:

- One query variable to represent pregnancy (P)
- Three evidence variables to represent the results of various tests: scanning test (S), blood test (B), and urine test (U)
- One intermediary variable to represent progesterone level (L).

Moreover, common understanding of causal relationships in this domain suggests the causal structure in Figure 5.10, where pregnancy is a direct cause of both the scanning test and progesterone level, which in turn is the direct cause of the blood and urine tests. Some of the independencies implied by the constructed structure are:

- The blood and urine tests are independent, given the progesterone level.
- The scanning test is independent of the blood and urine tests, given the status of pregnancy.

Note, however, that blood and urine tests are not independent even if we know the status of pregnancy since the result of one test will affect our belief in progesterone level, which will then affect our belief in the second test's outcome. The CPTs for this problem can be specified directly from the problem statement as shown in Figure 5.10.

Suppose now that we inseminate a cow, wait for a few weeks, and then perform the three tests, which all come out negative. Hence, the evidence we have is

$$\text{e:} \quad S = -\text{ve}, \ B = -\text{ve}, \ U = -\text{ve}.$$

If we compute the posterior marginal for pregnancy given this evidence, we get

P	Pr(P|e)
yes	10.21%
no	89.79%

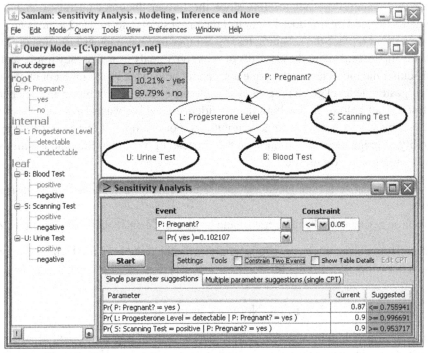

Figure 5.11: Sensitivity analysis in Samlam: What are the single-parameter changes necessary to ensure that the probability of pregnancy is no more than 5% given three negative tests?

Note that even though the probability of pregnancy is reduced from 87% to 10.21%, it is still relatively high given that all three tests came out negative.

5.3.3 Sensitivity analysis

Suppose now that a farmer is not too happy with this result and would like three negative tests to drop the probability of pregnancy to no more than 5%. Moreover, the farmer is willing to replace the test kits for this purpose but needs to know the false positive and negative rates of the new tests, which would ensure the constraint. This is a problem of sensitivity analysis, discussed in Chapter 16, in which we try to understand the relationship between the parameters of a Bayesian network and the conclusions drawn based on the network. For a concrete example of this type of analysis, Figure 5.11 depicts a screenshot of Samlam in which the following question is posed to the sensitivity analysis engine:

> Which network parameter do we have to change, and by how much, to ensure that the probability of pregnancy would be no more than 5% given three negative tests?

The previous query is implicitly asking for a single parameter change and Figure 5.11 portrays three possible changes, each of which is guaranteed to satisfy the constraint:[6]

1. If the false negative rate for the scanning test were about 4.63% instead of 10%
2. If the probability of pregnancy given insemination were about 75.59% instead of 87%
3. If the probability of a detectable progesterone level given pregnancy were about 99.67% instead of 90%.

---

[6] If multiple parameters can change simultaneously, the results would be different; see Chapter 16 for details.

The last two changes are not feasible since the farmer does not intend to change the insemination procedure nor does he control the progesterone level. Hence, he is left with only one option: replace the scanning test by another that has a lower false negative rate.

What is interesting about these results of sensitivity analysis is that they imply that improving either the blood test or the urine test cannot help. That is, the inherent uncertainty in the progesterone level given pregnancy is such that even a perfect blood test or a perfect urine test cannot help us in reaching the confidence level we want. However, these tests would become relevant if we were less ambitious. For example, if our goal is to drop the probability of pregnancy to no more than 8% (instead of 5%), then Samlam identifies the following additional possibilities:

- The false negative for the blood test should be no more than about 12.32% instead of 30%.

- The false negative for the urine test should be no more than about 8.22% instead of 20%.

As is clear from this example, sensitivity analysis can be quite important when developing Bayesian networks. We discuss this mode of analysis in some depth in Chapter 16.

5.3.4 Network granularity

The pregnancy problem provides an opportunity to discuss one of the central issues that arises when building Bayesian networks (and models in general): How fine-grained should the network be?

Specifically, consider again the network in Figure 5.10 and note that progesterone level (L) is neither a query variable nor an evidence variable. That is, we cannot observe the value of this variable nor are we interested in making inferences about it. The question then is: Why do we need to include it in the network?

Progesterone level is an intermediary variable that helps in modeling the relationship between the blood and urine tests on the one hand and pregnancy on the other. It is therefore a modeling convenience as it would be more difficult to build the model without including it explicitly. For example, the supplier of these tests may have only provided their false positive and negative rates with respect to progesterone level and we may have obtained the numbers relating progesterone to pregnancy from another source. Hence, the inclusion of this intermediary variable in the network helps in integrating these two pieces of information in a modular way. But now that we have the network in Figure 5.10, we are able to compute the following quantities:

$$\Pr(B = -\text{ve} | P = \text{yes}) = 36\%$$
$$\Pr(B = +\text{ve} | P = \text{no}) = 10.6\%$$
$$\Pr(U = -\text{ve} | P = \text{yes}) = 27\%$$
$$\Pr(U = +\text{ve} | P = \text{no}) = 10.7\%,$$

which allow us to build the network in Figure 5.12, where the progesterone level is no longer represented explicitly. The question now is whether this simpler network is equivalent to the original one from the viewpoint of answering queries.

By examining the two structures, one can immediately detect a major discrepancy: The simpler network in Figure 5.12 finds the blood and urine tests independent given pregnancy, while the original one in Figure 5.10 does not. One practical implication of this difference is that two blood and urine tests that are negative will count more in ruling out a pregnancy in the simpler network than they would in the original one. Specifically,

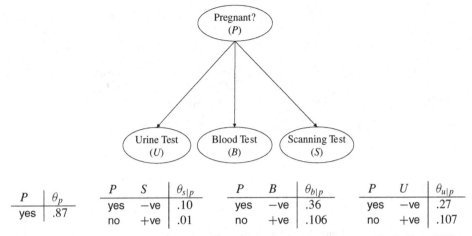

P	θ_p
yes	.87

P	S	$\theta_{s\|p}$
yes	−ve	.10
no	+ve	.01

P	B	$\theta_{b\|p}$
yes	−ve	.36
no	+ve	.106

P	U	$\theta_{u\|p}$
yes	−ve	.27
no	+ve	.107

Figure 5.12: A Bayesian network for detecting pregnancy based on three tests. Redundant CPT rows have been omitted. Note: This is another example of a naive Bayes structure.

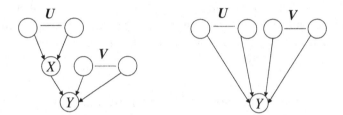

Figure 5.13: Bypassing the intermediary variable X in a Bayesian network.

the probability of pregnancy given these two negative tests is about 45.09% in the simpler network, while it is about 52.96% in the original. Similarly, two positive tests will count more in establishing a pregnancy in Figure 5.12 than they would in Figure 5.10. The difference is not as dramatic in this case though – about 99.61% in the simpler network versus 99.54% in the original one.

The moral of the previous example is that intermediary variables cannot be bypassed in certain cases as that may lead to changing the model in some undesirable ways. Here, the term "bypass" refers to the process of removing a variable, redirecting its parents to its children, and then updating the CPTs of these children (as they now have different parents).

As it turns out, one can identify a general case in which an intermediary variable can be bypassed without affecting *model accuracy,* a concept that we will define formally next. Suppose that Pr(.) is the distribution induced by a Bayesian network and let Pr'(.) be the distribution induced by the new network after bypassing an intermediary variable. The bypass procedure does not affect model accuracy in the case $\Pr(\mathbf{q}, \mathbf{e}) = \Pr'(\mathbf{q}, \mathbf{e})$ for all instantiations of query variables $\mathbf{Q}$ and evidence variables $\mathbf{E}$. This also implies that Pr(.) and Pr'(.) will agree on every query formulated using these variables.

Suppose now that X is a variable that is neither a query variable nor an evidence variable. Then X can be bypassed as long as it has a single child Y (see Figure 5.13). In this case, the CPT for variable Y must be updated as follows:

$$\theta'_{y|\mathbf{uv}} = \sum_x \theta_{y|x\mathbf{v}}\theta_{x|\mathbf{u}}. \tag{5.1}$$

Here $\mathbf{U}$ are the parents of variable X and $\mathbf{V}$ are the parents of variable Y other than X. This bypass can be justified using the techniques we introduce in Chapter 6 (see Exercise 6.4).

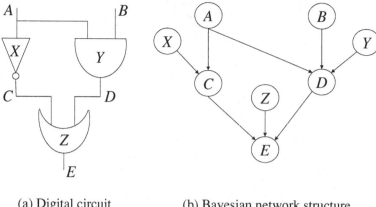

(a) Digital circuit   (b) Bayesian network structure

Figure 5.14: Bayesian network from design.

We will also see some concrete examples of it in some of the problems that we discuss later. We finally note that even though a variable may be bypassed without affecting the model accuracy, one may wish not to bypass it simply because the bypass procedure will lead to a large CPT. For example, if X and Y have five parents each, then Y will end up having nine parents after the bypass.

5.3.5 Diagnosis III: Model from design

We now turn to another reasoning problem from the domain of diagnosis that differs from previous problems in a fundamental way. Specifically, the Bayesian network model we develop for this problem is quite general to the point that it can be generated automatically for similar instances of the considered problem. The problem statement is as follows:

> Consider the digital circuit Figure 5.14(a). Given some values for the circuit primary inputs and output (test vector), our goal is to decide whether the circuit is behaving normally. If not, our goal is to decide the most likely health states of its components.

The evidence variables for this problem are the primary inputs and output of the circuit, A, B, and E, since we can observe their values. Given that our goal is to reason about the health of components, we need to include a query variable for each of these components: X, Y, and Z. That leaves the question of whether we need any intermediary variables. The obvious candidates for such variables are the states of the internal wires, C and D. As it turns out, modeling the circuit becomes much easier if we include these variables, especially if we are dealing with more realistic circuits that may have hundreds or thousands of components – it would be infeasible to model such circuits without explicitly representing the states of internal wires. These choices lead to the variables shown in the structure in Figure 5.14(b).

The edges of this structure are decided as follows. There are no direct causes for the health state of each component, hence variables X, Y, and Z have no parents – a more refined model may include other conditions, such as circuit power, that may end up being a direct cause of such variables. Similarly, there are no direct causes for the circuit primary inputs, A and B, which is why they have no parents in the given structure. Consider now variable D, which is the output of the and-gate. The direct causes of this variable are the gate inputs, A and B, and its state of health, Y. Hence, these are the parents of D in the network structure. For the same reason, A and X are the parents of C, while C, D, and Z are the parents of E. It should be clear that the developed structure generalizes easily to other circuits regardless of the number and types of their gates. In fact, it generalizes to any system that is composed of function blocks, where the outputs of each block are determined by its inputs and its state of health – as long as the system does not contain feedback loops, as that would lead to a cyclic structure.[7]

To completely specify the Bayesian network, we need to specify its CPTs. We also have to decide on the values of different variables, which we avoided until now for a good reason. First, the values of variables representing circuit wires – whether primary inputs, outputs, or internal wires – are simply one of low or high. The choice of values for health variables is not as obvious. The two choices are as follows. First, for each component its health variable can only take one of two values, ok or faulty. However, the problem with this choice is that the value faulty is too vague, as a component may fail in a number of modes. For example, it is common to talk about stuck-at-zero faults in which the gate will generate a low output regardless of its inputs. Similarly, one can have stuck-at-one faults or input-output-short faults in which an inverter would simply short its input to its output. From the viewpoint of precision, it is more appropriate to represent fault modes. Yet this choice may seem to put more demands on us when specifying the CPTs, as we discuss next.

First, note that the CPTs for this structure fall in one of three classes: CPTs for variables representing primary inputs (A, B), CPTs for variables representing gate outputs (C, D, E), and CPTs for variables representing component health (X, Y, Z). We will consider each of these next.

The CPTs for health variables depend on the values we choose for these variables. If we choose the values ok and faulty, then the CPT for each component, say, X would look like this:

X	θ_x
ok	.99
faulty	.01

Hence, if we have the probability of a fault in each component, then all such CPTs are determined immediately. If we choose to represent fault modes, say, stuckat0 and stuckat1, then the CPT would look like this:

X	θ_x
ok	.99
stuckat0	.005
stuckat1	.005

which implies that we know the probabilities of various fault modes. Clearly, we can assume that all fault modes are equally likely, in which case the probability of a faulty component will again be enough to specify the CPT.

The CPTs for component outputs are straightforward in case we represent fault modes since the probability of each possible output is then guaranteed to be either 0 or 1 (i.e., deterministic CPT) and can be determined directly from the gate's functionality.

---

[7] Systems with feedback loops can be modeled using Bayesian networks but require a different structure. See Section 5.3.7 and the discussion on convolutional codes for an example of representing such systems using Bayesian networks.

For example, the following is the CPT for the inverter X (we are omitting redundant rows):

A	X	C	$\theta_{c|a,x}$
high	ok	high	0
low	ok	high	1
high	stuckat0	high	0
low	stuckat0	high	0
high	stuckat1	high	1
low	stuckat1	high	1

The CPTs for the other two gates can be specified similarly. If we choose to have only two values for health variables, ok and faulty, then we need to decide on the probabilities in case the gate is faulty:

A	X	C	$\theta_{c|a,x}$
high	ok	high	0
low	ok	high	1
high	faulty	high	?
low	faulty	high	?

It is common to use a probability of .50 in this case and we show later that this choice is equivalent in a precise sense to the previous choice of assigning equal probabilities to fault modes.

We now move to the CPTs for primary inputs such as A, which require that we specify tables such as this:

A	θ_a
high	.5
low	.5

We assumed here that a high input at A is equally likely as a low input. This appears arbitrary at first but the good news is that the choice for these CPTs does not matter for the class of queries in which we are interested. That is, if our goal is to compute the probability of some health state x, y, z given some test vector a, b, e, then this probability is independent of $\Pr(a)$ and $\Pr(b)$, which can be chosen arbitrarily as long as they are not extreme. To prove this in general, let the primary inputs be $\mathbf{I}$, the primary outputs be $\mathbf{O}$, and the health variables be $\mathbf{H}$. We then have

$$\Pr(\mathbf{h}|\mathbf{i}, \mathbf{o}) = \frac{\Pr(\mathbf{h}, \mathbf{i}, \mathbf{o})}{\Pr(\mathbf{i}, \mathbf{o})} \quad \text{by Bayes conditioning}$$

$$= \frac{\Pr(\mathbf{o}|\mathbf{i}, \mathbf{h})\Pr(\mathbf{i}|\mathbf{h})\Pr(\mathbf{h})}{\Pr(\mathbf{o}|\mathbf{i})\Pr(\mathbf{i})} \quad \text{by the chain rule}$$

$$= \frac{\Pr(\mathbf{o}|\mathbf{i}, \mathbf{h})\Pr(\mathbf{i})\Pr(\mathbf{h})}{\Pr(\mathbf{o}|\mathbf{i})\Pr(\mathbf{i})} \quad \text{since } \mathbf{I} \text{ and } \mathbf{H} \text{ are d-separated}$$

$$= \frac{\Pr(\mathbf{o}|\mathbf{i}, \mathbf{h})\Pr(\mathbf{h})}{\Pr(\mathbf{o}|\mathbf{i})}.$$

Since both $\mathbf{I}$ and $\mathbf{H}$ are roots, $\Pr(\mathbf{o}|\mathbf{i}, \mathbf{h})$ does not depend on the CPTs for primary inputs $\mathbf{I}$ or health variables $\mathbf{H}$ (see Exercise 5.12). Similarly, $\Pr(\mathbf{o}|\mathbf{i})$ does not depend on the CPTs for primary inputs **I**. Moreover, Pr(**h**) depends only on the CPTs for health variables **H** since these variables are independent of each other. Note that this proof implicitly assumed that Pr(**i**, **o**) ≠ 0.

Note, however, that if our goal is to use the Bayesian network to predict the probability that a certain wire, say, E is high, then the CPTs for primary inputs matter considerably. But if this is our goal, it would then be reasonable to expect that we have some distribution on the primary inputs; otherwise, we do not have enough information to answer the query of interest.

Fault modes revisited

We now return to the two choices we considered when modeling component faults. According to the first choice, the health of each component, say, X had only two values, ok and faulty, which leads to the following CPTs for the component health and output:

X	θ_x
ok	.99
faulty	.01

A	X	C	$\theta_{c\mid a,x}$
high	ok	high	0
low	ok	high	1
high	faulty	high	.5
low	faulty	high	.5

According to the second choice, the health of each component had three values, ok, stuckat0, and stuckat1, leading to the following CPTs:

X	θ_x
ok	.99
stuckat0	.005
stuckat1	.005

A	X	C	$\theta_{c\mid a,x}$
high	ok	high	0
low	ok	high	1
high	stuckat0	high	0
low	stuckat0	high	0
high	stuckat1	high	1
low	stuckat1	high	1

We now show that these two choices are equivalent in the following sense. Since each health variable has a single child (see Figure 5.14), we can bypass these variables as suggested in Section 5.3.4. In particular, if we bypass variable X, then its single child C will have only one parent A and the following CPT:

$$Pr(c\mid a) = \sum_x Pr(c\mid a, x)Pr(x).$$

If we bypass variable X, assuming it has values ok and faulty, we get the following CPT for C:

A	C	$\theta_{c\mid a}$
high	high	$.005 = (0 * .99) + (.5 * .01)$
low	high	$.995 = (1 * .99) + (.5 * .01)$

Similarly, if we bypass variable X, assuming it has values ok, stuckat0, and stuckat1, we get the following CPT for C:

A	C	$\theta_{c\mid a}$
high	high	$.005 = (0 * .99) + (0 * .005) + (1 * .005)$
low	high	$.995 = (1 * .99) + (0 * .005) + (1 * .005)$

Hence, the two CPTs for variable C are the same. This would also be the case if we bypass health variables Y and Z, leading to equivalent CPTs for each of variables D and E. What this means is that the two Bayesian networks for the circuit in Figure 5.14 are equivalent in the following sense: Any query that involves only the wires A, B, C, D, and E is guaranteed to have the same answer with respect to either network. In fact, one can even prove a more direct equivalence with respect to diagnosis tasks (see Exercise 5.15).

A diagnosis example

Suppose now that we observed the following test vector,

$$\mathbf{e}: \quad A = \text{high}, \quad B = \text{high}, \quad E = \text{low},$$

and we wish to compute MAP over health variables X, Y, and Z under this observation. According to the network with fault modes, we get two MAP instantiations:

MAP given e	X	Y	Z
	ok	stuckat0	ok
	ok	ok	stuckat0

each with a probability of $\approx 49.4\%$. We get effectively the same two instantiations with respect to the second network with no fault modes:

MAP given e	X	Y	Z
	ok	faulty	ok
	ok	ok	faulty

where each MAP instantiation has also a probability of $\approx 49.4\%$. That is, we have two most likely instantiations of the health variables, with the and-gate Y being faulty in one and the or-gate Z being faulty in the other. Note here that we have assumed that all three components have the same reliability of 99%.

Posterior marginals

It is instructive to examine the posterior marginals over the health variables X, Y, Z in this case:

State	X	Y	Z	$\Pr(X, Y, Z \mid \mathbf{e})$
1	ok	ok	ok	0
2	faulty	ok	ok	0
3	ok	faulty	ok	.49374
4	ok	ok	faulty	.49374
5	ok	faulty	faulty	.00499
6	faulty	ok	faulty	.00499
7	faulty	faulty	ok	.00249
8	faulty	faulty	faulty	.00005

This table reveals a number of interesting observations. First, State 2, in which X is faulty but Y and Z are ok, is impossible; this follows from the circuit description. Second, double fault scenarios are not all equally likely. For example, a double fault involving Y and Z is more likely than one involving Y and X under the given evidence.[8]

---

[8] If Y and Z are faulty, we have two possible states for C and D ($C = $ low, D either low or high). If Y and X are faulty, we have only one possible state for C and D ($C = $ low and $D = $ low).

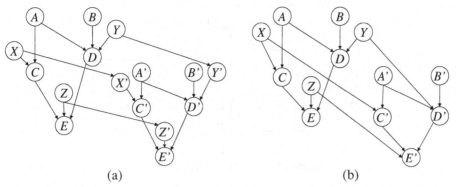

Figure 5.15: Two Bayesian network structures for diagnosing a circuit using two test vectors.

Due to this lack of symmetry, we have

$$\Pr(Z = \text{faulty}|\mathbf{e}) \approx 50.38\% \quad > \quad \Pr(Y = \text{faulty}|\mathbf{e}) \approx 50.13\%.$$

That is, among all possible states of the system states in which Z is faulty are more likely than states in which Y is faulty. Hence, even though the two faults are symmetric when considering most likely states of health variables (MAP), they are not symmetric when considering posterior marginals.

Integrating time

We now turn to an extension of the diagnosis problem we considered thus far in which we assume that we have two test vectors instead of only one. For example, to resolve the ambiguity that results from the MAP query considered previously, suppose that we now perform another test in which we apply two low inputs to the circuit and observe another abnormal low output. Our goal is then to find the most likely state of health variables given these two test vectors.

The key point to realize here is that we now have six evidence variables instead of only three as we need to capture the second test vector. This leads to three additional evidence variables, A', B' and E'. The same applies to the intermediary variables, leading to two additional variables, C' and D', which are needed to relate the elements of the second test vector (see Figure 5.15). Whether we need to include additional health variables depends on whether the health of a component stays the same during each of the two tests. If we want to allow for the possibility of intermittent faults, where the health of a component can change from one test to another, then we need to include additional health variables, X', Y', and Z', as shown in Figure 5.15(a). Otherwise, the original health variables are sufficient, leading to the structure in Figure 5.15(b).

Assuming this latter structure, let us revisit our previous example with the following two test vectors:

$$\mathbf{e}: \quad A = \text{high}, \quad B = \text{high}, \quad E = \text{low}$$

and

$$\mathbf{e}': \quad A = \text{low}, \quad B = \text{low}, \quad E = \text{low}.$$

If we compute MAP over health variables in this case, we obtain one instantiation:

MAP given $\mathbf{e}, \mathbf{e}'$	X	Y	Z
	ok	ok	faulty

that has a probability of $\approx 97.53\%$.

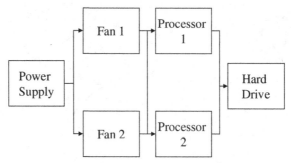

Figure 5.16: A reliability block diagram.

If we decide to allow intermittent faults, then we need a new class of CPTs to completely specify the resulting structure in Figure 5.15(a). In particular, for each component, say, X we now need to specify a CPT such as this one:

X	X'	$\theta_{x'|x}$
ok	ok	.99
ok	faulty	.01
faulty	ok	.001
faulty	faulty	.999

which represents a *persistence model* for the health of various components. For example, this table says that there is a 99% chance that a healthy component would remain healthy and there is a .1% chance that a faulty component would become healthy again (intermittent fault).

We close this section by noting that the structures depicted in Figure 5.15 are known as *dynamic Bayesian network* (DBN) structures since they include multiple copies of the same variable, where the different copies represent different states of the variable over time. We see more examples of dynamic Bayesian networks in future examples.

5.3.6 Reliability: Model from design

Consider the following problem from the domain of system reliability analysis:

> Figure 5.16 depicts a *reliability block diagram* (RBD) of a computer system, indicating conditions under which the system is guaranteed to be functioning normally (available). At 1,000 days since initial operation, the reliability of different components are as follows: power supply is 99%, fan is 90%, processor is 96%, and hard drive is 98%. What is the overall system reliability at 1,000 days since operation?

To address this problem, we need to provide an interpretation of an RBD. There are many variations on RBDs but we focus here on the simplest type consisting of a DAG that has a single leaf node and in which every node represents a block as given in Figure 5.16. We interpret each block B as representing a subsystem that includes the component B and the subsystems feeding into B. Moreover, for the subsystem represented by block B to be available component B and at least one of the subsystems feeding into it must also be available (see Exercise 5.9 for a more general model of availability). In Figure 5.16, the block labeled "Processor 1" represents a subsystem that includes this processor, the

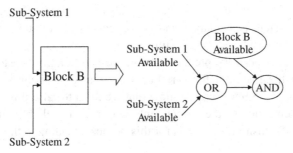

Figure 5.17: A Bayesian network fragment for a reliability block.

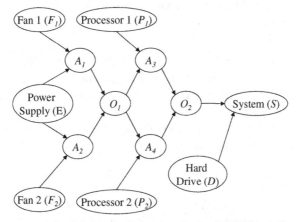

Figure 5.18: A Bayesian network structure for a reliability block diagram.

two fans, and the power supply. Moreover, the block labeled "Hard Drive" represents the whole system, as it includes all components.

This interpretation suggests the construction in Figure 5.17 for converting a reliability block into a Bayesian network fragment. To apply this construction to the RBD in Figure 5.16, we need variables to represent the availability of each system component: E for power supply, F_1/F_2 for the fans, P_1/P_2 for the processors, and D for the hard drive. We also need a variable S that represents the availability of the whole system and some intermediary variables to represent conjunctions and disjunctions, as suggested by Figure 5.17. This leads to the Bayesian network structure in Figure 5.18.

Let us now consider the CPTs for this network. The root variables correspond to system components, hence, their CPTs capture their reliability. For example, for the root E we have

E	θ_e
avail	99%

The CPTs for other roots (components) are similar. Intermediary variables $A_1, \ldots, A_4$ all represent and-gates. For example,

E	F_1	A_1	$\theta_{a_1|e,f_1}$
avail	avail	true	1
avail	un_avail	true	0
un_avail	avail	true	0
un_avail	un_avail	true	0

The CPT for variable S (system is available) is also an and-gate. Finally, the CPTs for O_1 (either fan subsystem is available) and O_2 (either processor subsystem is available) represent or-gates and can be specified similarly.

Given the Bayesian network presented here, we can compute system reliability by simply computing the marginal for variable S (system is available). In this case, the system reliability is $\approx 95.9\%$. Suppose now that we need to raise this system reliability to 96.5% by replacing one of the components with a more reliable one. What are our choices? We can use sensitivity analysis for this purpose, leading to three choices:

- Increase the reliability of the hard drive to $\approx 98.6\%$
- Increase the reliability of the power supply to $\approx 99.6\%$
- Increase the reliability of either fan to $\approx 96.2\%$.

What if we want to raise the system reliability to 97%? Sensitivity analysis tells us that we have only one choice in this case: Increase the reliability of the hard drive to $\approx 99.1\%$. Raising the system reliability to 98% would not be possible unless we change more than one component simultaneously.

Suppose now that we found the system to be functioning abnormally at day 1,000. We can then use MAP to find the most likely explanation of this abnormality. We get a single MAP answer in this case:

E	F_1	F_2	P_1	P_2	D	$Pr(.\|S = \text{un\_avail})$
avail	avail	avail	avail	avail	un_avail	36%

Therefore, our MAP solution blames the hard drive. It is interesting to consider the next two most likely explanations in this case:

E	F_1	F_2	P_1	P_2	D	$Pr(.\|S = \text{un\_avail})$
avail	un_avail	un_avail	avail	avail	avail	21.8%
un_avail	avail	avail	avail	avail	avail	17.8%

Note that having two faulty fans is more likely than a power failure in this case yet not as likely as having a hard drive failure. The prior example shows that we can use MAP queries to identify the mostly likely component failures in case of an overall system failure.

Logical constraints

Suppose now that we have a system constraint that precludes the first fan from ever operating concurrently with the first processor. We would expect the overall system reliability to be less than 95.9% in this case and our goal now is to compute this new reliability.

The described situation involves a logical constraint over some network variables, $\neg(F_1 = \text{avail} \wedge P_1 = \text{avail})$, which amounts to precluding some system states from being possible. The most general way to impose this constraint is to introduce an auxiliary variable, say, C in the network to represent this constraint (see Figure 5.19).

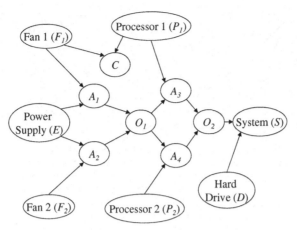

Figure 5.19: A Bayesian network structure for a reliability block diagram involving a constraint over two components.

The CPT for this variable is deterministic and given here:

F_1	P_1	C	$\theta_{c \mid f_1, p_1}$
avail	avail	true	0
avail	un_avail	true	1
un_avail	avail	true	1
un_avail	un_avail	true	1

That is, $C = $ true if and only if the constraint is satisfied. To enforce the constraint, we must therefore set C to true before we compute the overall system reliability, which comes out to 88.8% in this case.

Lifetime distributions and component reliability

We assumed previously that we are analyzing the system reliability at a given time (1,000 days) since the start of system operation. This allowed us to specify the reliability of each component, which depends on the time the component has been in operation. The dependence of component reliability on time is usually specified by a *lifetime distribution*, R. In particular, if we let t be a continuous variable that represents time, then $R(t)$ gives the probability that the component will be functioning normally at time t. Hence, $R(t)$ is known as the component *reliability* at time t. A simple yet quite common lifetime distribution is the *exponential distribution*, $R(t) = e^{-\lambda t}$, where λ represents the number of failures per unit time (i.e., failure rate) – see Figure 5.20.

More generally, a life distribution $R(t)$ is usually induced by a PDF $f(t)$ that captures unreliability information. In particular, the CDF $F(t)$ induced by $f(t)$,

$$F(t) = \int_0^t f(x)dx,$$

represents the probability that the component will fail by time t. This is called the component *unreliability*. The component reliability is then

$$R(t) = 1 - F(t) = 1 - \int_0^t f(x)dx.$$

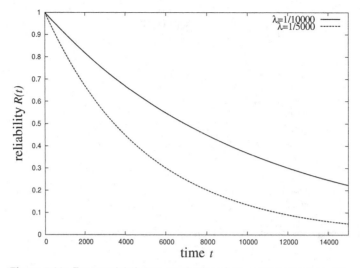

Figure 5.20: Exponential lifetime distributions for two different failure rates.

For example, the PDF for the exponential distribution is $f(t) = \lambda e^{-\lambda t}$. This leads to the following reliability function:

$$R(t) = 1 - \int_0^t \lambda e^{-\lambda x} dx = 1 - (1 - e^{-\lambda t}) = e^{-\lambda t}.$$

5.3.7 Channel coding

Consider the following problem from the domain of channel coding:

> We need to send four bits U_1, U_2, U_3, and U_4 from a source S to a destination D over a noisy channel where there is a 1% chance that a bit will be inverted before it gets to the destination. To improve the reliability of this process, we add three redundant bits X_1, X_2, and X_3 to the message where X_1 is the XOR of U_1 and U_3, X_2 is the XOR of U_2 and U_4, and X_3 is the XOR of U_1 and U_4. Given that we received a message containing seven bits at destination D, our goal is to restore the message generated at the source S.

In channel coding terminology, the bits $U_1, \ldots, U_4$ are known as *information bits,* $X_1, \ldots, X_3$ are known as *redundant bits,* and $U_1, \ldots, U_4, X_1, \ldots, X_3$ is known as the *code word* or *channel input.* Moreover, the message received at the destination $Y_1, \ldots, Y_7$ is known as the *channel output.* Our goal then is to restore the channel input given some channel output.

As we have seen in previous examples, query and evidence variables are usually determined immediately from the problem statement. In this case, evidence variables are $Y_1, \ldots, Y_7$ and they represent the bits received at destination D. Moreover, query variables are $U_1, \ldots, U_4$ and they represent the bits originating at source S. One can also include the redundant bits $X_1, \ldots, X_3$ in query variables or view them as constituting the set of intermediary variables. We shall see later that this choice does not matter much so we will include these bits in the query variables.

The causal structure for this problem is shown in Figure 5.21, where edges have been determined based on a basic understanding of causality in this domain. Specifically, the

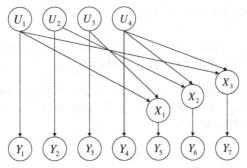

Figure 5.21: A Bayesian network structure for modeling a coding problem.

direct causes of each redundant bit are its two corresponding information bits, and the direct cause of each bit on the channel output is the corresponding bit on the channel input. Information bits have no parents since they are not directly caused by any of the other bits.

There are three CPT types in the problem. First, the CPT for each redundant bit, say, X_1 is deterministic and given as follows:

U_1	U_3	X_1	$\theta_{x_1|u_1,u_3}$
1	1	1	0
1	0	1	1
0	1	1	1
0	0	1	0

This CPT simply captures the functional relationship between X_1 and the corresponding information bits U_1 and U_3. That is, $\Pr(x_1|u_1, u_3) = 1$ iff $x_1 = u_1 \oplus u_3$ ($\oplus$ is the XOR function).

The CPT for a channel output bit, say, Y_1 is as follows:

U_1	Y_1	$\theta_{y_1|u_1}$
1	0	.01
0	1	.01

This CPT is then capturing the simple noise model given in the problem statement but we later discuss a more realistic noise model based on Gaussian distributions.

Finally, the CPTs for information bits such as U_1 capture the distribution of messages sent out from the source S. Assuming a uniform distribution, we can then use the following CPT:

U_1	θ_{u_1}
1	.5
0	.5

MAP or posterior-marginal (PM) decoders?

Now that we have completely specified a Bayesian network for this decoding problem, we need to decide on the specific query to pose. Our goal is to restore the channel input given channel output but there are two ways for achieving this:

1. Compute a MAP for the channel input $U_1, \ldots, U_4, X_1, \ldots, X_3$ given channel output $Y_1, \ldots, Y_7$.[9]

2. Compute the PM for each bit U_i / X_i in the channel input given channel output $Y_1, \ldots, Y_7$, and then select the value of U_i / X_i that is most probable.

The choice between MAP and PM decoders is a matter of the performance measure one is interested in optimizing. We discuss two such measures in the following section and relate them to MAP and PM decoders.

Evaluating decoders

Suppose that we have a *decoder,* which returns some channel input $u_1, \ldots, u_4, x_1, \ldots, x_3$ whenever it is given a channel output $y_1, \ldots, y_7$. Suppose further that our goal is to evaluate the performance of this decoder on a given set of channel inputs $\alpha_1, \ldots, \alpha_n$. There are two possible quality measures that we can use for this purpose:

- *Word Error Rate (WER):* Suppose that we send each input α_i into the channel, collect the corresponding (noisy) output β_i, feed it into the decoder, and finally collect the decoder output γ_i. We then compare each decoder output γ_i with corresponding channel input α_i. Let m be the number of channel inputs that are recovered incorrectly by the decoder, that is, there is a mismatch on some bit between α_i and γ_i. The word error rate for that decoder is then m/n.

- *Bit Error Rate (BER):* We perform the same experiment as for WER, except that when comparing the decoder output γ_i with the original channel input α_i, we count the number of bits on which they disagree. Let k be the total number of bits recovered incorrectly and let l be the total number of bits sent across the channel. The bit error rate for the decoder is then k/l.

Which performance measure to choose will depend on the application at hand. Suppose for example that the information bits represent pixels in an image that contains the photo of an individual to be recognized by a human when it arrives at the destination. Consider now two situations. In the first, we have a few bits off in each image we decode. In the second, we have many images that are perfectly decoded but a few that have massive errors in them. The BER would tend to be lower than the WER in the first situation, while it would tend to be larger in the second. Hence, our preference for one situation over the other will imply a preference for one performance measure over the other.

The choice between MAP and PM decoders can therefore be thought of as a choice between these performance measures. In particular, decoders based on MAP queries minimize the average probability of word error, while decoders based on PM queries minimize the average probability of bit error.

Noise models and soft evidence

Our previous discussion assumed a simple noise model according to which a channel input bit x_i is received as a channel output bit $y_i \neq x_i$ with 1% probability. A more realistic and common noise model is to assume that we are transmitting our code bits x_i through a channel that adds Gaussian noise with mean x_i and standard deviation σ

---

[9] This is actually an MPE query since MAP variables include all variables except those for evidence. Even if the MAP variables contain $U_1, \ldots, U_4$ only, this MAP query can be obtained by projecting an MPE on the information bits $U_1, \ldots, U_4$ since the redundant bits X_1, X_2, X_3 are functionally determined by the information bits $U_1, \ldots, U_4$ (see Exercise 5.11).

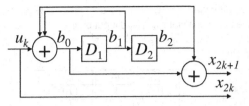

Figure 5.22: An example convolutional encoder. Each node denoted with a "+" represents a binary addition, and each box D_i represents a delay where the output of D_i is the input of D_i from the previous encoder state.

(see Section 3.7.1). Specifically, we will assume that the channel output Y_i is a continuous variable governed by a conditional density function:

$$f(y_i|x_i) = \frac{1}{\sqrt{2\pi\sigma^2}} e^{-(y_i-x_i)^2/2\sigma^2}.$$

As we have shown in Section 3.7.3, this more sophisticated noise model can be implemented by interpreting the continuous channel output y_i as soft evidence on the channel input $X_i = 0$ with a Bayes factor,

$$k = e^{(1-2y_i)/2\sigma^2}.$$

For example, if $\sigma = .5$ and we receive a channel output $y_i = .1$, we interpret that as a soft evidence on channel input $X_i = 0$ with a Bayes factor $k \approx 5$.

As shown in Section 5.2.2, this soft evidence can be integrated in our Bayesian network by adding a child, say, S_i of X_i and then setting its CPT such that

$$\frac{\Pr(S_i = \text{true}|X_i = 0)}{\Pr(S_i = \text{true}|X_i = 1)} = k = 5.$$

For example, either of the following CPTs will work:

X_i	S_i	$\theta_{S_i|x_i}$		X_i	S_i	$\theta_{S_i|x_i}$
0	true	.75		0	true	.5
0	false	.25		0	false	.5
1	true	.15		1	true	.1
1	false	.85		1	false	.9

as long as we emulate the channel output by setting the value of S_i to true.

Convolutional codes

We will now discuss two additional types of coding networks: convolutional-code networks and turbo-code networks. The difference between these networks and the one we discussed previously lies in the manner in which the redundant bits are generated. Moreover, both convolutional and turbo codes provide examples of modeling systems with feedback loops using dynamic Bayesian networks.

In Figure 5.22, we see an example encoder for generating the redundant bits of a convolutional code. This encoder has a state captured by three bits b_0, b_1, and b_2, leading to eight possible states. If we feed this encoder an information bit u_k, it will do two things. First, it will change its state, and second, it will generate two bits x_{2k} and x_{2k+1}. Here $x_{2k} = u_k$ is the same information bit we fed to the encoder, while x_{2k+1} is the redundant bit. Hence, if we feed the bit sequence $u_0 \ldots u_{n-1}$ to the encoder, it will generate the bit sequence $x_0 x_1 \ldots, x_{2n-2} x_{2n-1}$, where $x_0, x_2, \ldots, x_{2n-2}$ are our original information bits and $x_1, x_3, \ldots, x_{2n-1}$ are the redundant bits.

Table 5.1: Look-up tables for the encoder in Figure 5.22, to identify the current state s_k and redundant bit x_{2k+1} given previous state s_{k-1} and input bit u_k. According to the semantics of this encoder, we have $x_{2k+1} = s_k^0 + s_k^2$, $s_k^0 = s_{k-1}^0 + s_{k-1}^1 + u_k$, $s_k^1 = s_{k-1}^0$, and $s_k^2 = s_{k-1}^1$. Here s^i is the ith bit in state s.

s_{k-1}	u_k	s_k		s_{k-1}	u_k	s_k		s_k	x_{2k+1}
000	0	000		100	0	110		000	0
000	1	100		100	1	010		001	1
001	0	000		101	0	110		010	0
001	1	100		101	1	010		011	1
010	0	101		110	0	011		100	1
010	1	001		110	1	111		101	0
011	0	101		111	0	011		110	1
011	1	001		111	1	111		111	0

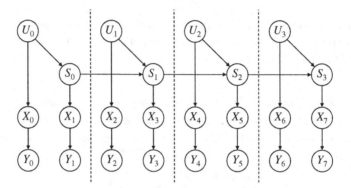

Figure 5.23: A Bayesian network for a convolutional code.

Suppose for example that we want to determine the current state of the encoder $s_k = b_0 b_1 b_2$ given input $u_k = 1$ and the previous state of the encoder $s_{k-1} = 010$. The last two bits of s_k are simply the first two bits of s_{k-1}. We then have $b_0 = u_k + b_1 + b_2 = 1 + 0 + 1 = 0$, and thus our current state s_k is 001. Given the current state, we can then determine that the encoder outputs $x_{2k} = u_k$ and $x_{2k+1} = b_0 + b_2 = 0 + 1 = 1$.

We can easily implement an encoder using two look-up tables, one for determining the new state s_k given the old state s_{k-1} and bit u_k, and another for determining the redundant bit x_{2k+1} given state s_k (x_{2k} is simply u_k). These look-up tables are shown in Table 5.1 and will prove useful as we next develop a Bayesian network for representing convolutional codes.

Consider Figure 5.23, which depicts a Bayesian network for a convolutional code. The network can be viewed as a sequence of replicated slices where slice k is responsible for generating the codeword bits x_{2k} and x_{2k+1} for the information bit u_k. Note also that each slice has a variable S_k that represents the state of the encoder at that slice. Moreover, this state variable is determined by the previous state variable S_{k-1} and the information bit U_k. Hence, the network in Figure 5.23 is another example of dynamic Bayesian networks that we encountered in Section 5.3.5.

Let us now parameterize this network structure. Root variables U_k corresponding to information bits are assumed to have uniform priors as before. Moreover, channel output variables Y_k are assumed to be parameterized as shown previously, depending on the noise model we assume. This leaves the CPTs for state variables S_k and for the codeword bits X_k.

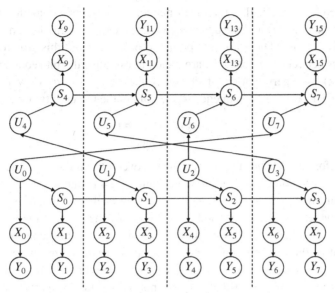

Figure 5.24: A Bayesian network for a turbo code.

The CPTs for state variables $S_k, k > 0$, are deterministic and given as follows (based on Table 5.1):

$$\theta_{s_k|u_k,s_{k-1}} = \begin{cases} 1, & \text{if the encoder transitions from } s_{k-1} \text{ to } s_k \text{ given } u_k \\ 0, & \text{otherwise.} \end{cases}$$

The CPT for variable S_0 can be determined similarly while assuming some initial state for the decoder.

The CPTs for variables X_{2k} and X_{2k+1} are also deterministic and given as follows (based also on Table 5.1):

$$\theta_{x_{2k}|u_k} = \begin{cases} 1, & \text{if } x_{2k} = u_k \\ 0, & \text{otherwise} \end{cases}$$

$$\theta_{x_{2k+1}|s_k} = \begin{cases} 1, & \text{if the encoder outputs } x_{2k+1} \text{ given } s_k \\ 0, & \text{otherwise.} \end{cases}$$

We can then decode a channel output $y_1, \ldots, y_n$ as we discussed in the previous section by computing the posterior marginals $\Pr(u_k|y_1, \ldots, y_n)$ of variables U_k or by computing MAP over these variables.

Turbo codes

Suppose now that we have four information bits $u_0, \ldots, u_3$. In a convolutional code, we will generate four redundant bits leading to a codeword with eight bits. In a turbo code, we apply a convolutional code twice, once on the original bit sequence u_0, u_1, u_2, u_3 and another time on some permutation of it, say, u_1, u_3, u_2, u_0. This leads to eight redundant bits and a codeword with twelve bits.[10]

The structure of a Bayesian network that captures this scenario is given in Figure 5.24. This network can be viewed as consisting of two networks, each representing a

---

[10] This gives a rate $1/3$ code (ratio of information bits to total bits). In principle, we can drop some of the redundant bits, leading to codes with different rates.

convolutional code. In particular, the lower network represents a convolutional code for the bit sequence $u_0, \ldots, u_3$ and the upper network represents a convolutional code for the bit sequence $u_4, \ldots, u_7$. There are two points to observe about this structure. First, the edges that cross between the networks are meant to establish the bit sequence $u_4, \ldots, u_7$ (upper network) as a permutation of the bit sequence $u_0, \ldots, u_3$ (lower network). In particular, the CPTs for the bit sequence $u_4, \ldots, u_7$ in the upper network are given by

$$\theta_{u_k | u_j} = \begin{cases} 1, & \text{if } u_k = u_j \\ 0, & \text{otherwise.} \end{cases}$$

This CPT therefore establishes the equivalence between U_k in the upper network and U_j in the lower.[11] The second observation about Figure 5.24 is that the upper network does not copy the information bits $u_4, \ldots, u_7$ to the output as these are simply a permutation of $u_0, \ldots, u_3$, which are already copied to the output by the lower network.

It should be noted here that networks corresponding to convolutional codes are *singly connected*; that is, there is only one (undirected) path between any two variables in the network (these networks are also called *polytrees*). Networks corresponding to turbo codes are *multiply connected* in that they do not satisfy this property. This has major computational implications that we discuss in future chapters.

5.3.8 Commonsense knowledge

Consider the following commonsense reasoning problem:

> When SamBot goes home at night, he wants to know if his family is home before he tries the doors. (Perhaps the most convenient door to enter is double locked when nobody is home.) Often when SamBot's wife leaves the house, she turns on an outdoor light. However, she sometimes turns on this light if she is expecting a guest. Also, SamBot's family has a dog. When nobody is home, the dog is in the back yard. The same is true if the dog has bowel trouble. Finally, if the dog is in the back yard SamBot will probably hear her barking, but sometimes he can be confused by other dogs barking. SamBot is equipped with two sensors, a light sensor for detecting outdoor lights and a sound sensor for detecting the barking of dogs. Both of these sensors are not completely reliable and can break. Moreover, they both require SamBot's battery to be in good condition.

Our goal is then to build a Bayesian network that SamBot will use to reason about this situation. Specifically, given sensory input SamBot needs to compute his beliefs in whether his family is home and whether any of his hardware is broken.

This problem is less structured than any of the problems we have examined so far. The choice of evidence and query variables remain relatively obvious. We only have two evidence variables in this case:

> LightSensor: Is SamBot's light sensor detecting a light (outdoor light)?
>
> SoundSensor: Is SamBot's sound sensor detecting a sound (barking)?

We also have four query variables:

> FamilyHome: Is SamBot's family (wife) home?
>
> LightSensorBroken: Is SamBot's light sensor broken?

---

[11] In principle, one does not need the U_k variables in the upper network as these can simply be the U_j variables in the lower network. Our choice of separating the two was meant to emphasize the two convolutional codes used to compose a turbo code.

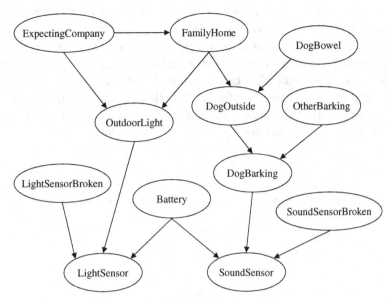

Figure 5.25: A Bayesian network structure for the SamBot problem.

SoundSensorBroken: Is SamBot's sound sensor broken?

Battery: Is SamBot's battery in good condition?

Finally, we have six intermediary variables:

ExpectingCompany: Is SamBot's family (wife) expecting company?

OutdoorLight: Is the outdoor light on?

DogOut: Is SamBot's dog outside?

DogBarking: Is some dog barking?

DogBowel: Is SamBot's dog having bowel problems?

OtherBarking: Are other dogs barking?

The network structure corresponding to these choices is shown in Figure 5.25. Note that all intermediary variables except for ExpectingCompany have a single child each. Hence, they can be easily bypassed using the technique discussed in Section 5.3.4.

Parameterizing this structure can be accomplished based on a combination of sources:

- Statistical information, such as reliabilities of sensors and battery
- Subjective beliefs relating to how often the wife goes out, guests are expected, the dog has bowel trouble, and so on
- Objective beliefs regarding the functionality of sensors.

One can also imagine the robot recording his experiences each evening and then constructing a data table similar to the one discussed in Section 5.3.1, which can then be used to estimate the network parameters as discussed in Chapters 17 and 18.

5.3.9 Genetic linkage analysis

Before we can state the problem of genetic linkage analysis and how Bayesian networks can be used to solve it, we need to provide some background.

A *pedigree* is a structure that depicts a group of individuals while explicating their sexes and identifying their children (see Figure 5.26). A pedigree is useful in reasoning about heritable characteristics that are determined by *genes,* where different genes are responsible for the expression of different characteristics. A gene may occur in different states called *alleles.* Each individual carries two alleles of each gene, one received from their mother and the other from their father. The alleles of an individual are called the *genotype*, while the heritable characteristic expressed by these alleles (such as hair color, blood type, and so on) are called the *phenotype* of the individual.

For example, consider the ABO gene, which is responsible for determining blood type. This gene has three alleles: A, B, and O. Since each individual must have two alleles for this gene, we have six possible genotypes in this case. Yet there are only four different blood types, as some of the different genotypes lead to the same phenotype:

Genotype	Phenotype
A/A	Blood type A
A/B	Blood type AB
A/O	Blood type A
B/B	Blood type B
B/O	Blood type B
O/O	Blood type O

Hence, if someone has the blood type A, they could have the pair of alleles A/A or the pair A/O for their genotype.

The phenotype is not always determined precisely by the genotype. Suppose for example that we have a disease gene with two alleles, H and D. There are three possible genotypes here yet none may guarantee the disease will show up:

Genotype	Phenotype
H/H	healthy
H/D	healthy
D/D	ill with probability .9

The conditional probability of observing a phenotype (e.g., healthy, ill) given the genotype (e.g., H/H, H/D, D/D) is known as a *penetrance*. In the ABO gene, the penetrance is always 0 or 1. However, for this gene, the penetrance is .9 for the phenotype *ill* given the genotype D/D.

Recombination events

The alleles received by an individual from one parent are called a *haplotype*. Hence, each individual has two haplotypes, one paternal and another maternal. Consider now the pedigree in Figure 5.26, which explicates two genes G_1 and G_2 for each individual where G_1 has two alleles A and a and gene G_2 has the alleles B and b.

Given the genotype of Mary in this pedigree, she can pass only one haplotype to her child, Jack: AB. Similarly, John can pass only one haplotype to Jack: ab. On the other hand, Jack can pass one of four haplotypes to his children: AB, Ab, aB, ab. Two of these haplotypes, AB and ab, were received from his parents but the haplotypes Ab and aB were not. For example, if Jack were to pass on the haplotype AB to an offspring, then this haplotype would have come exclusively from Jack's mother, Mary. However, if Jack were to pass on the haplotype Ab, then part of this haplotype would have come from Mary and the other part from Jack's father, John. In such a case, we say that a *recombination*

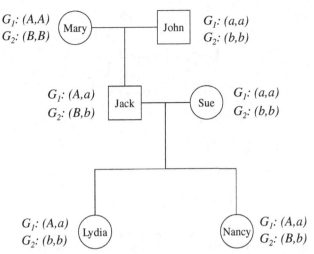

Figure 5.26: A pedigree involving six individuals. Squares represent males and circles represent females. Horizontal edges connect spouses and vertical edges connect couples to their children. For example, Jack and Sue are a couple with two daughters, Lydia and Nancy.

event has occurred between the two genes G_1 and G_2. We also say that the child receiving this haplotype is a *recombinant*. In Figure 5.26, Lydia must be a recombinant. If Lydia is not a recombinant, then she must have received the haplotype AB or ab from Jack and the haplotype ab from Sue. This means that Lydia's genotype would have been either of $G_1 = (A, a)$, $G_2 = (B, b)$ or $G_2 = (a, a)$, $G_2 = (b, b)$. Yet Lydia has neither of these genotypes.

Genetic linkage and gene maps

If two genes are inherited independently, the probability of a recombination is expected to be $1/2$. However, we sometimes observe that two alleles that were passed in the haplotype from a grandparent to a parent tend to be passed again in the same haplotype from the parent to a child. This phenomena is called *genetic linkage*, and one goal of genetic linkage analysis is to estimate the extent to which two genes are linked. More formally, the extent to which genes G_1 and G_2 are linked is measured by a *recombination fraction* or *frequency*, θ, which is the probability that a recombination between G_1 and G_2 will occur. Genes that are inherited independently are characterized by a recombination frequency $\theta = 1/2$ and are said to be unlinked. On the other hand, linked genes are characterized by a recombination frequency $\theta < 1/2$.

Linkage between genes is related to their locations on a chromosome within the cell nucleus. These locations are typically referred to as *loci* (singular: *locus*) – see Figure 5.27. In particular, for genes that are closely located on a chromosome, linkage is inversely proportional to the distance between their locations: the closer the genes, the more linked they are. The recombination frequency can then provide direct evidence on the distance between genes on a chromosome, making it a useful tool for mapping genes onto a chromosome. In fact, the recombination frequency is sometimes measured in units called *centimorgans*, where a 1% recombination frequency is equal to 1 centimorgan.

In the rest of this section, we will assume that we have a set of closely linked genes whose relative order on a given chromosome is already known. This allows us to produce a distance map for these genes on the chromosome by simply focusing on the recombination frequency of each pair of adjacent genes (loci) (see Figure 5.27).

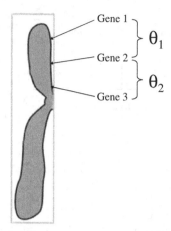

Figure 5.27: Genes correspond to locations on a chromosome within the cell nucleus. The figure depicts three genes on a chromosome and some hypotheses on their recombination frequencies.

The likelihood of a hypothesis

Given a pedigree, together with some information about the genotypes and phenotypes of involved individuals, we want to develop a Bayesian network that can be used to assess the likelihood of a particular recombination frequency. By developing such a network, we can discriminate between various hypotheses and even search for the most plausible hypothesis.

More formally, let $\mathbf{e}$ be the observed genotypes and phenotypes and let θ be a recombination frequency that we wish to investigate. We will then develop a Bayesian network (G, Θ) that induces a distribution $\Pr(.)$ and use it to compute $\Pr(\mathbf{e})$. The parametrization Θ of this network will be predicated on the recombination frequency θ, making $\Pr(\mathbf{e})$ correspond to the likelihood of hypothesis θ. To compute the likelihood of another hypothesis θ', we will generate another parametrization Θ' predicated on θ' that induces another distribution $\Pr'$, leading to another likelihood $\Pr'(\mathbf{e})$. We would then prefer hypothesis θ' over θ if its likelihood $\Pr'(\mathbf{e})$ is greater than the likelihood $\Pr(\mathbf{e})$ of θ.

From pedigrees to Bayesian networks

We now discuss a systematic process for constructing a Bayesian network from a given pedigree. The network will include variables to capture both phenotype and genotype, allowing one to capture such information as evidence on the developed network.

Figure 5.28 provides the basis of such a construction, as it depicts the Bayesian network corresponding to three individuals numbered 1, 2, and 3, with 3 being the child of 1 and 2. The network assumes three genes for each individual, where gene j of individual i is represented by two variables, GP_{ij} and GM_{ij}. Here GP_{ij} represents the paternal allele and GM_{ij} represents the maternal allele. In addition, a variable P_{ij} is included to represent the phenotype for individual i caused by gene j.

For an individual i who is not a founder (i.e., his parents are included in the pedigree), the network includes two selector variables for each gene j, SP_{ij} and SM_{ij}. These variables are meant to determine the method by which individual i inherits his alleles from his parents. In particular, variable SP_{ij} determines how i will inherit from his father: if $SP_{ij} = p$, then i will inherit the allele that his father obtained from the grandfather, while if $SP_{ij} = m$, then i will inherit the allele that his father obtained from the grandmother. The selector SM_{ij} is interpreted similarly.

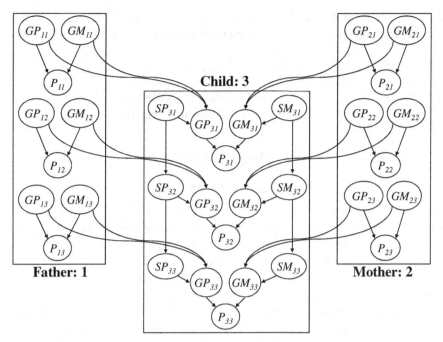

Figure 5.28: A Bayesian network structure corresponding to a simple pedigree involving three individuals numbered 1, 2, and 3. Here 3 is the child of father 1 and mother 2. Moreover, each individual has three genes numbered 1, 2, and 3, which are assumed to be in this order on a chromosome.

To parameterize the network in Figure 5.28, we need four types of CPTs. First, for a founder i we need the prior probability for the genotype variables GP_{ij} and GM_{ij} for each gene j. This is usually obtained from population statistics that are typically collected by geneticists. Second, for each individual i and gene j, we need a CPT for the phenotype P_{ij}. This may be a deterministic CPT or a probabilistic CPT, as we have seen previously. Third, for each nonfounder i, we need the CPTs for genotype variables GP_{ij} and GM_{ij}. These CPTs are deterministic and follow from the semantics of selector variables that we have discussed previously. For example, if individual i has father k, then the CPT for GP_{ij} is given by

$$\theta_{gp_{ij}|gp_{kj},gm_{kj},sp_{ij}} = \begin{cases} 1, & \text{if } sp_{ij} = p \text{ and } gp_{ij} = gp_{kj} \\ 1, & \text{if } sp_{ij} = m \text{ and } gp_{ij} = gm_{kj} \\ 0, & \text{otherwise.} \end{cases}$$

That is, if $SP_{ij} = p$, then the allele GP_{ij} for individual i will be inherited from the paternal haplotype of his father k, GP_{kj}. However, if $SP_{ij} = m$, then the allele GP_{ij} will be inherited from the maternal haplotype of his father k, GM_{kj}. The CPT for GM_{ij} is specified in a similar fashion.

The final type of CPTs concern selector variables, and it is these CPTs that will host our hypotheses about recombination frequencies. Note here that we are assuming an ordering of genes 1, 2, and 3 on the given chromosome. Hence, to produce a distance map for these genes, all we need is the distance between genes 1 and 2 and the distance between genes 2 and 3, which can be indicated by the corresponding recombination frequencies θ_{12} and θ_{23}.

The selectors of the first gene SP_{31} and SM_{31} will have uniform CPTs, indicating that the parents will pass either their paternal or maternal alleles with equal probability for this gene. For the second gene, the CPTs for selectors SP_{32} and SM_{32} will be a function of the recombination frequency θ_{12} between the first and second gene. For example:

SP_{31}	SP_{32}	$\theta_{sp_{32}|sp_{31}}$	
p	p	$1 - \theta_{12}$	
p	m	θ_{12}	recombination between genes 1 and 2
m	p	θ_{12}	recombination between genes 1 and 2
m	m	$1 - \theta_{12}$	

The CPTs for other selector variables can be specified similarly.

Putting the network to use

The Bayesian network described previously contains variables for both genotype and phenotype. It also contains CPT entries for every recombination frequency θ_{ij} between two adjacent genes i and j on a chromosome. Suppose now that this network induces a distribution $Pr(.)$ and let $\mathbf{g}$ be some evidence about the genotype and $\mathbf{p}$ be some evidence about the phenotype. The probability $Pr(\mathbf{g}, \mathbf{p})$ will then represent the likelihood of recombination frequencies included in the network's CPTs. By simply changing the CPTs for selector variables (which host the recombination frequencies) and recomputing $Pr(\mathbf{g}, \mathbf{p})$, we will be able to compute the likelihoods of competing hypotheses about genetic linkage.[12] We can even conduct a search in the space of such hypotheses to identify the one that maximizes likelihood while using the developed network and corresponding probabilities $Pr(\mathbf{g}, \mathbf{p})$ to guide the search process. We will have more to say about such a search process when we discuss parameter estimation in Chapter 17.

5.4 Dealing with large CPTs

One of the major issues that arise when building Bayesian network models is the potentially large size of CPTs. Suppose for example, that we have a variable E with parents $C_1, \ldots, C_n$ and suppose further that each one of these variables has only two values. We then need 2^n independent parameters to completely specify the CPT for variable E. The following table gives a concrete feel of this CPT size for different values of n:

Number of Parents: n	Parameter Count: 2^n
2	4
3	8
6	64
10	1,024
20	1,048,576
30	1,073,741,824

Both modeling and computational problems will arise as the number of parents n gets larger but the modeling problem will obviously manifest first. Specifically, a CPT with 1,024 entries is rarely a concern from a computational viewpoint but imagine trying to commit a medical expert to specifying 1,024 numbers in order to quantify the relationship

---

[12] For a given hypothesis θ_{ij}, the score $\log Pr^{\theta_{ij}}(\mathbf{g}, \mathbf{p})/Pr^{.5}(\mathbf{g}, \mathbf{p})$ is typically used to quantify the support for this hypothesis, which is meant to be normalized across different pedigrees. Here $Pr^{\theta_{ij}}$ is the distribution induced by the network where θ_{ij} is the recombination frequency between genes i and j, while $Pr^{.5}$ is the distribution induced by the network where .5 is the recombination frequency between i and j (no linkage).

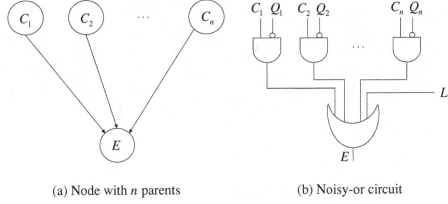

(a) Node with n parents   (b) Noisy-or circuit

Figure 5.29: Illustrating noisy-or semantics for a node with n parents.

between headache and ten different medical conditions that may cause it. There are two different types of solutions to this problem of large CPTs, which we discuss next.

5.4.1 Micro models

The first approach for dealing with large CPTs is to try to develop a *micro model* that details the relationship between the parents $C_1, \ldots, C_n$ and their common child E. The goal here is to reveal the local structure of this relationship in order to specify it using a number of parameters that is smaller than 2^n.

One of the most common micro models for this purpose is known as the *noisy-or* model, depicted in Figure 5.29(b). To understand this model, it is best to interpret parents $C_1, \ldots, C_n$ as causes and variable E as their common effect. The intuition here is that each cause C_i is capable of establishing the effect E on its own, regardless of other causes, except under some unusual circumstances that are summarized by the suppressor variable Q_i. That is, when the suppressor Q_i of cause C_i is active, cause C_i is no longer able to establish E. Moreover, the leak variable L is meant to represent all other causes of E that were not modelled explicitly. Hence, even when none of the causes C_i are active, the effect E may still be established by the leak variable L. Given this interpretation of the noisy-or model, one would then expect the probabilities of suppressors and leak to be usually small in practice.

The noisy-or model in Figure 5.29(b) can then be specified using $n + 1$ parameters, which is remarkable from a modeling viewpoint. For example, to model the relationship between headache and ten different conditions that may cause it, all we need are the following numbers:

- $\theta_{q_i} = \Pr(Q_i = \text{active})$: the probability that the suppressor of cause C_i is active
- $\theta_l = \Pr(L = \text{active})$: the probability that the leak variable is active.

The noisy-or model contains enough information to completely specify the conditional probability of variable E given any instantiation α of the parents $C_1, \ldots, C_n$. Hence, the model can be used to completely specify the CPT for variable E in Figure 5.29(a). To show this, let I_α be the indices of causes that are active in α. For example, if

$$\alpha: \ C_1 = \text{active}, \ C_2 = \text{active}, \ C_3 = \text{passive}, \ C_4 = \text{passive}, \ C_5 = \text{active},$$

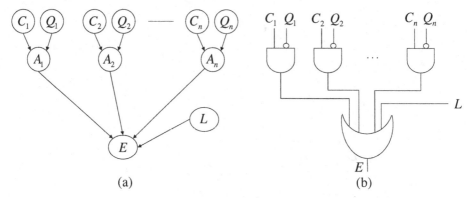

Figure 5.30: A Bayesian network for a noisy-or circuit.

then I_α is the set containing indices $1, 2$, and 5. Using this notation, we have

$$\Pr(E = \text{passive}|\alpha) = (1 - \theta_l) \prod_{i \in I_\alpha} \theta_{q_i}. \tag{5.2}$$

From this equation, we also get $\Pr(E = \text{active}|\alpha) = 1 - \Pr(E = \text{passive}|\alpha)$. Hence, the full CPT for variable E with its 2^n independent parameters can be induced from the $n + 1$ parameters associated with the noisy-or model.

One can derive (5.2) in a number of ways. The more intuitive derivation is that given the status α of causes $C_1, \ldots, C_n$, the effect E will be passive only if the leak was passive and all suppressors Q_i, for $i \in I_\alpha$, were active. Since the leak and suppressors are assumed to be independent, the probability of that happening is simply given by (5.2).

Another way to derive (5.2) is to build a *micro Bayesian network*, as given in Figure 5.30(a), which explicitly represents the noisy-or model. This network will have $3n + 2$ variables, where the CPTs for all variables except causes $C_1, \ldots, C_n$ are determined from the noisy-or model. Note here that variables $L, Q_1, \ldots, Q_n$ have a single child each. Hence, we can bypass each of them, as discussed in Section 5.3.4, while updating the CPT for variable E after bypassing each variable. We can then bypass variables $A_1, \ldots, A_n$, since each of them has a single child E. If we bypass all such variables, we get the CPT given by (5.2).

To consider a concrete example of noisy-or models, let us revisit the medical diagnosis problem from Section 5.3.1. Sore throat (S) has three causes in this problem: cold (C), flu (F), and tonsillitis (T). If we assume that S is related to its causes by a noisy-or model, we can then specify the CPT for S by the following four probabilities:

- The suppressor probability for cold, say, .15
- The suppressor probability for flu, say, .01
- The suppressor probability for tonsillitis, say, .05
- The leak probability, say, .02.

The CPT for sore throat is then determined completely as follows:

C	F	T	S	$\theta_{s|c,f,t}$	Equation 5.2
true	true	true	true	.9999265	$1 - (1 - .02)(.15)(.01)(.05)$
true	true	false	true	.99853	$1 - (1 - .02)(.15)(.01)$
true	false	true	true	.99265	$1 - (1 - .02)(.15)(.05)$
$\vdots$	$\vdots$	$\vdots$	$\vdots$	$\vdots$	
false	false	false	true	.02	$1 - (1 - .02)$

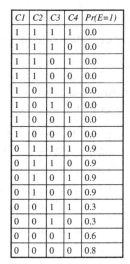

C1	C2	C3	C4	Pr(E=1)
1	1	1	1	0.0
1	1	1	0	0.0
1	1	0	1	0.0
1	1	0	0	0.0
1	0	1	1	0.0
1	0	1	0	0.0
1	0	0	1	0.0
1	0	0	0	0.0
0	1	1	1	0.9
0	1	1	0	0.9
0	1	0	1	0.9
0	1	0	0	0.9
0	0	1	1	0.3
0	0	1	0	0.3
0	0	0	1	0.6
0	0	0	0	0.8

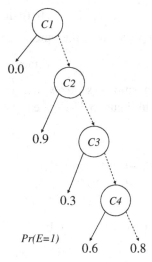

Figure 5.31: A CPT and its corresponding decision tree representation (also known as a probability tree). Solid edges represent 1-values and dotted edges represent 0-values.

5.4.2 Other representations of CPTs

The noisy-or model is only one of several other models for local structure. Each of these models is based on some assumption about the way parents $C_1, \ldots, C_n$ interact with their common child E. If the assumption corresponds to reality, then one can use these models for local structure. Otherwise, the resulting Bayesian network will be an inaccurate model of that reality (but it could be a good approximation).

Most often, we have some local structure in the relationship between a node and its parents but that structure does not fit precisely into any of the existing micro models such as noisy-or. Consider the CPT in Figure 5.31. Here we have a node with four parents and a CPT that exhibits a considerable amount of structure. For example, the probability of $E=1$ given $C_1=1$ is 0 regardless of the values assumed by parents C_2, C_3, and C_4. Moreover, given that $C_1=0$ and $C_2=1$, the probability of $E=1$ is .9 regardless of the values of other parents. Even with all of this local structure, the CPT of this node does not correspond to the assumptions underlying a noisy-or model and, hence, cannot be generated by such a model.

For this type of irregular structure, there are several nontabular representations that are not necessarily exponential in the number of parents. We discuss some of these representations next.

Decision trees and graphs

One of the more popular representations for this purpose is the decision tree, an example of which is shown in Figure 5.31. The basic idea here is that we start at the root of the tree and then branch downward at each node depending on the value of the variable attached to that node. The decision tree in Figure 5.31 represents the probability of $E=1$ under every possible instantiation of the parents $C_1, \ldots, C_4$ except that these instantiations are not represented explicitly. For example, if $C_1=1$ then the probability of $E=1$ is immediately decided to be 0, as shown on the very left of this decision tree. Obviously, the decision tree can have a size that is linear in the number of parents if there is enough structure in the CPT. But it may also be exponential in size if no such structure exists in the given CPT. We discuss in Chapter 13 a generalization of decisions trees called decision graphs that can be exponentially more compact than trees.

If-then rules

A CPT for variable E can be represented using a set of if-then rules of the form

$$\text{If } \alpha_i \text{ then } \Pr(e) = p_i,$$

where α_i is a propositional sentence constructed using the parents of variable E. For example, the CPT in Figure 5.31 can be represented using the following rules:

If $C_1 = 1$		then	$\Pr(E = 1) = 0$
If $C_1 = 0 \wedge C_2 = 1$		then	$\Pr(E = 1) = .9$
If $C_1 = 0 \wedge C_2 = 0 \wedge C_3 = 1$		then	$\Pr(E = 1) = .3$
If $C_1 = 0 \wedge C_2 = 0 \wedge C_3 = 0 \wedge C_4 = 1$	then	$\Pr(E = 1) = .6$
If $C_1 = 0 \wedge C_2 = 0 \wedge C_3 = 0 \wedge C_4 = 0$	then	$\Pr(E = 1) = .8$

For the rule-based representation to be complete and consistent, the set of rules

$$\text{If } \alpha_i \text{ then } \Pr(e) = p_i$$

for a given value e of E must satisfy two conditions:

- The premises α_i must be mutually exclusive. That is, $\alpha_i \wedge \alpha_j$ is inconsistent for $i \neq j$. This ensures that the rules will not conflict with each other.
- The premises α_i must be exhaustive. That is, $\bigvee_i \alpha_i$ must be valid. This ensures that every CPT parameter $\theta_{e|...}$ is implied by the rules.

We also need to have one set of rules for all but one value e of variable E. Again, the rule-based representation can be very efficient if the CPT has enough structure yet may be of exponential size when no such structure exists.

Deterministic CPTs

A *deterministic* or functional CPT is one in which every probability is either 0 or 1. These CPTs are very common in practice and we have seen a number of them in Sections 5.3.5 and 5.3.7. When a node has a deterministic CPT, the node is said to be *functionally determined* by its parents.

Deterministic CPTs can be represented compactly using propositional sentences. In particular, suppose that we have a deterministic CPT for variable E with values $e_1, \ldots, e_m$. We can then represent this CPT by a set of propositional sentences of the form

$$\Gamma_i \iff E = e_i,$$

where we have one rule for each value e_i of E and the premises Γ_i are mutually exclusive and exhaustive. The CPT for variable E is then given by

$$\theta_{e_i|\alpha} = \begin{cases} 1, & \text{if parent instantiation } \alpha \text{ is consistent with } \Gamma_i \\ 0, & \text{otherwise.} \end{cases}$$

Consider for example the following deterministic CPT from Sections 5.3.5:

A	X	C	$\theta_{c|a,x}$
high	ok	high	0
low	ok	high	1
high	stuckat0	high	0
low	stuckat0	high	0
high	stuckat1	high	1
low	stuckat1	high	1

We can represent this CPT as follows:

$$(X = \text{ok} \land A = \text{high}) \lor X = \text{stuckat0} \iff C = \text{low}$$

$$(X = \text{ok} \land A = \text{low}) \lor X = \text{stuckat1} \iff C = \text{high}$$

This representation can be very effective in general, especially when the number of parents is quite large.

Expanding CPT representations

We close this section with a word of caution on how the prior representations of CPTs are sometimes used by Bayesian network tools. Many of these tools will expand these structured representations into tabular representations before they perform inference. In such cases, these structured representations are only being utilized in addressing the modeling problem since the size of expanded representations is still exponential in the number of parents. However, Chapter 13 discusses algorithms that can operate directly on some structured representations of CPTs without having to expand them.

5.5 The significance of network parameters

Bayesian network parameters can be viewed as *local beliefs*, as each parameter $\theta_{x|\mathbf{u}}$ represents the belief in variable X given its parents $\mathbf{U}$ (direct causes). On the other hand, queries posed to a Bayesian network can be viewed as *global beliefs* as the query $\Pr(\mathbf{y}|\mathbf{e})$ represents our belief in some variables $\mathbf{Y}$ given the state of other variables $\mathbf{E}$ that can be distantly related to them (i.e., their indirect causes, indirect effects, and so on). One of the more practical issues when modeling and reasoning with Bayesian networks is that of understanding the relationship between global beliefs $\Pr(\mathbf{y}|\mathbf{e})$ and local beliefs $\theta_{x|\mathbf{u}}$. Next, we present some known relationships between these two quantities that can provide valuable insights when building Bayesian network models. Additional relationships are discussed in Chapter 16, which is dedicated to the subject of sensitivity analysis.

Suppose that X is a variable that has two values, x and $\bar{x}$, and a set of parents $\mathbf{U}$. We must then have

$$\theta_{x|\mathbf{u}} + \theta_{\bar{x}|\mathbf{u}} = 1$$

for any parent instantiation $\mathbf{u}$. Therefore, if we change either of these parameters we must also change the other parameter to ensure that their sum continues to be 1. Now let $\tau_{x|\mathbf{u}}$ be a metaparameter such that:

$$\theta_{x|\mathbf{u}} = \tau_{x|\mathbf{u}}$$

$$\theta_{\bar{x}|\mathbf{u}} = 1 - \tau_{x|\mathbf{u}}.$$

By changing the metaparameter $\tau_{x|\mathbf{u}}$, we are then simultaneously changing both parameters $\theta_{x|\mathbf{u}}$ and $\theta_{\bar{x}|\mathbf{u}}$ in a consistent way. Given this new tool, let us consider the following result, which provides a bound on the partial derivative of query $\Pr(\mathbf{y}|\mathbf{e})$ with respect to metaparameter $\tau_{x|\mathbf{u}}$:

$$\left| \frac{\partial \Pr(\mathbf{y}|\mathbf{e})}{\partial \tau_{x|\mathbf{u}}} \right| \leq \frac{\Pr(\mathbf{y}|\mathbf{e})(1 - \Pr(\mathbf{y}|\mathbf{e}))}{\Pr(x|\mathbf{u})(1 - \Pr(x|\mathbf{u}))}. \tag{5.3}$$

Note that this bound is independent of the Bayesian network under consideration; that is, it applies to any Bayesian network regardless of its structure and parametrization. The plot of this bound against the current value of the metaparameter, $\Pr(x|\mathbf{u})$, and the current

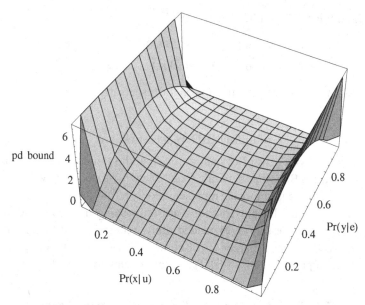

Figure 5.32: An upper bound on the partial derivative $|\partial \Pr(\mathbf{y}|\mathbf{e})/\partial \tau_{x|\mathbf{u}}|$ as a function of the query value $\Pr(\mathbf{y}|\mathbf{e})$ and the parameter value $\Pr(x|\mathbf{u})$.

value of the query, $\Pr(\mathbf{y}|\mathbf{e})$, is shown in Figure 5.32. A number of observations are in order about this plot:

1. The bound approaches infinity for extreme values of parameter $\Pr(x|\mathbf{u})$ and attains its smallest value when $\Pr(x|\mathbf{u}) = .5$.

2. The bound approaches 0 for extreme values of query $\Pr(\mathbf{y}|\mathbf{e})$ and attains its highest value when $\Pr(\mathbf{y}|\mathbf{e}) = .5$.

Therefore, according to this bound extreme queries tend to be robust when changing nonextreme parameters yet nonextreme queries may change considerably when changing extreme parameters.

Bound (5.3) can be used to show an even more specific relationship between parameters and queries. Specifically, let $O(x|\mathbf{u})$ denote the odds of variable X given its parents $\mathbf{U}$,

$$O(x|\mathbf{u}) = \Pr(x|\mathbf{u})/(1 - \Pr(x|\mathbf{u})),$$

and let $O(\mathbf{y}|\mathbf{e})$ denote the odds of variables $\mathbf{Y}$ given evidence $\mathbf{E}$:

$$O(\mathbf{y}|\mathbf{e}) = \Pr(\mathbf{y}|\mathbf{e})/(1 - \Pr(\mathbf{y}|\mathbf{e})).$$

Let $O'(x|\mathbf{u})$ and $O'(\mathbf{y}|\mathbf{e})$ denote these odds after having applied an arbitrary change to the metaparameter $\tau_{x|\mathbf{u}}$. We then have

$$|\ln(O'(\mathbf{y}|\mathbf{e})) - \ln(O(\mathbf{y}|\mathbf{e}))| \leq |\ln(O'(x|\mathbf{u})) - \ln(O(x|\mathbf{u}))|. \tag{5.4}$$

The inequality (5.4) allows us to bound the amount of change in a query value using only the amount of change we applied to a parameter without requiring any information about the Bayesian network under consideration. This inequality can be very useful in practice as it allows one to assess the impact of a parameter change on some query very efficiently (in constant time).

Consider for example the screenshot in Figure 5.3 on Page 79, where the evidence **e** indicates a patient with positive x-ray and no dyspnoea. The belief in this patient visiting

Asia, $\Pr(A = \text{yes}|\mathbf{e})$, is about 1.17% in this case. Moreover, the belief in this patient having cancer, $\Pr(C = \text{yes}|\mathbf{e})$, is about 25.23%. Consider now the parameter $\theta_{C=\text{yes}|S=\text{yes}}$, which represents our local belief in cancer given smoking. This parameter is currently set to 10% and we would like to change its value to 5%. Our interest here is in assessing the impact of this change on the probability of having visited Asia. Using bound (5.4), we have

$$\left| \ln\left(\frac{p}{1-p}\right) - \ln\left(\frac{1.17}{98.83}\right) \right| \leq \left| \ln\left(\frac{5}{95}\right) - \ln\left(\frac{10}{90}\right) \right|,$$

where $p = \Pr'(A = \text{yes}|\mathbf{e})$ is the new probability in a visit to Asia after having changed the parameter $\theta_{C=\text{yes}|S=\text{yes}}$ from 10% to 5%. Solving for p, we get

$$.56\% \leq \Pr'(A = \text{yes}|\mathbf{e}) \leq 2.44\%$$

If we actually change the parameter and perform inference, we find that the exact value of $\Pr'(A = \text{yes}|\mathbf{e})$ is 1.19%, which is within the bound as expected.

We can use the same technique to bound the change in our belief in cancer after the same parameter change, which gives

$$13.78\% \leq \Pr'(C = \text{yes}|\mathbf{e}) \leq 41.60\%$$

Note that the bound is looser in this case, which is not surprising since the query under consideration is less extreme.

Consider now the parameter $\theta_{B=\text{yes}|S=\text{yes}}$ that represents our local belief in bronchitis given smoking. This parameter is currently set to 60% and we would like to reduce it to 50%. We now have the following bounds for query change:

$$.78\% \leq \Pr'(A = \text{yes}|\mathbf{e}) \leq 1.74\%$$

$$18.36\% \leq \Pr'(C = \text{yes}|\mathbf{e}) \leq 33.61\%$$

These bounds are tighter than these for parameter $\theta_{C=\text{yes}|S=\text{yes}}$, which is not surprising since parameter $\theta_{B=\text{yes}|S=\text{yes}}$ is less extreme.

We finally note that the bound in (5.4) assumes that the parameter we are changing concerns a variable with only two values. This bound has a generalization to nonbinary variables but we defer the discussion of this generalization to Chapter 16, where we discuss sensitivity analysis in greater technical depth.

Bibliographic remarks

The Asia network of Section 5.2 is due to Lauritzen and Spiegelhalter [1988]. The pregnancy network of Section 5.3.2 is due to Jensen [1996]. The SamBot network of Section 5.3.8 is a slight modification on the one in Charniak [1991]. The connection between channel coding and graphical models, including Bayesian networks, is discussed in McEliece et al. [1998a], Frey and MacKay [1997], Frey [1998]. Our treatment of genetic linkage analysis is based on Fishelson and Geiger [2002; 2003]. Some of the early examples for using Bayesian networks in medical diagnosis include: The Quick Medical Reference (QMR) model [Miller et al., 1986], which was later reformulated as a Bayesian network model [Shwe et al., 1991]; the CPCS-PM network [Pradhan et al., 1994; Parker and Miller, 1987], which simulates patient scenarios in the medical field of hepatobiliary disease; and the MUNIN model for diagnosing neuromuscular disorders from data acquired by electromyographic (EMG) examinations [Andreassen et al., 1987;

1989; 2001]. Dynamic Bayesian networks were first discussed in Dean and Kanazawa [1989].

The noisy-or model and some of its generalizations are discussed in Pearl [1988], Henrion [1989], Srinivas [1993], and Díez [1993]. Nontabular representations of CPTs are discussed in Friedman and Goldszmidt [1996], Hoey et al. [1999], Nielsen et al. [2000], Poole and Zhang [2003], Sanner and McAllester [2005], Mateescu and Dechter [2006], and Chavira and Darwiche [2007]. Our discussion on the impact of network parameters is based on Chan and Darwiche [2002].

5.6 Exercises

5.1. Joe's x-ray test comes back positive for lung cancer. The test's false negative rate is $f_n = .40$ and its false positive rate is $f_p = .02$. We also know that the prior probability of having lung cancer is $c = .001$. Describe a Bayesian network and a corresponding query for computing the probability that Joe has lung cancer given his positive x-ray. What is the value of this probability? Use sensitivity analysis to identify necessary and sufficient conditions on each of f_n, f_p, and c that guarantee the probability of cancer to be no less than 10% given a positive x-ray test.

5.2. We have three identical and independent temperature sensors that will trigger in:

- 90% of the cases where the temperature is high
- 5% of the cases where the temperature is nominal
- 1% of the cases where the temperature is low.

The probability of high temperature is 20%, nominal temperature is 70%, and low temperature is 10%. Describe a Bayesian network and corresponding queries for computing the following:

(a) Probability that the first sensor will trigger given that the other two sensors have also triggered

(b) Probability that the temperature is high given that all three sensors have triggered

(c) Probability that the temperature is high given that at least one sensor has triggered

5.3. Suppose that we apply three test vectors to the circuit in Figure 5.14, where each gate is initially ok with probability .99. As we change the test vector, a gate that is ok may become faulty with probability .01, and a gate that is faulty may become ok with probability .001.

(a) What are the posterior marginals for the health variables given the following test vectors?

- $A =$ high, $B =$ high, $E =$ low
- $A =$ low, $B =$ low, $E =$ high
- $A =$ low, $B =$ high, $E =$ high

(b) What about the following test vectors?

- $A =$ high, $B =$ high, $E =$ low
- $A =$ low, $B =$ low, $E =$ high
- $A =$ low, $B =$ high, $E =$ low

(c) What are the MPE and MAP (over health variables) for each of the cases in (a) and (b)?

Assume that the test vectors are applied in the order given.

5.4. We have two sensors that are meant to detect extreme temperature, which occurs 20% of the time. The sensors have identical specifications with a false positive rate of 1% and a false negative rate of 3%. If the power is off (dead battery), the sensors will read negative regardless of the temperature. Suppose now that we have two sensor kits: Kit A where both sensors receive power from the same battery and Kit B where they receive power from independent batteries. Assuming that each battery has a .9 probability of power availability, what is the probability of extreme temperature given each of the following scenarios:

(a) The two sensors read negative

(b) The two sensors read positive

(c) One sensor reads positive while the other reads negative.

Answer the previous questions with respect to each of the two kits.

5.5. Jack has three coins C_1, C_2, and C_3 with p_1, p_2, and p_3 as their corresponding probabilities of landing heads. Jack flips coin C_1 twice and then decides, based on the outcome, whether to flip coin C_2 or C_3 next. In particular, if the two C_1 flips come out the same, Jack flips coin C_2 three times next. However, if the C_1 flips come out different, he flips coin C_3 three times next. Given the outcome of Jack's last three flips, we want to know whether his first two flips came out the same. Describe a Bayesian network and a corresponding query that solves this problem. What is the solution to this problem assuming that $p_1 = .4$, $p_2 = .6$, and $p_3 = .1$ and the last three flips came out as follows:

(a) tails, heads, tails

(b) tails, tails, tails

5.6. Lisa is given a fair coin C_1 and asked to flip it eight times in a row. Lisa also has a biased coin C_2 with a probability .8 of landing heads. All we know is that Lisa flipped the fair coin initially but we believe that she intends to switch to the biased coin and that she tends to be 10% successful in performing the switch. Suppose that we observe the outcome of the eight coin flips and want to find out whether Lisa managed to perform a coin switch and when. Describe a Bayesian network and a corresponding query that solves this problem. What is the solution to this problem assuming that the flips came out as follows:

(a) tails, tails, tails, heads, heads, heads, heads, heads

(b) tails, tails, heads, heads, heads, heads, heads, heads

5.7. Consider the system reliability problem in Section 5.3.6 and suppose that the two fans depend on a common condition C that materializes with a probability 99.5%. In particular, as long as the condition is established, each fan will have a reliability of 90%. However, if the condition is not established, both fans will fail. Develop a Bayesian network that corresponds to this scenario and compute the overall system reliability in this case.

5.8. Consider the electrical network depicted in Figure 5.33 and assume that electricity can flow in either direction between two adjacent stations S_i and S_j (i.e., connected by an edge), and that electricity is flowing into the network from sources I_1 and I_2. For the network to be

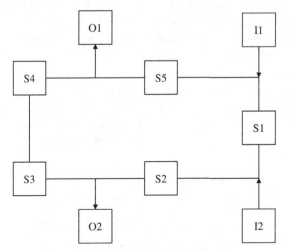

Figure 5.33: An electrical network system.

operational, electricity must also flow out of either outlets O_1 or O_2. Describe a Bayesian network and a corresponding query that allows us to compute the reliability of this network, given the reliability r_{ij} of each connection between stations S_i and S_j. What is the reliability of the network if $r_{ij} = .99$ for all connections?

5.9. Consider Section 5.3.6 and suppose we extend the language of RBDs to include k-out-of-n blocks. In particular, a block C is said to be of type k-out-of-n if it has n components pointing to it in the diagram, and at least k of them must be available for the subsystem represented by C to be available. Provide a systematic method for converting RBDs with k-out-of-n blocks into Bayesian networks.

5.10 (After Jensen). Consider a cow that may be infected with a disease that can possibly be detected by performing a milk test. The test is performed on five consecutive days, leading to five outcomes. We want to determine the state of the cow's infection over these days given the test outcomes. The prior probability of an infection on day one is $1/10,000$; the test false positive rate is $5/1,000$; and its false negative rate is $1/1,000$. Moreover, the state of infection at a given day depends only on its state at the previous day. In particular, the probability of a new infection on a given day is $2/10,000$, while the probability that an infection would persist to the next day is $7/10$.

(a) Describe a Bayesian network and a corresponding query that solves this problem. What is the most likely state of the cow's infection over the five days given the following test outcomes:

(1) positive, positive, negative, positive, positive

(2) positive, negative, negative, positive, positive

(3) positive, negative, negative, negative, positive

(b) Assume now that the original false negative and false positive rates double on a given day in case the test has failed on the previous day. Describe a Bayesian network that captures this additional information.

5.11. Let $\mathbf{E}$ be the evidence variables in a Bayesian network, $\mathbf{M}$ be the MAP variables, and let $\mathbf{Y}$ be all other variables. Suppose that $\Pr(\mathbf{m}, \mathbf{e}) > 0$ implies that $\Pr(\mathbf{m}, \mathbf{e}, \mathbf{y}) \neq 0$ for exactly one instantiation $\mathbf{y}$. Show that the projection of an MPE solution on the MAP variables $\mathbf{M}$ is also a MAP solution.

5.12. Let $\mathbf{R}$ be some root variables in a Bayesian network and let $\mathbf{Q}$ be some nonroots. Show that the probability $\Pr(\mathbf{q}|\mathbf{r})$ is independent of the CPTs for roots $\mathbf{R}$ for all $\mathbf{q}$ and $\mathbf{r}$ such that $\Pr(\mathbf{r}) \neq 0$.

5.13. Consider the two circuit models of Section 5.3.5 corresponding to two different ways of representing health variables. We showed in that section that these two models are equivalent as far as queries involving variables A, B, C, D, and E. Does this equivalence continue to hold if we extend the models to two test vectors as we did in Section 5.3.5? In particular, will the two models be equivalent with respect to queries involving variables $A, \ldots, E, A', \ldots, E'$? Explain your answer.

5.14. Consider the two circuit models of Section 5.3.5 corresponding to two different ways of representing health variables. We showed in that section that these two models are equivalent as far as queries involving variables A, B, C, D, and E. Show that this result generalizes to any circuit structure as long as the two models agree on the CPTs for primary inputs and the CPTs corresponding to components satisfy the following conditions:

$$\theta_{H=\text{ok}} = \theta'_{H=\text{ok}}$$

$$\theta_{O=0|i, H=\text{faulty}} = \frac{\theta'_{H=\text{stuckat0}}}{\theta'_{H=\text{stuckat0}} + \theta'_{H=\text{stuckat1}}}$$

$$\theta_{O=1|i, H=\text{faulty}} = \frac{\theta'_{H=\text{stuckat1}}}{\theta'_{H=\text{stuckat0}} + \theta'_{H=\text{stuckat1}}}.$$

Here H is the health of the component, O is its output, and $\mathbf{I}$ are its inputs. Moreover, θ are the network parameters when health variables have states ok and faulty, and θ' are the network parameters when health variables have states ok, stuckat0, and stuckat1.

5.15. Consider Exercise 5.14. Let $\mathbf{H}$ and $\mathbf{H}'$ be the health variables in corresponding networks and let $\mathbf{X}$ be all other variables in either network. Let $\mathbf{h}$ be an instantiation of variables $\mathbf{H}$, assigning either ok or faulty to each variable in $\mathbf{H}$. Let $\mathbf{h}'$ be defined as follows:

$$\mathbf{h}' \stackrel{def}{=} \left[\bigwedge_{\mathbf{h} \models H=ok} (H' = ok) \right] \wedge \left[\bigwedge_{\mathbf{h} \models H=faulty} (H' = \text{stuckat0}) \vee (H' = \text{stuckat1}) \right].$$

Show that $\Pr(\mathbf{x}, \mathbf{h}) = \Pr'(\mathbf{x}, \mathbf{h}')$ for all $\mathbf{x}$ and $\mathbf{h}$, where $\Pr$ is the distribution induced by the network with health states ok/faulty and $\Pr'$ is the distribution induced by the network with health states ok/stuckat0/stuckat1.

5.16. Consider a DAG G with one root node S and one leaf node T, where every edge $U \to X$ represents a communication link between U and X – a link is up if U can communicate with X and down otherwise. In such a model, nodes S and T can communicate iff there exists a directed path from S to T where all links are up. Suppose that each edge $U \to X$ is labeled with a probability p representing the reliability of communication between U and X. Describe a Bayesian network and a corresponding query that computes the reliability of communication between S and T. The Bayesian network should have a size that is proportional to the size of the DAG G.

6

Inference by Variable Elimination

We present in this chapter one of the simplest methods for general inference in Bayesian networks, which is based on the principle of variable elimination: A process by which we successively remove variables from a Bayesian network while maintaining its ability to answer queries of interest.

6.1 Introduction

We saw in Chapter 5 how a number of real-world problems can be solved by posing queries with respect to Bayesian networks. We also identified four types of queries: probability of evidence, prior and posterior marginals, most probable explanation (MPE), and maximum a posterior hypothesis (MAP). We present in this chapter one of the simplest inference algorithms for answering these types of queries, which is based on the principle of variable elimination. Our interest here will be restricted to computing the probability of evidence and marginal distributions, leaving the discussion of MPE and MAP queries to Chapter 10.

We start in Section 6.2 by introducing the process of eliminating a variable. This process relies on some basic operations on a class of functions known as factors, which we discuss in Section 6.3. We then introduce the variable elimination algorithm in Section 6.4 and see how it can be used to compute prior marginals in Section 6.5. The performance of variable elimination will critically depend on the order in which we eliminate variables. We discuss this issue in Section 6.6, where we also provide some heuristics for choosing good elimination orders. We then expand the scope of variable elimination to posterior marginals and probability of evidence in Section 6.7. The complexity of variable elimination is sensitive to the network structure and specific queries of interest. We study the effect of these two factors on the complexity of inference in Sections 6.8 and 6.9, respectively. We conclude the chapter in Section 6.10 with a discussion of a common variant on variable elimination known as bucket elimination.

6.2 The process of elimination

Consider the Bayesian network in Figure 6.1 and suppose that we are interested in computing the following marginal:

D	E	$\Pr(D, E)$
true	true	.30443
true	false	.39507
false	true	.05957
false	false	.24093

The algorithm of variable elimination will compute this marginal by summing out variables A, B, and C from the given network to construct a marginal distribution over

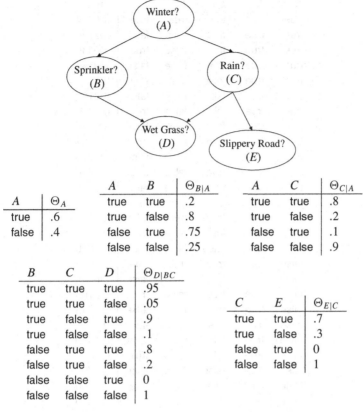

A B C D E

A	B	$\Theta_{B\vert A}$
true	true	.2
true	false	.8
false	true	.75
false	false	.25

A	Θ_A
true	.6
false	.4

A	C	$\Theta_{C\vert A}$
true	true	.8
true	false	.2
false	true	.1
false	false	.9

B	C	D	$\Theta_{D\vert BC}$
true	true	true	.95
true	true	false	.05
true	false	true	.9
true	false	false	.1
false	true	true	.8
false	true	false	.2
false	false	true	0
false	false	false	1

C	E	$\Theta_{E\vert C}$
true	true	.7
true	false	.3
false	true	0
false	false	1

Figure 6.1: A Bayesian network.

the remaining variables D and E. To explain this process of summing out variables, consider the joint probability distribution in Figure 6.2, which is induced by the network in Figure 6.1. To sum out a variable, say, A from this distribution is to produce a marginal distribution over the remaining variables B, C, D, and E. This is done by merging all rows that agree on the values of variables B, C, D, and E. For example, the following rows in Figure 6.2

A	B	C	D	E	Pr(.)
true	true	true	true	true	.06384
false	true	true	true	true	.01995

are merged into the row

B	C	D	E	Pr(.)
true	true	true	true	.08379 = .06384 + .01995

As we merge rows, we drop reference to the summed-out variable A and add up the probabilities of merged rows. Hence, the result of summing out variable A from the distribution Pr in Figure 6.2, which has thirty-two rows, is another distribution Pr$'$ that does not mention A and that has sixteen rows. The important property of summing variables out is that the new distribution is as good as the original one as far as answering queries that do not mention variable A. That is, Pr$'(\alpha) =$ Pr(α) for any event α that does not mention variable A. Therefore, if we want to compute the marginal distribution over, say, variables D and E, all we have to do then is sum out variables A, B, and C from the joint distribution.

A	B	C	D	E	Pr(.)
true	true	true	true	true	.06384
true	true	true	true	false	.02736
true	true	true	false	true	.00336
true	true	true	false	false	.00144
true	true	false	true	true	0
true	true	false	true	false	.02160
true	true	false	false	true	0
true	true	false	false	false	.00240
true	false	true	true	true	.21504
true	false	true	true	false	.09216
true	false	true	false	true	.05376
true	false	true	false	false	.02304
true	false	false	true	true	0
true	false	false	true	false	0
true	false	false	false	true	0
true	false	false	false	false	.09600
false	true	true	true	true	.01995
false	true	true	true	false	.00855
false	true	true	false	true	.00105
false	true	true	false	false	.00045
false	true	false	true	true	0
false	true	false	true	false	.24300
false	true	false	false	true	0
false	true	false	false	false	.02700
false	false	true	true	true	.00560
false	false	true	true	false	.00240
false	false	true	false	true	.00140
false	false	true	false	false	.00060
false	false	false	true	true	0
false	false	false	true	false	0
false	false	false	false	true	0
false	false	false	false	false	.0900

Figure 6.2: A joint probability distribution induced by the Bayesian network in Figure 6.1.

This procedure will always work but its complexity is exponential in the number of variables in the Bayesian network. The key insight underlying the method of variable elimination is that one can sometimes sum out variables without having to construct the joint probability distribution explicitly. In particular, variables can be summed out while keeping the original distribution and all successive distributions in some factored form. This allows the procedure to sometimes escape the exponential complexity of the brute-force method discussed previously.

Before we discuss the method of variable elimination, we first need to discuss its central component: the factor.

6.3 Factors

A *factor* is a function over a set of variables, mapping each instantiation of these variables to a non-negative number. Figure 6.3 depicts two factors in tabular form, the first of which is over three variables B, C, and D. Each row of this factor has two components: an instantiation and a corresponding number. In some cases, the number represents the probability of the corresponding instantiation, as in factor f_2 of Figure 6.3, which

B	C	D	f_1
true	true	true	.95
true	true	false	.05
true	false	true	.9
true	false	false	.1
false	true	true	.8
false	true	false	.2
false	false	true	0
false	false	false	1

D	E	f_2
true	true	.448
true	false	.192
false	true	.112
false	false	.248

Figure 6.3: Two factors: $f_1(b, c, d) = \Pr(d|b, c)$ and $f_2(d, e) = \Pr(d, e)$.

represents a distribution over variables D and E. In other cases, the number represents some conditional probability that relates to the instantiation, as in factor f_1 of Figure 6.3, which represents the conditional probability of D given B and C. Hence, it is important to stress that a factor does not necessarily represent a probability distribution over the corresponding variables. However, most of the computations we perform on factors will start with factors that represent conditional probabilities and end up with factors that represent marginal probabilities. In the process we may have a mixture of factors with different interpretations. The following is the formal definition of a factor.

Definition 6.1. A *factor* f over variables $\mathbf{X}$ is a function that maps each instantiation $\mathbf{x}$ of variables $\mathbf{X}$ to a non-negative number, denoted $f(\mathbf{x})$.[1]   ∎

We will use vars(f) to denote the variables over which the factor f is defined. We will also write $f(X_1, \ldots, X_n)$ to indicate that $X_1, \ldots, X_n$ are the variables over which factor f is defined. Finally, we will allow factors over an empty set of variables. Such factors are called *trivial* as they assign a single number to the trivial instantiation $\top$.

There are two key operations that are commonly applied to factors. The first is summing out a variable from a factor and the second is multiplying two factors. We will next define these operations and discuss their complexity as they represent the building blocks of many algorithms for inference with Bayesian networks, including variable elimination. We already discussed the summing-out operation informally in the previous section, so here we present the formal definition.

Definition 6.2. Let f be a factor over variables $\mathbf{X}$ and let X be a variable in $\mathbf{X}$. The result of *summing out* variable X from factor f is another factor over variables $\mathbf{Y} = \mathbf{X} \setminus \{X\}$, which is denoted by $\sum_X f$ and defined as

$$\left(\sum_X f \right)(\mathbf{y}) \stackrel{def}{=} \sum_x f(x, \mathbf{y}).$$ ∎

To visualize this summing-out operation, consider factor f_1 in Figure 6.3. The result of summing out variable D from this factor is then

B	C	$\sum_D f_1$
true	true	1
true	false	1
false	true	1
false	false	1

---

[1] A factor is also known as a *potential*.

Algorithm 1 SumOutVars($f(\mathbf{X})$, $\mathbf{Z}$)

---

input:

$f(\mathbf{X})$:   factor over variables $\mathbf{X}$

$\mathbf{Z}$:   a subset of variables $\mathbf{X}$

output: a factor corresponding to $\sum_{\mathbf{Z}} f$

main:

1: $\mathbf{Y} \leftarrow \mathbf{X} - \mathbf{Z}$
2: $f' \leftarrow$ a factor over variables $\mathbf{Y}$ where $f'(\mathbf{y}) = 0$ for all $\mathbf{y}$
3: **for** each instantiation $\mathbf{y}$ **do**
4:      **for** each instantiation $\mathbf{z}$ **do**
5:          $f'(\mathbf{y}) \leftarrow f'(\mathbf{y}) + f(\mathbf{yz})$
6:      **end for**
7: **end for**
8: **return** f'

Note that if we sum out variables B and C from the previous factor, we get a trivial factor that assigns the number 4 to the trivial instantiation:

$$\begin{array}{c|c} & \sum_B \sum_C \sum_D f_1 \\ \hline \top & 4 \end{array}$$

The summing-out operation is commutative; that is,

$$\sum_Y \sum_X f = \sum_X \sum_Y f.$$

Hence, it is meaningful to talk about summing out multiple variables from a factor without fixing the variable order. This also justifies the notation $\sum_{\mathbf{X}} f$, where $\mathbf{X}$ is a set of variables. Summing out variables $\mathbf{X}$ is also known as *marginalizing* variables $\mathbf{X}$. Moreover, if $\mathbf{Y}$ are the other variables of factor f, then $\sum_{\mathbf{X}} f$ is also called the result of *projecting* factor f on variables $\mathbf{Y}$.

Algorithm 1 provides pseudocode for summing out any number of variables from a factor within $O(\exp(w))$ time and space, where w is the number of variables over which the factor is defined. It is important to keep this complexity in mind as it is essential for analyzing the complexity of various inference algorithms based on variable elimination.

We now discuss the second operation on factors, which is called multiplication. Consider the two factors, $f_1(B, C, D)$ and $f_2(D, E)$, in Figure 6.3. To multiply these two factors is to construct a factor over the union of their variables B, C, D, and E, which is partially shown here:

B	C	D	E	$f_1(B, C, D) f_2(D, E)$
true	true	true	true	$.4256 = (.95)(.448)$
true	true	true	false	$.1824 = (.95)(.192)$
true	true	false	true	$.0056 = (.05)(.112)$
$\vdots$	$\vdots$	$\vdots$	$\vdots$	$\vdots$
false	false	false	false	$.2480 = (1)(.248)$

Note that each instantiation b, c, d, e of the resulting factor is compatible with exactly one instantiation in factor f_1, b, c, d, and exactly one instantiation in factor f_2, d, e.

Algorithm 2 `MultiplyFactors(`$f_1(\mathbf{X}_1), \ldots, f_m(\mathbf{X}_m)$`)`

---

input:

   $f_1(\mathbf{X}_1), \ldots, f_m(\mathbf{X}_m)$:   factors

output: a factor corresponding to the product $\prod_{i=1}^m f_i$

main:

  1: $\mathbf{Z} \leftarrow \bigcup_{i=1}^m \mathbf{X}_i$
  2: $f \leftarrow$ a factor over variables $\mathbf{Z}$ where $f(\mathbf{z}) = 1$ for all $\mathbf{z}$
  3: **for** each instantiation $\mathbf{z}$ **do**
  4:     **for** $i = 1$ to m **do**
  5:        $\mathbf{x}_i \leftarrow$ instantiation of variables $\mathbf{X}_i$ consistent with $\mathbf{z}$
  6:        $f(\mathbf{z}) \leftarrow f(\mathbf{z}) f_i(\mathbf{x}_i)$
  7:     **end for**
  8: **end for**
  9: **return** f

The value assigned by the new factor to instantiation b, c, d, e is then the product of numbers assigned by factors f_1 and f_2 to these compatible instantiations. The following is the formal definition of factor multiplication.

Definition 6.3. The result of *multiplying* factors $f_1(\mathbf{X})$ and $f_2(\mathbf{Y})$ is another factor over variables $\mathbf{Z} = \mathbf{X} \cup \mathbf{Y}$, which is denoted by $f_1 f_2$ and defined as

$$(f_1 f_2)(\mathbf{z}) \stackrel{def}{=} f_1(\mathbf{x}) f_2(\mathbf{y}),$$

where $\mathbf{x}$ and $\mathbf{y}$ are compatible with $\mathbf{z}$; that is, $\mathbf{x} \sim \mathbf{z}$ and $\mathbf{y} \sim \mathbf{z}$. ∎

Factor multiplication is commutative and associative. Hence, it is meaningful to talk about multiplying a number of factors without specifying the order of this multiplication process.

Algorithm 2 provides pseudocode for multiplying m factors within $O(m \exp(w))$ time and space, where w is the number of variables in the resulting factor. Again, it is important to keep this complexity in mind as factor multiplication is central to many algorithms for inference in Bayesian networks.

6.4 Elimination as a basis for inference

Consider again the Bayesian network in Figure 6.1 and suppose that our goal is to compute the joint probability distribution for this network, which is given in Figure 6.2. We can do this in two ways. First, we can use the chain rule for Bayesian networks, which allows us to compute the probability of each instantiation a, b, c, d, e as a product of network parameters:

$$\Pr(a, b, c, d, e) = \theta_{e|c}\, \theta_{d|bc}\, \theta_{c|a}\, \theta_{b|a}\, \theta_a.$$

Another more direct method is to multiply the CPTs for this Bayesian network, viewing each CPT as a factor. In particular, it is easy to verify that the factor

$$\Theta_{E|C}\, \Theta_{D|BC}\, \Theta_{C|A}\, \Theta_{B|A}\, \Theta_A$$

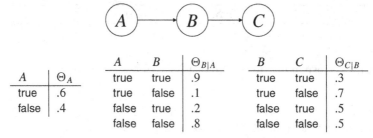

A	B	$\Theta_{B\|A}$
true	true	.9
true	false	.1
false	true	.2
false	false	.8

B	C	$\Theta_{C\|B}$
true	true	.3
true	false	.7
false	true	.5
false	false	.5

A	Θ_A
true	.6
false	.4

Figure 6.4: A Bayesian network.

is indeed the joint probability distribution given in Figure 6.2. This shows one of the key applications of factor multiplication, as it allows us to express the joint probability distribution of any Bayesian network as a product of its CPTs.

Suppose now that our goal is to compute the marginal distribution over variables D and E in the previous Bayesian network. We know that this marginal can be obtained by summing out variables A, B, and C from the joint probability distribution. Hence, the marginal we want corresponds to the following factor:

$$\Pr(D, E) = \sum_{A,B,C} \Theta_{E|C}\, \Theta_{D|BC}\, \Theta_{C|A}\, \Theta_{B|A}\, \Theta_A.$$

This equation shows the power of combining the operation for summing out variables with the one for multiplying factors as they are all we need to compute the marginal over any set of variables. However, there is still the problem of complexity since the multiplication of all CPTs takes time exponential in the number of network variables. Fortunately, the following result shows that such a multiplication is not necessary in general.

Theorem 6.1. *If f_1 and f_2 are factors and if variable X appears only in f_2, then*

$$\sum_X f_1 f_2 = f_1 \sum_X f_2. \qquad \blacksquare$$

Therefore, if $f_1, \ldots, f_n$ are the CPTs of a Bayesian network and if we want to sum out variable X from the product $f_1 \ldots f_n$, it may not be necessary to multiply these factors first. For example, if variable X appears only in factor f_n, then we do not need to multiply any of the factors before we sum out X since

$$\sum_X f_1 \ldots f_n = f_1 \ldots f_{n-1} \sum_X f_n.$$

However, if variable X appears in two factors, say, f_{n-1} and f_n, then we only need to multiply these two factors before we can sum out X since

$$\sum_X f_1 \ldots f_n = f_1 \ldots f_{n-2} \sum_X f_{n-1} f_n.$$

In general, to sum out variable X from the product $f_1 \ldots f_n$, all we need to multiply are factors f_k that include X and then sum out variable X from the resulting factor $\prod_k f_k$.

Let us consider an example with respect to the Bayesian network in Figure 6.4. Our goal here is to compute the prior marginal on variable C, $\Pr(C)$, by first eliminating variable A and then variable B. There are two factors that mention variable A, Θ_A and

$\Theta_{B|A}$. We must multiply these factors first and then sum out variable A from the resulting factor. Multiplying Θ_A and $\Theta_{B|A}$, we get

A	B	$\Theta_A \Theta_{B|A}$
true	true	.54
true	false	.06
false	true	.08
false	false	.32

Summing out variable A, we get

B	$\sum_A \Theta_A \Theta_{B|A}$
true	$.62 = .54 + .08$
false	$.38 = .06 + .32$

We now have two factors, $\sum_A \Theta_A \Theta_{B|A}$ and $\Theta_{C|B}$, and we want to eliminate variable B. Since B appears in both factors, we must multiply them first and then sum out B from the result. Multiplying,

B	C	$\Theta_{C|B} \sum_A \Theta_A \Theta_{B|A}$
true	true	.186
true	false	.434
false	true	.190
false	false	.190

Summing out,

C	$\sum_B \Theta_{C|B} \sum_A \Theta_A \Theta_{B|A}$
true	.376
false	.624

This factor is then the prior marginal for variable C, $\Pr(C)$. Therefore, according to the Bayesian network in Figure 6.4, the probability of $C =$ true is .376 and the probability of $C =$ false is .624.

6.5 Computing prior marginals

Algorithm 3, VE_PR1, provides pseudocode for computing the marginal over some variables $\mathbf{Q}$ in a Bayesian network based on the previous elimination method. The algorithm takes as input a Bayesian network $\mathcal{N}$, variables $\mathbf{Q}$, and an elimination order π over remaining variables. Here $\pi(1)$ is the first variable in the order, $\pi(2)$ is the second variable, and so on. The algorithm iterates over each variable $\pi(i)$ in the order, identifying all factors f_k that contain variable $\pi(i)$, multiplying them to yield factor f, summing out variable $\pi(i)$ from f, and finally replacing factors f_k by factor $\sum_{\pi(i)} f$. When all variables in the order π are eliminated, we end up with a set of factors over variables $\mathbf{Q}$. Multiplying these factors gives the answer to our query, $\Pr(\mathbf{Q})$. From now on, we will use the phrase *eliminate variable $\pi(i)$* to denote the multiplication of factors f_k on Line 3, followed by summing out variable $\pi(i)$ on Line 4.

The question that presents itself now is: How much work does algorithm VE_PR1 actually do? As it turns out, this is an easy question to answer once we observe that the real work done by the algorithm is on Line 3 and Line 4. Each of the steps on these lines takes time and space that is linear in the size of factor f_i constructed on Line 4. Note that

---

Algorithm 3 VE_PR1($\mathcal{N}$, **Q**, π)

---

input:

  $\mathcal{N}$:   Bayesian network

  Q: variables in network $\mathcal{N}$

  π: ordering of network variables not in **Q**

output: the prior marginal Pr(**Q**)

main:

  1: $S \leftarrow$ CPTs of network $\mathcal{N}$
  2: **for** $i = 1$ to length of order π **do**
  3:    $f \leftarrow \prod_k f_k$, where f_k belongs to S and mentions variable $\pi(i)$
  4:    $f_i \leftarrow \sum_{\pi(i)} f$
  5:    replace all factors f_k in S by factor f_i
  6: **end for**
  7: **return** $\prod_{f \in S} f$

---

factor f_i on Line 4 and factor f on Line 3 differ by only one variable $\pi(i)$. In the example of Figure 6.4 where we eliminated variable A first and then variable B, the largest factor f_i we had to construct had one variable in it. This can be seen in the following expression, which explicates the number of variables appearing in each factor f_i constructed on Line 4 of VE_PR1:

$$\sum_B \Theta_{C|B} \overbrace{\sum_A \Theta_A \Theta_{B|A}}^{1} .$$

However, suppose that we eliminate variable B first and then variable A. Our computation would then be

$$\sum_A \Theta_A \overbrace{\sum_B \Theta_{B|A} \Theta_{C|B}}^{2}$$

which involves constructing a factor f_i with two variables. Therefore, although any order for variable elimination will do, the particular order we use is typically significant computationally. Some orders are better than others in that they lead to constructing smaller intermediate factors on Line 4. Therefore, to minimize the resources consumed by VE_PR1 (both time and space) we must choose the "best" order, a subject that we consider in the next section.

Before we show how to construct good elimination orders, we first show how to formally measure the quality of a particular elimination order. We start with the following result.

Theorem 6.2. *If the largest factor constructed on Line 4 of Algorithm 3,* VE_PR1, *has w variables, the complexity of Lines 3–5 is then $O(n \exp(w))$, where n is the number of variables in the Bayesian network.* ∎

The number w is known as the *width* of used order π and is taken as a measure of the order quality. Therefore, we want to choose an order that has the smallest possible width.

Note that the total time and space complexity of VE_PR1 is $O(n \exp(w) + n \exp(|\mathbf{Q}|))$ as we finally construct a factor over variables $\mathbf{Q}$ on Line 7, which can be done in $O(n \exp(|\mathbf{Q}|))$ time. If the number of variables $\mathbf{Q}$ is bounded by a constant, then the complexity of the algorithm drops to $O(n \exp(w))$. We may also choose to skip the multiplication of factors on Line 7 and simply return the factors in $\mathcal{S}$. In this case, we are keeping the marginal for variables $\mathbf{Q}$ in factored form and the complexity of VE_PR1 is $O(n \exp(w))$ regardless of variables $\mathbf{Q}$. Finally, note that this complexity analysis assumes that we can identify factors that mention variable $\pi(i)$ on Line 3 in time linear in the number of such factors. This can be accomplished using an indexing scheme that we discuss in Section 6.10, leading to a variation on algorithm VE_PR1 known as bucket elimination.

6.6 Choosing an elimination order

Suppose that we are presented with two orders π_1 and π_2 and we need to choose one of them. We clearly want to choose the one with the smaller width but how can we compute the width of each order? One straightforward but inefficient method is to modify VE_PR1 in order to keep track of the number of variables appearing in factor f_i on Line 4. To compute the width of a particular order, we simply execute the algorithm on that order and return the maximum number of variables that any factor f_i ever contained. This will work but we can do much better than this, as we shall see.

Consider the network in Figure 6.1 and suppose that we want to compute the marginal for variable E by eliminating variables according to the order B, C, A, D. The following listing provides a trace of VE_PR1:

i	$\pi(i)$	$\mathcal{S}$	f_i	w
		$\Theta_A \; \Theta_{B|A} \; \Theta_{C|A} \; \Theta_{D|BC} \; \Theta_{E|C}$		
1	B	$\Theta_A \; \Theta_{C|A} \; \Theta_{E|C} \; f_1(A, C, D)$	$f_1 = \sum_B \Theta_{B|A} \; \Theta_{D|BC}$	3
2	C	$\Theta_A \; f_2(A, D, E)$	$f_2 = \sum_C \Theta_{C|A} \; \Theta_{E|C} \; f_1(A, C, D)$	3
3	A	$f_3(D, E)$	$f_3 = \sum_A \Theta_A \; f_2(A, D, E)$	2
4	D	$f_4(E)$	$f_4 = \sum_D f_3(D, E)$	1

The second column lists variables according to their elimination order. The third column lists the set of factors $\mathcal{S}$ computed by the algorithm at the end of each iteration i. The fourth column lists the factor f_i constructed on Line 4 at iteration i, and the final column lists the size of this constructed factor as measured by the number of its variables. The maximum of these sizes is the width of the given order, which is 3 in this case. Note that such an algorithm trace can be constructed without having to execute VE_PR1. That is, to eliminate variable $\pi(i)$ that appears in factors $f(\mathbf{X}_k)$, we simply replace such factors by a newly constructed factor over the variables $\bigcup_k \mathbf{X}_k \setminus \{\pi(i)\}$.

We can also compute the width of an order by simply operating on an undirected graph that explicates the interactions between the Bayesian network CPTs. Such a graph is defined formally here.

Definition 6.4. Let $f_1, \ldots, f_n$ be a set of factors. The *interaction graph* G of these factors is an undirected graph constructed as follows. The nodes of G are the variables that appear in factors $f_1, \ldots, f_n$. There is an edge between two variables in G iff those variables appear in the same factor. ∎

Another way to visualize the interaction graph G is to realize that the variables $\mathbf{X}_i$ of each factor f_i form a clique in G, that is, the variables are pairwise adjacent.

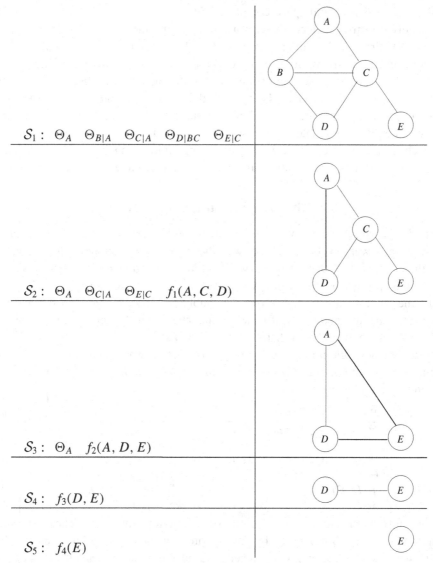

$\mathcal{S}_1:\ \Theta_A\quad\Theta_{B|A}\quad\Theta_{C|A}\quad\Theta_{D|BC}\quad\Theta_{E|C}$

$\mathcal{S}_2:\ \Theta_A\quad\Theta_{C|A}\quad\Theta_{E|C}\quad f_1(A,C,D)$

$\mathcal{S}_3:\ \Theta_A\quad f_2(A,D,E)$

$\mathcal{S}_4:\ f_3(D,E)$

$\mathcal{S}_5:\ f_4(E)$

Figure 6.5: Interaction graphs resulting from the elimination of variables B, C, A, D.

Figure 6.5 depicts the interaction graph that corresponds to each iteration of the above trace of VE_PR1. There are two key observations about these interaction graphs:

1. If G is the interaction graph of factors $\mathcal{S}$, then eliminating a variable $\pi(i)$ from $\mathcal{S}$ leads to constructing a factor over the neighbors of $\pi(i)$ in G. For example, eliminating variable B from the factors $\mathcal{S}_1$ in Figure 6.5 leads to constructing a factor over variables A, C, D, which are the neighbors of B in the corresponding interaction graph.

2. Let $\mathcal{S}'$ be the factors that result from eliminating variable $\pi(i)$ from factors $\mathcal{S}$. If G' and G are the interaction graphs of $\mathcal{S}'$ and $\mathcal{S}$, respectively, then G' can be obtained from G as follows:

    (a) Add an edge to G between every pair of neighbors of variable $\pi(i)$ that are not already connected by an edge.

    (b) Delete variable $\pi(i)$ from G.

Algorithm 4 `OrderWidth`($\mathcal{N}, \pi$)

input:

   $\mathcal{N}$:   Bayesian network

   π: ordering of the variables in network $\mathcal{N}$

output: the width of elimination order π

main:

  1: $G \leftarrow$ interaction graph of the CPTs in network $\mathcal{N}$

  2: $w \leftarrow 0$

  3: **for** $i = 1$ to length of elimination order π **do**

  4:     $w \leftarrow \max(w, d)$, where d is the number of $\pi(i)$'s neighbors in G

  5:     add an edge between every pair of non-adjacent neighbors of $\pi(i)$ in G

  6:     delete variable $\pi(i)$ from G

  7: **end for**

  8: **return** w

Algorithm 5 `MinDegreeOrder`($\mathcal{N}, \mathbf{X}$)

input:

   $\mathcal{N}$:   Bayesian network

   $\mathbf{X}$:   variables in network $\mathcal{N}$

output: an ordering π of variables $\mathbf{X}$

main:

  1: $G \leftarrow$ interaction graph of the CPTs in network $\mathcal{N}$

  2: **for** $i = 1$ to number of variables in $\mathbf{X}$ **do**

  3:     $\pi(i) \leftarrow$ a variable in $\mathbf{X}$ with smallest number of neighbors in G

  4:     add an edge between every pair of non-adjacent neighbors of $\pi(i)$ in G

  5:     delete variable $\pi(i)$ from G and from $\mathbf{X}$

  6: **end for**

  7: **return** π

In fact, (a) corresponds to multiplying all factors that contain variable $\pi(i)$ in $\mathcal{S}$, as the resulting factor must be over variable $\pi(i)$ and all its neighbors in G. Moreover, (b) corresponds to summing out variable $\pi(i)$ from the resulting factor.

Algorithm 4 provides pseudocode for computing the width of an order and a corresponding Bayesian network. It does this by maintaining an interaction graph G for the set of factors $\mathcal{S}$ maintained by VE_PR1 during each iteration. One can use Algorithm `OrderWidth` to measure the quality of a particular ordering before using it.

Computing the width of a particular variable order is useful when we have to choose between a small number of orders. However, when the number of orders is large we need to do better than simply computing the width of each potential order. As it turns out, computing an optimal order is an NP-hard problem, but there are a number of heuristic approaches that tend to generate relatively good orders.

One of the more popular heuristics is also one of the simplest: Always eliminate the variable that leads to constructing the smallest factor possible. If we are maintaining the interaction graph as we eliminate variables, this basically means that we always eliminate the variable that has the smallest number of neighbors in the current interaction graph. This heuristic method is given in Algorithm 5 and is known as the *min-degree* heuristic. It is also

---

Algorithm 6 `MinFillOrder(N, X)`

---

input:

  $\mathcal{N}$:   Bayesian network

  X: variables in network $\mathcal{N}$

output: an ordering π of variables **X**

main:

  1: $G \leftarrow$ interaction graph of the CPTs in network $\mathcal{N}$

  2: **for** $i = 1$ to number of variables in **X do**

  3:     $\pi(i) \leftarrow$ a variable in **X** that adds the smallest number of edges on Line 4

  4:     add an edge between every pair of non-adjacent neighbors of $\pi(i)$

  5:     delete variable $\pi(i)$ from G and from **X**

  6: **end for**

  7: **return** π

---

known that min-degree is optimal when applied to a network that has some elimination order of width ≤ 2. Another popular heuristic for constructing elimination orders, which is usually more effective than min-degree, is to always eliminate the variable that leads to adding the smallest number of edges on Line 4 of `MinDegreeOrder` (called fill-in edges). This heuristic method is given in Algorithm 6 and is known as the *min-fill* heuristic. Algorithms for constructing elimination orders are further discussed in Chapter 9.

6.7 Computing posterior marginals

We now present a generalization of Algorithm 3, `VE_PR1`, for computing the posterior marginal for any set of variables. For example, if we take $\mathbf{Q} = \{D, E\}$ and $\mathbf{e}$: $A =$ true, $B =$ false in the network of Figure 6.1, we want to compute the following factor:

D	E	$Pr(\mathbf{Q}|\mathbf{e})$
true	true	.448
true	false	.192
false	true	.112
false	false	.248

where the third row asserts that

$$Pr(D = \text{false}, E = \text{true} | A = \text{true}, B = \text{false}) = .112$$

More generally, given a Bayesian network $\mathcal{N}$, a set of variables **Q**, and an instantiation **e**, we want to compute the posterior marginal $Pr(\mathbf{Q}|\mathbf{e})$ for variables **Q**. Recall that prior marginals are a special case of posterior marginals when **e** is the trivial instantiation.

We find it more useful to compute a variation on posterior marginals called *joint marginals*, $Pr(\mathbf{Q}, \mathbf{e})$. That is, instead of computing the probability of **q** given **e**, $Pr(\mathbf{q}|\mathbf{e})$, we compute the probability of **q** and **e**, $Pr(\mathbf{q}, \mathbf{e})$. If we take $\mathbf{Q} = \{D, E\}$ and $\mathbf{e}$: $A =$ true, $B =$ false in the network of Figure 6.1, the joint marginal is

D	E	$Pr(\mathbf{Q}, \mathbf{e})$
true	true	.21504
true	false	.09216
false	true	.05376
false	false	.11904

For example, the third row says that

$$\Pr(D=\text{false}, E=\text{true}, A=\text{true}, B=\text{false}) = .05376$$

If we add up the probabilities in this factor we get .48, which is nothing but the probability of evidence **e**: $A=\text{true}$, $B=\text{false}$. This is always the case since $\sum_q \Pr(\mathbf{q}, \mathbf{e}) = \Pr(\mathbf{e})$ by case analysis. Hence, by adding up the probabilities that appear in the joint marginal, we will always get the probability of evidence **e**. This also means that we can compute the posterior marginal $\Pr(\mathbf{Q}|\mathbf{e})$ by simply normalizing the corresponding joint marginal $\Pr(\mathbf{Q}, \mathbf{e})$. Moreover, the probability of evidence **e** is obtained for free.

The method of variable elimination can be extended to compute joint marginals if we start by zeroing out those rows in the joint probability distribution that are inconsistent with evidence **e**.

Definition 6.5. The *reduction* of factor $f(\mathbf{X})$ given evidence **e** is another factor over variables $\mathbf{X}$, denoted by $f^\mathbf{e}$, and defined as

$$f^\mathbf{e}(\mathbf{x}) \overset{def}{=} \begin{cases} f(\mathbf{x}), & \text{if } \mathbf{x} \sim \mathbf{e} \\ 0, & \text{otherwise.} \end{cases} \qquad \blacksquare$$

For example, given the factor

D	E	f
true	true	.448
true	false	.192
false	true	.112
false	false	.248

and evidence **e**: $E=\text{true}$, we have

D	E	$f^\mathbf{e}$
true	true	.448
true	false	0
false	true	.112
false	false	0

We often omit the zeroed-out rows, writing

D	E	$f^\mathbf{e}$
true	true	.448
false	true	.112

Consider now the network of Figure 6.1 and let $\mathbf{Q} = \{D, E\}$ and **e**: $A=\text{true}$, $B=\text{false}$. The joint marginal $\Pr(\mathbf{Q}, \mathbf{e})$ can be computed as follows:

$$\Pr(\mathbf{Q}, \mathbf{e}) = \sum_{A,B,C} \left(\Theta_{E|C} \, \Theta_{D|BC} \, \Theta_{C|A} \, \Theta_{B|A} \, \Theta_A \right)^\mathbf{e}. \qquad (6.1)$$

Although this provides a systematic method for computing joint marginals, we still have the problem of complexity as (6.1) requires that we multiply all CPTs before we start eliminating variables. Fortunately, this is not needed, as shown by the following result.

Theorem 6.3. *If f_1 and f_2 are two factors and **e** is an instantiation, then*

$$(f_1 f_2)^\mathbf{e} = f_1^\mathbf{e} f_2^\mathbf{e}. \qquad \blacksquare$$

Hence (6.1) reduces to

$$\Pr(\mathbf{Q} = \{D, E\}, \mathbf{e}) = \sum_{A,B,C} \Theta^e_{E|C} \, \Theta^e_{D|BC} \, \Theta^e_{C|A} \, \Theta^e_{B|A} \, \Theta^e_{A},$$

which keeps the joint probability distribution in factored form, therefore allowing us to use VE_PR1 on the reduced CPTs.

Consider now the Bayesian network in Figure 6.4. Let $\mathbf{Q} = \{C\}$, $\mathbf{e} : A = \text{true}$, and suppose that we want to compute the joint marginal $\Pr(\mathbf{Q}, \mathbf{e})$ by eliminating variable A first and then variable B. We first need to reduce the network CPTs given evidence $\mathbf{e}$, which gives

A	Θ^e_A
true	.6

A	B	$\Theta^e_{B|A}$
true	true	.9
true	false	.1

B	C	$\Theta^e_{C|B}$
true	true	.3
true	false	.7
false	true	.5
false	false	.5

The formula we need to evaluate is then

$$\Pr(\mathbf{Q}, \mathbf{e}) = \sum_B \sum_A \Theta^e_A \, \Theta^e_{B|A} \, \Theta^e_{C|B}$$

$$= \sum_B \Theta^e_{C|B} \sum_A \Theta^e_A \, \Theta^e_{B|A}.$$

All intermediate factors needed to evaluate this formula are shown here:

A	B	$\Theta^e_A \Theta^e_{B|A}$
true	true	.54
true	false	.06

B	$\sum_A \Theta^e_A \Theta^e_{B|A}$
true	.54
false	.06

B	C	$\Theta^e_{C|B} \sum_A \Theta^e_A \Theta^e_{B|A}$
true	true	.162
true	false	.378
false	true	.030
false	false	.030

C	$\sum_B \Theta^e_{C|B} \sum_A \Theta^e_A \Theta^e_{B|A}$
true	.192
false	.408

Therefore,

$$\Pr(C = \text{true}, \ A = \text{true}) = .192$$
$$\Pr(C = \text{false}, \ A = \text{true}) = .408$$
$$\Pr(A = \text{true}) = .600$$

To compute the posterior marginal $\Pr(C|A = \text{true})$, all we have to do is normalize the previous factor, which gives

C	$\Pr(C|A = \text{true})$
true	.32
false	.68

Therefore, $\Pr(C = \text{true}|A = \text{true}) = .32$ and $\Pr(C = \text{false}|A = \text{true}) = .68$.

Algorithm 7, VE_PR2, provides pseudocode for computing the joint marginal for a set of variables $\mathbf{Q}$ with respect to a Bayesian network $\mathcal{N}$ and evidence $\mathbf{e}$. The algorithm

---

Algorithm 7 VE_PR2($\mathcal{N}$, **Q**, **e**, π)

---

input:

   $\mathcal{N}$:   Bayesian network

   Q: variables in network $\mathcal{N}$

   e: instantiation of some variables in network $\mathcal{N}$

   π: an ordering of network variables not in **Q**

output: the joint marginal Pr(**Q**, **e**)

main:

1: $\mathcal{S} \leftarrow \{f^{\mathbf{e}} : f$ is a CPT of network $\mathcal{N}\}$

2: **for** $i = 1$ to length of order π **do**

3:    $f \leftarrow \prod_k f_k$, where f_k belongs to $\mathcal{S}$ and mentions variable $\pi(i)$

4:    $f_i \leftarrow \sum_{\pi(i)} f$

5:    replace all factors f_k in $\mathcal{S}$ by factor f_i

6: **end for**

7: **return** $\prod_{f \in \mathcal{S}} f$

---

is a simple modification of Algorithm 3, VE_PR1, where we reduce the factors of a Bayesian network before we start eliminating variables. By normalizing the output of this algorithm, we immediately obtain an algorithm for computing posterior marginals, Pr(**Q**|**e**). Moreover, by adding up the numbers returned by this algorithm, we immediately obtain an algorithm for computing the probability of evidence, Pr(**e**). It is not uncommon to run VE_PR2 with **Q** being the empty set. In this case, the algorithm will eliminate all variables in the Bayesian network, therefore returning a trivial factor, effectively a number, that represents the probability of evidence **e**.

6.8 Network structure and complexity

Suppose we have two Bayesian networks each containing, say, a hundred variables. The best elimination order for the first network has width 3, which means that variable elimination will do very well on this network if passed an optimal order. The best elimination order for the second network has width 25, which means that variable elimination will do relatively poorly on this network regardless of which order it is passed. Why is the second network more difficult for variable elimination even though both networks have the same number of variables?

The answer to this question lies in this notion of *treewidth*, which is a number that quantifies the extent to which a network resembles a tree structure. In particular, the more that the network resembles a tree structure, the smaller its treewidth is. Treewidth is discussed at length in Chapter 9 but we point out here that no complete elimination order can have a width less than the network treewidth. Moreover, there is an elimination order whose width equals the network treewidth yet determining such an order is known to be NP-hard. Figure 6.6 depicts some networks with their treewidths.

We should point out here that when we say an "elimination order" in the context of defining treewidth, we mean a complete order that includes all network variables. Hence, the treewidth of a network can be defined as the width of its best complete elimination order (i.e., the one with the smallest width). Again, we treat the notion of treewidth more

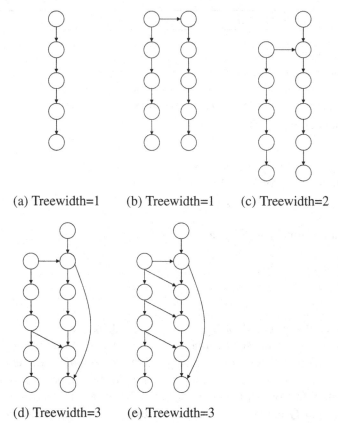

(a) Treewidth=1   (b) Treewidth=1   (c) Treewidth=2

(d) Treewidth=3   (e) Treewidth=3

Figure 6.6: Networks with different treewidth. Determining network treewidth is discussed in Chapter 9.

formally in Chapter 9 but we next present a number of observations about it to further our intuition about this notion:

- The number of nodes has no genuine effect on treewidth. For example, the network in Figure 6.6(a) has treewidth 1. The network in Figure 6.6(b) is obtained by doubling the number of nodes yet the treewidth remains 1.

- The number of parents per node has a direct effect on treewidth. If the number of parents per node can reach k, the treewidth is no less than k. The network in Figure 6.6(c) was obtained from the one in Figure 6.6(b) by adding one node and one edge. This addition increased the maximum number of parents per node from 1 to 2, leading also to an increase in the treewidth (see Exercise 6.15).

- Loops tend to increase treewidth. The network in Figure 6.6(d) was obtained from the one in Figure 6.6(c) by creating loops. Note that the number of parents per node did not increase yet the treewidth has increased from 2 to 3.

- The number of loops per se does not have a genuine effect on treewidth. It is the nature of these loops which does; their interaction in particular. The network in Figure 6.6(e) has more loops than the one in Figure 6.6(d) yet it has the same treewidth.

We also point out two important classes of networks with known treewidth. First is the class of *polytree networks*, also known as *singly connected* networks. These are networks in which there is at most one (undirected) path between any two nodes. The treewidth of such networks is k, where k is the maximum number of parents that any node may have. The network in Figure 6.6(c) is singly connected. We also have *tree networks,* which are

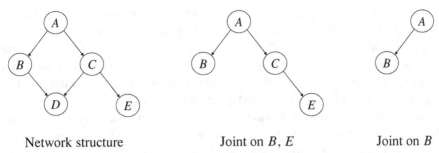

Network structure   Joint on B, E Joint on B

Figure 6.7: Pruning nodes in a Bayesian network given two different queries.

polytrees where each node has at most one parent, leading to a treewidth of at most 1. The networks in Figure 6.6(a) and Figure 6.6(b) are trees. We finally note that networks which are not singly connected are known as *multiply connected*. Figure 6.6(d) and Figure 6.6(e) contain two examples.

6.9 Query structure and complexity

Network structure has a major impact on the performance of variable elimination and on the performance of most algorithms we shall discuss later. This is why such algorithms are sometimes called *structure-based algorithms*. However, network structure can be simplified based on another important factor: query structure. In general, a query is a pair $(\mathbf{Q}, \mathbf{e})$ where $\mathbf{e}$ is an instantiation of evidence variables $\mathbf{E}$ and $\mathbf{Q}$ is the set of query variables, where the goal is to compute the joint marginal $\Pr(\mathbf{Q}, \mathbf{e})$.[2] As we discuss next, the complexity of inference can be very much affected by the number and location of query and evidence variables within the network structure. The effect of query structure on the complexity of inference is independent of the used inference algorithm. In particular, for a given query $(\mathbf{Q}, \mathbf{e})$ we next provide two transformations that simplify a Bayesian network, making it more amenable to inference yet preserving its ability to compute the joint marginal $\Pr(\mathbf{Q}, \mathbf{e})$ correctly.

6.9.1 Pruning nodes

Given a Bayesian network $\mathcal{N}$ and query $(\mathbf{Q}, \mathbf{e})$, one can remove any leaf node (with its CPT) from the network as long as it does not belong to variables $\mathbf{Q} \cup \mathbf{E}$ yet not affect the ability of the network to answer the query correctly. What makes this pruning operation powerful is that it can be applied iteratively, possibly leading to the pruning of many network nodes. The result of removing leaf nodes as suggested is denoted by pruneNodes$(\mathcal{N}, \mathbf{Q} \cup \mathbf{E})$.

Theorem 6.4. *Let $\mathcal{N}$ be a Bayesian network and let $(\mathbf{Q}, \mathbf{e})$ be a corresponding query. If $\mathcal{N}' = $ pruneNodes$(\mathcal{N}, \mathbf{Q} \cup \mathbf{E})$, then $\Pr(\mathbf{Q}, \mathbf{e}) = \Pr'(\mathbf{Q}, \mathbf{e})$ where $\Pr$ and $\Pr'$ are the probability distributions induced by networks $\mathcal{N}$ and $\mathcal{N}'$, respectively.* ∎

Figure 6.7 depicts a Bayesian network and two of its prunings. In the first case, we are interested in the marginal over variables B and E with no evidence. Therefore,

---

[2] It is possible that we have no evidence, $\mathbf{E} = \emptyset$, in which case we are interested in the prior marginal for variables $\mathbf{Q}$. It is also possible that we have no query variables, $\mathbf{Q} = \emptyset$, in which case we are interested in computing the probability $\Pr(\mathbf{e})$ of evidence $\mathbf{e}$.

D is a leaf node that can be pruned. After this pruning, all leaf nodes appear in the query and, therefore, cannot be pruned. In the second case, we are interested in the marginal over variable B with no evidence. Therefore, D and E are leaf nodes that can be pruned. However, after pruning them node C becomes a leaf node that can also be pruned since it does not appear in the query. Note that the network in Figure 6.7(a) has treewidth 2 yet the pruned networks in Figures 6.7(b) and 6.7(c) have treewidth 1.

Pruning nodes can lead to a significant reduction in network treewidth if variables $\mathbf{Q} \cup \mathbf{E}$ appear close to the network roots. In the worst case, all leaf nodes appear in variables $\mathbf{Q} \cup \mathbf{E}$ and no pruning is possible. In the best case, variables $\mathbf{Q} \cup \mathbf{E}$ contains only root nodes that permit the pruning of every node except for those in $\mathbf{Q} \cup \mathbf{E}$.

6.9.2 Pruning edges

Given a Bayesian network $\mathcal{N}$ and a query $(\mathbf{Q}, \mathbf{e})$, one can also eliminate some of the network edges and reduce some of its CPTs without affecting its ability to compute the joint marginal $\Pr(\mathbf{Q}, \mathbf{e})$ correctly. In particular, for each edge $U \to X$ that originates from a node U in $\mathbf{E}$, we can:

1. Remove the edge $U \to X$ from the network.
2. Replace the CPT $\Theta_{X|U}$ for node X by a smaller CPT, which is obtained from $\Theta_{X|U}$ by assuming the value u of parent U given in evidence $\mathbf{e}$. This new CPT corresponds to $\sum_U \Theta_{X|U}^u$.

The result of this operation is denoted by pruneEdges($\mathcal{N}, \mathbf{e}$) and we have the following result.

Theorem 6.5. *Let $\mathcal{N}$ be a Bayesian network and let $\mathbf{e}$ be an instantiation. If $\mathcal{N}' = $ pruneEdges($\mathcal{N}, \mathbf{e}$), then $\Pr(\mathbf{Q}, \mathbf{e}) = \Pr'(\mathbf{Q}, \mathbf{e})$ where $\Pr$ and $\Pr'$ are the probability distributions induced by networks $\mathcal{N}$ and $\mathcal{N}'$, respectively.* ■

Figure 6.8 depicts the result of pruning edges in the network of Figure 6.1 given evidence $C = \mathsf{false}$. The two edges originating from node C were deleted and CPTs $\Theta_{D|BC}$ and $\Theta_{E|C}$ were modified. In particular, all rows inconsistent with $C = \mathsf{false}$ were removed and the reference to C was dropped from these factors. It is important to stress that the pruned network is only good for answering queries of the form $\Pr(\mathbf{q}, C = \mathsf{false})$. If the instantiation $C = \mathsf{false}$ does not appear in the query, the answers returned by the pruned and original networks may disagree.

6.9.3 Network pruning

The result of pruning nodes and edges for a network will be called *pruning* the network given query $(\mathbf{Q}, \mathbf{e})$ and denoted by pruneNetwork($\mathcal{N}, \mathbf{Q}, \mathbf{e}$). Figure 6.9 depicts a pruning of the Bayesian network in Figure 6.1 given the query $\mathbf{Q} = \{D\}$ and $\mathbf{e} : A = \mathsf{true}, C = \mathsf{false}$. Pruning leads to removing node E and the edges originating from nodes A and C, and modifying the CPTs $\Theta_{B|A}$, $\Theta_{C|A}$ and $\Theta_{D|BC}$. Note that the pruned network in Figure 6.9 has a treewidth of 1, whereas the original network had a treewidth of 2. In general, network pruning may lead to a significant reduction in treewidth, which suggests the following definition.

Definition 6.6. *The effective treewidth* for a Bayesian network $\mathcal{N}$ with respect to query $(\mathbf{Q}, \mathbf{e})$ is the treewidth of pruneNetwork($\mathcal{N}, \mathbf{Q}, \mathbf{e}$). ■

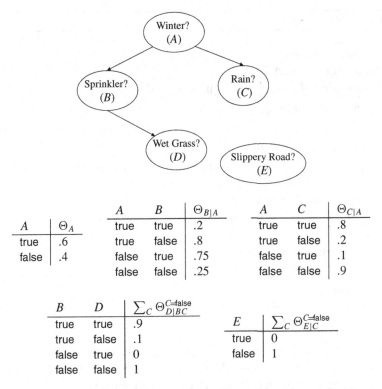

A	B	$\Theta_{B|A}$
true	true	.2
true	false	.8
false	true	.75
false	false	.25

A	Θ_A
true	.6
false	.4

A	C	$\Theta_{C|A}$
true	true	.8
true	false	.2
false	true	.1
false	false	.9

B	D	$\sum_C \Theta_{D|BC}^{C=\text{false}}$
true	true	.9
true	false	.1
false	true	0
false	false	1

E	$\sum_C \Theta_{E|C}^{C=\text{false}}$
true	0
false	1

Figure 6.8: Pruning edges in the network of Figure 6.1, where $\mathbf{e} : C = \text{false}$.

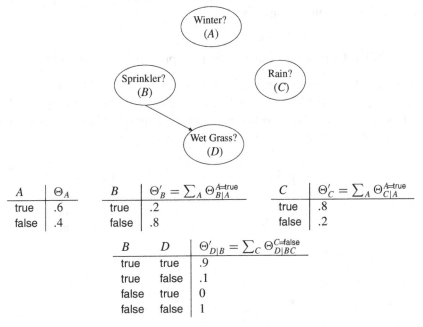

A	Θ_A
true	.6
false	.4

B	$\Theta'_B = \sum_A \Theta_{B|A}^{A=\text{true}}$
true	.2
false	.8

C	$\Theta'_C = \sum_A \Theta_{C|A}^{A=\text{true}}$
true	.8
false	.2

B	D	$\Theta'_{D|B} = \sum_C \Theta_{D|BC}^{C=\text{false}}$
true	true	.9
true	false	.1
false	true	0
false	false	1

Figure 6.9: Pruning the Bayesian network in Figure 6.1 given the query $\mathbf{Q} = \{D\}$ and $\mathbf{e} : A = \text{true}$, $C = \text{false}$.

Algorithm 8 VE_PR($\mathcal{N}$, **Q**, **e**)

---

input:

$\mathcal{N}$:   Bayesian network

Q: variables in network $\mathcal{N}$

e: instantiation of some variables in network $\mathcal{N}$

output: the joint marginal $\Pr(\mathbf{Q}, \mathbf{e})$

main:

1:   $\mathcal{N}' \leftarrow$ pruneNetwork($\mathcal{N}$, **Q**, **e**)
2:   $\pi \leftarrow$ an ordering of variables not in **Q** computed with respect to network $\mathcal{N}'$
3:   $\mathcal{S} \leftarrow \{f^{\mathbf{e}} : f$ is a CPT of network $\mathcal{N}'\}$
4:   **for** $i = 1$ to length of order π **do**
5:      $f \leftarrow \prod_k f_k$, where f_k belongs to $\mathcal{S}$ and mentions variable $\pi(i)$
6:      $f_i \leftarrow \sum_{\pi(i)} f$
7:      replace all factors f_k in $\mathcal{S}$ by factor f_i
8:   **end for**
9:   **return** $\prod_{f \in \mathcal{S}} f$

It is important to realize that pruning a Bayesian network can be accomplished in time that is linear in the size of the network (the size of its CPTs). Therefore, it is usually worthwhile to prune a Bayesian network before answering queries.

Algorithm 8, VE_PR, depicts the most general variable elimination algorithm of this chapter. Given a query (**Q**, **e**), the algorithm prunes the Bayesian network before it starts eliminating variables. The elimination order used by the algorithm is computed based on the pruned network, not the original one.

6.9.4 Computing marginals after pruning: An example

We now apply VE_PR to the network in Figure 6.1 with $\mathbf{Q} = \{D\}$ and $\mathbf{e} : A =$ true, $C =$ false. The pruning of this network given the query is depicted in Figure 6.9. The eliminating order $\pi = A, C, B$ is consistent with the min-degree heuristic. Reducing the network CPTs given evidence **e** leads to the following factors:

A	$\Theta^{\mathbf{e}}_A$
true	.6

B	$\Theta'^{\mathbf{e}}_B$
true	.2
false	.8

C	$\Theta'^{\mathbf{e}}_C$
false	.2

B	D	$\Theta'^{\mathbf{e}}_{D|B}$
true	true	.9
true	false	.1
false	true	0
false	false	1

VE_PR will then evaluate the following expression:

$$\Pr(D, A =\text{true}, C =\text{false}) = \sum_B \sum_C \sum_A \Theta^{\mathbf{e}}_A \; \Theta'^{\mathbf{e}}_B \; \Theta'^{\mathbf{e}}_C \; \Theta'^{\mathbf{e}}_{D|B}$$

$$= \left(\sum_A \Theta^{\mathbf{e}}_A \right) \left(\sum_B \Theta'^{\mathbf{e}}_B \; \Theta'^{\mathbf{e}}_{D|B} \right) \left(\sum_C \Theta'^{\mathbf{e}}_C \right).$$

All intermediate factors constructed during this process are shown here:

B	D	$\Theta'^e_B \Theta'^e_{D|B}$
true	true	.18
true	false	.02
false	true	0
false	false	.80

	$\sum_A \Theta^e_A$
$\top$	.6

D	$\sum_B \Theta'^e_B \Theta'^e_{D|B}$
true	.18
false	.82

	$\sum_C \Theta'^e_C$
$\top$	.2

The final factor returned by VE_PR is then

D	$\left(\sum_A \Theta^e_A\right)\left(\sum_B \Theta'^e_B \Theta'^e_{D|B}\right)\left(\sum_C \Theta'^e_C\right)$
true	$.0216 = (.6)(.18)(.2)$
false	$.0984 = (.6)(.82)(.2)$

which is the joint marginal $\Pr(D, A=\text{true}, C=\text{false})$. From this factor, we conclude that the probability of evidence, $\Pr(A=\text{true}, C=\text{false})$, is .12. Note how trivial factors act as scaling constants when multiplied by other factors.

6.10 Bucket elimination

The complexity analysis of Algorithm 8, VE_PR, assumes that we can identify all factors f_k that mention a particular variable $\pi(i)$ in time linear in the number of such factors. One method for achieving this is to arrange the factors maintained by the algorithm into *buckets*, where we have one bucket for each network variable. Consider the network in Figure 6.1 as an example, and suppose that we want to eliminate variables according to the order E, B, C, D, A. We can do this by constructing the following buckets, which are initially populated with network CPTs:

Bucket Label	Bucket Factors
E	$\Theta_{E|C}$
B	$\Theta_{B|A}, \quad \Theta_{D|BC}$
C	$\Theta_{C|A}$
D	
A	Θ_A

That is, each CPT is placed in the first bucket (from top) whose label appears in the CPT. For example CPT $\Theta_{C|A}$ is placed in the bucket with label C because this is the first bucket whose label C appears in $\Theta_{C|A}$. The only other bucket whose label appears in $\Theta_{C|A}$ is the one for variable A but that comes later in the order.

Given these buckets, we eliminate variables by processing buckets from top to bottom. When processing the bucket corresponding to some variable $\pi(i)$, we are guaranteed that the factors appearing in that bucket are exactly the factors that mention variable $\pi(i)$. This is true initially and remains true after processing each bucket for the following reason. When processing the bucket of variable $\pi(i)$, we multiply all factors in that bucket, sum out variable $\pi(i)$, and then place the resulting factor f_i in the first next bucket whose label appears in f_i. For example, after processing the bucket for variable E, the resulting factor $\sum_E \Theta_{E|C}$ is placed in the bucket for variable C:

Bucket Label	Bucket Factors
E	
B	$\Theta_{B|A}, \ \Theta_{D|BC}$
C	$\Theta_{C|A}, \ \sum_E \Theta_{E|C}$
D	
A	Θ_A

If our goal is to obtain the marginal over variables D and A, $\Pr(D, A)$, then we only process the first three buckets, E, B, and C. After such processing, the buckets for D and A will contain a factored representation of the marginal over these two variables. Again, we can either multiply these factors or simply keep them in factored form.

Another variation on VE_PR is in how evidence is handled. In particular, given evidence, say, $\mathbf{e}: B =$ true, $E =$ false we do not reduce CPTs explicitly. Instead, we create two new factors,

B	λ_B
true	1
false	0

E	λ_E
true	0
false	1

and then add these factors to their corresponding buckets:

Bucket Label	Bucket Factors
E	$\Theta_{E|C}, \ \lambda_E$
B	$\Theta_{B|A}, \ \Theta_{D|BC}, \ \lambda_B$
C	$\Theta_{C|A}$
D	
A	Θ_A

If we process buckets E, B, and C, the last two buckets for D and A will then contain the joint marginal for these two variables, $\Pr(D, A, \mathbf{e})$. Again, we can either multiply the factors or keep them in factored form. The factors λ_B and λ_E are known as *evidence indicators*. Moreover, the previous variation on VE_PR is known as the method of *bucket elimination*.

Bibliographic remarks

The variable elimination algorithm was first formalized in Zhang and Poole [1994], although its traces go back to Shachter et al. [1990]. The bucket elimination algorithm was introduced in Dechter [1996; 1999]. Variable elimination heuristics are discussed in Kjaerulff [1990]. Pruning network edges and nodes was initially proposed in Shachter [1990; 1986]. More sophisticated pruning techniques have also been proposed in Lin and Druzdzel [1997].

6.11 Exercises

6.1. Consider the Bayesian network in Figure 6.1 on Page 127.

    (a) Use variable elimination to compute the marginals $\Pr(\mathbf{Q}, \mathbf{e})$ and $\Pr(\mathbf{Q}|\mathbf{e})$ where $\mathbf{Q} = \{E\}$ and $\mathbf{e}: D =$ false. Use the min-degree heuristic for determining the elimination order, breaking ties by choosing variables that come first in the alphabet. Show all steps.

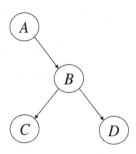

A	Θ_A
true	.2
false	.8

A	B	$\Theta_{B\mid A}$
true	true	.5
true	false	.5
false	true	.0
false	false	1.0

B	C	$\Theta_{C\mid B}$
true	true	1.0
true	false	.0
false	true	.5
false	false	.5

B	D	$\Theta_{D\mid B}$
true	true	.75
true	false	.25
false	true	.3
false	false	.7

Figure 6.10: A Bayesian network.

(b) Prune the network given the query $\mathbf{Q} = \{A\}$ and evidence $\mathbf{e} : E =$ false. Show the steps of node and edge pruning separately.

6.2. Consider the Bayesian network in Figure 6.10. Use variable elimination with ordering D, C, A to compute $\Pr(B, C =$ true$)$, $\Pr(C =$ true$)$, and $\Pr(B\mid C =$ true$)$.

6.3. Consider a chain network $C_0 \to C_1 \to \cdots \to C_n$. Suppose that variable C_t, for $t \geq 0$, denotes the health state of a component at time t. In particular, let each C_t take on states ok and faulty. Let C_0 denote component birth where $\Pr(C_0 =$ ok$) = 1$ and $\Pr(C_0 =$ faulty$) = 0$. For each $t > 0$, let the CPT of C_t be

$$\Pr(C_t = \text{ok}\mid C_{t-1} = \text{ok}) = \lambda$$
$$\Pr(C_t = \text{faulty}\mid C_{t-1} = \text{faulty}) = 1.$$

That is, if a component is healthy at time $t - 1$, then it remains healthy at time t with probability λ. If a component is faulty at time $t - 1$, then it remains faulty at time t with probability 1.

(a) Using variable elimination with variable ordering C_0, C_1, compute $\Pr(C_2)$.

(b) Using variable elimination with variable ordering $C_0, C_1, \ldots, C_{n-1}$, compute $\Pr(C_n)$.

6.4. Prove the technique of bypassing nodes as given by Equation 5.1 on Page 91.

6.5. Consider a naive Bayes structure with edges $X \to Y_1, \ldots, X \to Y_n$.

(a) What is the width of variable order $Y_1, \ldots, Y_n, X$?

(b) What is the width of variable order $X, Y_1, \ldots, Y_n$?

6.6. Consider a two-layer Bayesian network $\mathcal{N}$ with nodes $\mathbf{X} \cup \mathbf{Y}, \mathbf{X} \cap \mathbf{Y} = \emptyset$, where each $X \in \mathbf{X}$ is a root node and each $Y \in \mathbf{Y}$ is a leaf node with at most k parents. In such a network, all edges in $\mathcal{N}$ are directed from a node in $\mathbf{X}$ to a node in $\mathbf{Y}$. Suppose we are interested in computing $\Pr(Y)$ for all $Y \in \mathbf{Y}$. What is the effective treewidth for $\mathcal{N}$ for each one of these queries?

6.7. Prune the network in Figure 6.11 given the following queries:

(a) $\mathbf{Q} = \{B, E\}$ and $\mathbf{e} : A =$ true

(b) $\mathbf{Q} = \{A\}$ and $\mathbf{e} : B =$ true, $F =$ true

Show the steps of node and edge pruning separately.

6.8. What is the width of order A, B, C, D, E, F, G, H with respect to the network in Figure 6.11?

6.9. Compute an elimination order for the variables in Figure 6.11 using the min-degree method. In case of a tie, choose variables that come first alphabetically.

6.10. What is the treewidth of the network in Figure 6.11? Justify your answer.

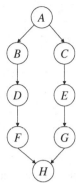

Figure 6.11: A Bayesian network structure.

6.11. Given a Bayesian network that has a tree structure with at least one edge, describe an efficient algorithm for obtaining an elimination order that is guaranteed to have width 1.

6.12. Given an elimination order π that covers all network variables, show how we can use this particular order and Algorithm 8, VE_PR, to compute the marginal $\Pr(X, \mathbf{e})$ for every network variable X and some evidence $\mathbf{e}$. What is the total complexity of computing all such marginals?

6.13. Prove the following: For factors f_i, f_j, and evidence $\mathbf{e}$: $(f_i f_j)^{\mathbf{e}} = f_i^{\mathbf{e}} f_j^{\mathbf{e}}$.

6.14. Prove the following: If $\mathcal{N}' = \text{pruneEdges}(\mathcal{N}, \mathbf{e})$, then $\Pr(\mathbf{Q}, \mathbf{e}) = \Pr'(\mathbf{Q}, \mathbf{e})$ for every $\mathbf{Q}$. Hint: Prove that the joint distributions of $\mathcal{N}$ and $\mathcal{N}'$ agree on rows that are consistent with evidence $\mathbf{e}$.

6.15. Suppose we have a Bayesian network containing a node with k parents. Show that every variable order that contains all network variables must have width at least k.

6.16. Consider the naive Bayes structure $C \rightarrow A_1, \ldots, C \rightarrow A_m$, where all variables are binary. Show how the algorithm of variable elimination can be used to compute a closed form for the conditional probability $\Pr(c|a_1, \ldots, a_m)$.

6.17. Suppose we have a Bayesian network $\mathcal{N}$ and evidence $\mathbf{e}$ with some node X having parents $U_1, \ldots, U_n$.

(a) Show that if X is a logical OR node that is set to false in $\mathbf{e}$, we can prune all edges incoming into X and assert hard evidence on each parent.

(b) Show that if X is a noisy OR node that is set to false in $\mathbf{e}$, we can prune all edges incoming into X and assert soft evidence on each parent.

In particular, for each case identify a network $\mathcal{N}'$ and evidence $\mathbf{e}'$ where all edges incoming into X have been pruned from $\mathcal{N}$ and where $\Pr(\mathbf{x}, \mathbf{e}) = \Pr'(\mathbf{x}, \mathbf{e}')$ for every network instantiation $\mathbf{x}$.

6.18. Suppose that f_1 is a factor over variables XY and f_2 is a factor over variables XZ. Show that $\left(\sum_X f_1\right)\left(\sum_X f_2\right)$ is an upper bound on $\sum_X f_1 f_2$ in the following sense:

$$\left(\left(\sum_X f_1\right)\left(\sum_X f_2\right)\right)(\mathbf{u}) \geq \left(\sum_X f_1 f_2\right)(\mathbf{u}),$$

for all instantiations $\mathbf{u}$ of $\mathbf{U} = \mathbf{Y} \cup \mathbf{Z}$. Show how this property can be used to produce an approximate version of VE_PR that can have a lower complexity yet is guaranteed to produce an upper bound on the true marginals.

6.12 Proofs

PROOF OF THEOREM 6.1. Let f_1 and f_2 be over variables $\mathbf{X}_1$ and $\mathbf{X}_2$, respectively, where $X \notin \mathbf{X}_1$ and $X \in \mathbf{X}_2$. Let $\mathbf{Y} = \mathbf{X}_2 \setminus \{X\}$ and $\mathbf{Z} = \mathbf{X}_1 \cup \mathbf{Y}$. If for some $\mathbf{z}$, $\mathbf{x}_1 \sim \mathbf{z}$ and $\mathbf{y} \sim \mathbf{z}$, then

$$\left(\sum_X f_1 f_2 \right) (\mathbf{z}) = \sum_x f_1(\mathbf{x}_1) f_2(x\mathbf{y})$$

$$= f_1(\mathbf{x}_1) \sum_x f_2(x\mathbf{y})$$

$$= f_1(\mathbf{x}_1) \left(\sum_X f_2 \right) (\mathbf{y}).$$

Hence, $\sum_X f_1 f_2 = f_1 \sum_X f_2$. ∎

PROOF OF THEOREM 6.2. Note that n is also the number of network CPTs and, hence, is the initial size of set $\mathcal{S}$. Let $\mathbf{R}$ be the network variables other than $\mathbf{Q}$. Suppose that we have to multiply m_i factors when eliminating variable $\pi(i)$. The complexity of Lines 3–5 is then

$$\sum_{i=1}^{|\mathbf{R}|} O(m_i \exp(w))$$

since $O(m_i \exp(w))$ is the complexity of eliminating variable $\pi(i)$. When we are about to eliminate this variable, the number of factors in the set $\mathcal{S}$ is $n - \sum_{k=1}^{i-1}(m_k - 1)$. Hence, $m_i \leq n - \sum_{k=1}^{i-1}(m_k - 1)$ and $\sum_{k=1}^{i} m_k \leq n + (i - 1)$. Therefore, $\sum_{i=1}^{|\mathbf{R}|} m_i = O(n)$ and the complexity of Lines 3–5 is $O(n \exp(w))$. ∎

PROOF OF THEOREM 6.3. Left to Exercise 6.13. ∎

PROOF OF THEOREM 6.4. For any CPT $\Theta_{X|\mathbf{U}}$, the result of summing out variable X from $\Theta_{X|\mathbf{U}}$ is a factor that assigns 1 to each of its instantiations:

$$\left(\sum_X \Theta_{X|\mathbf{U}} \right) (\mathbf{u}) = 1.$$

Multiplying this factor by any other factor f that includes variables $\mathbf{U}$ will give factor f back. Therefore, if a leaf variable X does not belong to $\mathbf{Q}$ nor to $\mathbf{E}$, we can sum it out first, leading to the identity factor. This is why we can always prune such a leaf variable from the network. ∎

PROOF OF THEOREM 6.5. Left to Exercise 6.14. ∎

7

Inference by Factor Elimination

We present in this chapter a variation on the variable elimination algorithm, known as the *jointree algorithm,* which can be understood in terms of factor elimination. This algorithm improves on the complexity of variable elimination when answering multiple queries. It also forms the basis for a class of approximate inference algorithms that we discuss in Chapter 14.

7.1 Introduction

Consider a Bayesian network and suppose that our goal is to compute the posterior marginal for each of its n variables. Given an elimination order of width w, we can compute a single marginal using variable elimination in $O(n \exp(w))$ time and space, as we explained in Chapter 6. To compute all these marginals, we can then run variable elimination $O(n)$ times, leading to a total complexity of $O(n^2 \exp(w))$.

For large networks, the n^2 factor can be problematic even when the treewidth is small. The good news is that we can avoid this complexity and compute marginals for all networks variables in only $O(n \exp(w))$ time and space. This can be done using a more refined algorithm known as the *jointree algorithm,* which is the main subject of this chapter.[1] The jointree algorithm will also compute the posterior marginals for other sets of variables, including all network families, where a family consists of a variable and its parents in the Bayesian network. Family marginals are especially important for sensitivity analysis, as discussed in Chapter 16, and for learning Bayesian networks, as discussed in Chapters 17 and 18.

There are a number of ways to derive the jointree algorithm. The derivation we adopt in this chapter is based on eliminating factors instead of eliminating variables and using *elimination trees* instead of elimination orders. We start by presenting a simple factor elimination algorithm in Section 7.2 and then discuss elimination trees in Section 7.3. Two refinements on the algorithm will be given in Sections 7.4 and 7.5, leading to a message-passing formulation that achieves the desired computational complexity. We then introduce jointrees in Section 7.6 as a tool for generating efficient elimination trees. We finally provide a more classical treatment of the jointree algorithm in Section 7.7, where we express it in terms of jointrees as is commonly done in the literature. We also discuss two important variations on the algorithm in this section that can vary in their time and space complexity.

---

[1] The algorithm is also called the *clique-tree algorithm* or the *tree-clustering algorithm.* The reasons for these names will become more obvious in Chapter 9.

Algorithm 9 FE1($\mathcal{N}$, Q)

input:

   $\mathcal{N}$:   a Bayesian network

   Q: a variable in network $\mathcal{N}$

output: the prior marginal $\Pr(Q)$

main:

  1: $S \leftarrow$ CPTs of network $\mathcal{N}$

  2: $f_r \leftarrow$ a factor in S that contains variable Q

  3: **while** S has more than one factor **do**

  4:     remove a factor $f_i \neq f_r$ from set S

  5:     $\mathbf{V} \leftarrow$ variables that appear in factor f_i but not in S

  6:     $f_j \leftarrow f_j \sum_{\mathbf{V}} f_i$ for some factor f_j in S

  7: **end while**

  8: **return** project(f_r, Q)

7.2 Factor elimination

Suppose that we wish to compute the prior marginal over some variable Q in a Bayesian network. A variable elimination algorithm will compute this marginal by eliminating every other variable from the network. On the other hand, a factor elimination algorithm will compute this marginal by eliminating all factors except for one that contains the variable Q.

> **Definition 7.1.** The elimination of factor f_i from a set of factors S is a two-step process. We first eliminate all variables $\mathbf{V}$ that appear only in factor f_i and then multiply the result $\sum_{\mathbf{V}} f_i$ by some other factor f_j in the set S. ∎

Algorithm 9, FE1, provides the pseudocode for computing the marginal over a variable Q using factor elimination. This algorithm makes use of the factor operation project(f, $\mathbf{Q}$), which simply sums out all variables not in $\mathbf{Q}$:

$$\text{project}(f, \mathbf{Q}) \stackrel{def}{=} \sum_{\text{vars}(f) - \mathbf{Q}} f.$$

The correctness of FE1 is easy to establish as it can be viewed as a variation on variable elimination. In particular, while variable elimination will eliminate one variable at a time factor elimination will eliminate a set of variables $\mathbf{V}$ at once. Since these variables appear only in factor f_i, all we have to do is replace the factor f_i by a new factor $\sum_{\mathbf{V}} f_i$ as suggested by Theorem 6.1 of Chapter 6. However, factor elimination takes one extra step, which is multiplying this new factor by some other factor f_j. Note that after each iteration of the algorithm, the number of factors in S will decrease by one. After enough iterations, S will contain a single factor f_r that contains the variable Q. Projecting this factor on Q provides the answer to our query.

As is clear from this elimination strategy, there are two choices to be made at each iteration:

1. Choosing a factor f_i to be eliminated on Line 4
2. Choosing a factor f_j to be multiplied into on Line 6

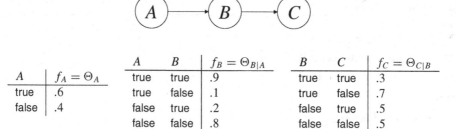

A	B	$f_B = \Theta_{B\mid A}$		B	C	$f_C = \Theta_{C\mid B}$
true	true	.9		true	true	.3
true	false	.1		true	false	.7
false	true	.2		false	true	.5
false	false	.8		false	false	.5

A	$f_A = \Theta_A$
true	.6
false	.4

Figure 7.1: A Bayesian network.

As with eliminating variables, any set of choices will provide a valid answer to our query but some choices will be better than others computationally. We return to this issue at a later stage.

Let us now consider the network in Figure 7.1 and suppose we want to compute the marginal over variable C using FE1. Initially, we have three factors in $\mathcal{S}$:

A	f_A
true	.6
false	.4

A	B	f_B		B	C	f_C
true	true	.9		true	true	.3
true	false	.1		true	false	.7
false	true	.2		false	true	.5
false	false	.8		false	false	.5

If we remove factor f_A from $\mathcal{S}$, we get $\mathbf{V} = \emptyset$ and $\sum_\emptyset f_A = f_A$. If we multiply this factor into factor f_B, the set $\mathcal{S}$ becomes

A	B	$f_A f_B$		B	C	f_C
true	true	.54		true	true	.3
true	false	.06		true	false	.7
false	true	.08		false	true	.5
false	false	.32		false	false	.5

Let us now remove factor $f_A f_B$ from $\mathcal{S}$, which leads to $\mathbf{V} = \{A\}$ and

B	$\sum_A f_A f_B$
true	.62
false	.38

Multiplying this factor into f_C leads to the following new set $\mathcal{S}$:

B	C	$f_C \sum_A f_A f_B$
true	true	.186
true	false	.434
false	true	.190
false	false	.190

The last step of FE1 will project the previous factor on variable C, leading to

C	project($f_C \sum_A f_A f_B, C$)
true	.376
false	.624

which is the answer to our query.

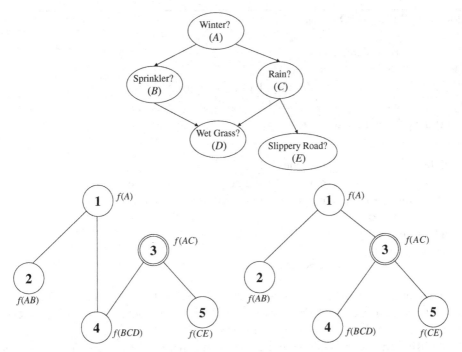

Figure 7.2: Two elimination trees for the CPTs associated with the network structure at the top.

Our discussion here was restricted to computing the marginal over a single variable. However, suppose that we wish to compute the marginal over a set of variables **Q** that are not contained in any existing factor. The simplest way to do this is by including an auxiliary factor $f(\mathbf{Q})$, where $f(\mathbf{q}) = 1$ for all instantiations **q**. We show later, however, that this may not be necessary as our final version of factor elimination will compute marginals over sets of variables that may not be contained in any factor.

7.3 Elimination trees

In variable elimination, the notion of an *elimination order* was used to specify a strategy for controlling the elimination process. Moreover, the amount of work performed by variable elimination was determined by the quality (width) of the used order.

In factor elimination, we appeal to trees for specifying an elimination strategy. Specifically, we will show that each organization of factors into a tree structure represents a particular factor elimination strategy. Moreover, we will define a quality measure for such trees (also called width) that can be used to quantify the amount of work performed by elimination algorithms driven by these trees. Figure 7.2 depicts two such trees, which we call *elimination trees*, for the same set of factors.

> **Definition 7.2.** An *elimination tree* for a set of factors $\mathcal{S}$ is a pair $(\mathcal{T}, \phi)$ where $\mathcal{T}$ is a tree. Each factor in $\mathcal{S}$ is assigned to exactly one node in tree $\mathcal{T}$, where ϕ_i denotes the product of factors assigned to node i in tree $\mathcal{T}$. We also use vars(i) to denote the variables appearing in factor ϕ_i. ∎

In Figure 7.2, the elimination tree $(\mathcal{T}, \phi)$ on the left has five nodes $\{1, \ldots, 5\}$, which are in one-to-one correspondence with the given factors. For example, $\phi_2 = f(AB)$ and $\phi_4 = f(BCD)$. Moreover, vars(2) = $\{A, B\}$ and vars(4) = $\{B, C, D\}$. In general, a node

---

Algorithm 10 FE2($\mathcal{N}$, **Q**, ($\mathcal{T}$, ϕ), r)

---

input:

   $\mathcal{N}$:   Bayesian network

   Q: some variables in network $\mathcal{N}$

   ($\mathcal{T}$, ϕ):   elimination tree for the CPTs of network $\mathcal{N}$

   r: a node in tree $\mathcal{T}$ where $\mathbf{Q} \subseteq \text{vars}(r)$

output: the prior marginal Pr(**Q**)

main:

1: **while** tree $\mathcal{T}$ has more than one node **do**
2:    remove a node $i \neq r$ having a single neighbor j from tree $\mathcal{T}$
3:    $\mathbf{V} \leftarrow$ variables appearing in ϕ_i but not in remaining tree $\mathcal{T}$
4:    $\phi_j \leftarrow \phi_j \sum_{\mathbf{V}} \phi_i$
5: **end while**
6: **return** project(ϕ_r, **Q**)

---

in an elimination tree may have multiple factors assigned to it or no factors at all.[2] For many of the concrete examples we examine, there will be a one-to-one correspondence between factors and nodes in an elimination tree.

When using an elimination tree for computing the marginal over variables **Q**, we need to choose a special node r, called a *root*, such that $\mathbf{Q} \subseteq \text{vars}(r)$. For example, if our goal is to compute the marginal over variable C in Figure 7.2, then nodes 3, 4 or 5 can all act as roots. This condition on root variables is not strictly needed but will simplify the current discussion. We say more about this later.

Given an elimination tree and a corresponding root r, our elimination strategy will proceed as follows. We eliminate a factor ϕ_i only if it has a single neighbor j and only if $i \neq r$. To eliminate the factor ϕ_i, we first sum out variables **V** that appear in ϕ_i but not in the rest of the tree, and then multiply the result $\sum_{\mathbf{V}} \phi_i$ into the factor ϕ_j associated with its single neighbor j.

Algorithm 10, FE2, which is a refinement of FE1, makes its elimination choices based on a given elimination tree and root. At each iteration, the algorithm eliminates a factor ϕ_i and its corresponding node i. After all nodes $i \neq r$ have been eliminated, projecting the factor ϕ_r on variables **Q** yields the answer to our query. Note that we still need to make a choice on Line 2 of FE2 since we may have more than one node i in the tree that satisfies the stated properties. However, it shall become clear later that the choice made at this step does not affect the amount of work done by the algorithm.

Figure 7.3 depicts a trace of FE2 for computing the marginal over variable C. The four elimination steps are as follows:

    Step 1: Eliminate f_2 and update $f_1 \leftarrow f_1 \sum_{\emptyset} f_2$.
    Step 2: Eliminate f_1 and update $f_4 \leftarrow f_4 \sum_{\emptyset} f_1$.
    Step 3: Eliminate f_4 and update $f_3 \leftarrow f_3 \sum_{BD} f_4$.
    Step 4: Eliminate f_5 and update $f_3 \leftarrow f_3 \sum_{E} f_5$.

The final factor f_3 is over variables A, C. Projecting it over C gives the desired result.

---

[2] If no factors are assigned to node i, then ϕ_i is a trivial factor that assigns the number 1 to the trivial instantiation.

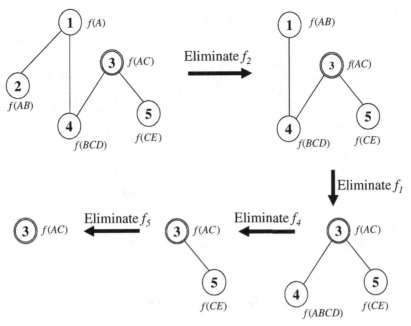

Figure 7.3: A trace of factor elimination with node 3 as the root.

When using variable elimination to compute marginals, any elimination order will lead to correct results yet the specific order we choose may have a considerable effect on the amount of work performed by the algorithm. The situation is similar with factor elimination. That is, any elimination tree will lead to correct results yet some trees will lead to less work than others. We address this point toward the end of the chapter. In the next two sections, we focus on another aspect of factor elimination that allows it to have a better complexity than standard variable elimination. In particular, we first introduce two notions, clusters and separators, that allow us to better understand the amount of work performed by factor elimination. We then show that factor elimination can cache some of its intermediate results and then re-use them when computing multiple marginals. It is this ability to save intermediate results that allows factor elimination to have a better complexity than standard variable elimination.

7.4 Separators and clusters

In this section, we define a set of variables for each edge in an elimination tree, called a *separator*, and a set of variables for each node in the tree, called a *cluster*. These sets will prove very helpful for the final statement of the algorithm and for analyzing its complexity.

Definition 7.3. The *separator* of edge i–j in an elimination tree is a set of variables defined as follows:

$$\mathbf{S}_{ij} \stackrel{def}{=} \text{vars}(i, j) \cap \text{vars}(j, i),$$

where $\text{vars}(i, j)$ are variables that appear in factors on the i-side of edge i–j and $\text{vars}(j, i)$ are variables that appear in factors on the j-side of edge i–j. ∎

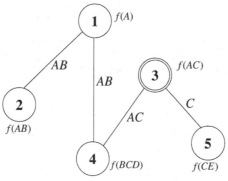

Figure 7.4: An elimination tree with separators.

Figure 7.4 depicts an elimination tree with each edge labeled with its separator. For example, since variables A, B appear in factors f_1, f_2, we have

$$\text{vars}(1, 4) = \{A, B\}.$$

Moreover, since variables A, B, C, D, E appear in factors f_3, f_4, f_5, we have

$$\text{vars}(4, 1) = \{A, B, C, D, E\}.$$

Therefore,

$$\mathbf{S}_{14} = \mathbf{S}_{41} = \{A, B\} \cap \{A, B, C, D, E\} = \{A, B\}.$$

The importance of separators stems from the following observation regarding Line 4 of FE2:

$$\sum_{\mathbf{V}} \phi_i = \text{project}(\phi_i, \mathbf{S}_{ij}). \tag{7.1}$$

That is, when variables $\mathbf{V}$ are summed out of factor ϕ_i before it is eliminated, the resulting factor is guaranteed to be over separator $\mathbf{S}_{ij}$ (see Exercise 7.4). Consider for example the four elimination steps with respect to Figure 7.3 and the corresponding separators in Figure 7.4:

Eliminate f_2: $\sum_{\emptyset} f_2 = \text{project}(f_2, AB)$.
Eliminate f_1: $\sum_{\emptyset} f_1 = \text{project}(f_1, AB)$.
Eliminate f_4: $\sum_{BD} f_4 = \text{project}(f_4, AC)$.
Eliminate f_5: $\sum_{E} f_5 = \text{project}(f_5, C)$.

This observation has a number of implications. First, it leads to a more compact statement of FE2, which we present later. Second, it allows us to bound the size of factors that are constructed during the factor elimination process. Both of these implications are best realized after we introduce the additional notion of a cluster.

Definition 7.4. The *cluster* of a node i in an elimination tree is a set of variables defined as follows:

$$\mathbf{C}_i \overset{def}{=} \text{vars}(i) \cup \bigcup_j \mathbf{S}_{ij}.$$

The *width* of an elimination tree is the size of its largest cluster minus one. ∎

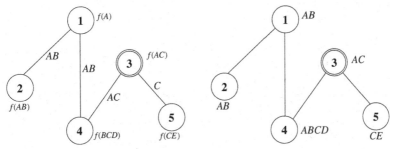

Figure 7.5: An elimination tree (left) and its corresponding clusters (right).

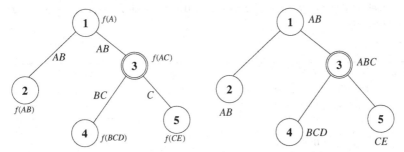

Figure 7.6: An elimination tree (left) and its corresponding clusters (right).

Figures 7.5 and 7.6 depict two elimination trees with corresponding clusters for each node. The elimination tree in Figure 7.5 has width 3 and the one in Figure 7.6 has width 2. We come back to this notion of width later but suffice it to say here that we can always construct an elimination tree of width w given an elimination order of width w.

We close this section by making two key observations about clusters. First, when we are about to eliminate node i on Line 2 of FE2, the variables of factor ϕ_i are exactly the cluster of node i, $\mathbf{C}_i$ (see Exercise 7.5). Moreover, the factor ϕ_r on Line 6 of FE2 must be over the cluster of root r, $\mathbf{C}_r$. Hence, FE2 can be used to compute the marginal over any subset of cluster $\mathbf{C}_r$. These observations allow us to rephrase FE2 as given in Algorithm 11, FE3. The new formulation takes advantages of both separators and clusters.

7.5 A message-passing formulation

We now provide our final refinement on factor elimination where we rephrase FE3 using a message-passing paradigm that allows us to execute the algorithm without destroying the elimination tree in the process. This is important when computing multiple marginals as it allows us to save intermediate computations and reuse them across different queries. This reuse will be the key to achieving the complexity we promised previously in the chapter. In particular, given an elimination tree of width w we will be able to compute the marginal over every cluster in $O(m \exp(w))$ time and space, where m is the number of nodes in the elimination tree. As a side effect, we will be able to compute the marginal over every network variable (and family) within the same complexity.

The message-passing formulation is based on the following observations given an elimination tree $(\mathcal{T}, \phi)$ with root r:

- For each node $i \neq r$ in the elimination tree, there is a unique neighbor of i that is closest to root r. In Figure 7.7, tree edges are directed so that each node i points to its neighbor closest to the root.

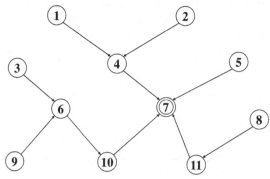

Figure 7.7: An elimination tree where edges have been directed so that each node points to its neighbor closest to the root node 7.

Algorithm 11 FE3($\mathcal{N}$, **Q**, $(\mathcal{T}, \phi)$, r)
$\mathbf{C}_i$ is the cluster of node i in tree $\mathcal{T}$
$\mathbf{S}_{ij}$ is the separator of edge i–j in tree $\mathcal{T}$

---

input:

$\mathcal{N}$:	Bayesian network
Q:	some variables in network $\mathcal{N}$
$(\mathcal{T}, \phi)$:	elimination tree for the CPTs of network $\mathcal{N}$
r:	node in tree $\mathcal{T}$ where $\mathbf{Q} \subseteq \mathbf{C}_r$

output: the prior marginal Pr(**Q**)

main:

1: **while** tree $\mathcal{T}$ has more than one node **do**
2:     remove a node $i \neq r$ having a single neighbor j from tree $\mathcal{T}$
3:     $\phi_j \leftarrow \phi_j \text{project}(\phi_i, \mathbf{S}_{ij})$
4: **end while**
5: **return** project(ϕ_r, **Q**)

- A node i will be eliminated from the tree only after all its neighbors, except the one closest to the root, have been eliminated. For example, node 4 will be eliminated from Figure 7.7 only after nodes 1 and 2 are eliminated.

- When a node i is about to be eliminated, it will have a single neighbor j. Moreover, its current factor will be projected over the separator between i and j and then multiplied into the factor of node j. In Figure 7.7, when node 4 is eliminated its current factor is projected onto the separator with node 7 and then multiplied into the factor of node 7.

Suppose now that we view the elimination of node i with single neighbor j as a process of passing a message M_{ij} from node i to neighbor j. We can then make the following observations:

1. When j receives the message, it multiplies it into its current factor ϕ_j.

2. Node i cannot send the message to j until it has received all messages from neighbors $k \neq j$.

3. After i receives these messages, its current factor will be

$$\phi_i \prod_{k \neq j} M_{ki}$$

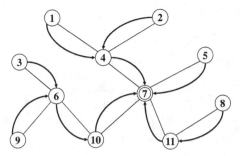

Figure 7.8: Inward (pull, collect) phase: Messages passed toward the root node 7.

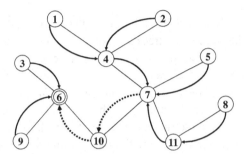

Figure 7.9: Inward (pull, collect) phase: Messages passed toward the root node 6.

and the message it sends to j will be

$$M_{ij} \stackrel{def}{=} \text{project}\left(\phi_i \prod_{k \neq j} M_{ki}, \mathbf{S}_{ij}\right). \tag{7.2}$$

In Figure 7.7, node 4 cannot send its message to node 7 until it receives messages from nodes 1 and 2. Moreover, after receiving such messages, its factor will be

$$\phi_4 M_{14} M_{24}$$

and the message it sends to node 7 will be

$$\text{project}(\phi_4 M_{14} M_{24}, \mathbf{S}_{47}).$$

We can now formulate factor elimination as a message-passing algorithm. Specifically, to compute the marginal over some variables $\mathbf{Q}$, we select a root r in the elimination tree such that $\mathbf{Q} \subseteq \mathbf{C}_r$. We then push messages toward the root r. When all messages into the root are available, we multiply them by ϕ_r and project onto $\mathbf{Q}$. If our elimination tree has m nodes, it will have $m-1$ edges and a total of $m-1$ messages will need to be passed. Figure 7.8 depicts an elimination tree with ten messages directed toward the root node 7.

7.5.1 Multiple marginals and message reuse

Suppose now that we want to compute the marginal over some other cluster $\mathbf{C}_i$, $i \neq r$. All we have to do is choose i as the new root and repeat the previous message-passing process. This requires some additional messages to be passed but not as many as $m-1$ messages, assuming that we saved the messages passed when node r was the root. Consider Figure 7.8 again and suppose that we want node 6 to be the root in this case. Out of the ten messages we need to direct toward node 6, eight messages have already been computed when node 7 was the root (see Figure 7.9).

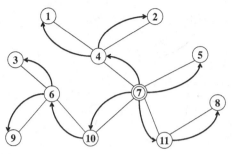

Figure 7.10: Outward (push, distribute) phase: Messages passed away from the root node 7.

The key observation here is that if we compute the marginals over every cluster by choosing every node in the elimination tree as a root, the total number of messages we have to pass is exactly $2(m - 1)$. This follows because we have $m - 1$ edges and two distinct messages per edge. These messages are usually computed in two phases with each phase computing $m - 1$ messages. In the first phase, known as the *inward, pull*, or *collect phase*, we direct messages toward some root node r. In the second phase, known as the *outward, push*, or *distribute phase*, we direct messages away from the root r. Figure 7.8 depicts the messages passed in the inward phase with node 7 as the root. Figure 7.10 depicts the messages passed in the outward phase in this case.

7.5.2 The cost of passing messages

To assess the cost of passing these messages, examine Equation 7.2 for computing a message from i to j. According to this equation, we need to first multiply a number of factors and then project the result on a separator. The factor that results from the multiplication process must be over the cluster of node i. Hence, the complexity of both multiplication and projection are $O(\exp(w))$, where w is the size of cluster $\mathbf{C}_i$. This assumes that node i has a bounded number of neighbors but we address this assumption later.

Recall that the width of an elimination tree is the size of its maximal cluster minus one. Hence, if w is the width of the given elimination tree, then the cost of any message is bounded by $O(\exp(w))$. Since we have a total of $2(m - 1)$ messages, the cost of computing all cluster marginals is then $O(m \exp(w))$. We later show that if we have a Bayesian network with n variables and treewidth w, then there exists an elimination tree with $O(n)$ edges, width w, and a bounded number of neighbors for each node. Hence, the complexity of computing all cluster marginals will be $O(n \exp(w))$ given this tree. This is indeed the major benefit of factor elimination over variable elimination, which would require $O(n^2 \exp(w))$ time and space to compute marginals over individual network variables.

7.5.3 Joint marginals and evidence

Before we discuss the generation of elimination trees in Section 7.6, we need to settle the issue of handling evidence, which is necessary for computing joint marginals. In particular, given some evidence $\mathbf{e}$ we want to use factor elimination to compute the joint marginal $\Pr(\mathbf{C}_i, \mathbf{e})$ for each cluster $\mathbf{C}_i$ in the elimination tree. As in variable elimination, this can be done in two ways:

1. We reduce each factor f given the evidence $\mathbf{e}$, leading to a set of reduced factors $f^\mathbf{e}$. We then apply factor elimination to the reduced set of factors.

2. We introduce an evidence indicator λ_E for every variable E in evidence **e**. Here λ_E is a factor over variable E that captures the value of E in evidence **e**: $\lambda_E(e) = 1$ if e is consistent with evidence **e** and $\lambda_E(e) = 0$ otherwise. We then apply factor elimination to the extended set of factors.

The first method is more efficient if we plan to compute marginals with respect to only one piece of evidence **e**. However, it is not uncommon to compute marginals with respect to multiple pieces of evidence, $\mathbf{e}_1, \ldots, \mathbf{e}_n$, while trying to reuse messages across different pieces of evidence. In this case, the second method is more efficient if applied carefully. This method is implemented by assigning the evidence indicator λ_E to a node i in the elimination tree while ensuring that $E \in \mathbf{C}_i$. As a result, the clusters and separators of the elimination tree will remain intact and so will its width.

Algorithm 12, FE, is our final refinement on factor elimination and uses the second method for accommodating evidence. This version computes joint marginals using two phases of message passing, as discussed previously. If one saves the messages across different runs of the algorithm, then one can reuse these messages as long as they are not invalidated when the evidence changes. In particular, when the evidence at node i changes in the elimination tree, we need to invalidate all messages that depend on the factor at that node. These messages happen to be the ones directed away from node i in the elimination tree (see Figure 7.10).

7.5.4 The polytree algorithm

An interesting special case of Algorithm 12, FE, arises when the Bayesian network has a polytree structure. In this case, one can use an elimination tree that corresponds to the polytree structure as given in Figure 7.11. This special case of Algorithm 12 is known as the *polytree algorithm* or *belief propagation algorithm* and is discussed in more detail in Chapter 14. We note here that if k is the maximum number of parents attained by any node in the polytree, then k will also be the width of the elimination tree. Hence, the time and

---

Algorithm 12 FE($\mathcal{N}, (\mathcal{T}, \phi), \mathbf{e}$)

---

input:

   $\mathcal{N}$:   Bayesian network

   $(\mathcal{T}, \phi)$:   elimination tree for the CPTs of network $\mathcal{N}$

   $\mathbf{e}$:   evidence

output: the joint marginal $\mathrm{Pr}(\mathbf{C}_i, \mathbf{e})$ for each node i in elimination tree

main:

1: **for** each variable E in evidence **e do**
2:    $i \leftarrow$ node in tree $\mathcal{T}$ such that $E \in \mathbf{C}_i$
3:    $\lambda_E \leftarrow$ evidence indicator for variable E {$\lambda_E(e) = 1$ if $e \sim \mathbf{e}$ and $\lambda_E(e) = 0$ otherwise}
4:    $\phi_i \leftarrow \phi_i \lambda_E$ {entering evidence at node i}
5: **end for**
6: Choose a root node r in the tree $\mathcal{T}$
7: Pull/collect messages towards root r using Equation 7.2
8: Push/distribute messages away from root r using Equation 7.2
9: **return** $\phi_i \prod_k M_{ki}$ for each node i in tree $\mathcal{T}$ {joint marginal $\mathrm{Pr}(\mathbf{C}_i, \mathbf{e})$}

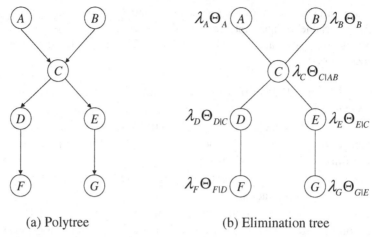

(a) Polytree (b) Elimination tree

Figure 7.11: There is a one-to-one correspondence between the polytree nodes and the elimination tree nodes. Moreover, the CPT $\Theta_{X|U}$ and evidence indicator λ_X of node X in the polytree are assigned to its corresponding node in the elimination tree.

space complexity of the polytree algorithm is $O(n \exp(k))$, where n is the number of nodes in the polytree. This means that the algorithm has a linear time and space complexity since the size of CPTs in the polytree is also $O(n \exp(k))$. Exercises 7.13 and 7.14 reveal some additional properties of the polytree algorithm.

7.6 The jointree connection

Constructing an elimination tree for a set of factors is straightforward: we simply construct a tree and assign each factor to one of its nodes. Any elimination tree constructed in this fashion will be good enough to drive algorithm FE. However, our interest is in constructing low-width elimination trees, as this leads to minimizing the amount of work performed by FE.

There are different methods for constructing elimination trees but the method we discuss next will be based on an influential tool known as a *jointree*. It is this tool that gives factor elimination its traditional name: the *jointree algorithm*. The connection between elimination trees and jointrees is so tight that it is possible to phrase the factor elimination algorithm directly on jointrees without explicit mention of elimination trees. This is indeed how the algorithm is classically described and we provide such a description in Section 7.7, where we also discuss some of the common variations on the jointree algorithm.

We start by defining jointrees.

Definition 7.5. A *jointree* for a DAG G is a pair $(\mathcal{T}, \mathbf{C})$ where $\mathcal{T}$ is a tree and $\mathbf{C}$ is a function that maps each node i in tree $\mathcal{T}$ into a label $\mathbf{C}_i$, called a *cluster*. The jointree must satisfy the following properties:

1. The cluster $\mathbf{C}_i$ is a set of nodes from the DAG G.

2. Each family in the DAG G must appear in some cluster $\mathbf{C}_i$.

3. If a node appears in two clusters $\mathbf{C}_i$ and $\mathbf{C}_j$, it must also appear in every cluster $\mathbf{C}_k$ on the path connecting nodes i and j in the jointree. This is known as the *jointree property*.

The *separator* of edge i–j in a jointree is denoted by $\mathbf{S}_{ij}$ and defined as $\mathbf{C}_i \cap \mathbf{C}_j$. The *width* of a jointree is defined as the size of its largest cluster minus one. ■

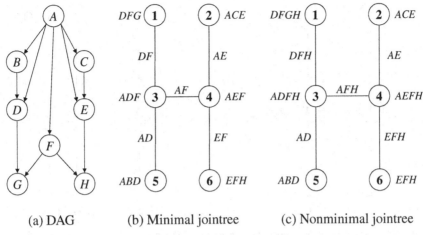

(a) DAG   (b) Minimal jointree   (c) Nonminimal jointree

Figure 7.12: Two jointrees for the same DAG.

Figure 7.12(a) depicts a DAG and Figure 7.12(b) depicts a corresponding jointree that has six nodes: $1, \ldots, 6$. For this jointree, the cluster of node 1 is $\mathbf{C}_1 = DFG$, the separator of edge 1–3 is $\mathbf{S}_{13} = DF$, and the width is 2. A jointree for DAG G is said to be *minimal* if it ceases to be a jointree for G once we remove a variable from one of its clusters. The jointree in Figure 7.12(b) is minimal. The one in Figure 7.12(c) is not minimal as we can remove variable H from clusters 1, 3 and 4.

Jointrees are studied in more depth in Chapter 9 but we point out here that the treewidth of a DAG can be defined as the width of its best jointree (i.e., the one with the smallest width). Recall that we had a similar definition in Chapter 6 for elimination orders, where the treewidth of a DAG was defined as the width of its best elimination order. Therefore, the best elimination order and best jointree for a given DAG must have equal widths. Polytime, width-preserving transformations between elimination orders and jointrees are provided in Chapter 9.

We next provide two results that show the tight connection between jointrees and elimination trees. According to the first result, every elimination tree induces a jointree of equal width.

Theorem 7.1. *The clusters of an elimination tree satisfy the three properties of a jointree stated in Definition 7.5.* ∎

Figure 7.13 depicts two elimination trees that have the same set of clusters, shown in Figure 7.12(b). We can verify that these clusters satisfy the three properties of a jointree.

According to our second result, a jointree can easily be used to construct an elimination tree of no greater width.

Definition 7.6. Let $(\mathcal{T}, \mathbf{C})$ be a jointree for network $\mathcal{N}$. An elimination tree $(\mathcal{T}, \phi)$ for the CPTs of network $\mathcal{N}$ is said to be *embedded* in the jointree if the variables of factor ϕ_i are contained in the jointree cluster $\mathbf{C}_i$. ∎

Hence, to construct an elimination tree that is embedded in a jointree $(\mathcal{T}, \mathbf{C})$, all we need to do is adopt the tree structure $\mathcal{T}$ of the jointree and then assign each CPT to some node i in tree $\mathcal{T}$ while ensuring that the CPT variables are contained in cluster $\mathbf{C}_i$. Figure 7.13 depicts two elimination trees that are embedded in the jointree of Figure 7.12(b) and also in the jointree of Figure 7.12(c).

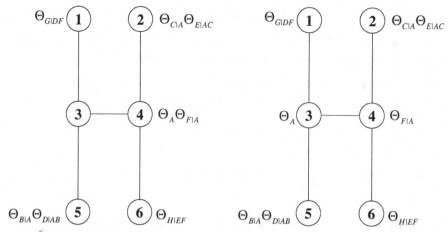

Figure 7.13: Two elimination trees that have identical clusters, as shown in Figure 7.12(b).

Theorem 7.2. *Let $\mathbf{C}_i$ and $\mathbf{S}_{ij}$ be the clusters and separators of a jointree and let $\mathbf{C}'_i$ and $\mathbf{S}'_{ij}$ be the clusters and separators of an embedded elimination tree. Then $\mathbf{C}'_i \subseteq \mathbf{C}_i$ and $\mathbf{S}'_{ij} \subseteq \mathbf{S}_{ij}$. Moreover, the equalities hold when the jointree is minimal.* ■

Hence, the width of an elimination tree is no greater than the width of an embedding jointree. The elimination trees in Figure 7.13 both have width 2. These trees are embedded in the jointree of Figure 7.12(b), which has width 2. They are also embedded in the jointree of Figure 7.12(c), which has width 3.

Given these results, we can immediately generate low-width elimination trees if we have an ability to generate low-width jointrees (as discussed in Chapter 9). However, note here that the classical description of the jointree algorithm does not refer to elimination trees. Instead, it immediately starts with the construction of a jointree and then assigns CPTs to the jointree clusters, as suggested by Definition 7.6. This is also the case for the classical semantics of the jointree algorithm and its classical proof of correctness, which do not make reference to elimination trees either and are therefore not based on the concept of factor elimination as shown here.

7.7 The jointree algorithm: A classical view

In this section, we provide a more classical exposition of the jointree algorithm where we discuss two of its most common variations known as the *Shenoy-Shafer* and *Hugin* architectures. The key difference between these architectures is due to the type of information they store and the way they compute messages, which leads to important implications on time and space complexity. We see later that factor elimination as derived in this chapter corresponds to the Shenoy-Shafer architecture and, hence, inherits its properties. The classical description of a jointree algorithm is as follows:

1. Construct a jointree $(\mathcal{T}, \mathbf{C})$ for the given Bayesian network. Figure 7.14 depicts a Bayesian network and a corresponding jointree.

2. Assign each network CPT $\Theta_{X|\mathbf{U}}$ to a cluster that contains X and $\mathbf{U}$. Figure 7.14(b) depicts factor assignments to jointree clusters.

3. Assign each evidence indicator λ_X to a cluster that contains X. Figure 7.14(b) depicts evidence indicator assignments to jointree clusters.

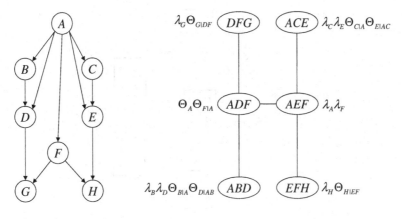

(a) Bayesian network   (b) Corresponding jointree

Figure 7.14: CPTs and evidence indicators are assigned to jointree clusters.

Note that Step 2 corresponds to the generation of an elimination tree as suggested by Definition 7.6, although the elimination tree is left implicit here.

A jointree algorithm starts by entering the given evidence **e** through evidence indicators. That is, $\lambda_X(x)$ is set to 1 if x is consistent with evidence **e** and to 0 otherwise. The algorithm then propagates messages between clusters. After passing two messages per edge in the jointree, we can compute the marginals $\Pr(\mathbf{C}, \mathbf{e})$ for every cluster **C**.

There are two main methods for propagating messages in a jointree, known as the Shenoy-Shafer architecture and the Hugin architecture. The methods differ in both their space and time complexity. In particular, the Shenoy-Shafer architecture would generally require less space but more time on an arbitrary jointree. However, the time complexity of both methods can be made equivalent if we restrict ourselves to a special type of jointree, as we see next.

7.7.1 The Shenoy-Shafer architecture

Shenoy-Shafer propagation corresponds to Algorithm 12, FE, and proceeds as follows. First, evidence **e** is entered into the jointree through evidence indicators. A cluster is then selected as the root and message propagation proceeds in two phases, inward and outward. In the inward phase, messages are passed toward the root. In the outward phase, messages are passed away from the root. The inward phase is also known as the *collect* or *pull* phase, and the outward phase is known as the *distribute* or *push* phase. Node i sends a message to node j only when it has received messages from all its other neighbors k. A message from node i to node j is a factor M_{ij} defined as follows:

$$M_{ij} \stackrel{def}{=} \text{project}\left(\Phi_i \prod_{k \neq j} M_{ki}, \mathbf{S}_{ij}\right), \tag{7.3}$$

where Φ_i is the product of factors (including evidence indicators) assigned to node i.

Note that cluster $\mathbf{C}_i$ includes exactly the variables of factor $\Phi_i \prod_{k \neq j} M_{ki}$. Hence, projecting this factor on variables $\mathbf{S}_{ij}$ is the same as summing out variables $\mathbf{C}_i \setminus \mathbf{S}_{ij}$ from

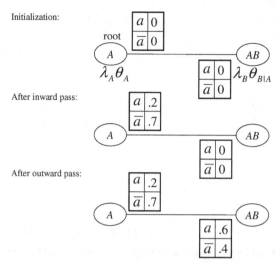

Figure 7.15: Shenoy-Shafer propagation illustrated on a simple jointree under evidence b. The factors on the left represent the content of the message directed toward the root. The factors on the right represent the content of the message directed away from the root. The jointree is for network $A \rightarrow B$, where $\theta_a = .6$, $\theta_{b|a} = .2$ and $\theta_{b|\bar{a}} = .7$.

this factor. This is why (7.3) is more commonly written as follows in the literature:

$$M_{ij} \stackrel{def}{=} \sum_{\mathbf{C}_i \setminus \mathbf{S}_{ij}} \Phi_i \prod_{k \neq j} M_{ki}. \tag{7.4}$$

Once message propagation is finished in the Shenoy-Shafer architecture, we have the following for each cluster i in the jointree:

$$\Pr(\mathbf{C}_i, \mathbf{e}) = \Phi_i \prod_k M_{ki}. \tag{7.5}$$

Hence, we can compute the joint marginal for any subset of variables that is included in a cluster (see also Exercise 7.6). Figure 7.15 illustrates Shenoy-Shafer propagation on a simple example.

7.7.2 Using nonminimal jointrees

The Shenoy-Shafer architecture corresponds to Algorithm 12, FE, when the jointree is minimal as the clusters and separators of the jointree match the ones induced by the embedded elimination tree. However, consider the jointree in Figure 7.12(c). This jointree is not minimal as we can remove variable H from clusters 1, 3, and 4, leading to the minimal jointree in Figure 7.12(b). Suppose now that we assign CPTs to these jointrees as given on the left side of Figure 7.13. If we apply the Shenoy-Shafer architecture to the nonminimal jointree with this CPT assignment, the factor Φ_1 will be over variables DFH, the separator $\mathbf{S}_{13} = DFH$, and the cluster $\mathbf{C}_1 = DFGH$. Hence, when computing the message from node 1 to node 3 using (7.3), we are projecting factor Φ_1 on variables DFH even though the factor does not contain variable H. Similarly, if we compute the message using (7.4), we are summing out variable H from factor Φ_1 even though it does not appear in that factor. We can simply ignore these superfluous variables when projecting or summing out, which leads to the same messages passed by the minimal jointree in Figure 7.12(b).

However, these variables are not superfluous when computing other messages. Consider for example the message sent from node 6 to node 4. The factor Φ_6 is over variables EFH in this case. In the minimal jointree, variable H is summed out from this factor before it is sent to node 4. However, in the nonminimal jointree the factor Φ_6 is sent intact to node 4. Hence, the nonminimal jointree insists on carrying the information about variable H as messages travel from node 6 to node 4, then to node 3, and finally to node 1. As a result, the nonminimal jointree ends up computing marginals over variable sets $AEFH$, $ADFH$, and $DFGH$, which cannot be computed if we use the minimal jointree. This is indeed one of the main values of using nonminimal jointrees as they allow us to compute marginals over sets of variables that may not be contained in the clusters of minimal jointrees.

7.7.3 Complexity of the Shenoy-Shafer architecture

Let us now look at the time and space requirements of the Shenoy-Shafer architecture, where we provide a more refined analysis than the one given in Section 7.5.1. In particular, we relax here the assumption that each node in the jointree has a bounded number of neighbors. The space requirements are those needed to store the messages computed by (7.4). That is, we need two factors for each separator $\mathbf{S}_{ij}$, one factor stores the message from cluster i to cluster j and the other stores the message from j to i. It needs to be stressed here that (7.4) can be evaluated without the need to construct a factor over all cluster variables (see Exercise 7.11). Hence, the space complexity of the Shenoy-Shafer architecture is not exponential in the size of jointree clusters but only in the size of jointree separators. This is a key difference with the Hugin architecture, to be discussed later.

Moving to the time requirements of the Shenoy-Shafer architecture, suppose that we have a jointree with n clusters and width w and let n_i be the number of neighbors that cluster i has in the jointree. For each cluster i, (7.4) has to be evaluated n_i times and (7.5) has to be evaluated once. Each evaluation of (7.4) leads to multiplying n_i factors, whose variables are all in cluster $\mathbf{C}_i$. Moreover, each evaluation of (7.5) leads to multiplying $n_i + 1$ factors, whose variables are also all in cluster $\mathbf{C}_i$. The total complexity is then

$$\sum_i O(n_i^2 \exp(|\mathbf{C}_i|) + (n_i + 1) \exp(|\mathbf{C}_i|)),$$

which reduces to

$$\sum_i O((n_i^2 + n_i + 1) \exp(w))$$

where w is the jointree width. Since $\sum_i n_i = 2(n - 1)$, this further reduces to

$$O((\alpha + 3n - 2) \exp(w))$$

where $\alpha = \sum_i n_i^2$ is a term that ranges from $O(n)$ to $O(n^2)$ depending on the jointree structure. For example, we may have what is known as a *binary jointree* in which each cluster has at most three neighbors, leading to $\alpha = O(n)$. Or we may have a jointree with one cluster having the other $n - 1$ clusters as its neighbors, leading to $\alpha = O(n^2)$.

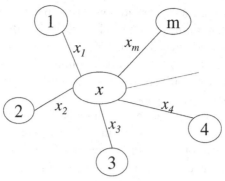

Figure 7.16: An illustration of the division technique in the Hugin architecture.

We see in Chapter 9 that if we are given a Bayesian network with n variables and an elimination order of width w, then we can always construct a binary jointree for the network with the following properties:

- The jointree width is w.
- The jointree has no more than $2n - 1$ clusters.

Hence, we can always avoid the quadratic complexity suggested previously by a careful construction of the jointree.

To summarize, the space complexity of the Shenoy-Shafer architecture is exponential in the size of separators but not exponential in the size of clusters. Moreover, its time complexity depends not only on the width and number of clusters in a jointree but also on the number of neighbors per node in the jointree. However, with an appropriate jointree the time complexity is $O(n \exp(w))$, where n is the number of networks variables and w is the network treewidth.

7.7.4 The Hugin architecture

We now discuss another variation on the jointree algorithm known as the Hugin architecture. This architecture has a space complexity that is exponential in the size of clusters. Yet its time complexity depends only on the width and number of clusters in the jointree, not the number of neighbors per cluster.

The Hugin architecture uses a new operation that divides one factor by another. We therefore motivate and define this operation before we introduce and analyze this architecture. Consider first Figure 7.16, which depicts a node x with neighbors $1, \ldots, m$, where each edge between x and its neighbor i is labeled with a number x_i (x is also a number). Suppose now that node x wants to send a message to each of its neighbors i, where the content of this message is the number:

$$x \prod_{j \neq i} x_j.$$

There are two ways to do this. First, we can compute the product for each neighbor i, which corresponds to the Shenoy-Shafer architecture. Second, we can compute the product $p = x \prod_{j=1}^{m} x_j$ only once and then use it to compute the message to each neighbor i as p/x_i. The second method corresponds to the Hugin architecture and is clearly more efficient as it only requires one division for each message (after some initialization), while the first method requires m multiplications per message. However, the second method requires that $x_i \neq 0$, otherwise p/x_i is not defined. But if the message p/x_i is later multiplied by an expression of the form $x_i \alpha$, then we can define $p/0$ to be 0, or any other number for that matter, and our computations will be correct since $(p/x_i)x_i \alpha = 0$ regardless of how $p/0$ is defined in this case. This is basically the main insight behind the Hugin architecture, except that the prior analysis is applied to factors instead of numbers.

Definition 7.7. Let f_1 and f_2 be two factors over the same set of variables $\mathbf{X}$. The *division* of factor f_1 by factor f_2 is a factor f over variables $\mathbf{X}$ denoted by f_1/f_2 and defined as follows:

$$f(\mathbf{x}) \stackrel{def}{=} \begin{cases} f_1(\mathbf{x})/f_2(\mathbf{x}) & \text{if } f_2(\mathbf{x}) \neq 0 \\ 0 & \text{otherwise.} \end{cases} \qquad \blacksquare$$

Hugin propagation proceeds similarly to Shenoy-Shafer by entering evidence $\mathbf{e}$ using evidence indicators, selecting a cluster as root, and propagating messages in two phases, inward and outward. However, the Hugin message propagation scheme differs in some major ways. First, it maintains over each separator $\mathbf{S}_{ij}$ a single factor Ψ_{ij}, with each entry of Ψ_{ij} initialized to 1. It also maintains over each cluster $\mathbf{C}_i$ a factor Ψ_i, which is initialized to $\Phi_i \prod_j \Psi_{ij}$ where Φ_i is the product of factors (including evidence indicators) assigned to node i.

Node i passes a message to neighboring node j only when i receives messages from all its other neighbors k. When node i is ready to send a message to node j, it does the following:

- Saves the factor Ψ_{ij} into Ψ_{ij}^{old}.
- Computes a new factor $\Psi_{ij} \leftarrow \sum_{\mathbf{C}_i \backslash \mathbf{S}_{ij}} \Psi_i$.
- Computes a message to node j: $M_{ij} = \Psi_{ij}/\Psi_{ij}^{old}$.
- Multiplies the computed message into the factor at node j: $\Psi_j \leftarrow \Psi_j M_{ij}$.

It is important to stress here that the factor saved with the edge i–j is Ψ_{ij}, which is different from the message sent from node i to node j, $\Psi_{ij}/\Psi_{ij}^{old}$. The message is not saved, which is contrary to the Shenoy-Shafer architecture.

After the inward and outward passes of Hugin propagation are completed, we have the following for each node i in the jointree:

$$\Pr(\mathbf{C}_i, \mathbf{e}) = \Psi_i.$$

Hence, we can compute the joint marginal for any set of variables as long as that set is included in a cluster. The Hugin propagation scheme also guarantees the following for each edge i–j:

$$\Pr(\mathbf{S}_{ij}, \mathbf{e}) = \Psi_{ij}.$$

That is, the separator factors contain joint marginals over the variables of these separators (see Exercises 7.6). Figure 7.17 illustrates Hugin propagation on a simple example.

7.7.5 Complexity of the Hugin architecture

The space requirements for the Hugin architecture are those needed to store cluster and separator factors: one factor for each cluster and one factor for each separator. Note that cluster factors are usually much larger than separator factors, leading to a much larger

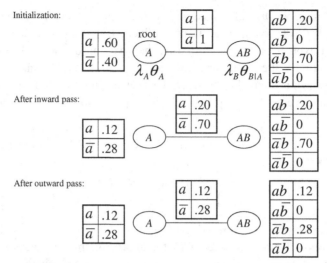

Figure 7.17: Hugin propagation illustrated on a simple jointree under evidence b, where one factor is associated with each cluster and with each separator. The jointree is for network $A \rightarrow B$, where $\theta_a = .6$, $\theta_{b|a} = .2$ and $\theta_{b|\bar{a}} = .7$.

demand on space than that required by the Shenoy-Shafer architecture (recall that the space complexity of the Shenoy-Shafer architecture is exponential only in the size of separators). This is the penalty that the Hugin architecture pays for the time complexity, as we discuss next.

Suppose that we have a jointree with n clusters and width w. Suppose further that the initial factors Ψ_i and Ψ_{ij} are already available for each cluster and separator. Let us now bound the amount of work performed by the inward and outward passes of the Hugin architecture, that is, the work needed to pass a message from each cluster i to each of its neighbors j. Saving the old separator factor takes $O(\exp(|\mathbf{S}_{ij}|))$, computing the message takes $O(\exp(|\mathbf{C}_i|) + \exp(|\mathbf{S}_{ij}|))$, and multiplying the message into the factor of cluster j takes $O(\exp(|\mathbf{C}_j|))$. Hence, if each cluster i has n_i neighbors j, the total complexity is

$$\sum_i \sum_j O(\exp(|\mathbf{C}_i|) + 2\exp(|\mathbf{S}_{ij}|) + \exp(|\mathbf{C}_j|)),$$

which reduces to

$$O(n \exp(w))$$

where w is the jointree width. Note that this result holds regardless of the number of neighbors per node in a jointree, contrary to the Shenoy-Shafer architecture, which needs to constrain the number of neighbors to achieve a similar complexity.

Bibliographic remarks

The Shenoy-Shafer architecture was introduced in Shenoy and Shafer [1990] and the Hugin architecture was introduced in Jensen et al. [1990]. Both architectures are based on Lauritzen and Spiegelhalter [1988], which introduced the first jointree algorithm. All three architectures are discussed and compared in Lepar and Shenoy [1998]. Another architecture, called *zero-conscious Hugin*, is proposed in Park and Darwiche [2003c], which combines some of the benefits attained by the Shenoy-Shafer and Hugin architectures. The notion of a binary jointree was introduced in Shenoy [1996]. A procedural description of the Hugin architecture is given in Huang and Darwiche [1996], laying out some of the techniques used in developing efficient implementations. The jointree algorithm is quite versatile in allowing other types of queries, including MAP and MPE [Jensen, 2001; Cowell et al., 1999], and a framework for time-space tradeoffs [Dechter and Fattah, 2001]. Jointrees have been referred to as *junction trees* in Jensen et al. [1990], *clique trees* in Lauritzen and Spiegelhalter [1988], *qualitative Markov trees* in Shafer [1987], and *hypertrees* in Shenoy and Shafer [1990]. However, we should mention that many definitions of jointrees in the literature are based on specific procedures that construct only a subset of the jointrees as given by Definition 7.5. We also note that the polytree algorithm as discussed in Section 7.5.4 precedes the jointree algorithm and was derived independently. The formulation we gave corresponds to the one proposed in Peot and Shachter [1991], which is a slight modification on the original polytree algorithm described in Pearl [1986b].

7.8 Exercises

7.1. Answer the following queries with respect to the Bayesian network in Figure 7.18:

    1. $\Pr(B, C)$.

    2. $\Pr(C, D = \text{true})$.

    3. $\Pr(A \mid D = \text{true}, E = \text{true})$.

You may prune the network before attempting each computation and use any inference method you find most appropriate.

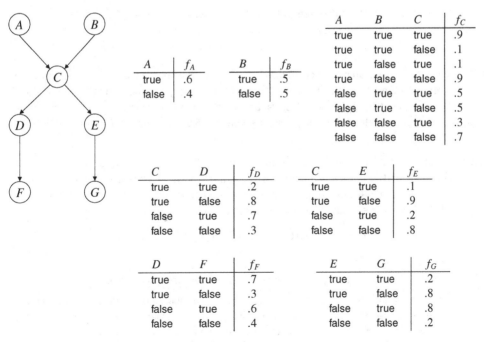

A	f_A
true	.6
false	.4

B	f_B
true	.5
false	.5

A	B	C	f_C
true	true	true	.9
true	true	false	.1
true	false	true	.1
true	false	false	.9
false	true	true	.5
false	true	false	.5
false	false	true	.3
false	false	false	.7

C	D	f_D
true	true	.2
true	false	.8
false	true	.7
false	false	.3

C	E	f_E
true	true	.1
true	false	.9
false	true	.2
false	false	.8

D	F	f_F
true	true	.7
true	false	.3
false	true	.6
false	false	.4

E	G	f_G
true	true	.2
true	false	.8
false	true	.8
false	false	.2

Figure 7.18: A Bayesian network.

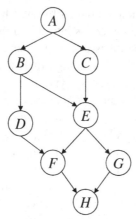

Figure 7.19: A Bayesian network structure.

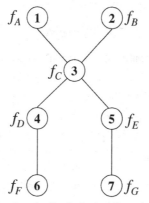

Figure 7.20: An elimination tree for the factors of Bayesian network in Figure 7.18.

7.2. Consider the Bayesian network in Figure 7.19. Construct an elimination tree for the Bayesian network CPTs that has the smallest width possible and assigns at most one CPT to each tree node. Compute the separators, clusters, and width of the elimination tree. It may be useful to know that this network has the following jointree: $ABC—BCE—BDE—DEF—EFG—FGH$.

7.3. Consider the Bayesian network in Figure 7.18 and the corresponding elimination tree in Figure 7.20, and suppose that the evidence indicator for each variable is assigned to the node corresponding to that variable (e.g., λ_C is assigned to node 3). Suppose we are answering the following queries according to the given order:

$$\Pr(G=\text{true}), \quad \Pr(G, F=\text{true}), \quad \Pr(F, A=\text{true}, F=\text{true}),$$

using Algorithm 12, FE.

  1. Compute the separators, clusters, and width of the given elimination tree.

  2. What messages are computed while answering each query according to the previous sequence? State the origin, destination, and value of each message. Use node 7 as the root to answer the first two queries, and node 6 as the root to answer the last query. For each query, compute only the messages directed toward the corresponding root.

3. What messages are invalidated due to new evidence as we attempt each new query?

4. What is the answer to each of the previous queries?

7.4. Prove Equation 7.1. Hint: Prove by induction, assuming first that node i has only a single neighbor and then prove for an arbitrary node i.

7.5. Let i be a node in an elimination tree. Show that for any particular neighbor k of i, we have

$$\mathbf{S}_{ik} \subseteq \text{vars}(i) \cup \bigcup_{j \neq k} \mathbf{S}_{ij}$$

and hence

$$\mathbf{C}_i = \text{vars}(i) \cup \bigcup_{j \neq k} \mathbf{S}_{ij}.$$

7.6. Prove the following statement with respect to Algorithm 12, FE:

$$M_{ij} = \text{project}(\phi_{ij}, \mathbf{S}_{ij}),$$

where ϕ_{ij} is the product of all factors assigned to nodes on the i-side of edge $i-j$ in the elimination tree. Use this result to show that

$$M_{ij} M_{ji} = \text{Pr}(\mathbf{S}_{ij}, \mathbf{e})$$

for every edge $i-j$ in the elimination tree.

7.7. Prove that for every edge $i-j$ in an elimination tree, $\mathbf{S}_{ij} = \mathbf{C}_i \cap \mathbf{C}_j$.

7.8. Let $\mathcal{N}$ be a Bayesian network and let $(\mathcal{T}, \phi)$ be an elimination tree of width w for the CPTs of network $\mathcal{N}$. Show how to construct an elimination order for network $\mathcal{N}$ of width $\leq w$. Hint: Consider the order in which variables are eliminated in the context of factor elimination.

7.9. Consider the following set of factors: $f(ABE)$, $f(ACD)$, and $f(DEF)$. Show that the optimal elimination tree (the one with smallest width) for this set of factors must have more than three nodes (hence, the set of nodes in the elimination tree cannot be in one-to-one correspondence with the factors).

7.10. A *cutset* $\mathbf{C}$ for a DAG G is a set of nodes that renders G a polytree when all edges outgoing from nodes $\mathbf{C}$ are removed. Let k be the maximum number of parents per node in the DAG G. Show how to construct an elimination tree for G whose width is $\leq k + |\mathbf{C}|$.

7.11. Show that the message defined by Equation 7.4 can be computed in space that is exponential only in the size of separator $\mathbf{S}_{ij}$, given messages M_{ki}, $k \neq j$, and the factors assigned to node i.

7.12. Consider the elimination tree on the left of Figure 7.13. Using factor elimination on this tree, one cannot compute the marginal over $AEFH$ as these variables are not contained in any cluster. Construct an elimination tree with width 3 that allows us to compute the marginal over these variables. Construct another elimination tree with width 3 that allows us to compute the marginal over variables GH. Note: You may need to introduce auxiliary factors.

7.13. Consider the polytree algorithm as discussed in Section 7.5.4, and let $X \to Y$ be an edge in the polytree. Show that the messages M_{XY} and M_{YX} sent across this edge must be over variable X.

7.14. Consider the polytree algorithm as discussed in Section 7.5.4, and let $\mathbf{e}$ be some given evidence. Let $X \to Y$ be an edge in the polytree, $\mathbf{e}_{XY}^+$ be the evidence assigned to nodes on the X-side of this edge, and $\mathbf{e}_{XY}^-$ be the evidence assigned to nodes on the Y-side of the edge (hence, $\mathbf{e} = \mathbf{e}_{XY}^+, \mathbf{e}_{XY}^-$). Show that the messages passed by Algorithm 12, FE, across edges $X \to Y$ have the following meaning:

$$M_{XY} = \text{Pr}(X, \mathbf{e}_{XY}^+)$$

and

$$M_{YX} = \Pr(\mathbf{e}_{XY}^-|X).$$

Moreover, show that $M_{XY}M_{YX} = \Pr(X, \mathbf{e})$.

7.15. Definition 7.7 showed how we can divide two factors f_1 and f_2 when each is over the same set of variables $\mathbf{X}$. Let us define division more generally while assuming that factor f_2 is over variables $\mathbf{Y} \subseteq \mathbf{X}$. The result is a factor f over variables $\mathbf{X}$ defined as follows:

$$f(\mathbf{x}) \stackrel{def}{=} \begin{cases} f_1(\mathbf{x})/f_2(\mathbf{y}) & \text{if } f_2(\mathbf{y}) \neq 0 \text{ for } \mathbf{y} \sim \mathbf{x} \\ 0 & \text{otherwise.} \end{cases}$$

Show that

$$\sum_{\mathbf{X}\backslash\mathbf{Y}} f_1/f_2 = \left(\sum_{\mathbf{X}\backslash\mathbf{Y}} f_1\right)/f_2.$$

Use this fact to provide a different definition for the messages passed by the Hugin architecture.

7.9 Proofs

PROOF OF THEOREM 7.1. The first two properties of a jointree are immediately satisfied by the definition of clusters for an elimination tree. To show the third property, suppose that some variable X belongs to clusters $\mathbf{C}_i$ and $\mathbf{C}_j$ of an elimination tree, and let $i\!-\!k \ldots l\!-\!j$ be the the path between i and j (we may have $k = l$, or $k = j$ and $i = l$). By the result in Exercise 7.5, $X \in \mathbf{C}_i$ implies that $X \in \text{vars}(i)$ or $X \in \mathbf{S}_{io}$ for some $o \neq k$. Similarly, $X \in \mathbf{C}_j$ implies that $X \in \text{vars}(j)$ or $X \in \mathbf{S}_{jo}$ for some $o \neq l$. This means that X must appear in some factor on the i-side of edge $i\!-\!k$ and X must appear in some factor on the j-side of edge $l\!-\!j$. Hence, X must belong to the separator of every edge on the path between i and j. Moreover, X must belong to every cluster on the path between i and j. ∎

PROOF OF THEOREM 7.2. By definition of an elimination tree separator, every variable $X \in \mathbf{S}'_{ij}$ must appear in some factor assigned to a node on the i-side of edge $i\!-\!j$ and also in some factor assigned to a node on the j-side of the edge. By the assumptions of this theorem, variable X must then appear in some jointree cluster on the i-side of edge $i\!-\!j$ and some jointree cluster on the j-side of edge $i\!-\!j$. By the jointree property, variable X must also appear in clusters $\mathbf{C}_i$ and $\mathbf{C}_j$. This means that X must appear in separator $\mathbf{S}_{ij} = \mathbf{C}_i \cap \mathbf{C}_j$ and, hence, $\mathbf{S}'_{ij} \subseteq \mathbf{S}_{ij}$. This leads to $\mathbf{C}'_i \subseteq \mathbf{C}_i$ since $\mathbf{C}'_i$ is the union of separators $\mathbf{S}'_{ij}$ and the variables of factor ϕ_i (which must be contained in $\mathbf{C}_i$ by the assumptions of this theorem).

Suppose now that $\mathbf{C}'_i \neq \mathbf{C}_i$ for some node i; then $X \in \mathbf{C}_i$ and $X \notin \mathbf{C}'_i$ for some variable X. We now show that the jointree cannot be minimal. Since $X \notin \mathbf{C}'_i$, then $X \notin \text{vars}(i)$ and $X \notin \mathbf{S}'_{ij}$ for all neighbors j of i. Hence, X can appear only in factors that are assigned to a node on the j-side of edge $i\!-\!j$ for a single neighbor j of i. Consider now the connected subtree of jointree clusters that contain variable X.[3] Consider now a leaf cluster $\mathbf{C}_k$ in this subtree that lies on the i-side of edge $i\!-\!j$. Then X can be removed from cluster $\mathbf{C}_k$ without destroying any of the jointree properties of Definition 7.5. The first property cannot be destroyed by removing variables from clusters. The third property cannot be destroyed

---

[3] The clusters of every variable must form a connected subtree by the jointree property.

by removing a variable from a leaf cluster. The only thing we need to consider now is the second property, that the variables of every network CPT must be contained in some jointree cluster. For this, we note that no CPT that mentions variable X is assigned to node k; otherwise, $X \in \mathbf{S}'_{ij}$ and $X \in \mathbf{C}'_i$, which we know is not the case. Hence, by removing X from cluster $\mathbf{C}_k$, the variables of every network CPT will still be contained in some jointree cluster.   ∎

8

Inference by Conditioning

We discuss in this chapter a class of inference algorithms that are based on the concept of conditioning, also known as case analysis. Conditioning algorithms are marked by their flexible space requirements, allowing a relatively smooth tradeoff between time and space resources.

8.1 Introduction

Reasoning by cases or assumptions is a common form of human reasoning, which is also quite dominant in mathematical proofs. According to this form of reasoning, one can simplify a problem by considering a number of cases where each corresponds to a particular assumption. We then solve each of the cases under its corresponding assumption and combine the results to obtain a solution to the original problem. In probabilistic reasoning, this is best illustrated by the identity,

$$\Pr(\mathbf{x}) = \sum_{\mathbf{c}} \Pr(\mathbf{x}, \mathbf{c}). \tag{8.1}$$

Here we are computing the probability of instantiation $\mathbf{x}$ by considering a number of cases $\mathbf{c}$, computing the probability of $\mathbf{x}$ with each case $\mathbf{c}$, and then adding up the results to get the probability of $\mathbf{x}$.

In general, solving a problem can always be made easier if we make the correct assumptions. For example, we saw in Chapter 6 how evidence can be used to prune network edges, possibly reducing the network treewidth and making it more amenable to inference algorithms. If the given evidence does not lead to enough edge pruning, one can always use case analysis to assume more evidence that leads to the necessary pruning. We present two fundamental applications of this principle in this chapter, one leading to the algorithm of cutset conditioning in Section 8.2 and the other leading to the algorithm of recursive conditioning in Section 8.3. The main property of conditioning algorithms is their flexible space requirements, which can be controlled to allow a smooth tradeoff between space and time resources. This is discussed in Section 8.4 using the algorithm of recursive conditioning. We then turn in Section 8.5 to show how this algorithm can be used to answer multiple queries as we did using the jointree algorithm of Chapter 7. We finally address in Section 8.6 the problem of optimizing the use of available space resources in order to minimize the running time of probabilistic inference.

8.2 Cutset conditioning

Consider the Bayesian network in Figure 8.1 and suppose that we want to answer the query $\Pr(E, D=\text{true}, B=\text{true})$. As we know from Chapter 6, we can prune the edge outgoing from node B in this case, leading to the network in Figure 8.2(a). This network is a polytree

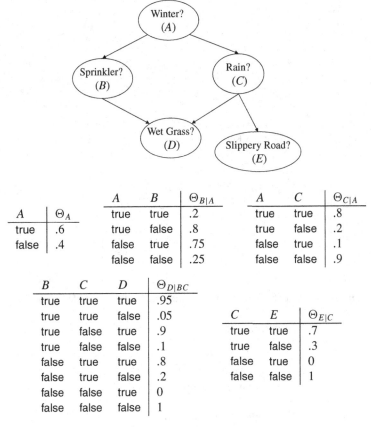

A	Θ_A
true	.6
false	.4

A	B	$\Theta_{B|A}$
true	true	.2
true	false	.8
false	true	.75
false	false	.25

A	C	$\Theta_{C|A}$
true	true	.8
true	false	.2
false	true	.1
false	false	.9

B	C	D	$\Theta_{D|BC}$
true	true	true	.95
true	true	false	.05
true	false	true	.9
true	false	false	.1
false	true	true	.8
false	true	false	.2
false	false	true	0
false	false	false	1

C	E	$\Theta_{E|C}$
true	true	.7
true	false	.3
false	true	0
false	false	1

Figure 8.1: A Bayesian network.

and is equivalent to the one in Figure 8.1 as far as computing $\Pr(E, D{=}\text{true}, B{=}\text{true})$. Hence, we can now answer our query using the polytree algorithm from Chapter 7, which has a linear time and space complexity.

The ability to use the polytree algorithm in this case is due to the specific evidence we have. For example, we cannot use this algorithm to answer the query $\Pr(E, D{=}\text{true})$ since the evidence does not permit the necessary edge pruning. However, if we perform case analysis on variable B we get two queries, $\Pr(E, D{=}\text{true}, B{=}\text{true})$ and $\Pr(E, D{=}\text{true}, B{=}\text{false})$, each of which can be answered using the polytree algorithm. Figure 8.2 depicts the two polytrees $\mathcal{N}_1$ and $\mathcal{N}_2$ corresponding to these queries, respectively. The first query with respect to polytree $\mathcal{N}_1$ leads to the following joint marginal:

E	$\Pr(E, D{=}\text{true}, B{=}\text{true})$
true	.08379
false	.30051

and the second query with respect to polytree $\mathcal{N}_2$ leads to

E	$\Pr(E, D{=}\text{true}, B{=}\text{false})$
true	.22064
false	.09456

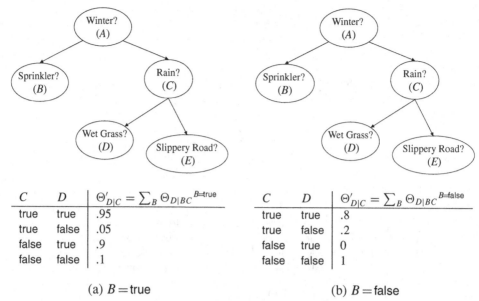

C	D	$\Theta'_{D|C} = \sum_B \Theta_{D|BC}{}^{B=true}$
true	true	.95
true	false	.05
false	true	.9
false	false	.1

C	D	$\Theta'_{D|C} = \sum_B \Theta_{D|BC}{}^{B=false}$
true	true	.8
true	false	.2
false	true	0
false	false	1

(a) $B = \text{true}$ (b) $B = \text{false}$

Figure 8.2: Two polytrees which result from setting the value of variable B.

Adding up the corresponding entries in these factors, we get

E	$\Pr(E, D = \text{true})$
true	.30443
false	.39507

which is the joint marginal for our original query.

We can always use this technique to reduce a query with respect to an arbitrary network into a number of queries that can be answered using the polytree algorithm. In general, we may need to perform case analysis on more than one variable, as shown by the following definition.

Definition 8.1. A set of nodes $\mathbf{C}$ is a *loop-cutset* for a Bayesian network $\mathcal{N}$ if removing the edges outgoing from nodes $\mathbf{C}$ will render the network a polytree. ∎

Every instantiation $\mathbf{c}$ of the loop-cutset allows us to reduce the network $\mathcal{N}$ to a polytree $\mathcal{N}_\mathbf{c}$. We can then compute the marginal over every network variable X as follows:

$$\Pr(X, \mathbf{e}) = \sum_\mathbf{c} \Pr_\mathbf{c}(X, \mathbf{e}, \mathbf{c}),$$

where $\Pr_\mathbf{c}$ is the distribution induced by the polytree $\mathcal{N}_\mathbf{c}$. This method of inference is known as *cutset conditioning* and is one of the first methods developed for inference with Bayesian networks.

Figure 8.3 depicts a few networks and some examples of loop-cutsets. Given a Bayesian network $\mathcal{N}$ with n nodes and a corresponding loop-cutset $\mathbf{C}$ of size s, the method of cutset conditioning requires $O(\exp(s))$ invocations to the polytree algorithm. Moreover, each of these invocations takes $O(n \exp(k))$ time, where k is the maximum number of parents per node in the polytree (k is also the treewidth of resulting polytree). Therefore, cutset conditioning takes $O(n \exp(k + s))$ time, which is exponential in the size of used cutset. Computing a loop-cutset of minimal size is therefore an important task in the context of cutset conditioning, but such a computation is known to be NP-hard.

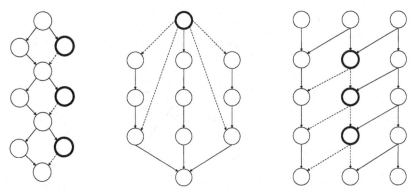

Figure 8.3: Networks and corresponding loop-cutsets (bold circles).

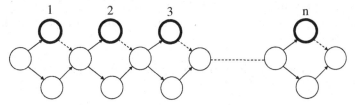

Figure 8.4: A Bayesian network with a loop-cutset that grows linearly with the network size.

The main advantage of cutset conditioning is its modest space requirements. In particular, the algorithm only needs to store the accumulated sum of joint marginals computed by the different calls to the polytree algorithm. Therefore, the space complexity of cutset conditioning is only $O(n \exp(k))$, which is also the space complexity of the polytree algorithm. This is quite important as the space complexity of elimination algorithms that we discussed in Chapters 6 and 7 are exponential in the network treewidth, which can be much larger than k.

8.3 Recursive conditioning

The main problem with cutset conditioning is that a large loop-cutset will lead to a blow up in the number of cases that it has to consider. In Figure 8.4, for example, the depicted loop-cutset contains n variables, leading cutset conditioning to consider 2^n cases (when all variables are binary). However, it is worth mentioning that elimination methods can solve this network in linear time as it has a bounded treewidth.

We now discuss another conditioning method that exploits assumptions differently than cutset conditioning. Specifically, instead of using assumptions to generate a polytree network, we use such assumptions to decompose the network. By decomposition, we mean the process of splitting the network into smaller, disconnected pieces that can be solved independently. Figure 8.5 shows how we can decompose network $\mathcal{N}$ into two subnetworks by performing a case analysis on variable B. That is, if variable B is included in the evidence, then pruning the network will lead to removing the edges outgoing from variable B and then decomposing the network. Figure 8.5 also shows how we can further decompose one of the subnetworks by performing a case analysis on variable C. Note that one of the resulting subnetworks contains a single node and cannot be decomposed further.

We can always use this recursive decomposition process to reduce a query with respect to some network $\mathcal{N}$ into a number of queries with respect to single-node networks.

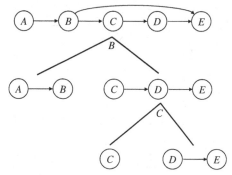

Figure 8.5: Decomposing a Bayesian network by performing a case analysis on variable B and then on variable C.

Specifically, let $\mathbf{C}$ be a set of variables such that pruning the network $\mathcal{N}$ given query $\Pr(\mathbf{e}, \mathbf{c})$ leads to decomposing it into subnetworks $\mathcal{N}_\mathbf{c}^l$ and $\mathcal{N}_\mathbf{c}^r$ with corresponding distributions $\Pr_\mathbf{c}^l$ and $\Pr_\mathbf{c}^r$. We then have

$$\Pr(\mathbf{e}) = \sum_\mathbf{c} \Pr(\mathbf{e}, \mathbf{c}) = \sum_\mathbf{c} \Pr_\mathbf{c}^l(\mathbf{e}^l, \mathbf{c}^l)\Pr_\mathbf{c}^r(\mathbf{e}^r, \mathbf{c}^r), \tag{8.2}$$

where $\mathbf{e}^l/\mathbf{c}^l$ and $\mathbf{e}^r/\mathbf{c}^r$ are the subsets of instantiation $\mathbf{e}/\mathbf{c}$ pertaining to subnetworks $\mathcal{N}_\mathbf{c}^l$ and $\mathcal{N}_\mathbf{c}^r$, respectively. The variable set $\mathbf{C}$ will be called a *cutset* for network $\mathcal{N}$ in this case, to be contrasted with a loop-cutset. Note that each of the networks $\mathcal{N}_\mathbf{c}^l$ and $\mathcal{N}_\mathbf{c}^r$ can be decomposed using the same method recursively until we reach queries with respect to single-node networks.

This is a universal process that can be used to compute the probability of any instantiation. Yet there are many ways in which we can decompose a Bayesian network into disconnected subnetworks. The question then is which decomposition should we use? As it turns out, any decomposition will be valid but some decompositions will lead to less work than others. The key is therefore to choose decompositions that will minimize the amount of work done and to bound it in some meaningful way. We address this issue later but we first provide a formal tool for capturing a certain decomposition policy, which is the subject of the following section.

Before we conclude this section, we highlight three key differences between cutset conditioning and recursive conditioning. First, the role of a cutset is different. In cutset conditioning, it is used to generate a polytree network; in recursive conditioning, it is used to decompose a network into disconnected subnetworks. In Figure 8.1, for example, variable B constitutes a valid loop-cutset since it would render the network a polytree when instantiated. However, instantiating variable B will not decompose the network into smaller subnetworks; hence, B is not a valid cutset in recursive conditioning. Next, there is a single cutset in cutset conditioning that is used at the very top level to generate a number of polytree networks. But there are many cutsets in recursive conditioning, each of which is used at a different level of the decomposition. Finally, the boundary condition in cutset conditioning is that of reaching a polytree network but the boundary condition in recursive conditioning is that of reaching a single-node network.

8.3.1 Recursive decomposition

The method of recursive conditioning employs the principle of divide-and-conquer, which is quite prevalent in computer algorithms. However, the effectiveness of this method is

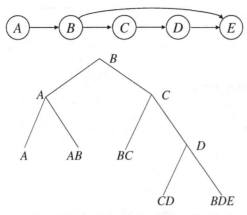

Figure 8.6: A dtree for a Bayesian network. Only CPT variables (families) are shown next to each leaf node. The cutset of each nonleaf node is also shown.

very much dependent upon our choice of cutsets at each level of the recursive process. Recall that the number of cases we have to consider at each level is exponential in the size of the cutset. Therefore, we want to choose our cutsets to minimize the total number of considered cases. Before we can address this issue, we need to introduce a formal tool for capturing the collection of cutsets employed by recursive conditioning.

Definition 8.2. A *dtree* for a Bayesian network is a full binary tree, the leaves of which correspond to the network CPTs. ∎

Recall that a full binary tree is a binary tree where each node has 2 or 0 children. Figure 8.6 depicts an example dtree. Following standard conventions on trees, we will often not distinguish between a tree node T and the tree rooted at that node. That is, T will refer both to a tree and the root of that tree. We will also use vars(T) to denote the set of variables that appear at the leaves of tree T. Moreover, we will use T^p, T^l, and T^r to refer to the parent, left child, and right child of node T, respectively. Finally, an *internal* dtree node is a node that is neither leaf (no children) nor root (no parent).

A dtree T suggests that we decompose its associated Bayesian network by instantiating variables that are shared by its left and right subtrees, T^l and T^r, vars(T^l) ∩ vars(T^r). In Figure 8.6, variable B is the only variable shared by the left and right subtrees of the root node. Performing a case analysis on this variable splits the network into two disconnected networks $\mathbf{N}^l$ and $\mathbf{N}^r$, each of which can be solved independently. What is most important is that subtrees T^l and T^r are guaranteed to be dtrees for the subnetworks $\mathbf{N}^l$ and $\mathbf{N}^r$, respectively. Therefore, each of these subnetworks can be decomposed recursively using these subtrees. The process continues until we reach single-node networks, which cannot be decomposed further.

Algorithm 13, RC1, provides the pseudocode for an implementation of (8.2) that uses dtree T to direct the decomposition process. RC1 is called initially with a dtree T of the Bayesian network and will return the probability of evidence **e** with respect to this network. The algorithm does not compute cutsets dynamically but assumes that they have been precomputed as follows.

Definition 8.3. The *cutset* of a nonleaf node T in a dtree is defined as follows:

$$\text{cutset}(T) \overset{def}{=} (\text{vars}(T^l) \cap \text{vars}(T^r)) \setminus \text{acutset}(T),$$

where acutset(T), called the *a-cutset* of T, is the union of all cutsets associated with ancestors of node T in the dtree. ∎

Algorithm 13 RC1(T, **e**)

---

input:
  T: dtree node
  e: evidence
output: probability of evidence **e**
main:
  1: **if** T is a leaf node **then**
  2:    **return** LOOKUP(T, **e**)
  3: **else**
  4:    $p \leftarrow 0$
  5:    **C** $\leftarrow$ cutset(T)
  6:    **for** each instantiation **c** that is compatible with evidence **e** (**c** $\sim$ **e**) **do**
  7:       $p \leftarrow p +$ RC1(T^l, **ec**)RC1(T^r, **ec**)
  8:    **end for**
  9:    **return** p
 10: **end if**

LOOKUP(T, **e**)
  1: $\Theta_{X|\mathbf{U}} \leftarrow$ CPT associated with dtree node T
  2: **u** $\leftarrow$ instantiation of **U** compatible with evidence **e** (**u** $\sim$ **e**)
  3: **if** X is instantiated to x in evidence **e then**
  4:    **return** $\theta_{x|\mathbf{u}}$
  5: **else**
  6:    **return** $1 \; \{= \sum_x \theta_{x|\mathbf{u}}\}$
  7: **end if**

For the root T of a dtree, we have acutset(T) $= \emptyset$ and cutset(T) is simply vars(T^l) $\cap$ vars(T^r). But for a nonroot node T, the cutsets associated with ancestors of T are excluded from vars(T^l) $\cap$ vars(T^r) since these cutsets are guaranteed to be instantiated when RC1 is called on node T.

Note that the larger the evidence **e** is, the less work that RC1 will do since that would reduce the number of instantiations **c** it has to consider on Line 6. The only space used by algorithm RC1 is that needed to store the dtree in addition to the space used by the recursion stack. The time complexity of RC1 can be assessed by bounding the number of recursive calls it makes as this count is proportional to its running time. For this, we need the following definitions.

Definition 8.4. The *cutset width* of a dtree is the size of its largest cutset. The *a-cutset width* of a dtree is the size of its largest a-cutset. ∎

Moreover, $\mathbf{X}^{\#}$ will denote the number of instantiations of variables **X**.

Theorem 8.1. *The total number of recursive calls made by* RC1 *to a nonroot node T is* $\leq$ acutset(T)$^{\#} = O(\exp(dw))$, *where w is the cutset width of the dtree and d is the depth of node T.* ∎

In Figure 8.7, the cutset width of each dtree is 1. However, the a-cutset width is 7 for the first dtree and is 3 for the second. In general, for a chain of n variables both dtrees will have a cutset width of 1 but the unbalanced dtree will have an a-cutset width of $O(n)$ and

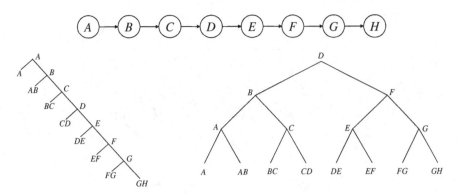

Figure 8.7: Two dtrees for a chain network, with their cutsets explicated. We are only showing the variables of CPTs (families) next to each leaf node.

the balanced dtree will have an a-cutset width of $O(\log n)$. Therefore, RC1 can make an exponential number of recursive calls to some node in the first dtree but will make only a linear number of recursive calls to each node in the second dtree. This example illustrates the impact of the used dtree on the complexity of recursive conditioning. Theorem 8.1 leads to the following complexity of recursive conditioning.

Theorem 8.2. *Given a balanced dtree with n nodes and cutset width w, the time complexity of* RC1 *is $O(n \exp(w \log n))$ and the space it consumes is $O(wn)$.* ■

We provide in Chapter 9 an algorithm that converts an elimination order of width w into a dtree with cutset width $\leq w + 1$. We also describe a method for balancing the dtree while keeping its cutset width $\leq w + 1$. Note that by using such an elimination order, the algorithm of variable elimination will take $O(n \exp(w))$ time to compute the probability of evidence. These results show that RC1 will then take $O(n \exp(w \log n))$ time given such an order. Note, however, that variable elimination will use $O(n \exp(w))$ space as well, whereas RC1 will only use $O(wn)$ space.

We note here that the time complexity of RC1 is not comparable to the time complexity of cutset conditioning (see Exercise 8.4). We also point out that when the width w is bounded, $n \exp(w \log n)$ becomes bounded by a polynomial in n. Therefore, with an appropriate dtree RC1 takes polynomial time on any network with bounded treewidth.

8.3.2 Caching computations

The time complexity of RC1 is clearly not optimal. This is best seen by observing RC1 run on the dtree in Figure 8.8, where all variables are assumed to be binary. Consider the node T marked with the bullet •. This node can be called by RC1 up to sixteen different times, once for each instantiation of acutset$(T) = ABCD$. Note, however, that only variable D appears in the subtree rooted at T. Hence, the sixteen calls to T fall in one of two equivalence classes depending on the value of variable D. This means that the subnetwork corresponding to node T will have only two distinct instances depending on the value of variable D. But RC1 does not recognize this fact, forcing it to solve sixteen instances of this subnetwork even though it can afford to solve only two.

In general, each node T in a dtree corresponds to a number of subnetwork instances. All of these instances share the same structure, which is determined by node T. But each instance will have a different set of (reduced) CPTs and a different evidence depending

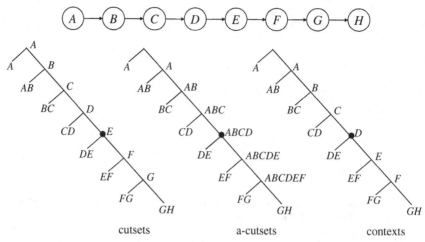

$$\text{cutsets} \qquad\qquad \text{a-cutsets} \qquad\qquad \text{contexts}$$

Figure 8.8: The dtree node labeled with ● can be called sixteen different times by RC1, once for each instantiation of variables $ABCD$.

on the instantiation $\mathbf{e}$ involved in the recursive call RC1(T, $\mathbf{e}$). However, we can bound the number of distinct instances using the following notion.

Definition 8.5. The *context* of node T in a dtree is defined as follows:

$$\text{context}(T) \stackrel{def}{=} \text{vars}(T) \cap \text{acutset}(T).$$

Moreover, the *context width* of a dtree is the size of its maximal context. ∎

Figure 8.8 depicts the context of each node in the given dtree.

The number of distinct instances solved for the subnetwork represented by node T cannot exceed context$(T)^{\#}$. That is, even though node T may be called as many as acutset$(T)^{\#}$ times, these calls will produce no more than context$(T)^{\#}$ distinct results. This is because only the instantiation of vars(T) will actually matter for the subnetwork represented by node T.

Since each distinct instance is characterized by an instantiation of context(T), all RC1 needs to do is save the result of solving each instance indexed by the instantiation of context(T). Any time a subnetwork instance is to be solved, RC1 will check its memory first to see if it has solved this instance previously. If it did, it will simply return the cached answer. If it did not, it will recurse on T, saving its computed solution at the end. This simple caching mechanism will actually drop the number of recursive calls considerably, as we discuss later, but at the expense of using more space.

Algorithm 14, RC2, presents the second version of recursive conditioning which caches its previous computations. All we had to do is include a cache with each node T in the dtree, which is used to store the answers returned by calls to T. RC2 will not recurse on a node T before it checks the cache at T first.

It should be clear that the size of cache$_T$ in RC2 is bounded by context$(T)^{\#}$. In Figure 8.8, the cache stored at each node in the dtree will have at most two entries. Therefore, RC2 will consume only a linear amount of space in addition to what is consumed by RC1. Interestingly enough, this additional space will drop the complexity of recursive conditioning from exponential to linear on this network.

Theorem 8.3. *The number of recursive calls made to a nonroot node T by* RC2 *is* $\leq$ cutset$(T^p)^{\#}$context$(T^p)^{\#}$. ∎

Algorithm 14 RC2(T, **e**)

Each dtree node T has an associated cache cache$_T$ which is indexed by instantiations of context(T). All cache entries are initialized to nil.

---

input:

  T: dtree node

  e: evidence

output: probability of evidence **e**

main:

1: **if** T is a leaf node **then**
2:    **return** LOOKUP(T, **e**)
3: **else**
4:    $\mathbf{Y} \leftarrow$ context(T)
5:    $\mathbf{y} \leftarrow$ instantiation of $\mathbf{Y}$ compatible with evidence **e**, $\mathbf{y} \sim \mathbf{e}$
6:    **if** cache$_T$[**y**] $\neq$ nil **then**
7:      **return** cache$_T$[**y**]
8:    **else**
9:      $p \leftarrow 0$
10:     $\mathbf{C} \leftarrow$ cutset(T)
11:     **for** each instantiation **c** compatible with evidence **e**, $\mathbf{c} \sim \mathbf{e}$ **do**
12:       $p \leftarrow p +$ RC2(T^l, **ec**)RC2(T^r, **ec**)
13:     **end for**
14:     cache$_T$[**y**] $\leftarrow p$
15:     **return** p
16:    **end if**
17: **end if**

In Figure 8.8, each cutset has one variable and each context has no more than one variable. Therefore, RC2 will make no more than four recursive calls to each node in the dtree.

We now define an additional notion that will be quite useful in analyzing the behavior of recursive conditioning.

Definition 8.6. The *cluster* of a dtree node is defined as follows:

$$\text{cluster}(T) \;\overset{def}{=}\; \begin{cases} \text{vars}(T), & \text{if } T \text{ is a leaf node} \\ \text{cutset}(T) \cup \text{context}(T), & \text{otherwise.} \end{cases}$$

The *width* of a dtree is the size of its largest cluster minus one. ■

Lemma 8.1 in the proofs appendix provides some interesting relationships between cutsets, contexts, and clusters. One of these relations is that the cutset and context of a node are always disjoint. This means that cutset(T)$^\#$context(T)$^\#$ = cluster(T)$^\#$. Hence, the following result.

Theorem 8.4. *Given a dtree with n nodes and width w, the time complexity of* RC2 *is* $O(n \exp(w))$ *and the space it consumes is* $O(n \exp(w))$. ■

We present a polytime algorithm in Chapter 9 that constructs a dtree of width $\leq w$ given an elimination order of width w. Together with Theorem 8.4, this shows that recursive conditioning under full caching has the same time and space complexity attained by algorithms based on variable elimination that we discussed in Chapter 6 and 7.

Algorithm 15 RC(T, **e**)

---

input:
  T: dtree node
  e: evidence
output: probability of evidence **e**
main:

  1: **if** T is a leaf node **then**
  2:    **return** LOOKUP(T, **e**)
  3: **else**
  4:    **Y**←context(T)
  5:    **y**← instantiation of **Y** compatible with evidence **e**, **y** ∼ **e**
  6:    **if** cache$_T$[**y**] ≠ nil **then**
  7:       **return** cache$_T$[**y**]
  8:    **else**
  9:       p←0
 10:       **C**←cutset(T)
 11:       **for** each instantiation **c** compatible with evidence **e**, **c** ∼ **e do**
 12:          p←p+RC(T^l, **ec**)RC(T^r, **ec**)
 13:       **end for**
 14:       when cache?(T, **y**), cache$_T$[**y**]←p
 15:       **return** p
 16:    **end if**
 17: **end if**

8.4 Any-space inference

We have presented two extremes of recursive conditioning thus far. On one extreme, no computations are cached, leading to a space complexity of $O(wn)$ and a time complexity of $O(n \exp(w \log n))$, where w is the width of a given dtree and n is the network size. On the other extreme, all previous computations are cached, dropping the time complexity to $O(n \exp(w))$ and increasing the space complexity to $O(n \exp(w))$.

These behaviors of recursive conditioning are only two extremes of an any-space version, which can use as much space as is made available to it. Specifically, recursive conditioning can cache as many computations as available space would allow and nothing more. By changing one line in RC2, we obtain an any-space version, which is given in Algorithm 15, RC. In this version, we include an extra test on Line 14 that is used to decide whether to cache a certain computation. One of the simplest implementations of this test is based on the availability of global memory. That is, cache?(T, **y**) will succeed precisely when global memory has not been exhausted and will fail otherwise. A more refined scheme will allocate a certain amount of memory to be used by each cache. We can control this amount using the notion of a cache factor.

> **Definition 8.7.** A *cache factor* for a dtree is a function cf that maps each node T in the dtree into a number $0 \le cf(T) \le 1$.   ■

The intention here is for $cf(T)$ to be the fraction of cache entries that will be filled by Algorithm RC at node T. That is, if $cf(T) = .2$, then we will only use 20% of the total cache entries required by cache$_T$. Note that Algorithm RC1 corresponds to the case where $cf(T) = 0$ for every node T. Moreover, Algorithm RC2 corresponds to the case where $cf(T) = 1$. For each of these cases, we provided a count of the recursive calls made by recursive conditioning. The question now is: What can we say about the number of recursive calls made by RC under a particular cache factor cf?

As it turns out, the number of recursive calls made by RC under the memory committed by cf will depend on the particular instantiations of context(T) that will be cached on Line 14. However, if we assume that any given instantiation $\mathbf{y}$ of context(T) is equally likely to be cached, then we can compute the average number of recursive calls made by RC and, hence, its average running time.

Theorem 8.5. *If the size of* cache$_T$ *in Algorithm* RC *is limited to* $cf(T)$ *of its full size and if each instantiation of* context(T) *is equally likely to be cached on Line 14 of* RC, *the average number of calls made to a nonroot node* T *in Algorithm* RC *is*

$$\text{ave}(T) \leq \text{cutset}(T^p)^{\#} \left[cf(T^p)\text{context}(T^p)^{\#} + (1 - cf(T^p))\text{ave}(T^p) \right]. \tag{8.3}$$

∎

This theorem is quite important practically as it allows one to estimate the running time of RC under any given memory configuration. All we have to do is add up ave(T) for every node T in the dtree. Note that once ave(T^p) is computed, we can compute ave(T) in constant time. Therefore, we can compute and sum ave(T) for every node T in the dtree in time linear in the dtree size.

Before we further discuss the practical utility of Theorem 8.5, we mention two important points. First, when the cache factor is such that $cf(T) = 0$ or $cf(T) = 1$ for all dtree nodes, we say it is a *discrete* cache factor. In this case, Theorem 8.5 provides an exact count of the number of recursive calls made by RC. In fact, the running time of RC1 and RC2 follow as corollaries of Theorem 8.5:[1]

- When $cf(T) = 0$ for all T:

$$\text{ave}(T) \leq \text{cutset}(T^p)^{\#}\text{ave}(T^p),$$

  and the solution to this recurrence is ave$(T) \leq \text{acutset}(T)^{\#}$. This is basically the result of Theorem 8.1.

- When $cf(T) = 1$ for all T:

$$\text{ave}(T) \leq \text{cutset}(T^p)^{\#}\text{context}(T^p)^{\#},$$

  which is the result of Theorem 8.3.

One of the key questions relating to recursive conditioning is that of identifying the cache factor which would minimize the running time according to Theorem 8.5. We return to this issue later after first discussing an extension of recursive conditioning that allows us to compute probabilistic quantities beyond the probability of evidence.

8.5 Decomposition graphs

A *decomposition graph (dgraph)* is a set of dtrees that share structure (see Figure 8.9). Running RC on a dgraph amounts to running it on each dtree in the graph. Suppose, for

---

[1] The inequalities become equalities when the evidence is empty.

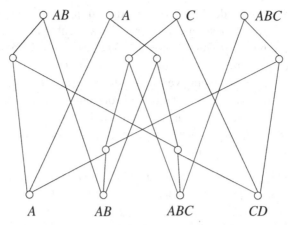

Figure 8.9: A dgraph. The cutset of each root node is shown next to the node.

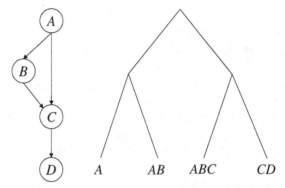

Figure 8.10: A Bayesian network and a corresponding dtree.

example, that we have a dgraph with dtrees $T_1, \ldots, T_n$ and evidence $\mathbf{e}$. Although each call $\text{RC}(T_1, \mathbf{e}), \ldots, \text{RC}(T_n, \mathbf{e})$ will return the same probability of evidence, we may still want to make all calls for the following reason. When RC is applied to a dtree under evidence $\mathbf{e}$, it not only computes the probability of $\mathbf{e}$ but also the marginal over variables in the cutset of the dtree root. Specifically, if $\mathbf{C}$ is the root cutset, then RC will perform a case analysis over all possible instantiations $\mathbf{c}$ of $\mathbf{C}$, therefore computing $\Pr(\mathbf{c}, \mathbf{e})$ as a side effect. Running RC on different dtrees then allow us to obtain different marginals. Consider the dgraph in Figure 8.9, which depicts the cutset $\mathbf{C}_i$ associated with each root node T_i in the dgraph. The call $\text{RC}(T_i, \mathbf{e})$ will then compute the marginal $\Pr(\mathbf{C}_i, \mathbf{e})$ as a side effect.

Since the dtrees of a dgraph share structure, the complexity of RC on a dgraph is better than the sum of its complexity on the isolated dtrees. We later quantify the dgraph complexity in precise terms.

Given a dtree T for a Bayesian network, we can always construct a dgraph that has enough root cutsets to allow the computation of all family marginals for the network. In particular, if node X is not a leaf node in the Bayesian network, then the dgraph will have a root cutset corresponding to its family $X\mathbf{U}$. In this case, running RC on the root will compute the marginal $\Pr(X\mathbf{U}, \mathbf{e})$, as discussed previously. However, if node X is a leaf node, then the dgraph will have a root cutset corresponding to its parents $\mathbf{U}$. In this case, running RC on the root will compute the marginal $\Pr(\mathbf{U}, \mathbf{e})$. But as X is a leaf node, the marginal $\Pr(X\mathbf{U}, \mathbf{e})$ can be easily obtained from $\Pr(\mathbf{U}, \mathbf{e})$. Figure 8.10 depicts a Bayesian

---

Algorithm 16 DT2DG(T)

Uses a cache cache(., .) that maps two dtree nodes to another dtree node. All cache entries initialized to nil.

---

input:

   T: dtree with ≥ 5 nodes

output: the roots of a decomposition graph for dtree T

main:

  1: *Leaves* ← leaf nodes of dtree T
  2: *Tree* ← undirected tree obtained from dtree T by removing edge directions and then removing the dtree root and connecting its neighbors
  3: *Roots* ← ∅ {roots of constructed dgraph}
  4: **for** each leaf node P in *Leaves* **do**
  5:   C ← single neighbor of node P in *Tree*
  6:   R ← a new dtree node with children P and ORIENT(C, P)
  7:   add R to *Roots*
  8: **end for**
  9: **return** *Roots*

ORIENT(C, P)

  1: **if** cache(C, P) ≠ nil **then**
  2:   **return** cache(C, P)
  3: **else if** C is a node in *Leaves* **then**
  4:   R ← C
  5: **else**
  6:   N_1, N_2 ← neighbors of node C in *Tree* such that $N_1 \neq P$ and $N_2 \neq P$
  7:   R ← a new dtree node with children ORIENT(N_1, C) and ORIENT(N_2, C)
  8: **end if**
  9: cache(C, P) ← R
10: **return** R

---

network and a corresponding dtree. Figure 8.9 depicts a dgraph for this Bayesian network that satisfies these properties.

Algorithm 16, DT2DG, takes a dtree for a given Bayesian network and returns a corresponding dgraph satisfying these properties. The algorithm generates an undirected version of the dtree that is then used to induce the dgraph. In particular, for each leaf node P in the dtree associated with CPT $\Theta_{X|\mathbf{U}}$, the algorithm constructs a dtree with its root R having P as one of its children. This guarantees that the cutset of root R will be either $X\mathbf{U}$ or $\mathbf{U}$, depending on whether variable X is a leaf node in the original Bayesian network. The construction of such a dtree can be viewed as orienting the undirected tree toward leaf node P. We will therefore say that Algorithm DT2DG works by orienting the tree towards each of its leaf nodes.

Figure 8.11 depicts a partial trace of Algorithm DT2DG. In particular, it depicts the undirected dtree constructed initially by the algorithm together with the dtree constructed by the algorithm as a result of orienting the tree toward the leaf node labelled with family AB. Figure 8.9 depicts the full dgraph constructed by the algorithm. Note that orienting the tree toward the first leaf node constructs a new dtree. However, successive orientations will reuse parts of the previously constructed dtrees. In fact, one can provide the following guarantee on Algorithm DT2DG.

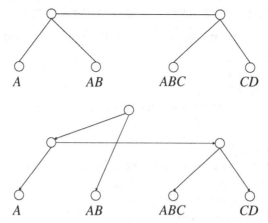

Figure 8.11: An undirected tree constructed by Algorithm DT2DG, and a corresponding dtree that results from orienting the undirected tree toward the leaf node with family AB.

Theorem 8.6. *If Algorithm DT2DG is passed a dtree with $n \geq 5$ nodes and width w, it will return a dgraph with $(5n - 7)/2$ nodes and $4(n - 2)$ edges. Moreover, every dtree in the dgraph will have width w.[2]* ∎

This means that running RC2 on either the dtree or the dgraph will have the same time and space complexity of $O(n \exp(w))$ (see also Exercise 8.8). The constant factors for the dgraph run will be larger as it will generate more recursive calls and will need to maintain more caches.

As we mentioned previously, we present a polytime algorithm in Chapter 9 that constructs a dtree of width $\leq w$ from an elimination order of width w. Given this result, we can then construct a dgraph of width w in this case, allowing recursive conditioning to compute all family marginals in $O(n \exp(w))$ time and space. This is the same complexity achieved by the jointree algorithm of Chapter 7 for computing family marginals.

8.6 The cache allocation problem

We consider in this section the problem of finding a cache factor that meets some given memory constraints while minimizing the running time of recursive conditioning. We restrict ourselves to discrete cache factors where we have full or no caching at each dgraph node. We also discuss both optimal and greedy methods for obtaining discrete cache factors that satisfy some given memory constraints.

We first observe that not all caches are equally useful from a computational viewpoint. That is, two dtree nodes may have equally sized caches yet one of them may increase the running time more than the other if we decide to stop caching at that node. An extreme case of this concerns *dead caches*, whose entries would never be looked up after the cache was filled. In particular, one can verify that if a dtree node T satisfies

$$\text{context}(T) = \text{cluster}(T^p), \tag{8.4}$$

then the cache at node T is dead as its entries would never be looked up if we also cache at its parent T^p (see Exercise 8.9). The cache at a dgraph node T is dead if it has a single

---

[2] If $n < 5$, then $n = 3$ (two node network) or $n = 1$ (single node network) and any dtree for these networks can already compute all marginals. Therefore, there is no need for a dgraph in this case.

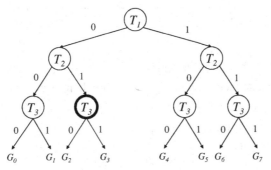

Figure 8.12: Search tree for a dgraph with three internal nodes.

parent and that parent satisfies the previous condition (see Exercise 8.10). We assume that dead caches are removed from a dgraph and, hence, the search for a cache factor applies only to nodes with live caches. It is also common to bypass caching at leaf dgraph nodes especially when the CPTs associated with these leaf nodes have a tabular form, as the CPT can be viewed as a cache in this case (see Exercise 8.11).

To search for a cache factor that minimizes running time, we need an efficient way to compute the running time of RC under a given cache factor. For this, we use the following extension of (8.3) which applies to dgraphs:

$$\text{calls}(T) = \sum_{T^p} \text{cutset}(T^p)^{\#} \Big(cf(T^p)\text{context}(T^p)^{\#} + (1 - cf(T^p))\text{calls}(T^p) \Big). \qquad (8.5)$$

That is, we simply add up the number of calls that a node receives from each of its parents.

8.6.1 Cache allocation by systematic search

The cache allocation problem can be phrased as a systematic search problem in which states in the search space correspond to partial cache factors, that is, a factor that maps each dgraph node into $\{0, 1, ?\}$. The *initial state* in this space is the empty cache factor in which no caching decisions have been made for any nodes in the dgraph. The *goal states* are then complete cache factors where a caching decision was made for every dgraph node. Suppose for example that we are searching for a cache factor over three dgraph nodes T_1, T_2, T_3. This will lead to the search tree in Figure 8.12. In this figure, each node n in the search tree represents a partial cache factor cf. For example, the node in bold corresponds to the partial cache factor $cf(T_1) = 0$, $cf(T_2) = 1$, and $cf(T_3) = ?$. Moreover, if node n is labeled with a dgraph node T_i, then the children of n represent two possible extensions of the cache factor cf: one in which dgraph node T_i will cache all computations (1-child) and another in which dgraph node T_i will cache no computations (0-child). Finally, if node n represents a partial cache factor, then the leaf nodes below n represent all possible completions of this factor.

According to the search tree in Figure 8.12, one always makes a decision on dgraph node T_1 followed by a decision on dgraph node T_2 and then on node T_3. A fixed ordering of dgraph nodes is not necessary as long as the following condition is met: a decision should be made on a dgraph node T_i only after decisions have been made on all its ancestors in the dgraph. We will explain the reason for this constraint later.

In the search tree depicted in Figure 8.12, the leftmost leaf (G_0) represents no caching and the rightmost leaf (G_7) represents full caching. The search trees for this problem have a maximum depth of d, where d is the number of considered nodes in the dgraph.

Algorithm 17 OPTIMAL_CF(Σ, M)

---

input:

Σ: a set of dgraph nodes

M: bound on number of cache entries

output: an optimal cache factor that assigns no more than M cache entries

main:

1:   $cf^o \leftarrow$ a cache factor {global variable}

2:   $c^o \leftarrow \infty$ {global variable}

3:   $cf \leftarrow$ a cache factor that maps each node in Σ to '?'

4:   OPTIMAL_CF_AUX(Σ, cf)

5:   **return** cache factor cf^o

OPTIMAL_CF_AUX(Σ, cf)

1:   **if** cf allocates more than M cache entries or $lower\_bound(cf) \geq c^0$ **then**

2:     **return** {prune node}

3:   **else if** Σ is empty **then** {cf is a complete cache factor}

4:     $c \leftarrow$ number of recursive calls under cache factor cf {Equation 8.5}

5:     **if** $c < c^0$, **then** $c^0 \leftarrow c$ and $cf^0 \leftarrow cf$

6:   **else** {search both extensions of the cache factor}

7:     $T \leftarrow$ choose a dgraph node in Σ that has no ancestors in Σ

8:     $d_1, d_2 \leftarrow$ distinct decisions from $\{0, 1\}$

9:     $cf(T) \leftarrow d_1$, OPTIMAL_CF_AUX($\Sigma \setminus \{T\}$, cf)

10:    $cf(T) \leftarrow d_2$, OPTIMAL_CF_AUX($\Sigma \setminus \{T\}$, cf)

11:    $cf(T) \leftarrow$?

12: **end if**

Given this property, depth-first branch-and-bound is a good search algorithm given its optimality and linear space complexity. It is also an anytime algorithm, meaning that it can always return its best result so far if interrupted, and if run to completion will return the optimal solution. Hence, we will focus on developing a depth-first branch-and-bound search algorithm. It should be noted that the search for a cache factor needs to be done only once per dtree and then can be used to answer multiple queries.

A lower bound

The branch-and-bound algorithm requires a function, $lower\_bound(cf)$, which provides a lower bound on the number of recursive calls made by RC on any completion of the partial cache factor cf. Consider now the completion cf' of a cache factor cf in which we decide to cache at each dgraph node on which cf did not make a decision. This cache factor cf' is the best completion of cf from the viewpoint of running time but it may violate the constraint given on total memory. Yet we will use the number of recursive calls for cf' as a value for $lower\_bound(cf)$ since no completion of the cache factor cf will lead to a smaller number of recursive calls than cf'.

Algorithm 17, OPTIMAL_CF, depicts the pseudocode for our search algorithm. One important observation is that once the caching decision is made on the ancestors of dgraph node T we can compute exactly the number of recursive calls that will be made to dgraph node T; see (8.5). Therefore, when extending a partial cache factor, we always insist on making a decision regarding a dgraph node T for which decisions have been made on all its ancestors, which explains Line 7 of OPTIMAL_CF_AUX. This strategy also leads to

---

Algorithm 18 GREEDY_CF(Σ, M)

---

input:
- Σ: a set of dgraph nodes
- M: bound on number of cache entries

output: a cache factor that assigns no more than M cache entries

main:

1: $cf \leftarrow$ cache factor that maps each node in Σ to 0
2: **while** $M > 0$ and $\Sigma \neq \emptyset$ **do**
3:     compute a score for each dgraph node in Σ
4:     $T \leftarrow$ dgraph node in Σ with largest score
5:     **if** $M \geq \text{context}(T)^{\#}$ **then**
6:         $cf(T) \leftarrow 1$
7:         $M \leftarrow M - \text{context}(T)^{\#}$
8:     **end if**
9:     remove T from Σ
10: **end while**
11: **return** cf

---

improving the quality of the lower bound monotonically as we search deeper in the tree. It also allows us to compute this lower bound for a node T in constant time given that we have the lower bound for its parent in the search tree.

Even though we make caching decisions on parent dgraph nodes before their children, there is still a lot of flexibility with respect to the choice on Line 7. In fact, the specific choice we make here (the order in which we visit dgraph nodes in the search tree) turns out to have a dramatic effect on the efficiency of search. Experimentation has shown that choosing the dgraph node T with the largest $\text{context}(T)^{\#}$ (i.e., the largest cache) can be significantly more efficient than some other basic ordering heuristics.

Algorithm OPTIMAL_CF leaves one more choice to be made: which child of a search tree node to expand first, determined by the specific values of d_1 and d_2 on Line 8 of OPTIMAL_CF_AUX. Experimental results suggest that a choice of $d_1 = 1$ and $d_2 = 0$ tend to work better, in general. This corresponds to trying to cache at particular node before trying not to cache at that node.

8.6.2 Greedy cache allocation

This section proposes a greedy cache allocation method that runs in quadratic time. This is considerably more efficient than the systematic search Algorithm OPTIMAL_CF, which can take exponential time in the worst case. However, the greedy method is not guaranteed to produce optimal cache allocations.

The greedy method starts with no memory allocated to any of the dgraph caches. It then chooses a dgraph node T (one at a time) and allocates $M = \text{context}(T)^{\#}$ cache entries to node T. Suppose now that c_1 is the number of recursive calls made by RC before memory is allocated to the cache at node T. Suppose further that c_2 is the number of recursive calls made by RC after memory has been allocated to the cache at T ($c_2 \leq c_1$). The node T will be chosen greedily to maximize $(c_1 - c_2)/M$: the number of reduced calls per memory unit.

The pseudocode for this method is shown in Algorithm 18, GREEDY_CF. The while-loop will execute $O(n)$ times, where n is the number of dgraph nodes. Note that (8.5) can be evaluated for all nodes in $O(n)$ time, which gives us the total number of recursive calls made by RC under any cache factor cf. Hence, the score of each dgraph node T can be computed in $O(n)$ time by simply evaluating (8.5) twice for all nodes: once while caching at T and another time without caching at T. Under this method, Line 3 will take $O(n^2)$ time, leading to a total time complexity of $O(n^3)$ for Algorithm GREEDY_CF.

However, we will now show that the scores of all candidates can be computed in only $O(n)$ time, leading to a total complexity of $O(n^2)$. The key idea is to maintain for each dgraph node T two auxiliary scores:

- $calls^{cf}(T)$: the number of calls made to node T under cache factor cf as given by (8.5)
- $cpc^{cf}(T)$: the number of calls made to descendants of node T for each call made to T (inclusive of that call) under cache factor cf:

$$cpc^{cf}(T) = \begin{cases} 1, & \text{if } T \text{ is leaf or } cf(T)=1 \\ 1 + cutset(T)^{\#}(cpc^{cf}(T^l) + cpc^{cf}(T^r)), & \text{otherwise.} \end{cases} \quad (8.6)$$

Let cf_2 be the cache factor that results from caching at node T in cache factor cf_1, and let c_1 and c_2 be the total number of recursive calls made by RC under cache factor cf_1 and cf_2, respectively. The score of node T under cache factor cf_1 is then given by (see Exercise 8.14):

$$score^{cf_1}(T) = \frac{c_1 - c_2}{context(T)^{\#}}$$
$$= \frac{cutset(T)^{\#}(calls^{cf_1}(T) - context(T)^{\#})(cpc^{cf_1}(T^l) + cpc^{cf_1}(T^r))}{context(T)^{\#}}. \quad (8.7)$$

Therefore, if we have the auxiliary scores calls(.) and cpc(.) for each node in the dgraph, we can obtain the scores for all dgraph nodes in $O(n)$ time. To initialize calls for each node, we traverse the dgraph such that parent nodes are visited prior to their children. At each node T, we compute calls(T) using (8.5), which can be obtained in constant time since the number of calls to each parent is already known. To initialize cpc for each node, we visit children prior to their parents and compute cpc(T) using (8.6).

To update these auxiliary scores, we first note that the update is triggered by a single change in the cache factor at node T. Therefore, the only affected scores are for nodes that are ancestors and descendants of node T. In particular, for the descendants of node T only calls(.) needs to be updated. Moreover, for node T and its ancestors only cpc(.) needs to be updated.

Bibliographic remarks

Cutset conditioning was the first inference algorithm proposed for arbitrary Bayesian networks [Pearl, 1986a; 1988]. Several refinements were proposed on the algorithm for the purpose of improving its time complexity but at the expense of increasing its space requirements [Darwiche, 1995; Díez, 1996]. Some other variations on cutset conditioning were also proposed as approximate inference techniques (e.g., [Horvitz et al., 1989]). The relation between cutset conditioning and the jointree algorithm was discussed early in Shachter et al. [1994]. The combination of conditioning and variable elimination algorithms was discussed in Dechter [1999; 2003], and Mateescu and Dechter [2005]. The computation of loop-cutsets is discussed in Suermondt et al. [1991], Becker and Geiger [1994],

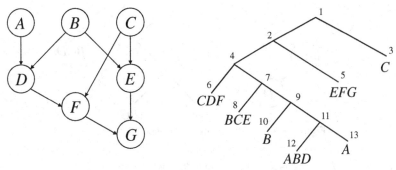

Figure 8.13: A network and a corresponding dtree.

and Becker et al. [1999]. Recursive conditioning was introduced in Darwiche [2001], yet the use of recursive decomposition in Bayesian network inference goes back to Cooper [1990a]. Cache allocation using systematic search was proposed in Allen and Darwiche [2004], and using greedy search in Allen et al. [2004]. Time-space tradeoffs have also been achieved by combining elimination and conditioning algorithms as suggested in Suermondt et al. [1991] and Dechter and Fattah [2001].

8.7 Exercises

8.1. Consider the Bayesian network and corresponding dtree given in Figure 8.13:

    (a) Find $\text{vars}(T)$, $\text{cutset}(T)$, $\text{acutset}(T)$, and $\text{context}(T)$ for each node T in the dtree.

    (b) What is the dtree width?

8.2. Consider the dtree in Figure 8.13. Assuming that all variables are binary:

    (a) How many recursive calls will RC1 make when run on this dtree with no evidence?

    (b) How many recursive calls will RC2 make when run on this dtree with no evidence?

    (c) How many cache hits will occur at node 9 when RC2 is run with no evidence?

    (d) Which of the dtree nodes have dead caches, if any?

    All of these questions can be answered without tracing the recursive conditioning algorithm.

8.3. Figure 8.13 depicts a Bayesian network and a corresponding dtree with height 6. Find a dtree for this network whose height is 3 and whose width is no worse than the width of the original dtree.

8.4. Show a class of networks on which the time complexity of Algorithm RC1 is worse than the time complexity of cutset conditioning. Show also a class of networks on which the time complexity of cutset conditioning is worse than RC1.

8.5. Show that for networks whose loop-cutset is bounded, Algorithm RC2 will have time and space complexity that are linear in the network size if RC2 is run on a carefully chosen dtree.

8.6. Show that if a network is pruned as given in Section 6.9 before applying RC1, then Line 6 of algorithm LOOKUP will never be reached. Recall that pruning a network can only be done under a given query.

8.7. Consider the Bayesian network and dtree shown in Figure 8.14. Create a dgraph for this network by orienting the given dtree with respect to each of its leaf nodes.

8.8. Suppose that Algorithm DT2DG is passed a dtree with n nodes and height $O(\log n)$. Will the generated dgraph also have height $O(\log n)$?

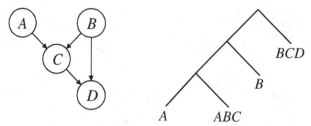

Figure 8.14: A network and a corresponding dtree.

8.9. Let $T_1, T_2, \ldots, T_n$ be a descending path in a dtree where

$$cf(T_i) = \begin{cases} 1, & \text{for } i = 1 \text{ and } i = n \\ 0, & \text{otherwise.} \end{cases}$$

Show that each entry of cache$_{T_n}$ will be retrieved no more than

$$\left(\left(\text{context}(T_1) \cup \bigcup_{i=1}^{n-1} \text{cutset}(T_i)\right) \setminus \text{context}(T_n)\right)^{\#} - 1$$

times after it has been filled by Algorithm RC. Show also that the definition of a dead dtree cache given by Equation 8.4 follows as a special case.

8.10. Show that the definition of a dead cache given by Equation 8.4 is not sufficient for a cache at a dgraph node T. That is, show an example where this condition is satisfied for every parent of dgraph node T yet cache entries at T are retrieved by RC after the cache has been filled.

8.11. Assume that CPTs support an implementation of LOOKUP that takes time and space that are linear in the number of CPT variables (instead of exponential). Provide a class of networks that have an unbounded treewidth yet on which RC will take time and space that are linear in the number of network variables.

8.12. Suppose that you are running recursive conditioning under a limited amount of space. You have already run the depth-first branch-and-bound algorithm and found the optimal discrete cache factor for your dgraph. Suddenly, the amount of space available to you increases. You want to find the new optimal discrete cache factor as quickly as possible.

   (a) What is wrong with the following idea? Simply run the branch-and-bound algorithm on the set of nodes that are not included in the current cache factor, finding the subset of these nodes that will most efficiently fill up the new space. Then add these nodes to the current cache factor.

   (b) How can we use our current cache factor to find the new optimal cache factor more quickly than if we had to start from scratch?

8.13. Consider the dtree in Figure 8.13. Assuming all variables are binary, which internal node will the greedy cache allocation algorithm select first for caching? Show your work.

8.14. Prove Equation 8.7.

8.8 Proofs

The proofs in this section will make use of the following lemma, which is presented in Chapter 9 as Theorem 9.13.

Lemma 8.1. *The following relationships hold:*

(a) $\text{cutset}(T) \cap \text{context}(T) = \emptyset$ *for nonleaf node T*

(b) $\text{context}(T) \subseteq \text{cluster}(T^p)$

(c) $\text{cutset}(T^p) \subseteq \text{context}(T)$

(d) cutset(T_1) $\cap$ cutset(T_2) $= \emptyset$ *for nonleaf nodes* $T_1 \neq T_2$

(e) context(T) $=$ cluster(T) $\cap$ cluster(T^p)

(f) context(T^l) $\cup$ context(T^r) $=$ cluster(T)

PROOF OF THEOREM 8.1. That the number of calls is $\leq$ acutset(T)$^{\#}$ follows from Theorem 8.5 – see the discussion after the theorem statement. To show acutset(T)$^{\#}$ $=$ $O(\exp(dw))$, we note the following:

- The cutsets associated with the ancestors of T are pairwise disjoint by Lemma 8.1(d).
- The size of any of these cutsets is no greater than w.
- acutset(T) is the union of cutset(T'), where T' is an ancestor of T.

Hence, the size of acutset(T) is bounded by dw and acutset(T)$^{\#}$ $= O(\exp(dw))$. ∎

PROOF OF THEOREM 8.2. The height of a balanced dtree is $O(\log n)$ and its a-cutset width must be $O(w \log n)$. Therefore, the number of recursive calls made by RC1 to any node is $O(\exp(w \log n))$. The total number of recursive calls made by RC1 is then $O(n \exp(w \log n))$. As far as the space requirements, the only space used by RC1 is for the recursion stack and dtree storage. ∎

PROOF OF THEOREM 8.3. Follows as a corollary of Theorem 8.5 – see discussion after the theorem statement. ∎

PROOF OF THEOREM 8.4. We have $O(n)$ caches and the size of each cache is $\leq$ context(T)$^{\#}$. Since the dtree has width w, we have context(T)$^{\#}$ $= O(\exp(w))$. Hence, the size of all caches is $O(n \exp(w))$. By Theorem 8.3, the number of recursive calls to each node T is $\leq$ cutset(T^p)$^{\#}$context(T^p)$^{\#}$. Note also that the dtree has width w, cluster(T^p) $=$ cutset(T^p) $\cup$ context(T^p), and the cutset and context are disjoint by Lemma 8.1(a). Hence, cutset(T^p)$^{\#}$context(T^p)$^{\#}$ $= O(\exp(w))$ and the total number of recursive calls is $O(n \exp(w))$. ∎

PROOF OF THEOREM 8.5. We will assume that RC is called on an empty evidence $\mathbf{e} =$ true, leading to a worst-case complexity.

The central concept in this proof is the notion of a T-*type* for a given node T in the dtree. This is basically the set of all calls to node T that agree on the instantiation of context(T) at the time the calls are made. Calls of a particular T-type are guaranteed to return the same probability. In fact, the whole purpose of cache$_T$ is to save the result returned by one member of each T-type so the result can be looked up when other calls in the same T-type are made. Each T-type is identified by a particular instantiation $\mathbf{y}$ of context(T). Hence, there are context(T)$^{\#}$ different T-types, each corresponding to one instantiation of context(T). We further establish the following definitions and observations:

- acpt(T) is defined as the average number of calls of a particular T-type.
- ave(T) is defined as the average number of calls to node T and equals ave(T) $=$ acpt(T)context(T)$^{\#}$.
- A T-type $\mathbf{y}$ is either cached or not cached depending on whether the test cache?($T, \mathbf{y}$) succeeds.
- We have $cf(T)$context(T)$^{\#}$ cached T-types and $(1 - cf(T))$context(T)$^{\#}$ T-types that are not cached.[3]

---

[3] In algorithm RC1, all T-types are noncached ($cf(T)=0$). In RC2, all T-types are cached ($cf(T) = 1$).

- A T^p-type $\mathbf{x}$ is consistent with T-type $\mathbf{y}$ iff instantiations $\mathbf{x}$ and $\mathbf{y}$ agree on the values of their common variables context(T^p) $\cap$ context(T). Calls in a particular T-type $\mathbf{y}$ will be generated recursively only by calls in a consistent T^p-type $\mathbf{x}$.

- There are (context(T^p) \ context(T))$^{\#}$ T^p-types that are consistent with a given T-type $\mathbf{y}$. On average,
  - $cf(T^p)$(context(T^p) \ context(T))$^{\#}$ of them are cached, and
  - $(1 - cf(T^p))$(context(T^p) \ context(T))$^{\#}$ are not cached.

  This follows because each T^p-type is equally likely to be cached. Moreover,
  - On average, a cached T^p-type $\mathbf{x}$ will generate cutset(T^p)$^{\#}$ calls to node T since RC(T^p) will recurse on only one call per cached T^p-type. Only one of these calls is consistent with a particular T-type $\mathbf{y}$ since cutset(T^p) $\subseteq$ context(T) by Lemma 8.1(c).
  - On average, a noncached T^p-type $\mathbf{x}$ will generate acpt(T^p)cutset(T^p)$^{\#}$ calls to node T since RC(T^p) will recurse on every call in a noncached T^p-type. Only acpt(T^p) of these calls are consistent with a particular T-type $\mathbf{y}$.

- acpt(T) can be computed for a particular T-type $\mathbf{y}$ by considering the average number of calls of T^p-types that are consistent with $\mathbf{y}$:

$$\text{acpt}(T) = \alpha\beta + \gamma\sigma$$
$$= (\text{context}(T^p) \setminus \text{context}(T))^{\#} \left[cf(T^p) + (1 - cf(T^p))\text{acpt}(T^p) \right]$$

where

$\alpha = cf(T^p)$(context(T^p) \ context(T))$^{\#}$ (number of cached T^p-types consistent with $\mathbf{y}$)

$\beta = 1$ (number of calls of T-type $\mathbf{y}$ each generates)

$\gamma = (1 - cf(T^p))$(context(T^p) \ context(T))$^{\#}$ (number of noncached T^p-types

   consistent with $\mathbf{y}$)

$\sigma = $ acpt(T^p) (number of calls of T-type $\mathbf{y}$ each generates)

Hence,

$\text{ave}(T)$

$= \text{acpt}(T)\text{context}(T)^{\#}$

$= (\text{context}(T^p) \setminus \text{context}(T))^{\#} \left[cf(T^p) + (1 - cf(T^p))\text{acpt}(T^p) \right] \text{context}(T)^{\#}$

$= (\text{cluster}(T^p) \setminus \text{context}(T))^{\#} \left[cf(T^p) + (1 - cf(T^p))\text{acpt}(T^p) \right] \text{context}(T)^{\#}$

   by Lemma 8.1(b,c)

$= \text{cluster}(T^p)^{\#} \left[cf(T^p) + (1 - cf(T^p))\text{acpt}(T^p) \right]$

   by Lemma 8.1(b)

$= \text{cutset}(T^p)^{\#}\text{context}(T^p)^{\#} \left[cf(T^p) + (1 - cf(T^p))\text{acpt}(T^p) \right]$

   by Lemma 8.1(a,b)

$= \text{cutset}(T^p)^{\#} \left[cf(T^p)\text{context}(T^p)^{\#} + (1 - cf(T^p))\text{acpt}(T^p)\text{context}(T^p)^{\#} \right]$

$= \text{cutset}(T^p)^{\#} \left[cf(T^p)\text{context}(T^p)^{\#} + (1 - cf(T^p))\text{ave}(T^p) \right]$. ∎

PROOF OF THEOREM 8.6. A dtree with n nodes has $(n + 1)/2$ leaves and $(n + 1)/2 - 2$ internal nodes (which are neither leaves nor root). The dgraph generated by Algorithm 16 will have $(n + 1)/2$ leaves corresponding to the dtree leaves and $(n + 1)/2$ roots, one for each leaf node. As for internal dgraph nodes, the algorithm will construct a node on Line 7 of Algorithm ORIENT only if node C is a nonleaf node in the undirected tree *Tree* and if the test cache(C, P) fails. There are $(n + 1)/2 - 2$ nonleaf nodes C in the undirected tree and the test cache(C, P) will fail exactly three times, one time for each neighbor P of C. Hence, the number of internal dgraph nodes constructed is $3((n + 1)/2 - 2)$, leading to a total number of dgraph nodes:

$$\frac{n+1}{2} + \frac{n+1}{2} + 3\left(\frac{n+1}{2} - 2\right) = (5n - 7)/2.$$

Each nonleaf dgraph node will have two outgoing edges. Hence, the total number of dgraph edges is

$$2\left(\frac{n+1}{2} + 3\left(\frac{n+1}{2} - 2\right)\right) = 4(n - 2).$$

Now consider the width of dtrees in the generated dgraph. Consider a dtree T' that results from orienting dtree T toward a leaf node with CPT $\Theta_{X|\mathbf{U}}$. Each node in the resulting dtree T' must then fall into one of these categories:

- A root node: Its cluster must be contained in each of its children's clusters, by Lemma 8.1(c) and since the context of a root node is empty.

- A leaf node: Its cluster in dtree T' is the same as its cluster in dtree T (variables of the CPT associated with the node).

- An internal node R: This node must be constructed on Line 7 of Algorithm ORIENT and correspond to a node C in the original dtree T. We can verify that the variables connected to node R through one of its neighbors in dtree T' are exactly the set of variables connected to node C through one of its neighbors in dtree T. Hence, the cluster of node R in dtree T' is the same as the cluster of node C in dtree T by Lemma 9.5 of Chapter 9.

This shows that the width of dtree T' is the same as the width of dtree T.   ∎

9

Models for Graph Decomposition

We consider in this chapter three models of graph decomposition: elimination orders, jointrees and dtrees, which underly the key inference algorithms we discussed thus far. We present formal definitions of these models, provide polytime, width-preserving transformations between them, and show how the optimal construction of each of these models corresponds in a precise sense to the process of optimally triangulating a graph.

9.1 Introduction

We presented three inference algorithms in previous chapters whose complexity can be exponential only in the network treewidth: variable elimination, factor elimination (jointree), and recursive conditioning. Each one of these algorithms can be viewed as decomposing the Bayesian network in a systematic manner, allowing us to reduce a query with respect to some network into a query with respect to a smaller network. In particular, variable elimination removes variables one at a time from the network, while factor elimination removes factors one at a time and recursive conditioning partitions the network into smaller pieces. We also saw how the decompositional choices made by these algorithms can be formalized using elimination orders, elimination trees (jointrees), and dtrees, respectively. In fact, the time and space complexity of each of these algorithms was characterized using the width of its corresponding decomposition model, which is lower-bounded by the treewidth.

We provide a more comprehensive treatment of decomposition models in this chapter including polytime, width-preserving transformations between them. These transformations allow us to convert any method for constructing low-width models of one type into low-width models of other types. This is important since heuristics that may be obvious in the context of one model may not be obvious in the context of other models.

We start in Section 9.2 by providing some graph-theoretic preliminaries that we use in the rest of the chapter. We then treat elimination orders in Section 9.3, jointrees in Section 9.4, and dtrees in Section 9.5. Our treatment of decomposition models also relates them to the class of triangulated graphs in Section 9.6. In particular, we show that the construction of an optimal elimination order, an optimal jointree, or an optimal dtree are all equivalent to the process of constructing an optimal triangulation of a graph.

9.2 Moral graphs

When discussing a decomposition model for a Bayesian network, we will work with the interaction graph of its factors (CPTs). Recall that an interaction graph for factors $f_1, \ldots, f_n$ is an undirected graph whose nodes correspond to the variables appearing in these factors and whose edges connect variables that appear in the same factor. If the

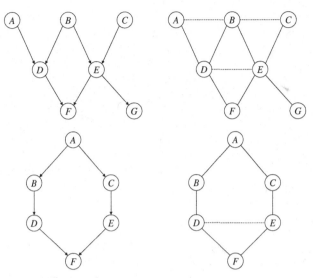

Figure 9.1: DAGs (left) and their corresponding moral graphs (right).

factors $f_1, \ldots, f_n$ are the CPTs of a Bayesian network with DAG G, the interaction graph for these factors can be obtained directly from G by a process known as *moralization*.

Definition 9.1. The *moral graph* of a DAG G is an undirected graph obtained as follows:

- Add an undirected edge between every pair of nodes that share a common child in G.
- Convert every directed edge in G to an undirected edge. ∎

Figure 9.1 depicts two DAGs and their corresponding moral graphs.

The notion of treewidth, which was central to our complexity analysis of inference algorithms, is usually defined for undirected graphs in the graph-theoretic literature. We give this definition in the next section but we note here that the definition can be extended formally to DAGs through their moral graphs.

Definition 9.2. The *treewidth* of a DAG G is the treewidth of its moral graph. ∎

When we say "graph G" in this chapter, we mean an undirected graph; otherwise, we say "DAG G" to mean a directed acyclic graph. The following are more definitions we adopt. A *neighbor* of node X in graph G is a node Y connected to X by an edge. We also say in this case that nodes X and Y are *adjacent*. The *degree* of node X in graph G is the number of neighbors that X has in G. A *clique* in graph G is a set of nodes that are pairwise adjacent, that is, every pair of nodes in the clique are connected by an edge. A *maximal clique* is a clique that is not strictly contained in another clique. Finally, a graph G is *complete* if its nodes form a clique.

9.3 Elimination orders

We discuss the generation of low-width elimination orders in this section using both heuristic and optimal search methods. We also provide polytime, width-preserving algorithms for converting jointrees and dtrees into elimination orders. We start with a formal

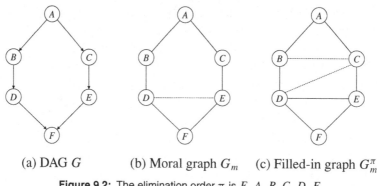

(a) DAG G (b) Moral graph G_m (c) Filled-in graph G_m^π

Figure 9.2: The elimination order π is F, A, B, C, D, E.

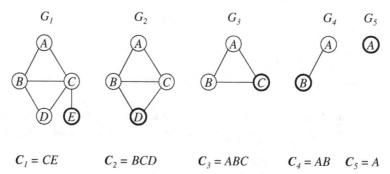

$C_1 = CE$ $C_2 = BCD$ $C_3 = ABC$ $C_4 = AB$ $C_5 = A$

Figure 9.3: The graph and cluster sequence induced by elimination order $\pi = E, D, C, B, A$.

definition of elimination orders and some of their properties, including a definition of treewidth based on such orders.

An *elimination order* for graph G is a total ordering π of the nodes of G, where $\pi(i)$ denotes the ith node in the ordering. To define the properties of elimination orders and to define treewidth based on elimination orders, it is best to first define the notion of eliminating a node from a graph.

> **Definition 9.3.** Let G be a graph and X be a node in G. The result of *eliminating* node X from graph G is another graph obtained from G by first adding an edge between every pair of nonadjacent neighbors of X and then deleting node X from G. The edges that are added during the elimination process are called *fill-in edges*.   ∎

The elimination of node X from graph G ensures that X's neighbors are made into a clique before X is deleted from the graph. Let E be all of the fill-in edges that result from eliminating nodes from graph G according to order π. We will then use G^π to denote the graph that results from adding these fill-in edges to G and write $G^\pi = G + E$. We will also refer to G^π as the *filled-in graph* of G (see Figure 9.2). We also find it useful to define the sequence of graphs and clusters that are induced by an elimination order.

> **Definition 9.4.** The elimination of nodes from graph G according to order π induces a *graph sequence* $G_1, G_2, \ldots, G_n$, where $G_1 = G$ and graph G_{i+1} is obtained by eliminating node $\pi(i)$ from graph G_i. Moreover, the elimination process induces a *cluster sequence* $C_1, \ldots, C_n$, where C_i consists of node $\pi(i)$ and its neighbors in graph G_i.   ∎

Figure 9.3 depicts a graph together with the corresponding graph and cluster sequence induced by the elimination order E, D, C, B, A.

We can now formally define the width of an elimination order in terms of the largest cluster it induces.

Definition 9.5. Let π be an elimination order for graph G and let $\mathbf{C}_1, \ldots, \mathbf{C}_n$ be the cluster sequence induced by applying the elimination order π to graph G. The *width* of elimination order π with respect to graph G is

$$width(\pi, G) \overset{def}{=} \max_{i=1}^{n} |\mathbf{C}_i| - 1.$$

We also extend the definition to DAGs: the width of elimination order π with respect to a DAG is its width with respect to the moral graph of this DAG. ∎

Considering Figure 9.3, the elimination order E, D, C, B, A has width 2 since the largest cluster it induces contains three variables.

Now that we have defined the width of an elimination order, we can also define the treewidth of a graph as the width of its best elimination order.

Definition 9.6. The *treewidth* of a graph G is

$$treewidth(G) \overset{def}{=} \min_{\pi} width(\pi, G),$$

where π is an elimination order for graph G. ∎

When the width of an elimination order π equals the treewidth of graph G, we say that the order is *optimal*. Hence, by finding an optimal elimination order one is also determining the treewidth of the underlying graph.

When the elimination order π does not lead to any fill-in edges when applied to graph G, we say that π is a *perfect elimination order* for graph G. Not every graph admits a perfect elimination order. However, graphs that admit such orders are quite special as they allow us to construct optimal elimination orders in polytime. More on this is presented in Section 9.6.

9.3.1 Elimination heuristics

Since the computation of an optimal elimination order is known to be NP-hard, a number of greedy elimination heuristics have been proposed in literature, suggesting ways to eliminate nodes from a graph G based on local considerations. The following are two of the more common heuristics:

- *min-degree:* Eliminate the node having the smallest number of neighbors.
- *min-fill:* Eliminate the node that leads to adding the smallest number of fill-in edges.

Figure 9.4 depicts a graph where node C has a min-degree score of 4 (number of neighbors) and a fill-in score of 1 (number of fill-in edges). The min-fill heuristic is known to produce better elimination orders than the min-degree heuristic. Moreover, the min-degree heuristic is known to be optimal for graphs whose treewidth is ≤ 2.

It is quite common in practice to combine heuristics. For example, we first select the most promising node to eliminate based on the min-fill heuristic, breaking ties with the min-degree heuristic. We can also apply min-degree first and then break ties using

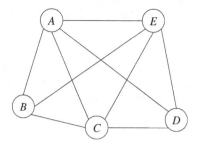

Figure 9.4: Variable C has four neighbors but will add one min-fill edge if eliminated.

min-fill. Stochastic techniques have also proven quite powerful in combining heuristics. These techniques can be applied in two ways:

- The same elimination heuristic is used to eliminate every node but ties are broken stochastically.
- Different elimination heuristics are used to eliminate different nodes, where the choice of a heuristic at each node is made stochastically.

9.3.2 Optimal elimination prefixes

A *prefix* of elimination order π is a sequence of variables τ that occurs at the beginning of order π. For example, if π is the order A, B, C, D, E, then A, B, C is a prefix of π and so is A, B. If τ is a prefix of some optimal elimination order π, we say that τ is an *optimal elimination prefix* as it can be completed to yield an optimal elimination order. The notion of width can be extended to elimination prefixes in the obvious way, that is, by considering the cluster sequence that results from applying the elimination prefix to a graph.

We now discuss four rules for preprocessing undirected graphs to generate optimal prefixes. That is, the preprocessing rules will eliminate a subset of the variables in a graph, while guaranteeing that they represent the prefix of some optimal elimination order. These rules are not complete for arbitrary graphs in the sense that we cannot always use them to produce a complete elimination order. Yet one can use these rules to eliminate as many nodes as possible before continuing the elimination process using heuristic or optimal elimination methods.

As we apply these rules, which can be done in any order, a lower bound (*low*) is maintained on the treewidth of the given graph. Some of the rules will update this bound, while others will use it as a condition for applying the rule. If we start with a graph G and a lower bound *low*, the rules will guarantee the following invariant. If graph G' is the result of applying any of these rules to G and if *low* is updated accordingly, then

$$treewidth(G) = \max(treewidth(G'), low).$$

Therefore, these rules can be used to reduce the computation of treewidth for graph G into the computation of treewidth for a smaller graph G'. Moreover, they are guaranteed to generate only optimal elimination prefixes.

In the following, we assume that graph G has at least one edge and, hence, its treewidth is ≥ 1. We therefore assume that *low* is set initially to 1 unless we have some information

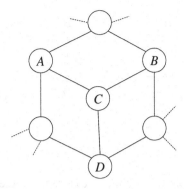

Figure 9.5: Nodes A, B, C, D forming a cube. The dashed edges indicate optional connections to nodes not in the figure.

about the treewidth of G that allows us to set *low* to a higher value, as we discuss in Section 9.3.3.

Some of the rules deal with simplicial and almost simplicial nodes. A *simplicial node* is one for which all of its neighbors are pairwise adjacent, forming a clique. An *almost simplicial node* is one for which all but one neighbor form a clique. The four rules are given next, with proofs of correctness omitted:

- *Simplicial rule:* Eliminate any simplicial node with degree d, updating *low* to max(*low*, d).
- *Almost simplicial rule:* Eliminate any almost simplicial node with degree d as long as *low* $\geq d$.
- *Buddy rule:* If *low* ≥ 3, eliminate any pair of nodes X and Y that have degree 3 each and share the same set of neighbors.
- *Cube rule:* If *low* ≥ 3, eliminate any set of four nodes A, B, C, D forming the structure in Figure 9.5.

We point out here that these four rules are known to be complete for graphs of treewidth ≤ 3.

Some of these rules have well-known special cases. For example, the simplicial rule has these special cases:

- *Islet rule:* Eliminate nodes with degree 0.
- *Twig rule:* Eliminate nodes with degree 1.

These follow since nodes of degree 0 and 1 are always simplicial. The almost simplicial rule has two special cases:

- *Series rule:* Eliminate nodes with degree 2 if *low* ≥ 2.
- *Triangle rule:* Eliminate nodes with degree 3 if *low* ≥ 3 and if at least two of the neighbors are connected by an edge.

We close this section by pointing out that preprocessing rules can be extremely important in practice as the application of these rules may reduce the graph size considerably. In turn, this can improve the running time of expensive algorithms that attempt to obtain optimal elimination orders, as given in Section 9.3.4. It can also improve the quality of elimination orders obtained by elimination heuristics.

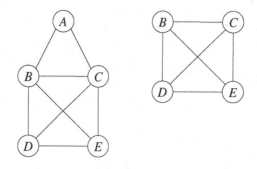

(a) Graph degree is 2   (b) Graph degree is 3

Figure 9.6: The degree of a graph (a) is smaller than the degree of a subgraph (b).

9.3.3 Lower bounds on treewidth

We discuss several lower bounds on treewidth in this section that can be used to empower the preprocessing rules discussed in the previous section. These lower bounds are also critical for algorithms that search for optimal elimination orders, which we discuss in the next section.

Our first lower bound is based on the cliques of a graph.

Theorem 9.1. *If graph G has a clique of size n, then treewidth(G) $\geq n - 1$.*   ■

Another lower bound is the degree of a graph (see Exercise 9.12), which is easier to compute.

> **Definition 9.7.** The *degree* of a graph is the minimum number of neighbors attained by any of its nodes.   ■

Both of the previous bounds are typically too weak. A better bound can be based on the following observations. First, the treewidth of any subgraph cannot be larger than the treewidth of the graph containing it. Second, the degree of a subgraph may be higher than the degree of the graph containing it. Figure 9.6 depicts such an example. These two observations lead to a lower bound called *graph degeneracy*.

> **Definition 9.8.** The *degeneracy* of a graph is the maximum degree attained by any of its subgraphs.   ■

The degeneracy of a graph is also known as the *maximum minimum degree* (MMD). The MMD lower bound is easily computed by generating a sequence of subgraphs, starting with the original graph and then obtaining the next subgraph by removing a minimum-degree node. The MMD is then the maximum degree attained by any of the generated subgraphs (see Exercise 9.14). Consider for example the graph in Figure 9.6(a). To compute the MMD lower bound for this graph, we generate subgraphs by removing nodes according to the order A, B, C, D, E. The resulting subgraphs have the respective degrees $2, 3, 2, 1, 0$. Hence, the MMD lower bound is 3, which is also the graph degeneracy.

An even better lower bound can be obtained by observing that one can contract edges in a graph without raising its treewidth, where contracting edge $X–Y$ corresponds to replacing its nodes X and Y with a new node that is adjacent to the union of their neighbors (see Exercise 9.13). Figure 9.7 depicts an example of edge contraction.

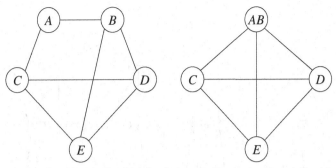

Figure 9.7: Contracting the edge A–B, which leads to removing nodes A and B, while adding the new node AB. Contracting the edge increases the graph degree from 2 to 3 in this case.

Definition 9.9. A graph *minor* is obtained by any combination of removing nodes, removing edges, or contracting edges in a graph. ∎

Definition 9.10. The *contraction degeneracy* of a graph is the maximum degree attained by any of its minors. ∎

The contraction degeneracy lower bound is also known as the *MMD+* lower bound. Although MMD+ provides tighter bounds than MMD, it is unfortunately NP-hard to compute. However, there are heuristic approximations of MMD+ that are relatively easy to compute yet can still provide tighter bounds than MMD. These approximations consider only a small subset of graph minors, which are obtained by contracting edges. The two dominant approximations work by contracting an edge incident to a minimum-degree node. This includes the *MMD+(min-d)* approximation, which works by contracting the edge between a minimum-degree node and one of its minimum-degree neighbors. The other approximation is *MMD+(least-c)*, which works by contracting the edge between a minimum-degree node and a neighbor with which it shares the least number of common neighbors. In practice, MMD+(least-c) leads to better bounds but MMD+(min-d) can be computed more efficiently.

9.3.4 Optimal elimination orders

In this section, we consider two algorithms for computing optimal elimination orders. The first algorithm is based on depth-first search, which is marked by its modest space requirements and its anytime behavior. The second algorithm is based on best-first search, which has a better time complexity but consumes more space. The two algorithms can be motivated by the different search spaces they explore.

Depth-first search

Figure 9.8 depicts the search space explored by depth-first search, which is a tree with leaf nodes corresponding to distinct variable orders. This tree will then have size $O(n!)$, where n is the total number of variables. One can explore this tree in a depth-first manner, which can be implemented in $O(n)$ space. However, one can improve the performance of the algorithm by using lower bounds on treewidth to prune some parts of the search tree. Suppose for example that we already have an elimination order π with width w_π and are currently exploring an elimination prefix τ whose width is w_τ. Suppose further that we have a lower bound b on the treewidth of subgraph G_τ, which results from applying the

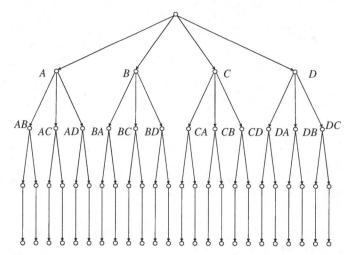

Figure 9.8: The search tree for an elimination order over four variables.

prefix τ to graph G. If $\max(w_\tau, b) \geq w_\pi$, then we clearly cannot improve on the order π, since every completion of prefix τ is guaranteed to have an equal or higher width. In this case, we can simply abandon the exploration of prefix τ and the corresponding search subtree.

Algorithm 19, DFS_OEO, provides the pseudocode for the proposed algorithm. The global order π is a seed to the algorithm, which can be chosen based on elimination heuristics such as min-fill. The better this seed is, the more efficient the algorithm will be as this will lead to more pruning on Line 5. Algorithm DFS_OEO is an anytime algorithm as it can be stopped at any point during its execution, while guaranteeing that the global variable π will be set to the best elimination order found thus far.

Best-first search

As mentioned previously, DFS_OEO has a linear space complexity. However, its main disadvantage is its time complexity that stems from the tree it needs to search. In particular, if the algorithm is given a graph G with n variables, it may have to fully explore a tree of size $O(n!)$ (the number of elimination orders for n variables is $n!$). One can improve the time complexity of Algorithm DFS_OEO considerably if one exploits the following theorem.

Theorem 9.2. *If τ_1 and τ_2 are two elimination prefixes that contain the same set of variables, then applying these prefixes to a graph G will lead to identical subgraphs, G_{τ_1} and G_{τ_2}.* ∎

Given this result, the search tree of Algorithm DFS_OEO will contain many replicated parts. For example, the subtree that results from eliminating variable A and then variable B will be the same as the subtree that results from eliminating variable B and then variable A (see Figure 9.8). If we merge these identical subtrees, we reach the graph structure given in Figure 9.9. Each node in this graph structure corresponds to a set of variables that can be eliminated in any order. However, regardless of what order τ is used to eliminate these variables, the subgraph G_τ will be the same and, hence, this subgraph need not be solved multiple times as is done by Algorithm DFS_OEO.

One can avoid these redundant searches using a best-first search. The basic idea here is to maintain two lists of search nodes: an open list and a closed list. The open list contains search nodes that need to be explored, while the closed list contains search nodes

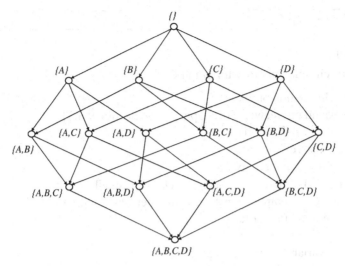

Figure 9.9: The search graph for an elimination order over four variables.

Algorithm 19 DFS_OEO(G)

input:

   G: graph

output: optimal elimination order for graph G

main:

   $\pi \leftarrow$ some elimination order for graph G {global variable}
   $w_\pi \leftarrow$ width of order π {global variable}
   $\tau \leftarrow$ empty elimination prefix
   $w_\tau \leftarrow 0$
   DFS_OEO_AUX(G, τ, w_τ)
   return π

DFS_OEO_AUX(G_τ, τ, w_τ)

1: **if** subgraph G_τ is empty **then** {τ is a complete elimination order}
2:    **if** $w_\tau < w_\pi$, **then** $\pi \leftarrow \tau$ and $w_\pi \leftarrow w_\tau$ {found better elimination order}
3: **else**
4:    $b \leftarrow$ lower bound on treewidth of subgraph G_τ {see Section 9.3.3}
5:    **if** $\max(w_\tau, b) \geq w_\pi$, **return** {prune as we cannot improve on order π}
6:    **for** each variable X in subgraph G_τ **do**
7:       $d \leftarrow$ number of neighbors X has in subgraph G_τ
8:       $G_\rho \leftarrow$ result of eliminating variable X from subgraph G_τ
9:       $\rho \leftarrow$ result of appending variable X to prefix τ
10:      $w_\rho \leftarrow \max(w_\tau, d)$
11:      DFS_OEO_AUX(G_ρ, ρ, w_ρ)
12:   **end for**
13: **end if**

Algorithm 20 BFS_OEO(G)

---

input:

   G: graph

output: optimal elimination order for graph G

  1: $\tau \leftarrow$ empty elimination prefix

  2: $b \leftarrow$ lower bound on treewidth of graph G {see Section 9.3.3}

  3: $OL \leftarrow \{(G, \tau, 0, b)\}$ {open list}

  4: $CL \leftarrow$ empty list {closed list}

  5: **while** open list OL not empty **do**

  6:     $(G_\tau, \tau, w_\tau, b_\tau) \leftarrow$ node from open list OL with smallest $\max(w_\tau, b_\tau)$

  7:     **if** subgraph G_τ is empty **then** {τ is a complete and optimal order}

  8:        **return** elimination order τ

  9:     **else**

 10:       **for** each variable X in subgraph G_τ **do**

 11:          $d \leftarrow$ number of neighbors X has in subgraph G_τ

 12:          $G_\rho \leftarrow$ result of eliminating variable X from subgraph G_τ

 13:          $\rho \leftarrow$ result of appending variable X to prefix τ

 14:          $w_\rho \leftarrow \max(w_\tau, d)$

 15:          $b_\rho \leftarrow$ lower bound on treewidth of subgraph G_ρ {see Section 9.3.3}

 16:          **if** OL contains $(G_{\rho'}, \rho', w_{\rho'}, b_{\rho'})$ and $G_{\rho'} = G_\rho$ **then**

 17:            **if** $w_\rho < w_{\rho'}$ **then** {prefix ρ is better}

 18:              remove $(G_{\rho'}, \rho', w_{\rho'}, b_{\rho'})$ from open list OL

 19:              add $(G_\rho, \rho, w_\rho, b_\rho)$ to open list OL

 20:            **end if**

 21:          **else if** CL does not contain $(G_{\rho'}, \rho', w_{\rho'}, b_{\rho'})$ where $G_{\rho'} = G_\rho$ **then**

 22:            add $(G_\rho, \rho, w_\rho, b_\rho)$ to open list OL {G_ρ never visited before}

 23:          **end if**

 24:       **end for**

 25:       add $(G_\tau, \tau, w_\tau, b_\tau)$ to closed list CL

 26:     **end if**

 27: **end while**

---

that have already been explored. Algorithm 20, BFS_OEO, provides the pseudocode for best-first search, which represents a search node by a tuple $(G_\tau, \tau, w_\tau, b_\tau)$. Here τ is an elimination prefix, w_τ is its width, G_τ is the subgraph that results from applying the prefix τ to the original graph G, and b_τ is a lower bound on the treewidth of subgraph G_τ.[1] Algorithm BFS_OEO iterates by choosing a most promising node from the open list, that is, a node $(G_\tau, \tau, w_\tau, b_\tau)$ that minimizes $\max(w_\tau, b_\tau)$. This corresponds to choosing an elimination prefix τ that leads to the most optimistic estimate of treewidth. If the prefix τ is complete, the algorithm terminates while declaring that τ is an optimal elimination order. Otherwise, the algorithm will generate the children $(G_\rho, \rho, w_\rho, b_\rho)$ of node $(G_\tau, \tau, w_\tau, b_\rho)$, which result from eliminating one variable from subgraph G_τ.

Before adding the new node $(G_\rho, \rho, w_\rho, b_\rho)$ to the open list, the algorithm will check if the subgraph G_ρ appears on either the closed list or the open list. If no duplicate subgraph

---

[1] In a practical implementation, one does not keep track of the full prefix τ but just a pointer back to the parent of the search node. The prefix can be recovered by following these pointers to the root node of the search graph.

is found, the node is added to the open list and the search continues. If a duplicate subgraph is found on the closed list, then it has already been expanded and the node $(G_\rho, \rho, w_\rho, b_\rho)$ will be discarded. If a duplicate subgraph is found on the open list and it turns out to have a worse prefix than ρ, then the duplicate is removed and the new node $(G_\rho, \rho, w_\rho, b_\rho)$ is added to the open list; otherwise, the new node will be discarded. Note that a duplicate cannot exist on both the open and closed lists simultaneously (see Exercise 9.15). Proving the correctness of this algorithm is left to Exercise 9.16.

We note here that although the search graph explored by BFS_OEO has size $O(2^n)$ – which is a considerable improvement over the search tree of size $O(n!)$ explored by DFS_OEO – Algorithm BFS_OEO may have to store $O(2^n)$ nodes in the worst case. This is to be contrasted with the linear number of nodes stored by Algorithm DFS_OEO.

We close this section by emphasizing again the importance of preprocessing rules that we discussed in Section 9.3.2. In particular, by using these rules one can generate an optimal prefix τ and then run Algorithm DFS_OEO or Algorithm BFS_OEO on the smaller subgraph G_τ instead of the original graph G. This can lead to exponential savings in some cases as it may considerably reduce the size of search spaces explored by these algorithms. These preprocessing rules can also be used at each node in the search space. That is, when considering a search node $(G_\tau, \tau, w_\tau, b_\tau)$, we can run these preprocessing rules to find an optimal prefix ϱ of subgraph G_τ and then continue the search using the subgraph $G_{\tau\varrho}$ and prefix $\tau\varrho$. This can reduce the search space considerably but it may also increase the computational overhead associated with the processing at each search node. It may then be necessary to apply only a select subset of preprocessing rules at each search node to balance the preprocessing cost with the savings that result from searching a smaller space.

9.3.5 From jointrees to elimination orders

Jointrees were introduced in Chapter 7 and are given a more comprehensive treatment in Section 9.4. Here we define a polytime algorithm for converting a jointree to an elimination order of no greater width. In particular, given a DAG G and a corresponding jointree, Algorithm 21, JT2EO, will return an elimination order for G whose width is no greater than the jointree width.

Algorithm 21 JT2EO$(\mathcal{T}, \mathbf{C})$

input:

　$(\mathcal{T}, \mathbf{C})$:　　jointree for DAG G

output: elimination order π for DAG G where $width(\pi, G)$ is no greater than the width of jointree $(\mathcal{T}, \mathbf{C})$

main:

1: $\pi \leftarrow$ empty elimination order
2: **while** there is more than one node in tree $\mathcal{T}$ **do**
3: 　　remove a node i from $\mathcal{T}$ that has a single neighbor j
4: 　　append variables $\mathbf{C}_i \setminus \mathbf{C}_i \cap \mathbf{C}_j$ to order π
5: **end while**
6: append variables $\mathbf{C}_r$ to order π, where r is the remaining node in tree $\mathcal{T}$
7: **return** elimination order π

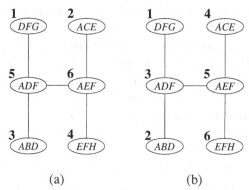

(a) (b)

Figure 9.10: A jointree with two numberings of the clusters according to the order in which JT2EO may visit them.

JT2EO is effectively simulating the process of factor elimination, as discussed in Chapter 7. In particular, at each step JT2EO picks up a leaf cluster $\mathbf{C}_i$ that has a single neighbor $\mathbf{C}_j$ and eliminates those variables that appear in cluster $\mathbf{C}_i$ but nowhere else in the tree. Note that if a variable appears in cluster $\mathbf{C}_i$ and in some other cluster $\mathbf{C}_k$ in the tree, it must also appear in the neighbor $\mathbf{C}_j$ of $\mathbf{C}_i$ and, hence, in $\mathbf{C}_i \cap \mathbf{C}_j$. This is why JT2EO eliminates variables $\mathbf{C}_i \setminus \mathbf{C}_i \cap \mathbf{C}_j$.

As stated, JT2EO leaves a number of choices undetermined: choosing node i to remove next from the jointree and choosing the order in which variables $\mathbf{C}_i \setminus \mathbf{C}_i \cap \mathbf{C}_j$ are appended to the elimination order. None of these choices actually matter to the guarantee provided by the algorithm. Hence, JT2EO can be thought of as defining a class of elimination orders whose width is no greater than the given jointree width. Consider Figure 9.10 as an example. The figure contains a jointree with two numberings of the clusters according to the order in which JT2EO may remove them. The ordering in Figure 9.10(a) gives rise to the elimination order $\pi = G, C, B, H, D, \{AEF\}$, where $\{AEF\}$ means that these variables can be in any order. The numbering in Figure 9.10(b) leads to the elimination order $\pi = G, B, D, C, A, \{EFH\}$. These orderings have width 2, which is also the width of the given jointree.

Note that JT2EO may generate elimination orders whose width is less than the width of the jointree. This can only happen when the jointree is not optimal, that is, the jointree width is greater than the treewidth of the corresponding graph. Exercise 9.17 suggests a method for proving the correctness of JT2EO.

9.3.6 From dtrees to elimination orders

Dtrees were introduced in Chapter 8 and are given a more comprehensive treatment in Section 9.5. Here we present a polytime algorithm for converting a dtree into an elimination order of no greater width. In particular, we show that each dtree specifies a partial elimination order and any total order consistent with it is guaranteed to have no greater width.

Definition 9.11. A variable X is *eliminated* at a dtree node T precisely when X belongs to cluster$(T) \setminus$ context(T). ∎

Note that if T is a nonleaf node, then cluster$(T) \setminus$ context(T) is precisely cutset(T). Figures 9.11(b) and 9.12(b) depict two dtrees and the variables eliminated at each of their nodes.

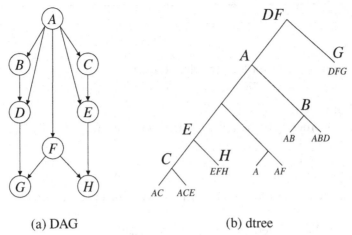

(a) DAG   (b) dtree

Figure 9.11: Converting a dtree into an elimination order. The variables eliminated at a dtree node are shown next to the node.

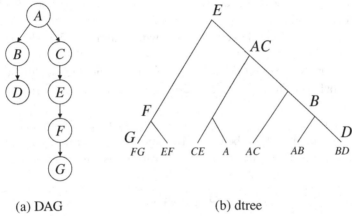

(a) DAG   (b) dtree

Figure 9.12: Converting a dtree into an elimination order. The variables eliminated at a dtree node are shown next to the node.

Theorem 9.3. *Given a dtree for DAG G, every variable in G is eliminated at some unique node in the dtree.* ∎

Theorem 9.3 allows us to view each dtree as inducing a partial elimination order.

Definition 9.12. A dtree induces the following partial elimination order on its variables: For every pair of variables X and Y, we have $X < Y$ if the dtree node at which X is eliminated is a descendant of the dtree node at which Y is eliminated. We also have $X = Y$ if the two variables are eliminated at the same dtree node. ∎

In the dtree of Figure 9.11(b), we have $C < E < A < D$ and $D = F$. We also have $H < E$, $B < A$, $G < D$, and $G < F$. Any total elimination order consistent with these constraints will have a width that is no greater than the dtree width.

Theorem 9.4. *Given a dtree of width w for DAG G, let π be a total elimination order for G which is consistent with the partial elimination order defined by the dtree. We then have $width(\pi, G) \leq w$.* ∎

Algorithm 22 DT2EO(T)
___
input:

   T: dtree

output: elimination order π for the variables of dtree T

main:

  1: **if** T is a leaf node **then**

  2:    **return** any ordering of variables cluster(T) \ context(T)

  3: **else**

  4:    $\pi_l \leftarrow$ DT2EO(T^l)

  5:    $\pi_r \leftarrow$ DT2EO(T^r)

  6:    $\pi \leftarrow$ a merge of suborders π_l and π_r preserving the order of variables within each suborder

  7:    append variables cluster(T) \ context(T) to order π

  8:    **return** elimination order π

  9: **end if**
___

The following two orders are consistent with the dtree in Figure 9.11(b): $\pi_1 = C, H, E, B, A, G, D, F$ and $\pi_2 = H, C, B, E, G, A, F, D$. For another example, consider Figure 9.12(b), which depicts a dtree with width 2. The elimination order $\pi = G, F, D, B, A, C, E$ has width 1 and is consistent with the dtree. An elimination order consistent with a dtree will have a width lower than the dtree width only when the dtree is not optimal. The dtree in Figure 9.12(b) is not optimal as the corresponding DAG has treewidth 1.

Algorithm 22, DT2EO, provides pseudocode for generating an elimination order from a dtree based on the method described here. The algorithm performs a post-order traversal of the dtree in which a dtree node is visited after each of its children has been visited.

9.4 Jointrees

We discussed jointrees in Chapter 7, where we showed how they represent the basis of the jointree algorithm. We discuss jointrees in more detail in this section, starting with a repetition of their definition from Chapter 7.

Definition 9.13. A *jointree* for a DAG G is a pair $(\mathcal{T}, \mathbf{C})$ where $\mathcal{T}$ is a tree and $\mathbf{C}$ is a function that maps each node i in tree $\mathcal{T}$ into a label $\mathbf{C}_i$ called a *cluster*. The jointree must satisfy the following properties:

  1. The cluster $\mathbf{C}_i$ is a set of nodes from the DAG G.

  2. Each family in the DAG G must appear in some cluster $\mathbf{C}_i$.

  3. If a node appears in two clusters $\mathbf{C}_i$ and $\mathbf{C}_j$, it must also appear in every cluster $\mathbf{C}_k$ on the path connecting nodes i and j in the jointree. This is known as the *jointree property*.

The *separator* of edge $i-j$ in a jointree is defined as $\mathbf{S}_{ij} = \mathbf{C}_i \cap \mathbf{C}_j$. The *width* of a jointree is defined as the size of its largest cluster minus one. ∎

A jointree is sometimes called a *junction tree*.

Figure 9.13 depicts a DAG and two corresponding jointrees. The jointree in Figure 9.13(b) has three nodes: 1, 2, 3. Moreover, the cluster of node 1 is $\mathbf{C}_1 = ABC$, the

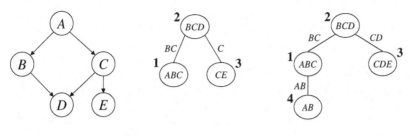

(a) DAG (b) Minimal jointree (c) Nonminimal jointree

Figure 9.13: A DAG and two corresponding jointrees.

separator of edge 1–2 is $\mathbf{S}_{12} = BC$, and the jointree width is 2. The jointree Figure 9.13(c) has four nodes and width 2. Jointrees can also be defined for undirected graphs, as given in Exercise 9.25. According to this definition, a jointree for the moral graph G_m of DAG G will also be a jointree for DAG G.

To gain more insight into jointrees, we note that the following transformations preserve all three properties of a jointree for DAG G:

- *Add variable*: We can add a variable X of G to a cluster $\mathbf{C}_i$ as long as $\mathbf{C}_i$ has a neighbor $\mathbf{C}_j$ that contains X.
- *Merge clusters*: We can merge two neighboring clusters $\mathbf{C}_i$ and $\mathbf{C}_j$ into a single cluster $\mathbf{C}_k = \mathbf{C}_i \cup \mathbf{C}_j$, where $\mathbf{C}_k$ will inherit the neighbors of $\mathbf{C}_i$ and $\mathbf{C}_j$.
- *Add cluster*: We can add a new cluster $\mathbf{C}_j$ and make it a neighbor of an existing cluster $\mathbf{C}_i$ as long as $\mathbf{C}_j \subseteq \mathbf{C}_i$.
- *Remove cluster*: We can remove a cluster $\mathbf{C}_j$ if it has a single neighbor $\mathbf{C}_i$ and $\mathbf{C}_j \subseteq \mathbf{C}_i$.

The jointree in Figure 9.13(c) results from applying two transformations to the jointree in Figure 9.13(b). The first transformation is adding the cluster $\mathbf{C}_4 = AB$. The second transformation is adding variable D to cluster $\mathbf{C}_3$.

These transformations have practical applications. For example, the addition of variable D as indicated previously allows the jointree algorithm to compute the marginal over variables CDE. This marginal will not be computed when the algorithm is applied to the jointree in Figure 9.13(b). Moreover, by merging two clusters we eliminate the separator connecting them from the jointree. Recall that the Shenoy-Shafer algorithm of Chapter 7 needs to create factors over each separator in the jointree. Hence, this transformation can be used to reduce the space requirements of the algorithm. This will typically increase the running time as the merging of clusters will typically lead to creating a larger cluster, and the algorithm's running time is exponential in the size of clusters. This transformation can therefore be the basis for time-space tradeoffs using the jointree algorithm.

We say that a jointree for DAG G is *minimal* if it ceases to be a jointree for G once we remove a variable from any of its clusters. The jointree in Figure 9.13(c) is therefore not minimal. As we mentioned previously, we may want to work with a nonminimal jointree as it allows us to obtain additional quantities that may not be obtainable from a minimal jointree (see also Section 10.3 for another application).

9.4.1 From elimination orders to jointrees

We now discuss a polytime, width-preserving algorithm for generating a jointree from an elimination order. The algorithm consists of two parts, where the first part is concerned

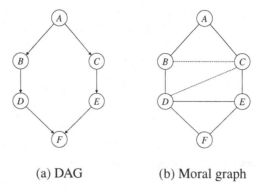

(a) DAG   (b) Moral graph

Figure 9.14: A DAG and its moral graph. The elimination order F, A, B, C, D, E has width 2 with respect to the DAG and its moral graph.

with the construction of jointree clusters and the second part is concerned with connecting them into a tree structure that satisfies the jointree property.

Constructing the clusters

Given a DAG G and a corresponding elimination order π, we show in this section how to generate a set of clusters with the following properties. First, the size of every cluster is $\leq width(\pi, G) + 1$. Second, the clusters satisfy Conditions 1 and 2 of Definition 9.13 for a jointree. Third, the clusters can be connected into a tree structure that satisfies Condition 3 of Definition 9.13 (the jointree property). However, the connection algorithm is given in the following section.

The method for generating such clusters is relatively simple.

Theorem 9.5. *Let $C_1, \ldots, C_n$ be the cluster sequence that results from applying the elimination order π to the moral graph G_m of DAG G. Every family of DAG G must be contained in some cluster of the sequence.* ∎

The clusters $C_1, \ldots, C_n$ will therefore satisfy the first two conditions of a jointree. Moreover, the size of each cluster must be $\leq width(\pi, G) + 1$ by Definition 9.5 of width. Hence, if we use these clusters to construct the jointree, the width of the jointree will be $\leq width(\pi, G)$.

Consider now Figure 9.14, which depicts a DAG G, its moral graph G_m, and an elimination order $\pi = F, A, B, C, D, E$ that has width 2. The cluster sequence induced by applying this order to the moral graph G_m is

$$\mathbf{C}_1 = FDE, \quad \mathbf{C}_2 = ABC, \quad \mathbf{C}_3 = BCD, \quad \mathbf{C}_4 = CDE, \quad \mathbf{C}_5 = DE, \quad \mathbf{C}_6 = E. \tag{9.1}$$

Every family of DAG G is contained in one of these clusters.

As we see later, the cluster sequence induced by an elimination order can always be connected into a tree structure that satisfies the jointree property. This is due to the following result.

Theorem 9.6. *Let $C_1, \ldots, C_n$ be the cluster sequence induced by applying elimination order π to graph G. For every $i < n$, the variables $C_i \cap (C_{i+1} \cup \ldots \cup C_n)$ are contained in some cluster C_j where $j > i$. This is known as the running intersection property of the cluster sequence.* ∎

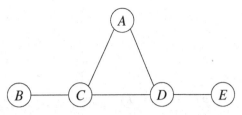

Figure 9.15: A graph.

Consider again the cluster sequence in (9.1). We have $C_1 \cap (C_2 \cup \ldots \cup C_6) = DE$. Moreover, the set DE is contained in cluster C_4. The same property can be verified for the remaining clusters in this sequence.

The cluster sequence induced by an elimination order may contain nonmaximal clusters, that is, ones that are contained in other clusters of the sequence. Note, however, that it is impossible for a cluster C_i to be contained in another cluster C_j that follows it in the sequence, $j > i$ (see Exercise 9.18). Yet it is possible that a cluster C_i will be contained in an earlier cluster C_j, $j < i$. In this case, we can remove cluster C_i from the sequence but we must reorder the sequence if we want to maintain the running intersection property (which is needed when connecting the clusters into a jointree at a later stage).

Consider, for example, the following cluster sequence that is induced by applying the elimination order $\pi = A, B, C, D, E$ to the graph in Figure 9.15:

$$C_1 = ACD, \quad C_2 = BC, \quad C_3 = CD, \quad C_4 = DE, \quad C_5 = E.$$

Cluster C_3 is nonmaximal as it is contained in cluster C_1. If we simply remove this cluster, we get the sequence

$$C_1 = ACD, \quad C_2 = BC, \quad C_4 = DE, \quad C_5 = E,$$

which does not satisfy the running intersection property since $C_1 \cap (C_2 \cup C_4 \cup C_5) = CD$ is not contained in any of the clusters that follow C_1. However, we can recover this property if we move cluster C_1 to the position that cluster C_3 used to assume:

$$C_2 = BC, \quad C_1 = ACD, \quad C_4 = DE, \quad C_5 = E.$$

More generally, we have the following result.

Theorem 9.7. *Let $C_1, \ldots, C_n$ be a cluster sequence satisfying the running intersection property. Suppose that $C_i \supseteq C_j$ where $i < j$ and i is the largest index satisfying this property. The following cluster sequence satisfies the running intersection property:*[2]

$$C_1, \ldots, C_{i-1}, C_{i+1}, \ldots, C_{j-1}, C_i, C_{j+1}, \ldots, C_n. \qquad \blacksquare$$

That is, we can remove the nonmaximal cluster C_j from the sequence and still maintain the running intersection property as long as we place cluster C_i in its position.

Assembling the jointree

Now that we have a cluster sequence that satisfies the first two conditions of a jointree, we will see how we can connect these clusters into a tree structure that satisfies the

---

[2] It is impossible to have another C_k such that $i < k \neq j$ and $C_i \supseteq C_k$, assuming that no cluster in the sequence can be contained in a following cluster. This last property continues to hold after removing a nonmaximal cluster, as suggested by the theorem.

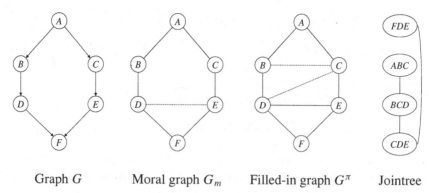

Graph G Moral graph G_m Filled-in graph G^π Jointree

Figure 9.16: The jointree is constructed by EO2JT_1 using order $\pi = F, A, B, C, D, E$. The clusters of the jointree are ordered from top to bottom so they satisfy the running intersection property.

Algorithm 23 EO2JT_1(G, π)

---

input:

G: DAG

π: elimination order for DAG G

output: jointree for DAG G with width equal to $width(\pi, G)$

main:

1: $G_m \leftarrow$ moral graph of DAG G
2: $\mathbf{C}_1, \ldots, \mathbf{C}_n \leftarrow$ cluster sequence induced by applying order π to graph G_m
3: $\Sigma \leftarrow$ a cluster sequence resulting from removing nonmaximal clusters from sequence $\mathbf{C}_1, \ldots, \mathbf{C}_n$ according to Theorem 9.7
4: **return** jointree assembled from cluster sequence Σ according to Theorem 9.8

---

third condition of a jointree (i.e., the jointree property). We provide two methods for this purpose, each with different properties. The first method is based on the following result.

Theorem 9.8. *Let* $\mathbf{C}_1, \ldots, \mathbf{C}_n$ *be a cluster sequence that satisfies the running intersection property. The following procedure will generate a tree of clusters that satisfies the jointree property: Start first with a tree that contains the single cluster* $\mathbf{C}_n$*. For* $i = n - 1, \ldots, 1$*, add cluster* $\mathbf{C}_i$ *to the tree by connecting it to a cluster* $\mathbf{C}_j$ *that contains* $\mathbf{C}_i \cap (\mathbf{C}_{i+1} \cup \ldots \cup \mathbf{C}_n)$*.* ∎

Algorithm 23, EO2JT_1, provides pseudocode for converting an elimination order into a jointree of equal width based on the method described here. Figure 9.16 depicts a jointree constructed by EO2JT_1. We can verify that this tree satisfies the conditions of a jointree (Definition 9.13). Figure 9.17 contains another example of a DAG and its moral graph, and Figure 9.18 depicts a jointree for this DAG constructed also using EO2JT_1.

The previous method for constructing jointrees was based on Theorems 9.5, 9.6, and 9.7 for constructing clusters, and on Theorem 9.8 for connecting them into a tree structure. A more general method for constructing jointrees is based on the following result, which bypasses Theorems 9.6 and 9.7 when constructing clusters and replaces the connection method of Theorem 9.8 by a more general method.

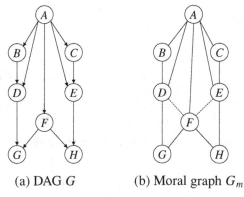

(a) DAG G (b) Moral graph G_m

Figure 9.17: A DAG and its moral graph.

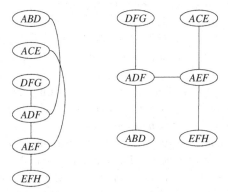

Figure 9.18: A jointree for the network in Figure 9.17 (with two different layouts) induced by the elimination order B, C, G, D, A, E, F, H. The clusters of the jointree on the left are ordered from top to bottom so they satisfy the running intersection property.

Algorithm 24 EO2JT_2(G,π)

input:

   G: DAG

   π: elimination order for DAG G

output: jointree for DAG G with width equal to $width(\pi, G)$

main:

  1: $G_m \leftarrow$ moral graph of DAG G
  2: $\mathbf{C}_1, \ldots, \mathbf{C}_n \leftarrow$ cluster sequence induced by applying order π to graph G_m
  3: $\mathcal{S} \leftarrow$ set of maximal clusters in the sequence $\mathbf{C}_1, \ldots, \mathbf{C}_n$
  4: **return** Jointree assembled from clusters in $\mathcal{S}$ according to Theorem 9.9

Theorem 9.9. *Let $\mathbf{C}_1, \ldots, \mathbf{C}_n$ be the set of maximal clusters that result from applying an elimination order to a graph. Define a cluster graph by including an edge $\mathbf{C}_i$–$\mathbf{C}_j$ between every pair of clusters and let $|\mathbf{C}_i \cap \mathbf{C}_j|$ be the cost of this edge. A tree that spans these clusters satisfies the jointree property if and only if it is a maximum spanning tree of the cluster graph.* ∎

Algorithm 24, EO2JT_2, provides pseudocode for a method EO2JT_2 that converts an elimination order into a jointree of equal width using this method. Figure 9.19 provides an example with two jointrees constructed for the same set of clusters using EO2JT_2.

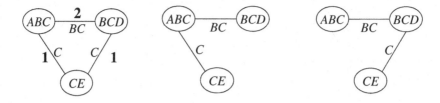

(a) Cluster graph   (b) Maximal spanning tree (c) Maximal spanning tree

Figure 9.19: Connecting clusters into a tree that satisfies the jointree property.

Algorithm EO2JT_2 provides an opportunity to generate jointrees that minimize some secondary cost measure. In particular, suppose that each separator has a secondary cost, depending for example on the cardinalities of variables involved. Suppose further that our goal is to generate a jointree that minimizes this secondary cost measure, which we assume is obtained by adding up the secondary costs of separators in a jointree. Algorithms for generating spanning trees can indeed be extended so they not only return the maximal spanning tree as described by Theorem 9.9 but also one that minimizes the secondary cost measure.

We note here that a maximum spanning tree can be computed using either Kruskal's algorithm, which can be implemented in $O(n^2 \log n)$ time, or Prim's algorithm, which can be implemented in $O(n^2 + n \log n)$ time, where n is the number of clusters in the jointree. Standard implementations of these algorithms require $O(n^2)$ space as they need to represent all possible edges and their weights. Even though algorithm EO2JT_2 is more general than algorithm EO2JT_1, the latter is more commonly used in practice as it can be implemented more efficiently. In particular, the assembly of a jointree using EO2JT_1 can be implemented in $O(n^2)$ time and $O(n)$ space.

Now that we have procedures for converting between elimination orders and jointrees in both directions while preserving width, we can define the treewidth of DAG G as the width of its best jointree. This also shows a strong connection between the complexity of the variable elimination algorithm of Chapter 6 and the jointree algorithm of Chapter 7.

9.4.2 From dtrees to jointrees

The following theorem provides a polytime, width-preserving method for converting a dtree into a jointree.

Theorem 9.10. *The clusters of a dtree satisfy the jointree property.* ∎

Since there is a one-to-one correspondence between the families of DAG G and the clusters of leaf nodes in a dtree, Theorem 9.10 shows that the clusters of a dtree are immediately a jointree with the same width. Figure 9.20 depicts a DAG and a corresponding dtree with its clusters explicated. One can verify that this tree satisfies all three conditions of a jointree. Note however that we have many nonmaximal clusters in this jointree. In fact, by applying the jointree transformations discussed previously, we can reduce this jointree to either of these in Figure 9.19. Even though the jointree induced by a dtree is usually not minimal, it is special in two ways:

- Each cluster has at most three neighbors, leading to a *binary jointree*.
- The tree contains exactly $2n - 1$ clusters, where n is the number of nodes in DAG G.

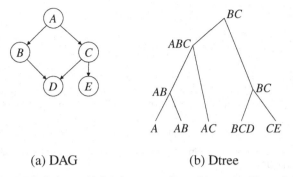

     (a) DAG   (b) Dtree

Figure 9.20: A dtree with its clusters explicated (see also Figure 9.22).

These properties are important for the Shenoy-Shafer algorithm given in Chapter 7, which needs a jointree with these properties to guarantee the complexity bounds discussed in that chapter.

9.4.3 Jointrees as a factorization tool

We close our discussion of jointrees by an important property, showing how we can read independence information from the jointree which are guaranteed to hold in the DAG for which it was constructed.

Theorem 9.11. *Let G be a DAG and let $(\mathcal{T}, \mathbf{C})$ be a corresponding jointree. For every edge $i{-}j$ in the jointree, let $\mathbf{Z} = \mathbf{C}_i \cap \mathbf{C}_j$, $\mathbf{X}$ be the union of clusters on the i-side of edge $i{-}j$, and $\mathbf{Y}$ be the union of clusters on the j-side of edge $i{-}j$. Then $\mathbf{X} \setminus \mathbf{Z}$ and $\mathbf{Y} \setminus \mathbf{Z}$ are d-separated by $\mathbf{Z}$ in DAG G.* ∎

Consider for example the jointree in Figure 9.18 and the clusters $\mathbf{C}_i = ADF$ and $\mathbf{C}_j = AEF$, leading to $\mathbf{Z} = AF$, $\mathbf{X} = ABDFG$ and $\mathbf{Y} = ACEFH$. Theorem 9.11 claims that $\mathbf{X} \setminus \mathbf{Z} = BDG$ is d-separated from $\mathbf{Y} \setminus \mathbf{Z} = CEH$ by $\mathbf{Z} = AF$ in the DAG of Figure 9.17(a). This can be verified since all paths between BDG and CEH are indeed blocked by AF.

The importance of Theorem 9.11 is due mostly to the following result, which shows how a jointree of DAG G can be used to factor any distribution that is induced by G.

Theorem 9.12. *Given a probability distribution $\Pr(\mathbf{X})$ that is induced by a Bayesian network and given a corresponding jointree, the distribution can be expressed in the following form:*

$$\Pr(\mathbf{X}) = \frac{\displaystyle\prod_{\text{jointree node } i} \Pr(\mathbf{C}_i)}{\displaystyle\prod_{\text{jointree edge } i{-}j} \Pr(\mathbf{C}_i \cap \mathbf{C}_j)}. \tag{9.2}$$

∎

This factored form of a probability distribution will prove quite useful in some of the approximate inference methods we discuss in Chapter 14. For an example, consider the jointree in Figure 9.18. According to Theorem 9.12, any probability distribution induced by the DAG in Figure 9.17(a) can be expressed as:

$$\Pr(A, B, C, D, E, F, G, H)$$
$$= \frac{\Pr(DFG)\Pr(ACE)\Pr(ADF)\Pr(AEF)\Pr(ABD)\Pr(EFH)}{\Pr(DF)\Pr(AE)\Pr(AF)\Pr(AD)\Pr(EF)}.$$

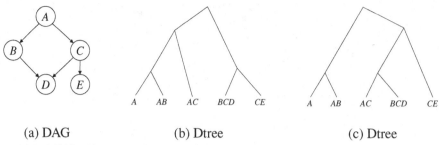

| (a) DAG | (b) Dtree | (c) Dtree |

Figure 9.21: A DAG with two corresponding dtrees. Each leaf node in a dtree is labeled with its corresponding family from the DAG.

9.5 Dtrees

We discussed dtrees in Chapter 8, where we showed the role they play in driving the recursive conditioning algorithm. In that chapter, a dtree was defined for a Bayesian network as a full binary tree whose leaf nodes are in one-to-one correspondence with the network CPTs. Here we provide a more general definition that is based on DAGs instead of Bayesian networks.

> **Definition 9.14.** A *dtree* for DAG G is a pair (T, vars) where T is a full binary tree whose leaf nodes are in one-to-one correspondence with the families of DAG G, and vars(.) is a function that maps each leaf node L in the dtree to the corresponding family vars(L) of DAG G. ∎

Figure 9.21 depicts a DAG with two of its dtrees. Dtrees can also be defined for undirected graphs, as given in Exercise 9.26.

Recall that a full binary tree is a binary tree where each node has 2 or 0 children. Hence, a full binary tree that has n leaf nodes must also have $n - 1$ nonleaf nodes. Following standard conventions on trees, we will often not distinguish between a tree node T and the tree rooted at that node, that is, T will refer both to a tree and the root of that tree. We also use T^p, T^l, and T^r to refer to the parent, left child, and right child of node T, respectively. Finally, an *internal* dtree node is one that is neither leaf (no children) nor root (no parent).

We extend the function vars(T) to nonleaf nodes in a dtree as follows:

$$\text{vars}(T) \stackrel{def}{=} \text{vars}(T^l) \cup \text{vars}(T^r).$$

We also recall the following definitions from Chapter 8:

$$\text{cutset}(T) \stackrel{def}{=} (\text{vars}(T^l) \cap \text{vars}(T^r)) \setminus \text{acutset}(T) \quad \text{for nonleaf node } T$$

$$\text{acutset}(T) \stackrel{def}{=} \bigcup_{T^\star \text{ ancestor of } T} \text{cutset}(T^\star)$$

$$\text{context}(T) \stackrel{def}{=} \text{vars}(T) \cap \text{acutset}(T)$$

$$\text{cluster}(T) \stackrel{def}{=} \begin{cases} \text{vars}(T), & \text{if } T \text{ is a leaf node} \\ \text{cutset}(T) \cup \text{context}(T), & \text{otherwise.} \end{cases}$$

The *width* of a dtree is defined as the size of its largest cluster minus one. Figure 9.22 depicts the cutsets, contexts, and clusters of a dtree.

The cutsets, contexts, and clusters associated with dtree nodes satisfy some important properties that were used in Chapter 8 and are appealed to in various proofs in this chapter.

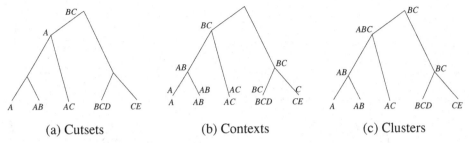

(a) Cutsets   (b) Contexts   (c) Clusters

Figure 9.22: The cutsets, contexts, and clusters of a dtree. Note that for a nonleaf node, the cluster is the union of cutset and context.

Algorithm 25 EO2DT(G,π)
___

input:

G: DAG

π: elimination order for G

output: dtree for DAG G having width $\leq width(\pi, G)$

main:

1: $\Sigma \leftarrow$ leaf dtree nodes corresponding to families of DAG G

2: **for** $i = 1$ to length of order π **do**

3:    $T_1, \ldots, T_n \leftarrow$ trees in Σ which contain variable $\pi(i)$

4:    remove $T_1, \ldots, T_n$ from Σ

5:    add $T = $ COMPOSE($T_1, \ldots, T_n$) to Σ

6: **end for**

7: **return** dtree which results from composing the dtrees in Σ

___

Theorem 9.13. *The following hold for dtree nodes:*

(a) cutset(T) $\cap$ context(T) $= \emptyset$ *for nonleaf node* T

(b) context(T) $\subseteq$ cluster(T^p)

(c) cutset(T^p) $\subseteq$ context(T)

(d) cutset(T_1) $\cap$ cutset(T_2) $= \emptyset$ *for nonleaf nodes* $T_1 \neq T_2$

(e) context(T) $=$ cluster(T) $\cap$ cluster(T^p)

(f) context(T^l) $\cup$ context(T^r) $=$ cluster(T).   ∎

Of particular importance are Property (a), which says that the cutset and context of a node are disjoint, and Property (d), which says that cutsets of various nodes are mutually disjoint.

We next treat three different subjects relating to dtrees. First, we provide a polytime, width-preserving algorithm for converting an elimination order into a dtree, leaving the conversion of a jointree to a dtree to Exercise 9.21. We then provide a more direct, heuristic method for constructing low-width dtrees based on the concept of hypergraph partitioning. We finally treat the subject of balancing dtrees, which was critical to some of the complexity results in Chapter 8.

9.5.1 From elimination orders to dtrees

In this section, we provide a polytime algorithm for converting an elimination order into a dtree of no greater width. The method, EO2DT, is given in Algorithm 25 and

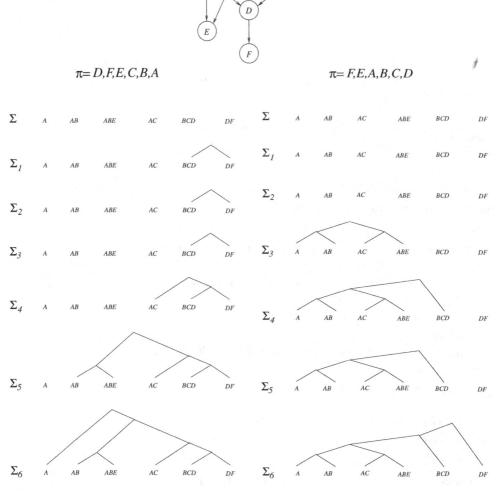

Figure 9.23: A step-by-step construction of dtrees for the included DAG using algorithm EO2DT and two different elimination orders. Each step i depicts the trees present in Σ of EO2DT after processing variable $\pi(i)$.

is based on the COMPOSE operator, which takes a set of binary trees $T_1, \ldots, T_n$ and connects them (arbitrarily) into a single binary tree COMPOSE$(T_1, \ldots, T_n)$. EO2DT starts initially by constructing a set of dtrees, each containing a single node and corresponding to one of the families in DAG G. It then considers variables $\pi(1), \pi(2), \ldots, \pi(n)$ in that order. Each time EO2DT considers a variable $\pi(i)$, it composes all binary trees that mention variable $\pi(i)$. It finally returns the composition of all remaining binary trees. Two examples of this algorithm are depicted in Figure 9.23. In the first example, we use the order $\pi = D, F, E, C, B, A$ of width 3 to generate a dtree of width 2. In the second example, we use the elimination order $\pi = F, E, A, B, C, D$ of width 2 and generate a dtree of the same width.

Theorem 9.14. *Let G be a DAG and let π be a corresponding elimination order of width w. The call* EO2DT(G, π) *returns a dtree of width $\leq w$ for DAG G.* ∎

Algorithm 26 HG2DT(H, E)

input:

H:	hypergraph
E:	hyperedges

output: dtree whose leaves correspond to the nodes of H

main:

1: $T \leftarrow$ new dtree node
2: **if** H has only one node $N_\mathbf{F}$ **then**
3:     vars(T)$\leftarrow$**F**
4: **else**
5:     $H^l, H^r \leftarrow$ two approximately equal parts of H that minimize $E^\star$ below
6:     $E^\star \leftarrow$ hyperedges that are not in E, yet include nodes in H^l and in H^r
7:     $T^l \leftarrow$HG2DT($H^l, E^\star \cup E$)
8:     $T^r \leftarrow$HG2DT($H^r, E^\star \cup E$)
9: **end if**
10: **return** dtree T

We now have width-preserving procedures for converting between elimination orders and dtrees in both directions, allowing us to define the treewidth of DAG G as the width of its best dtree. This also shows the strong connection between the complexity of variable elimination from Chapter 6 and the complexity of recursive conditioning from Chapter 8.

9.5.2 Constructing dtrees by hypergraph partitioning

In this section, we provide a heuristic method for constructing low-width dtrees based on hypergraph partitioning. Given our algorithms for converting dtrees to elimination orders and jointrees, the presented method will be immediately available for the construction of low-width elimination orders and jointrees.

A *hypergraph* is a generalization of a graph in which an edge is permitted to connect an arbitrary number of nodes rather than exactly two. The edges of a hypergraph are referred to as *hyperedges*. The problem of *hypergraph partitioning* is to find a way to split the nodes of a hypergraph into k approximately equal parts such that the number of hyperedges connecting vertices in different parts is minimized. Hypergraph partitioning algorithms are outside the scope of this chapter, so we restrict our discussion to how they can be employed in constructing dtrees.

Generating a dtree for a DAG using hypergraph partitioning is fairly straightforward. The first step is to express the DAG G as a hypergraph H:

- For each family **F** in DAG G, we add a node $N_\mathbf{F}$ to H.
- For each variable V in DAG G, we add a hyperedge to H that connects all nodes $N_\mathbf{F}$ such that $V \in \mathbf{F}$.

An example of this method is depicted in Figure 9.24. Notice that any full binary tree whose leaves correspond to the vertices of hypergraph H is a dtree for our DAG. This observation allows us to design a simple recursive procedure HG2DT using hypergraph partitioning to produce a dtree, which is given in Algorithm 26.

Algorithm HG2DT, which is called initially with $E = \emptyset$, attempts to minimize the cutset of each dtree node T it constructs. To see this, observe that every time we partition the

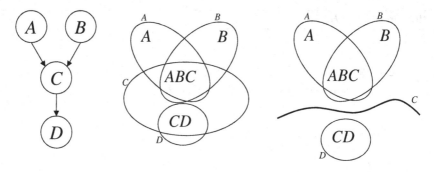

(a) From DAG to hypergraph   (b) Partitioned hypergraph

Figure 9.24: Partitioning a hypergraph.

hypergraph H into H^l and H^r, we attempt to minimize the number of hyperedges in $E^\star$. By construction, these hyperedges correspond to DAG variables that are shared by families in H^l and those in H^r (and have not already been cut by previous partitions). Hence, by attempting to minimize the hyperedges $E^\star$, we are actually attempting to minimize the cutset associated with dtree node T. Note that we do not make any direct attempt to minimize the width of the dtree, which depends on both the cutset and context of a dtree node. However, we see next that cutset minimization combined with a balanced partition is a good heuristic for width minimization. In particular, we next show that this method can be viewed as a relaxation of a method that is guaranteed to construct a dtree of width $\leq 4w + 1$ if the DAG has treewidth w.

Suppose now that every dtree node T satisfies the following conditions, which are guaranteed to hold for some dtree if the DAG has treewidth w:

- The cutset of T has no more than $w + 1$ variables.
- No more than two thirds of the variables in context(T) appear in either vars(T^l) or vars(T^r).

Under these conditions, the dtree is guaranteed to have a width $\leq 4w + 1$ (see Exercise 9.23). Note, however, that HG2DT does not generate dtrees that satisfy these conditions. Instead, it tries to minimize the cutset without ensuring that its size is bounded by $w + 1$. Moreover, it generates balanced partitions without necessarily ensuring that no more than two thirds of the context is in either part. Hence, HG2DT can be viewed as a relaxation of a method that constructs dtrees under these conditions.

9.5.3 Balancing dtrees

In this section, we present an algorithm for balancing a dtree while increasing its width by no more than a constant factor. The algorithm is similar to EO2DT except that the composition process is not driven by an elimination order. Instead, it is driven by applying an operation known as *tree contraction,* which is explained next.

The operation of tree contraction is applied to a directed tree, which is a tree identified with a root. Each node in the tree has a single parent, which is the neighbor of that node that is closest to the root (dtrees are directed trees). Contraction simply absorbs some of the tree nodes into their neighbors to produce a smaller tree. To absorb node N_1 into node N_2 is to transfer the neighbors of N_1 into neighbors of N_2 and to remove node N_1

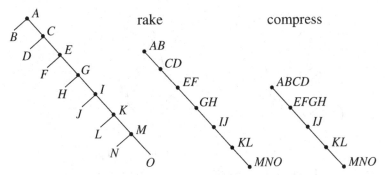

Figure 9.25: Demonstrating the tree-contraction operation.

from the tree. Contraction works by applying a rake operation to the tree, followed by a compress operation. The rake operation is simple: it absorbs each leaf node into its parent. The compress operation is more involved: it identifies all maximal chains $N_1, N_2, \ldots, N_k$ and then absorbs N_i into N_{i+1} for odd i. The sequence $N_1, N_2, \ldots, N_k$ is a chain if N_{i+1} is the only child of N_i for $1 \leq i < k$ and if N_k has exactly one child and that child is not a leaf. Contraction is a general technique that has many applications. Typically, each tree node N will have an application-specific label, $\mathsf{label}(N)$. When node N_1 is absorbed into its neighbor N_2, the label of N_2 is updated to $\mathsf{label}(N_1) \star \mathsf{label}(N_2)$ where "$\star$" is a label-specific operation.

Figure 9.25 depicts an example where contraction is applied to a tree where the labels of nodes are strings and the corresponding operation is string concatenation. The main property of contraction is that any tree can be reduced to a single node by only applying contraction $O(\log n)$ times, where n is the number of tree nodes.

We use the contraction operation to balance a dtree T as follows. First, we label each nonleaf node in T with the empty dtree. Second, we label each leaf node of T with itself. We then choose the label-specific operation to be COMPOSE as defined in Section 9.5.1. Finally, we apply contraction successively to the dtree until it is reduced to a single node and return the label of the final node. We refer to this algorithm as BAL_DT.

Theorem 9.15. *Let T be a dtree having n nodes and a largest context size of w. BAL_DT(T) will return a dtree of height $O(\log n)$, a cutset width $\leq w$, a context width $\leq 2w$, and a width $\leq 3w - 1$.* ∎

Given our method for converting dtrees to jointrees, algorithm BAL_DT can therefore be used to construct balanced jointrees as well. A balanced jointree with n clusters is one that has a root node r, where the path from root r to any other node has length $O(\log n)$.

9.6 Triangulated graphs

We discussed three models of graph decomposition in this chapter – elimination orders, jointrees, and dtrees – and measured the quality of each model by a corresponding notion of width. We provided an equivalence between these models in the sense that optimizing the width of one model is equivalent to optimizing the width of another. We also showed that the width of these models cannot be less than the treewidth of the corresponding DAG.

These equivalences can be understood at a more basic level by showing that the construction of each of these models corresponds to constructing a decomposable graph,

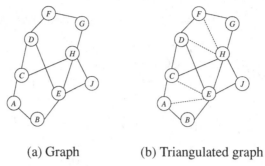

(a) Graph   (b) Triangulated graph

Figure 9.26: A graph and one of its triangulations.

and that minimizing the width of these models corresponds to minimizing the treewidth of this decomposable graph.

Intuitively, a *decomposable graph* is one for which we can construct an optimal elimination order in polytime and, hence, determine its treewidth in polytime. Decomposable graphs are characterized in a number of different ways in the literature. One of the more common characterizations is using the notion of perfect orders.

Definition 9.15. The elimination order π is *perfect* for graph G if and only if it does not add any fill-in edges when applied to G: $G = G^{\pi}$.   ∎

Theorem 9.16. *If graph G admits a perfect elimination order π, then the order π can be identified in polytime and treewidth$(G) = $ width(π, G).*   ∎

Not every graph admits a perfect elimination order. However, we can always add edges to a graph G so it admits a perfect elimination order. In particular, given an elimination order π the filled-in graph G^{π} is guaranteed to admit π as a perfect order (see Lemma 9.1 on Page 234).

The following is another characterization of decomposable graphs.

Definition 9.16. A graph is said to be *triangulated* precisely when every cycle of length ≥ 4 has a chord, that is, an edge connecting two nonconsecutive nodes in the cycle. Triangulated graphs are also called *chordal* graphs.   ∎

Figure 9.26(a) depicts a graph that is not triangulated, as it contains cycles of length four or more with no chords (e.g., the cycle A, B, E, H, C). Figure 9.26(b) depicts a triangulated graph that has no such cycles.

Theorem 9.17. *A graph is triangulated if and only if it admits a perfect elimination order.*   ∎

Recall that a filled-in graph G^{π} admits π as a perfect elimination order. Therefore, the graph G^{π} must be triangulated. This suggests that one can always triangulate a graph by adding edges to it. Figure 9.27 depicts a graph and two triangulations that result from adding the fill-in edges of two corresponding elimination orders.

We now have the following equivalence.

Theorem 9.18. *The following properties hold:*

- *Given a triangulation $G^{\star}$ for graph G, we can construct in polytime an elimination order π with width$(\pi, G) \leq$ treewidth$(G^{\star})$.*

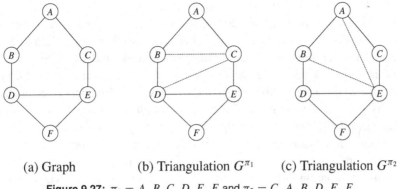

(a) Graph   (b) Triangulation G^{π_1} (c) Triangulation G^{π_2}

Figure 9.27: $\pi_1 = A, B, C, D, E, F$ and $\pi_2 = C, A, B, D, E, F$.

- *Given an elimination order π for graph G, we can construct in polytime a triangulation $G^\star$ for graph G with treewidth$(G^\star) \leq$ width(π, G).* ■

Therefore, finding an optimal triangulation for a graph is equivalent to constructing an optimal elimination order for that graph (jointrees and dtrees as well).

The classical treatment of jointrees makes a direct appeal to triangulated graphs. For example, it is quite common in the literature to describe the method of constructing jointree clusters as a method that starts by triangulating the moral graph of a Bayesian network and then identifying its maximal cliques as the jointree clusters. This is equivalent to the description we gave in Section 9.4.1 due to the following result.

Theorem 9.19. *Let $C_1, \ldots, C_n$ be the cluster sequence induced by applying elimination order π to graph G. The maximal clusters in $C_1, \ldots, C_n$ are precisely the maximal cliques of the triangulated graph G^π.* ■

Hence, the discussion of triangulation is not necessary for a procedural description of the jointree construction algorithm, since the cluster sequence already identifies the maximal cliques of a triangulated graph.

Bibliographic remarks

For an introductory treatment of graphs and some of their algorithms, such as maximal spanning trees, see Cormen et al. [1990].

The notion of treewidth, whose computation is NP-complete [Arnborg et al., 1987], was introduced in Robertson and Seymour [1986] based on the notion of *tree decompositions*, which are jointrees for undirected graphs (as defined in Exercise 9.25).[3] Other definitions of treewidth based on triangulated graphs are discussed in Gavril [1974] and Golumbic [1980], and a more recent overview of graph theoretic notions that are equivalent to treewidth is given in Bodlaender [1998]. The degeneracy lower bound on treewidth is attributed to Szekeres and Wilf [1968] and Lick and White [1970]. The contraction degeneracy lower bound was introduced and shown to be NP-hard in Bodlaender et al. [2004; 2006]. The heuristic version of contraction degeneracy referred to as MMD+ (min-d) was developed independently by Bodlaender et al. [2004] and, as minor-min-width, by Gogate and Dechter [2004]. A variety of other lower bounds on treewidth are

---

[3] See also the related notion of branch decompositions [Robertson and Seymour, 1991; 1995] as defined in Exercise 9.26.

studied by Bodlaender et al. [2005a] and Koster et al. [2005]. A survey of treewidth and related topics is given in Bodlaender [2005], including exact algorithms, approximation algorithms, upper bounds, and preprocessing rules; see also Bodlaender [2007; 2006].

Our treatment of elimination orders is based on Bertele and Brioschi [1972], who identify the notion of width using the term *dimension*. Our discussion of elimination prefixes and the associated preprocessing rules is based on Bodlaender et al. [2005b], which has its roots in Arnborg and Proskurowski [1986]. Elimination heuristics are discussed in Kjaerulff [1990]. The first algorithm to employ depth-first branch-and-bound on the elimination order search space was given in Gogate and Dechter [2004], who used the MMD+(min-d) lower bound on treewidth. The first best-first search algorithm for finding optimal elimination orders was given in Dow and Korf [2007], who also used the MMD+(min-d) lower bound. Our treatment of this algorithm is also based on Dow and Korf [2008].

The construction of jointrees according to Theorem 9.8 is based on Lauritzen [1996]. The construction of jointrees according to Theorem 9.9 is due to Jensen and Jensen [1994] and Shibata [1988]. The notion of a dtree was introduced in Darwiche [2001] and is closely related to branch decomposition in the graph-theoretic literature [Robertson and Seymour, 1991; 1995] (see Exercise 9.26). The construction of dtrees using hypergraph decomposition was introduced in Darwiche and Hopkins [2001] and its theoretical basis was given in Hopkins and Darwiche [2002]. For a treatment of the relation between elimination orders and triangulation, see Rose [1970] and Golumbic [1980].

9.7 Exercises

9.1. Construct a jointree for the DAG in Figure 9.28 using the elimination order $\pi = A, G, B, C, D, E, F$ and Algorithm 23.

9.2. Construct a jointree for the DAG in Figure 9.28 using the elimination order $\pi = A, G, B, C, D, E, F$ and Algorithm 24. In case of multiple maximum spanning trees, show all of them.

9.3. Convert the dtree in Figure 9.28 to a jointree and then remove all nonmaximal clusters.

9.4. Construct a total elimination order that is consistent with the partial elimination order induced by the dtree in Figure 9.28. When the relative order of two variables is not fixed by the dtree, place them in alphabetic order.

9.5. Construct a dtree for the DAG in Figure 9.28 using the elimination order $\pi = A, G, B, C, D, E, F$ and Algorithm 25. What is the width of this order? What is the width of the generated dtree?

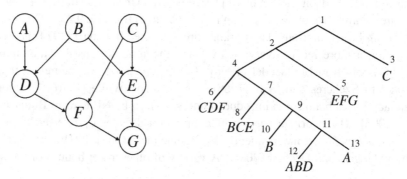

Figure 9.28: A network and a corresponding dtree.

9.6. Consider the networks in Figure 6.6(d) and Figure 6.6(e) on Page 142. Show that the treewidth of these networks is 3. Hint: Use the preprocessing rules for generating optimal elimination prefixes.

9.7. Show that the leaf nodes of a Bayesian network represent a prefix for an optimal elimination order.

9.8. Show that the root nodes of a Bayesian network, which have a single child each, represent a prefix for an optimal elimination order.

9.9. Show that the Islet and Twig rules are complete for graphs with treewidth 1; that is, they are sufficient to generate optimal elimination orders for such graphs.

9.10. Show that the Islet, Twig, and Series rules are complete for graphs with treewidth 2; that is, they are sufficient to generate optimal elimination orders for such graphs.

9.11. Show that the min-degree heuristic is optimal for graphs with treewidth ≤ 2.

9.12. Show that the degree of a graph (Definition 9.7) is a lower bound on the treewidth of the graph.

9.13. Consider the jointree for an undirected graph as defined in Exercise 9.25 and suppose that the treewidth of an undirected graph is the width of its best jointree (one with lowest width). Use this definition of treewidth to show that contracting an edge in a graph does not increase its treewidth.

9.14. Show that the degeneracy of a graph (Definition 9.8) can be computed by generating a sequence of subgraphs, starting with the original graph, and then generating the next subgraph by removing a minimum-degree node. The degeneracy is then the maximum degree attained by any of the generated subgraphs.

9.15. Show the following about Algorithm 20, BFS_OEO: At no point during the search can we have a node $(G_\rho, \rho, w_\rho, b_\rho)$ on the open list and another node $(G_{\rho'}, \rho', w_{\rho'}, b_{\rho'})$ on the closed list where $G_\rho = G_{\rho'}$.

9.16. Show that Algorithm 20, BFS_OEO, will not choose a node $(G_\tau, \tau, w_\tau, b_\tau)$ from the open list where τ is a complete yet suboptimal elimination order.

9.17. Prove the correctness of Algorithm 21, JT2EO. One way to prove this is to bound the size of factors constructed by the elimination Algorithm VE_PR from Chapter 6 while using the elimination order generated by JT2EO.

9.18. Consider a cluster sequence $\mathbf{C}_1, \ldots, \mathbf{C}_n$ induced by an elimination order π on graph G. Show that it is impossible for a cluster $\mathbf{C}_i$ to be contained in another cluster $\mathbf{C}_j$ where $j > i$.

9.19. Prove Lemma 9.5.

9.20. Consider a dtree generated from an elimination order π using Algorithm 25. Is it possible for the order not to be consistent with the dtree according to Definition 9.12, that is, the total order π is not compatible with the partial order induced by the dtree. Either show impossibility or provide a concrete example showing such a possibility.

9.21. Provide a polytime, width-preserving algorithm for converting a jointree into a dtree. Your algorithm should be direct, bypassing the notion of an elimination order.

9.22. Show the following: Given a probability distribution $\Pr(\mathbf{X})$ that is induced by a Bayesian network and given a corresponding dtree, the distribution can be expressed in the following form:

$$\Pr(\mathbf{X}) = \frac{\prod_{\substack{dtree\ node\ T}} \Pr(\mathrm{cluster}(T))}{\prod_{\substack{dtree\ node\ T}} \Pr(\mathrm{context}(T))}.$$

9.23. Show that a dtree will have width $\leq 4w + 1$ if each of its nodes T satisfies the following conditions:

- The cutset of T has no more than $w + 1$ variables.
- No more than two thirds of the variables in context(T) appear in either vars(T^l) or vars(T^r).

9.24. Use Algorithm BAL_DT of Section 9.5.3 to balance the dtree in Figure 9.28.

9.25. Define a jointree for an undirected graph G as a pair $(T, \mathbf{C})$, where T is tree and $\mathbf{C}$ is a function that maps each node i in the tree T to a label $\mathbf{C}_i$, called a cluster, that satisfies the following conditions:

- The cluster $\mathbf{C}_i$ is set of nodes in graph G.
- For every edge X–Y in graph G, the variables X and Y appear in some cluster $\mathbf{C}_i$.
- The clusters of tree T satisfy the jointree property.

Show that every clique of G must be contained in some cluster of the jointree. Show also that if G is the moral graph of some DAG $G^\star$, then $(T, \mathbf{C})$ is also a jointree for DAG $G^\star$. Note: This definition of a jointree is known as a tree decomposition (for graph G) in the graph-theoretic literature.

9.26. Define a dtree for an undirected graph G as a pair (T, vars), where T is a full binary tree whose leaves are in one-to-one correspondence with the graph edges and vars(.) is a function that maps each leaf node L in the dtree to the variables vars(L) of corresponding edge. Define the cutset, context, and cluster as they are defined for dtrees of DAGs. Show that the dtree clusters satisfy the jointree property. Show also that every clique of G must be contained in some cluster of the dtree. Note: This definition of a dtree is known as a branch decomposition (for graph G) in the graph-theoretic literature.

9.27. Let G be a DAG, G_m its moral graph, and consider a jointree for DAG G with width w. Let G_d be a graph that results from connecting in G_m every pair of variables that appear in some jointree cluster. Show that G_d is triangulated and that its treewidth is w.

9.28. Show that the treewidth of a triangulated graph equals the size of its maximal clique minus one.

9.8 Lemmas

This section contains a number of lemmas that are used in the proofs section.

Lemma 9.1. *Let G be a graph, π an elimination order for graph G, and let G^π be the corresponding filled-in graph. We then have:*

- *π is a perfect elimination order for G^π.*
- *The cluster sequence induced by applying order π to graph G is identical to the cluster sequence induced by applying order π to graph G^π.*
- *width(π, G) = width(π, G^π).*

PROOF. The third part follows immediately from the second part given the definition of width.

To prove the first two parts, let $E = E_1, \ldots, E_n$ be the fill-in edges of order π and graph G, where E_i are the edges added when eliminating node $\pi(i)$. The basic observation here is that edges $E_i, \ldots, E_n$ do not mention variables $\pi(1), \ldots, \pi(i)$. Hence, it suffices to show the following: Considering the graph sequences $G_1, G_2, \ldots, G_n$ and $G_1^\pi, G_2^\pi, \ldots, G_n^\pi$, the only difference between graphs G_i and G_i^π is that the latter graph has the extra edges $E_i, \ldots, E_n$. Since these edges do not mention node $\pi(i)$, eliminating this node from either graph G_i or G_i^π will generate the same cluster. The previous result follows immediately for $i = 1$. Suppose now that it holds for graphs G_i and G_i^π. Eliminating $\pi(i)$ from graph G_i will then add edges E_i. Eliminating it from graph G_i^π will add no edges. Hence, the only difference between graphs G_{i+1} and G_{i+1}^π is that the latter graph has the extra edges $E_{i+1}, \ldots, E_n$.   ■

Lemma 9.2. *If $G^\star$ is a graph that admits a perfect elimination order π, and if G is the result of removing some edges from $G^\star$, then width$(\pi, G) \leq$ width$(\pi, G^\star)$.*

PROOF. It is sufficient to prove that if $\mathbf{C}_1, \ldots, \mathbf{C}_n$ is the cluster sequence induced by applying order π to graph G and if $\mathbf{C}_1^\star, \ldots, \mathbf{C}_n^\star$ is the cluster sequence induced by applying order π to graph $G^\star$, then $\mathbf{C}_i \subseteq \mathbf{C}_i^\star$ for $i = 1, \ldots, n$. The proof is by induction on the size of elimination order π. The base case holds trivially for $n = 1$. Suppose now that it holds for elimination orders of size $n - 1$ and let us show that it holds for orders of size n. The neighbors that node $\pi(1)$ has in graph G are clearly a subset of its neighbors in graph $G^\star$, hence, $\mathbf{C}_1 \subseteq \mathbf{C}_1^\star$. Let G_1 be the result of eliminating node $\pi(1)$ from graph G and let $G_1^\star$ be the result of eliminating the node from graph $G^\star$. Since π is a perfect elimination order for $G^\star$, the neighbors of node $\pi(1)$ will form a clique in $G^\star$. Therefore, every fill-in edge that is added when eliminating node $\pi(1)$ from graph G is already an edge in $G^\star$. Hence, G_1 can be obtained by removing some edges from $G_1^\star$. Moreover, $\pi(2), \ldots, \pi(n)$ is a perfect elimination order for graph $G_1^\star$. By the induction hypothesis, $\mathbf{C}_i \subseteq \mathbf{C}_i^\star$ for $i = 2, \ldots, n$.   ■

Lemma 9.3. *The clusters $\mathbf{C}_1, \ldots, \mathbf{C}_n$ induced by a perfect elimination order π on graph G are all cliques in graph G.*

PROOF. Let $G_1 = G, \ldots, G_n$ be the graph sequence induced by applying order π to graph G. Recall that cluster $\mathbf{C}_i$ contains node $\pi(i)$ and its neighbors in graph G_i. Since order π is perfect, no edges are added between the neighbors of $\pi(i)$ when it is being eliminated. Hence, the neighbors of $\pi(i)$ form a clique in G, making cluster $\mathbf{C}_i$ also a clique in G.   ■

Lemma 9.4. *The clusters $\mathbf{C}_1, \ldots, \mathbf{C}_n$ induced by a perfect elimination order π on graph G include all of the maximal cliques in graph G.*

PROOF. Suppose that $\mathbf{C}$ is some maximal clique in graph G. Let $X = \pi(i)$ be the variable in $\mathbf{C}$ that appears first in the order π. When eliminating X, every node $Y \in \mathbf{C}$ is a neighbor of X unless $Y = X$ since $\mathbf{C}$ is a clique. Hence, $\mathbf{C} \subseteq \mathbf{C}_i$. Moreover, when eliminating X, every neighbor Z of X must be in $\mathbf{C}$ and, hence, $\mathbf{C}_i \subseteq \mathbf{C}$ for the following reason. If some neighbor Z is not in $\mathbf{C}$, we have one of two cases. First, Z is not adjacent to every node in $\mathbf{C}$. We must then add fill-in edges when eliminating X, which is a contradiction as π is a perfect elimination order. Second, Z is adjacent to every node in $\mathbf{C}$, then $\mathbf{C} \cup \{Z\}$ is a clique, which is a contradiction with $\mathbf{C}$ being a maximal clique. We must then have $\mathbf{C} = \mathbf{C}_i$.   ■

Lemma 9.5. *Consider a dtree node T and define vars$^\uparrow(T) = \emptyset$ if T is a root node; otherwise, vars$^\uparrow(T) = \bigcup_{T'}$ vars(T'), where T' is a leaf dtree node connected to node T*

through its parent. We have:

$$\text{cutset}(T) = \text{vars}(T^l) \cap \text{vars}(T^r) \setminus \text{vars}^\uparrow(T)$$

$$\text{context}(T) = \text{vars}(T) \cap \text{vars}^\uparrow(T)$$

$$\text{cluster}(T) = (\text{vars}(T^l) \cap \text{vars}(T^r)) \cup (\text{vars}(T^l) \cap \text{vars}^\uparrow(T)) \cup (\text{vars}(T^r) \cap \text{vars}^\uparrow(T)).$$

This implies that $X \in \text{cluster}(T)$ only if $X \in \text{vars}(T)$.

PROOF. Left to Exercise 9.19. ∎

Lemma 9.6. *Let π be an elimination order of DAG G and let $\Gamma = S_1, \ldots, S_n$ be the families of G. Define the elimination of variable $\pi(i)$ from collection Γ as replacing the sets $S_k \in \Gamma$ containing $\pi(i)$ by the set $(\bigcup_k S_k) \setminus \{\pi(i)\}$. If we eliminate variables according to order π, concurrently, from the moral graph G_m of G and from the collection Γ, we find the following: As we are about to eliminate variable $\pi(i)$, the set $(\bigcup_k S_k) \setminus \{\pi(i)\}$ contains exactly the neighbors of $\pi(i)$ in graph G_m.*

PROOF. (sketch). It suffices to show that at every stage of the elimination process, the following invariant holds: two nodes are adjacent in G_m if and only if they belong to some set in Γ. This holds initially and it is easy to show that it continues to hold after each elimination step. ∎

Lemma 9.7. *When processing variable $\pi(i)$ in EO2DT, let $T = \text{COMPOSE}(T_1, \ldots, T_n)$ and let $T^\star$ be a dtree node that is added in the process of composing trees $T_1, \ldots, T_n$. We then have $\text{cluster}(T^\star) \subseteq \text{vars}(T) \cap \{\pi(i), \ldots, \pi(n)\}$.*

PROOF. Suppose that a variable X belongs to $\text{cluster}(T^\star)$. Then by Lemma 9.5, X must either belong to two trees in $T_1, \ldots, T_n$ or belong to a tree in $T_1, \ldots, T_n$ and another tree in $\Sigma \setminus \{T_1, \ldots, T_n\}$. In either case, X cannot belong to $\{\pi(1), \ldots, \pi(i-1)\}$ since these variables have already been processed, so each can belong only to a single tree in Σ. Therefore, X must belong to $\pi(i), \ldots, \pi(n)$. Moreover, X must belong to at least one tree in $T_1, \ldots, T_n$. Hence, X must belong to T and $X \in \text{vars}(T) \cap \{\pi(i), \ldots, \pi(n)\}$. ∎

9.9 Proofs

PROOF OF THEOREM 9.1. Suppose we have a clique $\mathbf{C}$ of size n in graph G and let π be an optimal elimination order for G. Let $\pi(i)$ be the earliest node in order π such that $\pi(i) \in \mathbf{C}$. When $\pi(i)$ is about to be eliminated, all other nodes in $\mathbf{C}$ will be in the graph. These nodes are also neighbors of node $\pi(i)$ since $\mathbf{C}$ is a clique. Hence, the cluster $\mathbf{C}_i$ induced when eliminating node $\pi(i)$ must contain clique $\mathbf{C}$. This means that $|\mathbf{C}_i| \geq |\mathbf{C}|$, $width(\pi, G) \geq |\mathbf{C}| - 1 = n - 1$, and also $treewidth(G) \geq n - 1$ since the order π is optimal. ∎

PROOF OF THEOREM 9.2. This is known as the *Invariance theorem* in Bertele and Brioschi [1972]. We now show the following, which is sufficient to prove the theorem. Nodes A and B are adjacent in graph G_{τ_1} but not adjacent in graph G if and only if graph G contains a path

$$A, X_1, \ldots, X_m, B$$

connecting A and B, where all internal nodes X_i belong to prefix τ_1. This basically means that the set of edges that are added between nodes in G_{τ_1} after elimination prefix τ_1 depend only on the set of variables in this prefix and are independent of the order in which these variables are eliminated. This then guarantees $G_{\tau_1} = G_{\tau_2}$.

Let $G = G_1, \ldots, G_n = G_{\tau_1}$ be the graph sequence induced by eliminating prefix τ_1. Suppose now that we have a path $A, X_1, \ldots, X_m, B$ connecting nodes A and B in graph G_1, as discussed previously. Let G_i be the last graph in the sequence in which the above path is preserved. Graph G_{i+1} must then be obtained by eliminating some variable X_j from the path. This leads to adding an edge between the two variables before and after X_j on the path (if one does not already exist). Hence, G_{i+1} will continue to have a path connecting A and B with all its internal nodes belonging to prefix τ_1. This means that nodes A and B remain to be connected by such a path after each elimination. It also means that A and B are adjacent in graph G_{τ_1}.

Suppose now that A and B are adjacent in graph G_{τ_1} but are not adjacent in the initial graph G. Let G_i be the first graph in the sequence in which variables A and B became adjacent. This graph must then have resulted from eliminating a variable X_j that is adjacent to both A and B in G_{i-1}. This means that variables A and B are connected in G_{i-1} by a path whose internal nodes are in prefix τ_1. By repeated application of the same argument for edges A–X_j and B–X_j, it follows that A and B must be connected in G by a path whose internal nodes are in prefix τ_1. ∎

PROOF OF THEOREM 9.3. For any variable X, we have one of two cases:

1. Variable $X \in \text{vars}(T)$ for a unique leaf dtree node T. Variable X cannot appear in any cutset in this case. Moreover, $X \notin \text{context}(T)$ and $X \in \text{vars}(T) \setminus \text{context}(T) = \text{cluster}(T) \setminus \text{context}(T)$. Hence, variable X will be eliminated only at the unique leaf node T.

2. Variable $X \in \text{vars}(T)$ for multiple leaf nodes T. Variable X cannot be eliminated at any leaf node T because $X \in \text{vars}(T)$ implies $X \in \text{context}(T)$ in this case. Moreover, X must appear in some cutset since it appears in multiple leaf nodes. By Theorem 9.13(d), it must appear in a unique cutset and, hence, eliminated at a unique node. ∎

PROOF OF THEOREM 9.4. Given Theorem 9.10, the dtree nodes and their associated clusters form a jointree. Calling Algorithm 21 on this dtree (jointree) generates the same elimination orders characterized by Theorem 9.4 as long as the root of the dtree is removed last by Algorithm 21. To see this, let i be a node in the dtree and let j be the single neighbor of i when i is removed from the dtree by Algorithm 21. It then follows that j is the parent of i in the dtree and, hence, $\text{cluster}(i) \cap \text{cluster}(j) = \text{context}(i)$ by Theorem 9.13(e). Hence, when Algorithm 21 removes node i from the dtree, it appends variables $\text{cluster}(i) \setminus \text{context}(i)$ to the elimination order, which are precisely the variables eliminated at node i in the dtree. ∎

PROOF OF THEOREM 9.5. We first note that by the definition of a moral graph, every family of DAG G is a clique in its moral graph G_m. Let G_m^π be the filled-in graph of G_m. Every clique in the moral graph G_m is then a clique in G_m^π. Hence, every family of DAG G is a clique in G_m^π.

By Lemma 9.1, we have that π is a perfect elimination order for G_m^π and that applying this order to graph G_m^π must induce the cluster sequence $\mathbf{C}_1, \ldots, \mathbf{C}_n$. By Lemma 9.4, we now have that every maximal clique of G_m^π must appear in the cluster sequence $\mathbf{C}_1, \ldots, \mathbf{C}_n$. Hence, every family of DAG G must be contained in some cluster of the sequence. ∎

PROOF OF THEOREM 9.6. Without loss of generality, we assume that π is a perfect elimination order for graph G. If π is not perfect for G, replace G by its filled-in version G^π. By Lemma 9.1, π is perfect for G^π and applying it to G^π will induce the same cluster sequence $\mathbf{C}_1, \ldots, \mathbf{C}_n$.

Let $G = G_1, G_2, \ldots, G_n$ be the graph sequence induced by elimination order π. For each $i < n$, $S_i = \mathbf{C}_i \cap (\mathbf{C}_{i+1} \cup \ldots \cup \mathbf{C}_n)$ is the set of neighbors that variable $\pi(i)$ has in graph G_i. Since these neighbors form a clique in G_{i+1}, the set S_i must be contained in some maximal clique of G_{i+1}. Since $\pi(i + 1), \ldots, \pi(n)$ is a perfect elimination order for G_{i+1}, the maximal cliques of G_{i+1} must all appear in the sequence $\mathbf{C}_{i+1}, \ldots, \mathbf{C}_n$ by Lemma 9.4. Hence, the set S_i must be contained in some cluster in $\mathbf{C}_{i+1}, \ldots, \mathbf{C}_n$ and the running intersection property holds. ∎

PROOF OF THEOREM 9.7. Let $\mathbf{C}_i \cap (\mathbf{C}_{i+1} \cup \ldots \cup \mathbf{C}_n) \subseteq \mathbf{C}_k$ for some $k > i$ in accordance with the running intersection property. Since $\mathbf{C}_j \subseteq \mathbf{C}_i$ and $\mathbf{C}_j \subseteq (\mathbf{C}_{i+1} \cup \ldots \cup \mathbf{C}_n)$, we have

$$\mathbf{C}_j \subseteq \mathbf{C}_i \cap (\mathbf{C}_{i+1} \cup \ldots \cup \mathbf{C}_n) \subseteq \mathbf{C}_k$$

and, hence, $k \leq j$ since no cluster in the sequence can be contained in a following cluster. If $k < j$, i would not be the largest index, as given by the theorem; hence, $k = j$. This means that no variable in $\mathbf{C}_r = \mathbf{C}_i \setminus \mathbf{C}_j$ can appear in $\mathbf{C}_{i+1} \cup \ldots \cup \mathbf{C}_n$. In particular, no variable in $\mathbf{C}_r$ can appear in $\mathbf{C}_s$, for $i < s < j$. Hence, every cluster $\mathbf{C}_s$ continues to satisfy the running intersection property after $\mathbf{C}_j$ is replaced by $\mathbf{C}_i$ because the intersection $\mathbf{C}_s \cap (\mathbf{C}_{s+1} \cup \ldots \cup \mathbf{C}_n)$ does not change. Clusters other than $\mathbf{C}_s$ clearly continue to satisfy the running intersection property. ∎

PROOF OF THEOREM 9.8. Since the sequence $\mathbf{C}_1, \ldots, \mathbf{C}_n$ satisfies the running intersection property, for every cluster $\mathbf{C}_i$, $i < n$, there must exist a cluster $\mathbf{C}_j$, $j > i$, that includes $\mathbf{C}_i \cap (\mathbf{C}_{i+1} \cup \ldots \cup \mathbf{C}_n)$. Our proof will be by induction on i. For $i = n$, the tree consisting of cluster $\mathbf{C}_n$ will trivially satisfy the jointree property. Suppose now that we have assembled a tree of clusters T_i corresponding to the sequence $\mathbf{C}_i, \ldots, \mathbf{C}_n$ that satisfies the jointree property. Let T_{i-1} be the tree that results from connecting cluster $\mathbf{C}_{i-1}$ to a cluster $\mathbf{C}$ in T_i such that $\mathbf{C}_{i-1} \cap (\mathbf{C}_i \cup \ldots \cup \mathbf{C}_n) \subseteq \mathbf{C}$. We now show that tree T_{i-1} must also satisfy the jointree property by showing that the clusters of every variable form a connected subtree in T_{i-1}.[4] Consider a variable X. By the induction hypothesis, the clusters containing X in tree T_i must form a connected tree. If $X \notin \mathbf{C}_{i-1}$, then the clusters of X in T_{i-1} will also form a connected tree. If $X \in \mathbf{C}_{i-1}$, we have two cases. If X does not appear in T_i, then the clusters of X in T_{i-1} will also form a connected tree. If X appears in T_i, $X \in \mathbf{C}$ by the definition of $\mathbf{C}$ and the clusters of X in T_{i-1} will also form a connected tree. Hence, the tree T_{i-1} must satisfy the jointree property. ∎

PROOF OF THEOREM 9.9. A proof of this theorem is given in Jensen and Jensen [1994]. The more common statement of this result assumes that clusters $\mathbf{C}_1, \ldots, \mathbf{C}_n$ are the maximal cliques of a triangulated graph, which is equivalent to the given statement in light of Theorem 9.19. ∎

PROOF OF THEOREM 9.10. To prove the jointree property, we use Lemma 9.5. Suppose that l, m, and n are three nodes in a dtree. Suppose further that l is on the path connecting

---

[4] This is an equivalent condition to the jointree property.

m and n. Let X be a node in cluster(m) $\cap$ cluster(n). We want to show that X belongs to cluster(l). We consider two cases:

1. m is an ancestor of n. Hence, l is an ancestor of n. Since $X \in$ cluster(n), $X \in$ vars(n) and, hence, $X \in$ vars(l). Since $X \in$ cluster(m), either $X \in$ cutset(m) or $X \in$ context(m). If $X \in$ cutset(m), then $X \in$ vars(m^l) and $X \in$ vars(m^r). If $X \in$ context(m), then $X \in$ vars$^\uparrow$(m). In either case, we have $X \in$ vars$^\uparrow$(l), $X \in$ vars(l) $\cap$ vars$^\uparrow$(l) = context(l) and, hence, $X \in$ cluster(l).

2. m and n have a common ancestor o. Either $o = l$ or o is an ancestor of l. Therefore, it is sufficient to show that $X \in$ cluster(o) (given the above case). Without loss of generality, suppose that m is in the left subtree of o and n is in the right subtree. Since $X \in$ vars(m), $X \in$ vars(o^l). Since $X \in$ vars(n), $X \in$ vars(o^r). Therefore, $X \in$ cluster(o) by Lemma 9.5. ∎

PROOF OF THEOREM 9.11. Let G_m be the moral graph of DAG G and consider Exercise 4.24. We then have: If $\mathbf{X} \setminus \mathbf{Z}$ and $\mathbf{Y} \setminus \mathbf{Z}$ are intercepted by $\mathbf{Z}$ in graph G_m, then $\mathbf{X} \setminus \mathbf{Z}$ and $\mathbf{Y} \setminus \mathbf{Z}$ are d-separated by $\mathbf{Z}$ in DAG G. Consider now the graph $G^\star$ that results from connecting every pair of nodes that appear in some cluster of the given jointree. Then graph $G^\star$ contains the moral graph G_m and hence: If $\mathbf{X} \setminus \mathbf{Z}$ and $\mathbf{Y} \setminus \mathbf{Z}$ are intercepted by $\mathbf{Z}$ in graph $G^\star$, then $\mathbf{X} \setminus \mathbf{Z}$ and $\mathbf{Y} \setminus \mathbf{Z}$ are d-separated by $\mathbf{Z}$ in DAG G.

Let $X \in \mathbf{X} \setminus \mathbf{Z}$ and $Y \in \mathbf{Y} \setminus \mathbf{Z}$. X then appears only in clusters on the i-side of edge i–j and Y appears only in clusters on the j-side of the edge. We now show that any path between X and Y in graph $G^\star$ must be intercepted by a variable in $\mathbf{Z}$.

We first note that $\mathbf{X} \setminus \mathbf{Z}$ and $\mathbf{Y} \setminus \mathbf{Z}$ must be disjoint since $\mathbf{Z} = \mathbf{X} \cap \mathbf{Y}$ by the jointree property. This implies that X and Y cannot appear in a common jointree cluster and, hence, cannot be adjacent in $G^\star$. Suppose now that we have a path X–$Z_1 \ldots Z_k$–$Y, k \geq 1$. We now show by induction on k that any such path must be intercepted by $\mathbf{Z}$. If $k = 1$, then $Z_1 \in \mathbf{X}$ since it is adjacent to X (i.e., it must appear with X in some cluster) and $Z_1 \in \mathbf{Y}$ since it is adjacent to Y. Hence, $Z_1 \in \mathbf{X} \cap \mathbf{Y} = \mathbf{Z}$. Suppose now that $k > 1$. If $Z_1 \in \mathbf{Z}$, then the path is intercepted by $\mathbf{Z}$. Suppose that $Z_1 \notin \mathbf{Z}$. We have $Z_1 \in \mathbf{X}$ since X and Z_1 are adjacent. Hence, $Z_1 \in \mathbf{X} \setminus \mathbf{Z}$, $Y \in \mathbf{Y} \setminus \mathbf{Z}$, and the path Z_1–$Z_2 \ldots Z_k$–Y must be intercepted by $\mathbf{Z}$ given the induction hypothesis. ∎

PROOF OF THEOREM 9.12. Let $\mathbf{C}_k$ be any root cluster in the jointree and let us direct the jointree edges away from this root. If the edge $j \to i$ appears in the directed jointree, we say that cluster $\mathbf{C}_j$ is a parent of cluster $\mathbf{C}_i$. Since we have a tree structure, every cluster except the root will have a single parent.

Let $\mathbf{C}_1, \ldots, \mathbf{C}_n$ be an ordering of the jointree clusters such that $\mathbf{C}_n$ is the root cluster and every cluster appears before its parent in the order. Then for every i, clusters $\mathbf{C}_1, \ldots, \mathbf{C}_{i-1}$ must include all the descendants of $\mathbf{C}_i$ (i.e., clusters connected to $\mathbf{C}_i$ through a child) and $\mathbf{C}_{i+1}, \ldots, \mathbf{C}_n$ must be all nondescendants (i.e, clusters connected to $\mathbf{C}_i$ through its parent). Every cluster $\mathbf{C}_i, i \neq n$, can be partitioned into two sets $\mathbf{X}_i$ and $\mathbf{Y}_i = \mathbf{C}_i \cap \mathbf{C}_j$, where $\mathbf{C}_j$ is the parent of cluster $\mathbf{C}_i$. By Theorem 9.11 and the Decomposition axiom, we have

$$I_{\Pr}\left(\mathbf{X}_i, \mathbf{Y}_i, \left(\bigcup_{k=i+1}^{n} \mathbf{C}_k\right) \setminus \mathbf{Y}_i\right). \tag{9.3}$$

Note that the sets $\mathbf{Y}_i, i \neq n$, range over all separators in the jointree.

Let $c_1, \ldots, c_n$ be compatible instantiations of clusters $C_1, \ldots, C_n$, respectively. We then have

$$
\begin{aligned}
&\Pr(c_1, c_2, \ldots, c_n) \\
&= \Pr(x_1 y_1, x_2 y_2, \ldots, c_n) \\
&= \Pr(x_1 | y_1, x_2 y_2, \ldots, c_n) \Pr(y_1, x_2 y_2, \ldots, c_n) \\
&= \Pr(x_1 | y_1, x_2 y_2, \ldots, c_n) \Pr(x_2 y_2, \ldots, c_n) \text{ since } Y_i \subseteq X_{i+1} \cup Y_{i+1} \cup \ldots \cup C_n \\
&= \Pr(x_1 | y_1) \Pr(x_2 y_2, \ldots, c_n) \text{ by (9.3)} \\
&= \Pr(x_1 | y_1) \ldots \Pr(x_{n-1} | y_{n-1}) \Pr(c_n) \text{ by repeated application of the previous steps} \\
&= \frac{\Pr(x_1 y_1)}{\Pr(y_1)} \cdots \frac{\Pr(x_{n-1} y_{n-1})}{\Pr(y_{n-1})} \Pr(c_n) \\
&= \frac{\Pr(c_1)}{\Pr(y_1)} \cdots \frac{\Pr(c_{n-1})}{\Pr(y_{n-1})} \Pr(c_n) \\
&= \frac{\prod_{i=1}^{n} \Pr(c_i)}{\prod_{j=1}^{n-1} \Pr(y_j)}. \quad \blacksquare
\end{aligned}
$$

PROOF OF THEOREM 9.13. We have the following:

(a) Follows immediately from the definitions of $\text{context}(T) = \text{acutset}(T) \cap \text{vars}(T)$ and $\text{cutset}(T) = (\text{vars}(T^l) \cap \text{vars}(T^r)) \setminus \text{acutset}(T)$.

(b) Suppose $X \in \text{context}(T)$. Then $X \in \text{acutset}(T) \cap \text{vars}(T)$ and, hence, $X \in \text{vars}(T^p)$. We have two cases:

- $X \in \text{acutset}(T^p)$, then $X \in \text{context}(T^p)$.
- $X \notin \text{acutset}(T^p)$, then $X \in \text{cutset}(T^p)$ since $X \in \text{acutset}(T)$.

Therefore, $X \in \text{context}(T^p)$ or $X \in \text{cutset}(T^p)$.

(c) Let T^s be the sibling of T and suppose $X \in \text{cutset}(T^p)$. Then $X \in \text{acutset}(T)$ by definition of acutset and $X \in \text{vars}(T) \cap \text{vars}(T^s)$ by definition of a cutset. Therefore, $X \in \text{vars}(T)$, $X \in \text{acutset}(T)$ and, hence, $X \in \text{context}(T)$.

(d) Suppose first that T_1 is an ancestor of T_2. We have $\text{cutset}(T_1) \subseteq \text{acutset}(T_2)$ by definition of acutset. We also have $\text{cutset}(T_2) \cap \text{acutset}(T_2) = \emptyset$ by definition of cutset. Hence, $\text{cutset}(T_1) \cap \text{cutset}(T_2) = \emptyset$. Suppose now that T_1 and T_2 have a common ancestor and that $X \in \text{cutset}(T_1) \cap \text{cutset}(T_2)$ for some X. We then have $X \in \text{vars}(T_1)$ and $X \in \text{vars}(T_2)$. Moreover, if X_3 is the common ancestor closest to T_1 and T_2, then either $X \in \text{cutset}(T_3)$ or $X \in \text{acutset}(T_3)$ and, hence, $X \in \text{acutset}(T_3)$. This means that X is in the cutset of some common ancestor of T_1 and T_2, which is a contradiction with the first part.

(e) By definition of context, we have $\text{context}(T) \subseteq \text{cluster}(T)$. By (b), we have $\text{context}(T) \subseteq \text{cluster}(T^p)$. Hence, $\text{context}(T) \subseteq \text{cluster}(T) \cap \text{cluster}(T^p)$. Suppose that $X \in \text{cluster}(T) \cap \text{cluster}(T^p)$. Then $X \in \text{vars}(T)$ since $X \in \text{cluster}(T)$. Given $X \in \text{cluster}(T^p)$, we have one of two cases by (a):

- $X \in \text{cutset}(T^p)$, then $X \in \text{context}(T)$ by (c).
- $X \in \text{context}(T^p)$, then $X \in \text{acutset}(T^p)$ and $X \in \text{vars}(T^p)$. Therefore, $X \in \text{acutset}(T)$ and $X \in \text{context}(T)$.

(f) We have $\text{context}(T^l) \cup \text{context}(T^r) \subseteq \text{cluster}(T)$ by (b). Moreover, $\text{cutset}(T) \subseteq \text{context}(T^l)$ by (c) and $\text{cutset}(T) \subseteq \text{context}(T^l) \cup \text{context}(T^r)$. Suppose now that $X \in \text{context}(T)$. Then $X \in \text{vars}(T) \cap \text{acutset}(T)$, $X \in \text{vars}(T^l)$ or $X \in \text{vars}(T^r)$, $X \in \text{acutset}(T^l)$, and $X \in \text{acutset}(T^r)$. Hence, $X \in \text{context}(T^l)$ or $X \in \text{context}(T^r)$, and

$X \in \text{context}(T^l) \cup \text{context}(T^r)$. Therefore, $\text{context}(T) \subseteq \text{context}(T^l) \cup \text{context}(T^r)$ and $\text{cluster}(T) \subseteq \text{context}(T^l) \cup \text{context}(T^r)$. ■

PROOF OF THEOREM 9.14. The proof of this theorem will depend on Lemmas 9.6 and 9.7. EO2DT can be viewed as performing variable elimination on a collection of sets that initially contains the families of G as given by Lemma 9.6. We need to establish this correspondence first to prove our theorem. Consider the set of dtrees Σ maintained by EO2DT and let us assume that after processing variable $\pi(i)$, each dtree in Σ is associated with the following set of variables:

$$\mathcal{S}(T) \stackrel{def}{=} \text{vars}(T) \cap \{\pi(i+1), \ldots, \pi(n)\},$$

that is, variables in T that have not yet been processed. Initially, the trees in Σ correspond to families in DAG G since no variable has yet been processed. As we process variable $\pi(i)$, we collect all trees $T_1, \ldots, T_n$ such that $\pi(i) \in \mathcal{S}(T_1), \ldots, \mathcal{S}(T_n)$ and replace them by the tree $T = \text{COMPOSE}(T_1, \ldots, T_n)$. According to the prior definition of $\mathcal{S}(.)$, we have

$$\mathcal{S}(T = \text{COMPOSE}(T_1, \ldots, T_n)) = \mathcal{S}(T_1) \cup \ldots \cup \mathcal{S}(T_n) \setminus \{\pi(i)\},$$

and hence the correspondence we are seeking with the elimination process of Lemma 9.6.

From this correspondence and Lemma 9.6, we conclude that after processing variable $\pi(i)$, the tree $T = \text{COMPOSE}(T_1, \ldots, T_n)$ that is added to Σ is such that $\mathcal{S}(T)$ contains exactly the neighbors of variable $\pi(i)$ in the moral graph of DAG G after having eliminated $\pi(1), \ldots, \pi(i-1)$ from it. This means that the size of $\mathcal{S}(T)$ is $\leq \text{width}(\pi, G)$. Since $\mathcal{S}(T) = \text{vars}(T) \cap \{\pi(i+1), \ldots, \pi(n)\}$, the size of $\text{vars}(T) \cap \{\pi(i), \ldots, \pi(n)\}$ is $\leq \text{width}(\pi, G) + 1$. Given Lemma 9.7, this means that the cluster of any node that is added as a result of composing $T_1, \ldots, T_n$ cannot be larger than $\text{width}(\pi, G) + 1$. This proves that the width of constructed dtree is no more than the width of order π. ■

PROOF OF THEOREM 9.15. The proof of this theorem can be found in Darwiche [2001]. ■

PROOF OF THEOREM 9.16. Let $w = \text{width}(\pi, G)$. By Lemma 9.3, the clusters induced by order π are all cliques in G. Hence, graph G must have a clique of size $w + 1$. By Theorem 9.1, the treewidth of graph G must be $\geq w$. Since we have an order with width w, graph G must then have treewidth w.

To identify a perfect elimination order for G, all we have to do is identify a node in graph G whose neighbors form a clique (i.e., a simplicial node). If no simplicial node exists, the graph cannot have a perfect elimination order. If we find such a simplicial node X, we eliminate X from G and repeat the process until either all nodes have been eliminated, therefore leading to a perfect elimination order, or we fail to find a simplicial node, proving that the graph has no perfect elimination order. ■

PROOF OF THEOREM 9.17. The proof of this theorem can be found in Golumbic [1980]. ■

PROOF OF THEOREM 9.18. Suppose that we have a triangulation $G^\star$ of graph G where $\text{treewidth}(G^\star) = w$. By Theorem 9.17, $G^\star$ admits a perfect elimination order π. By Theorem 9.16, $\text{width}(\pi, G^\star) = w$ and the order π can be identified in polytime. By Lemma 9.2, $\text{width}(\pi, G) \leq \text{width}(\pi, G^\star)$ and, hence, $\text{width}(\pi, G) \leq w$. We can therefore identify in polytime an elimination order π for graph G such that $\text{width}(\pi, G) \leq w$.

Suppose we have an elimination order π for graph G where $width(\pi, G) = w$. By Lemma 9.1, π is a perfect elimination order for G^π and $width(\pi, G^\pi) = w$. By Theorem 9.16, $treewidth(G^\pi) = w$ and by Theorem 9.17, G^π must be triangulated. Hence, we can in polytime construct a triangulation for graph G having treewidth w. ∎

PROOF OF THEOREM 9.19. By Lemma 9.1, order π induces the same cluster sequence $\mathbf{C}_1, \ldots, \mathbf{C}_n$ when applied to either G or G^π. Since π is a perfect elimination order for G^π, Lemma 9.4 says that $\mathbf{C}_1, \ldots, \mathbf{C}_n$ contains all of the maximal cliques of G^π. Hence, the maximal clusters in $\mathbf{C}_1, \ldots, \mathbf{C}_n$ are the maximal cliques of G^π. ∎

10

Most Likely Instantiations

We consider in this chapter the problem of finding variable instantiations that have maximal probability under some given evidence. We present two classes of exact algorithms for this problem, one based on variable elimination and the other based on systematic search. We also present approximate algorithms based on local search.

10.1 Introduction

Consider the Bayesian network in Figure 10.1, which concerns a population that is 55% male and 45% female. According to this network, members of this population can suffer from a medical condition C that is more likely to occur in males. Moreover, two diagnostic tests are available for detecting this condition, T_1 and T_2, with the second test being more effective on females. The CPTs of this network also reveal that the two tests are equally effective on males.

One can partition the members of this population into four different groups depending on whether they are male or female and whether they have the condition or not. Suppose that a person takes both tests and all we know is that the two tests yield the same result, leading to the evidence $A = \text{yes}$. We may then ask: What is the most likely group to which this individual belongs? This query is therefore asking for the most likely instantiation of variables S and C given evidence $A = \text{yes}$, which is technically known as a *MAP instantiation*. We have already discussed this class of queries in Chapter 5, where we referred to variables S and C as the *MAP variables*. The MAP instantiation in this case is $S = \text{male}$ and $C = \text{no}$ with a posterior probability of about 49.3%.

The inference algorithms we presented in earlier chapters can be used to compute MAP instantiations when the number of MAP variables is relatively small. Under such a condition, we can simply compute the posterior marginal over MAP variables and then select the instantiation that has a maximal posterior probability. However, this method is guaranteed to be exponential in the number of MAP variables due to the size of the posterior marginal. Our goal in this chapter is to present algorithms that can compute MAP instantiations without necessarily being exponential in the number of MAP variables.

A notable special case of the MAP problem arises when the MAP variables contain all unobserved network variables. In the previous example, this corresponds to partitioning members of the population into sixteen different groups depending on whether they are male or female, whether they have the condition or not, and which of the four possible outcomes would be observed for the two tests. That is, we would be asking for the most

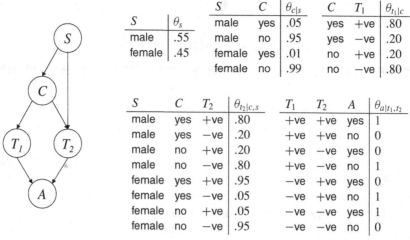

Figure 10.1: A Bayesian network. Variable S represents the gender of an individual and variable C represents a condition that is more likely in males. For males, tests T_1 and T_2 have the same false positive and false negative rates. For females, test T_2 has better rates. Variable A indicates the agreement between the two tests on a particular individual.

likely instantiation of variables S, C, T_1, and T_2 given the evidence $A =$ yes. The MAP instantiation in this case is

$$S = \text{female}, \quad C = \text{no}, \quad T_1 = -\text{ve}, \quad T_2 = -\text{ve},$$

with a posterior probability of about 47%.

This special class of MAP instantiations is known as *MPE instantiations*. As we shall see, computing MPE instantiations is much easier than computing MAP instantiations, which is one reason why this class of queries is distinguished by its own special name. It is worth mentioning here that projecting this MPE instantiation on variables S and C leads to $S =$ female and $C =$ no, which is not the MAP instantiation for variables S and C. Hence, one cannot generally obtain MAP instantiations by projecting MPE instantiations, although this technique is sometimes used as an approximation method for MAP.

We first consider the computation of MPE instantiations in Section 10.2, where we present algorithms based on variable elimination and systematic search. We then consider the computation of MAP instantiations in Section 10.3, where we present exact and approximate algorithms. The complexity classes of MAP and MPE queries is considered formally in Chapter 11.

10.2 Computing MPE instantiations

Suppose that we have a Bayesian network with variables **Q**. The *MPE probability* given evidence **e** is defined as

$$\text{MPE}_P(\mathbf{e}) \overset{def}{=} \max_{\mathbf{q}} \Pr(\mathbf{q}, \mathbf{e}).$$

There may be a number of instantiations $\mathbf{q}$ that attain this maximal probability. Each of these instantiations is then an *MPE instantiation,* where the set of all such instantiations is defined as

$$\text{MPE}(\mathbf{e}) \overset{def}{=} \underset{\mathbf{q}}{\text{argmax}}\, \Pr(\mathbf{q}, \mathbf{e}).$$

MPE instantiations can also be characterized as instantiations $\mathbf{q}$ that maximize the posterior probability $\Pr(\mathbf{q}|\mathbf{e})$ since $\Pr(\mathbf{q}|\mathbf{e}) = \Pr(\mathbf{q}, \mathbf{e})/\Pr(\mathbf{e})$ and $\Pr(\mathbf{e})$ is independent of instantiation $\mathbf{q}$.

We next define a variable elimination algorithm for computing the MPE probability and instantiations, and then follow with an algorithm based on systematic search. The complexity of the variable elimination algorithm is guaranteed to be $O(n\exp(w))$, where n is the number of network variables and w is the width of the elimination order. The algorithm based on systematic search does not have this complexity guarantee yet it can be more efficient in practice.

10.2.1 Computing MPE by variable elimination

Consider the joint probability distribution in Table 10.1, which has one MPE instantiation (assuming no evidence):

	S	C	T_1	T_2	A	Pr(.)
31	female	no	$-$ve	$-$ve	yes	.338580

Suppose for now that our goal is to compute the MPE probability, .338580. We can do this using the method of variable elimination that we discussed in Chapter 6 but when eliminating a variable, we maximize out that variable instead of summing it out. To maximize out variable S from the factor $f(S, C, T_1, T_2, A)$, we produce another factor over the remaining variables C, T_1, T_2, and A by merging all rows that agree on the values of these remaining variables. For example, the first and seventeenth rows in Table 10.1,

	S	C	T_1	T_2	A	Pr(.)
1	male	yes	$+$ve	$+$ve	yes	.017600
17	female	yes	$+$ve	$+$ve	yes	.003420

are merged as

C	T_1	T_2	A	
yes	$+$ve	$+$ve	yes	.017600 = max(.017600, .003420)

As we merge rows, we drop reference to the maximized variable S and assign to the resulting row the maximum probability associated with the merged rows.

The result of maximizing out variable S from factor f is another factor that we denote by $\max_S f$. Note that the factor $\max_S f$ does not mention variable S. Moreover, the new

Table 10.1: The joint probability distribution for the Bayesian network in Figure 10.1. Even rows are omitted as they all have zero probabilities.

	S	C	T_1	T_2	A	Pr(.)
1	male	yes	+ve	+ve	yes	.017600
3	male	yes	+ve	−ve	no	.004400
5	male	yes	−ve	+ve	no	.004400
7	male	yes	−ve	−ve	yes	.001100
9	male	no	+ve	+ve	yes	.020900
11	male	no	+ve	−ve	no	.083600
13	male	no	−ve	+ve	no	.083600
15	male	no	−ve	−ve	yes	.334400
17	female	yes	+ve	+ve	yes	.003420
19	female	yes	+ve	−ve	no	.000180
21	female	yes	−ve	+ve	no	.000855
23	female	yes	−ve	−ve	yes	.000045
25	female	no	+ve	+ve	yes	.004455
27	female	no	+ve	−ve	no	.084645
29	female	no	−ve	+ve	no	.017820
31	female	no	−ve	−ve	yes	.338580

factor $\max_S f$ agrees with the old factor f on the MPE probability. Hence, $\max_S f$ is as good as f for computing this probability. This means that we can continue to maximize variables out of $\max_S f$ until we are left with a trivial factor. The probability assigned by that factor is then the MPE probability. We show later how this method can be extended so that it returns an MPE instantiation in addition to computing its probability. But we first need to provide the formal definition of maximization.

Definition 10.1. Let $f(\mathbf{X})$ be a factor and let X be a variable in $\mathbf{X}$. The result of *maximizing out* variable X from factor f is another factor over variables $\mathbf{Y} = \mathbf{X} \setminus \{X\}$, which is denoted by $\max_X f$ and defined as

$$\left(\max_X f \right)(\mathbf{y}) \overset{def}{=} \max_x f(x, \mathbf{y}).$$ ∎

Similar to summation, maximization is commutative, which allows us to refer to maximizing out a set of variables without having to specify the order in which we maximize. Maximization is also similar to summation in the way it interacts with multiplication (see Exercise 10.6).

Theorem 10.1. *If f_1 and f_2 are factors and if variable X appears only in f_2, then*

$$\max_X f_1 f_2 = f_1 \max_X f_2.$$ ∎

This result justifies the use of Algorithm 27, VE_MPE, for computing the MPE probability. This algorithm resembles Algorithm 8, VE_PR, from Chapter 6 as it eliminates variables one at a time while multiplying only those factors that mention the variable being eliminated. The only difference with VE_PR is that:

- VE_MPE maximizes out variables instead of summing them out.
- VE_MPE does not prune nodes since every node in the network is relevant to the result.
- VE_MPE eliminates all variables from the network, leading to a trivial factor.

Algorithm 27 VE_MPE($\mathcal{N}$, **e**)

---

input:

  $\mathcal{N}$:   a Bayesian network

  e: evidence

output: trivial factor f, where $f(\top)$ is the MPE probability of evidence **e**

main:

1: $\mathcal{N}' \leftarrow$ pruneEdges($\mathcal{N}$, **e**) {see Section 6.9.2}

2: $\mathbf{Q} \leftarrow$ variables in network $\mathcal{N}'$

3: $\pi \leftarrow$ elimination order of variables $\mathbf{Q}$

4: $\mathcal{S} \leftarrow \{f^\mathbf{e} : f$ is a CPT of network $\mathcal{N}'\}$

5: **for** $i = 1$ to $|\mathbf{Q}|$ **do**

6:     $f \leftarrow \prod_k f_k$, where f_k belongs to $\mathcal{S}$ and mentions variable $\pi(i)$

7:     $f_i \leftarrow \max_{\pi(i)} f$

8:     replace all factors f_k in $\mathcal{S}$ by factor f_i

9: **end for**

10: **return** trivial factor $\prod_{f \in \mathcal{S}} f$

VE_MPE has the same complexity as VE_PR. That is, for a network with n variables and an elimination order of width w, the time and space complexity of VE_MPE is then $O(n \exp(w))$.

Recovering an MPE instantiation

Algorithm VE_MPE can be modified to compute an MPE instantiation in addition to its probability. The basic idea is to employ *extended factors*, which assign to each instantiation both a number and an instantiation. Consider for example the Bayesian network in Figure 10.2. An extended factor f with respect to this network will appear as

Y	O	$f(.)$	$f[.]$
true	false	.000095	$I =$ true, $X =$ true
false	false	.460845	$I =$ false, $X =$ false

This factor assigns the value .000095 to instantiation $Y =$ true, $O =$ false, but it also assigns the instantiation $I =$ true, $X =$ true to $Y =$ true, $O =$ false. We use $f[\mathbf{x}]$ to denote the instantiation that extended factor f assigns to $\mathbf{x}$ while continuing to use $f(\mathbf{x})$ for denoting the number it assigns to $\mathbf{x}$.

The instantiation $f[\mathbf{x}]$ is now used to record the MPE instantiation as it is being constructed.[1] Consider the following factor as an example:

X	Y	O		f
true	true	false	.0095	$I =$ true
true	false	false	.0205	$I =$ true
false	true	false	.0055	$I =$ false
false	false	false	.4655	$I =$ false

---

[1] Exercise 10.10 provides more precise semantics for the instantiation $f[\mathbf{x}]$.

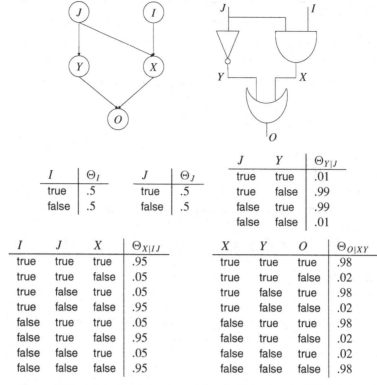

I	Θ_I
true	.5
false	.5

J	Θ_J
true	.5
false	.5

J	Y	$\Theta_{Y\mid J}$
true	true	.01
true	false	.99
false	true	.99
false	false	.01

I	J	X	$\Theta_{X\mid IJ}$
true	true	true	.95
true	true	false	.05
true	false	true	.05
true	false	false	.95
false	true	true	.05
false	true	false	.95
false	false	true	.05
false	false	false	.95

X	Y	O	$\Theta_{O\mid XY}$
true	true	true	.98
true	true	false	.02
true	false	true	.98
true	false	false	.02
false	true	true	.98
false	true	false	.02
false	false	true	.02
false	false	false	.98

Figure 10.2: A Bayesian network modeling the behavior of a digital circuit.

Maximizing out variable X now gives us the following factor:

Y	O	$\max\limits_{X} f$	
true	false	$.0095 = \max(.0095, .0055)$	$I = \text{true}, X = \text{true}$
false	false	$.4655 = \max(.0205, .4655)$	$I = \text{false}, X = \text{false}$

Note how we record the value true of X in the first row since this is the value of X that corresponds to the maximal probability .0095. Similarly, we record the value false of X in the second row for the same reason. There are situations where multiple values of the maximized variable lead to a maximal probability. Recording any of these values will do in such a case.

The following is the formal definition of operations on extended factors.

Definition 10.2. Let $f(\mathbf{X})$ be an extended factor, X be a variable in $\mathbf{X}$, and let $\mathbf{Y} = \mathbf{X} \setminus \{X\}$. We then define

$$\left(\max_{X} f\right)[\mathbf{y}] \overset{def}{=} x^{\star} f[x^{\star}, \mathbf{y}],$$

where $x^{\star} = \text{argmax}_x\, f(x, \mathbf{y})$. Moreover, let $f_1(\mathbf{X})$ and $f_2(\mathbf{Y})$ be extended factors and let $\mathbf{Z} = \mathbf{X} \cup \mathbf{Y}$. We then define

$$(f_1 f_2)[\mathbf{z}] \overset{def}{=} f_1[\mathbf{x}] f_2[\mathbf{y}],$$

where $\mathbf{x}$ and $\mathbf{y}$ are instantiation compatible with $\mathbf{z}$ ($\mathbf{x} \sim \mathbf{z}$ and $\mathbf{y} \sim \mathbf{z}$). ∎

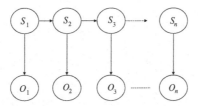

Figure 10.3: A hidden Markov model (discussed in Section 4.2).

Note that since each variable is eliminated only once, it will be recorded in only one factor. Hence, the instantiation $f[x^\star, \mathbf{y}]$ does not mention variable X. Similarly, the instantiations $f_1[\mathbf{x}]$ and $f_2[\mathbf{y}]$ do not mention a common variable.

Given extended factors and their operations, we can use VE_MPE to compute an MPE instantiation in addition to its probability. Specifically, we start the algorithm with each CPT f assigning the trivial instantiation to each of its rows: $f[.] = \top$. The trivial factor f returned by the algorithm will then contain the MPE probability, $f(\top)$, together with an MPE instantiation, $f[\top]$.

Before we consider an example of VE_MPE, we point out an important special case that arises from applying the algorithm to a class of Bayesian networks known as *hidden Markov models* (HMM) (see Figure 10.3). In particular, if we apply the algorithm to an HMM with evidence $o_1, \ldots, o_n$, and elimination order $\pi = O_1, S_1, O_2, S_2, \ldots, O_n, S_n$, we obtain the well-known Viterbi algorithm for HMMs. In the context of this algorithm, an MPE instantiation is known as a *most probable state path*. Moreover, if we compute the probability of evidence $o_1, \ldots, o_n$ using variable elimination and the previous order, we obtain the well known Forward algorithm for HMMs. Here the computed probability is known as the *sequence probability*. Finally, we note that the order $\pi = O_1, S_1, O_2, S_2, \ldots, O_n, S_n$ has width 1 with respect to an HMM. Hence, both the Viterbi and Forward algorithms have linear time and space complexity, which follow immediately from the complexity of variable elimination.

An example of computing MPE

Let us now consider an example of using VE_MPE to compute an MPE instantiation and its probability for the Bayesian network in Figure 10.2 given evidence $J=$true, $O=$false.

We first prune edges, leading to the network in Figure 10.4. Reducing network CPTs with the given evidence leads to the following extended factors (we are omitting rows that are assigned the value 0):

I	Θ_I^e	
true	.5	$\top$
false	.5	$\top$

J	Θ_J^e	
true	.5	$\top$

Y	Θ_Y^e	
true	.01	$\top$
false	.99	$\top$

I	X	$\Theta_{X\mid I}^e$	
true	true	.95	$\top$
true	false	.05	$\top$
false	true	.05	$\top$
false	false	.95	$\top$

X	Y	O	$\Theta_{O\mid XY}^e$	
true	true	false	.02	$\top$
true	false	false	.02	$\top$
false	true	false	.02	$\top$
false	false	false	.98	$\top$

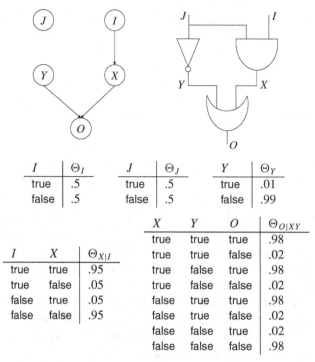

I	Θ_I
true	.5
false	.5

J	Θ_J
true	.5
false	.5

Y	Θ_Y
true	.01
false	.99

I	X	$\Theta_{X\mid I}$
true	true	.95
true	false	.05
false	true	.05
false	false	.95

X	Y	O	$\Theta_{O\mid XY}$
true	true	true	.98
true	true	false	.02
true	false	true	.98
true	false	false	.02
false	true	true	.98
false	true	false	.02
false	false	true	.02
false	false	false	.98

Figure 10.4: Pruning edges in the network of Figure 10.2 given the evidence J = true, O = false.

Note how each of these factors assigns the trivial instantiation $\top$ to each of its rows. Assuming the elimination order J, I, X, Y, O, Algorithm VE_MPE will then evaluate the following expression:

$$\max_{J,I,X,Y,O} \Theta_I^e \; \Theta_J^e \; \Theta_Y^e \; \Theta_{X\mid I}^e \; \Theta_{O\mid XY}^e$$

$$= \max_O \left(\max_Y \left(\max_X \left(\max_I \Theta_I^e \Theta_{X\mid I}^e \right) \Theta_{O\mid XY}^e \right) \Theta_Y^e \right) \left(\max_J \Theta_J^e \right).$$

All intermediate factors constructed during this evaluation are depicted in Figure 10.5. Therefore, an MPE instantiation given evidence $\mathbf{e} : J$ = true, O = false is

$$I = \text{false}, \quad J = \text{true}, \quad X = \text{false}, \quad Y = \text{false}, \quad O = \text{false}.$$

Moreover, the MPE probability is .2304225.

We can modify Algorithm VE_MPE further to enumerate the set of all MPE instantiations in time and space that are linear in the number of such instantiations (see Exercise 10.11). We can also adapt the algorithm of recursive conditioning from Chapter 8 for computing the MPE probability and instantiations, leading to an algorithm with a similar computational complexity to the one based on variable elimination (see Exercise 10.22).

10.2.2 Computing MPE by systematic search

In this section, we consider another class of algorithms for computing MPE that are based on systematic search and can be more efficient in practice than algorithms based on variable elimination.

Consider the Bayesian network in Figure 10.1 and suppose that our goal is to find an MPE instantiation given evidence A = true. One way of doing this is using depth-first

	$\max_{J} \Theta_J^e$	
⊤	.5	J = true

I	X	$\Theta_I^e \Theta_{X\|I}^e$	
true	true	.475	⊤
true	false	.025	⊤
false	true	.025	⊤
false	false	.475	⊤

X	$\max_{I} \Theta_I^e \Theta_{X\|I}^e$	
true	.475	I = true
false	.475	I = false

X	Y	O	$\left(\max_{I} \Theta_I^e \Theta_{X\|I}^e\right) \Theta_{O\|XY}^e$	
true	true	false	.0095	I = true
true	false	false	.0095	I = true
false	true	false	.0095	I = false
false	false	false	.4655	I = false

Y	O	$\max_{X}\left(\max_{I} \Theta_I^e \Theta_{X\|I}^e\right) \Theta_{O\|XY}^e$	
true	false	.0095	I = true, X = true
false	false	.4655	I = false, X = false

Y	O	$\left(\max_{X}\left(\max_{I} \Theta_I^e \Theta_{X\|I}^e\right) \Theta_{O\|XY}^e\right) \Theta_Y^e$	
true	false	.000095	I = true, X = true
false	false	.460845	I = false, X = false

O	$\max_{Y}\left(\max_{X}\left(\max_{I} \Theta_I^e \Theta_{X\|I}^e\right) \Theta_{O\|XY}^e\right) \Theta_Y^e$	
false	.460845	I = false, X = false, Y = false

	$\max_{O}\left(\max_{Y}\left(\max_{X}\left(\max_{I} \Theta_I^e \Theta_{X\|I}^e\right) \Theta_{O\|XY}^e\right) \Theta_Y^e\right)$	
⊤	.460845	I = false, X = false, Y = false, O = false

	$\max_{O}\left(\max_{Y}\left(\max_{X}\left(\max_{I} \Theta_I^e \Theta_{X\|I}^e\right) \Theta_{O\|XY}^e\right) \Theta_Y^e\right)\left(\max_{J} \Theta_J^e\right)$	
⊤	.2304225	J = true, I = false, X = false, Y = false, O = false

Figure 10.5: Intermediate factors of an MPE computation.

search on the tree depicted in Figure 10.6. The leaf nodes of this tree are in one-to-one correspondence with the instantiations of unobserved network variables. Moreover, each nonleaf node corresponds to a partial network instantiation. For example, the node marked by an arrow represents the instantiation S = male, C = yes. The children of this node correspond to extensions of this instantiation, which are obtained by assigning different values to the variable T_1. For example, the left child corresponds to instantiation S = male, C = yes, T_1 = −ve, while the right child corresponds to extension S = male, C = yes, T_1 = +ve.

We can traverse this search tree using depth-first search as given by Algorithm 28, DFS_MPE. Assuming that we have n unobserved network variables, DFS_MPE can be implemented to take $O(n)$ space and $O(n \exp(n))$ time. Note here that the probability $Pr(\mathbf{i})$ on Line 2 can be computed in time linear in the number of network variables using the chain rule of Bayesian networks.

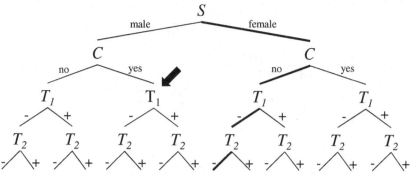

Figure 10.6: Searching for a most likely instantiation in the network of Figure 10.1 given evidence $A = $ yes. The instantiation marked in bold has the greatest probability in this case when combined with evidence $A = $ yes.

Algorithm 28 DFS_MPE($\mathcal{N}$, **e**)

input:

  $\mathcal{N}$:   Bayesian network

  e: evidence

output: an MPE instantiation for evidence **e**

main:

  Q ← network variables distinct from variables **E**

  s ← network instantiation compatible with evidence **e** {global variable}

  p ← probability of instantiation **s** {global variable}

  DFS_MPE_AUX(**e**, **Q**)

  return s

DFS_MPE_AUX(**i**,**X**)

  1: **if X** is empty **then** {**i** is a network instantiation}

  2:     **if** $\Pr(\mathbf{i}) > p$, **then** **s** ← **i** and p ← $\Pr(\mathbf{i})$

  3: **else**

  4:     X ← a variable in **X**

  5:     **for** each value x of variable X **do**

  6:        DFS_MPE_AUX(**i**x, **X** \ {X})

  7:     **end for**

  8: **end if**

Branch-and-bound search

We can improve the performance of Algorithm DFS_MPE by pruning parts of the search tree using an upper bound on the MPE probability. Suppose for example that we are exploring a search node corresponding to instantiation **i**. If we have already visited a leaf node corresponding to a network instantiation **s** with probability p and we know that every completion of instantiation **i** will not have a higher probability, we can then abandon the search node as it would not lead to instantiations that improve on the instantiation **s** found thus far.

Consider Figure 10.7, which depicts a search tree, and let us assume that the tree is traversed from left to right (we later explain how the upper bounds in this figure are computed). The first instantiation visited by depth-first search is then the one on the far left,

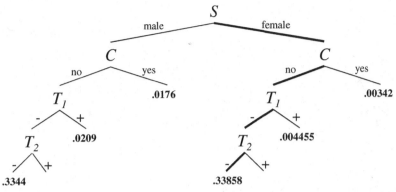

Figure 10.7: Pruning nodes while searching for a most likely instantiation in the network of Figure 10.1 given evidence $A =$ yes. Numbers associated with nonleaf nodes represent upper bounds on the MPE probability. For example, .0176 represents an upper bound on the MPE probability of evidence $S =$ male, $C =$ yes, and $A =$ true.

which has a probability of .3344. Using this instantiation as a baseline, the algorithm can now prune two subtrees as their upper bounds are lower than .3344. The next instantiation found by the algorithm has a probability of .33858, which is an improvement on the first instantiation. Using this new instantiation as a baseline, the algorithm prunes two more subtrees before terminating with the MPE instantiation

$$S = \text{female}, \quad C = \text{no}, \quad T_1 = -\text{ve}, \quad T_2 = -\text{ve}, \quad A = \text{yes},$$

which has an MPE probability of .33858.

The main point here is that our search algorithm did not have to visit every node in the search tree, which allows it to escape the exponential complexity in certain cases. If we let $\text{MPE}_P^u(\mathbf{i})$ stand for the computed upper bound on the MPE probability $\text{MPE}_P(\mathbf{i})$, we can then modify Algorithm DFS_MPE_AUX by inserting the following line just before Line 4:

if $\text{MPE}_P^u(\mathbf{i}) \le p$, return.

The efficiency of the resulting algorithm, which is known as depth-first branch-and-bound, will clearly depend on the tightness of computed upper bounds and the time it takes to compute them. In general, we want the tightest bounds possible and we would like to compute them efficiently, as we must compute one bound for each node in the search tree.

Generating upper bounds by node splitting

Instead of providing a specific upper bound on the MPE probability, we next discuss a technique that allows us to generate a spectrum of such bounds in which one can trade off the bound tightness with the time it takes to compute it.

Consider the network structure in Figure 10.8(a) and the corresponding transformation depicted in Figure 10.8(b). According to this transformation, the tail of edge $S \to T_2$ has been cloned by variable $\hat{S}$, that is, a variable that is meant to duplicate S by having the same set of values. Similarly, the tail of edge $T_1 \to A$ has now been cloned by variable $\hat{T}_1$. Here, both clone variables are roots and are assumed to have uniform CPTs, while all other network variables are assumed to maintain their original CPTs (except that we need to replace S by its clone $\hat{S}$ in the CPT of variable T_2 and replace T_1 by its clone $\hat{T}_1$ in the CPT of variable A).

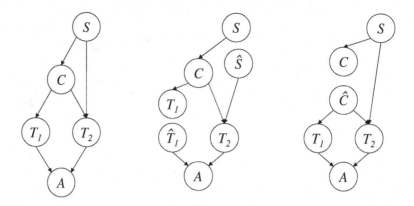

(a) Original network   (b) Splitting nodes S and T_1 (c) Splitting node C

Figure 10.8: Splitting nodes.

Transformations such as these can be used to reduce the treewidth of a network to a point where applying inference algorithms, such as variable elimination, becomes feasible. However, the transformed network does not induce the same distribution induced by the original network but is known to produce upper bounds on MPE probabilities. In particular, suppose that **e** is the given evidence and let **ê** be the instantiation of clone variables implied by evidence **e**. That is, for every variable X instantiated to x in evidence **e**, its clone $\hat{X}$ (if any) will also be instantiated to x in **ê**. The following is then guaranteed to hold:

$$\text{MPE}_P(\mathbf{e}) \leq \beta \cdot \text{MPE}'_P(\mathbf{e}, \hat{\mathbf{e}}),$$

where $\text{MPE}_P(\mathbf{e})$ and $\text{MPE}'_P(\mathbf{e}, \hat{\mathbf{e}})$ are MPE probabilities with respect to the original and transformed networks, respectively, and β is the total number of instantiations for the cloned variables. Hence, we can compute an upper bound on the MPE probability by performing inference on the transformed network, which usually has a low treewidth by design.

Consider Figure 10.8(b) as an example. If the evidence **e** is $S=\text{male}$ and $A=\text{yes}$, then **ê** is $\hat{S}=\text{male}$. Moreover,

$$\text{MPE}_P(\mathbf{e}) = .3344$$
$$\text{MPE}'_P(\mathbf{e}, \hat{\mathbf{e}}) = .0836$$
$$\beta = 4,$$

leading to

$$.3344 \leq (4)(.0836) = .3344.$$

Hence, the upper bound is exact in this case. Moreover, if the evidence **e** is simply $A=\text{yes}$, then **ê** is empty and we have

$$\text{MPE}_P(\mathbf{e}) = .33858$$
$$\text{MPE}'_P(\mathbf{e}, \hat{\mathbf{e}}) = .099275$$
$$\beta = 4,$$

leading to

$$.33858 < (4)(.099275) = .3971.$$

We later state this guarantee formally but we first need the following definition.

Definition 10.3. Let X be a node in a Bayesian network $\mathcal{N}$ with children $\mathbf{Y}$. We say that node X is *split according to children* $\mathbf{Z} \subseteq \mathbf{Y}$ when it results in a network that is obtained from $\mathcal{N}$ as follows:

- The edges outgoing from node X to its children $\mathbf{Z}$ are removed.
- A new root node $\hat{X}$, with the same values as X, is added to the network with nodes $\mathbf{Z}$ as its children.
- The node $\hat{X}$ is assigned a uniform CPT. The new CPT for a node in $\mathbf{Z}$ is obtained from its old CPT by replacing X with $\hat{X}$.

Here node $\hat{X}$ is called a *clone*. Moreover, the number of instantiations for split variables is called the *split cardinality*. ∎

In Figure 10.8(b), node S has been split according to its child T_2 and node T_1 has been split according to its child A, leading to a split cardinality of 4.

When a node X is split according to a single child Y, we say that we have deleted the edge $X \rightarrow Y$. Hence, the transformation in Figure 10.8(b) is the result of deleting two edges, $S \rightarrow T_2$ and $T_1 \rightarrow A$. Note, however, that in Figure 10.8(c) node C has been split according to both of its children, leading to a split cardinality of 2. Hence, this transformation cannot be described in terms of edge deletion. We now have the following theorem, which shows how splitting variables can be used to produce upper bounds on the MPE probability.

Theorem 10.2. *Let* $\mathcal{N}'$ *be the network that results from splitting variables in network* $\mathcal{N}$ *and let* β *be the split cardinality. For evidence* $\mathbf{e}$ *on network* $\mathcal{N}$, *let* $\hat{\mathbf{e}}$ *be the instantiation of split variables that is implied by* $\mathbf{e}$. *We then have*

$$\text{MPE}_P(\mathbf{e}) \leq \beta \cdot \text{MPE}'_P(\mathbf{e}, \hat{\mathbf{e}}),$$

where $\text{MPE}_P(\mathbf{e})$ *and* $\text{MPE}'_P(\mathbf{e}, \hat{\mathbf{e}})$ *are MPE probabilities with respect to the networks* $\mathcal{N}$ *and* $\mathcal{N}'$, *respectively.* ∎

We finally note that network transformations based on variable splitting can be cascaded. For example, a clone variable $\hat{X}$ that results from splitting variable X can later be split, producing its own clone. Moreover, each of the transformed networks produces upper bounds for all of the networks that precede it in the transformation sequence.

If variable splits are chosen carefully to reduce the network treewidth, then we can trade off the quality of the bounds with the time it takes to compute them. Typically, one chooses a treewidth that can be handled by the given computational resources and then splits enough variables to reach that treewidth.

Reducing the search space

When searching for an instantiation of variables $X_1, \ldots, X_n$, the size of the search tree will be $O(\exp(n))$, as we must have a leaf node for each variable instantiation. However, when using a split network for producing upper bounds we can reduce the search space significantly by searching only over the subset of variables that have been split. This is due to the following theorem.

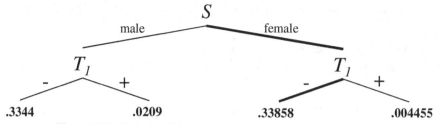

Figure 10.9: Reducing the search space for most likely instantiations.

Theorem 10.3. *Consider Theorem 10.2 and suppose that distributions* Pr *and* Pr′ *are induced by networks* $\mathcal{N}$ *and* $\mathcal{N}'$, *respectively. If the evidence* **e** *includes all split variables and if* **Q** *are the variables of* $\mathcal{N}$ *not in* **E**, *then*

$$\Pr(\mathbf{Q}, \mathbf{e}) = \beta \cdot \Pr'(\mathbf{Q}, \mathbf{e}, \hat{\mathbf{e}}).$$ ∎

This result is effectively showing that when the evidence instantiates all split variables, queries with respect to the split network are guaranteed to yield exact results. Hence, under evidence that instantiates all split variables we can perform exact inference in time and space that is exponential only in the treewidth of the split network.

Consider again the search tree in Figure 10.7, which is over four variables S, C, T_1, and T_2. The upper bounds for this search tree are generated by the network in Figure 10.8(b), which results from splitting two variables S and T_1. Hence, any time these variables are instantiated in the search tree, the bound produced by the split network is guaranteed to be exact. This means that one needs to only search over these two variables, leading to the smaller search tree shown in Figure 10.9. Consider for example the left-most leaf node, which corresponds to the instantiation S = male and T_1 = −ve. Since both split variables are instantiated in this case, Theorem 10.3 will then guarantee that

$$\mathrm{MPE}_P(\mathbf{e}) = 4 \cdot \mathrm{MPE}'_P(\mathbf{e}, \hat{\mathbf{e}}),$$

where **e** is the instantiation

$$S = \text{male}, \quad T_1 = -\text{ve}, \quad A = \text{yes},$$

and $\hat{\mathbf{e}}$ is the instantiation

$$\hat{S} = \text{male}, \quad \hat{T}_1 = -\text{ve}.$$

This means that once we reach this leaf node, there is no need to search deeper in the tree as we already know the exact MPE probability for instantiation **e**. Moreover, we can recover an MPE instantiation by calling Algorithm VE_MPE on the split network with evidence **e**, $\hat{\mathbf{e}}$ in this case.

Algorithm 29, BB_MPE, depicts the pseudocode for our search in this reduced space. BB_MPE uses depth-first search to find an instantiation **q** of the split variables for which the instantiation $\mathbf{s} = \mathbf{qe}$ has a greatest MPE probability p (this is done by calling BB_MPE_AUX). The algorithm then computes an MPE instantiation for the identified **s** using exact inference on the split network (this is done by calling VE_MPE). Note that inference is invoked on the split network in a number of places. Except in the case when Line 4 is reached, the results returned by the split network are guaranteed to be exact. This result follows because all such inferences are done while instantiating all of the split variables.

Algorithm 29 BB_MPE($\mathcal{N}$, **e**, $\mathcal{N}'$)

---

input:

   $\mathcal{N}$:   Bayesian network

   e: evidence

   $\mathcal{N}'$:   Bayesian network which results from splitting nodes in $\mathcal{N}$

output: MPE instantiation for network $\mathcal{N}$ and evidence **e**

main:

   Q$\leftarrow$ variables that were split in network $\mathcal{N}$ (assumes $\mathbf{Q} \cap \mathbf{E} = \emptyset$)

   q$\leftarrow$ an instantiation of split variables **Q**

   $\beta \leftarrow$ split cardinality

   s$\leftarrow$**qe** {current solution of BB_MPE_AUX}

   $p \leftarrow \beta \cdot \text{MPE}'_P(\mathbf{s}\hat{\mathbf{s}})$ {MPE probability of **s**}

   BB_MPE_AUX(**e**, **Q**) {modifies **s** and p}

   return MPE instantiation for evidence **s**$\hat{\mathbf{s}}$ and network $\mathcal{N}'$ using VE_MPE

BB_MPE_AUX(**i**, **X**)

  1: $b \leftarrow \beta \cdot \text{MPE}'_P(\mathbf{i}\mathbf{i})$ {bound on the MPE probability of **i**}

  2: **if X** is empty **then** {leaf node, bound b is exact}

  3:    **if** $b > p$, **then s**$\leftarrow$**i** and $p \leftarrow b$ {**i** better than current solution}

  4: **else if** $b > p$ **then**

  5:    $X \leftarrow$ a variable in **X**

  6:    **for** each state x of variable X **do**

  7:       BB_MPE_AUX(**i**x, **X** \ $\{X\}$)

  8:    **end for**

  9: **end if**

Complexity analysis

Suppose now that our original network has n variables and an elimination order of width w. Using variable elimination, we can solve an MPE problem for this network in time and space $O(n \exp(w))$. Suppose, however, that we wish to solve this MPE problem using BB_MPE, where we split m variables leading to a network with $n + m$ variables and an elimination order of width w'. Assuming that inference on the split network is performed using variable elimination, the space complexity of BB_MPE is now dominated by the space complexity of performing inference on the split network, which is $O((n + m) \exp(w'))$. This is also the time complexity for such inference, which must be performed for each node in the search tree. Since the search tree size is now reduced to $O(\exp(m))$ nodes, the total time complexity is then $O((n + m) \exp(w' + m))$.

This may not look favorable to BB_MPE but we should note the following. First, the space complexity of the BB_MPE is actually better as it is exponential in the reduced width w' instead of the original width w. Second, the time complexity of variable elimination is both a worst- and a best-case complexity. For BB_MPE however, this is only a worst-case complexity, leaving the possibility of a much better average-case complexity (due to pruning).

10.2.3 Reduction to W-MAXSAT

In Chapter 11, we consider a reduction of the MPE problem into the well-known W-MAXSAT problem, which can be solved using systematic and local search algorithms.

There is an extensive literature on these search methods that can be brought to bear on MPE, either directly or through the reduction to be discussed in Chapter 11.

10.3 Computing MAP instantiations

The *MAP probability* for variables **M** and evidence **e** is defined as

$$\text{MAP}_P(\mathbf{M}, \mathbf{e}) \stackrel{def}{=} \max_{\mathbf{m}} \Pr(\mathbf{m}, \mathbf{e}).$$

There may be a number of instantiations **m** that attain this maximal probability. Each of these instantiations is then a *MAP instantiation*, where the set of all such instantiations is defined as

$$\text{MAP}(\mathbf{M}, \mathbf{e}) \stackrel{def}{=} \underset{\mathbf{m}}{\text{argmax}} \, \Pr(\mathbf{m}, \mathbf{e}).$$

MAP instantiations can also be characterized as instantiations **m** that maximize the posterior probability $\Pr(\mathbf{m}|\mathbf{e})$ since $\Pr(\mathbf{m}|\mathbf{e}) = \Pr(\mathbf{m}, \mathbf{e})/\Pr(\mathbf{e})$ and $\Pr(\mathbf{e})$ is independent of instantiation **m**.

10.3.1 Computing MAP by variable elimination

We can compute the MAP probability $\text{MAP}_P(\mathbf{M}, \mathbf{e})$ using the algorithm of variable elimination by first summing out all non-MAP variables and then maximizing out MAP variables **M**. By summing out non-MAP variables, we effectively compute the joint marginal $\Pr(\mathbf{M}, \mathbf{e})$ in factored form. By maximizing out MAP variables **M**, we effectively solve an MPE problem over the resulting marginal. The proposed algorithm can therefore be thought of as a combination of Algorithm VE_PR from Chapter 6 and Algorithm VE_MPE that we presented previously for computing the MPE probability.

Algorithm 30, VE_MAP, provides the pseudocode for computing the MAP probability using variable elimination. There are two aspects of this algorithm that are worth noting. First, the elimination order used on Line 2 is special in the sense that MAP variables appear last in the order. Second, the algorithm performs both types of elimination, maximizing-out for MAP variables and summing-out for non-MAP variables. Algorithm VE_MAP can also be used to compute a MAP instantiation by using extended factors, just as when computing an MPE instantiation. We present an example of this later.

MAP and constrained width

The complexity of VE_MAP is similar to that of VE_MPE in the following sense. Given a Bayesian network with n variables and an elimination order of width w, the time and space complexity of VE_MAP is $O(n \exp(w))$. There is one key difference with VE_MPE, though. The variable order used on Line 2 of VE_MAP is constrained as it requires MAP variables **M** to appear last in the order. What this means is that we may not be able to use a good ordering (one with low width) simply because low-width orders may not satisfy this constraint. Consider the network in Figure 10.10, which has a polytree structure. The treewidth of this network is 2 since we have at most two parents per node. Suppose now that we want to compute MAP for variables $\mathbf{M} = \{Y_1, \ldots, Y_n\}$ with respect to this network. Any order in which variables **M** come last has a width $\geq n$, even though we have an unconstrained variable order with width 2. Hence, VE_MPE requires linear time in this case, while VE_MAP requires exponential time.

Algorithm 30 VE_MAP($\mathcal{N}$, **M**, **e**)

---

input:

   $\mathcal{N}$:   Bayesian network

   M: some variables in the network

   e: evidence ($\mathbf{E} \cap \mathbf{M} = \emptyset$)

output: trivial factor containing the MAP probability $\text{MAP}_P(\mathbf{M}, \mathbf{e})$

main:

1: $\mathcal{N}' \leftarrow$pruneNetwork($\mathcal{N}$, **M**, **e**) {see Section 6.9.3}

2: $\pi \leftarrow$ a variable elimination order for $\mathcal{N}'$ in which variables **M** appear last

3: $\mathcal{S} \leftarrow \{f^{\mathbf{e}} : f$ is a CPT of network $\mathcal{N}'\}$

4: **for** $i = 1$ to length of order π **do**

5:     $f \leftarrow \prod_k f_k$, where factor f_k belongs to $\mathcal{S}$ and mentions variable $\pi(i)$

6:     **if** $\pi(i) \in \mathbf{M}$ **then**

7:       $f_i \leftarrow \max_{\pi(i)} f$

8:     **else**

9:       $f_i \leftarrow \sum_{\pi(i)} f$

10:    **end if**

11:    replace all factors f_k in $\mathcal{S}$ by factor f_i

12: **end for**

13: **return** trivial factor $\prod_{f \in \mathcal{S}} f$

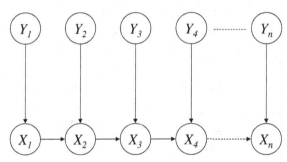

Figure 10.10: A polytree structure.

In general, we cannot use arbitrary elimination orders as we cannot interleave variables that we are summing out with those that we are maximizing out because maximization does not commute with summation, as shown by the following theorem.

Theorem 10.4. *Let f be a factor over disjoint variables X, Y, and $\mathbf{Z}$. We then have*

$$\left[\sum_X \max_Y f \right](\mathbf{z}) \geq \left[\max_Y \sum_X f \right](\mathbf{z})$$

for all instantiations $\mathbf{z}$. ■

The complexity of computing MAP using variable elimination is then at best exponential in the constrained treewidth, as defined next.

Definition 10.4. A variable order π is **M**-constrained iff variables **M** appear last in the order π. The **M**-*constrained treewidth* of a graph is the width of its best **M**-constrained variable order. ■

Computing MAP is therefore more difficult than computing MPE in the context of variable elimination. An interesting question is whether this difference in complexity is genuine or whether it is an idiosyncrasy of the variable elimination framework. We shed more light on this question when we discuss the complexity of probabilistic inference in Chapter 11.

An example of computing MAP

Let us now consider an example of using Algorithm VE_MAP to compute the MAP probability and instantiation for the Bayesian network of Figure 10.2 with MAP variables $\mathbf{M} = \{I, J\}$ and evidence $\mathbf{e} : O = \text{true}$. We use the constrained variable order $\pi = O, Y, X, I, J$ for this purpose. Summing out variables O, Y, and X, we obtain the following set of factors, which represent a factored representation of the joint marginal $\Pr(I, J, O = \text{true})$:

I	J	f_1	
true	true	.93248	⊤
true	false	.97088	⊤
false	true	.07712	⊤
false	false	.97088	⊤

I	f_2	
true	.5	⊤
false	.5	⊤

J	f_3	
true	.5	⊤
false	.5	⊤

We will now trace the rest of VE_MAP by maximizing out variables I and J. To eliminate variable I, we multiply its factors and then maximize:

I	J	$f_1 f_2$	
true	true	.466240	⊤
true	false	.485440	⊤
false	true	.038560	⊤
false	false	.485440	⊤

J	$\max_I f_1 f_2$	
true	.466240	$I = \text{true}$
false	.485440	$I = \text{true}$

To eliminate variable J, we multiply its factors and then maximize:

J	$\left(\max_I f_1 f_2\right) f_3$	
true	.233120	$I = \text{true}$
false	.242720	$I = \text{true}$

	$\max_J \left(\max_I f_1 f_2\right) f_3$	
⊤	.242720	$I = \text{true}, J = \text{false}$

Therefore, the instantiation $I = \text{true}, J = \text{false}$ is a MAP instantiation in this case. Moreover, .242720 is the MAP probability, $\Pr(I = \text{true}, J = \text{false}, O = \text{true})$.

10.3.2 Computing MAP by systematic search

MAP can be solved using depth-first branch-and-bound search, just as we did for MPE. The pseudocode for this is shown in Algorithm 31, BB_MAP, which resembles the one for computing MPE aside from two exceptions. First, the instantiation $\mathbf{i}$ on Line 2 does not cover all network variables (only MAP variables and evidence). Hence, computing its probability can no longer be performed using the chain rule of Bayesian networks and would therefore require inference on the given network. Second, although the upper bound needed for pruning on Line 3 can be computed based on a split network as we did for MPE, the quality of this bound has been observed to be somewhat loose in practice, at least compared to the MPE case. We therefore provide a different method for computing upper bounds on the MAP probability next that is based on the following theorem.

Algorithm 31 BB_MAP($\mathcal{N}$, **M**, **e**)

---

input:

$\mathcal{N}$:　　Bayesian network

M:　　some variables in the network

e:　　evidence ($\mathbf{E} \cap \mathbf{M} = \emptyset$)

output: MAP instantiation for variables **M** and evidence **e**

main:

　m ← some instantiation of variables **M** {global variable}

　p ← probability of instantiation **m**, **e** {global variable}

　BB_MAP_AUX(**e**, **M**)

　return m

BB_MAP_AUX(**i**, **X**)

　1:　**if X** is empty **then** {leaf node}

　2:　　**if** Pr(**i**) > p, **then m** ← **i** and p ← Pr(**i**)

　3:　**else if** MAP$_p^u$(**X**, **i**) > p **then**

　4:　　X ← a variable in **X**

　5:　　**for** each value x of variable X **do**

　6:　　　BB_MAP_AUX(**i**x, **X** \ {X})

　7:　　**end for**

　8:　**end if**

Theorem 10.5. *Consider Algorithm 30,* VE_MAP, *and let* Pr *be the distribution induced by the given Bayesian network. If we use an arbitrary elimination order on Line 2 of the algorithm, the number q it returns will satisfy*

$$\text{MAP}_P(\mathbf{M}, \mathbf{e}) \leq q \leq \text{Pr}(\mathbf{e}).$$　　■

That is, even though we cannot use an arbitrary elimination order for computing the MAP probability, we can use such an order for computing an upper bound on the MAP probability. As it turns out, some of these arbitrary orders produce better bounds than others, and our goal is to obtain an order that provides one of the better bounds. We discuss this issue next but only after analyzing the complexity of our search algorithm.

Suppose that we are given a network with n variables, an elimination order of width w, and a constrained elimination order of width $w + c$. We can compute MAP for this network using variable elimination in $O(n \exp(w + c))$ time and space. Suppose now that we use Algorithm BB_MAP for this purpose. The search tree has $O(\exp(m))$ nodes in this case, where m is the number of MAP variables. The inferences needed for a leaf node on Line 2 takes $O(n \exp(w))$ time and space, assuming the use of variable elimination. Computing the upper bound on Line 3 also requires a similar complexity. Hence, the total space complexity of the algorithm is $O(n \exp(w))$ and the total time complexity is $O(n \exp(w + m))$.

Comparing this to the use of variable elimination, VE_MAP, we find that the search algorithm has a better space complexity. As to the time complexity, it depends on the constrained width $w + c$ and the number of MAP variables m. Even if the number of MAP variables m is larger than c, the search algorithm may still perform better. Recall here that the complexity of variable elimination is for the best and worst case. However,

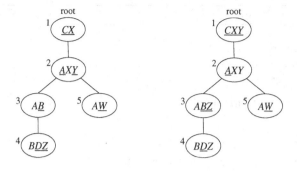

(a) Jointree   (b) Jointree with promoted variables

Figure 10.11: Variables that are underlined are eliminated in the corresponding clusters. The MAP variables are W, X, Y, and Z. Only variables Y and Z are promoted in this case. In particular, variable Y has been promoted from cluster 2 to cluster 1, and variable Z has been promoted from cluster 4 to cluster 3.

the complexity of search is only for the worst case, where the average complexity may be much better in practice.

Improving the bound

As it turns out, even though any elimination order can be used to produce an upper bound, some orders will produce tighter upper bounds than others. Intuitively, the closer the used order is to a constrained order, the tighter the bound is expected to be. We next discuss a technique for selecting one of the better (unconstrained) orders.

Our technique is based on elimination orders that are obtained from jointrees, as discussed in Section 9.3.5. For example, considering the jointree in Figure 10.11(a) and the root cluster $\mathbf{C}_1$, we can generate a number of elimination orders, including

$$\pi_1 = D, Z, B, W, A, Y, C, X$$
$$\pi_2 = Z, D, W, B, Y, A, X, C.$$

Suppose now that the MAP variables are W, X, Y, and Z. The elimination orders π_1 and π_2 are not constrained in this case. Note, however, that order π_1 will produce better bounds than order π_2 as the MAP variables appear later in the order.

We can easily transform a jointree of width w into another jointree of width w that induces elimination orders closer to a constrained order. The basic idea is to promote MAP variables toward the root without increasing the jointree width w. Specifically, let $\mathbf{C}_k$ and $\mathbf{C}_i$ be two adjacent clusters in the jointree where $\mathbf{C}_i$ is closer to the root. Any MAP variable M that appears in cluster $\mathbf{C}_k$ is added to cluster $\mathbf{C}_i$ as long as the new size of cluster $\mathbf{C}_i$ does not exceed $w + 1$. This transformation is guaranteed to preserve the jointree properties as discussed in Section 9.4.

Figure 10.11 illustrates a jointree before and after promotion of the MAP variables. The new jointree induces the following order:

$$\pi_3 = D, B, Z, W, A, C, X, Y,$$

which is closer to a constrained order than order π_1 given previously because the MAP variables Y and Z appear later in the order:

$$\pi_1 = D, Z, B, W, A, Y, C, X$$
$$\pi_3 = D, B, Z, W, A, C, X, Y.$$

Effectively, each time a MAP variable is promoted from cluster $\mathbf{C}_k$ to cluster $\mathbf{C}_i$ (which is closer to the root), the elimination of that variable is postponed, pushing it past all of the non-MAP variables that are eliminated in cluster $\mathbf{C}_i$. This typically has a monotonic effect on the upper bound, although in rare cases the bound may remain the same. We stress here that the promotion technique is meant to improve the bound computed by elimination orders that are induced by the jointree and a selected root. After such promotion, the quality of a bound computed by orders that are induced by some other root may actually worsen.

The performance of Algorithm 31, BB_MAP, can also be significantly improved if one employs heuristics for choosing variables and values on Lines 4 and 5, respectively. Exercise 10.21 suggests some heuristics for this purpose. Another technique that is known to improve the performance of branch-and-bound search concerns the choice of a seed instantiation with which to start the search. In particular, the greater the probability of this initial instantiation, the more pruning we expect during search. The next section discusses local search methods, which can be very efficient yet are not guaranteed to find the most likely instantiation. It is quite common to use these local search methods for producing high-quality seeds for branch-and-bound search.

10.3.3 Computing MAP by local search

A MAP instantiation can be approximated using local search, which can be more efficient than systematic search as presented in the previous section. In particular, given a network with n variables and an elimination order of width w, the local search algorithm we discuss next takes $O(r \cdot n \exp(w))$ time and space, where r is the number of search steps performed by the algorithm.

Similar to systematic search, local search is applied in the space of instantiations $\mathbf{m}$ of MAP variables $\mathbf{M}$. However, instead of systematically and exhaustively searching through this space, we simply start with an initial instantiation $\mathbf{m}_0$ and then visit one of its neighbors. A *neighbor* of instantiation $\mathbf{m}$ is defined as an instantiation that results from changing the value of a single variable X in $\mathbf{m}$. If the new value of X is x, we denote the resulting neighbor by $\mathbf{m} - X, x$. To perform local search efficiently, we need to compute the scores (probabilities) for all of the neighbors $\mathbf{m} - X, x$ efficiently. That is, we need to compute $\Pr(\mathbf{m} - X, x, \mathbf{e})$ for each $X \in \mathbf{M}$ and each of its values x not in $\mathbf{m}$. Computing the scores of all neighbors $\Pr(\mathbf{m} - X, x, \mathbf{e})$ can be done in $O(n \exp(w))$ time and space, as shown in Chapter 12.

A variety of local search methods can be used to navigate the instantiations of MAP variables $\mathbf{M}$. One particular approach is *stochastic hill climbing*, which is given in Algorithm 32, LS_MAP. Stochastic hill climbing proceeds by repeatedly either moving to the most probable neighbor of current instantiation $\mathbf{m}$ or changing a variable value at random in the current instantiation $\mathbf{m}$. This is repeated for a number of steps r before the algorithm terminates and returns the best instantiation visited in the process.

The quality of the solution returned by a local search algorithm depends to a large extent on which part of the search space it starts to explore. There are a number of possible initialization schemes that we could use for this purpose. Suppose that n is the number of network variables, w is the width of a given elimination order, and m is the number of MAP variables. We can then use any of the following initialization methods:

- *Random initialization*: For each MAP variable, we select one of its values with a uniform probability. This method takes $O(m)$ time.

Algorithm 32 LS_MAP($\mathcal{N}$, **M**, **e**)

---

input:

   $\mathcal{N}$:   Bayesian network

   M: some network variables

   e: evidence ($\mathbf{E} \cap \mathbf{M} = \emptyset$)

output: instantiation **m** of **M** which (approximately) maximizes $\Pr(\mathbf{m}|\mathbf{e})$

main:

  1: $r \leftarrow$ number of local search steps

  2: $P_f \leftarrow$ probability of randomly choosing a neighbor

  3: $\mathbf{m}^\star \leftarrow$ some instantiation of variables **M** {best instantiation}

  4: $\mathbf{m} \leftarrow \mathbf{m}^\star$ {current instantiation}

  5: **for** r times **do**

  6:     $p \leftarrow$ random number in $[0, 1]$

  7:     **if** $p \leq P_f$ **then**

  8:         $\mathbf{m} \leftarrow$ randomly selected neighbor of **m**

  9:     **else**

10:         compute the score $\Pr(\mathbf{m} - X, x, \mathbf{e})$ for each neighbor $\mathbf{m} - X, x$

11:         **if** no neighbor has a higher score than the score for **m then**

12:             $\mathbf{m} \leftarrow$ randomly selected neighbor of **m**

13:         **else**

14:             $\mathbf{m} \leftarrow$ a neighbor of **m** with a highest score

15:         **end if**

16:     **end if**

17:     **if** $\Pr(\mathbf{m}, \mathbf{e}) > \Pr(\mathbf{m}^\star, \mathbf{e})$, **then** $\mathbf{m}^\star \leftarrow \mathbf{m}$

18: **end for**

19: **return m***

- *MPE-based initialization*: Compute the MPE solution given the evidence. Then for each MAP variable, set its value according to the MPE instantiation. This method takes $O(n \exp(w))$ time.

- *Maximum marginal initialization*: For each MAP variable X, set its value to the instance x that maximizes $\Pr(x|\mathbf{e})$. This method takes $O(n \exp(w))$ time.

- *Sequential initialization*: This method considers the MAP variables $X_1, \ldots, X_m$, choosing each time a variable X_i that has the highest probability $\Pr(x_i|\mathbf{e}, \mathbf{y})$ for one of its values x_i, where **y** is the instantiation of MAP variables considered so far. This method takes $O(m \cdot n \exp(w))$ time.

The last initialization method is the most expensive but has also proven to be the most effective. Finally, when random initialization is used, it is not uncommon to use the technique of *random restarts*, where one runs the algorithm multiple times with a different initial, random instantiation in each run.

Bibliographic remarks

The use of variable elimination to solve MAP and MPE was proposed in Dechter [1999]. The Viterbi algorithm for solving MPE on HMMs is discussed in Viterbi [1967] and Rabiner [1989]. Constrained width was first introduced in Park and Darwiche [2004a], where it was used to analyze the complexity of variable elimination for solving MAP.

Solving MPE using branch-and-bound search was first proposed in Kask and Dechter [2001]; see also Marinescu et al. [2003] and Marinescu and Dechter [2006]. A more sophisticated algorithm based on a variant of recursive conditioning was proposed in Marinescu and Dechter [2005]. The upper bounds used in these algorithms are based on the minibuckets framework [Dechter and Rish, 2003], which is a relaxation of variable elimination that allows one to produce a spectrum of upper bounds that trade accuracy with efficiency. The upper bound based on splitting variables was proposed in Choi et al. [2007], where a correspondence was shown with the upper bounds produced by the minibuckets framework. However, the computation of these bounds based on split networks was shown to be more general as it allows one to use any algorithm for the computation of these bounds, such as the ones for exploiting local structure that we discuss in Chapter 13.

The use of branch-and-bound search for solving MAP was first proposed in Park and Darwiche [2003a], who also introduced the MAP upper bound discussed in this chapter. Arithmetic circuits, discussed in Chapter 12, were used recently for the efficient computation of this bound [Huang et al., 2006]. The use of stochastic local search for solving MAP was first proposed in Park and Darwiche [2001]. Other approximation schemes were proposed in Park and Darwiche [2004a], Yuan et al. [2004], and Sun et al. [2007]. Local search and other approximation schemes have also been proposed for solving MPE (e.g., [Kask and Dechter, 1999; Hutter et al., 2005; Wainwright et al., 2005; Kolmogorov and Wainwright, 2005]).

10.4 Exercises

10.1. Compute the MPE probability and a corresponding MPE instantiation for the Bayesian network in Figure 10.1, given evidence $A = $ no and using Algorithm 27, VE_MPE.

10.2. Consider the Bayesian network in Figure 10.1. What is the most likely outcome of the two tests T_1 and T_2 for a female on whom the tests came out different? Use Algorithm 30, VE_MAP, to answer this question.

10.3. Show that the MAP example in Section 10.3.1 admits another MAP instantiation with the same probability .242720.

10.4. Construct a factor f over variables X and Y such that

$$\sum_Y \max_X f \neq \max_X \sum_Y f.$$

10.5. Construct a factor f over variables X and Y such that

$$\sum_Y \max_X f = \max_X \sum_Y f.$$

10.6. Prove Theorem 10.1.

10.7. Consider a naive Bayes structure with edges $C \to A_1, \ldots, C \to A_n$. What is the complexity of computing the MPE probability for this network using Algorithm 27, VE_MPE? What is the complexity of computing the MAP probability for MAP variables $A_1, \ldots, A_n$ using Algorithm 30, VE_MAP? How does the complexity of these computations change when we have evidence on variable C?

10.8. True or false: We can compute a MAP instantiation MAP($\mathbf{M}, \mathbf{e}$) by computing the MAP instantiations $\mathbf{m}_x = $ MAP($\mathbf{M}, \mathbf{e}x$) for every value x of some variable $X \notin \mathbf{M}$ and then returning $\text{argmax}_{\mathbf{m}_x} \text{Pr}(\mathbf{m}_x, \mathbf{e})$. What if $X \in \mathbf{M}$? For each case, either prove or provide a counterexample.

10.9. Suppose that we have a jointree with n clusters and width w. Show that MAP can be solved in $O(n \exp(w))$ time and space if all MAP variables are contained in some jointree cluster.

10.10. Show that Algorithm 27, VE_MPE, is correct when run with extended factors. In particular, prove the following invariant for this algorithm. Let $\mathbf{X}$ be the variables appearing in the set S maintained by VE_MPE, $\mathbf{Y}$ be all other (eliminated) variables, and f be the product of factors in S. Then $f(\mathbf{x}) = \Pr(\mathbf{x}, f[\mathbf{x}], \mathbf{e})$ and $f(\mathbf{x}) = \max_{\mathbf{y}} \Pr(\mathbf{x}, \mathbf{y}, \mathbf{e})$. Show that this invariant holds before the algorithm reaches Line 5 and remains true after each iteration of Lines 6–8.

10.11. Extend Algorithm VE_MPE so it returns a structure Σ from which all MPE solutions can be enumerated in time linear in their count and linear in the size of Σ. The extended algorithm should have the same complexity as VE_MPE. Hint: Appeal to NNF circuits.

10.12. Prove Lemma 10.1 on Page 267.

10.13. Let $\mathcal{N}$ be a network with treewidth w and let $\mathcal{N}'$ be another network that results from splitting m variables in $\mathcal{N}$. Show that $w' \geq w - m$, where w' is the treewidth of network $\mathcal{N}'$. This means that to reduce the treewidth of network $\mathcal{N}$ by m, we must split at least m variables.

10.14. Let $\mathcal{N}$ be a Bayesian network and let $\mathbf{C}$ be a corresponding loop cutset. Provide tight lower and upper bounds on the treewidth of a network that results from splitting variables $\mathbf{C}$ in $\mathcal{N}$. Note: A variable $C \in \mathbf{C}$ can be split according to any number of children.

10.15. Suppose that we have a Bayesian network $\mathcal{N}$ with a corresponding jointree J. Let $\mathcal{N}'$ be a network that results from splitting some variable X in $\mathcal{N}$ according to its children (i.e., one clone is introduced). Show how we can obtain a jointree for network $\mathcal{N}'$ by modifying the clusters of jointree J. Aim for the best jointree possible (minimize its width). Show how this technique can be used to develop a greedy method for obtaining a split network that has a particular width.

10.16. Consider a Bayesian network $\mathcal{N}$, a corresponding jointree J, and assume that the CPTs for network $\mathcal{N}$ have been assigned to clusters in J. Consider a separator $\mathbf{S}_{ij}$ that contains variable X and suppose that the CPT of variable X has been assigned to a cluster on the j-side of edge i–j. Consider now a transformation that produces a new jointree J' as follows:

- Replace all occurrences of variable X by $\hat{X}$ on the i-side of edge i–j in the jointree.
- Remove all occurrences of X and $\hat{X}$ from clusters that have not been assigned CPTs mentioning X, as long as the removal will not destroy the jointree property.

Describe a network $\mathcal{N}'$ that results from splitting variables in $\mathcal{N}$ for which J' would be a valid jointree.

10.17. Let $\mathcal{N}'$ be a network that results from splitting nodes in network $\mathcal{N}$, and let $\Pr'$ and $\Pr$ be their corresponding distributions. Show that

$$\Pr(\mathbf{e}) \leq \beta \cdot \Pr'(\mathbf{e}, \hat{\mathbf{e}}),$$

where $\hat{\mathbf{e}}$ is the instantiation of clone variables that is implied by evidence $\mathbf{e}$ and β is the split cardinality.

10.18. Prove Theorem 10.3.

10.19. Consider the classical jointree algorithm as defined by Equations 7.4 and 7.5 in Chapter 7:

$$M_{ij} = \sum_{\mathbf{C}_i \setminus \mathbf{S}_{ij}} \Phi_i \prod_{k \neq j} M_{ki}$$

$$f_i(\mathbf{C}_i) = \Phi_i \prod_k M_{ki}.$$

Suppose that we replace all summations by maximization when computing messages,

$$M_{ij} = \max_{\mathbf{C}_i \setminus \mathbf{S}_{ij}} \Phi_i \prod_{k \neq j} M_{ki}.$$

What are the semantics of the factor $f_i(\mathbf{C}_i)$ in this case? In particular, can we use it to recover answers to MPE queries?

10.20. Consider the classical jointree algorithm as defined by Equations 7.4 and 7.5 in Chapter 7:

$$M_{ij} = \sum_{\mathbf{C}_i \setminus \mathbf{S}_{ij}} \Phi_i \prod_{k \neq j} M_{ki}$$

$$f_i(\mathbf{C}_i) = \Phi_i \prod_k M_{ki}.$$

Suppose that we replace all summations over MAP variables $\mathbf{M}$ by maximization when computing messages as follows:

$$M_{ij} = \max_{(\mathbf{C}_i \setminus \mathbf{S}_{ij}) \cap \mathbf{M}} \sum_{(\mathbf{C}_i \setminus \mathbf{S}_{ij}) \setminus \mathbf{M}} \Phi_i \prod_{k \neq j} M_{ki}.$$

What are the semantics of the factor $f_i(\mathbf{C}_i)$ in this case? In particular, can we use it to recover answers relating to MAP queries?

10.21. Consider Line 3 of Algorithm 31 and let

$$B_x = \text{MAP}_P^u(\mathbf{X} \setminus \{X\}, \mathbf{i}x).$$

Consider now the following heuristics:

- On Line 4, choose variable X that maximizes M_X / T_X, where

$$M_X = \max_x B_x$$

$$T_X = \sum_{B_x \geq p} B_x,$$

  and p is the probability on Line 2 of Algorithm 31.

- On Line 5, choose values x in decreasing order of B_x.

Implement a version of Algorithm 31 that employs these heuristics and compare its performance with and without the heuristics. Note: The jointree algorithm can be used to compute the bounds B_x efficiently (see Exercise 10.20).

10.22. We can modify Algorithm 13, RC1, from Chapter 8 to answer MPE queries by replacing summation with maximization, leading to RC_MPE shown in Algorithm 33. This algorithm computes the MPE probability but not the MPE instantiations.

(a) How can we modify Algorithm RC_MPE so that it returns the number of MPE instantiations?

(b) How can we modify Algorithm RC_MPE so that it returns an NNF circuit that encodes the set of MPE instantiations, that is, the circuit models are precisely the MPE instantiations?

10.5 Proofs

Lemma 10.1. *Let $\mathcal{N}'$ be the network resulting from splitting variables in network $\mathcal{N}$. Let Pr' and Pr be their corresponding distributions. We then have*

$$\text{Pr}(\mathbf{x}) = \beta \cdot \text{Pr}'(\mathbf{x}, \hat{\mathbf{x}}),$$

where $\mathbf{X}$ are the variables of network $\mathcal{N}$, $\hat{\mathbf{x}}$ is an instantiation of all clone variables that is implied by $\mathbf{x}$, and β is the split cardinality.

PROOF. Left to Exercise 10.12. ∎

PROOF OF THEOREM 10.2. Let $\mathcal{N}'$ be the network resulting from splitting variables in network $\mathcal{N}$. Let Pr' and Pr be their corresponding distributions. Suppose that

$$\text{MPE}_P(\mathbf{e}) > \beta \cdot \text{MPE}'_P(\mathbf{e}, \hat{\mathbf{e}}).$$

Algorithm 33 RC_MPE(T, **e**)

---

input:
   T: dtree node
   e: evidence

output: MPE probability for evidence **e**

main:
1: **if** T is a leaf node **then**
2:     $\Theta_{X|U} \leftarrow$ CPT associated with node T
3:     **u** $\leftarrow$ instantiation of parents **U** consistent with evidence **e**
4:     **if** X has value x in evidence **e then**
5:        **return** $\theta_{x|\mathbf{u}}$
6:     **else**
7:        **return** $\max_x \theta_{x|\mathbf{u}}$
8:     **end if**
9: **else**
10:    $p \leftarrow 0$
11:    $\mathbf{C} \leftarrow \text{cutset}(T)$
12:    **for** each instantiation **c** consistent with evidence **e**, $\mathbf{c} \sim \mathbf{e}$ **do**
13:       $p \leftarrow \max(p, \text{RC\_MPE}(T^l, \mathbf{ec})\,\text{RC\_MPE}(T^r, \mathbf{ec}))$
14:    **end for**
15:    **return** p
16: **end if**

We must then have a variable instantiation **x** that is compatible with evidence **e**, where

$$\Pr(\mathbf{x}) > \beta \cdot \text{MPE}'_P(\mathbf{e}, \hat{\mathbf{e}}).$$

By Lemma 10.1, we have

$$\Pr(\mathbf{x}) = \beta \cdot \Pr'(\mathbf{x}, \hat{\mathbf{x}}) > \beta \cdot \text{MPE}'_P(\mathbf{e}, \hat{\mathbf{e}}).$$

This is a contradiction because $\text{MPE}'_P(\mathbf{e}, \hat{\mathbf{e}})$ is the MPE probability for network $\mathcal{N}'$ and because **x** is compatible with **e** and $\hat{\mathbf{x}}$ is compatible with $\hat{\mathbf{e}}$. ■

PROOF OF THEOREM 10.3. Left to Exercise 10.18. ■

PROOF OF THEOREM 10.4. We are comparing here the two quantities

$$\sum_x \max_y f(xy\mathbf{z}) \quad \text{and} \quad \max_y \sum_x f(xy\mathbf{z}).$$

We first note that $\max_y f(xy\mathbf{z}) \geq f(xy^\star\mathbf{z})$ for any x and any $y^\star$. Summing over x, we get

$$\sum_x \max_y f(xy\mathbf{z}) \geq \sum_x f(xy^\star\mathbf{z}).$$

This is true for any value $y^\star$. It is then true for the particular value that maximizes $\sum_x f(xy\mathbf{z})$. Hence,

$$\sum_x \max_y f(xy\mathbf{z}) \geq \max_y \sum_x f(xy\mathbf{z}).$$

Note here that the equality holds only when there is some value $y^\star$ of variable Y such that $f(xy^\star\mathbf{z}) = \max_y f(xy\mathbf{z})$ for all values x of variable X. That is, for a given $\mathbf{z}$, the optimal value of variable Y is independent of variable X. ∎

PROOF OF THEOREM 10.5. Note first that from any elimination order π, a valid MAP order π' can be produced by successively commuting a MAP variable M with a non-MAP variable S whenever variable M is immediately before the variable S in the order. For example, consider MAP variables X, Y, and Z, non-MAP variables A, B, and C, and the order $\pi_0 = A, X, Y, B, C, Z$. This is not a valid order for MAP as the MAP variables do not appear last. Yet we can convert this order to the valid order $\pi_4 = A, B, C, X, Y, Z$ using the following commutations:

- Initial order: $\pi_0 = AXYBCZ$
- $\frac{YB}{BY} \rightarrow \pi_1 = AXBYCZ$
- $\frac{YC}{CY} \rightarrow \pi_2 = AXBCYZ$
- $\frac{XB}{BX} \rightarrow \pi_3 = ABXCYZ$
- $\frac{XC}{CX} \rightarrow \pi_4 = ABCXYZ$
- Final MAP order: π_4

Given Theorem 10.4, applying Algorithm VE_MAP to each of these orders will produce a number that is guaranteed to be no less than the number produced by the order following it in the sequence. For example, the first two orders, π_0 and π_1, give

$$\left(\max_Z \sum_C \sum_B \max_Y \max_X \sum_A f\right)(\mathsf{T}) \geq \left(\max_Z \sum_C \max_Y \sum_B \max_X \sum_A f\right)(\mathsf{T}).$$

Note that the number produced by the last order is the MAP probability. Hence, if we use the invalid order π_0 instead of the valid order π_4, we obtain a number q that is an upper bound on the MAP probability: $\text{MAP}_P(\mathbf{M}, \mathbf{e}) \leq q$.

For the second part of the theorem, note that for a factor f over disjoint variables X and $\mathbf{Z}$, we have

$$\left(\sum_X f\right)(\mathbf{z}) \geq \left(\max_X f\right)(\mathbf{z}).$$

Therefore, if we replace all maximizations by summations in Algorithm VE_MAP, we then produce a number greater than q. Moreover, now that all variables are eliminated by summation, the resulting number must be $\Pr(\mathbf{e})$; hence, $q \leq \Pr(\mathbf{e})$. We therefore have $\text{MAP}_P(\mathbf{M}, \mathbf{e}) \leq q \leq \Pr(\mathbf{e})$. ∎

11

The Complexity of Probabilistic Inference

We consider in this chapter the computational complexity of probabilistic inference. We also provide some reductions of probabilistic inference to well known problems, allowing us to benefit from specialized algorithms that have been developed for these problems.

11.1 Introduction

In previous chapters, we discussed algorithms for answering three types of queries with respect to a Bayesian network that induces a distribution $\Pr(\mathbf{X})$. In particular, given some evidence $\mathbf{e}$ we discussed algorithms for computing:

- The probability of evidence $\mathbf{e}$, $\Pr(\mathbf{e})$ (see Chapters 6–8)
- The MPE probability for evidence $\mathbf{e}$, $\mathrm{MPE}_P(\mathbf{e})$ (see Chapter 10)
- The MAP probability for variables $\mathbf{Q}$ and evidence $\mathbf{e}$, $\mathrm{MAP}_P(\mathbf{Q}, \mathbf{e})$ (see Chapter 10).

In this chapter, we consider the complexity of three decision problems that correspond to these queries. In particular, given a number p, we consider the following problems:

- D-PR: Is $\Pr(\mathbf{e}) > p$?
- D-MPE: Is there a network instantiation $\mathbf{x}$ such that $\Pr(\mathbf{x}, \mathbf{e}) > p$?
- D-MAP: Given variables $\mathbf{Q} \subseteq \mathbf{X}$, is there an instantiation $\mathbf{q}$ such that $\Pr(\mathbf{q}, \mathbf{e}) > p$?

We also consider a fourth decision problem that includes D-PR as a special case:

- D-MAR: Given variables $\mathbf{Q} \subseteq \mathbf{X}$ and instantiation $\mathbf{q}$, is $\Pr(\mathbf{q}|\mathbf{e}) > p$?

Note here that when $\mathbf{e}$ is the trivial instantiation, D-MAR reduces to asking whether $\Pr(\mathbf{q}) > p$, which is identical to D-PR.

We provide a number of results on these decision problems in this chapter. In particular, we show in Sections 11.2–11.4 that D-MPE is NP-complete, D-PR and D-MAR are PP-complete, and D-MAP is $\mathrm{NP}^{\mathrm{PP}}$-complete. We start in Section 11.2 with a review of these complexity classes and some of the prototypical problems that are known to be complete for them. We then show the hardness of the problems in Section 11.3 and their membership in Section 11.4.

Even though the decisions problems D-MPE, D-PR, and D-MAR are intractable in general, they can all be solved in polynomial time on networks whose treewidth is bounded. In Section 11.5, we show that D-MAP is NP-complete on polytrees with no more than two parents per node, that is, polytrees with treewidth ≤ 2.

The proofs we provide for various completeness results include reductions that can be quite useful in practice. In fact, we also provide additional reductions in Sections 11.6 and 11.7 that form the basis of state-of-the-art inference algorithms for certain classes in Bayesian networks. In particular, we show in Section 11.6 how to reduce the probability of evidence to a weighted model count on a CNF sentence. We then show in Section 11.7 how to reduce MPE to weighted MAXSAT, which is also a problem applied to CNF sentences.

11.2 Complexity classes

Proving that a problem P is complete for a particular complexity class C shows that P is among the hardest problems in this class. That is, if we know how to solve this problem, then we would know how to solve every other problem in the class. Proving completeness is therefore accomplished by proving two properties:

- Hardness: The problem P is as hard as any problem in the class C.
- Membership: The problem P is a member of the class C.

We show hardness by choosing a problem P' that is known to be complete for the class C and then provide an efficient reduction from P' to P. Intuitively, this shows that a box that solves P can also be used to solve P' and, hence, any member of the class C since P' is complete for class C. Note that hardness shows that problem P is as hard as any problem in class C but it leaves the possibility that P is actually harder than every problem in class C. Showing that problem P is a member of class C rules out this possibility.

To carry out our complexity proofs, we therefore need to choose problems that are known to be complete for the classes NP, PP, and NP^{PP}. The following definition provides three such problems. In this definition and in the rest of the chapter, we refer to an instantiation $x_1, \ldots, x_n$ of a set of Boolean variables $X_1, \ldots, X_n$ on which a propositional sentence α is defined. Each value x_i can be viewed as assigning a truth value to variable X_i. In particular, x_i can be viewed as assigning the value true to X_i, in which case it will correspond to the positive literal X_i, or assigning the value false to X_i, in which case it will correspond to the negative literal $\neg X_i$. In this sense, the instantiation $x_1, \ldots, x_n$ corresponds to a truth assignment (or a world), hence it is meaningful to talk about about whether the instantiation $x_1, \ldots, x_n$ will satisfy sentence α or not (see Chapter 2 for a review of satisfaction).

Definition 11.1. Given a propositional sentence α over Boolean variables $X_1, \ldots, X_n$, the following decision problems are defined:

- SAT: Is there a variable instantiation $x_1, \ldots, x_n$ that satisfies α?
- MAJSAT: Do the majority of instantiations over variables $X_1, \ldots, X_n$ satisfy α?
- E-MAJSAT: Given some $1 \leq k \leq n$, is there an instantiation $x_1, \ldots, x_k$ for which the majority of instantiations $x_1, \ldots, x_k, x_{k+1}, \ldots, x_n$ satisfy α? ■

These decision problems are known to be complete for the complexity classes of interest to us. In particular, SAT is NP-complete, MAJSAT is PP-complete, and E-MAJSAT is NP^{PP}-complete. This also holds when the propositional sentence is restricted to be in CNF. Recall that a CNF is a conjunction of clauses $\alpha_1 \wedge \ldots \wedge \alpha_n$ where each clause is a disjunction of literals $\ell_1 \vee \ldots \ell_m$ and each literal is a variable X_i or its negation $\neg X_i$.

Intuitively, to solve an NP-complete problem we have to search for a solution among an exponential number of candidates where it is easy to decide whether a given candidate constitutes a solution. For example, in SAT we are searching for a truth assignment that satisfies a sentence (testing whether a truth assignment satisfies a sentence can be done in time linear in the sentence size). Similarly, in D-MPE we are searching for a network instantiation that is compatible with the evidence and has a probability greater than some threshold. Note here that a network instantiation is a variable instantiation that assigns a value to each variable in the Bayesian network. Hence, computing the probability of a network instantiation can be performed in time linear in the Bayesian network size using the chain rule for Bayesian networks.

Intuitively, to solve a PP-complete problem we have to add up the weights of all solutions where it is easy to decide whether a particular candidate constitutes a solution and it is also easy to compute the weight of a solution. For example, in MAJSAT a solution is a truth assignment that satisfies the sentence and the weight of a solution is 1. And in D-PR a solution is a network instantiation that is compatible with evidence and the weight of a solution is its probability, which is easy to compute. Another characterization of PP-complete problems is as problems that permit polynomial time, randomized algorithms that can guess a solution to the problem while being correct with a probability greater than .5. Therefore, problems that are PP-complete can be solved to any fixed degree of accuracy by running a randomized, polynomial-time algorithm a sufficient (but unbounded) number of times. We use this particular characterization in one of our proofs later.

Finally, to solve an NP^{PP}-complete problem we have to search for a solution among an exponential number of candidates but we need to solve a PP-complete problem to decide whether a particular candidate constitutes a solution. For example, in E-MAJSAT we are searching for an instantiation $x_1, \ldots, x_k$ but to test whether an instantiation satisfies the condition we want, we must solve a MAJSAT problem. Moreover, in D-MAP we are searching for a variable instantiation $x_1, \ldots, x_k$ that is compatible with evidence and has a probability that exceeds a certain threshold. But to compute the probability of an instantiation $x_1, \ldots, x_k$, we need to solve a D-PR problem.[1]

The class NP is included in the class PP, which is also included in the class NP^{PP}. Moreover, these classes are strongly believed to be distinct. This distinction implies that D-MPE is strictly easier than D-PR, which is then strictly easier than D-MAP. This, for example, suggests that the use of variable elimination to solve D-MPE, as in Chapter 10, is actually an overkill since the amount of work that variable elimination does is sufficient to solve a harder problem, D-PR. It also suggests that the additional penalty we incur when using variable elimination to solve D-MAP is due to the intrinsic difficulty of D-MAP, as opposed to an idiosyncrasy of the variable elimination method.

11.3 Showing hardness

Suppose that we have the following propositional sentence:

$$\alpha : (X_1 \vee X_2 \vee \neg X_3) \wedge ((X_3 \wedge X_4) \vee \neg X_5). \tag{11.1}$$

We show in this section that we can solve SAT, MAJSAT, and E-MAJSAT for this and similar sentences by constructing a corresponding Bayesian network, $\mathcal{N}_\alpha$, and reducing the previous queries to D-MPE, D-PR, and D-MAP queries, respectively, on the constructed network. Figure 11.1 depicts the Bayesian network structure corresponding to the sentence α given in (11.1).

---

[1] Note, however, that if the instantiation $x_1, \ldots, x_k$ is complete, that is, covers every variable in the network, then computing its probability can be performed in linear time.

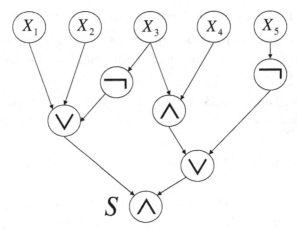

Figure 11.1: A Bayesian network representing a propositional sentence.

More generally, the Bayesian network $\mathcal{N}_\alpha$ for a propositional sentence α has a single leaf node S_α and is constructed inductively as follows:

- If α is a single variable X, its Bayesian network has a single binary node $S_\alpha = X$ with the following CPT: $\theta_x = 1/2$ and $\theta_{\bar{x}} = 1/2$.

- If α is of the form $\neg\beta$, then its Bayesian network is obtained from the Bayesian network for β by adding the node S_α with parent S_β and CPT (we omit redundant CPT rows):

S_β	S_α	$\Theta_{S_\alpha \mid S_\beta}$
true	true	0
false	true	1

- If α is of the form $\beta \vee \gamma$, then its Bayesian network is obtained from the Bayesian networks for β and γ by adding the node S_α with parents S_β and S_γ and CPT:

S_β	S_γ	S_α	$\Theta_{S_\alpha \mid S_\beta, S_\gamma}$
true	true	true	1
true	false	true	1
false	true	true	1
false	false	true	0

- If α is of the form $\beta \wedge \gamma$, then its Bayesian network is obtained from the Bayesian networks for β and γ by adding the node S_α with parents S_β and S_γ and CPT:

S_β	S_γ	S_α	$\Theta_{S_\alpha \mid S_\beta, S_\gamma}$
true	true	true	1
true	false	true	0
false	true	true	0
false	false	true	0

Suppose now that we have a propositional sentence α over variables $X_1, \ldots, X_n$ and let $\mathcal{N}_\alpha$ be a corresponding Bayesian network with leaf node S_α. The probability distribution Pr induced by network $\mathcal{N}_\alpha$ satisfies the following key property.

Theorem 11.1. *We have*

$$\Pr(x_1, \ldots, x_n, S_\alpha = \text{true}) = \begin{cases} 0, & \text{if } x_1, \ldots, x_n \models \neg\alpha \\ 1/2^n & \text{if } x_1, \ldots, x_n \models \alpha. \end{cases} \tag{11.2}$$

■

This theorem will be the basis for three reductions that we show next.

Theorem 11.2 (Reducing SAT to D-MPE). *There is a variable instantiation* $x_1, \ldots, x_n$ *that satisfies sentence* α *iff there is a variable instantiation* **y** *of network* $\mathcal{N}_\alpha$ *such that* $\Pr(\mathbf{y}, S_\alpha = \text{true}) > 0.$ ∎

Theorem 11.3 (Reducing MAJSAT to D-PR). *The majority of variable instantiations* $x_1, \ldots, x_n$ *satisfy* α *iff the probability of evidence* $S_\alpha = \text{true}$ *is greater than* $1/2$: $\Pr(S_\alpha = \text{true}) > 1/2.$ ∎

This reduction implies that MAJSAT can be reduced to D-MAR since D-PR is a special case of D-MAR.

Theorem 11.4 (Reducing E-MAJSAT to D-MAP). *There is a variable instantiation* $x_1, \ldots, x_k$, $1 \leq k \leq n$, *for which the majority of instantiations* $x_1, \ldots, x_k, x_{k+1}, \ldots, x_n$ *satisfy* α *iff there is a MAP instantiation* $x_1, \ldots, x_k$ *such that* $\Pr(x_1, \ldots, x_k, S_\alpha = \text{true}) > 1/2^{k+1}.$ ∎

11.4 Showing membership

In the previous section, we showed that D-MPE is NP-hard, D-PR and D-MAR are PP-hard, and D-MAP is NP^{PP}-hard. To show the completeness of these problems with respect to the mentioned classes, we need to establish the membership of each problem in the corresponding class. Establishing membership of D-MPE and D-MAP is relatively straightforward but establishing the membership of D-PR and D-MAR are more involved, so we handle them last.

Membership of D-MPE in NP

To show that D-MPE belongs to the class NP, all we have to show is that we can verify a potential solution for this problem in polynomial time. That is, suppose we are given an instantiation **x** of network variables and we want to check whether $\Pr(\mathbf{x}, \mathbf{e}) > p$ for some evidence **e** and threshold p. If **x** is inconsistent with **e**, then $\Pr(\mathbf{x}, \mathbf{e}) = 0$. If **x** is consistent with **e**, then $\mathbf{xe} = \mathbf{x}$ and $\Pr(\mathbf{x})$ can be computed in polynomial time using the chain rule of Bayesian networks. We can therefore perform the test $\Pr(\mathbf{x}, \mathbf{e}) > p$ in polynomial time, and D-MPE is then in the class NP.

Membership of D-MAP on polytrees in NP

The problem of D-MAP on polytrees with no more than two parents per node is also in the class NP. In this problem, verifying a solution corresponds to checking whether $\Pr(\mathbf{q}, \mathbf{e}) > p$ for a partial instantiation **q** of the network variables. We cannot use the chain rule to compute $\Pr(\mathbf{q}, \mathbf{e})$ since $\mathbf{q}, \mathbf{e}$ does not instantiate all network variables. Yet $\Pr(\mathbf{q}, \mathbf{e})$ can be computed using variable elimination in polynomial time since the network treewidth is bounded by 2. This shows the membership of D-MAP in NP for polytrees.

Membership of D-MAP in NP^{PP}

To show that general D-MAP belongs to the class NP^{PP} will require that we verify a potential solution to the problem in polynomial time, assuming that we have a PP-oracle.

Since verifying a potential D-MAP amounts to testing whether $\Pr(\mathbf{q}, \mathbf{e}) > p$, which is PP-complete, we can verify a potential D-MAP solution in polynomial time given the oracle.

Membership of D-MAR in PP

To show that D-MAR is in the class PP, we present a polynomial time algorithm that can guess a solution to D-MAR while guaranteeing that the guess will be correct with probability greater than .5. The algorithm for guessing whether $\Pr(\mathbf{q}|\mathbf{e}) > p$ is as follows:

1. Define the following probabilities as a function of the threshold p:

$$a(p) = \begin{cases} 1, & \text{if } p < .5 \\ 1/(2p), & \text{otherwise} \end{cases}$$

$$b(p) = \begin{cases} (1 - 2p)/(2 - 2p), & \text{if } p < .5 \\ 0, & \text{otherwise.} \end{cases}$$

2. Sample a variable instantiation $\mathbf{x}$ from the Bayesian network as given in Section 15.2. This can be performed in time linear in the network size.

3. Declare $\Pr(\mathbf{q}|\mathbf{e}) > p$ according to the following probabilities:

   - $a(p)$ if the instantiation $\mathbf{x}$ is compatible with $\mathbf{e}$ and $\mathbf{q}$
   - $b(p)$ if the instantiation $\mathbf{x}$ is compatible with $\mathbf{e}$ but not with $\mathbf{q}$
   - .5 if the instantiation $\mathbf{x}$ is not compatible with $\mathbf{e}$.

Theorem 11.5. *The previous procedure will declare* $\Pr(\mathbf{q}|\mathbf{e}) > p$ *correctly with probability greater than* .5.[2] ∎

This theorem shows that D-MAR is in the class PP and, consequently, that D-PR is also in the class PP.

11.5 Complexity of MAP on polytrees

We saw in Chapters 6 and 10 that networks with bounded treewidth can be solved in polynomial time using variable elimination to answer both probability of evidence and MPE queries. We also saw that variable elimination may take exponential time on such networks when answering MAP queries. We show in this section that this difficulty is probably due to an intrinsic property of the MAP problem, as opposed to some idiosyncrasy of the variable elimination algorithm. In particular, we show that D-MAP is NP-complete for polytree networks with no more than two parents per node (treewidth ≤ 2). Therefore, even though the complexity of D-MAP is improved for polytrees (NP-complete instead of NP^{PP}-complete), the problem remains intractable for this class of networks.

Membership in NP was shown in the previous section. To show NP-hardness, we reduce the MAXSAT problem, which is NP-complete, to D-MAP.

Definition 11.2 (MAXSAT). Given a set of clauses $\alpha_1, \ldots, \alpha_m$ over propositional variables $X_1, \ldots, X_n$ and an integer $0 \leq k < m$, is there an instantiation $x_1, \ldots, x_n$ that satisfies more than k of the clauses α_i? ∎

---

[2] This theorem and its proof are due to James D. Park.

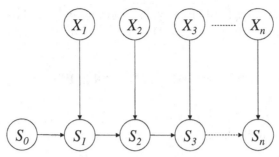

Figure 11.2: Structure used for reducing MAXSAT to MAP on polytrees.

The idea behind the reduction is to use a circuit whose structure is given in Figure 11.2. The circuit has $n + 1$ inputs. Input S_0 has the values $1, \ldots, m$ and is used to select a clause from the set $\alpha_1, \ldots, \alpha_m$ ($S_0 = i$ selects clause α_i). The other n inputs correspond to the propositional variables over which the clauses are defined, with each variable having two values true and false. The intermediate variables $S_j, 1 \leq j \leq n$ have values in $0, 1, \ldots, m$. The semantics of these intermediate variables is as follows. Suppose we set $S_0 = i$, therefore selecting clause α_i. Suppose also that we set the propositional variables $X_1, \ldots, X_n$ to some values $x_1, \ldots, x_n$. The behavior of the circuit is such that S_j will take the value 0 iff at least one of the values in $x_1, \ldots, x_j$ satisfies the clause α_i. If none of these values satisfy the clause, then S_j will take the value i. This is given by

$$Pr(s_j | x_j, s_{j-1}) = \begin{cases} 1, & \text{if } s_{j-1} = s_j = 0 \\ 1, & \text{if } s_{j-1} = i, s_j = 0 \text{ and } x_j \text{ satisfies } \alpha_i \\ 1, & \text{if } s_{j-1} = s_j = i \text{ and } x_j \text{ does not satisfy } \alpha_i \\ 0, & \text{otherwise.} \end{cases}$$

If we further assume that we have uniform priors for variable S_0, $\Pr(S_0 = i) = 1/m$, and uniform priors on inputs $X_1, \ldots, X_n$, $\Pr(x_i) = .5$, we get the following reduction.

Theorem 11.6 (Reducing MAXSAT to D-MAP). *There is an instantiation $x_1, \ldots, x_n$ that satisfies more than k of the clauses $\alpha_1, \ldots, \alpha_m$ iff there is an instantiation $x_1, \ldots, x_n$ such that $\Pr(x_1, \ldots, x_n, S_n = 0) > k/(m2^n)$.* ∎

This completes our proof that D-MAP is NP-complete for polytree networks with no more than two parents per node.

We present two more reductions in the rest of this chapter, allowing us to cast probabilistic inference on Bayesian networks in terms of inference on CNFs. In particular, we start in the following section by showing how we can compute the probability of evidence by solving the problem of weighted model counting on CNFs. We then follow by showing how we can compute the MPE probability (and MPE instantiations) by solving the problem of weighted MAXSAT on CNFs. We present these reductions with the goal of capitalizing on state-of-the-art algorithms for CNF inference.

11.6 Reducing probability of evidence to weighted model counting

We show in this section how we can compute the probability of evidence with respect to a Bayesian network by computing the weighted model count of a corresponding propositional sentence in CNF. We present two reductions for this purpose, each producing a different CNF encoding of the Bayesian network. One of these encodings will also be used in Chapter 12 when we discuss the compilation of Bayesian networks, and again in Chapter 13 when we discuss inference algorithms that exploit local structure.

We start by defining the weighted model counting problem.

Definition 11.3 (Weighted model counting, WMC). Let Δ be a propositional sentence over Boolean variables $X_1, \ldots, X_n$ and let Wt be a function that assigns a weight $Wt(x_i) \geq 0$ to each value x_i of variable X_i. The *weighted model count* of Δ is defined as the sum of weights assigned to its models:

$$\text{WMC}(\Delta) \overset{def}{=} \sum_{x_1,\ldots,x_n \models \Delta} Wt(x_1, \ldots, x_n),$$

where

$$Wt(x_1, \ldots, x_n) \overset{def}{=} \prod_{i=1}^{n} Wt(x_i). \qquad \blacksquare$$

We next describe two CNF encodings of Bayesian networks, allowing us to reduce the probability of evidence to a WMC. In particular, given a Bayesian network $\mathcal{N}$ that induces a distribution Pr and given evidence **e**, we show how to systematically construct a CNF Δ such that $\Pr(\mathbf{e}) = \text{WMC}(\Delta)$.

11.6.1 The first encoding

This CNF encoding employs two types of Boolean variables: indicators and parameters. In particular, for each network variable X with parents $\mathbf{U}$, we have

- A Boolean variable I_x, called an *indicator variable*, for each value x of network variable X.
- A Boolean variable $P_{x|\mathbf{u}}$, called a *parameter variable*, for each instantiation $x\mathbf{u}$ of the family $X\mathbf{U}$.

The network in Figure 11.3 generates the following indicator variables,

$$I_{a_1}, I_{a_2}, \quad I_{b_1}, I_{b_2}, \quad I_{c_1}, I_{c_2},$$

and the following parameter variables,

$$P_{a_1}, P_{a_2}, \quad P_{b_1|a_1}, P_{b_2|a_1}, P_{b_1|a_2}, P_{b_2|a_2}, \quad P_{c_1|a_1}, P_{c_2|a_1}, P_{c_1|a_2}, P_{c_2|a_2}.$$

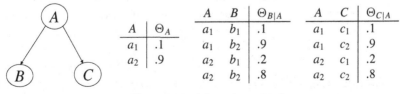

A	Θ_A
a_1	.1
a_2	.9

A	B	$\Theta_{B|A}$
a_1	b_1	.1
a_1	b_2	.9
a_2	b_1	.2
a_2	b_2	.8

A	C	$\Theta_{C|A}$
a_1	c_1	.1
a_1	c_2	.9
a_2	c_1	.2
a_2	c_2	.8

Figure 11.3: A Bayesian network.

Table 11.1: A CNF encoding of the Bayesian network in Figure 11.3.

Indicator Clauses		
A	$I_{a_1} \vee I_{a_2}$	$\neg I_{a_1} \vee \neg I_{a_2}$
B	$I_{b_1} \vee I_{b_2}$	$\neg I_{b_1} \vee \neg I_{b_2}$
C	$I_{c_1} \vee I_{c_2}$	$\neg I_{c_1} \vee \neg I_{c_2}$

Parameter Clauses		
A	$I_{a_1} \iff P_{a_1}$	
B	$I_{a_1} \wedge I_{b_1} \iff P_{b_1\|a_1}$	$I_{a_1} \wedge I_{b_2} \iff P_{b_2\|a_1}$
	$I_{a_2} \wedge I_{b_1} \iff P_{b_1\|a_2}$	$I_{a_2} \wedge I_{b_2} \iff P_{b_2\|a_2}$
C	$I_{a_1} \wedge I_{c_1} \iff P_{c_1\|a_1}$	$I_{a_1} \wedge I_{c_2} \iff P_{c_2\|a_1}$
	$I_{a_2} \wedge I_{c_1} \iff P_{c_1\|a_2}$	$I_{a_2} \wedge I_{c_2} \iff P_{c_2\|a_2}$

CNF clauses are also of two types: *indicator clauses* and *parameter clauses*. A set of indicator clauses is generated for each variable X with values $x_1, x_2, \ldots, x_k$ as follows:

$$I_{x_1} \vee I_{x_2} \vee \ldots \vee I_{x_k}$$

$$\neg I_{x_i} \vee \neg I_{x_j}, \quad \text{for } i < j. \tag{11.3}$$

These clauses ensure that exactly one indicator variable for variable X will be true. The network in Figure 11.3 generates the indicator clauses given in Table 11.1.

A set of clauses are also generated for each variable X and its parameter variable $P_{x|u_1,u_2,\ldots,u_m}$. These include an *IP clause*,

$$I_{u_1} \wedge I_{u_2} \wedge \ldots \wedge I_{u_m} \wedge I_x \implies P_{x|u_1,u_2,\ldots,u_m},$$

and a set of *PI clauses*,

$$P_{x|u_1,u_2,\ldots,u_m} \implies I_x$$
$$P_{x|u_1,u_2,\ldots,u_m} \implies I_{u_i}, \quad \text{for } i = 1, \ldots, m.$$

These clauses ensure that a parameter variable is true if and only if the corresponding indicator variables are true. We typically write these parameter clauses as one equivalence:

$$I_{u_1} \wedge I_{u_2} \wedge \ldots \wedge I_{u_m} \wedge I_x \iff P_{x|u_1,u_2,\ldots,u_m}. \tag{11.4}$$

The network in Figure 11.3 generates the parameter clauses given in Table 11.1. We now have the following reduction.

Theorem 11.7. *Let* $\mathcal{N}$ *be a Bayesian network inducing probability distribution* $\Pr$ *and let* $\Delta_{\mathcal{N}}$ *be its CNF encoding given by (11.3) and (11.4). For any evidence* $\mathbf{e} = e_1, \ldots, e_k$, *we have*

$$\Pr(\mathbf{e}) = \mathrm{WMC}(\Delta_{\mathcal{N}} \wedge I_{e_1} \wedge \ldots \wedge I_{e_k}),$$

given the following weights: $Wt(I_x) = Wt(\neg I_x) = Wt(\neg P_{x|\mathbf{u}}) = 1$ *and* $Wt(P_{x|\mathbf{u}}) = \theta_{x|\mathbf{u}}$. ∎

Table 11.2: Network instantiations and corresponding truth assignments for the network in Figure 11.3.

Network instantiation	Truth assignment sets these variables to true and all others to false	Weight of truth assignment
$a_1 b_1 c_1$	$\omega_0 : I_{a_1}\ I_{b_1}\ I_{c_1}\ P_{a_1}\ P_{b_1|a_1}\ P_{c_1|a_1}$	$.1 \cdot .1 \cdot .1 = .001$
$a_1 b_1 c_2$	$\omega_1 : I_{a_1}\ I_{b_1}\ I_{c_2}\ P_{a_1}\ P_{b_1|a_1}\ P_{c_2|a_1}$	$.1 \cdot .1 \cdot .9 = .009$
$a_1 b_2 c_1$	$\omega_2 : I_{a_1}\ I_{b_2}\ I_{c_1}\ P_{a_1}\ P_{b_2|a_1}\ P_{c_1|a_1}$	$.1 \cdot .9 \cdot .1 = .009$
$a_1 b_2 c_2$	$\omega_3 : I_{a_1}\ I_{b_2}\ I_{c_2}\ P_{a_1}\ P_{b_2|a_1}\ P_{c_2|a_1}$	$.1 \cdot .9 \cdot .9 = .081$
$a_2 b_1 c_1$	$\omega_4 : I_{a_2}\ I_{b_1}\ I_{c_1}\ P_{a_2}\ P_{b_1|a_1}\ P_{c_1|a_2}$	$.9 \cdot .2 \cdot .2 = .036$
$a_2 b_1 c_2$	$\omega_5 : I_{a_2}\ I_{b_1}\ I_{c_2}\ P_{a_2}\ P_{b_1|a_1}\ P_{c_2|a_2}$	$.9 \cdot .2 \cdot .8 = .144$
$a_2 b_2 c_1$	$\omega_6 : I_{a_2}\ I_{b_2}\ I_{c_1}\ P_{a_2}\ P_{b_2|a_1}\ P_{c_1|a_2}$	$.9 \cdot .8 \cdot .2 = .144$
$a_2 b_2 c_2$	$\omega_7 : I_{a_2}\ I_{b_2}\ I_{c_2}\ P_{a_2}\ P_{b_2|a_1}\ P_{c_2|a_2}$	$.9 \cdot .8 \cdot .8 = .576$

To get some intuition on why Theorem 11.7 holds, consider the CNF $\Delta_\mathcal{N}$ in Table 11.1 that encodes the network $\mathcal{N}$ in Figure 11.3. There is a one-to-one correspondence between the models of this CNF and the network instantiations, as shown in Table 11.2. Moreover, the weight of each model is precisely the probability of corresponding network instantiation. Consider now the evidence $\mathbf{e} = a_1 c_2$. By conjoining $I_{a_1} \wedge I_{c_2}$ with $\Delta_\mathcal{N}$, we are then dropping all CNF models that are not compatible with evidence $\mathbf{e}$ (see Table 11.2). We then get

$$\text{WMC}(\Delta_\mathcal{N} \wedge I_{a_1} \wedge I_{c_2}) = Wt(\omega_1) + Wt(\omega_3) = .009 + .081 = .09 = \text{Pr}(\mathbf{e}).$$

11.6.2 The second encoding

In this section, we discuss another CNF encoding of Bayesian networks that allows us to reduce the probability of evidence computation to a model count. This second encoding is somewhat less transparent semantically than the previous one, but it produces CNFs that have a smaller number of variables and clauses. However, the size of generated clauses may be larger in the presence of multivalued variables.

The encoding assumes some ordering on the values of each network variable X, writing $x' < x$ to mean that value x' comes before x in the ordering. The encoding uses variables of two types, indicators and parameters, defined as follows. For each network variable X with parents $\mathbf{U}$, we have:

- A Boolean variable I_x, called an *indicator variable*, for each value x of variable X, which is similar to the first encoding.
- A Boolean variable $Q_{x|\mathbf{u}}$, called a *parameter variable,* for each instantiation $x\mathbf{u}$ of the family $X\mathbf{U}$, assuming that x is not last in the value order of variable X. Note that these parameter variables do not correspond to those used in the first encoding. In particular, we do not have a parameter variable for each instantiation $x\mathbf{u}$ of the family $X\mathbf{U}$. Moreover, the semantics of these parameter variables are different, as we see later.

The network in Figure 11.4 generates the following parameter variables:

$$Q_{a_1}, Q_{a_2}, \quad Q_{b_1|a_1}, Q_{b_1|a_2}, Q_{b_1|a_3}.$$

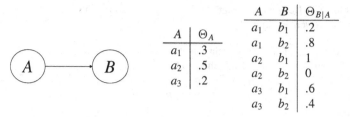

Figure 11.4: A Bayesian network.

CNF clauses are also of two types: *indicator clauses* and *parameter clauses*. A set of indicator clauses is generated for each variable X with values $x_1, x_2, \ldots, x_k$, as in the first encoding:

$$I_{x_1} \vee I_{x_2} \vee \ldots \vee I_{x_k}$$

$$\neg I_{x_i} \vee \neg I_{x_j}, \quad \text{for } i < j. \tag{11.5}$$

Suppose now that $x_1 < x_2 < \cdots < x_k$ is an ordering of X's values and let $\mathbf{u} = u_1, \ldots, u_m$ be an instantiation of X's parents. A set of parameter clauses is then generated for variable X as follows:

$$I_{u_1} \wedge \ldots \wedge I_{u_m} \wedge \neg Q_{x_1|\mathbf{u}} \wedge \ldots \wedge \neg Q_{x_{i-1}|\mathbf{u}} \wedge Q_{x_i|\mathbf{u}} \implies I_{x_i}, \quad \text{if } i < k$$

$$I_{u_1} \wedge \ldots \wedge I_{u_m} \wedge \neg Q_{x_1|\mathbf{u}} \wedge \ldots \wedge \neg Q_{x_{k-1}|\mathbf{u}} \implies I_{x_k}. \tag{11.6}$$

The network in Figure 11.4 generates the clauses given in Table 11.3. We now have the following result.

Theorem 11.8. *Let $\mathcal{N}$ be a Bayesian network inducing probability distribution* $\Pr$ *and let* $\Delta_{\mathcal{N}}$ *be its CNF encoding given by (11.5) and (11.6). For any evidence* $\mathbf{e} = e_1, \ldots, e_k$, *we have*

$$\Pr(\mathbf{e}) = \text{WMC}(\Delta_{\mathcal{N}} \wedge I_{e_1} \wedge \ldots \wedge I_{e_k}),$$

given the following weights:

$$Wt(I_x) = 1$$

$$Wt(\neg I_x) = 1$$

$$Wt(Q_{x|\mathbf{u}}) = \frac{\theta_{x|\mathbf{u}}}{1 - \sum_{x' < x} \theta_{x'|\mathbf{u}}}$$

$$Wt(\neg Q_{x|\mathbf{u}}) = 1 - Wt(Q_{x|\mathbf{u}}). \quad \blacksquare$$

For example, considering the encoding in Table 11.3, we have the following weights:

$$Wt(Q_{a_1}) = \theta_{a_1} = .3$$

$$Wt(Q_{a_2}) = \frac{\theta_{a_2}}{1 - \theta_{a_1}} = \frac{.5}{.7}$$

11.7 Reducing MPE to W-MAXSAT

In this section, we consider a reduction of MPE into a problem known as weighted MAXSAT (W-MAXSAT). This problem applies to a weighted CNF of the form

Table 11.3: A CNF encoding of the Bayesian network in Figure 11.4. We are assuming here that $a_1 < a_2 < a_3$ and $b_1 < b_2$.

Indicator Clauses				
A	$I_{a_1} \vee I_{a_2} \vee I_{a_3}$	$\neg I_{a_1} \vee \neg I_{a_2}$	$\neg I_{a_1} \vee \neg I_{a_3}$	$\neg I_{a_2} \vee \neg I_{a_3}$
B	$I_{b_1} \vee I_{b_2}$	$\neg I_{b_1} \vee \neg I_{b_2}$		

Parameter Clauses			
A	$Q_{a_1} \implies I_{a_1}$	$\neg Q_{a_1} \wedge Q_{a_2} \implies I_{a_2}$	$\neg Q_{a_1} \wedge \neg Q_{a_2} \implies I_{a_3}$
B	$I_{a_1} \wedge Q_{b_1|a_1} \implies I_{b_1}$	$I_{a_1} \wedge \neg Q_{b_1|a_1} \implies I_{b_2}$	
	$I_{a_2} \wedge Q_{b_1|a_2} \implies I_{b_1}$	$I_{a_2} \wedge \neg Q_{b_1|a_2} \implies I_{b_2}$	
	$I_{a_3} \wedge Q_{b_1|a_3} \implies I_{b_1}$	$I_{a_3} \wedge \neg Q_{b_1|a_3} \implies I_{b_2}$	

$\alpha_1^{w_1}, \ldots, \alpha_m^{w_m}$, where each α_i is a clause with weight $w_i \geq 0$. The following is an example weighted CNF over Boolean variables X, Y, and Z:

$$(X \vee \neg Y \vee \neg Z)^3, \ (\neg X)^{10.1}, \ (Y)^{.5}, \ (Z)^{2.5}. \tag{11.7}$$

Definition 11.4 (W-MAXSAT). Let $\alpha_1^{w_1}, \ldots, \alpha_m^{w_m}$ be a weighted CNF over Boolean variables $X_1, \ldots, X_n$. The weight of a truth assignment $x_1, \ldots, x_n$ is defined as

$$Wt(x_1, \ldots, x_n) \overset{def}{=} \sum_{x_1, \ldots, x_n \models \alpha_i} w_i.$$

The W-MAXSAT problem is that of finding a truth assignment with maximal weight. ∎

Considering the weighted CNF in (11.7), the truth assignment $X, Y, \neg Z$ has weight $3 + .5 = 3.5$ since it satisfies the first and third clauses but not the second and fourth. Moreover, the assignment $\neg X, \neg Y, Z$ has weight $3 + 10.1 + 2.5 = 15.6$, which is maximal, that is, no other assignment will have a higher weight.

We find it useful to define the *penalty* of a truth assignment as the weight of clauses that it does not satisfy:

$$Pn(x_1, \ldots, x_n) \overset{def}{=} \sum_{x_1, \ldots, x_n \not\models \alpha_i} w_i.$$

It then follows that

$$Wt(x_1, \ldots, x_n) + Pn(x_1, \ldots, x_n) = \psi,$$

where ψ is a constant and equals the sum of all weights appearing in the weighted CNF. Finding a truth assignment with a minimal penalty is then the same as finding one with a maximal weight, which allows us to define W-MAXSAT as the problem of finding a truth assignment with minimum penalty.

We find it useful to introduce a special weight, W, which we shall give to a clause when we want to ensure that it is satisfied by every maximal truth assignment. Intuitively, W is a very large weight that must be acquired by any truth assignment if it is optimal. We later suggest a method for choosing this weight. Clauses that receive this special weight are said to be *hard clauses*, while other clauses are said to be *soft clauses*.

We are now ready to show how MPE can be reduced to W-MAXSAT by encoding a Bayesian network as a weighted CNF. The encoding employs only one type of Boolean variables and two types of clauses. In particular, for each network variable X and value x we have a Boolean variable I_x, called an *indicator variable*. CNF clauses are of two types: *indicator clauses* and *parameter clauses*. A set of indicator clauses is generated for each variable X with values $x_1, x_2, \ldots, x_k$, just as in the previous encodings:

$$(I_{x_1} \vee I_{x_2} \vee \ldots \vee I_{x_k})^W \tag{11.8}$$

$$(\neg I_{x_i} \vee \neg I_{x_j})^W, \quad \text{for } i < j. \tag{11.9}$$

Note that all indicator clauses are hard clauses. Hence, they must be satisfied by every maximal truth assignment.

In addition to indictor clauses, we have one parameter clause for each parameter $\theta_{x|u_1,\ldots,u_m}$:

$$(\neg I_x \vee \neg I_{u_1} \vee \ldots \vee \neg I_{u_m})^{-\log \theta_{x|u_1,\ldots,u_m}}, \tag{11.10}$$

where $-\log 0$ is defined as W. Hence, if a parameter $\theta_{x|u_1,\ldots,u_m}$ equals zero, it will generate a hard clause.

Now that we have defined the set of all clauses generated by a Bayesian network, we can set the special weight W to be greater than the sum of weights assigned to all soft clauses. Hence, any truth assignment that violates even a single hard clause cannot be optimal.[3]

The network in Figure 11.4 will generate the following weighted CNF:

- Indicator clauses:

$$(I_{a_1} \vee I_{a_2} \vee I_{a_3})^W \quad (\neg I_{a_1} \vee \neg I_{a_2})^W \quad (\neg I_{a_1} \vee \neg I_{a_3})^W \quad (\neg I_{a_2} \vee \neg I_{a_3})^W$$
$$(I_{b_1} \vee I_{b_2})^W \qquad\qquad (\neg I_{b_1} \vee \neg I_{b_2})^W$$

- Parameter clauses:

$$(\neg I_{a_1})^{-\log.3} \qquad\qquad (\neg I_{a_2})^{-\log.5} \qquad\qquad (\neg I_{a_3})^{-\log.2}$$

$$(\neg I_{a_1} \vee \neg I_{b_1})^{-\log.2} \quad (\neg I_{a_1} \vee \neg I_{b_2})^{-\log.8} \quad (\neg I_{a_2} \vee \neg I_{b_1})^{-\log 1}$$
$$(\neg I_{a_2} \vee \neg I_{b_2})^W \qquad (\neg I_{a_3} \vee \neg I_{b_1})^{-\log.6} \quad (\neg I_{a_3} \vee \neg I_{b_2})^{-\log.4}$$

Suppose now that we have a Bayesian network that induces a distribution $\Pr(X_1, \ldots, X_n)$ and let $\alpha_1^{w_1}, \ldots, \alpha_m^{w_m}$ be the weighted CNF produced by this network according to (11.8)–(11.10). Let $x_1, \ldots, x_n$ be a network instantiation. We say that a truth assignment Γ corresponds to network instantiation $x_1, \ldots, x_n$ if and only if indictors $I_{x_1}, \ldots, I_{x_n}$ appear positively in Γ and all other indicators appear negatively in Γ. In the previous example, the truth assignment

$$\neg I_{a_1}, \neg I_{a_2}, I_{a_3}, I_{b_1}, \neg I_{b_2}$$

then corresponds to the network instantiation $a_3 b_1$. Given this definition, it should be clear than any truth assignment that does not correspond to a network instantiation will have a penalty $\geq W$ as it must violate one of the indicator clauses in (11.8) and (11.9). Hence, if a truth assignment has a minimal penalty (i.e., $< W$), it must correspond to a network instantiation.

---

[3] Note that the set of hard clauses generated by a Bayesian network is satisfiable. Hence, there is at least one truth assignment that satisfies each and every hard clause.

Consider now a truth assignment Γ that corresponds to a network instantiation $\mathbf{x}$ and let $\theta_{x|u_1,\ldots,u_k}$ be a network parameter that is compatible with Γ and $\mathbf{x}$, that is, the indicators $I_x, I_{u_1}, \ldots, I_{u_k}$ appear positively in Γ. Then Γ will violate the clause for parameter $\theta_{x|u_1,\ldots,u_k}$ and will therefore incur a penalty of $-\log \theta_{x|u_1,\ldots,u_k}$. In fact, the total penalty of truth assignment Γ will simply be the sum of $-\log \theta_{x|\mathbf{u}}$ over all parameters $\theta_{x|\mathbf{u}}$ that are compatible with Γ and $\mathbf{x}$. We therefore have

$$Pn(\Gamma) = \sum_{\theta_{x|\mathbf{u}} \sim \mathbf{x}} -\log \theta_{x|\mathbf{u}} = -\log \prod_{\theta_{x|\mathbf{u}} \sim \mathbf{x}} \theta_{x|\mathbf{u}} = -\log \Pr(\mathbf{x}).$$

That is, by choosing a truth assignment Γ with a minimum penalty, we are choosing a network instantiation $\mathbf{x}$ that has a maximal probability. Interestingly enough, the reduction given in this section continues to work even if we drop the indicator clauses given in (11.9) (see Exercise 11.10). Dropping such clauses can have a dramatic effect on the encoding size, especially when the cardinality of network variables is quite large.

We close this section by pointing out that evidence can be accommodated using the same technique adopted in the previous encodings. That is, if the evidence is $\mathbf{e} = e_1, \ldots, e_k$, all we have to do is add the hard clauses $I_{e_1}, \ldots, I_{e_k}$ to the weighted CNF. This will rule out any truth assignment that is not compatible with the evidence. For example, given the evidence $\mathbf{e} = a_1$ in our previous example, the maximal truth assignment will be

$$I_{a_1}, \neg I_{a_2}, \neg I_{a_2}, \neg I_{b_1}, I_{b_2}$$

which has a penalty of $-\log .8 - \log .3 = -\log(.8)(.3) = -\Pr(a_1, b_2)$. The corresponding network instantiation is a_1, b_2 in this case, which is then guaranteed to be an MPE instantiation given evidence $\mathbf{e} = a_1$.

Bibliographic remarks

The complexity of D-PR was initially studied in Cooper [1990b], where it was shown to be NP-hard, and then in Roth [1996], where the connection to model counting was first shown. The NP-hardness of D-MPE was shown in Shimony [1994] and the NP^{PP}-completeness of D-MAP was shown in Park and Darwiche [2004a]. That D-MAP remains NP-complete even for polytrees was shown in Park and Darwiche [2004a]. The CNF encoding of Section 11.6.1 is due to Darwiche [2002], and the one in Section 11.6.2 is due to Sang et al. [2005]. Reducing MPE to weighted MAXSAT is due to Park [2002].

11.8 Exercises

11.1. Prove Theorem 11.1.

11.2. Prove Theorem 11.2.

11.3. Consider the CPT in Table 11.4. Generate a CNF encoding for this CPT according to (11.3) and (11.4). Show the weights of all variables in the encoding.

11.4. Consider the CPT in Table 11.4. Generate a CNF encoding for this CPT according to (11.5) and (11.6). Show the weights of all variables in the encoding.

11.5. Consider Theorems 11.7 and 11.8. Provide a different weight function $Wt(.)$ that depends on evidence $\mathbf{e}$ for which the following would hold: $\Pr(\mathbf{e}) = \text{WMC}(\Delta_N)$.

11.6. Consider the CPT in Table 11.4. Generate a W-MAXSAT encoding for this CPT.

Table 11.4: A conditional probability table.

A	B	C	$\Theta_{C|A,B}$
a_1	b_1	c_1	.2
a_1	b_1	c_2	.1
a_1	b_1	c_3	.7
a_1	b_2	c_1	0
a_1	b_2	c_2	0
a_1	b_2	c_3	1
a_2	b_1	c_1	.5
a_2	b_1	c_2	.2
a_2	b_1	c_3	.3
a_2	b_2	c_1	.2
a_2	b_2	c_2	0
a_2	b_2	c_3	.8

11.7. Consider the class of Bayesian networks in which every variable is binary and every nonroot CPT is deterministic (that is, contains only zero/one parameters). Describe a corresponding reduction to WMC with a CNF encoding that includes a single Boolean variable for each network node, no variables for network parameters, and no more than one clause for each network parameter.

11.8. Prove Theorem 11.8.

11.9. Show how we can extend Theorems 11.7 and 11.8 to handle a more general type of evidence in which we may not know the exact value of a multivalued variable but only that some of its values are impossible.

11.10. Show that we can drop the indicator clauses given in (11.9) without affecting the correctness of the MPE to W-MAXSAT reduction given in Section 11.7.

11.9 Proofs

PROOF OF THEOREM 11.1. Left to Exercise 11.1.   ■

PROOF OF THEOREM 11.2. Left to Exercise 11.2.   ■

PROOF OF THEOREM 11.3. We first note that

$$\Pr(S_\alpha = \text{true})$$
$$= \sum_{x_1,\ldots,x_n} \Pr(x_1,\ldots,x_n, S_\alpha = \text{true})$$
$$= \sum_{x_1,\ldots,x_n \models \alpha} \Pr(x_1,\ldots,x_n, S_\alpha = \text{true}) + \sum_{x_1,\ldots,x_n \models \neg\alpha} \Pr(x_1,\ldots,x_n, S_\alpha = \text{true})$$
$$= \frac{1}{2^n} c + 0 \quad \text{by (11.2)}$$
$$= \frac{c}{2^n},$$

where c is the number of instantiations $x_1,\ldots,x_n$ that satisfy the sentence α. Since α has n variables, we have 2^n instantiations of these variables. The majority of these instantiations satisfy α precisely when $c > 2^n/2$. This is equivalent to $c/2^n > .5$, which is also equivalent to $\Pr(S_\alpha = \text{true}) > .5$.   ■

PROOF OF THEOREM 11.4. We first note that

$$\Pr(x_1, \ldots, x_k, S_\alpha = \text{true})$$

$$= \sum_{x_{k+1}, \ldots, x_n} \Pr(x_1, \ldots, x_k, x_{k+1}, \ldots, x_n, S_\alpha = \text{true})$$

$$= \sum_{\substack{x_{k+1}, \ldots, x_n \\ x_1, \ldots, x_n \models \alpha}} \Pr(x_1, \ldots, x_k, x_{k+1}, \ldots, x_n, S_\alpha = \text{true})$$

$$+ \sum_{\substack{x_{k+1}, \ldots, x_n \\ x_1, \ldots, x_n \models \neg\alpha}} \Pr(x_1, \ldots, x_k, x_{k+1}, \ldots, x_n, S_\alpha = \text{true})$$

$$= \frac{1}{2^n} c + 0 \quad \text{by (11.2)}$$

$$= \frac{c}{2^n},$$

where c is the number of instantiations $x_{k+1}, \ldots, x_n$ for which instantiation $x_1, \ldots,$ $x_k, x_{k+1}, \ldots, x_n$ satisfies α. There are 2^{n-k} instantiations of variables $X_{k+1}, \ldots, X_n$. A majority of these instantiations lead $x_1, \ldots, x_k, x_{k+1}, \ldots, x_n$ to satisfy α precisely when $c > 2^{n-k}/2$. This is equivalent to $c/2^n > 1/2^{k+1}$, which is also equivalent to $\Pr(x_1, \ldots, x_k, S_\alpha = \text{true}) > 1/2^{k+1}$.   ∎

PROOF OF THEOREM 11.5. The probability of declaring $\Pr(\mathbf{q}|\mathbf{e}) > p$ is given by

$$r = a(p)\Pr(\mathbf{q}, \mathbf{e}) + b(p)\Pr(\neg\mathbf{q}, \mathbf{e}) + 1/2(1 - \Pr(\mathbf{e}))$$

$$= a(p)\Pr(\mathbf{q}, \mathbf{e}) + b(p)\Pr(\neg\mathbf{q}, \mathbf{e}) + 1/2 - \Pr(\mathbf{e})/2.$$

Therefore, $r > .5$ if and only if

$$a(p)\Pr(\mathbf{q}, \mathbf{e}) + b(p)\Pr(\neg\mathbf{q}, \mathbf{e}) > \Pr(\mathbf{e})/2,$$

which is equivalent to

$$a(p)\Pr(\mathbf{q}|\mathbf{e}) + b(p)\Pr(\neg\mathbf{q}|\mathbf{e}) > .5.$$

Now consider two cases. If $p < .5$, we have the following equivalences:

$$a(p)\Pr(\mathbf{q}|\mathbf{e}) + b(p)\Pr(\neg\mathbf{q}|\mathbf{e}) > .5$$

$$\Pr(\mathbf{q}|\mathbf{e}) + (1 - 2p)/(2 - 2p)(1 - \Pr(\mathbf{q}|\mathbf{e})) > .5$$

$$\Pr(\mathbf{q}|\mathbf{e})(1 - (1 - 2p)/(2 - 2p)) > .5 - (1 - 2p)/(2 - 2p)$$

$$\Pr(\mathbf{q}|\mathbf{e})(1/(2 - 2p)) > p/(2 - 2p)$$

$$\Pr(\mathbf{q}|\mathbf{e}) > p$$

If $p \geq .5$, we have the following equivalences:

$$a(p)\Pr(\mathbf{q}|\mathbf{e}) + b(p)\Pr(\neg\mathbf{q}|\mathbf{e}) > .5$$

$$\Pr(\mathbf{q}|\mathbf{e})/(2p) > .5$$

$$\Pr(\mathbf{q}|\mathbf{e}) > p$$

Therefore, $r > .5$ if and only if $\Pr(\mathbf{q}|\mathbf{e}) > p$.   ∎

PROOF OF THEOREM 11.6. We first make some observations on the network in Figure 11.2. Note that setting the input variables $S_0, X_1, \ldots, X_n$ will functionally determine all other variables S_j. Moreover, according to the circuit behavior, $S_n = 0$ precisely when the selected clause α_i is satisfied by the input instantiation $x_1, \ldots, x_n$. More generally, if x_l is the first value in $x_1, \ldots, x_n$ that satisfies α_i, then we must have $S_1 = i, \ldots, S_{l-1} = i, S_l = 0, \ldots, S_n = 0$. And if no value in $x_1, \ldots, x_n$ satisfies α_i, then $S_1 = i, \ldots, S_n = i$.

We now have the following property of the network in Figure 11.2:

$$\Pr(S_0 = i, x_1, \ldots, x_n, S_n = 0) = \begin{cases} (1/m)(.5)^n, & \text{if } x_1, \ldots, x_n \text{ satisfies clause } \alpha_i \\ 0, & \text{otherwise.} \end{cases}$$

Moreover,

$$\Pr(x_1, \ldots, x_n, S_n = 0) = \sum_{i=1}^{m} \Pr(S_0 = i, x_1, \ldots, x_n, S_n = 0)$$

$$= c \frac{1}{m2^n},$$

where c is the number of clauses in $\alpha_1, \ldots, \alpha_m$ satisfied by the instantiation $x_1, \ldots, x_n$. Hence, more than k clauses are satisfied by this instantiation iff $c > k$, which is precisely when $\Pr(x_1, \ldots, x_n, S_n = 0) > k/(m2^n)$. ■

PROOF OF THEOREM 11.7. There is a one-to-one correspondence between the models of CNF $\Delta_{\mathcal{N}}$ and the variable instantiations of network $\mathcal{N}$. To see this, note first that there is a one-to-one correspondence between the instantiations of indicator variables in the CNF and instantiations of all variables in the Bayesian network (this follows from the indicator clauses). Moreover, for every instantiation of indicator variables, there is a single instantiation of parameter variables that is implied by it (this follows from parameter clauses). Finally, note that the model ω that corresponds to a network instantiation $\mathbf{x}$ sets to true only those parameter variables that are compatible with the instantiation $\mathbf{x}$. This implies that the weight of a model ω for CNF $\Delta_{\mathcal{N}}$ is precisely the probability of corresponding network instantiation $\mathbf{x}$. Moreover, by adding the indicators $I_{e_1} \wedge \ldots \wedge I_{e_k}$ to the CNF, we eliminate all CNF models (network instantiations) incompatible with the evidence. Hence, the weighted model count will be the sum of weights (probabilities) of models (network instantiations) compatible with given evidence. ■

PROOF OF THEOREM 11.8. Left to Exercise 11.8. ■

12

Compiling Bayesian Networks

We discuss in this chapter the compilation of Bayesian networks into arithmetic circuits. The compilation process takes place offline and is done only once per network. The resulting arithmetic circuit can then be used to answer multiple online queries through a simple process of circuit propagation.

12.1 Introduction

Consider the Bayesian network in Figure 12.1. We present an approach in this chapter for compiling such a network into an arithmetic circuit using an offline procedure that is applied only once. We then show how the compiled circuit can be used to answer multiple online queries using a simple process of circuit propagation.

Figure 12.2 depicts a circuit compilation of the network in Figure 12.1. The circuit has two types of inputs: the θ variables, which are called *parameters,* and the λ variables, which are called *indicators.* Parameter variables are set according to the network CPTs, while indicator variables are set according to the given evidence. Once the circuit inputs are set, it can be evaluated using a bottom-up pass, which proceeds from the circuit inputs to its output. The circuit output computed by this evaluation process is guaranteed to be the probability of given evidence. Figure 12.3 depicts the result of performing an evaluation pass on the given circuit under evidence $a\bar{c}$. The circuit output in this case, .1, is guaranteed to be the probability of evidence $a\bar{c}$.

We can perform a second pass on the circuit called a *differentiation pass,* which proceeds top-down from the circuit output toward the circuit inputs. This pass evaluates the partial derivatives of the circuit output with respect to each and every circuit input. Figure 12.3 depicts the result of performing a differentiation pass on the given circuit under evidence $a\bar{c}$. We see later that the circuit output is a linear function of each input. Hence, a derivative represents the change in the circuit output for each unit change in the circuit input. For example, the partial derivative .4 associated with input $\lambda_{\bar{a}}$ represents the amount by which the circuit output will change if the value of input $\lambda_{\bar{a}}$ changes from 0 to 1. We show later that using the values of these derivatives, we can compute many marginal probabilities efficiently without the need to re-evaluate the circuit. The values of partial derivatives also have important applications to sensitivity analysis which we discuss in Chapter 16. Finally, we note that the compiled circuits can be used to compute MPE and, if constructed carefully, can also be used to compute MAP.

The advantages of compiling Bayesian networks into arithmetic circuits can be summarized as follows. First, the separation of the inference process into offline and online phases allows us to push much of the computational overhead into the offline phase, which can then be amortized over many online queries. Next, the simplicity of the compiled arithmetic circuit and its propagation algorithms facilitate the development of online reasoning systems. Finally, compilation provides an effective framework for exploiting

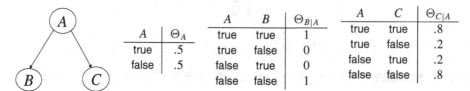

Figure 12.1: A Bayesian network.

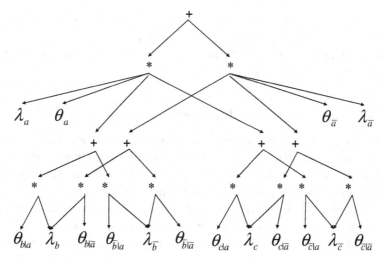

Figure 12.2: An arithmetic circuit for the Bayesian network in Figure 12.1.

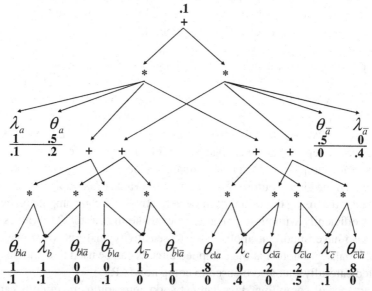

Figure 12.3: The result of circuit evaluation and differentiation under evidence $a\bar{c}$. There are two numbers below each leaf node. The first (top) is the value of that leaf node. The second (bottom) is the value of the partial derivative of the circuit output with respect to that circuit input.

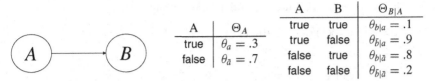

A	B	$\Theta_{B\mid A}$
true	true	$\theta_{b\mid a} = .1$
true	false	$\theta_{\bar{b}\mid a} = .9$
false	true	$\theta_{b\mid \bar{a}} = .8$
false	false	$\theta_{\bar{b}\mid \bar{a}} = .2$

A	Θ_A
true	$\theta_a = .3$
false	$\theta_{\bar{a}} = .7$

Figure 12.4: A Bayesian network.

the network local structure (i.e., the properties of network parameters), allowing an inference complexity that is not necessarily exponential in the network treewidth. As we see in Chapter 13, the techniques for exploiting local structure usually incur a nontrivial overhead that may not be justifiable unless they are pushed into the offline phase of a compilation process.

We discuss the semantics of compilation in Section 12.2 and provide algorithms for circuit propagation in Section 12.3. The compilation of Bayesian networks into arithmetic circuits is then discussed in Section 12.4.

12.2 Circuit semantics

The arithmetic circuit we compile from a Bayesian network is a compact representation of the probability distribution induced by the network. We show this correspondence more formally later but let us consider a concrete example first. According to the semantics of Bayesian networks, the probability distribution induced by the network in Figure 12.4 is

A	B	$\Pr(A, B)$
a	b	$\theta_a \theta_{b\mid a}$
a	$\bar{b}$	$\theta_a \theta_{\bar{b}\mid a}$
$\bar{a}$	b	$\theta_{\bar{a}} \theta_{b\mid \bar{a}}$
$\bar{a}$	$\bar{b}$	$\theta_{\bar{a}} \theta_{\bar{b}\mid \bar{a}}$

Let us now multiply each probability in this distribution by indicator variables, as follows:

A	B	$\Pr(A, B)$
a	b	$\lambda_a \lambda_b \theta_a \theta_{b\mid a}$
a	$\bar{b}$	$\lambda_a \lambda_{\bar{b}} \theta_a \theta_{\bar{b}\mid a}$
$\bar{a}$	b	$\lambda_{\bar{a}} \lambda_b \theta_{\bar{a}} \theta_{b\mid \bar{a}}$
$\bar{a}$	$\bar{b}$	$\lambda_{\bar{a}} \lambda_{\bar{b}} \theta_{\bar{a}} \theta_{\bar{b}\mid \bar{a}}$

That is, we multiply the indicator variable λ_v into the probability of each instantiation that includes value v. Let us finally take the sum of all probabilities in the distribution:

$$f = \lambda_a \lambda_b \theta_a \theta_{b\mid a} + \lambda_a \lambda_{\bar{b}} \theta_a \theta_{\bar{b}\mid a} + \lambda_{\bar{a}} \lambda_b \theta_{\bar{a}} \theta_{b\mid \bar{a}} + \lambda_{\bar{a}} \lambda_{\bar{b}} \theta_{\bar{a}} \theta_{\bar{b}\mid \bar{a}}. \tag{12.1}$$

The function f, called the *network polynomial,* can be viewed as a representation of the probability distribution induced by the network in Figure 12.4. In particular, we can use this polynomial to compute the probability of any evidence **e** by simply setting the indicator variables to 1 or 0, depending on whether they are consistent with evidence **e**. For example, given evidence $\mathbf{e} = \bar{a}$, we set the indicators as follows: $\lambda_a = 0, \lambda_{\bar{a}} = 1, \lambda_b = 1,$

and $\lambda_{\bar{b}} = 1$. The value of the polynomial under these settings is then

$$f(\mathbf{e} = \bar{a}) = (0)(1)\theta_a\theta_{b|a} + (0)(1)\theta_a\theta_{\bar{b}|a} + (1)(1)\theta_{\bar{a}}\theta_{b|\bar{a}} + (1)(1)\theta_{\bar{a}}\theta_{\bar{b}|\bar{a}}$$
$$= \theta_{\bar{a}}\theta_{b|\bar{a}} + \theta_{\bar{a}}\theta_{\bar{b}|\bar{a}}$$
$$= \Pr(\mathbf{e}).$$

For another example, consider the network in Figure 12.1. The polynomial of this network has eight terms, some of which are shown here:

$$f = \lambda_a\lambda_b\lambda_c\theta_a\theta_{b|a}\theta_{c|a} +$$
$$\lambda_a\lambda_b\lambda_{\bar{c}}\theta_a\theta_{b|a}\theta_{\bar{c}|a} +$$
$$\vdots$$
$$\lambda_{\bar{a}}\lambda_{\bar{b}}\lambda_{\bar{c}}\theta_{\bar{a}}\theta_{\bar{b}|\bar{a}}\theta_{\bar{c}|\bar{a}}. \tag{12.2}$$

In general, for a Bayesian network with n variables each term in the polynomial will contain $2n$ variables: n parameters and n indicators, where each of the variables has degree 1. Hence, the polynomial is a multilinear function (MLF), as it is a linear function in terms of each of its variables.[1]

The network polynomial has an exponential size as it includes a term for each instantiation of the network variables. Due to its size, we cannot work with the network polynomial directly. Instead, we will use the arithmetic circuit as a compact representation of the network polynomial. As we see later, there are interesting situations in which the size of an arithmetic circuit can be bounded even when the size of the polynomial it represents cannot. The generation of arithmetic circuits is discussed in Section 12.4. We first define formally the network polynomial and its circuit representation.

As a matter of notation, we write $\theta_{x|\mathbf{u}} \sim \mathbf{z}$ to mean that the subscript $x\mathbf{u}$ is consistent with instantiation $\mathbf{z}$, $x\mathbf{u} \sim \mathbf{z}$. Hence, $\prod_{\theta_{x|\mathbf{u}}\sim\mathbf{z}} \theta_{x|\mathbf{u}}$ denotes the product of all parameters $\theta_{x|\mathbf{u}}$ for which $x\mathbf{u}$ is consistent with $\mathbf{z}$. We similarly interpret the notation $\lambda_x \sim \mathbf{z}$.

Definition 12.1. Let $\mathcal{N}$ be a Bayesian network over variables $\mathbf{Z}$. For every variable X with parents $\mathbf{U}$ in the network, variable λ_x is called an *indicator* and variable $\theta_{x|\mathbf{u}}$ is called a *parameter*. The *polynomial* of network $\mathcal{N}$ is defined over indicator and parameter variables as

$$f \stackrel{def}{=} \sum_{\mathbf{z}} \prod_{\theta_{x|\mathbf{u}}\sim\mathbf{z}} \theta_{x|\mathbf{u}} \prod_{\lambda_x\sim\mathbf{z}} \lambda_x.$$

The *value* of network polynomial f at evidence $\mathbf{e}$, denoted by $f(\mathbf{e})$, is the result of replacing each indicator λ_x in f with 1 if x is consistent with $\mathbf{e}$, $x \sim \mathbf{e}$, and with 0 otherwise. ∎

The outer sum in the definition of f ranges over all instantiations $\mathbf{z}$ of the network variables. For each instantiation $\mathbf{z}$, the inner products range over parameter and indicator variables that are compatible with instantiation $\mathbf{z}$.

The following is another example for computing a value of the network polynomial in (12.1). If the evidence $\mathbf{e}$ is $a\bar{b}$, then $f(\mathbf{e})$ is obtained by applying the following substitutions to f: $\lambda_a = 1$, $\lambda_{\bar{a}} = 0$, $\lambda_b = 0$, and $\lambda_{\bar{b}} = 1$, leading to the probability $f(\mathbf{e}) = \Pr(\mathbf{e}) = \theta_a\theta_{\bar{b}|a}$.

---

[1] Linearity implies that the partial derivative $\partial f/\partial\lambda_x$ is independent of λ_x. Similarly, the partial derivative $\partial f/\partial\theta_{x|\mathbf{u}}$ is independent of $\theta_{x|\mathbf{u}}$.

Theorem 12.1. *Let* $\mathbf{N}$ *be a Bayesian network inducing probability distribution* $\Pr$ *and having polynomial* f. *For any evidence* $\mathbf{e}$, *we have* $f(\mathbf{e}) = \Pr(\mathbf{e})$.   ∎

As mentioned previously, we represent network polynomials by arithmetic circuits, which can be much smaller in size.

Definition 12.2. An *arithmetic circuit* over variables Σ is a rooted DAG whose leaf nodes are labeled with variables in Σ and whose other nodes are labeled with multiplication and addition operations. The *size* of an arithmetic circuit is the number of edges it contains.   ∎

Figure 12.2 depicts an arithmetic circuit representation of the network polynomial in (12.2). Note how the value of each node in the circuit is a function of the values of its children.

The compilation of Bayesian networks into arithmetic circuits provides a new measure for the complexity of inference, which is more refined than treewidth as it can be sensitive to the properties of network parameters (local structure).

Definition 12.3. The *circuit complexity* of a Bayesian network $\mathbf{N}$ is the size of the smallest arithmetic circuit that represents the network polynomial of $\mathbf{N}$.   ∎

For example, when the values of network parameters are known to have specific values, such as 0 and 1, or when some relationships exist between these parameters, such as equality, the arithmetic circuit can be simplified considerably, leading to a circuit complexity that could be much tighter than the complexity based on treewidth.

We next address two questions. First, assuming that we have a compact arithmetic circuit that represents the network polynomial, how can we use it to answer probabilistic queries? Second, how do we obtain a compact arithmetic circuit that represents a given network polynomial? The first question will be addressed in the following section and the second question will be addressed in Section 12.4.

12.3 Circuit propagation

Once we have an arithmetic circuit for a given Bayesian network, we can compute the probability of any evidence $\mathbf{e}$ by simply evaluating the circuit at that evidence. We can actually answer many more queries beyond the probability of evidence if we have access to the circuit's partial derivatives. Consider the circuit in Figure 12.3, for example, which has been evaluated and differentiated at evidence $\mathbf{e} = a\bar{c}$. The value of partial derivative $\partial f / \partial \lambda_{\bar{a}}$ equals .4 in this case. This derivative represents the amount of change in the circuit output for each unit change in the circuit input $\lambda_{\bar{a}}$. For example, if we change the input $\lambda_{\bar{a}}$ from the current value of 0 to 1, the circuit output changes from .1 to .5. Note, however, that changing the input $\lambda_{\bar{a}}$ from 0 to 1 corresponds to changing the evidence from $a\bar{c}$ to $\bar{c}$. Hence, from the value of this derivative we can conclude that the probability of evidence $\bar{c}$ is .5, without the need for re-evaluating the circuit under this new evidence.

We next present a theorem that gives a precise probabilistic meaning to circuit derivatives, allowing us to answer many interesting queries based on the values of these derivatives. But we first need the following notational convention. Let $\mathbf{e}$ be an instantiation and $\mathbf{X}$ be a set of variables. Then $\mathbf{e} - \mathbf{X}$ denotes the instantiation that results from erasing the values of variables $\mathbf{X}$ from instantiation $\mathbf{e}$. For example, if $\mathbf{e} = ab\bar{c}$, then $\mathbf{e} - A = b\bar{c}$ and $\mathbf{e} - AC = b$.

Before we present our next result, we note here that if f is a network polynomial, then $\partial f/\partial\lambda_x$ and $\partial f/\partial\theta_{x|\mathbf{u}}$ are also polynomials and, hence, can be evaluated at some evidence $\mathbf{e}$ in the same way that polynomial f is evaluated at $\mathbf{e}$. The quantities $\partial f/\partial\lambda_x(\mathbf{e})$ and $\partial f/\partial\theta_{x|\mathbf{u}}(\mathbf{e})$ are then well defined and Theorem 12.2 reveals their probabilistic semantics.

Theorem 12.2. *Let $\mathcal{N}$ be a Bayesian network representing probability distribution* $\Pr$ *and having polynomial f and let $\mathbf{e}$ be some evidence. For every indicator λ_x, we have*

$$\frac{\partial f}{\partial\lambda_x}(\mathbf{e}) = \Pr(x, \mathbf{e} - X). \tag{12.3}$$

Moreover, for every parameter $\theta_{x|\mathbf{u}}$ we have

$$\theta_{x|\mathbf{u}}\frac{\partial f}{\partial\theta_{x|\mathbf{u}}}(\mathbf{e}) = \Pr(x, \mathbf{u}, \mathbf{e}). \tag{12.4}$$

∎

We next provide some concrete examples of these derivatives to shed some light on their practical value.

Consider again the circuit in Figure 12.3, where evidence $\mathbf{e} = a\bar{c}$ and $\frac{\partial f}{\partial\lambda_{\bar{a}}}(\mathbf{e}) = .4$. Since $\mathbf{e} - A = \bar{c}$, we immediately conclude that

$$\frac{\partial f}{\partial\lambda_{\bar{a}}}(\mathbf{e}) = \Pr(\bar{a}, \mathbf{e} - A) = \Pr(\bar{a}\bar{c}) = .4.$$

Equation (12.3) can therefore be used to compute the probability of new evidence $\mathbf{e}'$ that results from flipping the value of some variable X in evidence $\mathbf{e}$. If variable X is not set in evidence $\mathbf{e}$, we have $\mathbf{e} - X = \mathbf{e}$. Hence, (12.3) can be used to compute the marginal probability $x, \mathbf{e}$ in this case.

Similarly, (12.4) can be used to compute all family marginals $\Pr(x, \mathbf{u}, \mathbf{e})$ from the values of circuit derivatives. Finally, note that (12.4) is commonly used in the context of standard algorithms, such as the jointree algorithm, to compute the values of partial derivatives:

$$\frac{\partial f}{\partial\theta_{x|\mathbf{u}}}(\mathbf{e}) = \frac{\Pr(x, \mathbf{u}, \mathbf{e})}{\theta_{x|\mathbf{u}}}, \quad \text{when } \theta_{x|\mathbf{u}} \neq 0. \tag{12.5}$$

That is, we could use a standard algorithm to compute the marginal $\Pr(x, \mathbf{u}, \mathbf{e})$ and then use (12.5) to evaluate the derivative $\frac{\partial f}{\partial\theta_{x|\mathbf{u}}}(\mathbf{e})$ given this marginal. This common technique is only valid when $\theta_{x|\mathbf{u}} \neq 0$, however. In the following section, we provide a more general technique that does not require this condition.

The derivative in (12.5) plays a key role in sensitivity analysis (Chapter 16) and in learning network parameters (Chapter 17). This derivative is also commonly expressed as

$$\frac{\partial f}{\partial\theta_{x|\mathbf{u}}}(\mathbf{e}) = \frac{\partial\Pr(\mathbf{e})}{\partial\theta_{x|\mathbf{u}}}, \tag{12.6}$$

where $\Pr$ is the distribution corresponding to the network polynomial f. We use this form in Chapters 16 and 17.

Algorithm 34 CircP1($\mathcal{AC}$, vr(), dr()). Assumes that the values of leaf circuit nodes v have been initialized in vr(v).

---

input:

  $\mathcal{AC}$:   arithmetic circuit

  vr():   array of value registers (one register for each circuit node)

  dr():   array of derivative registers (one register for each circuit node)

output: computes the value of circuit output v in vr(v) and computes derivatives of leaf nodes v in dr(v)

main:

1: **for** each circuit node v (visiting children before parents) **do**

2:    compute the value of node v and store it in vr(v)

3: **end for**

4: dr(v)$\leftarrow$0 for all non-root nodes v; dr(v)$\leftarrow$1 for root node v

5: **for** each circuit node v (visiting parents before children) **do**

6:    **for** each parent p of node v **do**

7:       **if** p is an addition node **then**

8:          dr(v)$\leftarrow$dr(v) + dr(p)

9:       **else**

10:         dr(v)$\leftarrow$dr(v) + dr(p) $\prod_{v' \neq v}$ vr(v'), where v' is a child of parent p

11:       **end if**

12:    **end for**

13: **end for**

12.3.1 Evaluation and differentiation passes

Evaluating an arithmetic circuit is straightforward: we simply traverse the circuit bottom-up, computing the value of a node after having computed the values of its children. The procedure for computing values of derivatives is also simple and is given in Algorithm 34, but the correctness of this procedure is not obvious and needs to be established. However, before we prove correctness we point to Figure 12.5, which contains an arithmetic circuit evaluated and differentiated under evidence $\mathbf{e} = a\bar{c}$ using Algorithm 34.

The algorithm uses two arrays of registers: vr(v) stores a value for each node v and dr(v) stores a partial derivative. We assume that the values of leaf nodes, which correspond to indicators and parameters, have been initialized. The algorithm starts by performing a bottom-up pass in which the value of each node v is computed and stored in the vr(v) register. It then initializes the dr(.) array and performs a second pass in which it fills the dr(.) array. To see how this array is filled, let us first use r to denote the root node (circuit output) and let v be an arbitrary circuit node. The key observation here is that the value of the root node vr(r) is a function of the value vr(v) of an arbitrary node v. Hence, it is meaningful to compute the partial derivative of vr(r) with respect to vr(v), ∂vr(r)$/\partial$vr(v). Algorithm 34 computes such a derivative for each node v and stores it in the register dr(v). Note that we are interested in the derivative dr(v) only for leaf nodes v, which correspond to parameter and indicator variables. However, computing these derivatives for every node makes things easier for the following reason: Once the derivatives are computed for the parents of node v, computing the derivative for node v becomes straightforward. This is indeed the basis of Algorithm 34, which proceeds top-down, computing the derivatives for parents before computing them for children.

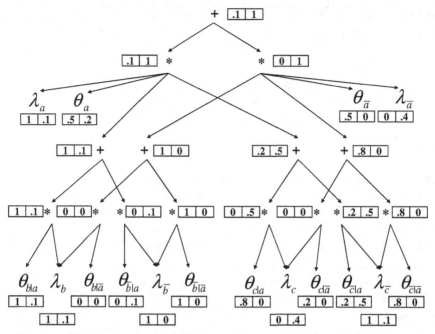

Figure 12.5: An arithmetic circuit for the Bayesian network in Figure 12.1 after it has been evaluated and differentiated under evidence $a\bar{c}$, using Algorithm 34. Registers vr(.) are shown on the left and registers dr(.) are shown on the right.

To further justify the particular update equations used by the algorithm, note first that $\partial\text{vr}(r)/\partial\text{vr}(r) = 1$ and r is the root, which is the reason why dr(r) is initialized to 1. For an arbitrary node $v \neq r$ with parents p, the chain rule of differential calculus gives

$$\frac{\partial\text{vr}(r)}{\partial\text{vr}(v)} = \sum_p \frac{\partial\text{vr}(r)}{\partial\text{vr}(p)} \frac{\partial\text{vr}(p)}{\partial\text{vr}(v)}.$$

Since the derivatives of the root r are stored in the dr(.) array, we have

$$\text{dr}(v) = \sum_p \text{dr}(p)\frac{\partial\text{vr}(p)}{\partial\text{vr}(v)}.$$

Suppose now that v' ranges over the children of parent p. If parent p is a multiplication node, then

$$\frac{\partial\text{vr}(p)}{\partial\text{vr}(v)} = \frac{\partial(\text{vr}(v)\prod_{v'\neq v}\text{vr}(v'))}{\partial\text{vr}(v)} = \prod_{v'\neq v}\text{vr}(v').$$

However, if parent p is an addition node, then

$$\frac{\partial\text{vr}(p)}{\partial\text{vr}(v)} = \frac{\partial(\text{vr}(v) + \sum_{v'\neq v}\text{vr}(v'))}{\partial\text{vr}(v)} = 1.$$

If we let $+p$ stand for an addition parent of v and let $\star p$ stand for a multiplication parent having children v', we then have

$$\text{dr}(v) = \sum_{+p}\text{dr}(+p) + \sum_{\star p}\text{dr}(\star p)\prod_{v'\neq v}\text{vr}(v').$$

Algorithm 34 uses this precise equation to fill in the dr(.) array.

Algorithm 35 CircP2($\mathcal{AC}$, vr(), dr()). Assumes the values of leaf circuit nodes v have been initialized in vr(v) and the circuit alternates between addition and multiplication nodes, with leaves having multiplication parents.

---

input:

   $\mathcal{AC}$:   arithmetic circuit

   vr():   array of value registers (one register for each circuit node)

   dr():   array of derivative registers (one register for each circuit node)

output: computes the value of circuit output v in vr(v) and computes derivatives of leaf nodes v in dr(v)

main:

1: **for** each non-leaf node v with children c (visit children before parents) **do**

2:    **if** v is an addition node **then**

3:       vr(v) $\leftarrow \sum_{c:\, \text{bit}(c)=0}$ vr(c) $\{$if bit(c) $= 1$, value of c is $0\}$

4:    **else**

5:       **if** v has a single child c' with vr(c') $= 0$ **then**

6:          bit(v) $\leftarrow 1$; vr(v) $\leftarrow \prod_{c \neq c'}$ vr(c)

7:       **else**

8:          bit(v) $\leftarrow 0$; vr(v) $\leftarrow \prod_{c}$ vr(c)

9:       **end if**

10:   **end if**

11: **end for**

12: dr(v) $\leftarrow 0$ for all non-root nodes v; dr(v) $\leftarrow 1$ for root node v

13: **for** each non-root node v (visit parents before children) **do**

14:   **for** each parent p of node v **do**

15:    **if** p is an addition node **then**

16:       dr(v) $\leftarrow$ dr(v) $+$ dr(p)

17:    **else**

18:       **if** vr(p) $\neq 0$ **then** $\{p$ has at most one child with zero value$\}$

19:          **if** bit(p) $= 0$ **then** $\{p$ has no zero children$\}$

20:             dr(v) $\leftarrow$ dr(v) $+$ dr(p)vr(p)/vr(v)

21:          **else if** vr(v) $= 0$ **then** $\{v$ is the single zero child$\}$

22:             dr(v) $\leftarrow$ dr(v) $+$ dr(p)vr(p)

23:          **end if**

24:       **end if**

25:    **end if**

26:   **end for**

27: **end for**

The bottom-up pass in Algorithm 34 clearly takes time linear in the circuit size, where size is defined as the number of circuit edges. However, the top-down pass takes linear time only when each multiplication node has a bounded number of children; otherwise, the time to evaluate the term $\prod_{v' \neq v}$ vr(v') cannot be bounded by a constant.

This is addressed by Algorithm 35, which is based on observing that the term $\prod_{v' \neq v}$ vr(v') equals vr(p)/vr(v) when vr(v) $\neq 0$ and, hence, the time to evaluate it can be bounded by a constant if we use division. Even the case vr(v) $= 0$ can be handled efficiently but that requires an additional bit per multiplication node p:

- bit(p) $= 1$ when exactly one child of node p has a zero value.

When this bit is set, the register $\mathsf{vr}(p)$ will not store the value of p, which must be zero. Instead, it will store the product of values for p's children, excluding the single child that has a zero value. The use of this additional bit leads to Algorithm 35, which takes time linear in the circuit size. Note that after finishing the bottom-up pass, we are guaranteed the following:

- The value of every addition node v is stored in $\mathsf{vr}(v)$.
- The value of every multiplication node v is stored in $\mathsf{vr}(v)$ if $\mathsf{bit}(v) = 0$, and the value is 0 otherwise.

Algorithm 35 assumes that the circuit alternates between addition and multiplication nodes with leaf nodes having multiplication parents. This can be easily relaxed but makes the statement of the algorithm somewhat more complicated as we would need to include more tests to decide the value of a node (based on its type and associated bit).

12.3.2 Computing MPEs

An arithmetic circuit can be easily modified into a maximizer circuit that computes the probability of MPEs.

Definition 12.4. The *maximizer circuit* $\mathcal{AC}^m$ for an arithmetic circuit $\mathcal{AC}$ is obtained by replacing each addition node in circuit $\mathcal{AC}$ with a maximization node. ∎

Figure 12.6 depicts a maximizer circuit obtained from the arithmetic circuit in Figure 12.2. A maximizer circuit computes the value of the maximum term in a network polynomial instead of adding up the values of these terms as done by an arithmetic circuit. In particular, if the arithmetic circuit $\mathcal{AC}$ represents the polynomial

$$f = \sum_{\mathbf{z}} \prod_{\theta_{x|\mathbf{u}} \sim \mathbf{z}} \theta_{x|\mathbf{u}} \prod_{\lambda_x \sim \mathbf{z}} \lambda_x,$$

then the maximizer circuit $\mathcal{AC}^m$ represents the following *maximizer polynomial:*

$$f^m \stackrel{def}{=} \max_{\mathbf{z}} \prod_{\theta_{x|\mathbf{u}} \sim \mathbf{z}} \theta_{x|\mathbf{u}} \prod_{\lambda_x \sim \mathbf{z}} \lambda_x.$$

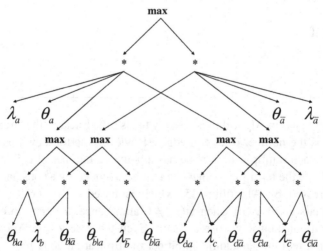

Figure 12.6: A maximizer circuit for the Bayesian network in Figure 12.1.

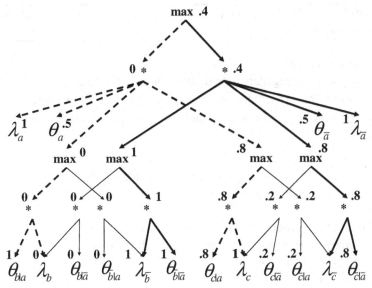

Figure 12.7: A maximizer circuit for the Bayesian network in Figure 12.1, evaluated at evidence $\bar{b}$.

Therefore, evaluating the maximizer circuit $\mathcal{AC}^m$ at evidence $\mathbf{e}$ gives the MPE probability, $\text{MPE}_P(\mathbf{e})$:

$$\mathcal{AC}^m(\mathbf{e}) = f^m(\mathbf{e}) = \text{MPE}_P(\mathbf{e}).$$

Figure 12.7 depicts a maximizer circuit that is evaluated at evidence $\mathbf{e} = \bar{b}$, leading to the MPE probability .4.

A maximizer circuit can also be used to recover one or all MPE instantiations. This is done using the notion of a complete subcircuit.

Definition 12.5. Let $\mathcal{AC}^m$ be a maximizer circuit. A *complete subcircuit* in $\mathcal{AC}^m$ is a subcircuit obtained by starting at the root of $\mathcal{AC}^m$ and moving downward from parents to children, including all children of a visited multiplication node and including exactly one child of a visited maximization node. Each complete subcircuit corresponds to a polynomial term obtained by taking the product of variables associated with leaf nodes in the subcircuit. The *value* of a subcircuit at evidence $\mathbf{e}$ is the value of its corresponding term at evidence $\mathbf{e}$. ∎

We therefore have a one-to-one correspondence between complete subcircuits and polynomial terms.

Figure 12.7 highlights two complete subcircuits, one in bold lines and the other in dashed bold lines. The subcircuit highlighted with bold lines corresponds to the term $\lambda_{\bar{a}}\lambda_{\bar{b}}\lambda_{\bar{c}}\theta_{\bar{a}}\theta_{\bar{b}|\bar{a}}\theta_{\bar{c}|\bar{a}}$ and has a value of .4 at evidence $\bar{b}$. The subcircuit highlighted in bold dashed lines corresponds to the term $\lambda_a\lambda_b\lambda_c\theta_a\theta_{b|a}\theta_{c|a}$ and has a value of 0 at this evidence. The maximizer circuit in Figure 12.6 has eight complete subcircuits corresponding to the eight terms of the network polynomial.

We can construct an MPE instantiation by choosing a complete subcircuit whose value is maximal at the given evidence $\mathbf{e}$. This can be done by ensuring that for each maximization node v in the subcircuit, the chosen child c of node v has the same value as v. Applying this procedure to Figure 12.7 leads to the subcircuit highlighted in bold lines, which corresponds to the term $\lambda_{\bar{a}}\lambda_{\bar{b}}\lambda_{\bar{c}}\theta_{\bar{a}}\theta_{\bar{b}|\bar{a}}\theta_{\bar{c}|\bar{a}}$ and MPE instantiation $\bar{a}\bar{b}\bar{c}$ with a probability of .4.

Algorithm 36 CircP_MPE($\mathcal{AC}$, vr(), dr()). Assumes that the values of leaf circuit nodes v have been initialized in vr(v).

---

input:

   $\mathcal{AC}$:   maximizer circuit

   vr():   array of value registers (one register for each circuit node)

   dr():   array of derivative registers (one register for each circuit node)

output: computes the value of circuit output v in vr(v) and computes derivatives of leaf nodes v in dr(v)

main:

  1: **for** each circuit node v (visiting children before parents) **do**

  2:     compute the value of node v and store it in vr(v)

  3: **end for**

  4: dr(v)←0 for all non-root nodes v; dr(v)←1 for root node v

  5: **for** each circuit node v (visiting parents before children) **do**

  6:     **for** each parent p of node v **do**

  7:         **if** p is a maximization node **then**

  8:            dr(v)← max(dr(v), dr(p))

  9:         **else**

10:            dr(v)← max(dr(v), dr(p) $\prod_{v' \neq v}$ vr(v')), where v' is a child of p

11:         **end if**

12:     **end for**

13: **end for**

In general, a maximization node v can have multiple children c with the same value as v, indicating the existence of multiple MPE instantiations. By choosing a different child c from this set we can induce different complete subcircuits, each corresponding to a different MPE instantiation.

We can also define a second pass on a maximizer circuit that traverses the circuit top-down from parents to children, as given by Algorithm 36.[2] This is very similar to the second pass of Algorithm 34 except that we replace additions by maximizations when computing the values of dr(.) registers. The values of these registers also have differential and probabilistic semantics similar to their arithmetic circuit counterparts. However, the derivatives are not with respect to the maximizer circuit but with respect to restrictions of this circuit, as we explain next.

Note first that the derivatives $\partial f^m / \partial \theta_{x|\mathbf{u}}$ and $\partial f^m / \partial \lambda_x$ are not well defined as the function f^m is not continuous in the variables $\theta_{x|\mathbf{u}}$ and λ_x. For example, the value of function f^m may stay constant for certain changes in variable $\theta_{x|\mathbf{u}}$ yet suddenly change its value when the change in $\theta_{x|\mathbf{u}}$ becomes large enough. However, these derivatives are well defined for restrictions of the maximizer polynomial, defined next.

Definition 12.6. The *restriction* of maximizer polynomial f^m to instantiation $\mathbf{e}$ is defined as

$$f_{\mathbf{e}}^m \overset{def}{=} \max_{\mathbf{z} \sim \mathbf{e}} \prod_{\theta_{x|\mathbf{u}} \sim \mathbf{z}} \theta_{x|\mathbf{u}} \prod_{\lambda_x \sim \mathbf{z}} \lambda_x,$$

where all symbols are as given by Definition 12.1.   ■

---

[2] We can improve the complexity of this algorithm by using an additional bit per multiplication node, as in Algorithm 35.

That is, instead of maximizing over all polynomial terms, we maximize over only those terms that are consistent with evidence **e**. Consider now the restriction $f_{x,\mathbf{u}}^m$. All terms of this maximizer polynomial contain the parameter $\theta_{x|\mathbf{u}}$, therefore $f_{x,\mathbf{u}}^m$ is continuous in terms of $\theta_{x|\mathbf{u}}$, leading to a well-defined partial derivative with respect to parameter $\theta_{x|\mathbf{u}}$. The same is true for the restriction f_x^m, leading to a well-defined partial derivative with respect to indicator λ_x.

Consider for example the following maximizer polynomial for the network in Figure 12.1,

$$f^m = \max(\lambda_a \lambda_b \lambda_c \theta_a \theta_{b|a} \theta_{c|a}, \lambda_a \lambda_b \lambda_{\bar{c}} \theta_a \theta_{b|a} \theta_{\bar{c}|a}, \ldots, \lambda_{\bar{a}} \lambda_{\bar{b}} \lambda_{\bar{c}} \theta_{\bar{a}} \theta_{\bar{b}|\bar{a}} \theta_{\bar{c}|\bar{a}})$$

and its restriction

$$f_{b,a}^m = \max(\lambda_a \lambda_b \lambda_c \theta_a \theta_{b|a} \theta_{c|a}, \lambda_a \lambda_b \lambda_{\bar{c}} \theta_a \theta_{b|a} \theta_{\bar{c}|a})$$
$$= \theta_{b|a} \max(\lambda_a \lambda_b \lambda_c \theta_a \theta_{c|a}, \lambda_a \lambda_b \lambda_{\bar{c}} \theta_a \theta_{\bar{c}|a}).$$

The derivative with respect to parameter $\theta_{b|a}$ is well defined in this case:

$$\partial f_{b,a}^m / \partial \theta_{b|a} = \max(\lambda_a \lambda_b \lambda_c \theta_a \theta_{c|a}, \lambda_a \lambda_b \lambda_{\bar{c}} \theta_a \theta_{\bar{c}|a}).$$

Given these definitions, we can now state the meaning of the registers dr(.) computed by Algorithm 36.

Theorem 12.3. *Let f^m be the maximizer polynomial represented by a maximizer circuit passed to Algorithm 36. The following holds after termination of Algorithm 36: For a leaf node v that corresponds to parameter $\theta_{x|\mathbf{u}}$, we have*

$$dr(v) = \frac{\partial f_{x,\mathbf{u}}^m}{\partial \theta_{x|\mathbf{u}}}(\mathbf{e}). \tag{12.7}$$

Moreover, for a leaf node v that corresponds to indicator λ_x, we have

$$dr(v) = \frac{\partial f_x^m}{\partial \lambda_x}(\mathbf{e}). \tag{12.8}$$

∎

Now that we have defined the differential semantics of the quantities computed by the second pass of Algorithm 36, let us reveal their probabilistic semantics.

Theorem 12.4. *Let f^m be a maximizer polynomial. We then have*

$$\frac{\partial f_x^m}{\partial \lambda_x}(\mathbf{e}) = \mathrm{MPE}_P(x, \mathbf{e} - X), \tag{12.9}$$

and

$$\theta_{x|\mathbf{u}} \frac{\partial f_{x,\mathbf{u}}^m}{\partial \theta_{x|\mathbf{u}}}(\mathbf{e}) = \mathrm{MPE}_P(\mathbf{e}, x, \mathbf{u}). \tag{12.10}$$

∎

Note the similarity between Theorem 12.4 and Theorem 12.2, which reveals the probabilistic semantics of arithmetic circuit derivatives.

The derivative with respect to parameter variables has applications in Chapter 16 on sensitivity analysis. The derivative with respect to indicator variables has a more direct application as it gives the probability of MPE after flipping the value of variable X in evidence **e** to x. If variable X is not set in **e**, then $\mathbf{e} - X = \mathbf{e}$ and the derivative gives the MPE marginal probability, $\mathrm{MPE}_P(x, \mathbf{e})$.

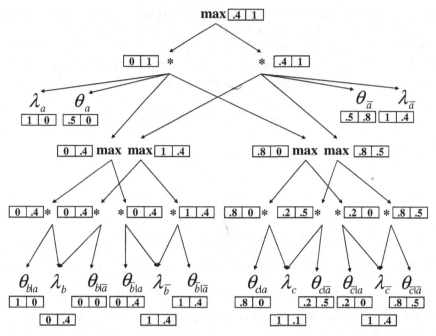

Figure 12.8: A maximizer circuit for the Bayesian network in Figure 12.1, evaluated and differentiated at evidence $\bar{b}$. Registers on the left contain node values and registers on the right contain node derivatives.

Figure 12.8 depicts a maximizer circuit evaluated and differentiated under evidence $\bar{b}$ using Algorithm 36. There is only one MPE instantiation in this case, $\bar{a}\bar{b}\bar{c}$. The following table lists the partial derivatives with respect to indicators together with their probabilistic semantics according to Theorem 12.4:

partial derivative	value	meaning
λ_a	0	$\mathrm{MPE}_P(a, \bar{b})$
$\lambda_{\bar{a}}$	.4	$\mathrm{MPE}_P(\bar{a}, \bar{b})$
λ_b	.4	$\mathrm{MPE}_P(b)$
$\lambda_{\bar{b}}$	.4	$\mathrm{MPE}_P(\bar{b})$
λ_c	.1	$\mathrm{MPE}_P(\bar{b}, c)$
$\lambda_{\bar{c}}$	.4	$\mathrm{MPE}_P(\bar{b}, \bar{c})$

12.4 Circuit compilation

We discuss two classes of algorithms for compiling arithmetic circuits, one class in this chapter and the other in Chapter 13. The algorithms discussed in this chapter are based on inference algorithms discussed previously. In particular, Section 12.4.1 describes a method for generating an arithmetic circuit by keeping a trace of the variable elimination algorithm, while Section 12.4.2 describes a method for extracting an arithmetic circuit from the structure of a jointree, and Section 12.4.3 describes a method based on CNF encodings. These methods are sensitive only to the network structure, leading to a circuit complexity that is independent of local structure (i.e., the specific values of network parameters). The second class of algorithms to be discussed in Chapter 13 will exploit the local structure of a Bayesian network and can be quite efficient even when the network treewidth is very large.

12.4.1 The circuits of variable elimination

We now describe a method for compiling a Bayesian network into an arithmetic circuit by keeping a trace of the variable elimination algorithm discussed in Chapter 6. In particular, instead of performing arithmetic operations as per the standard variable elimination algorithm, we perform circuit-construction operations that incrementally build up an arithmetic circuit in a bottom-up fashion.

To use variable elimination for constructing circuits, we need to work with circuit factors instead of standard factors. In a *circuit factor*, each variable instantiation is mapped to a circuit node instead of a number. Factor operations then need to be extended to work with circuit factors, which is accomplished by simply replacing the arithmetic operations of addition and multiplication by corresponding operations that construct circuit nodes. In particular, given circuit nodes n_1 and n_2, we use $+(n_1, n_2)$ to denote an addition node that has n_1 and n_2 as its children. Similarly, $\star(n_1, n_2)$ will denote a multiplication node that has n_1 and n_2 as its children. The multiplication of two circuit factors $f(\mathbf{X})$ and $f(\mathbf{Y})$ is then a factor over variables $\mathbf{Z} = \mathbf{X} \cup \mathbf{Y}$, defined as

$$f(\mathbf{z}) \stackrel{def}{=} \star(f(\mathbf{x}), f(\mathbf{y})), \quad \text{where } \mathbf{x} \sim \mathbf{z} \quad \text{and} \quad \mathbf{y} \sim \mathbf{z}.$$

The summing out of variable X from circuit factor $f(\mathbf{X})$ is defined similarly.

The algorithm we shall present starts by constructing a circuit factor for each network CPT. In particular, for every variable X with parents $\mathbf{U}$, a circuit factor is constructed over variables $X\mathbf{U}$. This factor maps each instantiation $x\mathbf{u}$ into a circuit node $\star(\lambda_x, \theta_{x|\mathbf{u}})$. Considering the network in Figure 12.4, the following circuit factors are constructed, where nodes $n_1, \ldots, n_6$ are also shown in Figure 12.9:

A	Θ_A	
true	n_1	$= \star(\lambda_a, \theta_a)$
false	n_2	$= \star(\lambda_{\bar{a}}, \theta_{\bar{a}})$

A	B	$\Theta_{B|A}$	
true	true	n_3	$= \star(\lambda_b, \theta_{b|a})$
true	false	n_4	$= \star(\lambda_{\bar{b}}, \theta_{\bar{b}|a})$
false	true	n_5	$= \star(\lambda_b, \theta_{b|\bar{a}})$
false	false	n_6	$= \star(\lambda_{\bar{b}}, \theta_{\bar{b}|\bar{a}})$

After constructing these factors, we apply the algorithm of variable elimination to eliminate every variable in the network. Just as in standard variable elimination, multiplying all resulting factors leads to a trivial factor with one entry, which in this case is the root to a circuit that represents the network polynomial.

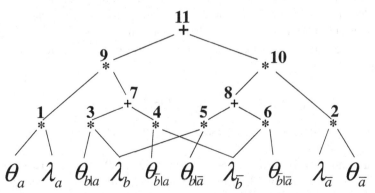

Figure 12.9: An arithmetic circuit for the Bayesian network in Figure 12.4 constructed by keeping a trace of variable elimination.

We now perform this elimination process using the order $\pi = B, A$. To eliminate variable B, we sum it out from factor $\Theta_{B|A}$, since it is the only factor containing B:

A	$\sum_B \Theta_{B|A}$	
true	n_7	$= +(n_3, n_4)$
false	n_8	$= +(n_5, n_6)$

This leads to constructing two new circuit nodes n_7 and n_8, shown in Figure 12.9.

To eliminate variable A, we must multiply the previous factor with factor Θ_A and then sum out variable A from the result. Multiplying leads to constructing two new circuit nodes, yielding

A	$\Theta_A \sum_B \Theta_{B|A}$	
true	n_9	$= \star(n_1, n_7)$
false	n_{10}	$= \star(n_2, n_8)$

Summing out constructs another circuit node, leading to

	$\sum_A \Theta_A \sum_B \Theta_{B|A}$	
$\top$	n_{11}	$= +(n_9, n_{10})$

Now that we have eliminated every variable, the resulting factor has a single entry n_{11} that is the root of the constructed circuit, shown in Figure 12.9. This circuit is guaranteed to correspond to the network polynomial.

The correctness of this algorithm follows immediately from the semantics of variable elimination, which evaluates the generated circuit in the process of computing the probability of evidence. The size of the resulting circuit is also bounded by the time complexity of variable elimination since the circuit nodes correspond to operations performed by the elimination algorithm. That is, if the elimination order used has n variables and width w, the size of the circuit and the time to generate it are bounded by $O(n \exp(w))$.

Recall that the algorithm of variable elimination is best suited for answering single queries, at least compared with the jointree algorithm, which can compute multiple queries within the same time complexity. One advantage of using variable elimination to compile arithmetic circuits is that we can use the resulting circuit to answer multiple queries in time linear in the circuit size, as shown in the previous section. In this sense, using variable elimination to compile arithmetic circuits provides the same computational advantages that we obtain from using the jointree algorithm.

We can also use the algorithm of recursive conditioning to compile out arithmetic circuits by keeping a trace of the operations it performs, just as with variable elimination. As such, both elimination and conditioning algorithms can be viewed as factorization algorithms as they factor the network polynomial into a corresponding arithmetic circuit representation.

12.4.2 Circuits embedded in a jointree

We now present another method for generating arithmetic circuits that is based on extracting them from jointrees.

Before a jointree is used to generate a circuit, each CPT $\Theta_{X|U}$ must be assigned to a cluster that contains family $X U$. Moreover, for each variable X an evidence indicator λ_X must be assigned to a cluster that contains X. Finally, a cluster in the jointree is chosen and designated as the root, allowing us to define parent/child relationships between

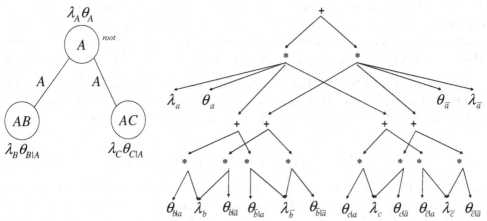

Figure 12.10: A jointree for the Bayesian network in Figure 12.1 and its corresponding arithmetic circuit.

neighboring clusters and separators. In particular, if two variable sets (clusters or separators) are adjacent in the jointree, the one closer to the root will be a parent of the other. The jointree in Figure 12.10 depicts the root cluster in addition to the assignment of CPTs and evidence indicators to various clusters. We show next that each jointree embeds an arithmetic circuit that represents the network polynomial.

Definition 12.7. Given a root cluster, a particular assignment of CPT, and evidence indicators to clusters, the arithmetic circuit *embedded* in a jointree is defined as follows. The circuit includes:

- One output addition node f
- An addition node $\mathbf{s}$ for each instantiation of a separator $\mathbf{S}$
- A multiplication node $\mathbf{c}$ for each instantiation of a cluster $\mathbf{C}$
- An input node λ_x for each instantiation x of variable X
- An input node $\theta_{x|\mathbf{u}}$ for each instantiation $x\mathbf{u}$ of family $X\mathbf{U}$.

The children of the output node f are the multiplication nodes $\mathbf{c}$ generated by the root cluster. The children of an addition node $\mathbf{s}$ are all compatible multiplication nodes $\mathbf{c}$, $\mathbf{c} \sim \mathbf{s}$, generated by the child cluster. The children of a multiplication node $\mathbf{c}$ are all compatible addition nodes $\mathbf{s}$, $\mathbf{s} \sim \mathbf{c}$, generated by child separators, in addition to all compatible inputs nodes $\theta_{x|\mathbf{u}}$ and λ_x, $x\mathbf{u} \sim \mathbf{c}$, for which CPT $\Theta_{X|\mathbf{U}}$ and evidence indicator λ_X are assigned to cluster $\mathbf{C}$. ∎

Figure 12.10 depicts a jointree and its embedded arithmetic circuit. Note the correspondence between addition nodes in the circuit (except the output node) and instantiations of separators in the jointree. Note also the correspondence between multiplication nodes in the circuit and instantiations of clusters in the jointree. One useful feature of the circuit embedded in a jointree is that it does not require that we represent its edges explicitly, as these can be inferred from the jointree structure. This leads to smaller space requirements but increases the time for evaluating and differentiating the circuit, given the overhead needed to infer these edges.[3] Another useful feature of the circuit embedded in a jointree is the guarantees one can offer on its size.

---

[3] Some optimized implementations of jointree algorithms maintain indices that associate cluster entries with compatible entries in their neighboring separators to reduce jointree propagation time. These algorithms are then representing both the nodes and edges of the embedded circuit explicitly.

Theorem 12.5. *Let J be a jointree for Bayesian network $\mathcal{N}$ with n clusters, a maximum cluster size c, and a maximum separator size s. The arithmetic circuit embedded in jointree J represents the network polynomial for $\mathcal{N}$ and has $O(n\exp(c))$ multiplication nodes, $O(n\exp(s))$ addition nodes, and $O(n\exp(c))$ edges.* ■

We saw in Chapter 9 that a Bayesian network with n nodes and treewidth w has a jointree with no more than n clusters and a maximum cluster size of $w + 1$. Theorem 12.5 is then telling us that the circuit complexity of such networks is $O(n\exp(w))$.

12.4.3 The circuits of CNF encodings

In Section 11.6, we showed that CNF encodings can be used to answer certain probabilistic queries (e.g., computing the probability of evidence by applying a weighted model counter to a CNF encoding). We show in this section that CNF encodings can also be used to generate arithmetic circuits for the corresponding Bayesian networks. In particular, we show that an arithmetic circuit can be immediately obtained once the CNF encoding (of Section 11.6.1) is converted into an equivalent NNF circuit that satisfies certain properties. Our proposed technique will consist of the following steps:

1. Encode the Bayesian network using a CNF Δ (see Section 11.6.1).
2. Convert the CNF Δ into an NNF circuit Γ that satisfies the properties of decomposability, determinism, and smoothness (see Section 2.7).
3. Extract an arithmetic circuit from the NNF circuit Γ.

We first illustrate this compilation technique using a concrete example and then discuss the reasons it works in general.

Consider the Bayesian network in Figure 12.4 and the CNF encoding scheme described in Section 11.6.1. If we apply this encoding scheme to the network, we obtain the following CNF:[4]

$$
\begin{array}{ccccccc}
I_a & \vee & I_{\bar{a}} & & I_b & \vee & I_{\bar{b}} \\
\neg I_a & \vee & \neg I_{\bar{a}} & & \neg I_b & \vee & \neg I_{\bar{b}}
\end{array}
$$

$$
\begin{array}{ccc}
I_a & \Longleftrightarrow & P_a \\
I_{\bar{a}} & \Longleftrightarrow & P_{\bar{a}}
\end{array}
$$

$$
\begin{array}{ccc}
I_a \wedge I_b & \Longleftrightarrow & P_{b|a} \\
I_a \wedge I_{\bar{b}} & \Longleftrightarrow & P_{\bar{b}|a} \\
I_{\bar{a}} \wedge I_b & \Longleftrightarrow & P_{b|\bar{a}} \\
I_{\bar{a}} \wedge I_{\bar{b}} & \Longleftrightarrow & P_{\bar{b},\bar{a}}
\end{array}
\tag{12.11}
$$

Figure 12.11(a) depicts an NNF circuit that is equivalent to this CNF and satisfies the properties of decomposability, determinism, and smoothness. Figure 12.11(b) depicts an arithmetic circuit obtained from this NNF circuit by applying the following substitutions (and some minor simplifications):

- Every or-node $\vee$ is replaced by an addition node $+$.
- Every and-node $\wedge$ is replaced by a multiplication node $*$.

---

[4] A sentence such as $I_a \wedge I_b \Longleftrightarrow P_{b|a}$ corresponds to a set of clauses $I_a \wedge I_b \Longrightarrow P_{b|a}$, $P_{b|a} \Longrightarrow I_a$, and $P_{b|a} \Longrightarrow I_b$.

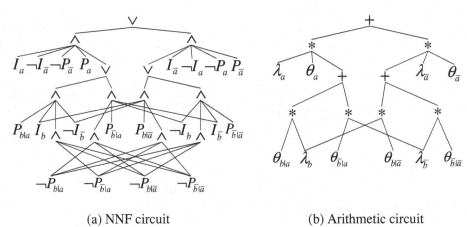

(a) NNF circuit   (b) Arithmetic circuit

Figure 12.11: Extracting an arithmetic circuit from an NNF circuit.

- Every negative literal of the form $\neg I_x$ or $\neg P_{x|u}$ is replaced by 1.
- Every positive literal I_x is replaced by the indicator λ_x.
- Every positive literal $P_{x|u}$ is replaced by the parameter $\theta_{x|u}$.

We can verify that the arithmetic circuit in Figure 12.11(b) does indeed represent the network polynomial of the Bayesian network given in Figure 12.4.

To see why this compilation technique works in general, we first show that every CNF can be interpreted as encoding an MLF with a one-to-one correspondence between the CNF models and the MLF terms.[5] Consider for example the CNF $\Delta = (V_A \vee \neg V_B) \wedge V_C$, which has three models:

model	V_A	V_B	V_C	encoded term t
ω_1	true	false	true	AC
ω_2	true	true	true	ABC
ω_3	false	false	true	C

Each of these models ω can be interpreted as encoding a term t in the following sense. A variable X appears in the term t if and only if the model ω sets the variable V_X to true. The CNF Δ then encodes an MLF that results from adding up all these terms: $AC + ABC + C$.

In fact, the MLF encoded by the CNF of a Bayesian network, as described in Section 11.6.1, is precisely the polynomial of this network (see the proof of Theorem 11.7). For an example, consider the network in Figure 12.4 and its polynomial

$$f = \lambda_a \lambda_b \theta_a \theta_{b|a} + \lambda_a \lambda_{\bar{b}} \theta_a \theta_{\bar{b}|a} + \lambda_{\bar{a}} \lambda_b \theta_{\bar{a}} \theta_{b|\bar{a}} + \lambda_{\bar{a}} \lambda_{\bar{b}} \theta_{\bar{a}} \theta_{\bar{b}|\bar{a}}.$$

We can show that the CNF in (12.11) does indeed encode this polynomial once we replace CNF variables I by indicators λ and CNF variables P by parameters θ.

Suppose now that we have a CNF Δ_f that encodes an MLF f. If Δ_f is converted into an equivalent NNF circuit Γ_f that satisfies the properties of decomposability, determinism,

---

[5] Recall that a multilinear function (MLF) over variables Σ is a function of the form $t_1 + t_2 + \cdots + t_n$, where each term t_i is a product of distinct variables from Σ. For example, if $\Sigma = A, B, C$, then $A + AB + AC + ABC$ is an MLF. Without loss of generality, we disallow duplicate terms in the representation of MLFs.

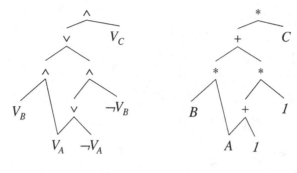

(a) NNF circuit　　　　(b) Arithmetic circuit

Figure 12.12: The NNF circuit is equivalent to the CNF $\Delta_f = (V_A \vee \neg V_B) \wedge V_C$, which encodes the MLF $f = AC + ABC + C$.

and smoothness, then we can extract an arithmetic circuit for the MLF f by applying the following substitutions to the NNF circuit Γ_f:

- Replace every conjunction by a multiplication and every disjunction by a summation.
- Replace every negative literal $\neg V_X$ by the constant 1.
- Replace every positive literal V_X by X.

Figure 12.12 provides an example of this conversion procedure whose correctness is left to Exercise 12.17. Note that the size of the resulting arithmetic circuit is proportional to the size of the NNF circuit. Hence, by minimizing the size of the NNF circuit, we also minimize the size of the generated arithmetic circuit. This means that the computational effort for compiling a Bayesian network is now shifted to the process of converting a CNF into an NNF circuit that satisfies the properties of decomposability, determinism, and smoothness.

Bibliographic remarks

The network polynomial and the semantics of its partial derivatives as discussed in this chapter are due to Darwiche [2000; 2003], although a more restricted version of the network polynomial was initially proposed in Castillo et al. [1996; 1997], and the derivatives with respect to network parameters were originally studied in Russell et al. [1995]. The representation of network polynomials using arithmetic circuits and the corresponding circuit propagation algorithms are due to Darwiche [2000; 2003]. The relationship between circuit propagation and jointree propagation was studied in Park and Darwiche [2003b; 2004b], where the circuit of a jointree was first defined. The generation of circuits using variable elimination was proposed in Darwiche [2000] and using CNF encodings in Darwiche [2002]. Maximizer circuits and their corresponding propagation algorithms were introduced in Chan and Darwiche [2006]. A state-of-the-art compiler for converting CNF to NNF circuits is discussed in Darwiche [2004] and is available for download at *http://reasoning.cs.ucla.edu/c2d/*.

12.5 Exercises

12.1. Consider the arithmetic circuit in Figure 12.13:

　(a) Construct the polynomial f represented by this arithmetic circuit.

　(b) Compute the partial derivatives $\partial f/\partial \lambda_{a_1}$, $\partial f/\partial \lambda_{a_2}$, $\partial f/\partial \theta_{c_1|a_1}$, and $\partial f/\partial \theta_{c_2|a_2}$.

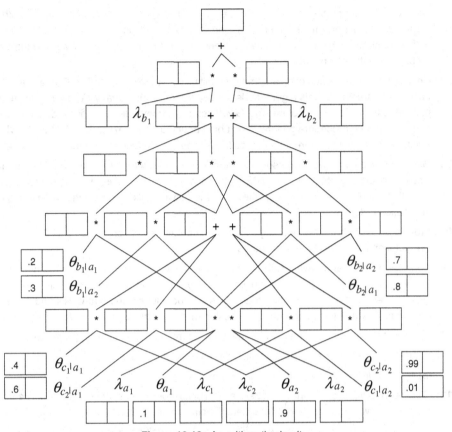

Figure 12.13: An arithmetic circuit.

(c) Evaluate the derivatives in (b) at evidence $\mathbf{e} = a_1 c_1$.

(d) What is the probabilistic meaning of these derivatives?

12.2. Consider the arithmetic circuit in Figure 12.13. Evaluate and differentiate this circuit at evidence $\mathbf{e} = a_1 c_1$. Perform the differentiation using both propagation schemes given by Algorithms 34 and 35.

12.3. Consider a Bayesian network with structure $A \rightarrow B \rightarrow C$, where all variables are binary. Construct an arithmetic circuit for this network using the method of variable elimination given in Section 12.4.1 and using elimination order C, B, A.

12.4. Show that the following partial derivatives are equal to zero for a network polynomial f:

(a) $\dfrac{\partial^2 f}{\partial \lambda_x \partial \lambda_{x'}}$, where x and x' are values (possibly equal) of the same variable.

(b) $\dfrac{\partial^2 f}{\partial \theta_{x|\mathbf{u}} \partial \theta_{x'|\mathbf{u}'}}$, where $x\mathbf{u}$ and $x'\mathbf{u}'$ are instantiations (possibly equal) of the same family.

What does this imply on the structure of the polynomial f?

12.5. Provide probabilistic semantics for the following second partial derivatives of the network polynomial:

$$\frac{\partial^2 f}{\partial \lambda_x \partial \lambda_y}(\mathbf{e}), \qquad \frac{\partial^2 f}{\partial \theta_{x|\mathbf{u}} \partial \lambda_y}(\mathbf{e}), \qquad \frac{\partial^2 f}{\partial \theta_{x|\mathbf{u}} \partial \theta_{y|\mathbf{v}}}(\mathbf{e}).$$

Provide a circuit propagation scheme that will compute these derivatives and discuss its time and space complexity.

12.6. Suppose we extend the notion of evidence to allow for constraining the value of a variable instead of fixing it. For example, if X is a variable with three values $x_1, x_2,$ and x_3, then a piece of evidence on variable X may be $X=x_1 \vee X=x_2$, which rules out value x_3 without committing to either values x_1 or x_2. Given this extended notion of evidence, known as a *finding*, show how we can evaluate a network polynomial so that its value equals the probability of the given findings.

12.7. Consider the construction of an arithmetic circuit using variable elimination. For each addition node n constructed by this algorithm, let var(n) stand for the variable X whose elimination has led to the construction of node n. Given some MAP variables **M** and evidence **e**, show that the following procedure generates an upper bound on the MAP probability $\text{MAP}_P(\mathbf{M}, \mathbf{e})$: Evaluate the circuit while treating an addition node n as a maximization node if var(n) $\in$ **M**.

12.8. Given a Bayesian network and some evidence **e**, show how to construct a Boolean formula whose models are precisely the MPE instantiations of evidence **e**. The complexity of your algorithm should be $O(n \exp(w))$, where n is the network size and w is the width of a given elimination order.

12.9. Provide an algorithm for generating circuits that can be used to compute MAP. Describe the computational complexity of the method.

12.10. Consider a Bayesian network with structure $A \rightarrow B \rightarrow C$, where all variables are binary and its jointree is $A - AB - BC$. Construct the arithmetic circuit embedded in this jointree as given in Section 12.4.2, assuming that BC is the root cluster and that CPTs and evidence indicators for variables A, B, and C are assigned to clusters A, AB, and BC, respectively.

12.11. Show that the arithmetic circuit embedded in a jointree has the following properties:

   (a) The circuit alternates between addition and multiplication nodes.

   (b) Each multiplication node has a single parent.

12.12. Given an arithmetic circuit that is embedded in a binary jointree, describe a circuit propagation scheme that will evaluate and differentiate the circuit under the following constraints:

   • The method can use only two registers for each addition or leaf node but no registers for multiplication nodes.

   • The time complexity of the algorithm is linear in the circuit size.

   Compare your developed scheme to the Shenoy-Shafer architecture for jointree propagation. Recall that a binary jointree is one in which each cluster has at most three neighbors.

12.13. Given an arithmetic circuit that is embedded in a jointree, describe a circuit propagation scheme that will evaluate and differentiate the circuit under the following constraints:

   • The method can use only one register dvr(v) for each circuit node v.

   • When the algorithm terminates, the register dvr(v) contains the product dr(v)vr(v), where dr(v) and vr(v) are as computed by Algorithm 34.

   • The time complexity of the algorithm is linear in the circuit size.

   Compare your developed scheme to the Hugin architecture for jointree propagation.

12.14. Consider the arithmetic circuit in Figure 12.13. Evaluate and differentiate this circuit at evidence $\mathbf{e} = b_2$ using the propagation scheme given by Algorithm 36. Compute all MPE instantiations given the evidence and describe the meaning of derivatives with respect to inputs λ_{a_1} and $\theta_{c_2|a_2}$ in this case.

12.15. Let X be a binary variable in a Bayesian network with maximizer polynomial f^m. Show that every MPE instantiation for evidence **e** includes $X=x$ if and only if

$$\frac{\partial f_x^m}{\partial \lambda_x}(\mathbf{e}) > \frac{\partial f_{\bar{x}}^m}{\partial \lambda_{\bar{x}}}(\mathbf{e}).$$

12.16. Show the MLF encoded by the propositional sentence $A \wedge (B \implies D) \wedge (C \implies B)$.

12.17. Let Δ_f be a propositional sentence encoding an MLF f. Let Γ_f be an equivalent NNF circuit that satisfies decomposability, determinism, and smoothness. Show that the arithmetic circuit extracted from Γ_f as given in Section 12.4.3 is a representation of the MLF f.

12.18. Prove Lemma 12.1 on Page 310.

12.19. Consider the network polynomial f for a Bayesian network and let $\theta_{x|u}$ be a set of parameters with equal values in the same CPT. Replace all these parameters in the polynomial f with a new variable η. What is the probabilistic meaning of $\partial f / \partial \eta(e)$ for a given evidence e?

12.20. Let f be an MLF and let f_m be another MLF obtained by including only the minimal terms of f. Here a term of f is minimal if the number of variables it contains is minimal among the terms of f. Suppose now that Δ_f is a CNF that encodes MLF f. Describe a procedure for obtaining an arithmetic circuit for MLF f_m. Hint: Consider Exercise 2.13.

12.6 Proofs

PROOF OF THEOREM 12.1. Definition 12.1 gives

$$f = \sum_{\mathbf{z}} \prod_{\theta_{x|u} \sim \mathbf{z}} \theta_{x|u} \prod_{\lambda_x \sim \mathbf{z}} \lambda_x,$$

and

$$f(\mathbf{e}) = \sum_{\mathbf{z}} \prod_{\theta_{x|u} \sim \mathbf{z}} \theta_{x|u} \prod_{\lambda_x \sim \mathbf{z}} \begin{cases} 1, & \text{if } x \sim \mathbf{e} \\ 0, & \text{otherwise} \end{cases}$$

$$= \sum_{\mathbf{z} \sim \mathbf{e}} \prod_{\theta_{x|u} \sim \mathbf{z}} \theta_{x|u}$$

$$= \sum_{\mathbf{z} \sim \mathbf{e}} \Pr(\mathbf{z})$$

$$= \Pr(\mathbf{e}). \qquad \blacksquare$$

PROOF OF THEOREM 12.2. By the definition of partial derivatives, we have

$$\frac{\partial f}{\partial \lambda_y} = \sum_{\mathbf{z} \sim y} \prod_{\theta_{x|u} \sim \mathbf{z}} \theta_{x|u} \prod_{\substack{\lambda_x \sim \mathbf{z} \\ x \neq y}} \lambda_x.$$

Definition 12.1 then gives us

$$\frac{\partial f}{\partial \lambda_y}(\mathbf{e}) = \sum_{\mathbf{z} \sim y} \prod_{\theta_{x|u} \sim \mathbf{z}} \theta_{x|u} \prod_{\substack{\lambda_x \sim \mathbf{z} \\ x \neq y}} \begin{cases} 1, & \text{if } x \sim \mathbf{e} \\ 0, & \text{otherwise} \end{cases}$$

$$= \sum_{\substack{\mathbf{z} \sim y \\ \mathbf{z} \sim \mathbf{e} - Y}} \prod_{\theta_{x|u} \sim \mathbf{z}} \theta_{x|u}$$

$$= \sum_{\substack{\mathbf{z} \sim y \\ \mathbf{z} \sim \mathbf{e} - Y}} \Pr(\mathbf{z})$$

$$= \Pr(y, \mathbf{e} - Y).$$

By the definition of partial derivative, we also have

$$\frac{\partial f}{\partial \theta_{y|v}} = \sum_{\mathbf{z} \sim yv} \prod_{\substack{\theta_{x|u} \sim \mathbf{z} \\ xu \neq yv}} \theta_{x|u} \prod_{\lambda_x \sim \mathbf{z}} \lambda_x.$$

Definition 12.1 then gives us

$$\frac{\partial f}{\partial \theta_{y|v}}(\mathbf{e}) = \sum_{\substack{\mathbf{z} \sim y\mathbf{v} \\ \theta_{x|\mathbf{u}} \sim \mathbf{z} \\ x\mathbf{u} \neq y\mathbf{v}}} \prod_{\theta_{x|\mathbf{u}} \sim \mathbf{z}} \theta_{x|\mathbf{u}} \prod_{\lambda_x \sim \mathbf{z}} \begin{cases} 1, & \text{if } x \sim \mathbf{e} \\ 0, & \text{otherwise} \end{cases}$$

$$= \sum_{\substack{\mathbf{z} \sim y\mathbf{v} \\ \mathbf{z} \sim \mathbf{e}}} \prod_{\substack{\theta_{x|\mathbf{u}} \sim \mathbf{z} \\ x\mathbf{u} \neq y\mathbf{v}}} \theta_{x|\mathbf{u}}.$$

Multiplying both sides by $\theta_{y|v}$, we get

$$\theta_{y|v} \frac{\partial f}{\partial \theta_{y|v}}(\mathbf{e}) = \sum_{\substack{\mathbf{z} \sim y\mathbf{v} \\ \mathbf{z} \sim \mathbf{e}}} \prod_{\theta_{x|\mathbf{u}} \sim \mathbf{z}} \theta_{x|\mathbf{u}}$$

$$= \sum_{\substack{\mathbf{z} \sim y\mathbf{v} \\ \mathbf{z} \sim \mathbf{e}}} \Pr(\mathbf{z})$$

$$= \Pr(y, \mathbf{v}, \mathbf{e}).$$ ∎

Lemma 12.1 (Path coefficients). *Consider a maximizer circuit AC^m evaluated at some evidence $\mathbf{e}$ and let α be a path from the circuit root to some leaf node n. Define the coefficient r of path α as the product of values attained by nodes c, where c is not on path α but has a multiplication parent on α. Then $r \cdot k$ is the maximum value attained by any complete subcircuit that includes path α, where k is the value of leaf node n. (The proof of this Lemma is left for Exercise 12.18.)*

PROOF OF THEOREM 12.3. By Lemma 12.1, the maximum coefficient value attained by any path from the circuit root to parameter $\theta_{x|\mathbf{u}}$ is also the maximum value attained by any complete subcircuit that includes parameter $\theta_{x|\mathbf{u}}$. Suppose now that $\alpha_1, \ldots, \alpha_m$ are all the paths from the root to parameter $\theta_{x|\mathbf{u}}$ and let $r_1, \ldots, r_m$ be their coefficients, respectively. We then have

$$\frac{\partial f_{x\mathbf{u}}^m}{\partial \theta_{x|\mathbf{u}}}(\mathbf{e}) = \max_{i=1}^{m} r_1, \ldots, r_m.$$

Therefore, if we can compute the maximum of these coefficients, we can also compute the derivative.

We can now reduce the problem to an all-pairs shortest path problem. In particular, let the weight of edge $v \rightarrow c$ be $0 = -\ln 1$ when v is a maximization node and let the weight of edge $v \rightarrow c$ be $-\ln \pi$ when v is a multiplication node, where π is the product of the values of the other children $c' \neq c$ of node v. The length of path α_i is then $-\ln r_i$, which is the sum of weights of α_i's edges.

We can easily verify that the second pass of Algorithm 36 is just the all-pairs shortest path algorithm with edge weights as defined previously. The same analysis applies to a leaf node corresponding to indicator λ_x. ∎

PROOF OF THEOREM 12.4. We have

$$f_y^m = \max_{\mathbf{z} \sim y} \prod_{\theta_{x|\mathbf{u}} \sim \mathbf{z}} \theta_{x|\mathbf{u}} \prod_{\lambda_x \sim \mathbf{z}} \lambda_x$$

$$= \lambda_y \max_{\mathbf{z} \sim y} \prod_{\theta_{x|\mathbf{u}} \sim \mathbf{z}} \theta_{x|\mathbf{u}} \prod_{\substack{\lambda_x \sim \mathbf{z} \\ x \neq y}} \lambda_x.$$

By the definition of partial derivatives, we have

$$\frac{\partial f_y^m}{\partial \lambda_y} = \max_{\mathbf{z} \sim y} \prod_{\theta_{x|\mathbf{u}} \sim \mathbf{z}} \theta_{x|\mathbf{u}} \prod_{\substack{\lambda_x \sim \mathbf{z} \\ x \neq y}} \lambda_x.$$

Evaluating the derivative at evidence $\mathbf{e}$,

$$\frac{\partial f_y^m}{\partial \lambda_y}(\mathbf{e}) = \max_{\mathbf{z} \sim y} \prod_{\theta_{x|\mathbf{u}} \sim \mathbf{z}} \theta_{x|\mathbf{u}} \prod_{\substack{\lambda_x \sim \mathbf{z} \\ x \neq y}} \begin{cases} 1, & \text{if } x \sim \mathbf{e} \\ 0, & \text{otherwise} \end{cases}$$

$$= \max_{\substack{\mathbf{z} \sim y \\ \mathbf{z} \sim \mathbf{e} - Y}} \prod_{\theta_{x|\mathbf{u}} \sim \mathbf{z}} \theta_{x|\mathbf{u}}$$

$$= \max_{\substack{\mathbf{z} \sim y \\ \mathbf{z} \sim \mathbf{e} - Y}} \Pr(\mathbf{z})$$

$$= \text{MPE}_P(y, \mathbf{e} - Y).$$

We also have

$$f_{y\mathbf{v}}^m = \max_{\mathbf{z} \sim y\mathbf{v}} \prod_{\theta_{x|\mathbf{u}} \sim \mathbf{z}} \theta_{x|\mathbf{u}} \prod_{\lambda_x \sim \mathbf{z}} \lambda_x$$

$$= \theta_{y|\mathbf{v}} \max_{\mathbf{z} \sim y\mathbf{v}} \prod_{\substack{\theta_{x|\mathbf{u}} \sim \mathbf{z} \\ x\mathbf{u} \neq y\mathbf{v}}} \theta_{x|\mathbf{u}} \prod_{\lambda_x \sim \mathbf{z}} \lambda_x.$$

By the definition of partial derivatives, we have

$$\frac{\partial f_{y\mathbf{v}}^m}{\partial \theta_{y|\mathbf{v}}} = \max_{\mathbf{z} \sim y\mathbf{v}} \prod_{\substack{\theta_{x|\mathbf{u}} \sim \mathbf{z} \\ x\mathbf{u} \neq y\mathbf{v}}} \theta_{x|\mathbf{u}} \prod_{\lambda_x \sim \mathbf{z}} \lambda_x.$$

Evaluating the derivative at evidence $\mathbf{e}$, we get

$$\frac{\partial f_{y\mathbf{v}}^m}{\partial \theta_{y|\mathbf{v}}}(\mathbf{e}) = \max_{\mathbf{z} \sim y\mathbf{v}} \prod_{\substack{\theta_{x|\mathbf{u}} \sim \mathbf{z} \\ x\mathbf{u} \neq y\mathbf{v}}} \theta_{x|\mathbf{u}} \prod_{\lambda_x \sim \mathbf{z}} \begin{cases} 1, & \text{if } x \sim \mathbf{e} \\ 0, & \text{otherwise} \end{cases}$$

$$= \max_{\substack{\mathbf{z} \sim y\mathbf{v} \\ \mathbf{z} \sim \mathbf{e}}} \prod_{\substack{\theta_{x|\mathbf{u}} \sim \mathbf{z} \\ x\mathbf{u} \neq y\mathbf{v}}} \theta_{x|\mathbf{u}}.$$

Multiplying both sides by $\theta_{y|\mathbf{v}}$, we get

$$\theta_{y|\mathbf{v}} \frac{\partial f_{y\mathbf{v}}^m}{\partial \theta_{y|\mathbf{v}}}(\mathbf{e}) = \max_{\substack{\mathbf{z} \sim y\mathbf{v} \\ \mathbf{z} \sim \mathbf{e}}} \prod_{\theta_{x|\mathbf{u}} \sim \mathbf{z}} \theta_{x|\mathbf{u}}$$

$$= \max_{\substack{\mathbf{z} \sim y\mathbf{v} \\ \mathbf{z} \sim \mathbf{e}}} \Pr(\mathbf{z})$$

$$= \Pr(y, \mathbf{v}, \mathbf{e}). \qquad \blacksquare$$

PROOF OF THEOREM 12.5. That the embedded arithmetic circuit represents the network polynomial follows from the semantics of the jointree algorithm, whose trace for computing the probability of evidence corresponds to the circuit (just pull messages toward the root cluster and then sum the entries of this cluster).

By Definition 12.7, there is a one-to-one correspondence between multiplication nodes and cluster instantiations; hence, the number of multiplication nodes is $O(n \exp(c))$. Similarly and except for the root node, there is a one-to-one correspondence between addition nodes and separator instantiations; hence, the number of addition nodes is $O(n \exp(s))$ since the number of jointree edges is $n - 1$.

As for the number of edges, note that the circuit alternates between addition and multiplication nodes, where input nodes are always children of multiplication nodes. Hence, we count edges by simply counting the total number of neighbors (parents and children) that each multiplication node has. By Definition 12.7, each multiplication node has a single parent. Moreover, the number of children that a multiplication node $\mathbf{c}$ has depends on the cluster $\mathbf{C}$ that generates it. Specifically, the node has one child $\mathbf{s}$ for each child separator $\mathbf{S}$, one child λ_x for each evidence table λ_X assigned to cluster $\mathbf{C}$, and one child $\theta_{x|\mathbf{u}}$ for each CPT $\theta_{X|\mathbf{U}}$ assigned to the same cluster.

Now let r be the root cluster, i be any cluster, c_i be the cluster size, n_i be the number of its neighbors, and e_i and p_i be the numbers of evidence indicators and CPTs assigned to the cluster, respectively. The total number of neighbors for multiplication nodes is then bounded by

$$\exp(c_r)(n_r + 1 + e_r + p_r) + \sum_{i \neq r} \exp(c_i)(n_i + e_i + p_i).$$

Note that a multiplication node generated by the root cluster has one addition parent and n_r addition children, while a multiplication node generated by a nonroot cluster has one addition parent and $n_i - 1$ addition children. Since, $c_i \leq c$ for all i, we can bound the number of edges by

$$\exp(c) + \exp(c) \sum_i (n_i + e_i + p_i).$$

Note also that the number of edges in a tree is one less than the number of nodes, leading to $\sum_i n_i = 2(n - 1)$. Moreover, we have $\sum_i e_i = n$ and $\sum_i p_i = n$ since we only have n evidence indicators and n CPTs. Hence, the total number of edges can be bounded by $(4n - 1) \exp(c)$, which is $O(n \exp(c))$. ∎

13

Inference with Local Structure

We discuss in this chapter computational techniques for exploiting certain properties of network parameters, allowing one to perform inference efficiently in some situations where the network treewidth can be quite large.

13.1 Introduction

We discussed in Chapters 6–8 two paradigms for probabilistic inference based on elimination and conditioning, showing how they lead to algorithms whose time and space complexity are exponential in the network treewidth. These algorithms are often called *structure-based* since their performance is driven by the network structure and is independent of the specific values attained by network parameters. We also presented in Chapter 11 some CNF encodings of Bayesian networks, allowing us to reduce probabilistic inference to some well-known CNF tasks. The resulting CNFs were also independent of the specific values of network parameters and are therefore also structure-based.

However, the performance of inference algorithms can be enhanced considerably if one exploits the specific values of network parameters. The properties of network parameters that lend themselves to such exploitation are known as *parametric* or *local structure*. This type of structure typically manifests in networks involving logical constraints, context-specific independence, or local models of interaction, such as the noisy-or model discussed in Chapter 5.

In this chapter, we present a number of computational techniques for exploiting local structure that can be viewed as extensions of inference algorithms discussed in earlier chapters. We start in Section 13.2 with an overview of local structure and the impact it can have on the complexity of inference. We then provide three sets of techniques for exploiting local structure. The first set concerns the encoding of Bayesian networks into CNFs, where we show in Section 13.3 how these CNFs can be refined so they encode local structure as well. The second set of techniques is discussed in Section 13.4 and is meant to refine conditioning algorithms so their performance is not necessarily exponential in the network treewidth. The third set of techniques is discussed in Section 13.5 and is meant to refine elimination algorithms for the same purpose.

13.2 The impact of local structure on inference complexity

Perhaps the simplest way to illustrate the impact of local structure on the complexity of inference is through the effect it has on the circuit complexity of Bayesian networks. Consider for example, Figure 13.1, which depicts a Bayesian network and two corresponding arithmetic circuits. The circuit in Figure 13.1(a) is compiled from the network as given in Chapter 12, that is, without exploiting the values of network parameters. The circuit in Figure 13.1(b) is obtained from the previous circuit by first substituting the values of

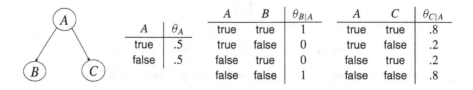

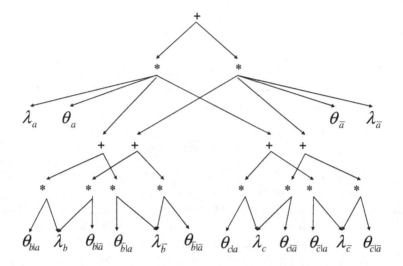

(a) Arithmetic circuit valid for any network parameters

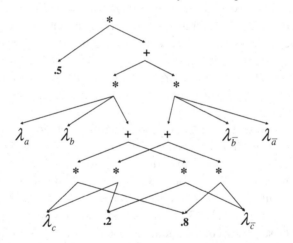

(b) Arithmetic circuit valid only for specific network parameters

Figure 13.1: A Bayesian network and two corresponding arithmetic circuits.

network parameters and then simplifying the circuit. As this example illustrates, the size of an arithmetic circuit can be quite dependent on the values of network parameters. For example, zero parameters can lead to substantial reductions in the circuit size and so does equality among the values of distinct parameters.

For another example, consider the network in Figure 13.2, which has a treewidth of n, making it inaccessible to structure-based algorithms when n is large enough. Suppose now that each variable has values in $\{0, 1\}$, that variables X_i have uniform distributions,

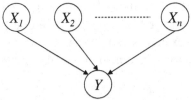

Figure 13.2: A Bayesian network with treewidth n.

and that node Y is a logical-or of its parents. Under these conditions, $\theta_{y|x_1,\ldots,x_n} = 1$ if and only if either:

- $y = 1$ and $x_i = 1$ for some x_i, or
- $y = 0$ and $x_i = 0$ for all x_i.

Given these parameter values, the network polynomial can be factored as follows:

$$f = \sum_{x_1,\ldots,x_n,y} \lambda_{x_1} \ldots \lambda_{x_n} \lambda_y \theta_{x_1} \ldots \theta_{x_n} \theta_{y|x_1,\ldots,x_n}$$

$$= \left(\frac{1}{2}\right)^n \left(\lambda_{y=0}\lambda_{x_1=0} \ldots \lambda_{x_n=0} + \lambda_{y=1} \sum_{\substack{x_1,\ldots,x_n \\ x_i=1 \text{ for some } i}} \lambda_{x_1} \ldots \lambda_{x_n} \right)$$

$$= \left(\frac{1}{2}\right)^n \left(\lambda_{y=0} \prod_{i=1}^{n} \lambda_{x_i=0} + \lambda_{y=1} \sum_{i=1}^{n} \left(\prod_{j=1}^{i-1} \lambda_{x_j=0} \right) \lambda_{x_i=1} \left(\prod_{j=i+1}^{n} (\lambda_{x_j=0} + \lambda_{x_j=1}) \right) \right). \tag{13.1}$$

Given this factorization, we can represent the polynomial using an arithmetic circuit of size $O(n)$ even though the underlying network has treewidth n (see Exercise 13.1). Hence, inference on this network can be done in time and space that are linear in its treewidth n.[1] In fact, this complexity continues to hold even if variables X_i do not have uniform distributions (see Exercise 13.3).

The CPT of variable Y in the previous example is deterministic, that is, all of its parameters are equal to 0 or 1. We can obtain a similar reduction in complexity even if the CPT is not deterministic. Suppose for example that Y is a soft-or of its parents, that is, if any of the parents is 1, then Y is 1 with probability ϵ_1. Similarly, if all parents are 0, then Y is 0 with probability ϵ_0. Under these conditions, the network polynomial factors as follows:

$$\left(\frac{1}{2}\right)^n \left((\epsilon_0 \lambda_{y=0} + (1 - \epsilon_0)\lambda_{y=1}) \prod_{i=1}^{n} \lambda_{x_i=0} \right.$$

$$\left. + ((1 - \epsilon_1)\lambda_{y=0} + \epsilon_1 \lambda_{y=1}) \sum_{i=1}^{n} \left(\prod_{j=1}^{i-1} \lambda_{x_j=0} \right) \lambda_{x_i=1} \left(\prod_{j=i+1}^{n} (\lambda_{x_j=0} + \lambda_{x_j=1}) \right) \right). \tag{13.2}$$

---

[1] The same reduction in complexity can be obtained by a technique known as *CPT decomposition*. In particular, it is well known that an n-input or-gate can be simulated by a number of two-input or-gates that are cascaded together. If we employ this technique, we can represent the network in Figure 13.2 by an equivalent network having treewidth 2. Again, this decomposition is only possible due to the specific values of network parameters.

This can also be represented by an arithmetic circuit of size $O(n)$, allowing us to perform inference in time and space that are linear in n (see Exercise 13.3).

The summary from these examples is that when network parameters exhibit a certain structure, exact inference can be performed efficiently even if the network treewidth is quite large.

13.2.1 Context-specific independence

The two networks discussed previously share a common type of local structure known as *context-specific independence*. In particular, given that some node X_i takes the value 1, the probability of Y becomes independent of other parents X_j for $j \neq i$:

$$\Pr(Y|x_i = 1) = \Pr(Y|x_1, \ldots, x_{i-1}, x_i = 1, x_{i+1}, \ldots, x_n),$$

for all values $x_1, \ldots, x_{i-1}, x_{i+1}, \ldots, x_n$. This type of independence is called context-specific as it is holds only for certain values of X_i, that is, the independence would not hold if X_i takes the value 0. Context-specific independence is therefore a function of network parameters and may be lost when changing the values of these parameters. This is to be contrasted with variable-based independence discussed in Chapters 3 and 4, which is a function of the network structure and would continue to hold for any values of network parameters.

The existence of context-specific independence can be sufficient for generating arithmetic circuits whose size is not exponential in the network treewidth yet one may attain such a complexity even without the existence of context-specific independence. For example, consider Figure 13.2 and suppose that Y is 1 iff an odd number of its parents are 1. In this case, the probability of Y remains dependent on a particular parent X_i even if all other parents X_j are known; yet the network still admits an arithmetic circuit of linear size (see Exercise 13.4).

13.2.2 Determinism

Consider the grid network in Figure 13.3, composed of $n \times n$ binary nodes. The treewidth of this network grows linearly in n yet if we assume that each node is a Boolean function of its parents, then we can describe an arithmetic circuit of size $O(n^2)$ for this network. To see this, note that setting the value of node I is guaranteed to imply the value of each and every other node in the network. Hence, the number of nonvanishing terms in the network polynomial must equal the number of values for node I and each term has size $O(n^2)$. The network polynomial will then have two terms, each of size $O(n^2)$.

For a more general characterization of this example and similar ones, consider Bayesian networks in which every nonroot node is *functionally determined* by its parents. That is, for every node X with parents $\mathbf{U} \neq \emptyset$, we have $\Pr(x|\mathbf{u}) = 1$ for each parent instantiation $\mathbf{u}$ and some value x. This means that $\Pr(x'|\mathbf{u}) = 0$ for all other values $x' \neq x$ and, hence, the value $\mathbf{u}$ of parents $\mathbf{U}$ implies the value x of child X. For these networks, called *functional networks*, the number of nonvanishing terms in the network polynomial is exponential only in the number of network roots, regardless of the network treewidth.

A more general type of local structure known as *determinism* occurs whenever network parameters take on zero values. Functional networks exhibit a strong type of determinism yet one may have this form of local structure even when a node is not functionally

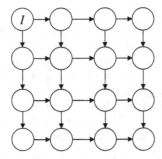

Figure 13.3: A Bayesian network with a grid structure having n^2 nodes. The treewidth of this class of networks grows linearly in n.

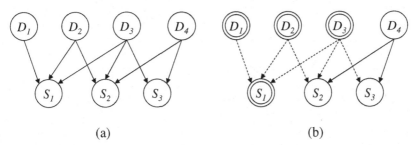

(a)   (b)

Figure 13.4: On the left, a Bayesian network where each leaf node is a logical-or of its parents. On the right, the result of pruning (dotted edges) the network given that S_1 is false and that S_2 and S_3 are true.

determined by its parents. For example, variable X may not be functionally determined by its parents $\mathbf{U}$ yet one of its values x may be impossible given the parent instantiation $\mathbf{u}$, $\theta_{x|\mathbf{u}} = 0$. The impossibility of x given $\mathbf{u}$ is known as a *logical constraint*. Logical constraints can significantly reduce the complexity of inference even when they do not correspond to functional dependencies.

13.2.3 Evidence

Local structure can be especially effective computationally in the presence of particular evidence. Consider the network in Figure 13.4(a) as an example and assume that each node S_i is a logical-or of its parents. Suppose now that we observe S_1 to be false and S_2 and S_3 to be true. Since S_1 is false and given that it is a logical-or of its parents D_1, D_2, and D_3, we can immediately conclude that all of these parents must also be false. Using the edge-pruning technique from Chapter 6, we can now prune all edges that are outgoing from these nodes, leading to the network in Figure 13.4(b). The key point here is that this pruning was enabled by the specific evidence that sets S_1 to false and by the specific relationship between S_1 and its parents. In particular, this pruning would not be possible if S_1 were set to true, neither would it be possible if S_1 were, say, a logical-and of its parents. More generally, we can show that certain inferences on networks of the type given in Figure 13.4 can be performed in time and space that is exponential only in the number of nodes S_i whose values are observed to be true, regardless of the network treewidth (see Exercises 13.19 and 13.20).

C_1	C_2	C_3	E	$\theta_{e|c_1,c_2,c_3}$
true	true	true	true	.9999265
true	true	false	true	.99853
true	false	true	true	.99265
true	false	false	true	.853
false	true	true	true	.99951
false	true	false	true	.9902
false	false	true	true	.951
false	false	false	true	.02

Figure 13.5: A CPT with no determinism or equal parameters.

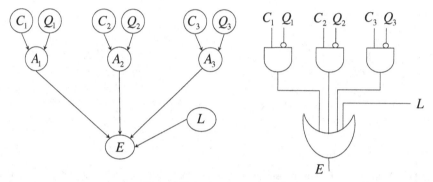

Figure 13.6: A noisy-or model.

13.2.4 Exposing local structure

Consider the CPT in Figure 13.5 relating a node E to its parents C_1, C_2, and C_3. The parameters of this CPT do not exhibit any of the structures discussed previously such as determinism, context-specific independence, or parameter equality.

As it turns out, this CPT is generated by a noisy-or model using the following parameters (see Section 5.4.1):

- The suppressor probability for C_1 is .15.
- The suppressor probability for C_2 is .01.
- The suppressor probability for C_3 is .05.
- The leak probability for E is .02.

Suppose that we now replace the family in Figure 13.5 by the network fragment in Figure 13.6 to explicate this noisy-or semantics (again, see Section 5.4.1). Given this expansion, the CPTs for E, A_1, A_2, A_3 are now all deterministic, showing much more local structure than was previously visible. In fact, the techniques we discuss in the rest of this chapter will not be effective on this network unless the corresponding local structure is exposed as we just discussed. The main point here is that we can expose local structure by decomposing CPTs. Alternatively, we can hide local structure by summing out variables from a Bayesian network (e.g., variables $Q_1, A_1, \ldots, Q_3, A_3$ and L in Figure 13.6), which can negatively impact the effectiveness of algorithms that attempt to exploit local structure.

We next present three sets of techniques for exploiting local structure that correspond to refinements on inference algorithms discussed in previous chapters. These include refinements on CNF-based algorithms (Sections 13.3), refinements on conditioning algorithms (Section 13.5), and refinements on elimination algorithms (Section 13.5).

13.3 CNF encodings with local structure

We proposed a CNF encoding of Bayesian networks in Section 11.6.1 and then presented two corresponding methods that use the encoding to perform inference on Bayesian networks. In particular, we showed in Section 11.6.1 how the CNF encoding can be used with a model counter to compute the probability of evidence. We then showed in Section 12.4.3 how the encoding can be used to compile out an arithmetic circuit for the corresponding network.

However, the CNF encoding of Section 11.6.1 was structure-based as it did not depend on the specific values of network parameters. We provide a more refined encoding in this section that exploits these values, leading to improved performance of both model counters and circuit compilers.

13.3.1 Encoding network structure

Consider the CNF encoding discussed in Section 11.6.1, which includes an indicator variable I_x for each network variable X and value x and a parameter variable $P_{x|u}$ for each network parameter $\theta_{x|u}$. If we apply this encoding to the network in Figure 13.1, we obtain a CNF that consists of two types of clauses. The first set of clauses, called *indicator clauses*, are contributed by network variables:

$$I_a \vee I_{\bar{a}} \qquad I_b \vee I_{\bar{b}} \qquad I_c \vee I_{\bar{c}}$$
$$\neg I_a \vee \neg I_{\bar{a}} \qquad \neg I_b \vee \neg I_{\bar{b}} \qquad \neg I_c \vee \neg I_{\bar{c}}$$

The second set of clauses, called parameter clauses, are contributed by network parameters:[2]

$$
\begin{aligned}
I_a &\iff P_a \\
I_{\bar{a}} &\iff P_{\bar{a}} \\[6pt]
I_a \wedge I_b &\iff P_{b|a} \\
I_a \wedge I_{\bar{b}} &\iff P_{\bar{b}|a} \\
I_{\bar{a}} \wedge I_b &\iff P_{b|\bar{a}} \\
I_{\bar{a}} \wedge I_{\bar{b}} &\iff P_{\bar{b}|\bar{a}} \\[6pt]
I_a \wedge I_c &\iff P_{c|a} \\
I_a \wedge I_{\bar{c}} &\iff P_{\bar{c}|a} \\
I_{\bar{a}} \wedge I_c &\iff P_{c|\bar{a}} \\
I_{\bar{a}} \wedge I_{\bar{c}} &\iff P_{\bar{c}|\bar{a}}
\end{aligned}
\tag{13.3}
$$

---

[2] Note here that each of these sentences corresponds to a set of clauses. For example, the sentence $I_a \wedge I_b \iff P_{b|a}$ corresponds to three clauses: $I_a \wedge I_b \implies P_{b|a}$, which is called an *IP clause*, and $P_{b|a} \implies I_a$ and $P_{b|a} \implies I_b$, which are called *PI clauses*.

We have already shown two particular uses of these CNF encodings in prior chapters:

- *Model counters* (Section 11.6.1): If we assign a weight of 1 to all literals I_x, $\neg I_x$, and $\neg P_{x|\mathbf{u}}$ and assign a weight of $\theta_{x|\mathbf{u}}$ to each literal $P_{x|\mathbf{u}}$, the weighted model count of $\Delta \wedge I_{e_1} \wedge \ldots \wedge I_{e_n}$ then corresponds to the probability $\Pr(e_1, \ldots, e_n)$. Hence, we can compute the probability of evidence by applying a model counter to the CNF encoding Δ.

- *Circuit compilers* (Section 12.4.3): If the CNF encoding Δ is converted to an NNF circuit that satisfies the properties of decomposability, determinism, and smoothness, then this NNF circuit can be immediately converted into an arithmetic circuit for the corresponding Bayesian network. Hence, we can compile an arithmetic circuit by applying an NNF-circuit compiler to the CNF encoding Δ.

Note that the CNF encoding discussed here does not exploit local structure, as this structure is only encoded in the weights assigned to literals. We next discuss a more refined encoding that captures this local structure directly into the CNF.

13.3.2 Encoding local structure

We now show how we can encode three different properties of network parameters in the CNF of a Bayesian network, leading to smaller CNFs that tend to be easier for model counters and NNF-circuit compilers.

Zero parameters

Consider the Bayesian network in Figure 13.1, which includes local structure, some of it in the form of determinism. Consider the parameter $\theta_{\bar{b}|a} = 0$ in particular, which adds the following clauses to the CNF encoding:

$$I_a \wedge I_{\bar{b}} \iff P_{\bar{b}|a}.$$

These clauses ensure that a model of the CNF sets the variable $P_{\bar{b}|a}$ to true if and only if it sets the variables I_a and $I_{\bar{b}}$ to true. Note, however, that the weight assigned to the positive literal $P_{\bar{b}|a}$ is 0 in this case. Hence, any model that sets $P_{\bar{b}|a}$ to true has a zero weight and does not contribute to the weighted model count. We can therefore replace the previous clauses with the single clause

$$\neg I_a \vee \neg I_{\bar{b}}$$

without affecting the weighted model count of any query (the clause will only eliminate models that have a zero weight). Note that this technique also has the affect of removing variable $P_{\bar{b}|a}$ from the CNF encoding.

More generally, for every zero parameter $\theta_{x|u_1,\ldots,u_n} = 0$, we can replace its clauses by the single clause

$$\neg I_{u_1} \vee \ldots \vee \neg I_{u_n} \vee \neg I_x,$$

and drop the variable $P_{x|u_1,\ldots,u_n}$ from the encoding.

One parameters

Consider now the parameter $\theta_{b|a} = 1$ for variable B in Figure 13.1. Given the value of this parameter, the positive literal $P_{b|a}$ has a weight of 1, which will not affect the weight of any model that sets variable $P_{b|a}$ to true. We can therefore drop the clauses of this variable without changing the weighted model count of any query. More generally, parameters that are equal to 1 need not generate any clauses or variables.

Equal parameters

The Bayesian network in Figure 13.1 exhibits another form of local structure known as *parameter equality*. For example, $\theta_{c|a} = \theta_{\bar{c}|\bar{a}} = .8$ in the CPT of variable C. This basically means that the positive literals $P_{c|a}$ and $P_{\bar{c}|\bar{a}}$ will have the same weight of .8. We can therefore replace their clauses

$$I_a \wedge I_c \iff P_{c|a}$$

$$I_{\bar{a}} \wedge I_{\bar{c}} \iff P_{\bar{c}|\bar{a}}$$

with the following sentence:

$$(I_a \wedge I_c) \vee (I_{\bar{a}} \wedge I_{\bar{c}}) \iff P_1,$$

where P_1 is a new variable that has the weight .8. Note that the sentence is not in CNF, so it needs to be converted to a set of clauses to keep the encoding in CNF (see Section 2.7.3).

More generally, let $\mathbf{F} = F_1, \ldots, F_n$ be the variables appearing in a CPT and let $\mathbf{f}_1, \ldots, \mathbf{f}_m$ be a set of instantiations of $\mathbf{F}$ that correspond to equal parameters $\theta_1, \ldots, \theta_m$. We can then replace these parameters with a new parameter η in the encoding. Moreover, we can replace their clauses with the sentence

$$(I_{\mathbf{f}_1} \vee \ldots \vee I_{\mathbf{f}_m}) \iff \eta,$$

where $I_{\mathbf{f}_i}$ denotes $I_{f_{i1}} \wedge \ldots \wedge I_{f_{in}}$ when $\mathbf{f}_i = f_{i1}, \ldots, f_{in}$.

Putting it all together

Applying these encoding techniques to the Bayesian network in Figure 13.1, we obtain the following CNF:

$$
\begin{array}{ccc}
I_a \vee I_{\bar{a}} & I_b \vee I_{\bar{b}} & I_c \vee I_{\bar{c}} \\
\neg I_a \vee \neg I_{\bar{a}} & \neg I_b \vee \neg I_{\bar{b}} & \neg I_c \vee \neg I_{\bar{c}}
\end{array}
$$

$$
\begin{array}{c}
\neg I_a \vee \neg I_{\bar{b}} \\
\neg I_{\bar{a}} \vee \neg I_b
\end{array} \tag{13.4}
$$

$$
\begin{array}{rcll}
(I_a \wedge I_c) \vee (I_{\bar{a}} \wedge I_{\bar{c}}) & \iff & P_1 & \text{(weight of } P_1 \text{ is .8)} \\
(I_a \wedge I_{\bar{c}}) \vee (I_{\bar{a}} \wedge I_c) & \iff & P_2 & \text{(weight of } P_2 \text{ is .2)} \\
I_a \vee I_{\bar{a}} & \iff & P_3 & \text{(weight of } P_3 \text{ is .5)}
\end{array}
$$

This is to be contrasted with the CNF in (13.3), which corresponds to the same Bayesian network but does not encode local structure.

Let us now use this CNF to compile an arithmetic circuit as described in Section 12.4.3. Figure 13.7(a) depicts an NNF circuit for this CNF, which satisfies the properties of decomposability, determinism, and smoothness. Figure 13.7(b) depicts an arithmetic circuit

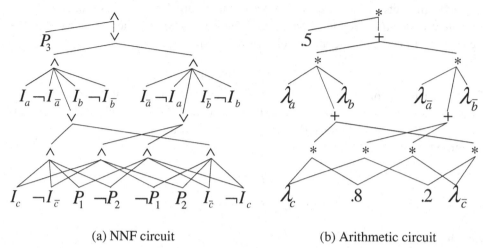

(a) NNF circuit   (b) Arithmetic circuit

Figure 13.7: Extracting an arithmetic circuit from an NNF circuit.

that is extracted from this NNF circuit (after some simplifications).[3] As expected, this circuit is smaller than the one in Figure 13.1(a), which was constructed without exploiting the specific values of network parameters.

There are other techniques for exploiting local structure beyond the ones discussed in this section. Some of these techniques are suggested in Exercises 13.21 and 13.22. The technique in Exercise 13.22 is known to produce the most efficient encodings in practice.

13.3.3 Encoding evidence

Suppose that we have a CNF encoding Δ of a Bayesian network. When using CNF Δ with a model counter, we must add the evidence to the CNF before calling the model counter. In particular, if the evidence is $e_1, \ldots, e_k$, then we must call the model counter on the extended CNF $\Delta \wedge I_{e_1} \wedge \ldots \wedge I_{e_k}$.

Consider now the use of a CNF to compile an arithmetic circuit. We have two choices here for handling evidence:

- Compile a circuit from the CNF before incorporating any evidence. When a piece of evidence arrives later, incorporate it into the circuit as discussed in Chapter 12. This is the normal mode of using arithmetic circuits as it involves a single compilation, leading to one circuit that is used to handle multiple pieces of evidence.

- Encode the evidence into the CNF Δ and then compile an arithmetic circuit. The circuit must then be recompiled each time the evidence changes.

As an example of the second choice, consider the CNF in (13.4) and suppose the evidence we have is $\bar{c}$. For the purpose of compiling this CNF into an arithmetic circuit, we incorporate this evidence by conditioning on the corresponding indicator $I_{\bar{c}}$ (that is, we

---

[3] Note here that we plugged in the actual weights of variables P_1, P_2, and P_3 in the circuit. We can keep the actual variables and compute their derivatives, as discussed in Chapter 12, but we need to be careful in how we interpret the values of these derivatives (see for example Exercise 12.19.)

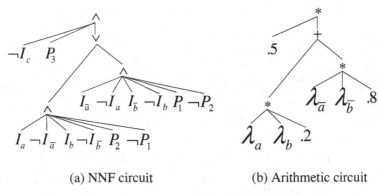

(a) NNF circuit   (b) Arithmetic circuit

Figure 13.8: Extracting an arithmetic circuit from an NNF circuit.

replace the literal $I_{\bar{c}}$ by true) and then simplify, leading to the CNF

$$
\begin{array}{ccc}
I_a \vee I_{\bar{a}} & I_b \vee I_{\bar{b}} & \\
\neg I_a \vee \neg I_{\bar{a}} & \neg I_b \vee \neg I_{\bar{b}} & \neg I_c
\end{array}
$$

$$
\begin{array}{c}
\neg I_a \vee \neg I_{\bar{b}} \\
\neg I_{\bar{a}} \vee \neg I_b
\end{array}
$$

$$
\begin{array}{ccc}
(I_a \wedge I_c) \vee I_{\bar{a}} & \Longleftrightarrow & P_1 \\
I_a \vee (I_{\bar{a}} \wedge I_c) & \Longleftrightarrow & P_2 \\
I_a \vee I_{\bar{a}} & \Longleftrightarrow & P_3
\end{array}
$$

Figure 13.8(a) depicts an NNF circuit for this CNF, which satisfies the properties of decomposability, determinism, and smoothness. Figure 13.8(b) depicts the corresponding arithmetic circuit.

The new arithmetic circuit is clearly smaller than the one in Figure 13.7(b), which was compiled without evidence. Yet the new circuit can only be used to answer queries in which $\bar{c}$ is part of the evidence, such as $a\bar{c}$ and $\bar{b}\bar{c}$. This may sound too restrictive at first but there are many situations where a certain piece of evidence needs to be part of every query posed. This includes, for example, genetic linkage analysis discussed in Chapter 5, where the phenotype and genotype correspond to such evidence. The same is also true for more general forms of inference such as sensitivity analysis, discussed in Chapter 16, where we search for parameter values under certain query constraints (evidence), and in MAP computations, discussed in Chapter 10, where we search for a variable instantiation with maximal probability given some fixed evidence.

If we have a piece of evidence that will be part of every query, it is then more effective to incorporate it in the CNF encoding before generating an arithmetic circuit. In fact, the size of resulting circuit may be exponentially smaller than the size of the circuit compiled without evidence.

13.4 Conditioning with local structure

In this section, we consider some techniques for exploiting local structure in the context of conditioning algorithms, recursive conditioning in particular.

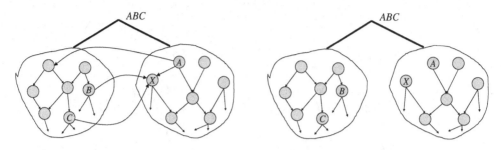

(a) X independent of B, C given $A = $ true   (b) Setting variable A to true

Figure 13.9: The role of local structure in reducing the number of cases considered by recursive conditioning. The set ABC is a cutset for the corresponding dtree node.

We show that in the presence of local structure, recursive conditioning can reduce the number of cases it needs to consider and the number of cache entries it has to maintain. This can lead to exponential savings in certain cases, allowing an inference complexity that is not necessarily exponential in the network treewidth.

13.4.1 Context-specific decomposition

Consider Figure 13.9(a) for an example that contains a dtree fragment with variables ABC as a root cutset. According to the recursive conditioning algorithm, we need to instantiate all three variables in order to decompose the network and recurse independently on the resulting subnetworks. This means that eight cases must be considered, each corresponding to one instantiation of the cutset. Suppose, however, that variable X is independent of variables BC given that A is true (context-specific independence). It is then sufficient in this case to set A to true in order to decompose the network without the need to instantiate variables B and C, as shown in Figure 13.9(b). That is, by setting A to true, not only can we delete edges outgoing from A but also other edges coming into X. This means that recursive conditioning needs to consider at most five cases instead of eight: one case for $A = $ true and up to four cases for $A = $ false. More generally, if local structure is exploited to apply context-specific decomposition as given previously, the complexity of recursive conditioning may not be exponential in the size of cutsets, leading to exponential savings in certain situations.

13.4.2 Context-specific caching

Consider now Figure 13.10(a) for another example where we have a dtree node T with context ABC (the node is marked with a •). According to the recursive conditioning algorithm, one needs to maintain a cache with eight entries at node T to store the values of eight distinct computations corresponding to the instantiations of variables ABC. Suppose, however, that variable X is independent of variables BC given $A = $ true. When A is set to true, the subnetwork corresponding to dtree node T will no longer be dependent on the values of B and C as shown in Figure 13.10(b). Hence, all four computations corresponding to $A = $ true give the same answer, which means that four of the cache entries at node T will be storing the same value. By accounting for this equivalence among cache entries, not only do we reduce the size of cache entries at node T from eight

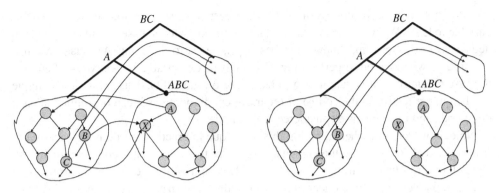

(a) X independent of B, C given $A = \text{true}$ (b) Setting variable A to true

Figure 13.10: The role of local structure in reducing the number of cache entries maintained by recursive conditioning. The sets BC and A are cutsets for the corresponding nodes. The set ABC is a context for the corresponding node.

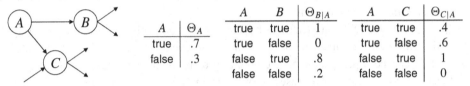

	Θ_A		A	B	$\Theta_{B\mid A}$		A	C	$\Theta_{C\mid A}$
A			true	true	1		true	true	.4
true	.7		true	false	0		true	false	.6
false	.3		false	true	.8		false	true	1
			false	false	.2		false	false	0

Figure 13.11: Exploiting determinism in recursive conditiong.

to at most five but we also reduce the number of recursions from node T from eight to at most five. Again, if local structure is exploited to apply *context-specific caching*, as given here, the complexity of recursive conditioning may not be exponential in the size of contexts. This can lead to exponential savings in certain situations, especially that the algorithm's complexity need not be exponential in cutset sizes either.

13.4.3 Determinism

One particular attraction of conditioning algorithms is the ease with which they can exploit determinism. In particular, we can preprocess the network to generate a propositional knowledge base Δ that captures the logical constraints implied by the network parameters and then use logical deduction on this knowledge base to reduce the amount of work performed by the algorithm. The knowledge base is generated by adding a logical constraint (clause) for each zero parameter $\theta_{x_n \mid x_1, \dots, x_{n-1}} = 0$ in the network:

$$\neg(X_1 = x_1) \vee \dots \vee \neg(X_{n-1} = x_{n-1}) \vee \neg(X_n = x_n).$$

For an example, consider the network fragment in Figure 13.11. There are two zero parameters in the given CPTs, $\theta_{B=\text{false}\mid A=\text{true}}$ and $\theta_{C=\text{false}\mid A=\text{false}}$, leading to the following knowledge base Δ:

$$\neg(A = \text{true}) \vee \neg(B = \text{false}), \quad \neg(A = \text{false}) \vee \neg(C = \text{false}).$$

These logical constraints can be simplified to

$$(A = \text{false}) \vee (B = \text{true}), \quad (A = \text{true}) \vee (C = \text{true}).$$

Suppose now that in the course of performing case analysis on variable B, we set this variable to false. We would then add $B =$ false to the knowledge base Δ and apply logical deduction to the resulting knowledge base. This leads to deducing $A =$ false and also $C =$ true. If we move on to performing case analysis on variable C, we would then skip the case $C =$ false as it is guaranteed to have a zero probability. This skipping technique can be quite effective in the course of recursive conditioning as it can be applied at each dtree node and for each case considered at that node.

Note, however, that when applying this technique in practice, we do not typically use general logical deduction on the knowledge base due to the associated computational cost. Instead, unit resolution (discussed in Chapter 2) is commonly used for this purpose as it can be implemented in time linear in the knowledge base size, even though it may not be able to find all possible implications of the knowledge base.

13.5 Elimination with local structure

In this section, we consider some techniques for exploiting local structure in the context of variable elimination algorithms.

The exploitation of local structure by elimination algorithms is relatively straightforward at the conceptual level. In a nutshell, the presence of local structure implies that factors can be represented more compactly using data structures that are more sophisticated than the tabular representation used in Chapter 6. As a result, the size of these factors will no longer be necessarily exponential in the number of variables appearing in a factor, which can have a dramatic effect on the complexity of elimination algorithms.

To elaborate on this point, recall that our complexity analysis of variable elimination in Chapter 6 produced the following result. Given an elimination order of width w, the time and space complexity of the algorithm is $O(n \exp(w))$ where n is the number of network variables. If we re-examines this complexity result, we find that a factor generated by variable elimination can contain as many as w variables. When factors are represented using tables, their size can then be exponential in w and the worst-case complexity of $O(n \exp(w))$ is reached. However, given a more sophisticated data structure for representing factors, their size may never be exponential in the number of their variables. In this case, the complexity of $O(n \exp(w))$ is only an upper bound and the average case complexity may be much better.

We can therefore exploit local structure in elimination algorithms by adopting a nontabular representation of factors and by supplying the necessary operations on this representation:

- *Multiplication*, where we compute the product of factors f_1 and f_2, $f_1 f_2$.
- *Summing out*, where we sum out variable X from factor f, leading to $\sum_X f$.[4]
- *Reduction*, where we reduce a factor f given evidence $\mathbf{e}$, leading to $f^{\mathbf{e}}$.

There are a number of nontabular representations of factors that have been proposed in the literature. In the rest of this chapter, we focus on one such representation based on decision diagrams. In particular, we describe this representation and its operations in Sections 13.5.1–13.5.2. We then show in Section 13.5.3 how it can be employed in the

---

[4] We also need *maximizing out* if we are computing most likely instantiations.

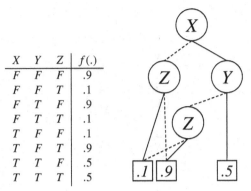

X	Y	Z	$f(.)$
F	F	F	.9
F	F	T	.1
F	T	F	.9
F	T	T	.1
T	F	F	.1
T	F	T	.9
T	T	F	.5
T	T	T	.5

Figure 13.12: A factor over binary variables X, Y, Z with a tabular representation (left) and an ADD representation (right).

context of variable elimination. We finally show in Section 13.5.4 how it can be used to compile arithmetic circuits by keeping a trace of variable elimination as we did in Chapter 12.

13.5.1 Algebraic decision diagrams

In this section, we describe a representation of factors using *algebraic decision diagrams* (ADDs), a data structure that provides support for a variety of factor operations including multiplication, summing out, and reduction given evidence.

Figure 13.12 depicts an example factor with its tabular and ADD representations. An ADD is a DAG with one root node and multiple leaf nodes. In the ADD of Figure 13.12, parents are drawn above their children, a layout convention that we adopt from here on. Each nonleaf node in an ADD is labeled with a binary variable having two children, a *high child* pointed to by a solid edge and a *low child* pointed to by a dotted edge. Each leaf node is called a *sink* and labeled with a real number. The ADD in Figure 13.12 has three sinks. The ADD must satisfy a variable ordering condition: the variables labeling nodes must appear in the same order along any path from the root to a leaf node. In the ADD of Figure 13.12, variables appear according to the order X, Y, Z. Note, however, that a path need not mention every variable in the order yet all paths must be consistent with a single total ordering of the ADD variables. An ADD is identified with its root node.

To see how an ADD represents a factor, let us identify the value assigned by the ADD in Figure 13.12 to the variable instantiation $X = F, Y = T, Z = T$. We always start at the ADD root, labeled with X in this case. We check the value of variable X according to the given instantiation. Since X has value F, we move to its low child, labeled with Z in this case. Since Z has the value T, we move to its high child, which is a sink labeled with .1. Hence, the factor assigns the value .1 to instantiation $X = F, Z = T$, independent of Y's value. That is, it assigns this value to both instantiations $X = F, Y = T, Z = T$ and $X = F, Y = F, Z = T$. Similarly, the factor assigns the value .9 to instantiation $X = T, Y = F, Z = T$.

The ADD representation of factors is interesting for a number of reasons. First, the ADD size can be exponentially smaller and never worse than the size of a tabular representation of the same factor – Figure 13.13 depicts an example showing an exponential difference

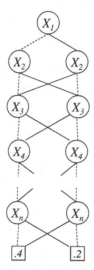

Figure 13.13: An ADD representing a factor $f(X_1, \ldots, X_n)$, where $f(x_1, \ldots, x_n) = .2$ if an odd number of values x_i are true and $f(x_1, \ldots, x_n) = .4$ otherwise. The ADD size is $O(n)$, while the tabular representation is $O(\exp(n))$.

in size. Second, ADD operations can be implemented efficiently. In particular, given two ADDs f_1 and f_2 of sizes n and m, respectively, the product $f_1 f_2$ can be computed in $O(nm)$ time, summing out $\sum_X f_1$ can be computed in $O(n^2)$ time, and the reduced factor f_1^e can be computed in $O(n)$ time. Summing out variables can also be accomplished in $O(n)$ time in some cases (see Exercise 13.17).

ADDs can contain redundant nodes. An ADD node is *redundant* if its high and low children are the same or if it has the same high and low children as another node in the ADD. In the first case, we simply remove the node from the ADD and direct all its parents to one of its identical children. In the second case, we also remove the node from the ADD and direct all its parents to the duplicate node. Figure 13.14 depicts an example of removing redundant nodes from an ADD. The resulting ADD is said to be *reduced* as it contains no redundant nodes. From now on, we assume that ADDs are reduced unless mentioned otherwise.

ADD representations satisfy another interesting property. Once we fix the variable ordering, each factor has a unique reduced ADD representation. Therefore, the corresponding ADD size is only a function of the variable order used in the ADD, which is why ADDs are said to be a *canonical* representation. However, we should stress that different variable orders can lead to significant differences in the ADD size. The difference can be exponential in the number of ADD variables in some cases. We also point out that the ADD variable order is independent and distinct from the variable order used by the variable elimination algorithm. However, experimental results suggest that using an ADD variable order that reverses the variable elimination order tends to produce good results (see Exercise 13.17).

13.5.2 ADD operations

We now discuss the three factor operations required by variable elimination, assuming that factors are represented by ADDs. We also discuss the automated conversion of tabular

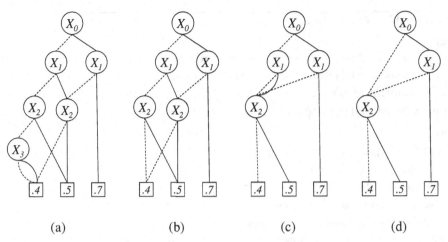

Figure 13.14: (a) An ADD with redundant nodes; (b) after removing the redundant node labeled with X_3; (c) after removing one of the redundant nodes labeled with X_2; and (d) after removing the redundant node labeled with X_1.

representations of factors into ADD representations. This allows a complete implementation of variable elimination using ADDs.

All ADD operations of interest rest on two primitive operations called *apply* and *restrict*, which we discuss next.

Apply

The APPLY operation takes two ADDs representing factors $f_1(\mathbf{X})$ and $f_2(\mathbf{Y})$ and a binary numeric operation $\odot$ and returns a new ADD representing the factor $f_1 \odot f_2$ over variables $\mathbf{Z} = \mathbf{X} \cup \mathbf{Y}$, defined as

$$(f_1 \odot f_2)(\mathbf{z}) \stackrel{def}{=} f_1(\mathbf{x}) \odot f_2(\mathbf{y}), \text{ where } \mathbf{x} \sim \mathbf{z} \text{ and } \mathbf{y} \sim \mathbf{z}.$$

For example, by taking $\odot$ to be numeric multiplication, we can use the APPLY operation to compute the product of two ADDs. Algorithm 37 provides pseudocode for this operation, which is guaranteed to run in $O(nm)$ time where n and m are the sizes of given ADDs (see also Exercise 13.16 for another bound on the size of ADD returned by APPLY).[5] Figure 13.15 provides an example of using the APPLY operation to compute the product of two ADDs.

The APPLY operation can also be used to reduce a factor f given some evidence $\mathbf{e}$, $f^{\mathbf{e}}$. All we have to do here is construct an ADD f' over variables $\mathbf{E}$, which maps instantiation $\mathbf{e}$ to 1 and all other instantiations to 0. The product ff' will then represent the reduced factor $f^{\mathbf{e}}$.

Restrict

The second primitive operation on ADDs is called *restrict* and can be used to implement the sum-out operation. Restrict takes an ADD representing factor $f(\mathbf{X}, \mathbf{E})$ and a variable instantiation $\mathbf{e}$ and then returns an ADD representing factor $f'(\mathbf{X}) = \sum_{\mathbf{E}} f^{\mathbf{e}}$, that is,

---

[5] The pseudocode of Algorithm 37 does not include standard optimizations which can have a dramatic effect on performance. These include checking for situations where one of the arguments to APPLY is a zero or identity element for the operation $\odot$.

Algorithm 37 APPLY($\varphi_1, \varphi_2, \odot$)

---

input:

  φ_1:   reduced ADD that respects variable order $\prec$

  φ_2:   reduced ADD that respects variable order $\prec$

  $\odot$:   numeric operation

output: reduced ADD $\varphi_1 \odot \varphi_2$

main:

  1: swap φ_1 and φ_2 if var(φ_2) $\prec$ var(φ_1)
  2: **if** cache(φ_1, φ_2) $\neq$ nil **then**
  3:     **return** cache(φ_1, φ_2)
  4: **else if** φ_1 and φ_2 are sinks **then**
  5:     $\varphi \leftarrow$ unique_sink(label(φ_1), label(φ_2), $\odot$)
  6: **else if** var(φ_1) = var(φ_2) **then**
  7:     $l \leftarrow$ APPLY(low(φ_1), low(φ_2), $\odot$)
  8:     $h \leftarrow$ APPLY(high(φ_1), high(φ_2), $\odot$)
  9:     $\varphi \leftarrow l$ if $l = h$ otherwise $\varphi \leftarrow$ unique_node(l, h, var(φ_1))
 10: **else** $\{$var(φ_1) $\prec$ var(φ_2)$\}$
 11:     $l \leftarrow$ APPLY(low(φ_1), φ_2, $\odot$)
 12:     $h \leftarrow$ APPLY(high(φ_1), φ_2, $\odot$)
 13:     $\varphi \leftarrow l$ if $l = h$ otherwise $\varphi \leftarrow$ unique_node(l, h, var(φ_1))
 14: **end if**
 15: cache(φ_1, φ_2) $\leftarrow \varphi$
 16: **return** φ

supporting functions: The functions var(φ), low(α), and high(α) return the variable of node φ, its low child, and its high child, respectively. If φ is a sink, then var(φ) is a variable that follows every other variable in the order. The function label(α) returns the label of sink node α. The function cache(φ_1, φ_2) remembers the result of calling apply on the ADDs φ_1 and φ_2. The function unique_sink($l_1, l_2, \odot$) returns a sink with label $l_1 \odot l_2$ if one already exists, otherwise it creates one. The function unique_node(φ_1, φ_2, V) returns a node labeled with variable V and having low child φ_1 and high child φ_2 if one exists, otherwise creates one.

$f'(\mathbf{x}) = f(\mathbf{x}, \mathbf{e})$. Algorithm 38 provides pseudocode for this operation, which runs in $O(n)$ time where n is the size of given ADD. Figure 13.16 provides an example of restricting an ADD to two different instantiations.

Suppose now that we wish to sum out variable X from a factor f. We can do this by first restricting f to $X = F$, then to $X = T$, and then adding up the results:

$$\sum_X f = \left(\sum_X f^{X=F} \right) + \left(\sum_X f^{X=T} \right).$$

This allows us to sum out a variable from an ADD by simply using the restrict operation twice followed by the apply operation with $\odot$ defined as numeric addition $+$. If the ADD has size n, then summing out will run in $O(n^2)$ time. If the summed-out variable appears last in the variable ordering, then we can perform the operation in $O(n)$ time (see Exercise 13.17). Figure 13.16 depicts an example of implementing the sum-out operation

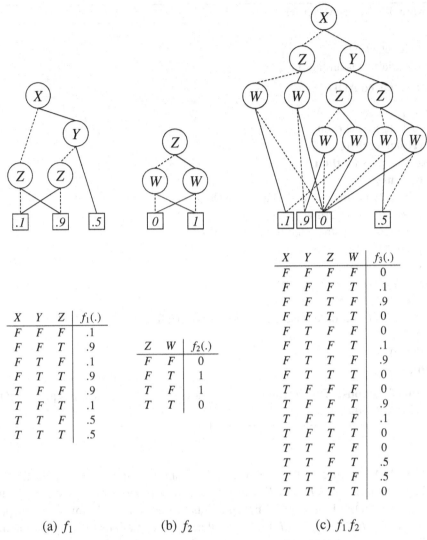

X	Y	Z	$f_1(.)$
F	F	F	.1
F	F	T	.9
F	T	F	.1
F	T	T	.9
T	F	F	.9
T	F	T	.1
T	T	F	.5
T	T	T	.5

Z	W	$f_2(.)$
F	F	0
F	T	1
T	F	1
T	T	0

X	Y	Z	W	$f_3(.)$
F	F	F	F	0
F	F	F	T	.1
F	F	T	F	.9
F	F	T	T	0
F	T	F	F	0
F	T	F	T	.1
F	T	T	F	.9
F	T	T	T	0
T	F	F	F	0
T	F	F	T	.9
T	F	T	F	.1
T	F	T	T	0
T	T	F	F	0
T	T	F	T	.5
T	T	T	F	.5
T	T	T	T	0

(a) f_1 (b) f_2 (c) $f_1 f_2$

Figure 13.15: Computing the product of two ADDs.

using a combination of restrict and apply, leading to an ADD that represents the following factor:

X	Y	W	
F	F	F	.9
F	F	T	.1
F	T	F	.9
F	T	T	.1
T	F	F	.1
T	F	T	.9
T	T	F	.5
T	T	T	.5

From tabular to ADD representations

We now show how the APPLY operation can be used to convert a tabular representation of a factor into an ADD representation. Consider Figure 13.17, which depicts a factor in tabular

---

Algorithm 38 RESTRICT(φ, **e**)

---

input:
  φ: reduced ADD
  e: variable instantiation

output: a reduced ADD $\sum_{\mathbf{E}} \varphi^{\mathbf{e}}$

main:

 1: **if** cache(φ) $\neq$ nil **then**
 2:     **return** cache(φ)
 3: **else if** φ is a sink **then**
 4:     **return** φ
 5: **else if** var(φ) is instantiated to true in **e then**
 6:     $\varphi' \leftarrow$ RESTRICT(high(φ), **e**)
 7: **else if** var(φ) is instantiated to false in **e then**
 8:     $\varphi' \leftarrow$ RESTRICT(low(φ), **e**)
 9: **else**
10:     $l \leftarrow$ RESTRICT(low(φ), **e**)
11:     $h \leftarrow$ RESTRICT(high(φ), **e**)
12:     $\varphi' \leftarrow l$ if $l = h$ otherwise $\varphi' \leftarrow$ unique_node(l, h, var(φ_1))
13: **end if**
14: cache(φ) $\leftarrow \varphi'$
15: **return** φ'

---

supporting functions: The functions cache(), var(), low(), high(), and unique_node() are as given by Algorithm 37.

---

form. The ADD in Figure 13.17(a) represents the first row in this table. That is, the ADD maps the instantiation $X = F, Y = F, Z = F$ to .1 and maps every other instantiation to 0. Similarly, the ADD in Figure 13.17(b) represents the second row in this table, mapping instantiation $X = F, Y = F, Z = T$ to .9 and all other instantiations to 0. By adding these two ADDs using the APPLY operation, we obtain the ADD in Figure 13.17(c), which represents the first two rows in the table. That is, this ADD maps these two rows to the corresponding values and maps every other row to 0. By constructing an ADD for each remaining row and adding up the resulting ADDs, we obtain an ADD corresponding to the given table. However, we can devise more efficient methods for converting tabular representations of factors into their ADD representations (see Exercise 13.12).

13.5.3 Variable elimination using ADDs

Now that we have a systematic method for converting tabular factors into their ADD representations and given the ADD operations for multiplying, summing out, and reducing ADDs, we are ready to provide a full implementation of variable elimination based on ADDs. This would be similar to Algorithm 8, VE_PR, of Chapter 6 except that we now use ADD representations of factors and the corresponding ADD operations. Note that the use of ADDs requires a variable ordering that must be respected by any ADDs on which the APPLY operation is called. Using the reverse of the variable elimination order has been

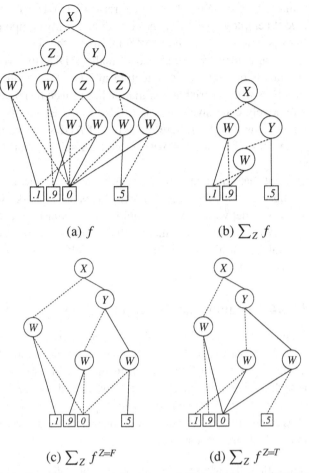

(a) f (b) $\sum_Z f$

(c) $\sum_Z f^{Z=F}$ (d) $\sum_Z f^{Z=T}$

Figure 13.16: Summing out a variable from an ADD by adding two of its restrictions.

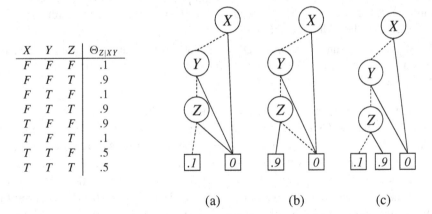

X	Y	Z	$\Theta_{Z|XY}$
F	F	F	.1
F	F	T	.9
F	T	F	.1
F	T	T	.9
T	F	F	.9
T	F	T	.1
T	T	F	.5
T	T	T	.5

(a)   (b)   (c)

Figure 13.17: From left to right: A tabular representation of a factor, an ADD representing its first row, an ADD representing its second row, and an ADD representing their summation.

observed empirically to give good results (see Exercise 13.17). However, a more sophisticated approach would employ ADD packages that dynamically compute variable orders within each APPLY operation with the intent of minimizing the size of resulting ADD.

Although dynamic variable ordering can lead to smaller ADDs, the overhead associated with it may not be justifiable unless the reduction in ADD size is quite significant. In general, the use of ADDs within variable elimination has proven beneficial only when the local structure is relatively excessive – this is needed to offset the overhead associated with ADD operations. One exception here is the use of ADDs and variable elimination to compile Bayesian networks into arithmetic circuits, a subject that we discuss in the following section.

Finally, we point out that our treatment has thus far assumed that all of our variables are binary, precluding the application of ADDs to Bayesian networks with multivalued variables. For this class of networks, we can employ multi-valued ADDs that are defined in a similar manner. We can also use binary-valued ADDs except that we must now represent each multivalued variable in the Bayesian network by a number of binary ADD variables (see Exercise 13.18).

13.5.4 Compiling arithmetic circuits using ADDs

We showed in Chapter 12 that variable elimination can be used to compile a Bayesian network into an arithmetic circuit by keeping a trace of the algorithm. We also showed that the time complexity of circuit compilation using standard variable elimination is exponential in the width of the used variable order. However, if we use ADDs to represent factors, the time complexity may not be necessarily exponential in the order width.

The use of ADDs to compile out circuits proceeds as in standard variable elimination with two exceptions, which are discussed next.

- We have to work with ADDs whose sinks are labeled with arithmetic circuit nodes instead of numeric constants (see Figure 13.19). This also requires that the operator $\odot$ passed to the APPLY operation must now be defined to operate on circuit nodes. For example, to multiply two ADDs, we define $\odot$ as an operator that takes two circuit nodes α and β and returns a new circuit node labeled with the multiplication operator $*$ and having α and β as its children. To sum two ADDs, we do the same except that the new circuit node will be labeled with the addition operator $+$.

- We need to include an *indicator* ADD for each network variable to capture evidence on that variable (see Figure 13.18). That is, for each variable X, we need an ADD $f(X)$ where $f(X = F) = \lambda_{x_0}$ and $f(X = T) = \lambda_{x_1}$.

Let us now consider an example where we compile an arithmetic circuit for the Bayesian network $X \rightarrow Y$ whose CPTs are depicted in Figure 13.18. The figure also depicts the initial ADDs we start with for the given Bayesian network: two ADDs for each network variable, one representing the variable CPT and another representing its indicators.

To construct an arithmetic circuit for this network, all we have to do is eliminate all network variables. Assuming that we eliminate variable Y first, we have to first multiply all ADDs that mention this variable, leading to the ADD in Figure 13.19(a). We can now sum out variable Y from this ADD, leading to the one in Figure 13.19(b). To eliminate variable X, we again have to multiply all ADDs that mention this variable, leading to the ADD in Figure 13.19(c). Summing out variable X from this ADD leads to the one in Figure 13.19(d). This final ADD contains a single sink, which is labeled

X	Y	$\Theta_{Y|X}$
x_0	y_0	0
x_0	y_1	1
x_1	y_0	.5
x_1	y_1	.5

X	Θ_X
x_0	.1
x_1	.9

CPT for X CPT for Y

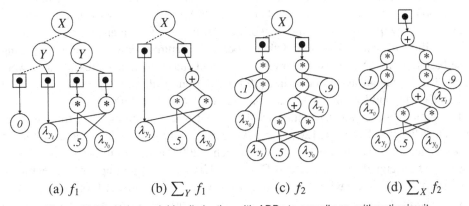

ADD for	ADD for	ADD for	ADD for
CPT of X	indicators of X	CPT of Y	indicators of Y

Figure 13.18: The CPTs and ADDs for a simple Bayesian network $X \rightarrow Y$.

(a) f_1 (b) $\sum_Y f_1$ (c) f_2 (d) $\sum_X f_2$

Figure 13.19: Using variable elimination with ADDs to compile an arithmetic circuit.

with an arithmetic circuit corresponding to the given network. Algorithm 39 depicts the pseudocode for compiling out an arithmetic circuit using variable elimination on factors that are represented by ADDs.

We conclude this section by pointing out that we can use ADDs in the context of variable elimination for computing probabilities or for compiling networks. As mentioned previously, the use of ADDs for computing probabilities will only be beneficial if the network has sufficient local structure to offset the overhead incurred by ADD operations. Note, however, that this overhead is incurred only once when compiling networks and is then amortized over many queries.

Algorithm 39 AC_VE_ADD($\mathcal{N}$)

---

input:

$\mathcal{N}$:   Bayesian network with binary variables

output: arithmetic circuit for Bayesian network $\mathcal{N}$

main:

1: $\Gamma \leftarrow$ the set of indicator and CPT ADDs for network $\mathcal{N}$
2: $\pi \leftarrow$ an ordering of the n network variables
3: **for** i from 1 to n **do**
4:      $\mathcal{S} \leftarrow$ the ADDs in Γ that mention variable $\pi(i)$
5:      $\varphi_i \leftarrow \sum_{\pi(i)} \prod_{\varphi \in \mathcal{S}} \varphi$
6:      $\Gamma \leftarrow (\Gamma \setminus \mathcal{S}) \cup \{\varphi_i\}$
7: **end for**
8: $\varphi \leftarrow \prod_{\varphi' \in \Gamma} \varphi'$
9: **return** label(φ) {ADD φ has a single (sink) node}

Bibliographic remarks

The role of determinism in improving the efficiency of inference was first observed in Jensen and Andersen [1990], where it was exploited in the context of jointree algorithms. Context-specific independence was formalized in Boutilier et al. [1996], who also observed its potential impact on the complexity of inference. The use of structured representations in the context of variable elimination was first reported in Zhang and Poole [1996]. ADDs were introduced in Bahar et al. [1993]. Their use was first reported in Hoey et al. [1999] for representing network CPTs and in Chavira and Darwiche [2007] for compiling Bayesian networks. Other types of structured representations, including those based on decision trees and graphs, rules, and sparse tabular representations were reported in Friedman and Goldszmidt [1996], Nielsen et al. [2000], Poole and Zhang [2003], Dechter and Larkin [2003], and Sanner and McAllester [2005].

The exploitation of local structure in the context of conditioning algorithms was reported in Allen and Darwiche [2003] and Bacchus et al. [2003]. The logical encoding of Bayesian networks was first proposed in Darwiche [2002] and later in Sang et al. [2005]. It was further refined in Chavira and Darwiche [2005; 2006] and applied to relational Bayesian networks in Chavira et al. [2006]; see Chavira and Darwiche [2008] for a recent survey. The exploitation of evidence in noisy-or networks was proposed in Heckerman [1989] and more generally in Chavira et al. [2005] and Sang et al. [2005].

Network preprocessing can also be quite effective in the presence of local structure, especially determinism, and is sometimes orthogonal to the techniques discussed in this chapter. For example, preprocessing has proven quite effective and critical for networks corresponding to genetic linkage analysis, allowing exact inference on networks with very large treewidth [Fishelson and Geiger, 2002; 2003; Allen and Darwiche, 2008]. A fundamental form of preprocessing is CPT decomposition in which one decomposes a CPT with local structure into a series of CPTs by introducing auxiliary variables [Díez and Galán, 2003; Vomlel, 2002]. This decomposition can reduce the network treewidth, allowing inference to be performed much more efficiently. The problem of finding an optimal CPT decomposition corresponds to the problem of determining tensor

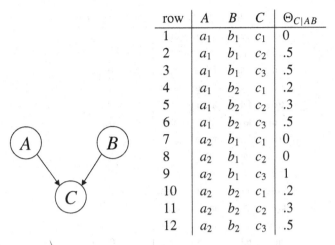

row	A	B	C	$\Theta_{C|AB}$
1	a_1	b_1	c_1	0
2	a_1	b_1	c_2	.5
3	a_1	b_1	c_3	.5
4	a_1	b_2	c_1	.2
5	a_1	b_2	c_2	.3
6	a_1	b_2	c_3	.5
7	a_2	b_1	c_1	0
8	a_2	b_1	c_2	0
9	a_2	b_1	c_3	1
10	a_2	b_2	c_1	.2
11	a_2	b_2	c_2	.3
12	a_2	b_2	c_3	.5

Figure 13.20: A Bayesian network with one of its CPTs.

rank [Savicky and Vomlel, 2006], which is NP-hard [Hrastad, 1990]. However, closed-form solutions are known for CPTs with a particular local structure [Savicky and Vomlel, 2006].

13.6 Exercises

13.1. Provide an arithmetic circuit of size $O(n)$ for the polynomial in Equation 13.1.

13.2. Consider Exercise 13.1. Show that a smaller circuit can be constructed for this polynomial assuming that the circuit can contain subtraction nodes.

13.3. Consider a Bayesian network consisting of binary nodes $X_1, \ldots, X_n, Y$, and edges $X_i \to Y$ for $i = 1, \ldots, n$. Assume that Y is true with probability ϵ_1 given that any of its parents are true and that it is false with probability ϵ_0 given that all its parents are false. Provide an arithmetic circuit for this network of size $O(n)$ while making no assumptions about the distributions over nodes X_i.

13.4. Consider a Bayesian network consisting of binary nodes $X_1, \ldots, X_n$, Y, and edges $X_i \to Y$ for $i = 1, \ldots, n$. Assume that Y is true if and only if an odd number of its parents X_i are true. Provide an arithmetic circuit for this network of size $O(n)$ while making no assumptions about the distributions over nodes X_i.

13.5. Construct two CNF encodings for the CPT in Figure 13.20, one that ignores local structure (Section 13.3.1) and another that accounts for local structure (Section 13.3.2).

13.6. Construct an arithmetic circuit for the network in Figure 13.20 while assuming that the instantiation a_2, b_1 is always part of the evidence (see Section 13.3.3). Assume that variables A and B have uniform CPTs.

13.7. Encode the CPT in Figure 13.21 as a CNF while ignoring local structure (Section 13.3.1). Show how the encoding would change if we account for determinism (Section 13.3.2). Show how this last encoding would change if we account for equal parameters (Section 13.3.2).

13.8. Construct an ADD for the CPT in Figure 13.21 using the variable order A, B, C, D.

13.9. Consider a factor f over binary variables $X_1, \ldots, X_n$, where $f(x_1, \ldots, x_n) = 1$ if exactly one value in $x_1, \ldots, x_n$ is true and $f(x_1, \ldots, x_n) = 0$ otherwise. Construct an ADD representation of this factor with size $O(n)$.

13.10. Reduce the ADD in Figure 13.22 (see also Figure 13.14).

A	B	C	D	$\Pr(D\mid A, B, C)$
true	true	true	true	.9
true	true	true	false	.1
true	true	false	true	.9
true	true	false	false	.1
true	false	true	true	.9
true	false	true	false	.1
true	false	false	true	.2
true	false	false	false	.8
false	true	true	true	.5
false	true	true	false	.5
false	true	false	true	.5
false	true	false	false	.5
false	false	true	true	0
false	false	true	false	1
false	false	false	true	0
false	false	false	false	1

Figure 13.21: A conditional probability table.

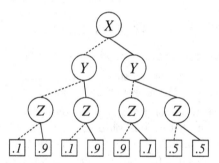

Figure 13.22: A decision tree representation of a factor (unreduced ADD).

13.11. Show how we can reduce an ADD with n nodes using an algorithm that takes $O(n \log n)$ time (see Figure 13.14).

13.12. Consider the method described in Section 13.5.2 for converting a tabular representation of a factor into its ADD representation. Consider now a second method in which we construct a decision tree to represent the factor (see Figure 13.22) and then reduce the ADD using the algorithm developed in Exercise 13.11. Implement and compare the efficiency of these methods.

13.13. Construct an ADD over variables A and B, which maps each instantiation to 1 if either A or B is true and to 0 otherwise. Multiply this ADD with the one constructed in Exercise 13.8.

13.14. Sum-out variable B from the ADD constructed in Exercise 13.8.

13.15. Restrict the ADD constructed in Exercise 13.8 to $C =$ false.

13.16. Let $f_1(\mathbf{X}_1)$ and $f_2(\mathbf{X}_2)$ be two factors and let φ_1 and φ_2 be their corresponding ADD representations using the same variable ordering. Show that the size of the ADD returned by APPLY$(\varphi_1, \varphi_2, \odot)$ is $O(\exp(|\mathbf{X}_1 \cup \mathbf{X}_2|))$.

13.17. We presented a $O(n^2)$ algorithm for summing out a variable from an ADD where n is the size of the given ADD. Assuming that the summed-out variable appears last in the ADD variable order, show how the sum-out operation can be implemented in $O(n)$. Show that this complexity applies to summing out multiple variables as long as they appear last in the ADD order.

13.18. Show how we can represent a factor over multivalued variables using an ADD with binary variables. Explain how the sum-out operation (of a multivalued variable) should be implemented in this case.

13.19. Consider Bayesian networks of the type given in Figure 13.4 and let $\mathbf{e}$ be some evidence on nodes S_i. Let m be the number of nodes S_i set to true by evidence $\mathbf{e}$ and let k be the number of network edges. Show that $\Pr(D_j|\mathbf{e})$ can be computed in $O(k\exp(m))$. Hint: Prune the network and appeal to the inclusion-exclusion principle.[6]

13.20. Consider Exercise 13.19. Show that the same complexity still holds if each node S_i is a noisy-or of its parents.

13.21. Consider the problem of encoding equal parameters, as discussed in Section 13.3.2. Show that the following technique can be adopted to deal with this problem:

- Do not drop clauses for parameters with value 1.

- Replace each set of equal parameters θ_i in the same CPT by a new parameter η and drop all PI clauses of parameters θ_i.

- Add the following clauses $\neg\eta_i \vee \neg\eta_j$ for $i \neq j$ and $\neg\eta_i \vee \neg\theta_j$ for all i, j. Here $\eta_1, \ldots, \eta_k$ are all the newly introduced parameters to a CPT and $\theta_1, \ldots, \theta_m$ are all surviving old parameters in the CPT.

In particular, show that the old and new CNF encodings agree on their weighted model counts.

13.22. Consider the problem of encoding equal parameters as discussed in Section 13.3.2. Consider the following technique for dealing with this problem:

- Do not drop clauses for parameters with value 1.

- Replace each set of equal parameters θ_i in the same CPT by a new parameter η and drop all the PI clauses of parameters θ_i.

Let f be the MLF encoded by resulting CNF Δ. Show that the minimal terms of f correspond to the network polynomial. Hence, when coupled with the procedure of Exercise 12.20, this method can be used as an alternative for exploiting equal parameters.

---

[6] This principle says that

$$\Pr(\alpha_1 \vee \ldots \vee \alpha_n) = \sum_{k=1}^{n} (-1)^{k-1} \sum_{I \subseteq \{1,\ldots,n\}, |I|=k} \Pr\left(\bigwedge_{i \in I} \alpha_i\right).$$

Note that there are $2^n - 1$ terms in this equation.

14

Approximate Inference by Belief Propagation

We discuss in this chapter a class of approximate inference algorithms which are based on belief propagation. These algorithms provide a full spectrum of approximations, allowing one to trade-off approximation quality with computational resources.

14.1 Introduction

The algorithm of belief propagation was first introduced as a specialized algorithm that applied only to networks having a polytree structure. This algorithm, which we treated in Section 7.5.4, was later applied to networks with arbitrary structure and found to produce high-quality approximations in certain cases. This observation triggered a line of investigations into the semantics of belief propagation, which had the effect of introducing a generalization of the algorithm that provides a full spectrum of approximations with belief propagation approximations at one end and exact results at the other.

We discuss belief propagation as applied to polytrees in Section 14.2 and then discuss its application to more general networks in Section 14.3. The semantics of belief propagation are exposed in Section 14.4, showing how it can be viewed as searching for an approximate distribution that satisfies some interesting properties. These semantics will then be the basis for developing generalized belief propagation in Sections 14.5–14.7. An alternative semantics for belief propagation will also be given in Section 14.8, together with a corresponding generalization. The difference between the two generalizations of belief propagation is not only in their semantics but also in the way they allow the user to trade off the approximation quality with the computational resources needed to produce them.

14.2 The belief propagation algorithm

Belief propagation is a message-passing algorithm originally developed for exact inference in polytree networks – this is why it is also known as the *polytree algorithm.*

There are two versions of belief propagation, one computing joint marginals and the other computing conditional marginals. In particular, for some evidence $\mathbf{e}$ the first version computes $\Pr(X, \mathbf{e})$ for every variable X in the polytree, while the second version computes $\Pr(X|\mathbf{e})$. The first version falls as a special case of the jointree algorithm and is discussed first. The second version is slightly different and is the one we pursue in this chapter.

Consider the polytree network in Figure 14.1 and suppose that our goal is to apply the jointree algorithm to this network under evidence $E = \text{true}$ using the jointree on the left of Figure 14.2. This jointree is special in the sense that its structure coincides with the polytree structure. That is, a node i in the jointree, which corresponds to variable X in the polytree, has its cluster as $\mathbf{C}_i = X\mathbf{U}$, where $\mathbf{U}$ are the parents of X in the polytree. Moreover, an undirected edge $i{-}j$ in the jointree, which corresponds to edge $X \to Y$ in the polytree, has its separator as $\mathbf{S}_{ij} = X$. This immediately implies that the jointree width

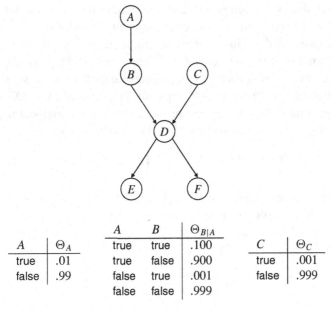

A	B	$\Theta_{B|A}$
true	true	.100
true	false	.900
false	true	.001
false	false	.999

A	Θ_A
true	.01
false	.99

C	Θ_C
true	.001
false	.999

B	C	D	$\Theta_{D|BC}$
true	true	true	.99
true	true	false	.01
true	false	true	.90
true	false	false	.10
false	true	true	.95
false	true	false	.05
false	false	true	.01
false	false	false	.99

D	E	$\Theta_{E|D}$
true	true	.9
true	false	.1
false	true	.3
false	false	.7

D	F	$\Theta_{F|D}$
true	true	.2
true	false	.8
false	true	.1
false	false	.9

Figure 14.1: A polytree network.

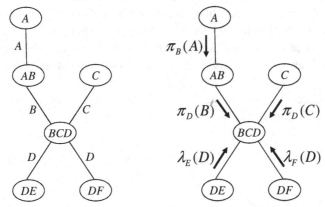

Figure 14.2: Message passing in a jointree corresponding to a polytree.

equals the treewidth of the given polytree. It also implies that each separator has a single variable and, hence, each jointree message is over a single variable.

Belief propagation is the jointree algorithm under these conditions, where messages are notated differently and based on the polytree structure. In particular, the message from node U to child X is denoted by $\pi_X(U)$ and called the *causal support* from U to X. Moreover, the message from node Y to parent X is denoted by $\lambda_Y(X)$ and called the *diagnostic support* from Y to X (see Figure 14.2). Given this notation, the joint marginal for the family of variable X with parents U_i and children Y_j is given by

$$\Pr(X\mathbf{U}, \mathbf{e}) = \lambda_{\mathbf{e}}(X)\Theta_{X|\mathbf{U}} \prod_i \pi_X(U_i) \prod_j \lambda_{Y_j}(X).$$

Here $\lambda_{\mathbf{e}}(X)$ is an evidence indicator where $\lambda_{\mathbf{e}}(x) = 1$ if x is consistent with evidence $\mathbf{e}$ and zero otherwise. This equation follows immediately from the jointree algorithm once we adjust for notational differences. Using this new notation, causal and diagnostic messages can also be defined as

$$\lambda_X(U_i) = \sum_{X\mathbf{U}\backslash\{U_i\}} \lambda_{\mathbf{e}}(X)\Theta_{X|\mathbf{U}} \prod_{k\neq i} \pi_X(U_k) \prod_j \lambda_{Y_j}(X)$$

$$\pi_{Y_j}(X) = \sum_{\mathbf{U}} \lambda_{\mathbf{e}}(X)\Theta_{X|\mathbf{U}} \prod_i \pi_X(U_i) \prod_{k\neq j} \lambda_{Y_k}(X).$$

A node can send a message to a neighbor only after it has received messages from all other neighbors. When a node has a single neighbor, it can immediately send a message to that neighbor. This includes a leaf node X with a single parent U, for which

$$\lambda_X(U) = \sum_X \lambda_{\mathbf{e}}(X)\Theta_{X|U}.$$

It also includes a root node X with a single child Y, for which

$$\pi_Y(X) = \lambda_{\mathbf{e}}(X)\Theta_X.$$

These are indeed the base cases for belief propagation, showing us the type of messages that can be computed immediately as they do not depend on the computation of any other message. Typically, messages are first propagated by pulling them toward a particular node, called a *root*, and then propagated again by pushing them away from the root. This particular order of propagating messages, called a *pull-push schedule*, guarantees that when a message is about to be computed, all messages it depends on would have already been computed.

Figure 14.2 depicts the messages propagated toward node D under evidence $E = \text{true}$. We have three π-messages in this case:

A	$\pi_B(A)$	B	$\pi_D(B)$	C	$\pi_D(C)$
true	.01	true	.00199	true	.001
false	.99	false	.99801	false	.999

We also have two λ-messages:

D	$\lambda_E(D)$	D	$\lambda_F(D)$
true	.9	true	1
false	.3	false	1

To compute the joint marginal for the family of variable D, we simply evaluate

$$\Pr(BCD, \mathbf{e}) = \Theta_{D|BC} \cdot \pi_D(B)\pi_D(C) \cdot \lambda_E(D)\lambda_F(D),$$

leading to the following:

B	C	D	$Pr(BCD, \mathbf{e})$
true	true	true	1.7731×10^{-6}
true	true	false	5.9700×10^{-9}
true	false	true	1.6103×10^{-3}
true	false	false	5.9640×10^{-5}
false	true	true	8.5330×10^{-4}
false	true	false	1.4970×10^{-5}
false	false	true	8.9731×10^{-3}
false	false	false	2.9611×10^{-1}

where all quantities are rounded to four decimal places. By summing all table entries, we find that $Pr(\mathbf{e}) \approx .3076$. We can also compute the joint marginal for variable C once we compute the message passed from D to C:

C	$\lambda_D(C)$
true	.8700
false	.3071

C	$Pr(C, \mathbf{e})$
true	.0009
false	.3067

Note that we could have also computed the joint marginal for variable C using the joint marginal for the family of D: $Pr(C, \mathbf{e}) = \sum_{BD} Pr(BCD, \mathbf{e})$.

To compute conditional marginals, we simply normalize joint marginals as in the jointree algorithm. However, another approach is to use the following alternative equations for belief propagation, in which $BEL(X\mathbf{U})$ denotes the conditional marginal $Pr(X\mathbf{U}|\mathbf{e})$:

$$BEL(X\mathbf{U}) = \eta \, \lambda_{\mathbf{e}}(X)\Theta_{X|\mathbf{U}} \prod_i \pi_X(U_i) \prod_j \lambda_{Y_j}(X)$$

$$\lambda_X(U_i) = \eta \sum_{X\mathbf{U}\backslash\{U_i\}} \lambda_{\mathbf{e}}(X)\Theta_{X|\mathbf{U}} \prod_{k\neq i} \pi_X(U_k) \prod_j \lambda_{Y_j}(X)$$

$$\pi_{Y_j}(X) = \eta \sum_{\mathbf{U}} \lambda_{\mathbf{e}}(X)\Theta_{X|\mathbf{U}} \prod_i \pi_X(U_i) \prod_{k\neq j} \lambda_{Y_k}(X).$$

Note that the only difference between these equations and the previous ones is in the use of the constant η, which we use generically as a constant that normalizes a factor to sum to one (to simplify the notation, we refrain from distinguishing between constants η that normalize different factors). We will indeed use this version of belief propagation as it helps prevent numerical underflow.[1]

14.3 Iterative belief propagation

Although belief propagation was designed as an exact algorithm for polytrees, it was later applied to multiply connected networks. However, this application poses some procedural and semantic difficulties. On the procedural side, recall that a message can be sent from a node X to its neighbor Y only after X has received messages from all its other neighbors. Suppose now that we need to apply belief propagation to the

---

[1] As we see in the following section, messages are updated iteratively from previously computed messages. As we iterate, messages become the product of increasingly many factors with values that become increasingly small, even though only the relative values of messages are needed to compute conditional marginals.

Algorithm 40 IBP($\mathcal{N}$, **e**)

---

input:

   $\mathcal{N}$:   a Bayesian network inducing distribution Pr

   e: an instantiation of some variables in network $\mathcal{N}$

output: approximate marginals, $BEL(X\mathbf{U})$, of $\Pr(X\mathbf{U}|\mathbf{e})$ for each family $X\mathbf{U}$ in $\mathcal{N}$

main:

1: $t \leftarrow 0$

2: initialize all messages π^0, λ^0 (uniformly)

3: **while** messages have not converged **do**

4:     $t \leftarrow t + 1$

5:     **for** each node X with parents $\mathbf{U}$ **do**

6:        **for** each parent U_i **do**

7:           $\lambda_X^t(U_i) = \eta \sum_{X\mathbf{U}\setminus\{U_i\}} \lambda_{\mathbf{e}}(X)\Theta_{X|\mathbf{U}} \prod_{k \neq i} \pi_X^{t-1}(U_k) \prod_j \lambda_{Y_j}^{t-1}(X)$

8:        **end for**

9:        **for** each child Y_j **do**

10:       $\pi_{Y_j}^t(X) = \eta \sum_{\mathbf{U}} \lambda_{\mathbf{e}}(X)\Theta_{X|\mathbf{U}} \prod_i \pi_X^{t-1}(U_i) \prod_{k \neq j} \lambda_{Y_k}^{t-1}(X)$

11:       **end for**

12:     **end for**

13: **end while**

14: **return** $BEL(X\mathbf{U}) = \eta \, \lambda_{\mathbf{e}}(X)\Theta_{X|\mathbf{U}} \prod_i \pi_X^t(U_i) \prod_j \lambda_{Y_j}^t(X)$ for families $X\mathbf{U}$

---

network in Figure 14.3. We can start off by sending message $\lambda_E(C)$ from node E to node C as the message does not depend on any other. But no other message can be propagated next, as each is dependent on others that are waiting to be propagated. On the semantic side, the correctness of belief propagation depends critically on the underlying polytree, possibly leading to incorrect results if applied to multiply connected networks. As we see later, these procedural difficulties can be addressed and the resulting algorithm, although no longer always correct, can still provide high-quality approximations in many cases.

Algorithm 40, IBP, depicts the application of belief propagation to multiply connected networks. The key observation here is that we start off by assuming some initial value to each message in the network. Given these initial values, every node will now be ready to send a message to each of its neighbors. Algorithm 40 assumes that message passing takes place in iterations and is the reason it is referred to as *iterative belief propagation* (IBP).[2] That is, at iteration t, every node X sends a message to its neighbors using the messages it received from its other neighbors at iteration $t-1$. Algorithm 40 continues iterating until messages converge, which we declare when the value of messages at the current iteration are within some threshold from their values at the previous iteration. When IBP converges, the values of its messages at convergence are called a *fixed point* (see Appendix C). In general, IBP may have multiple fixed points on a given network.

A natural question that we may ask is how fast IBP converges, or if we should even expect it to converge at all. Indeed, as described we can identify networks where the

---

[2] The algorithm is also commonly known as *loopy belief propagation*, as it is run in "loopy" networks.

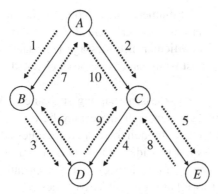

Figure 14.3: A Bayesian network, annotated with an ordering of IBP messages.

messages computed by IBP can oscillate, and if left to run without limit IBP could loop forever.

The convergence rate of IBP can depend crucially on the order in which messages are propagated, which is known as a *message schedule*. Algorithm 40 is said to use a *parallel schedule* since we wait until all messages for an iteration are computed before they are propagated (in parallel) in the following iteration. Thus, in a parallel message-passing schedule, the precise order we compute messages does not affect the dynamics of the algorithm. On the other hand, we can adopt a *sequential schedule* where messages are propagated as soon as they are computed. In this case, we are allowed much flexibility in when and how quickly information gets propagated across a network. Although one message-passing schedule may converge and others may not, all schedules in principle have the same fixed points (if IBP starts at a fixed point, it stays at a fixed point, independent of the schedule). Thus, for simplicity we assume parallel schedules beyond this section.

For a concrete example of sequential schedules, consider the network in Figure 14.3, where we compute messages in the following order:

$$\pi_B(A), \pi_C(A), \pi_D(B), \pi_D(C), \pi_E(C), \lambda_D(B), \lambda_B(A), \lambda_E(C), \lambda_D(C), \lambda_C(A).$$

When we are ready to compute the message $\pi_E(C)$ using messages $\pi_C(A)$ and $\lambda_D(C)$, we can use the most up-to-date ones: $\pi_C(A)$ from the current iteration and $\lambda_D(C)$ from the previous iteration. Since we use the most up-to-date message $\pi_C(A)$ to compute $\pi_E(C)$, information available at node A is able to propagate to E, two steps away, in the same iteration. Computing messages in parallel, this same information would take two iterations to reach E.

A sequential schedule could also vary the order in which it computes messages from one iteration to another and pass only a subset of the messages in each iteration. For example, for each iteration we could pick a different spanning tree embedded in a network and pass messages only on the spanning tree using a pull-push schedule. Considering Figure 14.3, we may use a message order

$$\pi_B(A), \pi_D(B), \lambda_D(C), \pi_E(C), \lambda_E(C), \pi_D(C), \lambda_D(B), \lambda_B(A)$$

in one iteration and another message order

$$\lambda_E(C), \lambda_D(C), \lambda_C(A), \lambda_B(A), \pi_B(A), \pi_C(A), \pi_D(C), \pi_E(C)$$

in the next. Such a schedule allows information to propagate from one end of the network to the other in a single iteration. To propagate the same information, a parallel schedule needs as many iterations as the diameter of the polytree. If a message-passing schedule updates a message in one iteration but not the next, we should ensure that each message is updated often enough. In particular, if a message is updated in a given iteration, any other message that uses it must be updated (or at least checked for convergence) in some future iteration.

Unfortunately, even a careful message-passing schedule may not guarantee convergence. Moreover, even if IBP converges there may be another fixed point that could provide a better approximation. Although there are techniques that can be used to counter oscillations, IBP often does not provide a good approximation in such problematic situations. We instead look to generalizations of belief propagation that can lead to more accurate approximations as well as more stable dynamics.

14.4 The semantics of IBP

We provide a semantics for Algorithm 40, IBP, in this section, showing how it can be viewed as searching for an approximate probability distribution $\Pr'$ that attempts to minimize the Kullback-Leibler divergence with the distribution $\Pr$ induced by the given Bayesian network.

14.4.1 The Kullback-Leibler divergence

Consider the Kullback-Leibler divergence, known as the *KL divergence*, between two distributions $\Pr$ and $\Pr'$ given that each has been conditioned on evidence $\mathbf{e}$:

$$KL(\Pr'(\mathbf{X}|\mathbf{e}), \Pr(\mathbf{X}|\mathbf{e})) = \sum_{\mathbf{x}} \Pr'(\mathbf{x}|\mathbf{e}) \log \frac{\Pr'(\mathbf{x}|\mathbf{e})}{\Pr(\mathbf{x}|\mathbf{e})}. \qquad (14.1)$$

$KL(\Pr'(\mathbf{X}|\mathbf{e}), \Pr(\mathbf{X}|\mathbf{e}))$ is non-negative and equal to zero if and only if $\Pr'(\mathbf{X}|\mathbf{e})$ and $\Pr(\mathbf{X}|\mathbf{e})$ are equivalent. However, the KL divergence is not a true distance measure in that it is not symmetric. In general,

$$KL(\Pr'(\mathbf{X}|\mathbf{e}), \Pr(\mathbf{X}|\mathbf{e})) \neq KL(\Pr(\mathbf{X}|\mathbf{e}), \Pr'(\mathbf{X}|\mathbf{e})).$$

Moreover, when computing $KL(\Pr'(\mathbf{X}|\mathbf{e}), \Pr(\mathbf{X}|\mathbf{e}))$ we say that we are weighting the KL divergence by the approximate distribution $\Pr'$ (as opposed to the true distribution $\Pr$). We indeed focus on the KL divergence weighted by the approximate distribution as it has some useful computational properties.

Theorem 14.1. *Let* $\Pr(\mathbf{X})$ *be a distribution induced by a Bayesian network* $\mathcal{N}$ *having families* $X\mathbf{U}$. *The KL divergence between* $\Pr$ *and another distribution* $\Pr'$ *can be written as a sum of three components:*

$$KL(\Pr'(\mathbf{X}|\mathbf{e}), \Pr(\mathbf{X}|\mathbf{e})) = -ENT'(\mathbf{X}|\mathbf{e}) - \sum_{X\mathbf{U}} AVG'(\log \lambda_{\mathbf{e}}(X)\Theta_{X|\mathbf{U}}) + \log \Pr(\mathbf{e}),$$

where

- $ENT'(\mathbf{X}|\mathbf{e}) = -\sum_{\mathbf{x}} \Pr'(\mathbf{x}|\mathbf{e}) \log \Pr'(\mathbf{x}|\mathbf{e})$ *is the entropy of the conditioned approximate distribution* $\Pr'(\mathbf{X}|\mathbf{e})$.
- $AVG'(\log \lambda_{\mathbf{e}}(X)\Theta_{X|\mathbf{U}}) = \sum_{x\mathbf{u}} \Pr'(x\mathbf{u}|\mathbf{e}) \log \lambda_{\mathbf{e}}(x)\theta_{x|\mathbf{u}}$ *is a set of expectations over the original network parameters weighted by the conditioned approximate distribution.* ∎

A number of observations are in order about this decomposition of the KL divergence. First, the component $\text{ENT}'(\mathbf{X}|\mathbf{e})$ depends only on the approximate distribution Pr' and, hence, our ability to compute it efficiently depends on the specific form of Pr'. Next, the component $\text{AVG}'(\log \lambda_{\mathbf{e}}(X)\Theta_{X|U})$ depends on both distributions but can be computed efficiently assuming that we can project the approximate distribution Pr' on the families of the original network $\mathcal{N}$. Finally, the component $\log \text{Pr}(\mathbf{e})$ is effectively a constant as it is independent of the approximate distribution Pr'.

From these observations, we see that evaluating the first two components of the KL divergence between Pr and Pr' requires:

- A computation of the entropy for Pr', and
- A computation of marginals according to Pr' for families in the original network $\mathcal{N}$.

Moreover, if our goal is to choose a specific instance Pr' that minimizes the KL divergence, then we need to consider only its first two components as the third component, $\log \text{Pr}(\mathbf{e})$, is independent of our choice of Pr'.

More specifically, we have now formulated the minimization of the KL divergence in terms of the following.

Corollary 2. *Consider Theorem 14.1. A distribution* $\text{Pr}'(\mathbf{X}|\mathbf{e})$ *minimizes the KL divergence* $\text{KL}(\text{Pr}'(\mathbf{X}|\mathbf{e}), \text{Pr}(\mathbf{X}|\mathbf{e}))$ *if it maximizes*

$$\text{ENT}'(\mathbf{X}|\mathbf{e}) + \sum_{X\mathbf{U}} \text{AVG}'(\log \lambda_{\mathbf{e}}(X)\Theta_{X|\mathbf{U}}). \tag{14.2}$$

■

This formulation thus reveals two competing properties of $\text{Pr}'(\mathbf{X}|\mathbf{e})$ that minimize the KL divergence:

- $\text{Pr}'(\mathbf{X}|\mathbf{e})$ should match the original distribution by giving more weight to more likely parameters $\lambda_{\mathbf{e}}(x)\theta_{x|\mathbf{u}}$ (i.e., maximize the expectations).
- $\text{Pr}'(\mathbf{X}|\mathbf{e})$ should not favor unnecessarily one network instantiation over another by being evenly distributed (i.e., maximize the entropy).

14.4.2 Optimizing the KL divergence

We can now pose the approximate inference problem as an optimization problem, where the goal is to search for an approximate distribution $\text{Pr}'(\mathbf{X}|\mathbf{e})$ that minimizes the KL divergence with $\text{Pr}(\mathbf{X}|\mathbf{e})$. In particular, we can assume a parameterized form for the approximate distribution $\text{Pr}'(\mathbf{X}|\mathbf{e})$ and try to search for the best instance of that form, that is, the best set of parameter values. Note that although we desire a solution that minimizes the KL divergence, depending on how we search for such a solution and what techniques we use we may only find a local extremum or, more generally, a stationary point of the KL divergence. See Appendix D for a review of concepts in constrained optimization that we employ here.

Regardless of our particular approach, we should expect to be able to compute the ENT and AVG components of the KL divergence. This in turn dictates that we choose a suitably restricted form for Pr' that facilitates such a computation. As we see next, the approximations computed by Algorithm 40, IBP, are based on assuming an approximate distribution $\mathrm{Pr}'(\mathbf{X})$ that factors as

$$\mathrm{Pr}'(\mathbf{X}|\mathbf{e}) = \prod_{XU} \frac{\mathrm{Pr}'(XU|\mathbf{e})}{\prod_{U \in \mathbf{U}} \mathrm{Pr}'(U|\mathbf{e})}. \tag{14.3}$$

Here XU ranges over the families of network $\mathcal{N}$ and U ranges over nodes that appear as parents in $\mathcal{N}$. Note how this form is in terms of only the marginals that Pr' assigns to parents and families. A number of observations are in order about this assumption.

First, this choice of $\mathrm{Pr}'(\mathbf{X}|\mathbf{e})$ is expressive enough to describe distributions $\mathrm{Pr}(\mathbf{X}|\mathbf{e})$ induced by polytree networks $\mathcal{N}$. That is, if $\mathcal{N}$ is a polytree, then the corresponding distribution $\mathrm{Pr}(\mathbf{X}|\mathbf{e})$ does indeed factor according to (14.3) (see Exercise 14.4). In the case where $\mathcal{N}$ is not a polytree, then we are simply trying to fit $\mathrm{Pr}(\mathbf{X}|\mathbf{e})$ into an approximation $\mathrm{Pr}'(\mathbf{X}|\mathbf{e})$ as if it were generated by a polytree network.

Second, the form in (14.3) allows us to express the entropy of distribution $\mathrm{Pr}'(\mathbf{X}|\mathbf{e})$ as

$$\mathrm{ENT}'(\mathbf{X}|\mathbf{e}) = -\sum_{XU}\sum_{x\mathbf{u}} \mathrm{Pr}'(x\mathbf{u}|\mathbf{e}) \log \frac{\mathrm{Pr}'(x\mathbf{u}|\mathbf{e})}{\prod_{u \sim \mathbf{u}} \mathrm{Pr}'(u|\mathbf{e})},$$

where XU ranges over the network families and U is a parent in $\mathbf{U}$. Again, note how the entropy is expressed in terms of only marginals over parents, $\mathrm{Pr}'(u|\mathbf{e})$, and families, $\mathrm{Pr}'(x\mathbf{u}|\mathbf{e})$. If we use μ_u and $\mu_{x\mathbf{u}}$ to denote these marginals, respectively, then our goal becomes that of searching for the values of these marginals which will hopefully minimize the KL divergence, and thus by Corollary 2 maximize its ENT and AVG components.

Suppose now that we have a fixed point of IBP, that is, a set of messages π and λ that satisfy the convergence conditions of Algorithm 40. The associated marginal approximations $BEL(U)$ and $BEL(XU)$ are in fact a solution to this optimization problem.

Theorem 14.2. *Let $\mathrm{Pr}(\mathbf{X})$ be a distribution induced by a Bayesian network $\mathcal{N}$ having families XU. Then IBP messages are a fixed point if and only if IBP marginals $\mu_u = BEL(u)$ and $\mu_{x\mathbf{u}} = BEL(x\mathbf{u})$ are a stationary point of*

$$\mathrm{ENT}'(\mathbf{X}|\mathbf{e}) + \sum_{XU} \mathrm{AVG}'(\log \lambda_{\mathbf{e}}(X)\Theta_{X|\mathbf{U}})$$

$$= -\sum_{XU}\sum_{x\mathbf{u}} \mu_{x\mathbf{u}} \log \frac{\mu_{x\mathbf{u}}}{\prod_{u \sim \mathbf{u}} \mu_u} + \sum_{XU}\sum_{x\mathbf{u}} \mu_{x\mathbf{u}} \log \lambda_{\mathbf{e}}(x)\theta_{x|\mathbf{u}}, \tag{14.4}$$

under normalization constraints,

$$\sum_u \mu_u = \sum_{x\mathbf{u}} \mu_{x\mathbf{u}} = 1$$

for each family XU and parent U, and under consistency constraints,

$$\sum_{x\mathbf{u}\sim y} \mu_{x\mathbf{u}} = \mu_y$$

for each family instantiation $x\mathbf{u}$ and value y of family member $Y \in XU$. ∎

That is, the parent marginals $\mu_u = BEL(u)$ and family marginals $\mu_{x\mathbf{u}} = BEL(x\mathbf{u})$ computed by IBP parameterize an approximate distribution $\mathrm{Pr}'(\mathbf{X}|\mathbf{e})$ that factorizes as in (14.3). Moreover, these marginal approximations are stationary points of the KL divergence between $\mathrm{Pr}'(\mathbf{X}|\mathbf{e})$ and $\mathrm{Pr}(\mathbf{X}|\mathbf{e})$ under constraints that ensure that they behave, at least locally, like true marginal distributions. Our normalization constraints ensure that marginals μ_u

and $\mu_{x\mathbf{u}}$ normalize properly and our consistency constraints ensure that node marginals μ_y are consistent with family marginals $\mu_{x\mathbf{u}}$, for each member Y of a family $X\mathbf{U}$.[3]

The previous correspondence only tells us that IBP fixed points are stationary points of the KL divergence: they may only be local minima or they may not be minima at all (see Appendix D). When IBP performs well, it often has fixed points that are indeed minima of the KL divergence. For problems where IBP does not behave as well, we next seek approximations Pr′ whose factorizations are more expressive than that of the polytree-based factorization of (14.3).

14.5 Generalized belief propagation

Not every probability distribution can be factored as given by (14.3). According to this equation, the distribution is a quotient of two terms: one is a product of family marginals and the other is a product of variable marginals. If we do not insist on marginals being over families and individual variables, we can devise a more general form that can cover every possible distribution. In particular, any distribution can be expressed as

$$\text{Pr}'(\mathbf{X}|\mathbf{e}) = \frac{\prod_{\mathbf{C}} \text{Pr}'(\mathbf{C}|\mathbf{e})}{\prod_{\mathbf{S}} \text{Pr}'(\mathbf{S}|\mathbf{e})}, \tag{14.5}$$

where $\mathbf{C}$ and $\mathbf{S}$ are sets of variables. If the approximate distribution Pr′ is assumed to take the form in (14.5), then its entropy can also be expressed as follows.

Theorem 14.3. *If a distribution* Pr′ *has the form*

$$\text{Pr}'(\mathbf{X}|\mathbf{e}) = \frac{\prod_{\mathbf{C}} \text{Pr}'(\mathbf{C}|\mathbf{e})}{\prod_{\mathbf{S}} \text{Pr}'(\mathbf{S}|\mathbf{e})},$$

then its entropy has the form

$$\text{ENT}'(\mathbf{X}|\mathbf{e}) = \sum_{\mathbf{C}} \text{ENT}'(\mathbf{C}|\mathbf{e}) - \sum_{\mathbf{S}} \text{ENT}'(\mathbf{S}|\mathbf{e}). \qquad \blacksquare$$

This immediately means that when the marginals Pr′$(\mathbf{C}|\mathbf{e})$ and Pr′$(\mathbf{S}|\mathbf{e})$ are readily available, the ENT component of the KL divergence can be computed efficiently. In fact, if we further assume that each family $X\mathbf{U}$ of the original Bayesian network is contained in some set $\mathbf{C}$ or set $\mathbf{S}$, then the AVE component of the KL divergence is also computable efficiently. Hence, given the functional form in (14.5), marginals that minimize the KL divergence will maximize

$$\text{ENT}'(\mathbf{X}|\mathbf{e}) + \sum_{X\mathbf{U}} \text{AVG}'(\log \lambda_{\mathbf{e}}(X)\Theta_{X|\mathbf{U}})$$

$$= -\sum_{\mathbf{C}} \sum_{\mathbf{c}} \mu_{\mathbf{c}} \log \mu_{\mathbf{c}} + \sum_{\mathbf{S}} \sum_{\mathbf{s}} \mu_{\mathbf{s}} \log \mu_{\mathbf{s}} + \sum_{X\mathbf{U}} \sum_{x\mathbf{u}} \mu_{x\mathbf{u}} \log \lambda_{\mathbf{e}}(x)\theta_{x|\mathbf{u}},$$

where $\mu_{\mathbf{c}}$, $\mu_{\mathbf{s}}$ and $\mu_{x\mathbf{u}}$ denote Pr′$(\mathbf{c}|\mathbf{e})$, Pr′$(\mathbf{s}|\mathbf{e})$, and Pr′$(x\mathbf{u}|\mathbf{e})$, respectively.

We saw in Section 9.4.3 that the probability distribution induced by a Bayesian network $\mathcal{N}$ can always be factored as given in (14.5) as long as the sets $\mathbf{C}$ correspond to the clusters of a jointree for $\mathcal{N}$ and the sets $\mathbf{S}$ correspond to the separators. As we shall see, if we base

---

[3] Note, however, that these normalization and consistency constraints are not sufficient in general to ensure that the marginals μ_u and $\mu_{x\mathbf{u}}$ are globally consistent, that is, that they correspond to some distribution.

our factorization on a jointree and assert some normalization and local consistency constraints among cluster and separator marginals, solving the previous optimization problem yields the same update equations of the jointree algorithm. Moreover, the quantities μ_c and μ_s obtained will correspond to the exact cluster and separator marginals.

A factorization based on a jointree leads to an expensive optimization problem whose complexity is not less than that of the jointree algorithm itself. Hence, the factorization used by IBP in (14.3) and the factorization based on jointrees can be viewed as two extremes: one being quite efficient but possibly quite approximate and one being expensive but leading to exact results. However, there is a spectrum of other factorizations that fall in between the two extremes, allowing a trade-off between the quality of approximations and the efficiency of computing them. The notion of a joingraph is one way to obtain such a spectrum of factorizations and is discussed next.

14.6 Joingraphs

Joingraphs are a generalization of jointrees that can be used to obtain factorizations according to (14.5). Joingraphs are also used in the following section to formulate a message-passing algorithm that is analogous to iterative belief propagation and is thus referred to as iterative joingraph propagation. We can define joingraphs in a manner similar to how we defined jointrees.

Definition 14.1. A *joingraph* G for network $\mathcal{N}$ is a graph where nodes i are labeled by clusters $\mathbf{C}_i$ and edges $i–j$ are labeled by separators $\mathbf{S}_{ij}$. Moreover, G satisfies the following properties:

1. Clusters $\mathbf{C}_i$ and separators $\mathbf{S}_{ij}$ are sets of nodes from network $\mathcal{N}$.
2. Each family in $\mathcal{N}$ must appear in some cluster $\mathbf{C}_i$.
3. If a node X appears in two clusters $\mathbf{C}_i$ and $\mathbf{C}_j$, then there exists a path connecting i and j in the joingraph such that X appears in every cluster and separator on that path.
4. For every edge $i–j$ in the joingraph, $\mathbf{S}_{ij} \subseteq \mathbf{C}_i \cap \mathbf{C}_j$.   ∎

We can think of a joingraph as a way of relaxing certain constraints asserted by a jointree. For example, suppose that two clusters $\mathbf{C}_i$ and $\mathbf{C}_j$ in a jointree share a set of variables $\mathbf{X}$. Then every cluster and every separator on the path connecting $\mathbf{C}_i$ and $\mathbf{C}_j$ must contain the set $\mathbf{X}$. We relax this constraint in a joingraph and assert only that each variable $X \in \mathbf{X}$ be contained in the clusters and separators on some path connecting $\mathbf{C}_i$ and $\mathbf{C}_j$ (Property 3). Although both properties imply that any variable X must be connected in the embedded graph induced by X, the jointree imposes a stronger constraint. Similarly, we do not require separators $\mathbf{S}_{ij}$ to be precisely the intersection of clusters $\mathbf{C}_i$ and $\mathbf{C}_j$ (Property 4), as is the case for jointrees.

Although a jointree induces an exact factorization of a distribution (see Section 9.4.3), a joingraph G induces an approximate factorization,

$$\text{Pr}'(\mathbf{X}|\mathbf{e}) = \frac{\prod_i \text{Pr}'(\mathbf{C}_i|\mathbf{e})}{\prod_{ij} \text{Pr}'(\mathbf{S}_{ij}|\mathbf{e})}, \tag{14.6}$$

which is a product of cluster marginals over a product of separator marginals. When the joingraph corresponds to a jointree, this factorization will be exact.

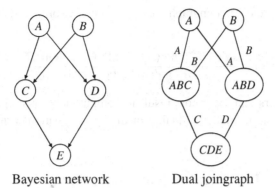

Figure 14.4: A Bayesian network and its corresponding dual joingraph.

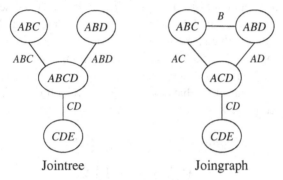

Figure 14.5: A jointree and a joingraph for the network in Figure 14.4.

If we use a special joingraph called the *dual joingraph,* the factorization in (14.6) reduces to that in (14.3), which is used by IBP. A dual joingraph G for network $\mathcal{N}$ is obtained as follows:

- G has the same undirected structure of network $\mathcal{N}$.
- For each family $X\mathbf{U}$ in network $\mathcal{N}$, the corresponding node i in joingraph G will have the cluster $\mathbf{C}_i = X\mathbf{U}$.
- For each $U \to X$ in network $\mathcal{N}$, the corresponding edge i–j in joingraph G will have the separator $\mathbf{S}_{ij} = U$.

In Figure 14.4, the dual joingraph is given on the right and induces the factorization

$$\Pr'(\mathbf{X}|\mathbf{e}) = \frac{\Pr'(A|\mathbf{e})\Pr'(B|\mathbf{e})\Pr'(ABC|\mathbf{e})\Pr'(ABD|\mathbf{e})\Pr'(CDE|\mathbf{e})}{\Pr'(A|\mathbf{e})^2\Pr'(B|\mathbf{e})^2\Pr'(C|\mathbf{e})\Pr'(D|\mathbf{e})},$$

which is the same factorization used by IBP. Hence, iterative joingraph propagation (which we discuss in the following section) subsumes iterative belief propagation. The jointree in Figure 14.5 induces the following factorization, which is exact:

$$\Pr'(\mathbf{X}|\mathbf{e}) = \frac{\Pr'(ABC|\mathbf{e})\Pr'(ABD|\mathbf{e})\Pr'(ABCD|\mathbf{e})\Pr'(CDE|\mathbf{e})}{\Pr'(ABC|\mathbf{e})\Pr'(ABD|\mathbf{e})\Pr'(CD|\mathbf{e})}.$$

Figure 14.5 depicts another joingraph for the given network, leading to the following factorization:

$$Pr'(\mathbf{X}|\mathbf{e}) = \frac{Pr'(ABC|\mathbf{e})Pr'(ABD|\mathbf{e})Pr'(ACD|\mathbf{e})Pr'(CDE|\mathbf{e})}{Pr'(B|\mathbf{e})Pr'(AC|\mathbf{e})Pr'(AD|\mathbf{e})Pr'(CD|\mathbf{e})}.$$

Since smaller clusters and separators result in computationally simpler problems, joingraphs allow us a way to trade the quality of the approximation with the complexity of computing it.

14.7 Iterative joingraph propagation

Suppose that we have a Bayesian network $\mathcal{N}$ that induces a distribution Pr and a corresponding joingraph that induces a factorization Pr', as given in (14.6). Suppose further that we want to compute cluster marginals $\mu_{\mathbf{c}_i} = Pr'(\mathbf{c}_i|\mathbf{e})$ and separator marginals $\mu_{\mathbf{s}_{ij}} = Pr'(\mathbf{s}_{ij}|\mathbf{e})$ that minimize the KL divergence between $Pr'(\mathbf{X}|\mathbf{e})$ and $Pr(\mathbf{X}|\mathbf{e})$. This optimization problem can be solved using a generalization of IBP called *iterative joingraph propagation* (IJGP), which is a message-passing algorithm that operates on a joingraph. In particular, the algorithm starts by assigning each network CPT $\Theta_{X|\mathbf{U}}$ and evidence indicator $\lambda_{\mathbf{e}}(X)$ to some cluster $\mathbf{C}_i$ that contains family $X\mathbf{U}$. It then propagates messages using the following equations:

$$BEL(\mathbf{C}_i) = \eta\ \Phi_i \prod_k M_{ki}$$

$$M_{ij} = \eta \sum_{\mathbf{C}_i \backslash \mathbf{S}_{ij}} \Phi_i \prod_{k \neq j} M_{ki},$$

where Φ_i is the product of all CPTs and evidence indicators assigned to cluster $\mathbf{C}_i$, M_{ij} is the message sent from cluster i to cluster j, η is a normalizing constant, and $BEL(\mathbf{C}_i)$ is the approximation to cluster marginal $Pr(\mathbf{C}_i|\mathbf{e})$. We can also use the algorithm to approximate the separator marginal $Pr(\mathbf{S}_{ij}|\mathbf{e})$ as follows:

$$BEL(\mathbf{S}_{ij}) = \eta\ M_{ij}M_{ji}.$$

IJGP is given in Algorithm 41 and resembles IBP as given in Algorithm 40 except that we only have one type of messages when operating on a joingraph. Note that we are using a parallel message-passing schedule in Algorithm 41 but we can use sequential schedules as in IBP. Note also that if IJGP is applied to the dual joingraph of the given network, it reduces to IBP. The semantics of IJGP is also a generalization of the semantics for IBP, as shown next.

Theorem 14.4. *Let* $Pr(\mathbf{X})$ *be a distribution induced by a Bayesian network* $\mathcal{N}$ *having families* $X\mathbf{U}$ *and let* $\mathbf{C}_i$ *and* $\mathbf{S}_{ij}$ *be the clusters and separators of a joingraph for* $\mathcal{N}$. *Then messages* M_{ij} *are a fixed point of* IJGP *if and only if* IJGP *marginals* $\mu_{\mathbf{c}_i} = BEL(\mathbf{c}_i)$ *and* $\mu_{\mathbf{s}_{ij}} = BEL(\mathbf{s}_{ij})$ *are a stationary point of*

$$ENT'(\mathbf{X}|\mathbf{e}) + \sum_{\mathbf{C}_i} AVG'(\log \Phi_i)$$

$$= -\sum_{\mathbf{C}_i}\sum_{\mathbf{c}_i} \mu_{\mathbf{c}_i} \log \mu_{\mathbf{c}_i} + \sum_{\mathbf{S}_{ij}}\sum_{\mathbf{s}_{ij}} \mu_{\mathbf{s}_{ij}} \log \mu_{\mathbf{s}_{ij}} + \sum_{\mathbf{C}_i}\sum_{\mathbf{c}_i} \mu_{\mathbf{c}_i} \log \Phi_i(\mathbf{c}_i),$$

Algorithm 41 IJGP(G, Φ)

---

input:

G: a joingraph

Φ: factors assigned to clusters of G

output: approximate marginal $BEL(\mathbf{C}_i)$ for each node i in the joingraph G

main:

1:   $t \leftarrow 0$

2:   initialize all messages M_{ij}^t (uniformly)

3:   **while** messages have not converged **do**

4:      $t \leftarrow t + 1$

5:      **for** each joingraph edge i–j **do**

6:          $M_{ij}^t \leftarrow \eta \sum_{\mathbf{C}_i \backslash \mathbf{S}_{ij}} \Phi_i \prod_{k \neq j} M_{ki}^{t-1}$

7:          $M_{ji}^t \leftarrow \eta \sum_{\mathbf{C}_j \backslash \mathbf{S}_{ij}} \Phi_j \prod_{k \neq i} M_{kj}^{t-1}$

8:      **end for**

9:   **end while**

10: **return** $BEL(\mathbf{C}_i) \leftarrow \eta \, \Phi_i \prod_k M_{ki}^t$ for each node i

---

under normalization constraints,

$$\sum_{\mathbf{c}_i} \mu_{\mathbf{c}_i} = \sum_{\mathbf{s}_{ij}} \mu_{\mathbf{s}_{ij}} = 1$$

for each cluster $\mathbf{C}_i$ and separator $\mathbf{S}_{ij}$, and under consistency constraints,

$$\sum_{\mathbf{c}_i \sim \mathbf{s}_{ij}} \mu_{\mathbf{c}_i} = \mu_{\mathbf{s}_{ij}} = \sum_{\mathbf{c}_j \sim \mathbf{s}_{ij}} \mu_{\mathbf{c}_j} \tag{14.7}$$

for each separator $\mathbf{S}_{ij}$ and neighboring clusters $\mathbf{C}_i$ and $\mathbf{C}_j$.   ■

We now have an algorithm that provides a spectrum of approximations. On one end is IBP, which results from applying IJGP to the dual joingraph of the given network. On the other end is the jointree algorithm, which results from applying IJGP to a jointree (as a joingraph). Between these two ends, we have a spectrum of joingraphs and corresponding factorizations, where IJGP seeks stationary points of the KL divergence between these factorizations and the original distribution.

One way to see the effect of a joingraph on the approximation quality is by considering the local consistency constraints given by (14.7) and the extent to which they are sufficient to ensure global consistency of the corresponding marginals. Consider, for example, the jointree in Figure 14.5. Since clusters ABC and $ABCD$ are consistent with respect to their marginals on variables AB and clusters $ABCD$ and ABD are consistent on variables AB, we can infer that clusters ABC and ABD are consistent on variables AB as well. However, when we consider the joingraph in Figure 14.5 we see that although clusters ABC and ABD are consistent on A and also consistent on B, we are not necessarily guaranteed they are consistent on variables AB. This lack of global consistency highlights the fact that although IBP and IJGP may be able to provide accurate approximations, the approximate marginals they produce may not correspond to any real distribution. We explore a more concrete example of this issue in Exercise 14.1.

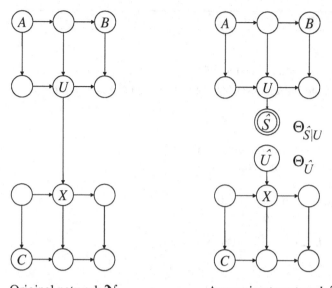

(a) Original network $\mathcal{N}$,
     original distribution Pr,
     original evidence **e**

(b) Approximate network $\mathcal{N}'$,
     approximate distribution Pr',
     approximate evidence **e'**

Figure 14.6: Deleting the edge $U \to X$. Network $\mathcal{N}$ comes with evidence $\mathbf{e} = \bar{a}, b, \bar{c}$. This evidence is copied to network $\mathcal{N}'$ in addition to the new evidence $\hat{s}$, leading to $\mathbf{e}' = \bar{a}, b, \bar{c}, \hat{s}$.

14.8 Edge-deletion semantics of belief propagation

We present an alternative semantics of belief propagation in this section and use it as a basis for an alternative formulation of generalized belief propagation.

Consider the network in Figure 14.6(a) and suppose that we delete the edge $U \to X$ as shown in Figure 14.6(b). That is, we first remove the edge and then add two new variables:

- A variable $\hat{U}$ that has the same values as U and is meant to be a *clone* of variable U.
- A variable $\hat{S}$ that has two values and is meant to assert *soft evidence* on variable U (hence, $\hat{S}$ is assumed to be observed).

We later provide some intuition on why we added these variables but the main question we raise now is as follows: To what extent can the network in Figure 14.6(b) approximate the one in Figure 14.6(a)? In particular, to what extent can a query on the original network be approximated by a query on the edge-deleted network? This question is significant because we can use this technique of deleting edges to reduce the treewidth of a given network to the point where exact inference can be applied efficiently. Hence, we can use this edge-deletion technique to cast the problem of approximate inference as a problem of exact inference on an approximate network. Interestingly enough, we show in this section that belief propagation can be understood as a degenerate case of this approximation paradigm. In particular, we show that belief propagation corresponds to deleting each and every edge in the Bayesian network. Not only will these semantics provide new insights into belief propagation but they also provide another formulation of generalized belief propagation with a specific method for trading the approximation quality with computational resources.

However, before we proceed we will need to settle some notational conventions that we use consistently in the rest of the chapter. We use $\mathcal{N}$, Pr, and **e** to represent an original Bayesian network, its induced probability distribution, and its corresponding evidence, respectively. We also use $\mathcal{N}'$, Pr$'$, and **e**$'$ to represent the corresponding approximate network, distribution, and evidence. Our goal here is to approximate queries of the form Pr$(\alpha|\mathbf{e})$ by queries of the form Pr$'(\alpha|\mathbf{e}')$. The evidence **e**$'$ always consists of the original evidence **e** and the value $\hat{s}$ for each variable $\hat{S}$ added to network $\mathcal{N}'$ during edge deletion (see Figure 14.6).

14.8.1 Edge parameters

Consider Figure 14.6 again, which depicts a network $\mathcal{N}$ and one of its approximations $\mathcal{N}'$. We cannot use the approximate network $\mathcal{N}'$ before specifying the CPTs for the newly added variables $\hat{U}$ and $\hat{S}$. These CPTs, $\Theta_{\hat{U}}$ and $\Theta_{\hat{S}|U}$, are called parameters for the deleted edge $U \to X$, or simply *edge parameters*.

Interestingly enough, if the deleted edge splits the network into two disconnected subnetworks, as is the case with Figure 14.6, then we can find edge parameters that guarantee exact node marginals in the approximate network.

Theorem 14.5. *Suppose that we delete a single edge $U \to X$ that splits the network into two disconnected subnetworks. Suppose further that the parameters of deleted edge $U \to X$ satisfy the following conditions:*

$$\Theta_{\hat{U}} = \text{Pr}'(U|\mathbf{e}' - \hat{S}) \tag{14.8}$$

$$\Theta_{\hat{S}|U} = \eta \, \text{Pr}'(\mathbf{e}'|\hat{U}), \text{ for some constant } \eta > 0. \tag{14.9}$$

It then follows that $\text{Pr}(Q|\mathbf{e}) = \text{Pr}'(Q|\mathbf{e}')$ *for every variable Q and evidence* **e**. ■

According to Theorem 14.5, if we choose the CPTs $\Theta_{\hat{U}}$ and $\Theta_{\hat{S}|U}$ carefully, then we can replace each query Pr$(Q|\mathbf{e})$ on the original network with a query Pr$'(Q|\mathbf{e}')$ on the approximate network while being guaranteed to obtain the same result. Recall that $\mathbf{e}' - \hat{S}$ denotes the evidence that results from retracting the value of variable $\hat{S}$ from evidence $\mathbf{e}'$. Note also that checking whether some edge parameters satisfy (14.8) and (14.9) can be accomplished by performing inference on the approximate network. That is, all we need to do is plug the edge parameters $\Theta_{\hat{U}}$ and $\Theta_{\hat{S}|U}$ into the approximate network $\mathcal{N}'$, compute the quantities Pr$'(U|\mathbf{e}' - \hat{S})$ and Pr$'(\mathbf{e}'|\hat{U})$ by performing inference on the approximate network, and finally check whether (14.8) and (14.9) are satisfied.

Consider now Figure 14.6, which leads to the following instance of (14.8) and (14.9):

$$\Theta_{\hat{U}} = \text{Pr}'(U|\bar{a}, b, \bar{c}) \tag{14.10}$$

$$\Theta_{\hat{S}|U} = \eta \, \text{Pr}'(\bar{a}, b, \bar{c}, \hat{s}|\hat{U}). \tag{14.11}$$

According to Exercise 14.8, these equations simplify to

$$\Theta_{\hat{U}} = \text{Pr}'(U|\bar{a}, b) \tag{14.12}$$

$$\Theta_{\hat{S}|U} = \eta \, \text{Pr}'(\bar{c}|\hat{U}). \tag{14.13}$$

Recall here that the edge $U \to X$ splits the network of Figure 14.6(a) into two disconnected subnetworks. Note also that the evidence $\bar{a}, b$ is part of one subnetwork (containing U), while the evidence $\bar{c}$ is part of the other subnetwork (containing $\hat{U}$). Hence, the CPT for clone $\hat{U}$ can be viewed as summarizing the impact of evidence $\bar{a}, b$ on variable U – this evidence is now disconnected from the subnetwork containing $\hat{U}$. Similarly, the CPT for variable $\hat{S}$ is summarizing the impact of evidence $\bar{c}$ on the clone $\hat{U}$ – this evidence is also disconnected from the subnetwork containing variable U. Hence, edge parameters are playing the role of communication devices between the disconnected subnetworks.

We finally point out that the edge parameters of Theorem 14.5 come with a stronger guarantee than the one suggested by the theorem. In particular, not only will node marginals be exact but also the marginal over any set of variables that appears on the U-side of edge $U \rightarrow X$ or on the X-side of that edge (see Exercise 14.14).

14.8.2 Deleting multiple edges

We have thus far considered an idealized case: deleting a single edge that splits the network into two disconnected subnetworks. We also provided edge parameters that guarantee exact results when computing node marginals in the edge-deleted network.

We now consider the more general case of deleting multiple edges, where each edge may or may not split the network. This leaves us with the question of which edge parameters to use in this case, as the conditions of Theorem 14.5 will no longer hold. As it turns out, if we use these edge parameters while deleting every edge in the network, we obtain the same node marginals that are obtained by iterative belief propagation. This result is shown by the following corollary of a more general theorem that we present later (Theorem 14.6).

Corollary 3. *Suppose that we delete all edges of a Bayesian network $\mathcal{N}$ and then set edge parameters according to (14.8) and (14.9). For each deleted edge $U \rightarrow X$, the message values $\pi_X(U) = \Theta_{\hat{U}}$ and $\lambda_X(U) = \Theta_{\hat{S}|U}$ represent a fixed point for iterative belief propagation on network $\mathcal{N}$. Moreover, under this fixed point, $BEL(X) = \Pr'(X|\mathbf{e}')$ for every variable X.* ∎

According to this result, iterative belief propagation corresponds to a degenerate case in which we delete every network edge. Therefore, we can potentially improve on the approximations of iterative belief propagation by working with an approximate network that results from deleting fewer edges. We address this topic in Section 14.8.4 but we first show how we can search for edge parameters that satisfy (14.8) and (14.9).

14.8.3 Searching for edge parameters

We now consider an iterative procedure for finding edge parameters that satisfy (14.8) and (14.9), assuming that an arbitrary number of edges have been deleted. We then provide a stronger correspondence between the resulting algorithm and iterative belief propagation.

According to this procedure, we start with an approximate network $\mathcal{N}'_0$ in which all edge parameters $\Theta^0_{\hat{U}}$ and $\Theta^0_{\hat{S}|U}$ are initialized, say, uniformly. Let $\Pr'_0$ be the distribution induced by this network. For each iteration $t > 0$, the edge parameters for network $\mathcal{N}'_t$ are determined by performing exact inference on the approximate network $\mathcal{N}'_{t-1}$ as follows:

$$\Theta^t_{\hat{U}} = \Pr'_{t-1}(U|\mathbf{e}' - \hat{S}) \tag{14.14}$$

$$\Theta^t_{\hat{S}|U} = \eta \, \Pr'_{t-1}(\mathbf{e}'|\hat{U}). \tag{14.15}$$

If the edge parameters for network $\mathcal{N}_t$ are the same as those for network $\mathcal{N}_{t-1}$ (or within some threshold), we stop and say the edge parameters we found represent a fixed point of the iterative algorithm. If not, we continue iterating until we reach a fixed point (if any).

Algorithm 42 ED_BP($\mathcal{N}$, **e**, Σ)

---

input:

   $\mathcal{N}$:   a Bayesian network

   e: an instantiation of some variables in network $\mathcal{N}$

   Σ: a set of edges in $\mathcal{N}$

output: approximate network $\mathcal{N}'$

main:

  1: $t \leftarrow 0$

  2: $\mathcal{N}'_0 \leftarrow$ result of deleting edges Σ in $\mathcal{N}$

  3: $\mathbf{e}' \leftarrow \mathbf{e}$ plus $\hat{s}$ for each added node $\hat{S}$ to $\mathcal{N}'$

  4: initialize all edge parameters $\Theta_{\hat{U}}^0$ and $\Theta_{\hat{s}|U}^0$ (uniformly)

  5: **while** edge parameters have not converged **do**

  6:    $t \leftarrow t + 1$

  7:    **for** each edge $U \rightarrow X$ in network $\mathcal{N}$ **do**

  8:       $\Theta_{\hat{U}}^t \leftarrow \text{Pr}'_{t-1}(U|\mathbf{e}' - \hat{S})$

  9:       $\Theta_{\hat{s}|U}^t \leftarrow \eta \, \text{Pr}'_{t-1}(\mathbf{e}'|\hat{U})$ $\{\eta$ is typically chosen to normalize $\Theta_{\hat{s}|U}^t$, that is, $\eta = 1/\sum_{\hat{u}} \text{Pr}'_{t-1}(\mathbf{e}'|\hat{u})\}$

 10:    **end for**

 11: **end while**

 12: **return** $\mathcal{N}'_t$

This iterative procedure, called ED_BP, is summarized in Algorithm 42. Figure 14.7 depicts a network that results from deleting an edge, and Figure 14.8 depicts the iterations of ED_BP as it searches for the parameters of this edge. Note that ED_BP converges after four iterations in this case.

Algorithm 42, ED_BP, corresponds to Algorithm 40, IBP, in the following sense.

Theorem 14.6. *Let $\mathcal{N}'$ be a Bayesian network that results from deleting every edge from network $\mathcal{N}$. Suppose we run IBP on network $\mathcal{N}$ and ED_BP on network $\mathcal{N}'$, where initially all $\pi_X^0(U) = \Theta_{\hat{U}}^0$ and all $\lambda_X^0(U) = \Theta_{\hat{s}|U}^0$. For each edge $U \rightarrow X$ in network $\mathcal{N}$ and each iteration t, we have*

- $\pi_X^t(U) = \Theta_{\hat{U}}^t$
- $\lambda_X^t(U) = \Theta_{\hat{s}|U}^t$.

Moreover, for all variables X in network $\mathcal{N}$ and each iteration t, we have

- $BEL_t(X) = \text{Pr}'_t(X|\mathbf{e}')$
- $BEL_t(X\mathbf{U}) = \text{Pr}'_t(X\hat{\mathbf{U}}|\mathbf{e}')$, *where $\mathbf{U}$ are the parents of variable X in network $\mathcal{N}$ and $\hat{\mathbf{U}}$ are its parents in network $\mathcal{N}'$.* ∎

This correspondence tells us that IBP is in fact searching for the edge parameters of a fully disconnected network. Moreover, the messages computed by IBP contain precisely the values of edge parameters computed by ED_BP.

Interestingly enough, we can obtain a similar correspondence between ED_BP and IBP as long as we delete enough edges to render the network a polytree. In particular, suppose the network $\mathcal{N}$ has n nodes. When deleting edges, all we need is to generate a polytree with

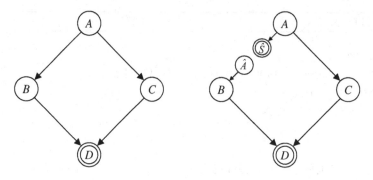

    (a) Evidence **e** : D=true   (b) Evidence **e'** : D=true, $\hat{S}$=true

A	Θ_A
true	.8
false	.2

A	B	$\Theta_{B\mid A} = \Theta_{B\mid \hat{A}}$
true	true	.8
true	false	.2
false	true	.4
false	false	.6

A	C	$\Theta_{C\mid A}$
true	true	.5
true	false	.5
false	true	1.0
false	false	.0

B	C	D	$\Theta_{D\mid BC}$
true	true	true	.1
true	true	false	.9
true	false	true	.3
true	false	false	.7
false	true	true	.9
false	true	false	.1
false	false	true	.8
false	false	false	.2

$\hat{A}$	$\Theta_{\hat{A}}$
true	.8262
false	.1738

A	$\hat{S}$	$\Theta_{\hat{S}\mid A}$
true	true	.3438
true	false	.6562
false	true	.6562
false	false	.3438

Figure 14.7: A network (a) and its approximation (b) that results from deleting edge $A \rightarrow B$ and then running Algorithm 42, ED_BP. The CPTs $\Theta_{\hat{A}}$ and $\Theta_{\hat{S}\mid A}$ are obtained after the convergence of ED_BP (see Figure 14.8).

		$t = 0$	$t = 1$	$t = 2$	$t = 3$	$t = 4$
$\Theta_{\hat{S}=\text{true}\mid A}$	A=true	.5000	.3496	.3440	.3438	.3438
	A=false	.5000	.6504	.6560	.6562	.6562
$\Theta_{\hat{A}}$	$\hat{A}$=true	.5000	.8142	.8257	.8262	.8262
	$\hat{A}$=false	.5000	.1858	.1743	.1738	.1738

Figure 14.8: Edge parameters computed by Algorithm 42, ED_BP, in the approximate network of Figure 14.7(b).

no more than $n - 1$ edges. If we keep exactly $n - 1$ original edges, we have a maximal polytree, which is a spanning tree of nodes in the original network. If we keep zero edges, we have a fully disconnected network as in Theorem 14.6. Between these extremes, there is a spectrum of polytrees (see Figure 14.9). Yet if we run ED_BP on any of these polytrees, the family marginals we obtain will correspond to those obtained by IBP. For an example consider Figure 14.7, which depicts a network $\mathcal{N}'$ that results from deleting a single edge $A \rightarrow B$ in network $\mathcal{N}$. Since the approximate network $\mathcal{N}'$ is a polytree, it yields family

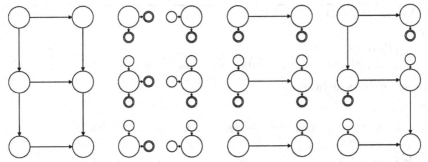

Figure 14.9: Three polytrees (right) that result from deleting edges from the Bayesian network on the far left. The polytree on the far right is maximal.

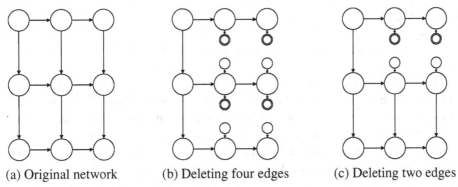

(a) Original network (b) Deleting four edges (c) Deleting two edges

Figure 14.10: Deleting edges in a Bayesian network.

marginals that correspond to those obtained by running belief propagation on network $\mathcal{N}$ (see also Exercise 14.10).

Intuitively, we expect that a polytree network that results from deleting fewer edges should in general lead to different (and better) approximations. This intuition is indeed correct but the difference appears only when considering the marginal for a set of variables that does not belong to any network family. We find a need for computing such marginals in the following section, leading us to favor maximal polytrees when applying Algorithm 42, ED_BP.

14.8.4 Choosing edges to delete (or recover)

Deleting every edge is obviously the coarsest approximation we can expect. In practic, we only need to delete enough edges to render the resulting network amenable to exact inference. Figure 14.10 depicts a network and two potential approximations. The approximate network in Figure 14.10(b) is a polytree and leads to the same approximations obtained by iterative belief propagation. The network in Figure 14.10(c) results from deleting fewer edges and leads to a better approximation.

Deciding which edges to delete in general requires inference, which is not possible on networks that we are interested in approximating. An alternative approach is to delete too many edges and then recover some of them. For example, the network in Figure 14.10(c) can be viewed as the result of recovering two edges in the network of Figure 14.10(b). The difference here is that deciding which edges to recover can be accomplished by performing

---

Algorithm 43 ER($\mathcal{N}$, **e**)

---

input:

   $\mathcal{N}$:   a Bayesian network

   e: an instantiation of some variables in network $\mathcal{N}$

output: approximate network $\mathcal{N}'$

main:

  1: $\Sigma \leftarrow$ a set of edges whose deletion renders $\mathcal{N}$ a maximal polytree

  2: $\mathcal{N}' \leftarrow$ ED_BP($\mathcal{N}$, **e**, Σ)

  3: **while** recovery of edges in $\mathcal{N}'$ is amenable to exact inference **do**

  4:     rank deleted edges $U \rightarrow X$ based on MI($U; \hat{U}|\mathbf{e}'$)

  5:     $\Sigma \leftarrow \Sigma \setminus \{$top k edges with the largest scores$\}$

  6:     $\mathcal{N}' \leftarrow$ ED_BP($\mathcal{N}$, **e**, Σ)

  7: **end while**

  8: **return** $\mathcal{N}'$

---

inference on an approximate network, which we know is feasible. Our strategy is then be as follows: We first delete enough edges to render the network a maximal polytree. We next perform inference on the approximate network to rank all deleted edges according to their impact on improving the approximation quality. We then recover some of the edges whose recovery will have the best impact on approximation quality. This process is repeated until we reach a network that becomes inaccessible to exact inference if more edges are added to it.

The key to this approach is that of assessing the impact a recovered edge will have on improving approximation quality. Before we proceed on this question, recall that when deleting an edge $U \rightarrow X$ that splits the network, Algorithm 42, ED_BP, can identify edge parameters that lead to exact node marginals. But what if deleting the edge $U \rightarrow X$ does not fully split the network yet comes close to this?

The intuition here is to rank edges based on the extent to which they split the network. One method for doing this is by measuring the mutual information between variable U and its clone $\hat{U}$ in the approximate network:

$$\text{MI}(U; \hat{U}|\mathbf{e}') = \sum_{u\hat{u}} \text{Pr}'(u\hat{u}|\mathbf{e}') \log \frac{\text{Pr}'(u\hat{u}|\mathbf{e}')}{\text{Pr}'(u|\mathbf{e}')\text{Pr}'(\hat{u}|\mathbf{e}')}.$$

If deleting edge $U \rightarrow X$ splits the network into two, the mutual information between U and $\hat{U}$ is zero. Since edge deletion leads to exact results in this case, there is no point in recovering the corresponding edge. On the other hand, if MI($U; \hat{U}|\mathbf{e}'$) is not zero, then edge $U \rightarrow X$ does not split the network. Moreover, the value of MI($U; \hat{U}|\mathbf{e}'$) can be viewed as a measure of the extent to which edge $U \rightarrow X$ splits the network, leading us to favor the recovery of edges that have a larger value of MI($U; \hat{U}|\mathbf{e}'$).

Algorithm 43, ER, summarizes this proposal for edge recovery. First, we choose an initial network based on a maximal polytree embedded in the given network $\mathcal{N}$ and parameterize the deleted edges using Algorithm 42, ED_BP. Next, we use the resulting approximation to compute the joint marginals $\text{Pr}'(u\hat{u}|\mathbf{e}')$ needed for the mutual information scores. Finally, we recover the top k edges using our mutual information heuristic and run ED_BP again on a more connected network $\mathcal{N}'$, resulting in a more structured

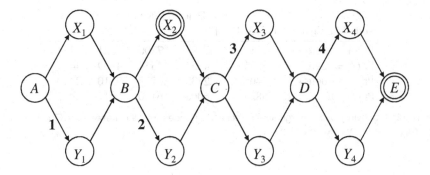

							X_1	Y_1	B	$\Theta_{B\mid X_1 Y_1}$
							true	true	true	1
							true	true	false	0
A	X_1	$\Theta_{X_1\mid A}$	A	Y_1	$\Theta_{Y_1\mid A}$		true	false	true	.1
true	true	.75	true	true	.9		true	false	false	.9
true	false	.25	true	false	.1		false	true	true	.2
false	true	.25	false	true	.1		false	true	false	.8
false	false	.75	false	false	.9		false	false	true	0
							false	false	false	1

Figure 14.11: Variables $X_1, \ldots, X_4$ have the same CPTs and so do variables $Y_1, \ldots, Y_4$ and variables B, C, D and E. Variable A has $\Pr(A = \text{true}) = .8$. Evidence e is $X_2 = \text{false}, E = \text{true}$.

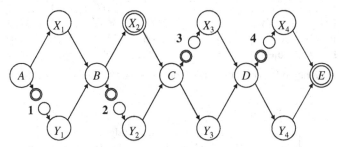

Figure 14.12: Deleting four edges in the network of Figure 14.11.

approximation. We can repeat this process of ranking deleted edges and recovering them as long as we can afford to perform exact inference on network $\mathbf{N}'$. Although we can recover as many edges as possible after the initial ranking of edges, we expect that our mutual information heuristic will become more accurate as more edges are recovered, leading to better quality approximations. On the other hand, we should also keep in mind that the cost of re-ranking edges increases as more edges are recovered. Exercise 14.15 proposes an efficient scheme for ranking deleted edges based on mutual information, which is important for a practical implementation of Algorithm 43.

Figure 14.13 illustrates an example where we recover edges into the network of Figure 14.12, one edge at a time, until all edges are recovered. Edge recovery is based on the mutual information heuristic as shown in Figure 14.14. Note that the edge labeled 2 does not improve any of the reported approximations. In fact, if we recovered this edge first, we would see no improvement in approximation quality. This is shown in Figures 14.15 and 14.16, where we recover edges with the smallest mutual information first. We see here that the approximations improve more modestly (if at all) than those in Figure 14.13.

Node Marginals	Deleted Edges				
	$\{1, 2, 3, 4\}$	$\{2, 3, 4\}$	$\{2, 3\}$	$\{2\}$	$\{\}$
$\Pr'(A=\text{true}\|e')$	.7114	.7290	.7300	.7331	.7331
$\Pr'(B=\text{true}\|e')$	.3585	.4336	.4358	.4429	.4429
$\Pr'(C=\text{true}\|e')$	.2405	.2733	.2775	.2910	.2910
$\Pr'(D=\text{true}\|e')$	.5824	.6008	.6100	.5917	.5917

Figure 14.13: Improving node marginals by recovering edges into the network of Figure 14.12. The marginals in the far right column are exact.

Edge Scores	Deleted Edges				
	$\{1, 2, 3, 4\}$	$\{2, 3, 4\}$	$\{2, 3\}$	$\{2\}$	$\{\}$
$A \rightarrow Y_1$ (1)	$\mathbf{1.13 \times 10^{-3}}$				
$B \rightarrow Y_2$ (2)	0	0	0	**0**	
$C \rightarrow X_3$ (3)	6.12×10^{-4}	7.26×10^{-4}	$\mathbf{6.98 \times 10^{-4}}$		
$D \rightarrow X_4$ (4)	1.12×10^{-3}	$\mathbf{1.08 \times 10^{-3}}$			

Figure 14.14: Scoring deleted edges in the network of Figure 14.12. Scores corresponding to largest mutual information are shown in bold. Based on these scores, edges are recovered according to the order 1, 4, 3, and then 2.

Node Marginals	Deleted Edges				
	$\{1, 2, 3, 4\}$	$\{1, 3, 4\}$	$\{1, 4\}$	$\{4\}$	$\{\}$
$\Pr'(A=\text{true}\|e')$	.7114	.7114	.7160	.7324	.7331
$\Pr'(B=\text{true}\|e')$	.3585	.3585	.3681	.4412	.4429
$\Pr'(C=\text{true}\|e')$	.2405	.2405	.2564	.2879	.2910
$\Pr'(D=\text{true}\|e')$	.5824	.5824	.5689	.5848	.5917

Figure 14.15: Recovering edges into the network of Figure 14.12. The marginals in the far right column are exact.

Edge Scores	Deleted Edges				
	$\{1, 2, 3, 4\}$	$\{1, 3, 4\}$	$\{1, 4\}$	$\{4\}$	$\{\}$
$A \rightarrow Y_1$ (1)	1.13×10^{-3}	1.13×10^{-3}	$\mathbf{9.89 \times 10^{-4}}$		
$B \rightarrow Y_2$ (2)	**0**				
$C \rightarrow X_3$ (3)	6.12×10^{-4}	$\mathbf{6.12 \times 10^{-4}}$			
$D \rightarrow X_4$ (4)	1.12×10^{-3}	1.12×10^{-3}	1.14×10^{-3}	$\mathbf{1.11 \times 10^{-3}}$	

Figure 14.16: Scoring deleted edges in the network of Figure 14.12. Scores corresponding to smallest mutual information are shown in bold. Based on these scores, edges are recovered according to the order 2, 3, 1 and then 4.

This highlights the impact that a good (or poor) recovery heuristic can have on the quality of approximations.

14.8.5 Approximating the probability of evidence

In this section, we consider the problem of approximating the probability of evidence, $\Pr(e)$, by performing inference on a network that results from deleting edges. We may consider approximating this probability using $\Pr'(e')$, the probability of extended evidence e' in the approximate network. However, this probability is not well defined given (14.9), since this equation does not specify a unique CPT for variable $\hat{S}$ and there-fore does not specify a unique value for $\mathrm{Pr}'(\mathbf{e}')$.[4] We next propose a correction to $\mathrm{Pr}'(\mathbf{e}')$ that addresses this problem. That is, the correction leads to an approximation that is in-variant to the CPT of node $\hat{S}$ as long as it satisfies (14.9). Moreover, it corresponds to a well-known approximation that is often computed by iterative belief propagation.

Consider the case where we delete a single edge $U \to X$ but where the mutual informa-tion $\mathrm{MI}(U; \hat{U}|\mathbf{e}')$ is zero in the resulting network. Let us call such an edge a zero-MI edge (an edge that splits the network is guaranteed to be zero-MI). According to Theorem 14.7, the approximate probability of evidence can be corrected to the true probability when a single zero-MI edge is deleted.

Theorem 14.7. *Let $\mathbf{N}'$ be a Bayesian network that results from deleting a single edge $U \to X$ in network $\mathbf{N}$. Suppose further that the edge parameters of network $\mathbf{N}'$ satisfy (14.8) and (14.9) and that $\mathrm{MI}(U; \hat{U}|\mathbf{e}') = 0$ in network $\mathbf{N}'$. Then*

$$\mathrm{Pr}(\mathbf{e}) = \mathrm{Pr}'(\mathbf{e}') \cdot \frac{1}{z_{UX}}, \quad where \quad z_{UX} = \sum_{u=\hat{u}} \theta_{\hat{u}} \theta_{\hat{s}|u}. \qquad \blacksquare$$

That is, if we delete an edge $U \to X$ and find out that U and $\hat{U}$ are independent in the approximate network $\mathbf{N}'$, we can correct the approximate probability of evidence $\mathrm{Pr}'(\mathbf{e}')$ using z_{UX} and recover the exact probability $\mathrm{Pr}(\mathbf{e})$.[5]

Even though Theorem 14.7 considers only the case of deleting a single zero-MI edge, it does suggest an approximate correction that applies to multiple edges whether zero-MI or not. In particular, we can adopt the correction $\mathrm{Pr}'(\mathbf{e}') \cdot \frac{1}{z}$, where

$$z = \prod_{U \to X} z_{UX} = \prod_{U \to X} \sum_{u=\hat{u}} \theta_{\hat{u}} \theta_{\hat{s}|u}, \qquad (14.16)$$

and $U \to X$ ranges over all deleted edges. This correction no longer recovers the true probability of evidence yet it corresponds to a well-known approximation that is typically computed by iterative belief propagation.

To formally state this connection, consider again Theorem 14.2 and Algorithm 40, IBP. According to this theorem, a fixed point of iterative belief propagation corresponds to a stationary point of (14.4):

$$F_\beta = -\mathrm{ENT}'(\mathbf{X}|\mathbf{e}) - \sum_{XU} \mathrm{AVG}'(\log \lambda_\mathbf{e}(X)\Theta_{X|U}).$$

The quantity $\exp\{-F_\beta\}$ (i.e., e^{-F_β}) is usually taken as an approximation to the probability of evidence, where F_β is known as the *Bethe free energy*.[6]

Theorem 14.8 shows that the Bethe free energy approximation can be formulated as a corrected probability of evidence.

---

[4] Note, however, that any CPT that satisfies (14.9) leads to the same marginals $\mathrm{Pr}'(.|\mathbf{e}')$, since these marginals are conditioned on evidence $\mathbf{e}'$ (see Exercise 14.9).

[5] Since $z_{UX} \leq 1$, this correction can only increase the value of $\mathrm{Pr}'(\mathbf{e}')$. Hence, $\mathrm{Pr}'(\mathbf{e}')$ is a lower bound on $\mathrm{Pr}(\mathbf{e})$ when $U \to X$ is a zero-MI edge.

[6] This term comes from the statistical physics literature. As a result, it is typically stated that the fixed points of IBP are stationary points of the Bethe free energy. The Bethe free energy F_β is an approximation to the (Helmholtz) free energy F where $\exp\{-F\} = \mathrm{Pr}(\mathbf{e})$ is the exact probability of evidence.

Theorem 14.8. *Let $\mathbf{N}'$ be a network that results from deleting every edge in network $\mathbf{N}$. Suppose further that the edge parameters of network $\mathbf{N}'$ satisfy (14.8) and (14.9). Then*

$$\exp\{-F_\beta\} = \text{Pr}'(\mathbf{e}') \cdot \frac{1}{z},$$

where F_β is the Bethe free energy and z is given by (14.16). ■

Note that the proposal for correcting $\text{Pr}'(\mathbf{e}')$ applies to any number of deleted edges. Yet the Bethe free energy corresponds to the extreme case of deleting every edge. We then expect to improve on the Bethe approximation by recovering some of the deleted edges. Note, however, that similar to the case with marginals, we only see improvements after we have recovered enough edges to go beyond a polytree structure.[7]

Consider again the example of Figure 14.11, where this time we use evidence $\mathbf{e}$: $X_2 =$ false, $E =$ false. Recovering edges back into the network of Figure 14.12, we find the following approximations to the probability of evidence:

	Deleted Edges				
	$\{1, 2, 3, 4\}$	$\{2, 3, 4\}$	$\{2, 3\}$	$\{2\}$	$\{\}$
$\text{Pr}'(\mathbf{e}') \cdot \frac{1}{z}$	.4417	.4090	.3972	.3911	.3911

When no edges are recovered, we have the Bethe approximation $\exp\{-F_\beta\} \approx .4417$. As we recover edges, the approximation improves until only the edge labeled 2 is deleted. This is a zero-MI edge since nodes B and $\hat{B}$ are d-separated, leading to an exact approximation. Hence, .3911 is the correct probability of evidence in this case and is obtained before we even recover all edges.

Bibliographic remarks

Belief propagation was originally proposed as an exact inference algorithm for polytree Bayesian networks [Kim and Pearl, 1983]. Belief propagation is an extension of a similar algorithm for exact inference in directed trees, where nodes have at most one parent [Pearl, 1982]. In Pearl [1988], a suggestion was made that belief propagation could still be applied to networks with loops, as an approximate algorithm, leading to iterative belief propagation, IBP. Frequently called *loopy belief propagation*, IBP did not enjoy the popularity it does today until some decoders for error correction were shown to be instances of IBP in Bayesian networks with loops; see for example McEliece et al. [1998b] and Frey and MacKay [1997].

Message-passing schedules of iterative belief propagation are discussed briefly in Wainwright et al. [2001], Tappen and Freeman [2003], and more extensively in Elidan et al. [2006]. The connection between fixed points of IBP and stationary points of the Bethe free energy in Theorem 14.2 was made in Yedidia et al. [2000]. This connection led to improved algorithms, such as the Kikuchi cluster variational method, and further to *generalized belief propagation* (GBP) [Yedidia et al., 2005]. For some background on the statistical physics that influenced these discoveries, see, for example, Yedidia [2001] and Percus et al. [2006]. Iterative joingraph propagation, IJGP, the particular flavor of GBP that we focused on here, is examined in Aji and McEliece [2001] and Dechter et al. [2002]. The edge-deletion semantics for IBP were given in Choi and Darwiche [2006; 2008], along with the correspondence between ED_BP and IJGP. Alternative

---

[7] This basically means that the correspondence of Theorem 14.8 continues to hold as long as we delete enough edges to render the network a polytree.

characterizations of IBP are also given by *tree-based reparameterization* [Wainwright et al., 2001] and *expectation propagation*, [Minka, 2001]. See also Jordan et al. [1999] and Jaakkola [2001] for tutorials on the closely related family of variational approximations. An alternative edge deletion approach is discussed in Suermondt [1992] and van Engelen [1997], which is explored in Exercise 14.17.

14.9 Exercises

14.1. Consider the Bayesian network in Figure 14.17 and suppose that we condition on evidence e: D=true. Suppose that we have run Algorithm 40, IBP, on the network, where it converges and yields the (partial) set of messages and family marginals given in Figure 14.18.

  (a) Fill in the missing values for IBP messages in Figure 14.18.

  (b) Fill in the missing values for family marginals in Figure 14.18.

  (c) Compute marginals $BEL(A)$ and $BEL(B)$ using the IBP messages in Figure 14.18 and those computed in (a).

  (d) Compute marginals $BEL(A)$ and $BEL(B)$ by summing out the appropriate variables from the family marginals $BEL(ABC)$ as well as $BEL(ABD)$.

  (e) Compute joint marginal $BEL(AB)$ by summing out the appropriate variables from family marginals $BEL(ABC)$ as well as $BEL(ABD)$.

Are the marginals computed in (d) consistent? What about those computed in (e)?

14.2. Consider the following function,

$$f(x) = \frac{-.21x + .42}{-.12x + .54}$$

and the problem of identifying a fixed point $x^\star$,

$$x^\star = f(x^\star)$$

using fixed point iteration. We start with some initial value x_0, then at a given iteration $t > 0$ we update our current value x_t using the value x_{t-1} from the previous iteration:

$$x_t = f(x_{t-1}).$$

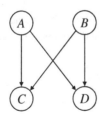

A	Θ_A
true	.5
false	.5

B	Θ_B
true	.25
false	.75

A	B	C	$\Theta_{C|AB}$
true	true	true	.9
true	true	false	.1
true	false	true	.8
true	false	false	.2
false	true	true	.7
false	true	false	.3
false	false	true	.6
false	false	false	.4

A	B	D	$\Theta_{D|AB}$
true	true	true	.6
true	true	false	.4
true	false	true	.4
true	false	false	.6
false	true	true	.3
false	true	false	.7
false	false	true	.3
false	false	false	.7

Figure 14.17: A Bayesian network.

A	$\pi_C(A)$	$\pi_D(A)$	$\lambda_C(A)$	$\lambda_D(A)$
true	.5	.5	.6	
false	.5	.5	.4	

B	$\pi_C(B)$	$\pi_D(B)$	$\lambda_C(B)$	$\lambda_D(B)$
true	.3	.25	.5	
false	.7	.75	.5	

A	B	C	$BEL(ABC)$
true	true	true	.162
true	true	false	.018
true	false	true	
true	false	false	.084
false	true	true	.084
false	true	false	.036
false	false	true	.168
false	false	false	.112

A	B	D	$BEL(ABD)$
true	true	true	.2
true	true	false	0
true	false	true	
true	false	false	0
false	true	true	.1
false	true	false	0
false	false	true	.3
false	false	false	0

Figure 14.18: (Partial) IBP messages and marginal approximations.

A	Θ_A
true	.7
false	.3

$\hat{A}$	$\Theta_{\hat{A}}$
true	θ
false	$1 - \theta$

A	$\hat{A}$	B	$\Theta_{B|A\hat{A}}$
true	true	true	.3
true	true	false	.7
true	false	true	.6
true	false	false	.4
false	true	true	.7
false	true	false	.3
false	false	true	.4
false	false	false	.6

Figure 14.19: CPTs for a Bayesian network over three variables: $A \to B$ and $\hat{A} \to B$ with evidence $\mathbf{e} = B =$ true.

Starting with $x_0 = .2$, we have $x_1 \approx .7326$ and $x_2 \approx .5887$. In this particular example, repeated iterations will approach the desired solution x^*.

(a) Continue evaluating x_t for $t \geq 3$ until the four most significant digits stop changing. Consider the Bayesian network in Figure 14.19 and the problem of identifying a parameter θ defining CPT $\Theta_{\hat{A}}$, such that

$$\theta = \Pr(A = \text{true}|\mathbf{e}).$$

(b) Suppose we set $\theta = .2$. What is $\Pr(A = \text{true}|\mathbf{e})$? Suppose we now reset θ to $\Pr(A = \text{true}|\mathbf{e})$. What is the new value of $\Pr(A = \text{true}|\mathbf{e})$?

(c) Design a fixed point iterative method to find such a θ.

14.3. Consider the modified belief propagation algorithm (with normalizing constants). For an edge $U \to X$, let $\mathbf{e}_{UX}^+$ be the evidence instantiating nodes on the U-side of edge $U \to X$ and let $\mathbf{e}_{UX}^-$ be the evidence instantiating nodes on the X-side of the edge. Prove the following:

$$\pi_X(U) = \Pr(U|\mathbf{e}_{UX}^+)$$
$$\lambda_X(U) = \eta \Pr(\mathbf{e}_{UX}^-|U),$$

where η is a constant that normalizes message $\lambda_X(U)$.

14.4. Consider a polytree network $\mathcal{N}$ with families $X\mathbf{U}$ that induces a distribution $Pr(\mathbf{X})$.

(a) Prove that the distribution $Pr(\mathbf{X}|\mathbf{e})$ factorizes as

$$Pr(\mathbf{X}|\mathbf{e}) = \prod_{X\mathbf{U}} \frac{Pr(X\mathbf{U}|\mathbf{e})}{\prod_{U \in \mathbf{U}} Pr(U|\mathbf{e})}.$$

(b) Prove that the factorization of (a) is equivalent to

$$Pr(\mathbf{X}|\mathbf{e}) = \prod_{X\mathbf{U}} \frac{Pr(X\mathbf{U}|\mathbf{e})}{Pr(X|\mathbf{e})^{n_X}},$$

where n_X is the number of children that variable X has in network $\mathcal{N}$.

14.5. Consider Theorem 14.1. Let $\mathcal{N}$ and $\mathcal{N}'$ be two Bayesian networks over the same set of variables $\mathbf{X}$, possibly having different structures. Prove that

$$\log Pr(\mathbf{e}) \geq \text{ENT}'(\mathbf{X}|\mathbf{e}) + \sum_{X\mathbf{U}} \text{AVG}'(\log \lambda_{\mathbf{e}}(X)\Theta_{X|\mathbf{U}}).$$

Thus, if a distribution $Pr'(\mathbf{X}|\mathbf{e})$ is induced by a sufficiently simple Bayesian network $\mathcal{N}'$, we can compute a lower bound on the probability of evidence $Pr(\mathbf{e})$.

14.6. Consider running Algorithm 40, IBP, on a network $\mathcal{N}$ that does not have any evidence. Further, suppose that all IBP messages are initialized uniformly.

(a) Show that all λ messages are neutral. That is, for any given message $\lambda_X(U)$, show that all values $\lambda_X(u)$ are the same.

(b) Argue that when there is no evidence, IBP need not propagate any λ messages.

(c) Design a sequential message passing schedule where IBP is guaranteed to converge in a single iteration.

Hint: It may be useful to analyze how Algorithm 42, ED_BP, parameterizes a fully disconnected network when the original network $\mathcal{N}$ has no evidence.

14.7. Let $\mathcal{N}$ and $\mathcal{N}'$ be two Bayesian networks over the same set of variables $\mathbf{X}$, where $\mathcal{N}'$ is fully disconnected. That is, $\mathcal{N}'$ induces the distribution

$$Pr'(\mathbf{X}) = \prod_{X \in \mathbf{X}} \Theta'_X.$$

Identify CPTs Θ'_X for network $\mathcal{N}'$ that minimize $KL(Pr, Pr')$.

14.8. Show that Equations 14.10 and 14.11 reduce to Equations 14.12 and 14.13.

14.9. Let $\mathcal{N}$ be a Bayesian network that induces a distribution $Pr(\mathbf{X})$ and let S be a leaf node in network $\mathcal{N}$ that has a single parent U. Show that the conditional distribution $Pr(\mathbf{X} \setminus \{S\}|s)$ is the same for any two CPTs $\Theta_{S|U}$ and $\Theta'_{S|U}$ of node S as long as $\Theta_{s|U} = \eta \cdot \Theta'_{s|U}$ for some constant $\eta > 0$.

14.10. Consider again Figure 14.7, which defines a network $\mathcal{N}$, and another network $\mathcal{N}'$ that results from deleting edge $A \to B$. Figure 14.8 depicts the edge parameters for $\mathcal{N}'$ computed using Algorithm 42, ED_BP. Figure 14.20 depicts the messages computed by Algorithm 40, IBP, in the original network $\mathcal{N}$.

(a) Identify how edge parameters in $\mathcal{N}'$ correspond to IBP messages in $\mathcal{N}$.

(b) Consider the following correspondence between the approximations for family marginals computed by IBP in $\mathcal{N}$ and by ED_BP in $\mathcal{N}'$:

A	B	$BEL(AB) = Pr'(\hat{A}B|\mathbf{e}')$
true	true	.3114
true	false	.4021
false	true	.0328
false	false	.2537

Compute $BEL(A) = Pr'(\hat{A}|\mathbf{e}')$.

Edge $A \to B$		
A	$\pi_B(A)$	$\lambda_B(A)$
true	.8262	.3438
false	.1738	.6562

Edge $A \to C$		
A	$\pi_C(A)$	$\lambda_C(A)$
true	.6769	.5431
false	.3231	.4569

Edge $B \to D$		
B	$\pi_D(B)$	$\lambda_D(B)$
true	.7305	.1622
false	.2695	.8378

Edge $C \to D$		
C	$\pi_D(C)$	$\lambda_D(C)$
true	.6615	.4206
false	.3384	.5794

Figure 14.20: Messages computed by Algorithm 40, IBP, after converging on the network of Figure 14.7(a).

(c) Given the results of (b), argue that we must have $\Pr'(\hat{A}|\mathbf{e}') = \Pr'(A|\mathbf{e}')$.

(d) Identify a pair of variables in $\mathcal{N}'$ whose joint marginal can be easily computed in $\mathcal{N}'$ but cannot be computed using IBP in $\mathcal{N}$.

14.11. Let $\mathcal{N}'$ be a network that results from deleting a single edge $U \to X$ from the network $\mathcal{N}$ and suppose that this edge splits the network $\mathcal{N}$ into two disconnected subnetworks. Show that $\Pr(\mathbf{e}_X|u) = \Pr'(\mathbf{e}_X|\hat{u})$, where $\mathbf{e}_X$ is evidence that instantiates nodes on the X-side of edge $U \to X$.

14.12. Consider Equations 14.8 and 14.9:

$$\Theta_{\hat{U}} = \Pr'(U \mid \mathbf{e}' - \hat{S})$$
$$\Theta_{\hat{s}|U} = \eta \Pr'(\mathbf{e}' \mid \hat{U}).$$

(a) Show that Equations 14.8 and 14.9 are equivalent to

$$\theta_{\hat{u}} = \frac{\partial \Pr'(\mathbf{e}')}{\partial \theta_{\hat{s}|u}}$$

$$\theta_{\hat{s}|u} = \frac{\partial \Pr'(\mathbf{e}')}{\partial \theta_{\hat{u}}},$$

where $u = \hat{u}$.

(b) Show that Equations 14.8 and 14.9 are equivalent to

$$\Pr'(U|\mathbf{e}') = \Pr'(\hat{U}|\mathbf{e}')$$
$$\Pr'(U|\mathbf{e}' - \hat{S}) = \Pr'(\hat{U}).$$

14.13. Let $\mathcal{N}$ be a Bayesian network and $\mathcal{N}'$ be the result of deleting edges in $\mathcal{N}$. Show how an ED-BP fixed point in $\mathcal{N}'$ corresponds to a fixed point of IJGP. In particular, show how to construct a joingraph that allows IJGP to simulate Algorithm 42.

14.14. Let $\mathcal{N}'$ be a Bayesian network that results from deleting an edge $U \to X$ that splits network $\mathcal{N}$ into two disconnected subnetworks: $\mathcal{N}_U$ containing U and $\mathcal{N}_X$ containing X. Let $\mathbf{X}_U$ be the variables of subnetwork $\mathcal{N}_U$ and $\mathbf{X}_X$ be the variables of subnetwork $\mathcal{N}_X$. If the parameters $\Theta_{\hat{U}}$ and $\Theta_{\hat{s}|U}$ are determined by Equations 14.8 and 14.9, show that the marginal distributions for each approximate subnetwork are exact:

$$\Pr'(\mathbf{X}_U|\mathbf{e}') = \Pr(\mathbf{X}_U|\mathbf{e})$$
$$\Pr'(\mathbf{X}_X|\mathbf{e}') = \Pr(\mathbf{X}_X|\mathbf{e}).$$

14.15. Let $\mathcal{N}'$ be a polytree that results from deleting edges in network $\mathcal{N}$ and suppose that the parameter edges of $\mathcal{N}'$ satisfy Equations 14.8 and 14.9. Suppose further that we are using the polytree algorithm (i.e., belief propagation) to compute the MI scores in Algorithm 43. To compute the MI score for each edge $U \to X$ that we delete, we need two types of values:

- Node marginals $\Pr'(u|\mathbf{e}')$ and $\Pr'(\hat{u}|\mathbf{e}')$
- Joint marginals $\Pr'(u\hat{u}|\mathbf{e}')$.

If network $\mathcal{N}$ has n nodes and m edges and since $\mathcal{N}'$ is a polytree, at most $n-1$ edges are left undeleted. Thus, we may need to score $O(n^2)$ deleted edges in the worst case. Luckily, to compute every node marginal we only need to run belief propagation once. However, if we naively computed joint marginals $\Pr'(u\hat{u}|\mathbf{e}')$, we could have run belief propagation $O(m \max_U |U|^2)$ times: for each of our $O(m)$ deleted edges, we could have run belief propagation once for each of the $|U|^2$ instantiations $u\hat{u}$. Consider the following:

$$\Pr'(u\hat{u}|\mathbf{e}') = \Pr'(\hat{u}|u, \mathbf{e}')\Pr'(u|\mathbf{e}').$$

Show that we can compute $\Pr'(\hat{u}|u, \mathbf{e}')$ for all instantiations $u\hat{u}$ using only $O(n \max_U |U|)$ runs of belief propagation, thus showing that we need only the same number of runs of belief propagation to score all edges in Algorithm 43.

14.16. Let $\mathcal{N}$ and $\mathcal{N}'$ be two Bayesian networks that have the same structure but possibly different CPTs. Prove that

$$\mathrm{KL}(\Pr, \Pr') = \sum_{XU} \sum_{\mathbf{u}} \Pr(\mathbf{u}) \cdot \mathrm{KL}(\Theta_{X|\mathbf{u}}, \Theta'_{X|\mathbf{u}})$$

$$= \sum_{XU} \sum_{\mathbf{u}} \Pr(\mathbf{u}) \cdot \sum_{x} \theta_{x|\mathbf{u}} \log \frac{\theta_{x|\mathbf{u}}}{\theta'_{x|\mathbf{u}}},$$

where $\Theta_{X|\mathbf{U}}$ are CPTs in network $\mathcal{N}$ and $\Theta'_{X|\mathbf{U}}$ are the corresponding CPTs in network $\mathcal{N}'$.

14.17. Suppose we have a network $\mathcal{N}$ with a variable X that has parents Y and $\mathbf{U}$. Suppose that deleting the edge $Y \to X$ results in a network $\mathcal{N}'$ where

- $\mathcal{N}'$ has the same structure as $\mathcal{N}$ except that edge $Y \to X$ is removed.
- The CPT for variable X in $\mathcal{N}'$ is given by

$$\theta'_{x|\mathbf{u}} \overset{def}{=} \Pr(x|\mathbf{u}).$$

- The CPTs for variables other than X in $\mathcal{N}'$ are the same as those in $\mathcal{N}$.

(a) Prove that when we delete a single edge $Y \to X$, we have

$$\mathrm{KL}(\Pr, \Pr') = \mathrm{MI}(X; Y|\mathbf{U}) = \sum_{xy\mathbf{u}} \Pr(xy\mathbf{u}) \log \frac{\Pr(xy|\mathbf{u})}{\Pr(x|\mathbf{u})\Pr(y|\mathbf{u})}.$$

(b) Prove that when we delete multiple edges but at most one edge $Y \to X$ incoming into X is deleted, the error is additive:

$$\mathrm{KL}(\Pr, \Pr') = \sum_{Y \to X} \mathrm{MI}(X; Y|\mathbf{U}).$$

(c) Identify a small network conditioned on some evidence $\mathbf{e}$ where the KL divergence $\mathrm{KL}(\Pr(X|\mathbf{e}), \Pr'(X|\mathbf{e}))$ can be made arbitrarily large even when divergence $\mathrm{KL}(\Pr, \Pr')$ can be made arbitrarily close to zero. Hint: A two-node network $A \to B$ suffices.

14.18. Let $\mathcal{N}'$ be a Bayesian network that results from deleting edges $U \to X$ from network $\mathcal{N}$. Show that the edge parameters of network $\mathcal{N}'$ satisfy Equations 14.8 and 14.9 if and only if the edge parameters are a stationary point of $\Pr'(\mathbf{e}) \cdot \frac{1}{z}$, where z is given by Equation 14.16.

14.19. Prove Equation 14.27 on Page 376.

14.20. Consider a Bayesian network with families $X\mathbf{U}$ and distribution $\Pr(\mathbf{X})$. Show that for evidence $\mathbf{e}$, we have $\log \Pr(\mathbf{e}) = \text{ENT} + \text{AVG}$ where

- $\text{ENT} = -\sum_{\mathbf{x}} \Pr(\mathbf{x}|\mathbf{e}) \log \Pr(\mathbf{x}|\mathbf{e})$ is the entropy of distribution $\Pr(\mathbf{X}|\mathbf{e})$.
- $\text{AVG} = \sum_{X\mathbf{U}} \sum_{x\mathbf{u}} \Pr(x\mathbf{u}|\mathbf{e}) \log \lambda_{\mathbf{e}}(x)\theta_{x|\mathbf{u}}$ is a sum of expectations over network parameters.

14.10 Proofs

PROOF OF THEOREM 14.1.

$$\text{KL}(\Pr'(\mathbf{X}|\mathbf{e}), \Pr(\mathbf{X}|\mathbf{e}))$$

$$= \sum_{\mathbf{x}} \Pr'(\mathbf{x}|\mathbf{e}) \log \frac{\Pr'(\mathbf{x}|\mathbf{e})}{\Pr(\mathbf{x}|\mathbf{e})}$$

$$= \sum_{\mathbf{x}} \Pr'(\mathbf{x}|\mathbf{e}) \log \Pr'(\mathbf{x}|\mathbf{e}) - \sum_{\mathbf{x}} \Pr'(\mathbf{x}|\mathbf{e}) \log \Pr(\mathbf{x}|\mathbf{e})$$

$$= \sum_{\mathbf{x}} \Pr'(\mathbf{x}|\mathbf{e}) \log \Pr'(\mathbf{x}|\mathbf{e}) - \sum_{\mathbf{x}} \Pr'(\mathbf{x}|\mathbf{e}) \log \frac{\Pr(\mathbf{x}, \mathbf{e})}{\Pr(\mathbf{e})}$$

$$= \sum_{\mathbf{x}} \Pr'(\mathbf{x}|\mathbf{e}) \log \Pr'(\mathbf{x}|\mathbf{e}) - \sum_{\mathbf{x}} \Pr'(\mathbf{x}|\mathbf{e}) \log \Pr(\mathbf{x}, \mathbf{e}) + \sum_{\mathbf{x}} \Pr'(\mathbf{x}|\mathbf{e}) \log \Pr(\mathbf{e})$$

$$= \sum_{\mathbf{x}} \Pr'(\mathbf{x}|\mathbf{e}) \log \Pr'(\mathbf{x}|\mathbf{e}) - \sum_{\mathbf{x}} \Pr'(\mathbf{x}|\mathbf{e}) \log \Pr(\mathbf{x}, \mathbf{e}) + \log \Pr(\mathbf{e}).$$

We now have

$$- \sum_{\mathbf{x}} \Pr'(\mathbf{x}|\mathbf{e}) \log \Pr'(\mathbf{x}|\mathbf{e}) = \text{ENT}'(\mathbf{X}|\mathbf{e}).$$

Moreover,

$$\sum_{\mathbf{x}} \Pr'(\mathbf{x}|\mathbf{e}) \log \Pr(\mathbf{x}, \mathbf{e}) = \sum_{\mathbf{x}} \Pr'(\mathbf{x}|\mathbf{e}) \log \prod_{x\mathbf{u}\sim\mathbf{x}} \lambda_{\mathbf{e}}(x)\theta_{x|\mathbf{u}}$$

$$= \sum_{\mathbf{x}} \sum_{x\mathbf{u}\sim\mathbf{x}} \Pr'(\mathbf{x}|\mathbf{e}) \log \lambda_{\mathbf{e}}(x)\theta_{x|\mathbf{u}}$$

$$= \sum_{X\mathbf{U}} \sum_{x\mathbf{u}} \sum_{\mathbf{x}\sim x\mathbf{u}} \Pr'(\mathbf{x}|\mathbf{e}) \log \lambda_{\mathbf{e}}(x)\theta_{x|\mathbf{u}}$$

$$= \sum_{X\mathbf{U}} \sum_{x\mathbf{u}} \log \lambda_{\mathbf{e}}(x)\theta_{x|\mathbf{u}} \sum_{\mathbf{x}\sim x\mathbf{u}} \Pr'(\mathbf{x}|\mathbf{e})$$

$$= \sum_{X\mathbf{U}} \sum_{x\mathbf{u}} \Pr'(x\mathbf{u}|\mathbf{e}) \log \lambda_{\mathbf{e}}(x)\theta_{x|\mathbf{u}}$$

$$= \sum_{X\mathbf{U}} \text{AVG}'(\log \lambda_{\mathbf{e}}(X)\Theta_{X|\mathbf{U}}).$$ ∎

Hence,

$$\text{KL}(\Pr'(\mathbf{X}|\mathbf{e}), \Pr(\mathbf{X}|\mathbf{e})) = -\text{ENT}'(\mathbf{X}|\mathbf{e}) - \sum_{X\mathbf{U}} \text{AVG}'(\log \lambda_{\mathbf{e}}(X)\Theta_{X|\mathbf{U}}) + \log \Pr(\mathbf{e}).$$

PROOF OF THEOREM 14.2. The proof of Theorem 14.2 is identical to the proof of Theorem 14.4 in the case where the joingraph is the dual joingraph of $\mathcal{N}$. ∎

PROOF OF THEOREM 14.3.

$$\text{ENT}(\mathbf{X}|\mathbf{e}) = -\sum_{\mathbf{x}} \Pr(\mathbf{x}|\mathbf{e}) \log \Pr(\mathbf{x}|\mathbf{e})$$

$$= -\sum_{\mathbf{x}} \Pr(\mathbf{x}|\mathbf{e}) \log \frac{\prod_{\mathbf{c} \sim \mathbf{x}} \Pr(\mathbf{c}|\mathbf{e})}{\prod_{\mathbf{s} \sim \mathbf{x}} \Pr(\mathbf{s}|\mathbf{e})}$$

$$= -\sum_{\mathbf{x}} \Pr(\mathbf{x}|\mathbf{e}) \log \prod_{\mathbf{c} \sim \mathbf{x}} \Pr(\mathbf{c}|\mathbf{e}) + \sum_{\mathbf{x}} \Pr(\mathbf{x}|\mathbf{e}) \log \prod_{\mathbf{s} \sim \mathbf{x}} \Pr(\mathbf{s}|\mathbf{e})$$

$$= -\sum_{\mathbf{x}} \sum_{\mathbf{c} \sim \mathbf{x}} \Pr(\mathbf{x}|\mathbf{e}) \log \Pr(\mathbf{c}|\mathbf{e}) + \sum_{\mathbf{x}} \sum_{\mathbf{s} \sim \mathbf{x}} \Pr(\mathbf{x}|\mathbf{e}) \log \Pr(\mathbf{s}|\mathbf{e})$$

$$= -\sum_{\mathbf{C}} \sum_{\mathbf{c}} \sum_{\mathbf{x} \sim \mathbf{c}} \Pr(\mathbf{x}|\mathbf{e}) \log \Pr(\mathbf{c}|\mathbf{e}) + \sum_{\mathbf{S}} \sum_{\mathbf{s}} \sum_{\mathbf{x} \sim \mathbf{s}} \Pr(\mathbf{x}|\mathbf{e}) \log \Pr(\mathbf{s}|\mathbf{e})$$

$$= -\sum_{\mathbf{C}} \sum_{\mathbf{c}} \Pr(\mathbf{c}|\mathbf{e}) \log \Pr(\mathbf{c}|\mathbf{e}) + \sum_{\mathbf{S}} \sum_{\mathbf{s}} \Pr(\mathbf{s}|\mathbf{e}) \log \Pr(\mathbf{s}|\mathbf{e})$$

$$= \sum_{\mathbf{C}} \text{ENT}(\mathbf{C}|\mathbf{e}) - \sum_{\mathbf{S}} \text{ENT}(\mathbf{S}|\mathbf{e}). \qquad \blacksquare$$

PROOF OF THEOREM 14.4. We want to show that a fixed point for IJGP is a stationary point of the KL divergence or, equivalently, a stationary point of

$$f = \text{ENT}'(\mathbf{X}|\mathbf{e}) + \sum_{\mathbf{C}_i} \text{AVG}'(\log \Phi_i)$$

$$= -\sum_{\mathbf{C}_i} \sum_{\mathbf{c}_i} \mu_{\mathbf{c}_i} \log \mu_{\mathbf{c}_i} + \sum_{\mathbf{S}_{ij}} \sum_{\mathbf{s}_{ij}} \mu_{\mathbf{s}_{ij}} \log \mu_{\mathbf{s}_{ij}} + \sum_{\mathbf{C}_i} \sum_{\mathbf{c}_i} \mu_{\mathbf{c}_i} \log \Phi_i(\mathbf{c}_i)$$

under the normalization constraints,

$$\sum_{\mathbf{c}_i} \mu_{\mathbf{c}_i} = \sum_{\mathbf{s}_{ij}} \mu_{\mathbf{s}_{ij}} = 1 \qquad (14.17)$$

for all clusters $\mathbf{C}_i$ and separators $\mathbf{S}_{ij}$, and under the consistency constraints,

$$\sum_{\mathbf{c}_i \sim \mathbf{s}_{ij}} \mu_{\mathbf{c}_i} = \mu_{\mathbf{s}_{ij}} = \sum_{\mathbf{c}_j \sim \mathbf{s}_{ij}} \mu_{\mathbf{c}_j} \qquad (14.18)$$

for each separator $\mathbf{S}_{ij}$ and neighboring clusters $\mathbf{C}_i$ and $\mathbf{C}_j$.

First, we construct the Lagrangian L from our objective function f (see Appendix D):

$$L = f + \sum_{\mathbf{C}_i} \gamma_i \left(\sum_{\mathbf{c}_i} \mu_{\mathbf{c}_i} - 1 \right) + \sum_{\mathbf{S}_{ij}} \gamma_{ij} \left(\sum_{\mathbf{s}_{ij}} \mu_{\mathbf{s}_{ij}} - 1 \right)$$

$$+ \sum_{\mathbf{S}_{ij}} \sum_{\mathbf{s}_{ij}} \kappa_{ij}(\mathbf{s}_{ij}) \left(\sum_{\mathbf{c}_j \sim \mathbf{s}_{ij}} \mu_{\mathbf{c}_j} - \mu_{\mathbf{s}_{ij}} \right) + \kappa_{ji}(\mathbf{s}_{ij}) \left(\sum_{\mathbf{c}_i \sim \mathbf{s}_{ij}} \mu_{\mathbf{c}_i} - \mu_{\mathbf{s}_{ij}} \right),$$

where Lagrangian multipliers γ_i and γ_{ij} enforce the normalization constraints and the multipliers $\kappa_{ij}(\mathbf{s}_{ij})$, $\kappa_{ji}(\mathbf{s}_{ij})$ enforce the consistency constraints.

Setting to zero the partial derivatives of L with respect to our parameters μ, γ, and κ, we want to solve for these same parameters. The partial derivatives of L with respect to Lagrange multipliers γ_i and γ_{ij} yield

$$\sum_{\mathbf{c}_i} \mu_{\mathbf{c}_i} - 1 = 0, \quad \sum_{\mathbf{s}_{ij}} \mu_{\mathbf{s}_{ij}} - 1 = 0,$$

giving us back the normalization constraints in (14.17). The partial derivatives of L with respect to Lagrange multipliers $\kappa_{ij}(\mathbf{s}_{ij})$ and $\kappa_{ji}(\mathbf{s}_{ij})$ yield

$$\sum_{\mathbf{c}_j \sim \mathbf{s}_{ij}} \mu_{\mathbf{c}_j} - \mu_{\mathbf{s}_{ij}} = 0, \qquad \sum_{\mathbf{c}_i \sim \mathbf{s}_{ij}} \mu_{\mathbf{c}_i} - \mu_{\mathbf{s}_{ij}} = 0,$$

giving us back our consistency constraints in (14.18).

When we take the partial derivatives of L with respect to cluster marginals $\mu_{\mathbf{c}_i}$ and separator marginals $\mu_{\mathbf{s}_i}$, we have, respectively,

$$-1 - \log \mu_{\mathbf{c}_i} + \log \Phi_i(\mathbf{c}_i) + \gamma_i + \sum_k \kappa_{ki}(\mathbf{s}_{ik}) = 0$$

$$1 + \log \mu_{\mathbf{s}_{ij}} + \gamma_{ij} - \kappa_{ji}(\mathbf{s}_{ij}) - \kappa_{ij}(\mathbf{s}_{ji}) = 0,$$

where k are neighbors of i. Solving for $\mu_{\mathbf{c}_i}$ and $\mu_{\mathbf{s}_i}$, we get

$$\mu_{\mathbf{c}_i} = \exp\{-1\} \cdot \exp\{\gamma_i\} \cdot \Phi_i(\mathbf{c}_i) \cdot \prod_k \exp\{\kappa_{ki}(\mathbf{s}_{ik})\} \tag{14.19}$$

$$\mu_{\mathbf{s}_{ij}} = \exp\{-1\} \cdot \exp\{-\gamma_{ij}\} \cdot \exp\{\kappa_{ji}(\mathbf{s}_{ij})\} \cdot \exp\{\kappa_{ij}(\mathbf{s}_{ij})\} \tag{14.20}$$

where $\exp\{x\}$ (equivalently e^x) is the exponential function. We now have expressions for the cluster and separator marginals at a stationary point of the KL divergence.

Applying our normalization constraints (14.17) on (14.19), we get

$$\sum_{\mathbf{c}_i} \mu_{\mathbf{c}_i} = \exp\{-1\} \cdot \exp\{\gamma_i\} \cdot \sum_{\mathbf{c}_i} \Phi_i(\mathbf{c}_i) \cdot \prod_k \exp\{\kappa_{ki}(\mathbf{s}_{ik})\} = 1$$

and thus

$$\exp\{\gamma_i\} = \exp\{1\} \cdot \left[\sum_{\mathbf{c}_i} \Phi_i(\mathbf{c}_i) \cdot \prod_k \exp\{\kappa_{ki}(\mathbf{s}_{ik})\} \right]^{-1}.$$

Substituting back into (14.19), we see that the role of $\exp\{\gamma_i\}$ is as a normalizing constant; similarly, for $\exp\{-\gamma_{ij}\}$ in (14.20).

We now establish a correspondence between these expressions for marginals and the ones computed by IJGP. In particular, if we substitute $M_{ki}(\mathbf{s}_{ik}) = \exp\{\kappa_{ki}(\mathbf{s}_{ik})\}$, (14.19) and (14.20) simplify to

$$\mu_{\mathbf{c}_i} = \eta \; \Phi_i(\mathbf{c}_i) \prod_k M_{ki}(\mathbf{s}_{ik}) \tag{14.21}$$

$$\mu_{\mathbf{s}_{ij}} = \eta \; M_{ji}(\mathbf{s}_{ij}) M_{ij}(\mathbf{s}_{ij}). \tag{14.22}$$

Applying the consistency constraint given by (14.18) to (14.21) and (14.22), we get

$$\sum_{\mathbf{c}_i \sim \mathbf{s}_{ij}} \Phi_i(\mathbf{c}_i) \prod_k M_{ki}(\mathbf{s}_{ik}) \propto M_{ji}(\mathbf{s}_{ij}) M_{ij}(\mathbf{s}_{ij}),$$

and thus

$$M_{ij}(\mathbf{s}_{ij}) = \eta \sum_{\mathbf{c}_i \sim \mathbf{s}_{ij}} \Phi_i(\mathbf{c}_i) \prod_{k \neq j} M_{ki}(\mathbf{s}_{ik}).$$

We have therefore derived a correspondence between IJGP marginals and the stationary points of the KL divergence. ∎

PROOF OF THEOREM 14.5. Let $\hat{S} = \hat{s}$ be the soft evidence introduced when deleting the edge $U \to X$. Let $\mathbf{e}_U, \hat{s}$ denote the evidence in the subnetwork of $\mathcal{N}'$ containing variable U and let $\mathbf{e}_X$ denote the evidence in the subnetwork containing variable X. Hence, $\mathbf{e} = \mathbf{e}_U, \mathbf{e}_X$ and $\mathbf{e}' = \hat{s}, \mathbf{e}_U, \mathbf{e}_X$.

Before showing $\Pr'(q|\mathbf{e}') = \Pr(q|\mathbf{e})$, we show the more specific result $\Pr'(u|\mathbf{e}') = \Pr(u|\mathbf{e})$. This is shown while observing that $\Pr(u, \mathbf{e}_U) = \Pr'(u, \mathbf{e}_U)$ and $\Pr(\mathbf{e}_X|u) = \Pr'(\mathbf{e}_X|\hat{u})$. The first equality follows immediately once we prune the networks $\mathcal{N}$ and $\mathcal{N}'$ for the corresponding queries (see Section 6.9). The second equality is the subject of Exercise 14.11. We now have

$$
\begin{aligned}
\Pr(u|\mathbf{e}) &\propto \Pr(\mathbf{e}|u)\Pr(u) \\
&= \Pr(\mathbf{e}_U|u)\Pr(\mathbf{e}_X|u)\Pr(u) && \mathbf{E}_U \text{ and } \mathbf{E}_X \text{ are d-separated by } U \\
&= \Pr(u, \mathbf{e}_U)\Pr(\mathbf{e}_X|u) \\
&= \Pr'(u, \mathbf{e}_U)\Pr'(\mathbf{e}_X|\hat{u}) && \text{see previous equalities} \\
&= \Pr'(u, \mathbf{e}_U)\frac{\Pr'(\mathbf{e}_X|\hat{u})\Pr'(\mathbf{e}_U, \hat{s}|\hat{u})}{\Pr'(\mathbf{e}_U, \hat{s}|\hat{u})} \\
&= \Pr'(u, \mathbf{e}_U)\frac{\Pr'(\mathbf{e}'|\hat{u})}{\Pr'(\mathbf{e}_U, \hat{s}|\hat{u})} && \mathbf{E}_X \text{ and } \hat{S}, \mathbf{E}_U \text{ d-separated by } \hat{U} \\
&= \Pr'(u, \mathbf{e}_U)\frac{\Pr'(\mathbf{e}'|\hat{u})}{\Pr'(\mathbf{e}_U, \hat{s})} && \hat{S}, \mathbf{E}_U \text{ and } \hat{U} \text{ d-separated} \\
&\propto \Pr'(u, \mathbf{e}_U)\frac{\theta_{\hat{s}|u}}{\Pr'(\mathbf{e}_U, \hat{s})} && \text{by (14.9)} \\
&= \frac{\Pr'(u, \mathbf{e}_U, \hat{s})}{\Pr'(\mathbf{e}_U, \hat{s})} && \theta_{\hat{s}|u} = \Pr'(\hat{s}|u, \mathbf{e}_U) \\
&= \Pr'(u|\mathbf{e}_U, \hat{s}.) \\
&= \Pr'(u|\mathbf{e}') && U \text{ and } \mathbf{E}_X \text{ d-separated by } \mathbf{E}_U, \hat{S}. \quad (14.23)
\end{aligned}
$$

To show that $\Pr'(q|\mathbf{e}') = \Pr(q|\mathbf{e})$ when Q is in the subnetwork of $\mathcal{N}'$ containing U, we have

$$
\begin{aligned}
\Pr(q|\mathbf{e}) &= \sum_u \Pr(q|u, \mathbf{e})\Pr(u|\mathbf{e}) \\
&= \sum_u \Pr(q|u, \mathbf{e}_U)\Pr(u|\mathbf{e}) && Q \text{ and } \mathbf{E}_X \text{ d-separated by } U, \mathbf{E}_U \\
&= \sum_u \Pr'(q|u, \mathbf{e}_U)\Pr(u|\mathbf{e}) && \text{equivalent after pruning } \mathcal{N} \text{ and } \mathcal{N}' \\
&= \sum_u \Pr'(q|u, \mathbf{e}_U)\Pr'(u|\mathbf{e}') && \text{by (14.23)} \\
&= \sum_u \Pr'(q|u, \mathbf{e}')\Pr'(u|\mathbf{e}') && Q \text{ and } \mathbf{E}_X, \hat{S} \text{ d-separated by } U, \mathbf{E}_U \\
&= \Pr'(q|\mathbf{e}').
\end{aligned}
$$

We can similarly show the equality when Q is in the subnetwork of $\mathcal{N}'$ containing X once we observe that $\Pr(u|\mathbf{e}) = \Pr'(\hat{u}|\mathbf{e}')$ (see Lemma 14.1). ∎

PROOF OF THEOREM 14.6. We show the correspondence between ED_BP and IBP by induction. Let a variable X in network $\mathcal{N}$ have parents U_i and children Y_j. Observe that X is the center of a star network in $\mathcal{N}'$ whose arms are auxiliary variables $\hat{U}_i$ and $\hat{S}_j$ introduced by deleting edges $U_i \rightarrow X$ and $X \rightarrow Y_j$, respectively (see Figure 14.21,

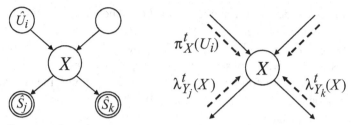

Figure 14.21: Correspondence between ED_BP parameter updates in a fully disconnected network and message passing in IBP.

left). For an iteration t, let $\Theta_{\hat{U}_i}^t$ parameterize clone variable $\hat{U}_i$ and let $\Theta_{\hat{S}_j|X}^t$ parameterize variable $\hat{S}_j$. Then at iteration $t = 0$, we are given that $\pi_X^0(U_i) = \Theta_{\hat{U}_i}^0$ for all edges $U_i \rightarrow X$ and $\lambda_{Y_j}^0(X) = \Theta_{\hat{S}_j|X}^0$ for all edges $X \rightarrow Y_j$.

We first want to show for an iteration $t > 0$ and for an edge $X \rightarrow Y_j$, the IBP message that variable X passes to its child Y_j is the same as the parameters for the clone $\hat{X}$ that was made a parent of Y_j. That is, we want to show $\pi_{Y_j}^t(X) = \Theta_{\hat{X}}^t$.

Assume that $\mathbf{e}_X'$ is the evidence in the star network of X in $\mathcal{N}'$. Starting from (14.14), we have

$$\Theta_{\hat{X}}^t = \mathrm{Pr}_{t-1}'(X|\mathbf{e}' - \hat{S}_j) = \mathrm{Pr}_{t-1}'(X|\mathbf{e}_X' - \hat{S}_j),$$

since X is independent of all evidence other than the evidence $\mathbf{e}_X'$ that is directly connected to X. Letting $\hat{\mathbf{U}}$ denote the set of clones that became parents of X in $\mathcal{N}'$, we have

$$\Theta_{\hat{X}}^t = \eta \, \mathrm{Pr}_{t-1}'(X, \mathbf{e}_X' - \hat{S}_j) = \eta \sum_{\hat{\mathbf{U}}} \mathrm{Pr}_{t-1}'(X\hat{\mathbf{U}}, \mathbf{e}_X' - \hat{S}_j)$$

where $\eta = [\mathrm{Pr}'(\mathbf{e}_X' - \hat{S}_j)]^{-1}$. We can now factorize into the subnetwork parameters of the star centered at X:

$$\Theta_{\hat{X}}^t = \eta \sum_{\hat{\mathbf{U}}} \lambda_{\mathbf{e}}(X)\Theta_{X|\hat{\mathbf{U}}} \prod_i \Theta_{\hat{U}_i}^{t-1} \prod_{k \neq j} \Theta_{\hat{S}_k|X}^{t-1}.$$

Finally, by our inductive hypothesis and by relabeling $\hat{\mathbf{U}}$ to $\mathbf{U}$, we have

$$\Theta_{\hat{X}}^t = \eta \sum_{\mathbf{U}} \lambda_{\mathbf{e}}(X)\Theta_{X|\mathbf{U}} \prod_i \pi_X^{t-1}(U_i) \prod_{k \neq j} \lambda_{Y_k}^{t-1}(X) = \pi_{Y_j}^t(X).$$

We can similarly show that $\lambda_{Y_j}^t(X) = \Theta_{\hat{S}_j|X}^t$, that $\mathrm{Pr}_t(X|\mathbf{e}) = \mathrm{Pr}_t'(X|\mathbf{e}')$, and that $\mathrm{Pr}_t(X\mathbf{U}|\mathbf{e}) = \mathrm{Pr}_t'(X\hat{\mathbf{U}}|\mathbf{e}')$. ∎

Lemma 14.1. *Let $\mathcal{N}'$ be a Bayesian network that results from deleting a single edge $U \rightarrow X$ in network $\mathcal{N}$. Suppose further that the edge parameters of network $\mathcal{N}'$ satisfy (14.8) and (14.9). Then*

$$\mathrm{Pr}'(u|\mathbf{e}') = \mathrm{Pr}'(\hat{u}|\mathbf{e}') = \frac{1}{z_{UX}} \cdot \theta_{\hat{u}}\theta_{\hat{s}|u}$$

for states $u = \hat{u}$, where

$$z_{UX} = \sum_{u=\hat{u}} \theta_{\hat{u}}\theta_{\hat{s}|u}.$$

PROOF. Noting (14.9), we have

$$\theta_{\hat{u}}\theta_{\hat{s}|u} = \theta_{\hat{u}} \cdot \eta \, \mathrm{Pr}'(\mathbf{e}'|\hat{u}) = \mathrm{Pr}'(\hat{u}, \mathbf{e}') \cdot \eta = \mathrm{Pr}'(\hat{u}|\mathbf{e}') \cdot \eta \, \mathrm{Pr}'(\mathbf{e}'). \qquad (14.24)$$

Using (14.8), we have

$$
\begin{aligned}
\theta_{\hat{u}}\theta_{\hat{s}|u} &= \Pr'(u|\mathbf{e}' - \hat{S})\theta_{\hat{s}|u} \\
&= \frac{\Pr'(u, \mathbf{e}' - \hat{S})\theta_{\hat{s}|u}}{\Pr'(\mathbf{e}' - \hat{S})} \\
&= \frac{\Pr'(u, \mathbf{e}' - \hat{S})\Pr'(\hat{s}|u, \mathbf{e}' - \hat{S})}{\Pr'(\mathbf{e}' - \hat{S})} \\
&= \frac{\Pr'(u, \mathbf{e}')}{\Pr'(\mathbf{e}' - \hat{S})} \\
&= \Pr'(u|\mathbf{e}') \cdot \frac{\Pr'(\mathbf{e}')}{\Pr'(\mathbf{e}' - \hat{S})}
\end{aligned}
\tag{14.25}
$$

Summing (14.24) and (14.25) over states $u = \hat{u}$ (as in z_{UX}) and equating, we find that $\eta = [\Pr'(\mathbf{e}' - \hat{S})]^{-1}$ and also $z_{UX} = \eta \Pr'(\mathbf{e}')$. Making this substitution in (14.24) and (14.25), we find that

$$
\theta_{\hat{u}}\theta_{\hat{s}|u} = \Pr'(\hat{u}|\mathbf{e}') \cdot z_{UX} = \Pr'(u|\mathbf{e}') \cdot z_{UX},
\tag{14.26}
$$

which yields our lemma.   ∎

PROOF OF THEOREM 14.7. Suppose that we replace the edge $U \to X$ in network $\mathcal{N}$ with a chain $U \to \hat{U} \to X$ where the edge $U \to \hat{U}$ denotes an equivalence constraint: $\theta_{\hat{u}|u} = 1$ iff $\hat{u} = u$. The resulting augmented network is equivalent to the original network over the original variables and, in particular, it yields the same probability of evidence. We thus observe first

$$
\Pr(\mathbf{e}) = \sum_{u\hat{u}} \Pr(u\hat{u}, \mathbf{e}) = \sum_{u=\hat{u}} \Pr(u\hat{u}, \mathbf{e}).
$$

Noting (12.5) and (12.6) and that $\theta_{\hat{u}|u} = 1$ when $u = \hat{u}$, we have

$$
\Pr(\mathbf{e}) = \sum_{u=\hat{u}} \frac{\partial \Pr(u\hat{u}, \mathbf{e})}{\partial \theta_{\hat{u}|u}} \theta_{\hat{u}|u} = \sum_{u=\hat{u}} \frac{\partial \Pr(u\hat{u}, \mathbf{e})}{\partial \theta_{\hat{u}|u}} = \sum_{u=\hat{u}} \frac{\partial \Pr'(u\hat{u}, \mathbf{e})}{\partial \theta_{\hat{u}}}.
$$

The last equality follows since $\Pr(u, \hat{u}, \mathbf{e})$ and $\Pr'(u, \hat{u}, \mathbf{e})$ differ only in the parameters $\theta_{\hat{u}|u}$ and $\theta_{\hat{u}}$. Noting (12.5) and (12.6) again, and going further, we have

$$
\begin{aligned}
\Pr(\mathbf{e}) &= \sum_{u=\hat{u}} \frac{\Pr'(u\hat{u}, \mathbf{e})}{\theta_{\hat{u}}} = \sum_{u=\hat{u}} \frac{\Pr'(u\hat{u}, \mathbf{e})\theta_{\hat{s}|u}}{\theta_{\hat{u}}\theta_{\hat{s}|u}} \\
&= \sum_{u=\hat{u}} \frac{\Pr'(u\hat{u}, \mathbf{e})\Pr'(\hat{s}|u\hat{u}, \mathbf{e})}{\theta_{\hat{u}}\theta_{\hat{s}|u}} = \sum_{u=\hat{u}} \frac{\Pr'(u\hat{u}, \mathbf{e}')}{\theta_{\hat{u}}\theta_{\hat{s}|u}}.
\end{aligned}
$$

Using (14.26) from the proof of Lemma 14.1, we have

$$
\Pr(\mathbf{e}) = \sum_{u=\hat{u}} \frac{\Pr'(u\hat{u}, \mathbf{e}')}{\Pr'(\hat{u}|\mathbf{e}') \cdot z_{UX}} = \Pr'(\mathbf{e}') \cdot \frac{1}{z_{UX}} \cdot \sum_{u=\hat{u}} \Pr'(u|\hat{u}, \mathbf{e}').
$$

Since we assumed that $\mathrm{MI}(U; \hat{U}|\mathbf{e}') = 0$, we have $\Pr(\mathbf{e}) = \Pr'(\mathbf{e}') \cdot \frac{1}{z_{UX}}$.   ∎

PROOF OF THEOREM 14.8. This proof is based on a number of observations. The first observation uses Theorem 14.6 to express the Bethe free energy F_β, given by (14.4), in terms of quantities in the approximate network $\mathcal{N}'$:

$$F_\beta = \sum_{X\hat{U}} \sum_{x\hat{u}} \Pr'(x\hat{u}|e') \log \frac{\Pr'(x\hat{u}|e')}{\prod_{\hat{u}\sim\hat{u}} \Pr'(\hat{u}|e')}$$

$$- \sum_{X\hat{U}} \sum_{x\hat{u}} \Pr'(x\hat{u}|e') \log \lambda_e(x)\theta_{x|\hat{u}},$$

where X ranges over variables in the original network $\mathcal{N}$ and $\hat{U}$ are the (cloned) parents of variable X in network $\mathcal{N}'$ (see Figure 14.21).

The second observation is based on Exercise 14.20, which shows that $\log \Pr'(e')$ can be expressed as a sum of two terms ENT + AVG, where ENT is the entropy of distribution $\Pr'(.|e')$. Since network $\mathcal{N}'$ is fully disconnected, this entropy decomposes as follows (see Exercise 14.19):

$$\text{ENT} = - \sum_{X\hat{U}} \sum_{x\hat{u}} \Pr'(x\hat{u}|e') \log \Pr'(x\hat{u}|e'). \tag{14.27}$$

The third observation underlying this proof concerns the second term AVG in $\log \Pr'(e') = \text{ENT} + \text{AVG}$. From the definition given in Exercise 14.20, we have

$$\text{AVG} = \sum_{X\hat{U}} \sum_{x\hat{u}} \Pr'(x\hat{u}|e') \log \lambda_e(x)\theta_{x|\hat{u}}$$

$$+ \sum_{U \to X} \sum_{\hat{u}} \Pr'(\hat{u}|e') \log \lambda_{e'}(\hat{u})\theta_{\hat{u}} + \sum_{U \to X} \sum_{u} \Pr'(u|e') \log \lambda_{e'}(\hat{s})\theta_{\hat{s}|u}.$$

Note that each term in this sum is ranging over different types of network parameters in the approximate network $\mathcal{N}'$: parameters $\theta_{x|\hat{u}}$ from the original network $\mathcal{N}$ and parameters $\theta_{\hat{u}}$ and $\theta_{\hat{s}|u}$ introduced by deleting edges $U \to X$ in network $\mathcal{N}'$. Note also that $\lambda_{e'}(\hat{u}) = 1$ for all $\hat{u}$ as we have no evidence on the clone $\hat{U}$. Moreover, $\lambda_{e'}(\hat{s}) = 1$ since $\hat{S}$ is observed to $\hat{s}$. We therefore drop these evidence indicators for simplicity.

Since $\Pr'(\hat{u}|e') = \Pr'(u|e')$ by Lemma 14.1, we now have

$$\text{AVG} = \sum_{X\hat{U}} \sum_{x\hat{u}} \Pr'(x\hat{u}|e') \log \lambda_e(x)\theta_{x|\hat{u}} + \sum_{U \to X} \sum_{u=\hat{u}} \Pr'(\hat{u}|e') \log \theta_{\hat{u}}\theta_{\hat{s}|u}.$$

By Lemma 14.1, we also have $\theta_{\hat{u}}\theta_{\hat{s}|u} = z_{UX}\Pr'(\hat{u}|e')$; thus,

$$\sum_{U \to X} \sum_{u=\hat{u}} \Pr'(\hat{u}|e') \log \theta_{\hat{u}}\theta_{\hat{s}|u} = \sum_{U \to X} \sum_{\hat{u}} \Pr'(\hat{u}|e') \log z_{UX}\Pr'(\hat{u}|e')$$

$$= \sum_{U \to X} \log z_{UX} + \sum_{U \to X} \sum_{\hat{u}} \Pr'(\hat{u}|e') \log \Pr'(\hat{u}|e').$$

Substituting this expression into AVG, we get

$$\text{AVG} = \sum_{X\hat{U}} \sum_{x\hat{u}} \Pr'(x\hat{u}|e') \log \lambda_e(x)\theta_{x|\hat{u}}$$

$$+ \sum_{U \to X} \log z_{UX} + \sum_{U \to X} \sum_{\hat{u}} \Pr'(\hat{u}|e') \log \Pr'(\hat{u}|e').$$

Adding this to the entropy term in (14.27), we get

$$\log \Pr'(\mathbf{e}') = \text{ENT} + \text{AVG}$$

$$= -\sum_{X\hat{U}} \sum_{x\hat{u}} \Pr'(x\hat{u}|\mathbf{e}') \log \Pr'(x\hat{u}|\mathbf{e}') + \sum_{X\hat{U}} \sum_{x\hat{u}} \Pr'(x\hat{u}|\mathbf{e}') \log \lambda_{\mathbf{e}}(x)\theta_{x|\hat{u}}$$

$$+ \sum_{U \rightarrow X} \log z_{UX} + \sum_{U \rightarrow X} \sum_{\hat{u}} \Pr'(\hat{u}|\mathbf{e}') \log \Pr'(\hat{u}|\mathbf{e}').$$

Since

$$\sum_{U \rightarrow X} \sum_{\hat{u}} \Pr'(\hat{u}|\mathbf{e}') \log \Pr'(\hat{u}|\mathbf{e}')$$

$$= \sum_{U \rightarrow X} \sum_{\hat{u}} \sum_{\substack{x\hat{u} \\ \hat{u}\sim\hat{u}}} \Pr'(x\hat{u}|\mathbf{e}') \log \Pr'(\hat{u}|\mathbf{e}')$$

$$= \sum_{X\hat{U}} \sum_{x\hat{u}} \sum_{\hat{u}\sim\hat{u}} \Pr'(x\hat{u}|\mathbf{e}') \log \Pr'(\hat{u}|\mathbf{e}')$$

$$= \sum_{X\hat{U}} \sum_{x\hat{u}} \Pr'(x\hat{u}|\mathbf{e}') \log \prod_{\hat{u}\sim\hat{u}} \Pr'(\hat{u}|\mathbf{e}'),$$

we have

$$\log \Pr'(\mathbf{e}') = \text{ENT} + \text{AVG}$$

$$= -\sum_{X\hat{U}} \sum_{x\hat{u}} \Pr'(x\hat{u}|\mathbf{e}') \log \frac{\Pr'(x\hat{u}|\mathbf{e}')}{\prod_{\hat{u}\sim\hat{u}} \Pr'(\hat{u}|\mathbf{e}')} + \sum_{X\hat{U}} \sum_{x\hat{u}} \Pr'(x\hat{u}|\mathbf{e}') \log \lambda_{\mathbf{e}}(x)\theta_{x|\hat{u}}$$

$$+ \sum_{U \rightarrow X} \log z_{UX}$$

$$= -F_\beta + \sum_{U \rightarrow X} \log z_{UX}$$

$$= -F_\beta + \log z.$$

Hence, $-F_\beta = \log \Pr'(\mathbf{e}') - \log z$ and $\exp\{-F_\beta\} = \Pr'(\mathbf{e}') \cdot \frac{1}{z}$ as desired. ∎

15

Approximate Inference by Stochastic Sampling

We discuss in this chapter a class of approximate inference algorithms based on stochastic sampling: a process by which we repeatedly simulate situations according to their probability and then estimate the probabilities of events based on the frequency of their occurrence in the simulated situations.

15.1 Introduction

Consider the Bayesian network in Figure 15.1 and suppose that our goal is to estimate the probability of some event, say, wet grass. *Stochastic sampling* is a method for estimating such probabilities that works by measuring the frequency at which events materialize in a sequence of situations simulated according to their probability of occurrence. For example, if we simulate 100 situations and find out that the grass is wet in 30 of them, we estimate the probability of wet grass to be $3/10$. As we see later, we can efficiently simulate situations according to their probability of occurrence by operating on the corresponding Bayesian network, a process that provides the basis for many of the sampling algorithms we consider in this chapter.

The statements of sampling algorithms are remarkably simple compared to the methods for exact inference discussed in previous chapters, and their accuracy can be made arbitrarily high by increasing the number of sampled situations. However, the design of appropriate sampling methods may not be trivial as we may need to focus the sampling process on a set of situations that are of particular interest. For example, if the goal is to estimate the probability of wet grass given a slippery road, we may need to only simulate situations in which the road is slippery to increase the rate at which our estimates converge to the true probabilities. Another potential complication with sampling algorithms concerns the guarantees we can offer on the quality of estimates they produce, which may require sophisticated mathematical analysis in certain cases.

We begin in the next section by presenting the simplest sampling method for computing (unconditional) probabilities but without providing any analysis of its properties. We then go over some estimation background in Section 15.3 that allows us to provide a formal treatment of this sampling method and some of its variants in Section 15.4. We then discuss the problem of estimating conditional probabilities in Section 15.5, leading to two key algorithms for this purpose that are discussed in Sections 15.6 and 15.7.

15.2 Simulating a Bayesian network

Suppose that we have a Bayesian network that induces a probability distribution $\Pr(\mathbf{X})$. To draw a *random sample* of size n from this distribution is to independently generate a sequence of instantiations $\mathbf{x}^1, \ldots, \mathbf{x}^n$ where the probability of generating instantiation $\mathbf{x}^i$ is $\Pr(\mathbf{x}^i)$. We will show in this section how we can efficiently draw a random sample from

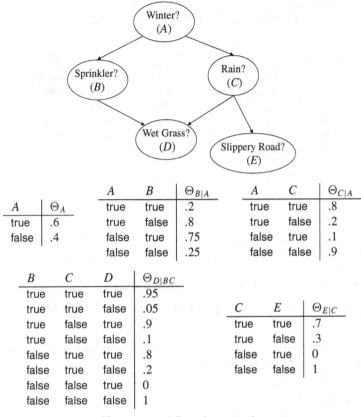

A	Θ_A
true	.6
false	.4

A	B	$\Theta_{B|A}$
true	true	.2
true	false	.8
false	true	.75
false	false	.25

A	C	$\Theta_{C|A}$
true	true	.8
true	false	.2
false	true	.1
false	false	.9

B	C	D	$\Theta_{D|BC}$
true	true	true	.95
true	true	false	.05
true	false	true	.9
true	false	false	.1
false	true	true	.8
false	true	false	.2
false	false	true	0
false	false	false	1

C	E	$\Theta_{E|C}$
true	true	.7
true	false	.3
false	true	0
false	false	1

Figure 15.1: A Bayesian network.

a probability distribution specified by a Bayesian network, a process known as *simulating the Bayesian network*.

As mentioned in the introduction, if we have an ability to draw random samples, then we can estimate the probability of event α by simply considering the fraction of instantiations at which α is true. For example, if we sample 100 instantiations and α happens to be true in 30 of them, then our estimate will be $30/100 = .3$. This very simple estimation process is analyzed formally in Section 15.4. However, in this section we simply focus on the process of drawing random samples from a distribution induced by a Bayesian network.

Consider the Bayesian network in Figure 15.1, which induces the distribution $\Pr(A, B, C, D, E)$. The basic idea for drawing a random instantiation from a Bayesian network is to traverse the network in topological order, visiting parents before children, and generate a value for each visited node according to the probability distribution of that node. In Figure 15.1, this procedure dictates that we start with variable A while sampling a value from its distribution $\Pr(A)$.[1] Suppose, for example, that we end up sampling the value a. We can now visit either variable B or C next. Suppose we visit B. We then have to sample a value for B from the distribution $\Pr(B|a)$ since a is the chosen value for variable A. Suppose that this value turns out to be $\bar{b}$ and that we also sample the value

---

[1] Since $\Pr(a) = .6$, this can be done by first choosing a random number r in the interval $[0, 1)$ and then selecting the value a if $r < .6$ and the value $\bar{a}$ otherwise. If a variable X has multiple values $x_1, \ldots, x_m$, we can generate a sample from $\Pr(X)$ as follows. We first generate a random number p in the interval $[0, 1)$ and then choose the value x_k if $\sum_{i=1}^{k-1} \Pr(x_i) \le p < \sum_{i=1}^{k} \Pr(x_i)$.

Table 15.1: A sample of size $n = 10$ generated from the network in Figure 15.1, where $\mathbf{X} = \{A, B, C, D, E\}$.

	A	B	C	E	D
$\mathbf{x}^1$	true	true	true	true	true
$\mathbf{x}^2$	true	false	true	true	false
$\mathbf{x}^3$	false	false	false	false	false
$\mathbf{x}^4$	false	true	false	false	true
$\mathbf{x}^5$	true	true	true	false	true
$\mathbf{x}^6$	true	true	true	true	true
$\mathbf{x}^7$	false	true	false	false	true
$\mathbf{x}^8$	false	false	true	true	true
$\mathbf{x}^9$	false	false	false	false	false
$\mathbf{x}^{10}$	true	false	false	false	false

Algorithm 44 SIMULATE_BN($\mathcal{N}$)

input:

$\mathcal{N}$:   A Bayesian network inducing distribution $\Pr(\mathbf{X})$

output: a network instantiation $\mathbf{x}$ sampled from the distribution $\Pr(\mathbf{X})$

main:

1: $\pi \leftarrow$ a total order of network variables in which parents appear before their children
2: $\Sigma \leftarrow \top$ {trivial variable instantiation}
3: $n \leftarrow$ number of network variables
4: **for** i from 1 to n **do**
5:     $X \leftarrow$ variable at position i in order π
6:     $\mathbf{u} \leftarrow$ value of X's parents in instantiation Σ
7:     $x \leftarrow$ value of variable X sampled from the distribution $\Pr(X|\mathbf{u})$
8:     $\Sigma \leftarrow \Sigma, x$ {appending value x to instantiation Σ}
9: **end for**
10: **return** Σ

---

c for variable C using a similar procedure. We can then sample a value for D from the distribution $\Pr(D|\bar{b}, c)$ and, finally, sample a value for variable E from $\Pr(E|c)$.

Algorithm 44, SIMULATE_BN, describes this procedure, which runs in time linear in the network size. Table 15.1 depicts a random sample of size $n = 10$ generated by this algorithm from the network in Figure 15.1. According to this sample, the probability of $A = \bar{a}$ is $5/10$, and the probability of $D = d$ is $6/10$.

Theorem 15.1. *Algorithm 44, SIMULATE_BN, generates an instantiation* $\mathbf{x}$ *with probability* $\Pr(\mathbf{x})$ *where* $\Pr(\mathbf{X})$ *is the distribution induced by the given Bayesian network.* ∎

Note also that the instantiations generated by Algorithm SIMULATE_BN are independent of each other. Hence, by repeated application of this algorithm we can generate a random sample of any size.

We next review some classical results from estimation theory, which we use in Section 15.4 to provide a more formal treatment of the sampling algorithm discussed in this section. These results will also provide the formal foundation for many of the algorithms discussed later in the chapter.

	Pr($\mathbf{X}$)	$f(\mathbf{X})$	$g(\mathbf{X})$
$\mathbf{x}_1$	.125	1	3
$\mathbf{x}_2$	.125	1	4
$\mathbf{x}_3$	.125	2	4
$\mathbf{x}_4$	.125	4	5
$\mathbf{x}_5$	.125	4	5
$\mathbf{x}_6$	.125	6	4
$\mathbf{x}_7$	.125	7	4
$\mathbf{x}_8$	.125	7	3

Figure 15.2: Two functions with the same expected value, 4, but different variances. The variance of f is 5.5 and the variance of g is .5.

15.3 Expectations

Consider a function $f(\mathbf{X})$ that takes its values depending on which instantiation $\mathbf{x}$ materializes. Since instantiations materialize according to some probability distribution $Pr(\mathbf{X})$, the values of function $f(\mathbf{X})$ also materialize according to some distribution.[2] We can define the *expected value* of function $f(\mathbf{X})$ as:

$$\text{Ex}(f) \overset{def}{=} \sum_{\mathbf{x}} f(\mathbf{x}) \cdot Pr(\mathbf{x}), \tag{15.1}$$

which is sometimes denoted by μ and called the *expectation* or *mean*. For an example, the expected value of function $f(\mathbf{X})$ in Figure 15.2 is 4.

All of our sampling algorithms are based on a central technique in which we formulate the probability of an event as an expected value of some function $f(\mathbf{X})$. Approximate inference then becomes a matter of estimating expectations, allowing us to provide guarantees on the quality of our approximations by capitalizing on results from the vast literature on estimating expectations. Our goal in this section is then to introduce this concept of an expectation and provide some of the fundamental techniques for estimating expectations and guaranteeing the quality of these estimates.

Continuing with the example in Figure 15.2, note that the function g has the same expected value as function f, that is, 4. Yet it should be clear that the values of function g are more concentrated around this expectation than the values of function f. This distinction is important when trying to estimate the expected value by observing some values of the function. For example, an observed value of function g is more likely to be close to the expectation 4 than an observed value of f. Therefore, we prefer observing the values of function g instead of function f when trying to estimate this expectation.

We can formalize the distinction between these two functions and the impact it has on the quality of estimates by using the notion of *variance*, which quantifies the extent to which an observed value of a function tends to deviate from its expected value:

$$\text{Va}(f) \overset{def}{=} \sum_{\mathbf{x}} (f(\mathbf{x}) - \text{Ex}(f))^2 \cdot Pr(\mathbf{x}). \tag{15.2}$$

In Figure 15.2, the variance of function f is 5.5 and the variance of function g is .5. Hence, the observed values of f tend to deviate from its expectation more than the values of function g do.

---

[2] This is why the value of $f(\mathbf{X})$ is typically called a *random variable*.

The variance is typically denoted by σ^2, where σ is also called the *standard deviation.*[3] The variance of a function can be used to offer some precise guarantees on the extent to which its observed values will deviate from its expectation.

Theorem 15.2 (Chebyshev's inequality). *Let μ and σ^2 be the expectation and variance of a function and let v be one of its observed values. For any $\epsilon > 0$, we have*

$$\mathbb{P}(|v - \mu| < \epsilon) \geq 1 - \frac{\sigma^2}{\epsilon^2}.$$ ∎

The main use of this theorem is as follows. Suppose that all we know is the variance of the function and wish to estimate its expectation. Suppose further that we observe a value v of our function and wish to use this value as an estimate for the expectation μ. What can we say about the quality of this estimate? In particular, what confidence do we have that the expectation μ lies in the interval $(v - \epsilon, v + \epsilon)$? Chebyshev's inequality says that our confidence is at least $1 - \sigma^2/\epsilon^2$. We say in this case that the inequality is used to provide a *confidence interval* for our estimate. We stress here that our confidence level in such intervals increases as the variance decreases, which highlights the importance of a low variance in producing high levels of confidence.[4] Considering Figure 15.2 and using only the variance of function g, we can immediately say that its expectation will lie in the interval $(v - 2.5, v + 2.5)$ with 92% confidence, where v is an observed value of the function. However, we can say the same thing about function f with only 12% confidence. Hence, if we initially know that the two functions have the same expectation and if our goal is to estimate this expectation, we clearly prefer to observe the values of function g as they allow us to provide tighter guarantees on the corresponding estimates.

Theorem 15.2 allows us to provide confidence intervals using only the variance of the function. If we also know how the values of the function are distributed, then we can provide tighter intervals, as shown by the following theorem.

Theorem 15.3. *Let μ and σ^2 be the expectation and variance of a function and let v be one of its observed values. If the values of the function are normally distributed, then*

$$\mathbb{P}(|v - \mu| < \epsilon) = \alpha,$$

where

$$\epsilon = \Phi^{-1}\left(\frac{1 + \alpha}{2}\right)\sigma$$

and $\Phi(.)$ is the CDF of the standard Normal distribution.   ∎

The main use of this theorem is as follows. We start with some confidence level, say, $\alpha = 95\%$, which leads to $\Phi^{-1}((1 + \alpha)/2) = 1.96$ based on standard tabulations of the function Φ^{-1}. We then get the guarantee $\mathbb{P}(|v - \mu| < 1.96\sigma) = .95$. That is, we can now say that the observed value v lies in the interval $(\mu - 1.96\sigma, \mu + 1.96\sigma)$ with

---

[3] The notions of expectation and variance can be extended to continuous distributions in the usual way. Suppose, for example, that $h(X)$ is a probability density function and suppose that $f(X)$ is a function that maps every value of X to a real number. The expectation of f is then $\mathrm{Ex}(f) \overset{def}{=} \int f(x)h(x)dx$ and its variance is $\mathrm{Va}(f) \overset{def}{=} \int (f(x) - \mathrm{Ex}(f))^2 h(x)dx$.

[4] Another use of Chebyshev's inequality is as follows. Suppose that we know both the expectation μ and variance σ^2 of a function. We can then guarantee that an observed value of this function will lie in the interval $(\mu - \epsilon, \mu + \epsilon)$ with a probability at least $1 - \sigma^2/\epsilon^2$.

95% confidence. This answer is better than the interval we can obtain from Chebyshev's inequality (see Exercise 15.3).

15.3.1 Probability as an expectation

All of our approximation algorithms are based on formulating the probability of an event as an expectation of some function. There are a number of ways for defining the probability of an event as an expectation, each leading to a different variance. We present several definitions in this chapter but begin with the simplest function we can define for this purpose.

Definition 15.1. The *direct sampling* function for event α, denoted $\breve{\alpha}(\mathbf{X})$, maps each instantiation $\mathbf{x}$ to a number in $\{0, 1\}$ as follows:

$$\breve{\alpha}(\mathbf{x}) \overset{def}{=} \begin{cases} 1, & \text{if } \alpha \text{ is true at instantiation } \mathbf{x} \\ 0, & \text{otherwise.} \end{cases} \quad \blacksquare$$

Theorem 15.4. *The direct sampling function $\breve{\alpha}(\mathbf{X})$ has the following expectation and variance with respect to distribution $\Pr(\mathbf{X})$:*

$$\mathrm{Ex}(\breve{\alpha}) = \Pr(\alpha) \tag{15.3}$$

$$\mathrm{Va}\,(\breve{\alpha}) = \Pr(\alpha)\Pr(\neg\alpha) = \Pr(\alpha) - \Pr(\alpha)^2. \tag{15.4}$$

$$\blacksquare$$

Hence, we can now formulate the problem of approximating a probability $\Pr(\alpha)$ as a problem of estimating the expectation $\mathrm{Ex}(\breve{\alpha})$. We discuss this estimation problem next but we first note that the variance of function $\breve{\alpha}$ gets smaller as the probability $\Pr(\alpha)$ becomes extreme, with the highest variance attained when $\Pr(\alpha) = 1/2$.

15.3.2 Estimating an expectation: Monte Carlo simulation

The basic technique for estimating the expectation of a function $f(\mathbf{X})$ is using *Monte Carlo simulation,* which works as follows. We first simulate a random sample $\mathbf{x}^1, \ldots, \mathbf{x}^n$ from the underlying distribution $\Pr(\mathbf{X})$ then evaluate the function at each instantiation of the sample, $f(\mathbf{x}^1), \ldots, f(\mathbf{x}^n)$, and finally compute the arithmetic average of attained values. This average is called the *sample mean* and defined as:

$$\mathrm{Av}_n(f) \overset{def}{=} \frac{1}{n} \sum_{i=1}^{n} f(\mathbf{x}^i). \tag{15.5}$$

Note that the sample mean is a function of the sample space yet the notation $\mathrm{Av}_n(f)$ keeps the sample $\mathbf{x}^1, \ldots, \mathbf{x}^n$ implicit for convenience. Moreover, the distribution over the sample space is known as the *sampling distribution.*

Since the sample mean is a function of the sample space, it has its own expectation and variance that are given by the following theorem.

Theorem 15.5. *Let $\mathrm{Av}_n(f)$ be a sample mean where the function f has expectation μ and variance σ^2. The expectation of the sample mean $\mathrm{Av}_n(f)$ is μ and its variance is σ^2/n.* $\blacksquare$

The first part of Theorem 15.5 provides a justification for using the sample mean $\mathrm{Av}_n(f)$ as an estimate of the expectation μ. In particular, we say here that the estimate $\mathrm{Av}_n(f)$ is *unbiased*, which is a general term used in estimation theory to indicate that the expectation of the estimate equals the quantity we are trying to estimate. The second part of the theorem shows that the variance of this estimate is inversely proportional to the sample size n. Hence, the quality of our estimates will monotonically improve as we increase the sample size.

A fundamental result known as the *law of large numbers* tells us that the sample mean is guaranteed to converge to the expectation of the function f as the sample size tends to infinity.

Theorem 15.6 (Law of Large Numbers). *Let $\mathrm{Av}_n(f)$ be a sample mean where the function f has expectation μ. For every $\epsilon > 0$, we then have*

$$\lim_{n \to \infty} \mathbb{P}(|\mathrm{Av}_n(f) - \mu| \le \epsilon) = 1. \qquad \blacksquare$$

Note that $|\mathrm{Av}_n(f) - \mu|$ is the absolute error of our estimate. Hence, we can guarantee that the absolute error is bounded by any given ϵ as the sample size tends to infinity. We say in this case that the estimate $\mathrm{Av}_n(f)$ is *consistent*, which is a general term used in estimation theory to indicate that an estimate converges to the quantity we are trying to estimate as the sample size tends to infinity.

Another fundamental result known as the *Central Limit Theorem* says roughly that the sample mean has a distribution that is approximately Normal. Before we state this result, we point out that the following statements are equivalent:

- The values of function f are Normally distributed with mean μ and variance σ^2/n.
- The values of function $\sqrt{n}(f - \mu)$ are Normally distributed with mean 0 and variance σ^2.

Although the second statement appears less intuitive, it is sometimes necessary as it refers to a Normal distribution that is independent of the sample size n.

Theorem 15.7 (Central Limit Theorem). *Let $\mathrm{Av}_n(f)$ be a sample mean where the function f has expectation μ and variance σ^2. As the sample size n tends to infinity, the distribution of $\sqrt{n}(\mathrm{Av}_n(f) - \mu)$ converges to a Normal distribution with mean 0 and variance σ^2. We say in this case that the estimate $\mathrm{Av}_n(f)$ is asymptotically Normal.* $\qquad \blacksquare$

The Central Limit Theorem is known to be robust, suggesting that the distribution of $\sqrt{n}(\mathrm{Av}_n(f) - \mu)$ can be approximated by a Normal distribution with mean 0 and variance σ^2. Equivalently, the distribution of estimate $\mathrm{Av}_n(f)$ can be approximated by a Normal distribution with mean μ and variance σ^2/n.

It is helpful here to contrast what Theorems 15.5 and 15.7 are telling us about the sample mean $\mathrm{Av}_n(f)$. Theorem 15.5 tells us that the sample mean has expectation μ and variance σ^2/n. On the other hand, Theorem 15.7 tells us that the sample mean is approximately Normal with mean μ and variance σ^2/n. Recall again that the sample mean $\mathrm{Av}_n(f)$ is meant as an estimate of the expectation μ, so we are typically interested in guarantees of the form, "The expectation μ lies in the interval $(\mathrm{Av}_n(f) - \epsilon, \mathrm{Av}_n(f) + \epsilon)$ with some confidence level α." Theorem 15.5 allows us to provide confidence intervals based on Chebyshev's inequality (Theorem 15.2) as this inequality requires that we only know the variance of the sample mean. However, Theorem 15.7 allows us to provide

---

Algorithm 45 DIRECT_SAMPLING($\alpha, n, \mathcal{N}$)

---

input:

   α: event

   n: sample size

   $\mathcal{N}$:   Bayesian network inducing distribution $\Pr(\mathbf{X})$

output: an estimate for the probability $\Pr(\alpha)$

main:

  1: $P \leftarrow 0$

  2: **for** $i = 1$ to n **do**

  3:     $\mathbf{x} \leftarrow$ SIMULATE_BN($\mathcal{N}$) {Algorithm 44}

  4:     $P \leftarrow P + \breve{\alpha}(\mathbf{x})$ {see Definition 15.1 for computing $\breve{\alpha}(\mathbf{x})$}

  5: **end for**

  6: **return** P/n {sample mean}

---

better confidence intervals based on Theorem 15.3, as this theorem requires the sample mean to be Normally distributed.

It is known that Theorem 15.7 continues to hold if we replace the variance σ^2 by what is known as the *sample variance*,

$$S^2{}_n(f) \stackrel{def}{=} \frac{1}{n-1} \sum_{i=1}^{n} \left(f(\mathbf{x}^i) - \mathrm{Av}_n(f) \right)^2. \tag{15.6}$$

This is quite important in practice as it allows us to compute confidence intervals even when we do not know the value of variance σ^2. Similar to the sample mean, the sample variance is also a function of the sample space. Moreover, the expectation of this function is known to be σ^2, which justifies using the sample variance as an estimate of σ^2. Finally, the square root of the sample variance is known as the *standard error*.

15.4 Direct sampling

We now have all the ingredients needed to provide a formal treatment of the method introduced in Section 15.2 for estimating a probability $\Pr(\alpha)$. We begin by providing a formal statement of this method, which we call *direct sampling*, and then follow with a discussion of its properties.

According to Theorem 15.4, the probability $\Pr(\alpha)$ can be formulated as an expectation of the function $\breve{\alpha}$ given by Definition 15.1. Hence, we can estimate this probability by estimating the expectation of $\breve{\alpha}$ using Monte Carlo simulation:

1. Simulate a sample $\mathbf{x}^1, \ldots, \mathbf{x}^n$ from the given Bayesian network.
2. Compute the values $\breve{\alpha}(\mathbf{x}^1), \ldots, \breve{\alpha}(\mathbf{x}^n)$.
3. Estimate the probability $\Pr(\alpha)$ using the sample mean,

$$\mathrm{Av}_n(\breve{\alpha}) = \frac{1}{n} \sum_{i=1}^{n} \breve{\alpha}(\mathbf{x}^i). \tag{15.7}$$

Consider Table 15.1, which depicts a sample drawn from the Bayesian network in Figure 15.1. Consider also the event α: the grass is wet or the road is slippery. The corresponding values of function $\breve{\alpha}$ are 1, 1, 0, 1, 1, 1, 1, 1, 0, 0, leading to an estimate of 7/10 for the probability of event α. Algorithm 45 provides the pseudocode for direct sampling.

The following result, which is a corollary of Theorems 15.4 and 15.5, provides some properties of direct sampling.

Corollary 4. *Consider the sample mean* $\mathrm{Av}_n(\breve{\alpha})$ *in (15.7). The expectation of this sample mean is* $\mathrm{Pr}(\alpha)$ *and its variance is* $\mathrm{Pr}(\alpha)\mathrm{Pr}(\neg\alpha)/n$. ∎

Using the Central Limit Theorem, we also conclude that the distribution of sample mean $\mathrm{Av}_n(\breve{\alpha})$ can be approximated by a Normal distribution with mean $\mathrm{Pr}(\alpha)$ and variance $\mathrm{Pr}(\alpha)\mathrm{Pr}(\neg\alpha)/n$. Note, however, that we cannot compute the variance $\mathrm{Pr}(\alpha)\mathrm{Pr}(\neg\alpha)$ in this case as we do not know the probability $\mathrm{Pr}(\alpha)$ (we are trying to estimate it). Yet as mentioned previously, we can still apply the Central Limit Theorem by using the sample variance $\mathrm{S}^2{}_n(\breve{\alpha})$ instead of the true variance. We next provide some guarantees on both the absolute and relative error of the estimates computed by direct sampling.

15.4.1 Bounds on the absolute error

The *absolute error* of an estimate $\mathrm{Av}_n(\breve{\alpha})$ is the absolute difference it has with the true probability $\mathrm{Pr}(\alpha)$ we are trying to estimate. We next provide two bounds on the absolute error of estimates computed by direct sampling.

The first bound is immediate from Corollary 4 and Chebyshev's inequality.

Corollary 5. *For any* $\epsilon > 0$, *we have*

$$\mathbb{P}(|\mathrm{Av}_n(\breve{\alpha}) - \mathrm{Pr}(\alpha)| < \epsilon) \geq 1 - \frac{\mathrm{Pr}(\alpha)\mathrm{Pr}(\neg\alpha)}{n\epsilon^2}.$$

∎

That is, the estimate $\mathrm{Av}_n(\breve{\alpha})$ computed by direct sampling falls within the interval $(\mathrm{Pr}(\alpha) - \epsilon, \mathrm{Pr}(\alpha) + \epsilon)$ with probability at least $1 - \mathrm{Pr}(\alpha)\mathrm{Pr}(\neg\alpha)/n\epsilon^2$. Figure 15.3 plots this bound as a function of the sample size n and probability $\mathrm{Pr}(\alpha)$. Note that we typically do not know the probability $\mathrm{Pr}(\alpha)$ yet we can still use this bound by assuming a worst-case scenario of $\mathrm{Pr}(\alpha) = 1/2$.

A sharper bound that does not depend on the probability $\mathrm{Pr}(\alpha)$ follows from the following result.

Theorem 15.8 (Hoeffding's inequality). *Let* $\mathrm{Av}_n(f)$ *be a sample mean where the function f has expectation μ and values in $\{0, 1\}$. For any* $\epsilon > 0$, *we have*

$$\mathbb{P}(|\mathrm{Av}_n(f) - \mu| \leq \epsilon) \geq 1 - 2e^{-2n\epsilon^2}.$$

∎

The second bound on the absolute error is immediate from Corollary 4 and Hoeffding's inequality.

Corollary 6. *For any* $\epsilon > 0$, *we have*

$$\mathbb{P}(|\mathrm{Av}_n(\breve{\alpha}) - \mathrm{Pr}(\alpha)| \leq \epsilon) \geq 1 - 2e^{-2n\epsilon^2}.$$

∎

That is, the estimate $\mathrm{Av}_n(\breve{\alpha})$ computed by direct sampling falls within the interval $(\mathrm{Pr}(\alpha) - \epsilon, \mathrm{Pr}(\alpha) + \epsilon)$ with probability at least $1 - 2e^{-2n\epsilon^2}$. Figure 15.4 plots this bound as a function of the sample size n.

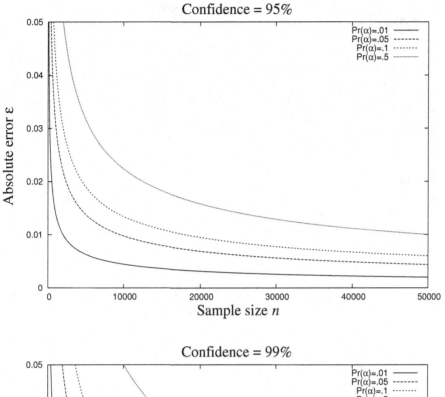

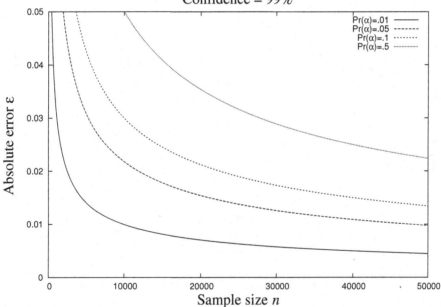

Figure 15.3: Absolute error ϵ as a function of the sample size n and event probability, according to Corollary 6. The confidence level represents the probability that the estimate will fall within the interval $(\Pr(\alpha) - \epsilon, \Pr(\alpha) + \epsilon)$.

15.4.2 Bounds on the relative error

The *relative error* of an estimate $Av_n(\breve{\alpha})$ is defined as

$$\frac{|Av_n(\breve{\alpha}) - \Pr(\alpha)|}{\Pr(\alpha)}.$$

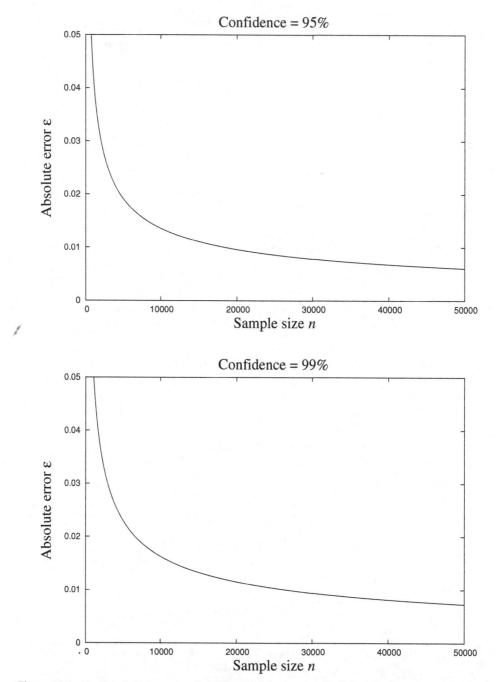

Figure 15.4: Absolute error ϵ as a function of the sample size n, according to Corollary 6. The confidence level represents the probability that the estimate will fall within the interval $(\Pr(\alpha) - \epsilon, \Pr(\alpha) + \epsilon)$.

Considering Figure 15.3, it should be clear that the bound on the absolute error becomes tighter as the probability of an event becomes more extreme. Yet the corresponding bound on the relative error becomes looser as the probability of an event becomes more extreme (see Figure 15.5). For example, for an event with probability .5 and a sample size of 10,000, there is a 95% chance that the relative error is about 4.5%. However, for the same confidence level the relative error increases to about 13.4% if the event has probability .1,

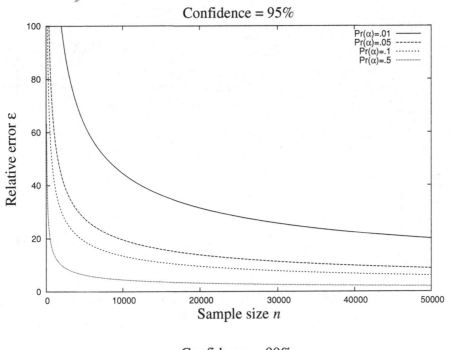

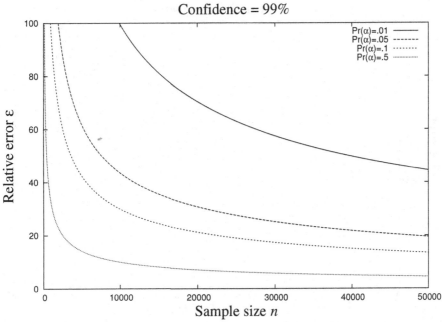

Figure 15.5: Percentage relative error ϵ as a function of the sample size n and event probability, according to Corollary 7. The confidence level represents the probability that the estimate will fall within the interval $(\mathrm{Pr}(\alpha) - \epsilon\,\mathrm{Pr}(\alpha), \mathrm{Pr}(\alpha) + \epsilon\,\mathrm{Pr}(\alpha))$.

and increases again to about 44.5% if the event has probability .01. We can quantify this more precisely based on Corollary 5.

Corollary 7. *For any $\epsilon > 0$, we have*

$$\mathbb{P}\left(\frac{|\mathrm{Av}_n(\breve{\alpha}) - \mathrm{Pr}(\alpha)|}{\mathrm{Pr}(\alpha)} < \epsilon\right) \geq 1 - \frac{\mathrm{Pr}(\neg\alpha)}{n\epsilon^2\mathrm{Pr}(\alpha)}. \qquad \blacksquare$$

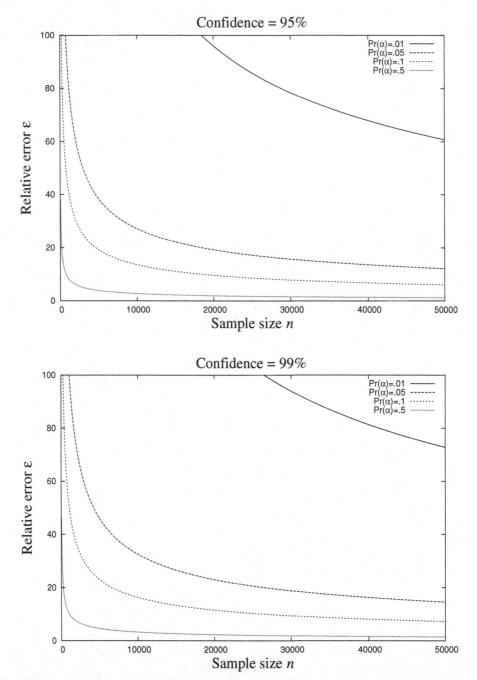

Figure 15.6: Percentage relative error ϵ as a function of the sample size n and event probability, according to Corollary 8. The confidence level represents the probability that the estimate will fall within the interval $(\Pr(\alpha) - \epsilon\Pr(\alpha), \Pr(\alpha) + \epsilon\Pr(\alpha))$.

This result, plotted in Figure 15.5, highlights the difficulty with bounding the relative error when estimating the probability of rare events, even when the sample size is large. We also have the following bound on the relative error, which follows directly from Corollary 6 and is plotted in Figure 15.6.

Corollary 8. *For any $\epsilon > 0$, we have*

$$\mathbb{P}\left(\frac{|\mathrm{Av}_n(\breve{\alpha}) - \mathrm{Pr}(\alpha)|}{\mathrm{Pr}(\alpha)} \leq \epsilon\right) \geq 1 - 2e^{-2n\epsilon^2\mathrm{Pr}(\alpha)^2}. \qquad \blacksquare$$

Note that both Corollaries 7 and 8 require the probability $\mathrm{Pr}(\alpha)$ or some lower bound on it.

15.4.3 Rao-Blackwell sampling

Direct sampling is the only method we currently have for estimating a probability $\mathrm{Pr}(\alpha)$. This method uses Monte Carlo simulation to estimate the expectation of the direct sampling function $\breve{\alpha}$ that has variance $\mathrm{Pr}(\alpha)\mathrm{Pr}(\neg\alpha)$ (see Theorem 15.4). We next define another estimation method called *Rao-Blackwell sampling*, which is based on the expectation of a different function and can have a smaller variance.

To reveal the intuition behind Rao-Blackwell sampling, suppose we have a Bayesian network over disjoint variables $\mathbf{X}$ and $\mathbf{Y}$, where our goal is to estimate the probability of some event α, $\mathrm{Pr}(\alpha)$. Suppose further that the computation of $\mathrm{Pr}(\alpha|\mathbf{y})$ can be done efficiently for any instantiation $\mathbf{y}$. Rao-Blackwell sampling exploits this fact to reduce the variance by sampling from the distribution $\mathrm{Pr}(\mathbf{Y})$ instead of the full distribution $\mathrm{Pr}(\mathbf{X}, \mathbf{Y})$. In particular, Rao-Blackwell sampling does the following:

1. Draw a sample $\mathbf{y}^1, \ldots, \mathbf{y}^n$ from the distribution $\mathrm{Pr}(\mathbf{Y})$.
2. Compute $\mathrm{Pr}(\alpha|\mathbf{y}^i)$ for each sampled instantiation $\mathbf{y}^i$.
3. Estimate the probability $\mathrm{Pr}(\alpha)$ using the average $(1/n)\sum_{i=1}^n \mathrm{Pr}(\alpha|\mathbf{y}^i)$.

As we see next, this estimate generally has a smaller variance than the one produced by direct sampling.

Rao-Blackwell sampling is formalized as follows.

Definition 15.2. The *Rao-Blackwell* function for event α and distribution $\mathrm{Pr}(\mathbf{X}, \mathbf{Y})$, denoted $\ddot{\alpha}(\mathbf{Y})$, maps each instantiation $\mathbf{y}$ into $[0, 1]$ as follows:

$$\ddot{\alpha}(\mathbf{y}) \stackrel{def}{=} \mathrm{Pr}(\alpha|\mathbf{y}). \qquad \blacksquare$$

Hence, if our sample is $\mathbf{y}^1, \ldots, \mathbf{y}^n$ and if we use Monte Carlo simulation to estimate the expectation of the Rao-Blackwell function $\ddot{\alpha}(\mathbf{Y})$, then our estimate will simply be the sample mean,

$$\mathrm{Av}_n(\ddot{\alpha}) = \frac{1}{n}\sum_{i=1}^n \mathrm{Pr}(\alpha|\mathbf{y}^i).$$

Theorem 15.9. *The expectation and variance of the Rao-Blackwell function $\ddot{\alpha}(\mathbf{Y})$ with respect to distribution $\mathrm{Pr}(\mathbf{Y})$ are*

$$\mathrm{Ex}(\ddot{\alpha}) = \mathrm{Pr}(\alpha)$$
$$\mathrm{Va}\,(\ddot{\alpha}) = \sum_{\mathbf{y}} \mathrm{Pr}(\alpha|\mathbf{y})^2\mathrm{Pr}(\mathbf{y}) - \mathrm{Pr}(\alpha)^2. \qquad \blacksquare$$

The variance of the newly defined function $\ddot{\alpha}$ ranges between zero and $\mathrm{Pr}(\alpha)\mathrm{Pr}(\neg\alpha)$ (see Exercise 15.13). Hence, the variance of Rao-Blackwell sampling is no greater than the variance of direct sampling and can actually be much smaller. Note, however, that for Rao-Blackwell sampling to be feasible the variables $\mathbf{Y}$ must be chosen carefully to allow for the efficient computation of the conditional probability $\Pr(\alpha|\mathbf{y})$ (see Exercise 15.11).

15.5 Estimating a conditional probability

Consider now the problem of estimating a conditional probability $\Pr(\alpha|\beta)$ when the distribution $\Pr(.)$ is induced by a Bayesian network. Since $\Pr(\alpha|\beta)$ corresponds to the expectation of the direct sampling function $\breve{\alpha}$ with respect to distribution $\Pr(.|\beta)$, we can estimate $\Pr(\alpha|\beta)$ by estimating the corresponding expectation. However, the problem with this approach is that sampling from the distribution $\Pr(.|\beta)$ is generally hard, which tends to preclude the use of Monte Carlo simulation for computing this expectation. That is, we typically cannot efficiently generate a sequence of independent instantiations $\mathbf{x}^1, \ldots, \mathbf{x}^n$ where the probability of generating instantiation $\mathbf{x}^i$ is $\Pr(\mathbf{x}^i|\beta)$.[5]

A common solution to this problem is based on estimating the probabilities $\Pr(\alpha \wedge \beta)$ and $\Pr(\beta)$ and then taking their ratio as an estimate for $\Pr(\alpha|\beta)$. For example, if $\gamma = \alpha \wedge \beta$ and if we are using direct sampling to estimate probabilities, our estimate for the conditional probability $\Pr(\alpha|\beta)$ is then the ratio $Av_n(\breve{\gamma})/Av_n(\breve{\beta})$.

When computing the ratio $Av_n(\breve{\gamma})/Av_n(\breve{\beta})$, it is quite common to generate one sample of size n from the distribution $\Pr(.)$ and then use it for computing the sample means $Av_n(\breve{\gamma})$ and $Av_n(\breve{\beta})$ simultaneously. In particular, let c_1 be the number of instantiations in the sample at which $\gamma = \alpha \wedge \beta$ is true and let c_2 be the number of instantiations at which β is true $(c_1 \leq c_2)$. Then $Av_n(\breve{\gamma})/Av_n(\breve{\beta})$ equals $(c_1/n)/(c_2/n) = c_1/c_2$, which is the estimate for $\Pr(\alpha|\beta)$. This method is called *rejection sampling* as it can be thought of as rejecting all sampled instantiations at which β is false (see Exercise 15.14 for a more formal explanation).

Theorem 15.10 sheds some light on the quality of estimates produced by rejection sampling.

Theorem 15.10. *Let α and β be two events and let $\gamma = \alpha \wedge \beta$. The estimate $Av_n(\breve{\gamma})/Av_n(\breve{\beta})$ is asymptotically Normal and its distribution can be approximated by a Normal distribution with mean $\Pr(\alpha|\beta)$ and variance*

$$\frac{\Pr(\alpha|\beta)\Pr(\neg\alpha|\beta)}{n\Pr(\beta)}. \qquad \blacksquare$$

According to this result, the variance of rejection sampling grows larger as the probability of β gets smaller. Hence, when $\Pr(\beta)$ is really small rejection sampling may not be an attractive method for estimating conditional probabilities, even when the sample size n is large.

We next present two alternative approaches for estimating conditional probabilities. The first method, called importance sampling, is based on formulating the probability as an expectation of yet another function. The second method, called Markov chain Monte Carlo simulation, allows us to compute expectations with respect to distributions that may be hard to sample from, such as $\Pr(.|\beta)$. These methods are discussed in Sections 15.6 and 15.7, respectively.

---

[5] Contrast this with the discussion in Section 15.2 where we provided an efficient procedure for sampling from the unconditional distribution $\Pr(\mathbf{X})$. That is, we showed how to efficiently generate a sequence of independent instantiations $\mathbf{x}^1, \ldots, \mathbf{x}^n$ where the probability of generating instantiation $\mathbf{x}^i$ is $\Pr(\mathbf{x}^i)$.

15.6 Importance sampling

Importance sampling is a technique that can be used to reduce the variance when estimating the probabilities of rare events or when estimating probabilities that are conditioned on rare events. The basic idea behind this technique is to sample from another distribution $\widetilde{\Pr}$ that emphasizes the instantiations consistent with the rare event. This is done by defining the probability of an event as an expectation of a new function as given next.

Definition 15.3. Given an event α and two distributions $\Pr(\mathbf{X})$ and $\widetilde{\Pr}(\mathbf{X})$, the *importance sampling* function for event α, denoted $\tilde{\alpha}(\mathbf{X})$, maps each instantiation $\mathbf{x}$ into a number as follows:

$$\tilde{\alpha}(\mathbf{x}) \stackrel{def}{=} \begin{cases} \Pr(\mathbf{x})/\widetilde{\Pr}(\mathbf{x}), & \text{if } \alpha \text{ is true at instantiation } \mathbf{x} \\ 0, & \text{otherwise.} \end{cases}$$

$\widetilde{\Pr}(\mathbf{X})$ is called the *importance* or *proposal* distribution and is required to satisfy the following condition: $\widetilde{\Pr}(\mathbf{x}) = 0$ only if $\Pr(\mathbf{x}) = 0$ for all instantiations $\mathbf{x}$ at which α is true. ■

Note that although a direct sampling function $\breve{\alpha}$ has values in $\{0, 1\}$ and a Rao-Blackwell function $\ddot{\alpha}$ has values in $[0, 1]$, an important sampling function $\tilde{\alpha}$ has values in $[0, \infty)$.

To estimate a probability $\Pr(\alpha)$, importance sampling simply estimates the expectation of the corresponding importance sampling function $\tilde{\alpha}$ using Monte Carlo simulation. That is, the method start by drawing a sample $\mathbf{x}^1, \ldots, \mathbf{x}^n$ from the importance distribution $\widetilde{\Pr}(\mathbf{X})$. It then computes the corresponding values $\tilde{\alpha}(\mathbf{x}^1), \ldots, \tilde{\alpha}(\mathbf{x}^n)$. It finally estimates the probability $\Pr(\alpha)$ using the sample mean,

$$\mathrm{Av}_n(\tilde{\alpha}) \stackrel{def}{=} \frac{1}{n} \sum_{i=1}^{n} \tilde{\alpha}(\mathbf{x}^i). \tag{15.8}$$

Importance sampling improves on direct sampling only when the importance distribution satisfies some conditions. To characterize these conditions, we first start with the following properties of the importance sampling function.

Theorem 15.11. *The expectation and variance of an importance sampling function $\tilde{\alpha}(\mathbf{X})$ with respect to the importance distribution $\widetilde{\Pr}(\mathbf{X})$ are*

$$\mathrm{Ex}(\tilde{\alpha}) = \Pr(\alpha)$$

$$\mathrm{Va}\,(\tilde{\alpha}) = \left(\sum_{\mathbf{x} \models \alpha} \frac{\Pr(\mathbf{x})^2}{\widetilde{\Pr}(\mathbf{x})} \right) - \Pr(\alpha)^2. \qquad ■$$

If $\widetilde{\Pr}(\mathbf{x}) \geq \Pr(\mathbf{x})$ for all instantiations $\mathbf{x}$ that are consistent with event α, the variance $\mathrm{Va}\,(\tilde{\alpha})$ ranges between zero and $\Pr(\alpha)\Pr(\neg\alpha)$ (see Exercise 15.19). Hence, under this condition the variance of importance sampling is no greater than the variance of direct sampling (see Theorem 15.4). Intuitively, this condition requires the importance distribution to emphasize the instantiations consistent with event α no less than they are emphasized by the original distribution. We later provide a concrete instance of importance sampling that satisfies this condition.

We next define an additional property of importance distributions that, although difficult to ensure in practice, provides an idealized case that reveals the promise of this method in estimating probabilities.

Definition 15.4. Two distributions $\Pr(\mathbf{X})$ and $\widetilde{\Pr}(\mathbf{X})$ are *proportional* at event α if and only if $\Pr(\mathbf{x})/\widetilde{\Pr}(\mathbf{x}) = c$ for some constant $c > 0$ and all instantiations $\mathbf{x}$ that are consistent with event α. ∎

Theorem 15.12. *If the importance and original distributions are proportional at event α, we have*

$$Va\,(\tilde{\alpha}) = \left(\frac{\Pr(\alpha)}{\widetilde{\Pr}(\alpha)}\right)\Pr(\alpha) - \Pr(\alpha)^2. \tag{15.9}$$

∎

Consider now the variance of direct sampling:

$$Va\,(\breve{\alpha}) = \Pr(\alpha) - \Pr(\alpha)^2.$$

If the importance distribution assigns a greater probability to event α, $\widetilde{\Pr}(\alpha) > \Pr(\alpha)$, importance sampling is guaranteed to have a smaller variance than direct sampling. Moreover, the reduction in variance is precisely tied to the extent to which event α is emphasized by the importance distribution. Note that when $\widetilde{\Pr}(\alpha) = 1$, the variance is zero and the importance distribution $\widetilde{\Pr}(.)$ equals $\Pr(.|\alpha)$. Hence, $\Pr(.|\alpha)$ can be viewed as the ideal importance distribution when estimating $\Pr(\alpha)$ yet we typically cannot use this distribution for the reasons mentioned in Exercise 15.20.

Let us now return to our original problem of estimating a conditional probability $\Pr(\alpha|\beta)$ when event β is rare. Suppose again that we estimate this conditional probability using rejection sampling, that is, using the ratio of estimates for $\Pr(\alpha, \beta)$ and $\Pr(\beta)$. Suppose, however, that we now use importance sampling to produce these estimates. Theorem 15.13 sheds some light on the quality of our estimate when the importance distribution satisfies the proportionality condition.

Theorem 15.13. *Let α and β be two events, let $\gamma = \alpha \wedge \beta$, and suppose that the original and importance distributions are proportional at event β as given by Definition 15.4. The estimate $Av_n(\tilde{\gamma})/Av_n(\tilde{\beta})$ is asymptotically Normal and its distribution can be approximated by a Normal distribution with mean $\Pr(\alpha|\beta)$ and variance*

$$\frac{\Pr(\alpha|\beta)\Pr(\neg\alpha|\beta)}{n\widetilde{\Pr}(\beta)}.$$

∎

Compare this with the estimate based on direct sampling (Theorem 15.10), for which the variance is

$$\frac{\Pr(\alpha|\beta)\Pr(\neg\alpha|\beta)}{n\Pr(\beta)}.$$

Importance sampling in this idealized case allows us to replace $\Pr(\beta)$ by $\widetilde{\Pr}(\beta)$ in the denominator, which in turn makes the variance independent of $\Pr(\beta)$.

This analysis reveals the promise of importance sampling in dealing with unlikely events as it allows us to make the variance independent of the probability of such events. However, we stress that using importance distributions that satisfy the condition of Theorem 15.12 is generally not feasible. We next discuss a weaker condition that is easy to ensure in practice yet is guaranteed to improve on the variance of direct sampling.

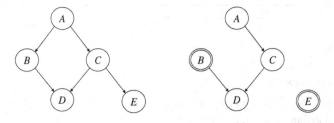

Bayesian network   Likelihood weighting network

Figure 15.7: A Bayesian network and its likelihood weighting network given evidence on variables B and E. Both networks have the same CPTs for variables A, C, and D. The CPTs for variables B and E in the second network depend on the available evidence. For example, if the evidence is $B = b$ and $E = \bar{e}$, then $\theta_b = 1$, $\theta_{\bar{b}} = 0$ and $\theta_e = 0$, $\theta_{\bar{e}} = 1$.

15.6.1 Likelihood weighting

Consider a Bayesian network N and some evidence $\mathbf{e}$, where the goal is to estimate some conditional probability $\Pr(\alpha|\mathbf{e})$. The method of *likelihood weighting* uses an importance distribution, which is defined as follows.

Definition 15.5. Let N be a Bayesian network and let $\mathbf{e}$ be a variable instantiation. The corresponding *likelihood-weighting network* $\widetilde{N}$ is obtained from N by deleting edges going into nodes $\mathbf{E}$ while setting the CPTs of these nodes as follows. If variable $E \in \mathbf{E}$ is instantiated to e in evidence $\mathbf{e}$, then $\widetilde{\theta}_e = 1$; otherwise, $\widetilde{\theta}_e = 0$. All other CPTs of network $\widetilde{N}$ are equal to those in network N. ∎

Figure 15.7 depicts a Bayesian network and a corresponding likelihood-weighting network given evidence on nodes B and E. Note here that the CPTs for variables A, C, and D are the same for both networks.

The variance of likelihood weighting is no greater than the variance of direct sampling due to Theorem 15.14.

Theorem 15.14. *Let N be a Bayesian network, $\mathbf{e}$ be some evidence, and let $\widetilde{N}$ be the corresponding likelihood-weighting network. Suppose that networks N and $\widetilde{N}$ induce distributions $\Pr(\mathbf{X})$ and $\widetilde{\Pr}(\mathbf{X})$, respectively, and that $\mathbf{x}$ is consistent with evidence $\mathbf{e}$. If $\theta_{e|\mathbf{u}}$ ranges over the parameters of variables $E \in \mathbf{E}$ in network N, where $e\mathbf{u}$ is consistent with instantiation $\mathbf{x}$, then*

$$\Pr(\mathbf{x})/\widetilde{\Pr}(\mathbf{x}) = \prod_{\theta_{e|\mathbf{u}}} \theta_{e|\mathbf{u}} \leq 1. \qquad \blacksquare$$

According to Theorem 15.14, $\widetilde{\Pr}(\mathbf{x}) \geq \Pr(\mathbf{x})$ for every instantiation $\mathbf{x}$ consistent with evidence $\mathbf{e}$. Hence, the variance of likelihood weighting cannot be larger than the variance of direct sampling (see Exercise 15.19). Theorem 15.14 also shows that the ratio $\Pr(\mathbf{x})/\widetilde{\Pr}(\mathbf{x})$ can be computed efficiently for any instantiation $\mathbf{x}$ as it corresponds to the product of all network parameters $\theta_{e|\mathbf{u}}$ that belong to the CPTs of evidence variables $\mathbf{E}$ and are consistent with instantiation $\mathbf{x}$. Consider Figure 15.7 for an example and assume that we have the evidence $B = b$ and $E = \bar{e}$. For instantiation $\mathbf{x} : \bar{a}, b, c, d, \bar{e}$, we have

$$\frac{\Pr(\bar{a}, b, c, d, \bar{e})}{\widetilde{\Pr}(\bar{a}, b, c, d, \bar{e})} = \frac{\theta_{\bar{a}} \theta_{b|\bar{a}} \theta_{c|\bar{a}} \theta_{d|bc} \theta_{\bar{e}|c}}{\theta_{\bar{a}}(1) \theta_{c|\bar{a}} \theta_{d|bc}(1)} = \theta_{b|\bar{a}} \theta_{\bar{e}|c}.$$

Algorithm 46 LIKELIHOOD_WEIGHTING($\mathbf{e}, n, \mathcal{N}$)

input:

    $\mathbf{e}$:   evidence

    n: sample size

    $\mathcal{N}$:   Bayesian network

output: an estimate for $\Pr(\mathbf{e})$ and $\Pr(x|\mathbf{e})$ for each value x of variable X in network $\mathcal{N}$, where $\Pr$ is the distribution induced by $\mathcal{N}$

main:

1: $\mathcal{N}' \leftarrow$ LW network for network $\mathcal{N}$ and evidence $\mathbf{e}$
2: $P \leftarrow 0$ {estimate for $\Pr(\mathbf{e})$}
3: $P[x] \leftarrow 0$ for each value x of variable X in network $\mathcal{N}$ {estimate for $\Pr(x, \mathbf{e})$}
4: **for** $i = 1$ to n **do**
5:    $\mathbf{x} \leftarrow$ SIMULATE_BN($\mathcal{N}'$)
6:    $W \leftarrow$ product of all network parameters $\theta_{e|\mathbf{u}}$ where $E \in \mathbf{E}$ and $e\mathbf{u} \sim \mathbf{x}$
7:    $P \leftarrow P + W$
8:    $P[x] \leftarrow P[x] + W$ for each variable X and its value x consistent with $\mathbf{x}$
9: **end for**
10: **return** P/n and $P[x]/P$ for each value x of variable X in network $\mathcal{N}$

Consider again the network in Figure 15.7 (its CPTs are shown in Figure 15.1). Suppose that our goal is to estimate the conditional probability $\Pr(\bar{d}|b, \bar{e})$ by estimating each of $\Pr(\bar{d}, b, \bar{e})$ and $\Pr(b, \bar{e})$ and then taking their ratio. The following table contains a sample of five instantiations generated from the likelihood-weighting network in Figure 15.7 using evidence $b, \bar{e}$.

Instantiation $\mathbf{x}$	$\Pr(\mathbf{x})/\widetilde{\Pr}(\mathbf{x})$		$\tilde{\gamma}(\mathbf{x})$	$\tilde{\beta}(\mathbf{x})$
$\mathbf{x}^1 : a, b, c, d, \bar{e}$	$\theta_{b|a}\theta_{\bar{e}|c}$	$= (.2)(.3)$	0	.060
$\mathbf{x}^2 : a, b, c, \bar{d}, \bar{e}$	$\theta_{b|a}\theta_{\bar{e}|c}$	$= (.2)(.3)$	.060	.060
$\mathbf{x}^3 : a, b, \bar{c}, \bar{d}, \bar{e}$	$\theta_{b|a}\theta_{\bar{e}|\bar{c}}$	$= (.2)(1)$	.200	.200
$\mathbf{x}^4 : \bar{a}, b, c, d, \bar{e}$	$\theta_{b|\bar{a}}\theta_{\bar{e}|c}$	$= (.75)(.3)$	0	.225
$\mathbf{x}^5 : a, b, c, d, \bar{e}$	$\theta_{b|a}\theta_{\bar{e}|c}$	$= (.2)(.3)$	0	.060

The table also shows the corresponding values of the importance sampling function for events $\gamma = \bar{d}, b, \bar{e}$ and $\beta = b, \bar{e}$. Hence, we have $\text{Av}_5(\tilde{\gamma}) = .260/5$ and $\text{Av}_5(\tilde{\beta}) = .605/5$, leading to $.260/.605$ as the estimate of conditional probability $\Pr(\bar{d}|b, \bar{e})$.

Note here that we used the same importance distribution for both events γ and β. In principle, we could use two distinct importance distributions, each targeted toward the corresponding event. Using the same distribution is more common in practice, especially when estimating $\Pr(X|\mathbf{e})$ for each node X in a Bayesian network. Algorithm 46 provides pseudocode for estimating these conditional probabilities using the method of likelihood weighting.

15.6.2 Particle filtering

Likelihood weighting can be applied to dynamic Bayesian networks (DBNs), leading to an instance of what is known as *sequential importance sampling* (SIS) (see Exercise 15.22). However, in this section we discuss a more sophisticated application of likelihood weighting to DBNs, known as *particle filtering*. We first describe particle filtering on HMMs and then on a more general class of DBNs.

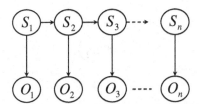

Figure 15.8: A hidden Markov model (HMM).

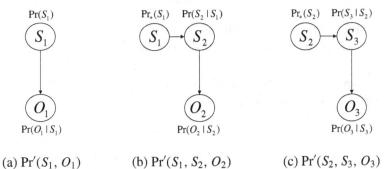

$$(a) \; \Pr'(S_1, O_1) \qquad (b) \; \Pr'(S_1, S_2, O_2) \qquad (c) \; \Pr'(S_2, S_3, O_3)$$

Figure 15.9: The networks used by particle filtering when performing inference on the HMM in Figure 15.8.

Consider the HMM in Figure 15.8 and suppose that our goal is to estimate the conditional probability $\Pr(S_t | O_1, \ldots, O_t)$ for each time t. The key insight behind particle filtering is to approximate this HMM using a number of smaller networks as shown in Figure 15.9. In particular, for each time step $t > 1$, particle filtering will work with a network that induces a distribution $\Pr'(S_{t-1}, S_t, O_t)$ specified by the following CPTs:

- A CPT for node S_{t-1}, $\Pr_\star(S_{t-1})$, which is specified as given next.
- A CPT for node S_t, $\Pr(S_t | S_{t-1})$, obtained from the original HMM.
- A CPT for node O_t, $\Pr(O_t | S_t)$, obtained from the original HMM.

Suppose now that the CPT for node S_{t-1} is set as

$$\Pr_\star(S_{t-1}) = \Pr(S_{t-1} | O_1, \ldots, O_{t-1}). \tag{15.10}$$

That is, the CPT is chosen to summarize the impact that past observations have on node S_{t-1}. This choice leads to the following distribution for the network fragment at time t (see Exercise 15.23):

$$\Pr'(S_{t-1}, S_t, O_t) = \Pr(S_{t-1}, S_t, O_t | O_1, \ldots, O_{t-1}). \tag{15.11}$$

Hence, the network fragment used by particle filtering at time t now integrates all the evidence obtained before time t. More precisely, this network fragment can be used to obtain the probability of interest, as we now have (see Exercise 15.23):

$$\Pr'(S_t | O_t) = \Pr(S_t | O_1, \ldots, O_t). \tag{15.12}$$

The only problem with this proposal is that we typically do not have the distribution $\Pr(S_{t-1} | O_1, \ldots, O_{t-1})$ in (15.10) as it is precisely this distribution that particle filtering is trying to compute. Particle filtering instead uses an estimate of this distribution when specifying the CPT $\Pr_\star(S_{t-1})$ for node S_{t-1}. Moreover, it obtains this estimate from the network fragment it has for time $t - 1$.

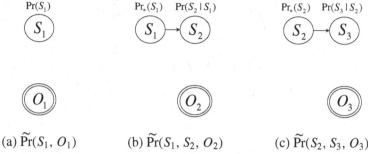

(a) $\widetilde{\Pr}(S_1, O_1)$ (b) $\widetilde{\Pr}(S_1, S_2, O_2)$ (c) $\widetilde{\Pr}(S_2, S_3, O_3)$

Figure 15.10: The likelihood-weighting networks used by particle filtering.

Let us consider a concrete example of how particle filtering works by considering the HMM in Figure 15.8 and the evidence

$$O_1 = T, O_2 = F, O_3 = F.$$

To estimate $\Pr(S_3 | O_1 = T, O_2 = F, O_3 = F)$, particle filtering performs the following computations:

- It estimates $\Pr'(S_1 | O_1 = T)$ using the network in Figure 15.9(a) and then uses the result to specify $\Pr_\star(S_1)$ in the network of Figure 15.9(b).
- It then estimates $\Pr'(S_2 | O_2 = F)$ using the network in Figure 15.9(b) and then uses the result to specify $\Pr_\star(S_2)$ in the network of Figure 15.9(c).
- It finally estimates $\Pr'(S_3 | O_3 = F)$ using the network in Figure 15.9(c).

This last estimate corresponds to the desired probability $\Pr(S_3 | O_1 = T, O_2 = F, O_3 = F)$; see (15.12).

Note that this process requires that we only pass the estimate of $\Pr'(S_{t-1} | O_{t-1})$ from time $t - 1$ to time t. Hence, the space requirements for particle filtering are independent of the time span, which is critical if t is large. This is indeed one of the main highlights of particle filtering.

Likelihood weighting

Note that particle filtering must estimate three conditional probabilities of the form $\Pr'(S_t | O_t)$ for $t = 1, 2, 3$. These estimates are computed using likelihood weighting on the network fragments corresponding to these times. Figure 15.10 depicts the likelihood-weighting networks and corresponding distributions $\widetilde{\Pr}(.)$ used by particle filtering.

In particular, at time $t > 1$ particle filtering generates the following sample from the likelihood-weighting network:

$$s_{t-1}^1, s_t^1, o_t, \quad s_{t-1}^2, s_t^2, o_t, \quad \ldots, \quad s_{t-1}^n, s_t^n, o_t,$$

where o_t is the value of O_t as given by the evidence. It then uses this sample to estimate the conditional probability $\Pr'(s_t | o_t)$ by first estimating the unconditional probabilities $\Pr'(s_t, o_t)$ and $\Pr'(o_t)$ and computing their ratio.

We can show that the estimate of $\Pr'(o_t)$ is given by the following average (see Exercise 15.24):

$$\frac{1}{n} \sum_{i=1}^{n} \Pr(o_t | s_t^i), \tag{15.13}$$

Algorithm 47 PARTICLE_FILTER($\{s_{t-1}^1, \ldots, s_{t-1}^n\}$, o_t, $\Pr(S_t|S_{t-1})$, $\Pr(O_t|S_t)$)

---

input:

$\{s_{t-1}^1, \ldots, s_{t-1}^n\}$:	particles passed from time $t-1$
o_t:	evidence for time t
$\Pr(S_t|S_{t-1})$:	transition distribution
$\Pr(O_t|S_t)$:	sensor distribution

output: an estimate of $\Pr'(S_t|o_t)$, and n particles passed to time $t+1$

main:

1: $P \leftarrow 0$ {estimate for $\Pr'(o_t)$}
2: $P[s_t] \leftarrow 0$ for each state s_t of variable S_t {estimate for $\Pr'(s_t, o_t)$}
3: **for** $i = 1$ to n **do**
4:     $s_t^i \leftarrow$ sampled value from $\Pr(S_t|s_{t-1}^i)$
5:     $P \leftarrow P + \Pr(o_t|s_t^i)$
6:     $P[s_t] \leftarrow P[s_t] + \Pr(o_t|s_t^i)$ for state $s_t = s_t^i$
7: **end for**
8: **return** $P[s_t]/P$ for each state s_t (an estimate of $\Pr'(s_t|o_t)$), and n particles sampled from the distribution $P[s_t]/P$ (passed to time $t+1$)

---

where $\Pr(o_t|s_t^i)$ is called the *weight* of state s_t^i. Moreover, we can show that the estimate of $\Pr'(s_t, o_t)$ is given by the average (see Exercise 15.24):

$$\frac{1}{n} \sum_{s_t^i = s_t} \Pr(o_t|s_t^i). \tag{15.14}$$

Hence, the estimate for the conditional probability $\Pr'(s_t|o_t)$ is given by

$$\frac{\sum_{s_t^i = s_t} \Pr(o_t|s_t^i)}{\sum_{s_t^i} \Pr(o_t|s_t^i)}. \tag{15.15}$$

Using particles

The standard implementation of particle filtering does not actually pass the estimate of $\Pr'(S_{t-1}|O_{t-1})$ from time $t-1$ to time t. Instead, a sample of size n is generated from this distribution and passed to the next time step since this is all we need to apply likelihood weighting at time t. Members of this sample are called *particles*.

The particles for a time step can then be generated from the particles at the previous time step as follows:

- For each of the n particles s_{t-1}^i passed from time $t-1$ to time t, sample a state s_t^i from the distribution $\Pr(S_t|s_{t-1}^i)$.
- Compute an estimate for $\Pr'(S_t|o_t)$ using the sampled states $s_t^1, \ldots, s_t^n$ as given by (15.15).
- Sample n states from the estimate of $\Pr'(S_t|o_t)$. These are the n particles to be passed from time t to time $t+1$.

Algorithm 47 provides the pseudocode for one iteration of particle filtering.[6]

---

[6] Note that when variable S_t has a very large number of states, the estimated probability for many of these states will be zero. In fact, with n particles no more than n states of variable S_t can have estimates greater than zero. This implies that computing an estimate for the distribution $\Pr'(S_t|o_t)$ can be done in $O(n)$ time and space. This

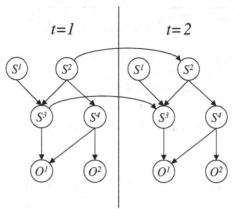

Figure 15.11: A dynamic Bayesian network.

Particle filtering on more general DBNs

Our treatment of particle filtering has thus far been focused on HMMs as given by Figure 15.8, which are specified by an initial distribution $\Pr(S_1)$, a transition distribution $\Pr(S_t|S_{t-1})$, and a sensor distribution $\Pr(O_t|S_t)$. The first and second distributions are used to generate particles, while the third distribution is used to compute the weights of these particles.

Particle filtering can be similarly applied to a larger class of DBNs with the following structure (see Figure 15.11):

- Each edge in the network connects two nodes at the same time t or extends from a node at time $t-1$ to a node at time t.
- The set of nodes at time t is partitioned into two sets $\mathbf{S}_t$ and $\mathbf{O}_t$, where nodes $\mathbf{O}_t$ are leaves having their parents in $\mathbf{S}_t$ and are guaranteed to be observed at time t.

These networks can be viewed as factored versions of HMMs, in which the hidden state S_t is now factored into a set of variables $\mathbf{S}_t$ and the observed variable O_t is factored into a set of variables $\mathbf{O}_t$. For this class of DBNs, the three relevant distributions, $\Pr(\mathbf{S}_1)$, $\Pr(\mathbf{S}_t|\mathbf{S}_{t-1})$, and $\Pr(\mathbf{O}_t|\mathbf{S}_t)$, can be represented using network fragments that allow us to efficiently perform the computations needed by particle filtering, as discussed next.

First, the distribution $\Pr(\mathbf{S}_1)$ is represented by the initial time slice ($t=1$) of the DBN as given in Figure 15.11. We can therefore sample an initial set of particles for time $t=1$ by applying Algorithm 44 to this network.

Second, the distribution $\Pr(\mathbf{S}_t|\mathbf{s}_{t-1})$ can be represented by a fragment of the DBN as given in Figure 15.12(a). This network fragment can then be used to generate particles for time t based on particles for time $t-1$. For example, in Figure 15.12(a) we can use each particle for time $t-1$ to set the values of variable S^2 and S^3 at time $t-1$ and then apply Algorithm 44 to sample values for variables S^1, S^2, S^3, S^4 at time t.

complexity is critical when applying particle filtering to the more general class of DBNs that we discuss next (see Figure 15.12). For these networks, the variable S_t is replaced by a set of variables $\mathbf{S}_t$. Hence, it is critical to compute an estimate for the distribution $\Pr'(\mathbf{S}_t|\mathbf{O}_t)$ in $O(n)$ time and space instead of $O(m)$, where m is the number of instantiations of variables $\mathbf{S}_t$.

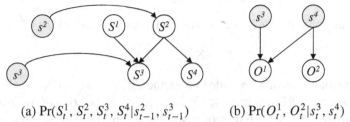

(a) $\Pr(S_t^1, S_t^2, S_t^3, S_t^4 | s_{t-1}^2, s_{t-1}^3)$ (b) $\Pr(O_t^1, O_t^2 | s_t^3, s_t^4)$

Figure 15.12: Fragments of a DBN. The fragment in (a) represents the distribution $\Pr(\mathbf{S}_t | \mathbf{S}_{t-1})$. It is constructed from the network slice at time t and the parents at time $t - 1$. The fragment in (b) represents the distribution $\Pr(\mathbf{O}_t | \mathbf{S}_t)$. It is a subset of the network slice at time t obtained by keeping only nodes in $\mathbf{O}_t$ and their parents in $\mathbf{S}_t$.

Third, the distribution $\Pr(\mathbf{O}_t | \mathbf{S}_t)$ can be represented by a fragment of the DBN as given in Figure 15.12(b). Using this fragment, we can efficiently compute the weight of a particle, $\Pr(\mathbf{o}_t | \mathbf{s}_t)$, which must correspond to a product of network parameters. This follows since the nodes in $\mathbf{O}_t$ are all leaf nodes in the network fragment with their parents in $\mathbf{S}_t$. For example, in Figure 15.12 $\Pr(O_t^1, O_t^2 | s_t^1, s_t^2, s_t^3, s_t^4)$ evaluates to $\Pr(O_t^1 | s_t^3, s_t^4)\Pr(O_t^2 | s_t^4)$, which is a simple product of network parameters.

Specifying the pseudocode for particle filtering using this more general class of DBNs is left to Exercise 15.25.

15.7 Markov chain simulation

Given a function $f(\mathbf{X})$ and an underlying distribution $\Pr(\mathbf{X})$, we present in this section a method for estimating the expectation of this function but without sampling directly from the distribution $\Pr(\mathbf{X})$. This method, known as *Markov chain Monte Carlo* (MCMC) simulation, provides an alternative to Monte Carlo simulation as the latter method requires an ability to sample from the distribution $\Pr(\mathbf{X})$.

MCMC first constructs a Markov chain,

$$\mathbf{X}_1 \rightarrow \mathbf{X}_2 \rightarrow \ldots \rightarrow \mathbf{X}_n.$$

It then generates a sample $\mathbf{x}_1, \mathbf{x}_2, \ldots, \mathbf{x}_n$ from the distributions $\mathbb{P}(\mathbf{X}_1), \mathbb{P}(\mathbf{X}_2 | \mathbf{x}_1), \ldots,$ $\mathbb{P}(\mathbf{X}_n | \mathbf{x}_{n-1})$, respectively, through a process known as *simulating the Markov chain*. If the Markov chain satisfies some specific properties, then MCMC estimates based on such a sample are consistent. That is, as the sample size n tends to infinity, the sample mean,

$$\frac{1}{n} \sum_{i=1}^{n} f(\mathbf{x}_i),$$

converges to the expectation of function f with respect to distribution $\Pr(\mathbf{X})$.

Note here that MCMC does not have to sample directly from the distribution $\Pr(\mathbf{X})$, which is a main advantage of this algorithm as it allows us to compute expectations with respect to distributions that may be hard to sample from. For example, we see later that MCMC can compute expectations with respect to a conditional distribution, $\Pr(.|\beta)$, even when sampling from this distribution may not be computationally feasible.

In the next section, we define some properties of Markov chains that guarantee the consistency of estimates produced by MCMC. We follow this by discussing a particular method for constructing Markov chains that satisfy these properties.

15.7.1 Markov chains

A *Markov chain* for variables $\mathbf{X}$ is a dynamic Bayesian network of the form

$$\mathbf{X}_1 \to \mathbf{X}_2 \to \ldots \to \mathbf{X}_n,$$

where the instantiations $\mathbf{x}$ of $\mathbf{X}$ are called *states*, the CPT for variable $\mathbf{X}_1$ is called the *initial distribution*, and the CPTs for variables $\mathbf{X}_2, \ldots, \mathbf{X}_n$ are called *transition distributions* or *transition matrices*. When all transition distributions are the same, the Markov chain is said to be *homogeneous*. We restrict our discussion in this section to homogeneous Markov chains and use $\mathbb{P}$ to denote the distribution induced by the chain.

Suppose now that we have a Markov chain where the initial distribution $\mathbb{P}(\mathbf{X}_1)$ is set to some given distribution $\Pr(\mathbf{X})$. If the chain maintains this distribution for all times, that is, $\mathbb{P}(\mathbf{X}_t) = \Pr(\mathbf{X})$ for $t > 1$, we say that $\Pr(\mathbf{X})$ is a *stationary distribution* for the Markov chain. We also say that a Markov chain is *irreducible* if every state $\mathbf{x}'$ is reachable from every other state $\mathbf{x}$, that is, if for every pair of states $\mathbf{x}$ and $\mathbf{x}'$, there is some time t such that $\mathbb{P}(\mathbf{X}_t = \mathbf{x}' | \mathbf{X}_1 = \mathbf{x}) > 0$. The states of the Markov chain are said to be *recurrent* in this case as each state is guaranteed to be visited an infinite number of times when we simulate the chain. Every Markov chain has at least one stationary distribution yet an irreducible Markov chain is guaranteed to have a unique stationary distribution.[7] We also have the following.

Theorem 15.15. *Let* $\mathbf{X}_1 \to \mathbf{X}_2 \to \ldots \to \mathbf{X}_n$ *be an irreducible Markov chain and let* $\Pr(\mathbf{X})$ *be its stationary distribution. Let* $f(\mathbf{X})$ *be a function and* $\mathbf{x}_1, \ldots, \mathbf{x}_n$ *be a sample simulated from the given Markov chain. The sample mean*

$$\mathrm{Av}_n(f) = \frac{1}{n} \sum_{i=1}^{n} f(\mathbf{x}_i)$$

will then converge to the expectation of function f,

$$\lim_{n \to \infty} \mathrm{Av}_n(f) = \mathrm{Ex}(f) = \sum_{\mathbf{x}} f(\mathbf{x}) \Pr(\mathbf{x}). \qquad \blacksquare$$

To use MCMC as suggested here, we must therefore construct an irreducible Markov chain that has an appropriate stationary distribution.

Consider now a Markov chain whose transition matrix stands in the following relationship with a distribution $\Pr(\mathbf{X})$:

$$\Pr(\mathbf{x})\mathbb{P}(\mathbf{X}_i = \mathbf{x}' | \mathbf{X}_{i-1} = \mathbf{x}) \quad = \quad \Pr(\mathbf{x}')\mathbb{P}(\mathbf{X}_i = \mathbf{x} | \mathbf{X}_{i-1} = \mathbf{x}'). \qquad (15.16)$$

This condition is known as *detailed balance*, and a Markov chain that satisfies detailed balance is said to be *reversible*. If a Markov chain is reversible, that is, satisfies (15.16), then $\Pr(\mathbf{X})$ is guaranteed to be a stationary distribution for the chain. Note, however, that reversibility is sufficient but not necessary for ensuring that the Markov chain has a particular stationary distribution (see Exercises 15.27 and 15.28).

We next provide a systematic method for constructing reversible Markov chains called Gibbs sampling, and then show how it can be applied to Bayesian networks.

---

[7] An irreducible Markov chain may or may not converge to its stationary distribution, yet Exercise 15.29 defines a condition called *aperiodicity*, which ensures this convergence.

15.7.2 Gibbs sampling

Given a distribution $\Pr(\mathbf{X})$, we can always construct a Markov chain that is guaranteed to have $\Pr(\mathbf{X})$ as its stationary distribution as long as we adopt the following transition matrix.

Definition 15.6. Given a distribution $\Pr(\mathbf{X})$, the corresponding *Gibbs transition matrix* is defined as follows, where m is the number of variables in $\mathbf{X}$:

$$\mathbb{P}(\mathbf{X}_i = \mathbf{x}' | \mathbf{X}_{i-1} = \mathbf{x})$$

$$= \begin{cases} 0, & \text{if } \mathbf{x} \text{ and } \mathbf{x}' \text{ disagree on more than one variable} \\[2ex] \dfrac{1}{m} \Pr(s' | \mathbf{x} - S), & \text{if } \mathbf{x} \text{ and } \mathbf{x}' \text{ disagree on a single variable } S, \\ & \text{which has value } s' \text{ in } \mathbf{x}' \\[2ex] \dfrac{1}{m} \displaystyle\sum_{S \in \mathbf{X}} \Pr(s_\mathbf{x} | \mathbf{x} - S), & \text{if } \mathbf{x} = \mathbf{x}' \text{ and } s_\mathbf{x} \text{ is the value of variable } S \text{ in } \mathbf{x}. \end{cases} \quad \blacksquare$$

A Markov chain with this transition matrix is called a *Gibbs chain.*

We next provide some intuition about this transition matrix and how we can sample from it efficiently, but let us first stress the following important point. To define the matrix, we only need to compute quantities of the form $\Pr(s | \mathbf{x} - S)$ with respect to the distribution Pr, where $\mathbf{x}$ is a complete variable instantiation. Moreover, we show later that if the distribution Pr is induced by a Bayesian network, then this computation can be performed efficiently using the chain rule of Bayesian networks.

For a concrete example of a Gibbs transition matrix, suppose that $\mathbf{X} = \{A, B, C\}$ and $\mathbf{x} = a, b, \bar{c}$. The following table depicts part of the Gibbs transition matrix for distribution $\Pr(\mathbf{X})$:

$\mathbf{x}'$	$\mathbb{P}(\mathbf{x}' \mid \mathbf{x} = a, b, \bar{c})$	Variables on which $\mathbf{x}'$ and $\mathbf{x}$ disagree
a, b, c	$\Pr(c\mid a, b)/3$	C
$a, b, \bar{c}$	$(\Pr(a\mid b, \bar{c}) + \Pr(b\mid a, \bar{c}) + \Pr(\bar{c}\mid a, b))/3$	
$a, \bar{b}, c$	0	B, C
$a, \bar{b}, \bar{c}$	$\Pr(\bar{b}\mid a, \bar{c})/3$	B
$\bar{a}, b, c$	0	A, C
$\bar{a}, b, \bar{c}$	$\Pr(\bar{a}\mid b, \bar{c})/3$	A
$\bar{a}, \bar{b}, c$	0	A, B, C
$\bar{a}, \bar{b}, \bar{c}$	0	A, B

We now have the following result.

Theorem 15.16. *The Gibbs transition matrix for distribution $\Pr(\mathbf{X})$ satisfies detailed balance*

$$\Pr(\mathbf{x})\mathbb{P}(\mathbf{X}_i = \mathbf{x}' | \mathbf{X}_{i-1} = \mathbf{x}) = \Pr(\mathbf{x}')\mathbb{P}(\mathbf{X}_i = \mathbf{x} | \mathbf{X}_{i-1} = \mathbf{x}').$$

Moreover, if the distribution $\Pr(\mathbf{X})$ is strictly positive, the Gibbs chain is irreducible and, hence, $\Pr(\mathbf{X})$ is its only stationary distribution. $\blacksquare$

If the distribution $\Pr(\mathbf{X})$ is not strictly positive, the Gibbs chain may or may not be irreducible yet it maintains $\Pr(\mathbf{X})$ as a stationary distribution.

Simulating a Gibbs chain

To simulate a Gibbs chain, we start with some initial state $\mathbf{x}_1$ that is sampled from the initial distribution $\mathbb{P}(\mathbf{X}_1)$.[8] To sample a state $\mathbf{x}_2$ from $\mathbb{P}(\mathbf{X}_2|\mathbf{x}_1)$, we perform the following (see Exercise 15.31):

- Choose a variable S from $\mathbf{X}$ at random.
- Sample a state s from the distribution $\Pr(S|\mathbf{x}_1 - S)$.
- Set the state $\mathbf{x}_2$ to $\mathbf{x}_1 - S, s$.

We can then repeat the same process to sample a state $\mathbf{x}_3$ from $\mathbb{P}(\mathbf{X}_3|\mathbf{x}_2)$ and so on. We use the term *Gibbs sampler* or *Gibbs simulator* to refer to any algorithm than can simulate a Gibbs chain as discussed here. Note that by definition of the Gibbs transition matrix, any consecutive states $\mathbf{x}_i$ and $\mathbf{x}_{i+1}$ disagree on at most one variable.

Computing Gibbs estimates

Now that we have a Gibbs sampler for a distribution $\Pr(\mathbf{X})$, we can use it to estimate the expectation of any function with respect to this distribution. The simplest example here is estimating the expectation of the direct sampling function $\breve{\alpha}$ for some event α. That is, given a sample $\mathbf{x}_1, \mathbf{x}_2, \ldots, \mathbf{x}_n$ simulated from the Markov chain, we simply estimate the probability $\Pr(\alpha)$ using the sample mean

$$\mathrm{Av}_n(\breve{\alpha}) = \frac{1}{n} \sum_{i=1}^{n} \breve{\alpha}(\mathbf{x}_i).$$

We can also estimate the conditional probability $\Pr(\alpha|\mathbf{e})$, where $\mathbf{e}$ is some evidence, by observing that it corresponds to the expectation of the direct sampling function $\breve{\alpha}$ with respect to the conditional distribution $\Pr(.|\mathbf{e})$. Hence, we can estimate $\Pr(\alpha|\mathbf{e})$ using the mean of a sample $\mathbf{x}_1, \mathbf{x}_2, \ldots, \mathbf{x}_n$ that is simulated using a Gibbs sampler for the conditional distribution $\Pr(\mathbf{X}|\mathbf{e})$ ($\mathbf{X}$ are the variables distinct from $\mathbf{E}$). We can construct such a sampler by passing the distribution $\Pr(\mathbf{X}|\mathbf{e})$ to Definition 15.6, which leads to the following Gibbs transition matrix:

$$\mathbb{P}(\mathbf{X}_i = \mathbf{x}'|\mathbf{X}_{i-1} = \mathbf{x})$$

$$= \begin{cases} 0, & \text{if } \mathbf{x} \text{ and } \mathbf{x}' \text{ disagree on more than one variable} \\[2mm] \dfrac{1}{m}\Pr(s'|\mathbf{x} - S, \mathbf{e}), & \text{if } \mathbf{x} \text{ and } \mathbf{x}' \text{ disagree on a single variable } S, \\ & \text{which has value } s' \text{ in } \mathbf{x}' \\[2mm] \dfrac{1}{m}\displaystyle\sum_{S\in\mathbf{X}} \Pr(s_{\mathbf{x}}|\mathbf{x} - S, \mathbf{e}), & \text{if } \mathbf{x} = \mathbf{x}' \text{ and } s_{\mathbf{x}} \text{ is the value of variable } S \text{ in } \mathbf{x}. \end{cases}$$

Again, this highlights the main advantage of Gibbs sampling as it allows us to compute expectations with respect to a conditional distribution $\Pr(.|\mathbf{e})$ even when sampling from this distribution may not be feasible computationally.

---

[8] The choice of initial distribution does not affect the consistency of estimates computed by MCMC but may affect its speed of convergence. Ideally, we want the initial distribution $\mathbb{P}(\mathbf{X}_1)$ to be the stationary distribution $\Pr(\mathbf{X})$. Note, however, that sampling from the stationary distribution is usually hard, otherwise we would not be using MCMC in the first place. Yet since we will need to sample only once from this distribution, it may be justifiable to expend some computational effort on this using, for example, rejection sampling as discussed in Exercise 15.14.

Algorithm 48 GIBBS_NEXT_STATE($\mathbf{x}, \mathbf{e}, \mathcal{N}$)

input:

$\mathbf{x}$:	instantiation
$\mathbf{e}$:	evidence
$\mathcal{N}$:	Bayesian network inducing distribution $\Pr(\mathbf{X}, \mathbf{E})$, $\mathbf{X} \cap \mathbf{E} = \emptyset$

output: a state sampled from $\mathbb{P}(\mathbf{X}_i | \mathbf{X}_{i-1} = \mathbf{x})$, where $\mathbb{P}(\mathbf{X}_i | \mathbf{X}_{i-1})$ is the Gibbs transition matrix for the distribution $\Pr(\mathbf{X}|\mathbf{e})$

main:

1:   $S \leftarrow$ a variable chosen randomly from $\mathbf{X}$
2:   **for** each state s of variable S **do**
3:     $\Sigma \leftarrow$ instantiation $\mathbf{x} - S, s, \mathbf{e}$
4:     $\mathbf{u} \leftarrow$ value attained by parents of node S in instantiation Σ
5:     $c_1, \ldots, c_k \leftarrow$ values attained by children of node S in instantiation Σ
6:     $\mathbf{u}_1, \ldots, \mathbf{u}_k \leftarrow$ values attained by parents of nodes $C_1, \ldots, C_k$ in instantiation Σ
7:     $P(s) \leftarrow \theta_{s|\mathbf{u}} \prod_{i=1}^{k} \theta_{c_i|\mathbf{u}_i}$
8:   **end for**
9:   $\eta \leftarrow \sum_s P(s)$ {normalizing constant}
10: $P(s) \leftarrow P(s)/\eta$ for each state s
11: $s \leftarrow$ a value for variable S sampled from the distribution $P(S)$
12: **return** instantiation $\mathbf{x} - S, s$

15.7.3 A Gibbs sampler for Bayesian networks

To apply Gibbs sampling to a Bayesian network that contains evidence $\mathbf{e}$, we need to construct a Gibbs sampler for the distribution $\Pr(\mathbf{X}|\mathbf{e})$, where $\mathbf{X}$ are the network variables distinct from $\mathbf{E}$. In particular, given an instantiation $\mathbf{x}$, we need to sample a next state from the distribution $\mathbb{P}(\mathbf{X}_i | \mathbf{X}_{i-1} = \mathbf{x})$, where $\mathbb{P}(\mathbf{X}_i | \mathbf{X}_{i-1})$ is the Gibbs transition matrix for distribution $\Pr(\mathbf{X}|\mathbf{e})$. Given our previous discussion, this amounts to choosing a variable S at random from $\mathbf{X}$, sampling a value s from the distribution $\Pr(S|\mathbf{x} - S, \mathbf{e})$, and then choosing $\mathbf{x} - S, s$ as the next state. Hence, all we need to show here is how to compute the distribution $\Pr(S|\mathbf{x} - S, \mathbf{e})$ so we can sample from it. This is given by Theorem 15.17.

Theorem 15.17. *Given a Bayesian network that induces a distribution* $\Pr(\mathbf{X}, \mathbf{E})$, $\mathbf{X} \cap \mathbf{E} = \emptyset$, *and given a variable* $S \in \mathbf{X}$, *we have*

$$\Pr(s|\mathbf{x} - S, \mathbf{e}) = \eta \cdot \theta_{s|\mathbf{u}} \prod_{i=1}^{k} \theta_{c_i|\mathbf{u}_i},$$

where η *is a normalizing constant, and*

- $\mathbf{U}$ *are the parents of* S *and* $\mathbf{u}$ *is their state in* $\mathbf{x} - S, s, \mathbf{e}$;
- $C_1, \ldots, C_k$ *are the children of* S *and* $c_1, \ldots, c_k$ *are their states in* $\mathbf{x} - S, s, \mathbf{e}$;
- $\mathbf{U}_1, \ldots, \mathbf{U}_k$ *are the parents of* $C_1, \ldots, C_k$ *and* $\mathbf{u}_1, \ldots, \mathbf{u}_k$ *are their states in* $\mathbf{x} - S, s, \mathbf{e}$.

                                                                    ■

Algorithm 48 provides pseudocode for a Gibbs sampler based on Theorem 15.17, which is used by Algorithm 49 for estimating node marginals in a Bayesian network.

Algorithm 49 GIBBS_MCMC(**e**, n, $\mathcal{N}$)

---

input:

  e: evidence

  n: sample size

  $\mathcal{N}$:   Bayesian network

output: estimate Pr($S|$**e**) for each node S in the network, where $S \notin$ **E**

main:

  1: **X** ← variables of network $\mathcal{N}$ that are distinct from **E**

  2: $P(s)$ ← 0 for each value s of variable $S \in$ **X** {estimate for Pr($S|$**e**)}

  3: $\mathbf{x}_1$ ← an instantiation of variables **X** {sampled from Pr(**X**|**e**) if possible}

  4: increment $P(s)$ for each variable S and its value s in instantiation $\mathbf{x}_1$

  5: **for** i from 2 to n **do**

  6:     $\mathbf{x}_i$ ← GIBBS_NEXT_STATE($\mathbf{x}_{i-1}$, **e**, $\mathcal{N}$)

  7:     increment $P(s)$ for each variable S and its value s in instantiation $\mathbf{x}_i$

  8: **end for**

  9: **return** $P(s)/n$ for each variable $S \in$ **X** and value s of S

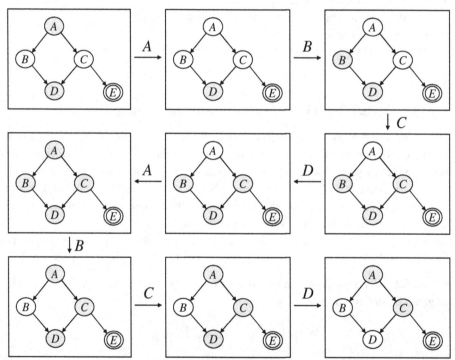

Figure 15.13: Simulating a Gibbs chain. Gray nodes have the value false and white nodes have the value true.

Figure 15.13 depicts an example of applying Algorithm 49. What we have here is a network with evidence $E = e$ where our goal is to estimate the conditional probabilities for variables A, B, C, and D given $E = e$. Gibbs sampling start with an initial instantiation of network variables in which $E = e$. This initial instantiation is $\bar{a}, b, c, \bar{d}, e$ in Figure 15.13. Gibbs sampling then picks a variable, say, A and then samples a value of this variable from the distribution $\Pr(A|b, c, \bar{d}, e)$. According to Figure 15.13, the value a is sampled in this case, leading to the next instantiation $a, b, c, \bar{d}, e$. Picking the variable B next and sampling a value from $\Pr(B|a, c, \bar{d}, e)$ leads to the instantiation $a, \bar{b}, c, \bar{d}, e$, and so on. Note that when picking variable D, the sampled value is the same as the current one, leaving the instantiation without change. The sample corresponding to Figure 15.13 consists of the following instantiations:

Instantiation	Sampled variable
$\bar{a}, b, c, \bar{d}, e$	
$a, b, c, \bar{d}, e$	A
$a, \bar{b}, c, \bar{d}, e$	B
$a, \bar{b}, \bar{c}, \bar{d}, e$	C
$a, \bar{b}, \bar{c}, \bar{d}, e$	D
$\bar{a}, \bar{b}, \bar{c}, \bar{d}, e$	A
$\bar{a}, b, \bar{c}, \bar{d}, e$	B
$\bar{a}, b, \bar{c}, \bar{d}, e$	C
$\bar{a}, b, \bar{c}, d, e$	D

Estimating a probability of some event, say, $C = \bar{c}$ using direct sampling is then a matter of counting the number of instantiations in which the event is true. For example, given the previous sample, the estimate for $\Pr(\bar{c}|e)$ is 6/9 and the estimate for $\Pr(c|e)$ is 3/9.

Bibliographic remarks

For introductory references on expectations and estimation, see DeGroot [2002] and Wasserman [2004], and on Markov chains, see Bertsekas and Tsitsiklis [2002]. For a survey of Monte Carlo methods, see Neal [1993]. For a more advanced and comprehensive coverage of these methods, see Robert and Casella [2004], Gilks et al. [1996], and Rubinstein [1981], and for their application to dynamic models, see Doucet et al. [2001].

The simulation of Bayesian networks was introduced in Henrion [1988], where rejection sampling was also introduced for these networks under the name of logic sampling. Likelihood weighting was introduced in Shachter and Peot [1989] and Fung and Chang [1989], yet the literature contains many other sampling algorithms that can be understood as applications of importance sampling to Bayesian networks (e.g., [Fung and del Favero, 1994; Hernandez et al., 1998; Salmeron et al., 2000]). Some of the more recent algorithms use belief propagation (see Chapter 14) for obtaining an importance distribution [Yuan and Druzdzel, 2003; 2006; Gogate and Dechter, 2005], while others resort to learning and adjusting the importance distribution throughout the inference process [Shachter and Peot, 1989; Ortiz and Kaelbling, 2000; Cheng and Druzdzel, 2000; Moral and Salmeron, 2003]. Some applications of Rao-Blackwell sampling are discussed in Doucet et al. [2000] and Bidyuk and Dechter [2006]. The application of Gibbs sampling to Bayesian networks was first introduced in Pearl [1987] and then analyzed in York [1992].

The complexity of approximating probabilistic inference is discussed in Dagum and Luby [1993], where it is shown that approximating both conditional and unconditional probabilities are NP-hard when zero probabilities (or probabilities arbitrarily close to zero) are present in the network.

15.8 Exercises

15.1. Let N_a be the number of students in a class having age a:

Age a	N_a
18	5
19	15
20	21
21	30
22	20
23	6
24	3

What is the expected age of a student chosen randomly from this class? Formulate this problem by defining a function f where the expected value of the function corresponds to the answer. Compute the variance of the identified function.

15.2. Show that the variance of function $f(\mathbf{X})$ with respect to distribution $\Pr(\mathbf{X})$ satisfies

$$\mathrm{Va}(f) = \mathrm{Ex}(f^2) - \mathrm{Ex}(f)^2.$$

15.3. Let μ and σ^2 be the expectation and variance of a function and let v be one of its observed values. Using Chebyshev's inequality (Theorem 15.2), what is the value of ϵ that allows us to state that μ lies in the interval $(v - \epsilon, v + \epsilon)$ with confidence $\geq 95\%$? Compare this with the value of ϵ based on Theorem 15.3.

15.4. Let f be a function with expectation μ and variance $\sigma^2 = 4$. Suppose we wish to estimate the expectation μ using Monte Carlo simulation (Equation 15.5) and a sample of size n. How large should n be if we want to guarantee that expectation μ falls in the interval $(\mathrm{Av}_n(f) - 1, \mathrm{Av}_n(f) + 1)$ with confidence $\geq 99\%$? Use Chebyshev's inequality (Theorem 15.2).

15.5. Prove the law of large numbers (Theorem 15.6).

15.6. Consider the Bayesian network in Figure 15.1 and the parameter $\theta_{\bar{a}}$ representing the probability of $A =$ false (i.e., it is not winter). For each of the following values of this parameter, .01, .4, and .99, do the following:

(a) Compute the probability $\Pr(d, e)$: wet grass and slippery road.

(b) Estimate $\Pr(d, e)$ using direct sampling with sample sizes ranging from $n = 100$ to $n = 15,000$.

(c) Generate a plot with n on the x-axis and the exact value of $\Pr(d, e)$ and the estimate for $\Pr(d, e)$ on the y-axis.

(d) Generate a plot with n on the x-axis and the exact variance of the estimate for $\Pr(d, e)$ and the sample variance on the y-axis.

15.7. Show that the sample variance of function $f(\mathbf{X})$ and sample $\mathbf{x}^1, \ldots, \mathbf{x}^n$ can be computed as follows:

$$S^2{}_n(f) = \frac{1}{n-1} T,$$

where

$$T = \sum_{i=1}^{n} (f(\mathbf{x}^i) - \mathrm{Av}_n(f))^2 = \sum_{i=1}^{n} f(\mathbf{x}^i)^2 - \frac{1}{n} \left[\sum_{i=1}^{n} f(\mathbf{x}^i) \right]^2.$$

Note that the first form of T given in this chapter suggests computation by a two-pass algorithm: compute the mean in one pass and compute the differences squared in another pass. The second form of T suggests computation by a one-pass algorithm that simply accumulates the sums of $f(\mathbf{x}^i)^2$ and $f(\mathbf{x}^i)$.

15.8. Suppose we want to simulate a Bayesian network $\mathcal{N}$ that has been conditioned on evidence **e**. Suppose further that we are given cluster marginals $\Pr(\mathbf{C}_i|\mathbf{e})$ and separator marginals $\Pr(\mathbf{S}_{ij}|\mathbf{e})$ computed by running the jointree algorithm on network $\mathcal{N}$ and evidence **e**. Give an efficient algorithm for simulating the network $\mathcal{N}$ conditioned on **e** given these cluster and separator marginals. That is, show how we can efficiently generate a sequence of independent network instantiations $\mathbf{x}^1, \ldots, \mathbf{x}^n$ where the probability of generating instantiation $\mathbf{x}^i$ is $\Pr(\mathbf{x}^i|\mathbf{e})$.

15.9. Show the following for an instantiation **x** returned by Algorithm 44, SIMULATE_BN:

    (a) The partial instantiation $x_1, \ldots, x_k$ of **x** is generated with probability $\Pr(x_1, \ldots, x_k)$, where X_i is the variable at position i in the used order π.

    (b) The value x assigned to variable X by instantiation **x** is generated with probability $\Pr(x)$.

    (c) The instantiation **c** assigned to variables $\mathbf{C} \subseteq \mathbf{X}$ by **x** is generated with probability $\Pr(\mathbf{c})$.

    Hint: You can use (a) to prove (b), and use (b) to prove (c).

15.10. Prove Theorem 15.9.

15.11. Given a Bayesian network over variables **X** and **Y** where $\mathbf{X} \cap \mathbf{Y} = \emptyset$ and **Y** is a loop-cutset, show how $\Pr(\mathbf{z}|\mathbf{y})$ can be computed in time polynomial in the network size where $\mathbf{Z} \subseteq \mathbf{X}$.

15.12. Given a Bayesian network over variables **X** and containing evidence **e**, show how we can construct a Gibbs sampler for the distribution $\Pr(\mathbf{Y}|\mathbf{e})$, $\mathbf{Y} \subseteq \mathbf{X} \setminus \mathbf{E}$, assuming that we can compute $\Pr(\mathbf{y}, \mathbf{e})$ for each instantiation **y** of variables **Y**. That is, we want a Gibbs sampler that allows us to compute expectations with respect to the distribution $\Pr(\mathbf{Y}|\mathbf{e})$.

15.13. Show that the variance of Theorem 15.9 ranges between zero and $\Pr(\alpha)\Pr(\neg\alpha)$. State a condition under which the variance reduces to zero and a condition under which it reduces to $\Pr(\alpha)\Pr(\neg\alpha)$.

15.14. Let $\Pr(\mathbf{X})$ be a distribution that is hard to sample from. Let $\Pr'(\mathbf{X})$ be another distribution that is easy to sample from, where $\Pr(\mathbf{x}) \leq c \cdot \Pr'(\mathbf{x})$ for all instantiations **x** and some constant $c > 0$. The method of rejection sampling performs the following steps to generate a sample of size n from distribution $\Pr(\mathbf{X})$:

    Repeat n times:

      1. Sample an instantiation **x** from distribution $\Pr'(\mathbf{X})$.

      2. Accept **x** with probability $\Pr(\mathbf{x})/c \cdot \Pr'(\mathbf{x})$.

      3. If **x** is not accepted (i.e., rejected), go to Step 1.

    We can show that the accepted instantiations represent a random sample from distribution $\Pr(\mathbf{X})$. Consider now the algorithm given in Section 15.5 for computing a conditional probability $\Pr(\alpha|\beta)$. Show how this algorithm can be formulated as an instance of rejection sampling by specifying the corresponding distribution $\Pr'$ and constant c.

15.15. Consider the bounds on the absolute and relative errors of direct sampling that we provided in Sections 15.4.1 and 15.4.2 (based on Chebyshev's inequality). Derive similar bounds based on this inequality for the absolute and relative errors of (idealized) importance sampling (Theorem 15.12). Can we use Hoeffding's inequality for this purpose? Why?

15.16. Consider a simple Bayesian network of the form $A \rightarrow B$, where A and B are binary variables. Provide a closed form for the variance of likelihood weighting when estimating $\Pr(a)$. Give a similar form for the estimate of $\Pr(b)$. Your forms must be expressed in terms of network parameters and the probabilities of a and b.

15.17. Prove Theorem 15.14.

15.18. Consider a Bayesian network in which all leaf nodes are deterministic (their CPTs contain only 0 and 1 entries) and let **e** be an instantiation of the leaf nodes. What is the variance of likelihood weighting when estimating $\Pr(\mathbf{e})$?

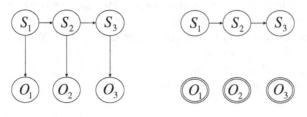

(a) HMM   (b) Likelihood weighting HMM

Figure 15.14: An HMM for three time steps and the corresponding likelihood weighting HMM given evidence on nodes O_1, O_2, and O_3.

15.19. Consider the functions $\breve{\alpha}$ and $\tilde{\alpha}$ given in Definitions 15.1 and 15.3, respectively. Show that $Va(\tilde{\alpha}) \leq Va(\breve{\alpha})$ if $\widetilde{Pr}(\mathbf{x}) \geq Pr(\mathbf{x})$ for all instantiations $\mathbf{x}$ consistent with α.

15.20. Show the following: If $Pr(.|\alpha)$ can be used as an importance distribution, then $Pr(\alpha)$ can be computed exactly after generating a sample of size 1.

15.21. Consider a Bayesian network $X_1 \rightarrow \ldots \rightarrow X_n$ and suppose that we want to estimate $Pr(x_n)$ using likelihood weighting. Find a closed form for the variance of this method in terms of the CPT for node X_n and the marginal distribution of node X_{n-1}. Identify conditions on the network that lead to a zero variance.

15.22. Consider the HMM in Figure 15.14 and suppose that our goal is to estimate the probability $Pr(S_t|o_1, \ldots, o_t)$ for each time t given evidence $o_1, \ldots, o_t$. Suppose that we use likelihood weighting for this purpose and let $\widetilde{Pr}(.)$ be the importance distribution. Show that for every instantiation $s_1, \ldots, s_t, o_1, \ldots, o_t$ that satisfies the given evidence, we have

$$\frac{Pr(s_1, \ldots, s_t, o_1, \ldots, o_t)}{\widetilde{Pr}(s_1, \ldots, s_t, o_1, \ldots, o_t)} = Pr(o_1, \ldots, o_t|s_1, \ldots, s_t).$$

Describe an implementation of this algorithm whose space complexity is independent of time t.

15.23. Show that Equations 15.11 and 15.12 are implied by Equation 15.10.

15.24. Prove Equations 15.13 and 15.14. That is, show that these are the estimates computed by likelihood weighing when applied to the network fragment at time $t > 1$.

15.25. Write the pseudocode for applying particle filtering to the class of DBNs discussed in Section 15.6.2 and Figure 15.12.

15.26. Show that if a Markov chain satisfies the detailed balance property given in Equation 15.16, then $Pr(\mathbf{X})$ must be a stationary distribution for the chain.

15.27. Provide a Markov chain over three states that has a stationary distribution yet does not satisfy the detailed balance property.

15.28. The Gibbs sampler can be implemented in two ways. In one case, the variable S whose state will be sampled is chosen at random. In another case, a particular sequence for variables S is predetermined and sampling is always performed according to that sequence. The second method is known to result in an irreducible Markov chain that does not satisfy the detailed balance property. Compare the performance of these methods empirically.

15.29. A Markov chain is said to be aperiodic[9] if and only if there exists a specific time $t > 1$ such that for every pair of states $\mathbf{x}$ and $\mathbf{x}'$, we have $\mathbb{P}(\mathbf{X}_t = \mathbf{x}'|\mathbf{X}_1 = \mathbf{x}) > 0$. If a Markov chain is aperiodic, it will also be irreducible and, hence, have a unique stationary distribution, say,

---

[9] The literature on Markov chains contains multiple definitions of the notion of aperiodicity.

$\Pr(\mathbf{X})$.[10] Moreover, if the chain is aperiodic, it will converge to its stationary distribution. That is,

$$\lim_{t \to \infty} \mathbb{P}(\mathbf{X}_t = \mathbf{x}' | \mathbf{X}_1 = \mathbf{x}) = \Pr(\mathbf{x}')$$

for all states $\mathbf{x}$ and $\mathbf{x}'$. Hence, when simulating the Markov chain, the simulated instantiations are eventually sampled from the stationary distribution $\Pr(\mathbf{X})$ and become independent of the initial state at time 1.

Consider now the Markov chain for a binary variable X with the transition matrix $\mathbb{P}(x | \bar{x}) = 1$ and $\mathbb{P}(\bar{x} | x) = 1$; hence, $\mathbb{P}(\bar{x} | \bar{x}) = 0$ and $\mathbb{P}(x | x) = 0$. Is this chain aperiodic? Is it irreducible? If it is, identify its unique stationary distribution. Will the chain converge to any distribution?

15.30. Show that the Gibbs transition matrix given in Definition 15.6 satisfies the following condition:

$$\sum_{\mathbf{x}'} \mathbb{P}(\mathbf{X}_i = \mathbf{x}' | \mathbf{X}_{i-1} = \mathbf{x}) = 1.$$

15.31. Consider the Gibbs transition matrix $\mathbb{P}(\mathbf{X}_i | \mathbf{X}_{i-1})$ given in Definition 15.6 and let $\mathbf{x}$ be a state of variables $\mathbf{X}$. Consider now the state $\mathbf{x}'$ generated as follows:

- Let S be a variable chosen randomly from $\mathbf{X}$.
- Let s be a state of variable S sampled from $\Pr(S | \mathbf{X} - S)$.
- Set state $\mathbf{x}'$ to $\mathbf{x} - S, s$.

Show that the state $\mathbf{x}'$ is generated with probability $\mathbb{P}(\mathbf{X}_i = \mathbf{x}' | \mathbf{X}_{i-1} = \mathbf{x})$.

15.9 Proofs

PROOF OF THEOREM 15.1. To prove that Algorithm 44 generates an instantiation $x_1, \ldots, x_n$ with probability $\Pr(x_1, \ldots, x_n)$, we need to recall the chain rule for Bayesian networks. In particular, let $\pi = X_1, \ldots, X_n$ be a total ordering of network variables as given in Algorithm 44 and let $x_1, \ldots, x_n$ be a corresponding variable instantiation. If $\mathbf{u}_i$ denote the instantiation of X_i's parents in $x_1, \ldots, x_n$, then

$$\begin{aligned} \Pr(x_1, \ldots, x_n) &= \Pr(x_n | x_{n-1}, \ldots, x_1)\Pr(x_{n-1} | x_{n-2}, \ldots, x_1) \ldots \Pr(x_1) \\ &= \Pr(x_n | \mathbf{u}_n)\Pr(x_{n-1} | \mathbf{u}_{n-1}) \ldots \Pr(x_1) \\ &= \prod_{i=1}^{n} \Pr(x_i | \mathbf{u}_i). \end{aligned}$$

Note that Algorithm 44 iterates over variables X_i according to order π, sampling a value x_i for each variable X_i from the distribution $\Pr(X_i | \mathbf{u}_i)$. Hence, the probability of generating the instantiation $x_1, \ldots, x_n$ is simply the product of probabilities used for generating the individual variable values, which equals $\Pr(x_1, \ldots, x_n)$ as given here. ∎

PROOF OF THEOREM 15.2. This is a classical result from statistics that follows immediately from another classical result known as Markov's inequality. For a proof of both inequalities, see DeGroot [2002]. ∎

PROOF OF THEOREM 15.3. Classical result; see DeGroot [2002] and Wasserman [2004]. ∎

---

[10] Note the subtle difference between aperiodicity and irreducibility, where the latter states that for every pair of states $\mathbf{x}$ and $\mathbf{x}'$, there exists a specific time $t > 1$ such that $\mathbb{P}(\mathbf{X}_t = \mathbf{x}' | \mathbf{X}_1 = \mathbf{x}) > 0$. As defined here, periodicity implies irreducibility but the converse is not true.

PROOF OF THEOREM 15.4. For the expectation, we have

$$\mathrm{Ex}(\breve{\alpha}) = \sum_{\mathbf{x} \models \alpha} \breve{\alpha}(\mathbf{x})\mathrm{Pr}(\mathbf{x}) + \sum_{\mathbf{x} \not\models \alpha} \breve{\alpha}(\mathbf{x})\mathrm{Pr}(\mathbf{x})$$

$$= \sum_{\mathbf{x} \models \alpha} (1)\mathrm{Pr}(\mathbf{x}) + \sum_{\mathbf{x} \not\models \alpha} (0)\mathrm{Pr}(\mathbf{x})$$

$$= \sum_{\mathbf{x} \models \alpha} \mathrm{Pr}(\mathbf{x})$$

$$= \mathrm{Pr}(\alpha).$$

For the variance, we have

$$\mathrm{Va}(\breve{\alpha}) = \sum_{\mathbf{x}} (\breve{\alpha}(\mathbf{x}) - \mathrm{Pr}(\alpha))^2 \mathrm{Pr}(\mathbf{x})$$

$$= \sum_{\mathbf{x} \models \alpha} (\breve{\alpha}(\mathbf{x}) - \mathrm{Pr}(\alpha))^2 \mathrm{Pr}(\mathbf{x}) + \sum_{\mathbf{x} \not\models \alpha} (\breve{\alpha}(\mathbf{x}) - \mathrm{Pr}(\alpha))^2 \mathrm{Pr}(\mathbf{x})$$

$$= \sum_{\mathbf{x} \models \alpha} (1 - \mathrm{Pr}(\alpha))^2 \mathrm{Pr}(\mathbf{x}) + \sum_{\mathbf{x} \not\models \alpha} (0 - \mathrm{Pr}(\alpha))^2 \mathrm{Pr}(\mathbf{x})$$

$$= (1 - \mathrm{Pr}(\alpha))^2 \mathrm{Pr}(\alpha) + \mathrm{Pr}(\alpha)^2 \mathrm{Pr}(\neg\alpha)$$

$$= (1 - \mathrm{Pr}(\alpha))^2 \mathrm{Pr}(\alpha) + \mathrm{Pr}(\alpha)^2 (1 - \mathrm{Pr}(\alpha))$$

$$= \mathrm{Pr}(\alpha) - \mathrm{Pr}(\alpha)^2$$

$$= \mathrm{Pr}(\alpha)\mathrm{Pr}(\neg\alpha). \quad \blacksquare$$

PROOF OF THEOREM 15.5. This is a classical result from statistics; see DeGroot [2002]. $\blacksquare$

PROOF OF THEOREM 15.6. Left to Exercise 15.5. $\blacksquare$

PROOF OF THEOREM 15.7. This is a classical result from statistics; see DeGroot [2002]. However, we point out that the more formal statement of this theorem is that $\sqrt{n}(\mathrm{Av}_n(f) - \mu)$ converges in distribution to a Normal with mean 0 and variance σ^2. That is, for all t, we have

$$\lim_{n \to \infty} \mathbb{P}(\sqrt{n}(\mathrm{Av}_n(f) - \mu) \leq t) = \Phi(t),$$

where $\Phi(t)$ is the CDF for a Normal distribution with mean 0 and variance σ^2. $\blacksquare$

PROOF OF THEOREM 15.8. This theorem is discussed in Wasserman [2004]. $\blacksquare$

PROOF OF THEOREM 15.9. Left to Exercise 15.10. $\blacksquare$

PROOF OF THEOREM 15.10. The more formal statement of this theorem is as follows. As the sample size n tends to infinity, the distribution of $\sqrt{n}(\mathrm{Av}_n(\breve{\gamma})/\mathrm{Av}_n(\breve{\beta}) - \mathrm{Pr}(\alpha|\beta))$ converges in distribution to a Normal with mean 0 and variance

$$\frac{\mathrm{Pr}(\alpha|\beta)\mathrm{Pr}(\neg\alpha|\beta)}{\mathrm{Pr}(\beta)}.$$

Hence, the estimate $\mathrm{Av}_n(\breve{\gamma})/\mathrm{Av}_n(\breve{\beta})$ is asymptotically Normal. Approximate normality follows from the robustness of the Central Limit Theorem.

Theorem 15.10 follows from the multivariate Delta method; see for example Wasserman [2004]. Roughly speaking, this method states that if a set of estimates are approximately Normal, then a function of these estimates is also approximately Normal.

Let $X = \check{\gamma}$ and $Y = \check{\beta}$ be two direct sampling functions, μ_X and μ_Y be their means, σ^2_X and σ^2_Y be their variances, σ_{XY} be their covariance, and let Σ be the variance-covariance matrix

$$\Sigma = \begin{pmatrix} \sigma^2_X & \sigma_{XY} \\ \sigma_{XY} & \sigma^2_Y \end{pmatrix}.$$

The multivariate Central Limit Theorem [Wasserman, 2004] shows that as n tends to infinity, the vector $\sqrt{n}(A - \mu)$, where

$$A = \begin{pmatrix} \mathrm{Av}_n(X) \\ \mathrm{Av}_n(Y) \end{pmatrix} \quad \text{and} \quad \mu = \begin{pmatrix} \mu_X \\ \mu_Y \end{pmatrix},$$

tends to a multivariate Normal distribution with mean 0 and variance matrix Σ. This result allows us to invoke the Delta method as follows.

Consider the function $g(X, Y) = X/Y$ and define

$$\nabla_{g(X,Y)} = \begin{pmatrix} \frac{\partial g}{\partial X} \\ \frac{\partial g}{\partial Y} \end{pmatrix}.$$

Let ∇_μ denote $\nabla_{g(X,Y)}$ evaluated at mean vector μ and assume that the elements of ∇_μ are nonzero. The Delta method then says that as n tends to infinity, the distribution of

$$\sqrt{n}\big(g(\mathrm{Av}_n(X), \mathrm{Av}_n(Y)) - g(\mu_X, \mu_Y)\big) = \sqrt{n}\left(\frac{\mathrm{Av}_n(X)}{\mathrm{Av}_n(Y)} - \frac{\mu_X}{\mu_Y}\right)$$

tends to a Normal distribution with mean 0 and variance $\nabla_\mu^T \Sigma \nabla_\mu$. This implies that the distribution of estimate $\mathrm{Av}_n(X)/\mathrm{Av}_n(Y)$ is approximately Normal with mean μ_X/μ_Y and variance $\nabla_\mu^T \Sigma \nabla_\mu / n$. All we need now is to evaluate the mean μ_X/μ_Y and variance $\nabla_\mu^T \Sigma \nabla_\mu / n$. We have

$$\frac{\partial}{\partial X}\left(\frac{X}{Y}\right) = \frac{1}{Y}$$

$$\frac{\partial}{\partial Y}\left(\frac{X}{Y}\right) = -\frac{X}{Y^2}$$

$$\mu_X = \mathrm{Pr}(\alpha \wedge \beta)$$

$$\mu_Y = \mathrm{Pr}(\beta)$$

$$\sigma^2_X = \mathrm{Pr}(\alpha \wedge \beta)(1 - \mathrm{Pr}(\alpha \wedge \beta))$$

$$\sigma^2_Y = \mathrm{Pr}(\beta)(1 - \mathrm{Pr}(\beta))$$

$$\sigma_{XY} = \mathrm{Pr}(\alpha \wedge \beta) - \mathrm{Pr}(\alpha \wedge \beta)\mathrm{Pr}(\beta).$$

The last step follows since $\sigma_{XY} = \mathrm{Ex}(XY) - \mathrm{Ex}(X)\mathrm{Ex}(Y)$, and $XY = \check{\gamma}\check{\beta} = \check{\gamma}$ since $\gamma = \alpha \wedge \beta$. We then have

$$\nabla_{g(X,Y)} = \begin{pmatrix} \frac{1}{Y} \\ -\frac{X}{Y^2} \end{pmatrix}$$

$$\nabla_\mu = \begin{pmatrix} \frac{1}{\mu_Y} \\ -\frac{\mu_X}{\mu_Y^2} \end{pmatrix}$$

Hence, the mean is

$$\frac{\mu_X}{\mu_Y} = \frac{\Pr(\alpha, \beta)}{\Pr(\beta)} = \Pr(\alpha|\beta).$$

Moreover, the variance is

$$\nabla_\mu^T \Sigma \nabla_\mu = \begin{pmatrix} \frac{1}{\mu_Y} & -\frac{\mu_X}{\mu_Y^2} \end{pmatrix} \begin{pmatrix} \sigma^2_X & \sigma_{XY} \\ \sigma_{XY} & \sigma^2_Y \end{pmatrix} \begin{pmatrix} \frac{1}{\mu_Y} \\ -\frac{\mu_X}{\mu_Y^2} \end{pmatrix},$$

which evaluates to

$$\nabla_\mu^T \Sigma \nabla_\mu = \frac{\sigma^2_X}{\mu_Y^2} - 2\frac{\mu_X \sigma_{XY}}{\mu_Y^3} + \frac{\mu_X^2 \sigma^2_Y}{\mu_Y^4}.$$

Substituting and simplifying leads to

$$\frac{\nabla_\mu^T \Sigma \nabla_\mu}{n} = \frac{\Pr(\alpha|\beta)\Pr(\neg\alpha|\beta)}{n\Pr(\beta)}. \qquad \blacksquare$$

PROOF OF THEOREM 15.11. We did not define $\Pr(\mathbf{x})/\widetilde{\Pr}(\mathbf{x})$ when $\widetilde{\Pr}(\mathbf{x}) = 0$. However, since $\Pr(\mathbf{x}) = 0$ in this case, the following derivations hold regardless of how this is defined.

We have

$$\begin{aligned}
\mathrm{Ex}(\tilde\alpha) &= \sum_{\mathbf{x} \models \alpha} \left(\frac{\Pr(\mathbf{x})}{\widetilde{\Pr}(\mathbf{x})}\right) \widetilde{\Pr}(\mathbf{x}) + \sum_{\mathbf{x} \not\models \alpha}(0)\widetilde{\Pr}(\mathbf{x}) \\
&= \sum_{\mathbf{x} \models \alpha} \Pr(\mathbf{x}) \\
&= \Pr(\alpha).
\end{aligned}$$

Using Exercise 15.2, we have

$$\begin{aligned}
\mathrm{Va}(\tilde\alpha) &= \sum_{\mathbf{x}} \tilde\alpha(\mathbf{x})^2 \cdot \widetilde{\Pr}(\mathbf{x}) - \Pr(\alpha)^2 \\
&= \sum_{\mathbf{x} \models \alpha} \tilde\alpha(\mathbf{x})^2 \cdot \widetilde{\Pr}(\mathbf{x}) + \sum_{\mathbf{x} \not\models \alpha} \tilde\alpha(\mathbf{x})^2 \cdot \widetilde{\Pr}(\mathbf{x}) - \Pr(\alpha)^2 \\
&= \sum_{\mathbf{x} \models \alpha} \frac{\Pr(\mathbf{x})^2}{\widetilde{\Pr}(\mathbf{x})^2} \cdot \widetilde{\Pr}(\mathbf{x}) + \sum_{\mathbf{x} \not\models \alpha} 0 \cdot \widetilde{\Pr}(\mathbf{x}) - \Pr(\alpha)^2 \\
&= \sum_{\mathbf{x} \models \alpha} \frac{\Pr(\mathbf{x})^2}{\widetilde{\Pr}(\mathbf{x})} - \Pr(\alpha)^2.
\end{aligned}$$

$\blacksquare$

PROOF OF THEOREM 15.12. This proof follows immediately from Theorem 15.11 and observing that $\Pr(\alpha)/\widetilde{\Pr}(\alpha) = \Pr(\mathbf{x})/\widetilde{\Pr}(\mathbf{x})$ for all instantiations $\mathbf{x}$ that are consistent with α.

$\blacksquare$

PROOF OF THEOREM 15.13. This proof parallels that for Theorem 15.10 using the Delta method, except that we now define $X = \tilde\gamma$ and $Y = \tilde\beta$, where $\gamma = \alpha \wedge \beta$. We then get

$$\mu_X = \Pr(\alpha \wedge \beta)$$

$$\mu_Y = \Pr(\beta)$$

$$\sigma^2{}_X = \frac{\Pr(\alpha \wedge \beta)^2 - \widetilde{\Pr}(\alpha \wedge \beta)\Pr(\alpha \wedge \beta)^2}{\widetilde{\Pr}(\alpha \wedge \beta)}$$

$$\sigma^2{}_Y = \frac{\Pr(\beta)^2 - \widetilde{\Pr}(\beta)\Pr(\beta)^2}{\widetilde{\Pr}(\beta)}$$

$$\sigma_{XY} = \frac{\Pr(\alpha \wedge \beta)\Pr(\beta)}{\widetilde{\Pr}(\beta)} - \frac{\Pr(\alpha \wedge \beta)\widetilde{\Pr}(\beta)\Pr(\beta)}{\widetilde{\Pr}(\beta)}.$$

These forms can be simplified further. However, using these specific forms makes further substitutions easier to manipulate and simplify.

Substituting and simplifying, we get

$$\frac{\nabla_\mu^T \Sigma \nabla_\mu}{n} = \frac{\Pr(\alpha|\beta)\Pr(\neg\alpha|\beta)}{n\widetilde{\Pr}(\beta)}. \qquad \blacksquare$$

PROOF OF THEOREM 15.14. Left to Exercise 15.17. $\qquad \blacksquare$

PROOF OF THEOREM 15.15. See Neal [2004] for a discussion of this result and some relevant pointers. $\qquad \blacksquare$

PROOF OF THEOREM 15.16. The detailed balance property holds immediately if $\mathbf{x} = \mathbf{x}'$. If $\mathbf{x}$ and $\mathbf{x}'$ disagree on more than one variable, both sides evaluate to zero. Suppose now that $\mathbf{x}$ and $\mathbf{x}'$ disagree on a single variable S, which has value s in $\mathbf{x}$ and value s' in $\mathbf{x}'$. We then have

$$\Pr(\mathbf{x})\mathbb{P}(\mathbf{x}'|\mathbf{x}) \overset{?}{=} \Pr(\mathbf{x}')\mathbb{P}(\mathbf{x}|\mathbf{x}')$$

$$\Pr(\mathbf{x})\mathbb{P}(s'|\mathbf{x} - S)/m \overset{?}{=} \Pr(\mathbf{x}')\mathbb{P}(s|\mathbf{x}' - S)/m$$

$$\Pr(\mathbf{x})\frac{\Pr(\mathbf{x}')}{m\Pr(\mathbf{x} - S)} = \Pr(\mathbf{x}')\frac{\Pr(\mathbf{x})}{m\Pr(\mathbf{x}' - S)}.$$

The last step follows since $\mathbf{x} - S$ is the same as $\mathbf{x}' - S$.

When $\Pr(\mathbf{X})$ is strictly positive, it follows immediately from the definition of a Gibbs matrix that any two states of $\mathbf{X}$ can be connected by a sequence of nonzero transitions. $\qquad \blacksquare$

PROOF OF THEOREM 15.17. Let $Z_1, \ldots, Z_m$ be all variables other than S and its children $C_1, \ldots, C_k$, and let $\mathbf{V}_1, \ldots, \mathbf{V}_m$ be their corresponding parents. Using the chain rule of Bayesian networks, we have

$$\Pr(s, \mathbf{x} - S, \mathbf{e}) = \theta_{s|\mathbf{u}} \prod_{i=1}^{k} \theta_{c_i|\mathbf{u}_i} \prod_{i=1}^{m} \theta_{z_i|\mathbf{v}_i},$$

where each $z_i, \mathbf{v}_i$ is compatible with instantiation $s, \mathbf{x} - S, \mathbf{e}$. Note that the variable S appears in exactly $k + 1$ CPTs: the one for S, $\theta_{s|\mathbf{u}}$ and the ones for its k children, $\theta_{c_i|\mathbf{u}_i}$. Hence, the product $\prod_{i=1}^{m} \theta_{z_i|\mathbf{v}_i}$ does not depend on the state s of variable S and we have

$$\Pr(s, \mathbf{x} - S, \mathbf{e}) \quad \propto \quad \theta_{s|\mathbf{u}} \prod_{i=1}^{k} \theta_{c_i|\mathbf{u}_i}.$$

Note also that

$$\Pr(\mathbf{x} - S, \mathbf{e}) = \sum_{s^*} \Pr(s^*, \mathbf{x} - S, \mathbf{e})$$

does not depend on s. Hence,

$$\Pr(s \mid \mathbf{x} - S, \mathbf{e}) = \frac{\Pr(s, \mathbf{x} - S, \mathbf{e})}{\Pr(\mathbf{x} - S, \mathbf{e})}$$

$$\propto \theta_{s \mid \mathbf{u}} \prod_{i=1}^{k} \theta_{c_i \mid \mathbf{u}_i}$$

$$= \eta \cdot \theta_{s \mid \mathbf{u}} \prod_{i=1}^{k} \theta_{c_i \mid \mathbf{u}_i}. \qquad \blacksquare$$

16

Sensitivity Analysis

We consider in this chapter the relationship between the values of parameters that quantify a Bayesian network and the values of probabilistic queries applied to these networks. In particular, we consider the impact of parameter changes on query values, and the amount of parameter change needed to enforce some constraints on these values.

16.1 Introduction

Consider a laboratory that administers three tests for detecting pregnancy: a blood test, a urine test, and a scanning test. Assume also that these tests relate to the state of pregnancy as given by the network of Figure 16.1 (we treated this network in Chapter 5). According to this network, the prior probability of pregnancy is 87% after an artificial insemination procedure. Moreover, the posterior probability of pregnancy given three negative tests is 10.21%. Suppose now that this level of accuracy is not acceptable: the laboratory is interested in improving the tests so the posterior probability is no greater than 5% given three negative tests. The problem now becomes one of finding a certain set of network parameters (corresponding to the tests' false positive and negative rates) that guarantee the required accuracy. This is a classic problem of sensitivity analysis that we address in Section 16.3 as it is concerned with controlling network parameters to enforce some constraints on the queries of interest.

Assume now that we replace one of the tests with a more accurate one, leading to a new Bayesian network that results from updating the parameters corresponding to that test. We would now like to know the impact of this parameter change on other queries of interest, for example, the probability of pregnancy given three positive tests. We can solve this problem by simply recomputing these queries to find out their new values but this approach could be infeasible if we are interested in a large number of queries. As we see in this chapter, we can apply techniques from sensitivity analysis to efficiently obtain a bound on the possible changes in query results by considering only the changes applied to network parameters. This part of sensitivity analysis is then concerned with the robustness of queries against parameter changes and is the subject of the next section.

16.2 Query robustness

We start in this section by addressing the problem of query *robustness*, which can be approached at two different levels depending on whether we are interested in network-independent or network-specific results. In network-independent sensitivity analysis, we obtain robustness results in the form of bounds on query results yet these bounds can be very efficiently computed. In network-specific sensitivity analysis, we can characterize precisely the relationship between a particular query and a network parameter by explicitly constructing the function that governs this relationship. However, the construction of this

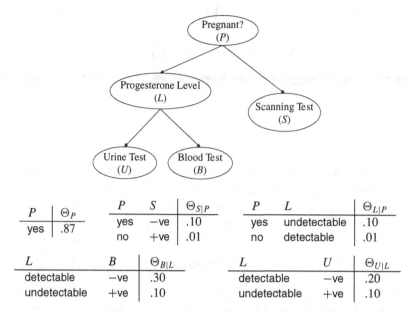

P	Θ_P
yes	.87

P	S	$\Theta_{S\mid P}$
yes	−ve	.10
no	+ve	.01

P	L	$\Theta_{L\mid P}$
yes	undetectable	.10
no	detectable	.01

L	B	$\Theta_{B\mid L}$
detectable	−ve	.30
undetectable	+ve	.10

L	U	$\Theta_{U\mid L}$
detectable	−ve	.20
undetectable	+ve	.10

Figure 16.1: A Bayesian network for detecting pregnancy based on three tests. Redundant CPT rows have been omitted.

function generally requires inference and is therefore more costly than the bounds obtained by network-independent sensitivity analysis. We consider both approaches next.

16.2.1 Network-independent robustness

Assume that we are given a Bayesian network $\mathcal{N}^0$ and we change some network parameters to obtain a new network $\mathcal{N}$. Consider now a general query of the form $\alpha\mid\beta$ that can have different probabilities, $\mathrm{Pr}^0(\alpha\mid\beta)$ and $\mathrm{Pr}(\alpha\mid\beta)$, with respect to the two networks $\mathcal{N}^0$ and $\mathcal{N}$. Our goal in this section is to try to characterize the change in the probability of query $\alpha\mid\beta$ as a result of the parameter change. Our first approach for this is based on computing a distance measure between the two distributions Pr^0 and Pr and then using the value of this distance to bound the new probability $\mathrm{Pr}(\alpha\mid\beta)$. We first introduce this distance measure and then discuss how to compute it and how to use it for obtaining the sought bounds.

Definition 16.1 (CD distance). Let $\mathrm{Pr}^0(\mathbf{X})$ and $\mathrm{Pr}(\mathbf{X})$ be two probability distributions and define the measure $D(\mathrm{Pr}^0, \mathrm{Pr})$ as

$$D(\mathrm{Pr}^0, \mathrm{Pr}) \stackrel{def}{=} \ln \max_{\mathbf{x}} \frac{\mathrm{Pr}(\mathbf{x})}{\mathrm{Pr}^0(\mathbf{x})} - \ln \min_{\mathbf{x}} \frac{\mathrm{Pr}(\mathbf{x})}{\mathrm{Pr}^0(\mathbf{x})},$$

where $0/0 \stackrel{def}{=} 1$ and $\infty/\infty \stackrel{def}{=} 1$. ∎

Table 16.1 depicts an example of computing this measure for two distributions.

This measure satisfies the three properties of distance and is therefore a *distance measure*. In particular, if Pr^0, Pr, and Pr' are three probability distributions over the same set of variables, we have:

- Positiveness: $D(\mathrm{Pr}^0, \mathrm{Pr}) \geq 0$ and $D(\mathrm{Pr}^0, \mathrm{Pr}) = 0$ iff $\mathrm{Pr}^0 = \mathrm{Pr}$
- Symmetry: $D(\mathrm{Pr}^0, \mathrm{Pr}) = D(\mathrm{Pr}, \mathrm{Pr}^0)$
- Triangle Inequality: $D(\mathrm{Pr}^0, \mathrm{Pr}) + D(\mathrm{Pr}, \mathrm{Pr}') \geq D(\mathrm{Pr}^0, \mathrm{Pr}')$.

Table 16.1: Two distributions with a CD distance equal to $1.61 = \ln 2 - \ln .4$.

A	B	C	$\Pr(a, b, c)$	$\Pr^0(a, b, c)$	$\Pr^0(a, b, c)/\Pr(a, b, c)$
true	true	true	.10	.20	2.00
true	true	false	.20	.30	1.50
true	false	true	.25	.10	.40
true	false	false	.05	.05	1.00
false	true	true	.05	.10	2.00
false	true	false	.10	.05	.50
false	false	true	.10	.10	1.00
false	false	false	.15	.10	.67

Our interest in the CD distance stems from two reasons. First, it can be easily computed for distributions that correspond to very similar Bayesian networks, that is, networks that result from a local perturbation to one another. Second, it allows us to bound query results computed with respect to one distribution in terms of query results computed with respect to the other.

Theorem 16.1. *Let* $\Pr^0$ *and* $\Pr$ *be two probability distributions over the same set of variables and let* α *and* β *be arbitrary events. Given the distance measure* $D(\Pr^0, \Pr)$ *between* $\Pr^0$ *and* $\Pr$, *we have the following tight bound:*

$$e^{-D(\Pr^0, \Pr)} \leq \frac{O(\alpha|\beta)}{O^0(\alpha|\beta)} \leq e^{D(\Pr^0, \Pr)},$$

where $O^0(\alpha|\beta)$ *and* $O(\alpha|\beta)$ *are the odds of* $\alpha|\beta$ *under distributions* $\Pr^0$ *and* $\Pr$, *respectively.* ∎

We can express the bound given by Theorem 16.1 in two other useful forms. First, we can use logarithms:

$$\left| \ln O(\alpha|\beta) - \ln O^0(\alpha|\beta) \right| \leq D(\Pr^0, \Pr). \tag{16.1}$$

Second, we can use probabilities instead of odds to express the bound:

$$\frac{e^{-d} p}{\left(e^{-d} - 1\right) p + 1} \leq \Pr(\alpha|\beta) \leq \frac{e^d p}{\left(e^d - 1\right) p + 1}, \tag{16.2}$$

where $p = \Pr^0(\alpha|\beta)$ and $d = D(\Pr^0, \Pr)$. Figure 16.2 plots the bounds on $\Pr(\alpha|\beta)$ as a function of the initial probability p for several values of the CD distance d. As is clear from this figure, the smaller the CD distance between two distributions, the tighter the bounds we can obtain. Moreover, for a given value d of the CD distance the bounds get tighter as the initial probability p becomes more extreme (tends to 0 or 1).

Before we provide concrete examples of how the CD distance can be used to address the query robustness problem of sensitivity analysis, we discuss a condition under which can efficiently compute the distance.

Theorem 16.2. *Let* $\mathbf{N}^0$ *and* $\mathbf{N}$ *be Bayesian networks, where network* $\mathbf{N}$ *is obtained from* $\mathbf{N}^0$ *by changing the conditional probability distribution of variable* X *given parent instantiation* $\mathbf{u}$ *from* $\Theta^0_{X|\mathbf{u}}$ *to* $\Theta_{X|\mathbf{u}}$, *that is, changing parameter value* $\theta^0_{x|\mathbf{u}}$ *to some new*

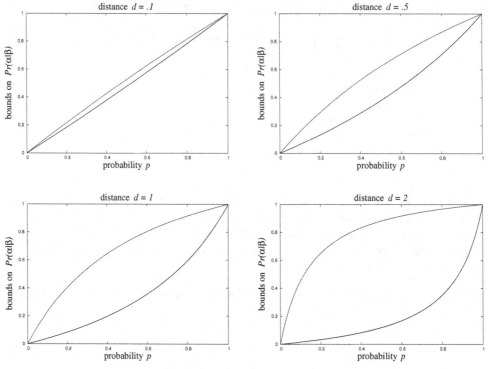

Figure 16.2: Plotting the CD distance bounds for several values of the distance.

value $\theta_{x|\mathbf{u}}$ for every x. Let Pr^0 and Pr be the distributions induced by networks $\mathcal{N}^0$ and $\mathcal{N}$, respectively. If $\mathrm{Pr}^0(\mathbf{u}) > 0$, then

$$D(\mathrm{Pr}^0, \mathrm{Pr}) = D(\Theta^0_{X|\mathbf{u}}, \Theta_{X|\mathbf{u}})$$

$$= \ln \max_x \frac{\theta_{x|\mathbf{u}}}{\theta^0_{x|\mathbf{u}}} - \ln \min_x \frac{\theta_{x|\mathbf{u}}}{\theta^0_{x|\mathbf{u}}}. \tag{16.3}$$

Moreover, if $\mathrm{Pr}^0(\mathbf{u}) = 0$, then $D(\mathrm{Pr}^0, \mathrm{Pr}) = 0$. ■

Theorem 16.2 shows that the CD distance between the global distributions induced by networks $\mathcal{N}^0$ and $\mathcal{N}$ is exactly the CD distance between the local conditional distributions $\Theta^0_{X|\mathbf{u}}$ and $\Theta_{X|\mathbf{u}}$ (assuming all other parameters in $\mathcal{N}^0$ and $\mathcal{N}$ are the same and that $\mathbf{u}$ has a nonzero probability). This theorem is important practically as it identifies a condition under which the bounds given by Theorem 16.1 can be computed efficiently.

To consider a concrete example, let us examine the network in Figure 16.3 under the evidence $\mathbf{e} = \neg S, R$, that is, there is no smoke but people are reported to be leaving. The probability of fire in this case is $\mathrm{Pr}^0(F|\neg S, R) = .029$. Suppose now that we change the CPT for variable Smoke as follows:

Fire (F)	Smoke (S)	$\Theta^0_{S|F}$
true	true	.90
true	false	.10
false	true	.01
false	false	.99

Fire (F)	Smoke (S)	$\Theta_{S|F}$
true	true	.92
true	false	.08
false	true	.01
false	false	.99

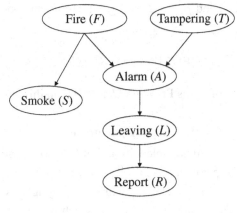

Fire (F)	Θ_F
true	.01

Tampering (T)	Θ_T
true	.02

Fire	Smoke (S)	$\Theta_{S\mid F}$
true	true	.9
false	true	.01

Fire	Tampering	Alarm (A)	$\Theta_{A\mid F,T}$
true	true	true	.5
true	false	true	.99
false	true	true	.85
false	false	true	.0001

Alarm	Leaving (L)	$\Theta_{L\mid A}$
true	true	.88
false	true	.001

Leaving	Report (R)	$\Theta_{R\mid L}$
true	true	.75
false	true	.01

Figure 16.3: A Bayesian network. Redundant CPT rows have been omitted.

According to Theorem 16.2, the CD distance between the initial and new distributions is then equal to the CD distance between the initial and new CPTs for Smoke:

$$D(\text{Pr}^0, \text{Pr}) = D(\Theta_{S\mid F}^0, \Theta_{S\mid F}) = \ln \frac{.10}{.08} - \ln \frac{.90}{.92} = .245.$$

Using (16.2) with $d = .245$ and $p = .029$, we get the following bound on the new probability for fire:

$$.023 \leq \text{Pr}(F\mid \neg S, R) \leq .037.$$

The exact new probability of fire is $\text{Pr}(F\mid \neg S, R) = .024$ in this case.

For another example, consider the impact of changing the CPT for Tampering as follows:

Tampering (T)	Θ_T^0
true	.02
false	.98

Tampering (T)	Θ_T
true	.036
false	.964

The CD distance between these CPTs for Tampering is

$$D(\text{Pr}^0, \text{Pr}) = D(\Theta_T^0, \Theta_T) = \ln \frac{.036}{.02} - \ln \frac{.964}{.98} = .604.$$

Using (16.2) with $d = .604$ and $p = .029$, we get the following bound on the new probability for fire:

$$.016 \leq \Pr(F|\neg S, R) \leq .052.$$

The exact new probability of fire is $\Pr(F|\neg S, R) = .021$ in this case.

Co-varying parameters

Suppose that X is a multivalued variable with initial CPT $\Theta^0_{X|\mathbf{U}}$. Suppose further that we wish to change a particular parameter value $\theta^0_{x|\mathbf{u}}$ to the new value $\theta_{x|\mathbf{u}}$. Since $\sum_x \theta_{x|\mathbf{u}} = 1$, we cannot change the value of parameter $\theta^0_{x|\mathbf{u}}$ without changing the values of its co-varying parameters $\theta^0_{x^\star|\mathbf{u}}, x^\star \neq x$. There are many ways in which we can change these co-varying parameters, but a common technique known as the *proportional scheme* is to change the values of co-varying parameters while maintaining their relative ratios.

As an example of this scheme, consider the following distribution for variable X:

$\theta^0_{x_1|\mathbf{u}}$	$\theta^0_{x_2|\mathbf{u}}$	$\theta^0_{x_3|\mathbf{u}}$
.6	.3	.1

and suppose that we wish to change the first parameter value from .6 to .8. We know in this case that a total change of $-.2$ must be applied to co-varying parameters. The proportional scheme will distribute this amount among co-varying parameters while preserving their ratios, leading to

$\theta_{x_1|\mathbf{u}}$	$\theta_{x_2|\mathbf{u}}$	$\theta_{x_3|\mathbf{u}}$
.8	.15	.05

Note here that $\theta_{x_3|\mathbf{u}}/\theta_{x_2|\mathbf{u}} = \theta^0_{x_3|\mathbf{u}}/\theta^0_{x_2|\mathbf{u}}$. From now on, we assume that co-varying parameters are changed according to this scheme, which is defined formally next.

Definition 16.2 (Single Parameter Change). Let $\Theta^0_{X|\mathbf{U}}$ be an initial CPT for variable X and suppose we want to change a single parameter value $\theta^0_{x|\mathbf{u}}$ to the new value $\theta_{x|\mathbf{u}}$. The co-varying parameters of $\theta^0_{x|\mathbf{u}}$ are changed simultaneously as follows, for all $x^\star \neq x$:

$$\theta_{x^\star|\mathbf{u}} \stackrel{def}{=} \rho(x, x^\star, \mathbf{u})(1 - \theta_{x|\mathbf{u}})$$

$$\rho(x, x^\star, \mathbf{u}) \stackrel{def}{=} \begin{cases} \frac{\theta^0_{x^\star|\mathbf{u}}}{1 - \theta^0_{x|\mathbf{u}}} & \text{if } \theta^0_{x|\mathbf{u}} \neq 1 \\ \frac{1}{|X|-1} & \text{if } \theta^0_{x|\mathbf{u}} = 1, \end{cases}$$

where $|X|$ is the number of values that variable X has. ∎

Note that when the changing parameter has an initial value of 1, all its co-varying parameters have initial values of 0. In this case, the proportional scheme distributes the parameter change equally among co-varying parameters.

More on single parameter changes

When changing a single parameter as given by Definition 16.2, Theorem 16.2 takes a more specific and intuitive form.

Theorem 16.3. *Consider Theorem 16.2 and suppose that the CPT $\Theta_{X|U}$ results from changing a single parameter $\theta^0_{x|\mathbf{u}}$ in the initial CPT $\Theta^0_{X|U}$. Equation 16.3 then reduces to the simpler form*

$$D(\mathrm{Pr}^0, \mathrm{Pr}) = \left| \ln O(x|\mathbf{u}) - \ln O^0(x|\mathbf{u}) \right|. \hspace{2cm} \blacksquare$$

That is, the CD distance between the old and new distributions is nothing but the absolute change in the log-odds of the changed parameter. Combining this result with (16.1), we get

$$\left| \ln O(\alpha|\beta) - \ln O^0(\alpha|\beta) \right| \leq \left| \ln O(x|\mathbf{u}) - \ln O^0(x|\mathbf{u}) \right|. \hspace{1.5cm} (16.4)$$

The new inequality suggests a particular method for measuring the amount of change that a parameter or query undergoes: the absolute change in log-odds. Moreover, the inequality shows that if the change is measured this way, the amount of change that a query undergoes can be no more than the amount of the corresponding parameter change.

For more insight into this method of measuring change, consider two parameter changes, one from .1 to .15, and another from .4 to .45. Both of these changes amount to the same absolute change of .05, however, the first change amounts to a log-odds change of .463 and the second change amounts to a log-odds change of .205. Therefore, the second change is smaller according to the log-odds measure even though it is an equal absolute change. Two parameter changes that amount to the same relative change can also lead to different amounts of log-odds change. For example, consider two parameter changes, one from .1 to .2, and another from .2 to .4. Both these changes double the initial parameter value. However, the first change amounts to a log-odds change of .811, while the second change amounts to a log-odds change of .981.

16.2.2 Network-specific robustness

We approached the robustness problem in the previous section from a network-independent viewpoint, which allowed us to provide some general guarantees on the amount of change that a query can undergo as a result of a parameter change. The ability to provide these guarantees independently of the given network has two implications. First, the guarantees themselves can be computed efficiently as they do not require inference. Second, the guarantees have the form of bounds on the query and these bounds get looser as the parameter change increases.

We can provide stronger guarantees on query changes if we take into consideration the specific network and query at hand. In particular, we can construct a specific function called the *sensitivity function* that relates any particular parameter to any particular query, allowing us to efficiently compute the exact effect that a parameter has on the query. However, the price we have to pay computationally is in constructing the sensitivity function itself as that requires performing inference on the given network.

The construction of a sensitivity function is based on the following result.

Theorem 16.4. *Let $\mathbf{N}^0$ and $\mathbf{N}$ be two Bayesian networks where $\mathbf{N}$ is obtained from $\mathbf{N}^0$ by changing a single parameter value $\theta^0_{x|\mathbf{u}}$ to the new value $\theta_{x|\mathbf{u}}$. Let Pr^0 and Pr be the two distributions induced by these networks. The value of a query $\mathrm{Pr}(\alpha)$ can be expressed in terms of the original network $\mathbf{N}^0$ and the new parameter value $\theta_{x|\mathbf{u}}$ as*

$$\mathrm{Pr}(\alpha) = \mu^\alpha_{x|\mathbf{u}} \cdot \theta_{x|\mathbf{u}} + \nu^\alpha_{x|\mathbf{u}},$$

where

$$\mu_{x|\mathbf{u}}^{\alpha} = \frac{\partial \Pr(\alpha)}{\partial \theta_{x|\mathbf{u}}} - \sum_{x^{\star} \neq x} \rho(x, x^{\star}, \mathbf{u}) \frac{\partial \Pr(\alpha)}{\partial \theta_{x^{\star}|\mathbf{u}}}, \qquad (16.5)$$

$$\nu_{x|\mathbf{u}}^{\alpha} = \sum_{x^{\star} \neq x} \rho(x, x^{\star}, \mathbf{u}) \frac{\partial \Pr(\alpha)}{\partial \theta_{x^{\star}|\mathbf{u}}} + \sum_{\mathbf{u}^{\star} \neq \mathbf{u}} \Pr^0(\mathbf{u}^{\star}, \alpha). \qquad (16.6)$$

Here $\rho(x, x^{\star}, \mathbf{u})$ is as given by Definition 16.2. ∎

According to Theorem 16.4, the value of query $\Pr(\alpha)$ is a linear function of the new parameter value $\theta_{x|\mathbf{u}}$. A key observation about Theorem 16.4 is that the quantities needed to compute the constants $\mu_{x|\mathbf{u}}^{\alpha}$ and $\nu_{x|\mathbf{u}}^{\alpha}$ can be obtained by performing inference on the initial network $\mathbf{N}^0$. We discussed the computation of derivatives in Chapter 12 but we recall here that[1]

$$\frac{\partial \Pr(\alpha)}{\partial \theta_{x|\mathbf{u}}} = \frac{\Pr(\alpha, x, \mathbf{u})}{\theta_{x|\mathbf{u}}}, \quad \text{when } \theta_{x|\mathbf{u}} \neq 0.$$

Therefore, if we have an algorithm that can compute in $O(f)$ time the probability of $\alpha, x, \mathbf{u}$, for a given α and all parameters $\theta_{x|\mathbf{u}}$, then we can also compute in $O(f)$ time the constants $\mu_{x|\mathbf{u}}^{\alpha}$ and $\nu_{x|\mathbf{u}}^{\alpha}$ for a given α and all parameters $\theta_{x|\mathbf{u}}$. This allows us to construct the sensitivity functions for a given query with respect to all network parameters simultaneously in $O(f)$ time.

For a conditional query $\Pr(\alpha|\beta)$, we can construct the sensitivity function as

$$\Pr(\alpha|\beta) = \frac{\Pr(\alpha, \beta)}{\Pr(\beta)} = \frac{\mu_{x|\mathbf{u}}^{\alpha,\beta} \cdot \theta_{x|\mathbf{u}} + \nu_{x|\mathbf{u}}^{\alpha,\beta}}{\mu_{x|\mathbf{u}}^{\beta} \cdot \theta_{x|\mathbf{u}} + \nu_{x|\mathbf{u}}^{\beta}}.$$

As an example, consider again the Bayesian network in Figure 16.3. The sensitivity function for the query $\Pr(F|S, \neg R)$ with respect to the parameter $\theta_{S|\neg F}$ is given by

$$\Pr(F|S, \neg R) = \frac{.003165}{.968357 \cdot \theta_{S|\neg F} + .003165},$$

which is plotted in Figure 16.4. We see that at the current parameter value of .01, the query value is .246 but if we decrease the parameter value to .00327, the query value increases to .500. This example shows that once a sensitivity function is constructed, we can immediately compute query changes that result from parameter changes without the need to perform further inference. Note, however, that if we were to use the bound given by (16.2), we would conclude that by changing the parameter from .01 to .00327 the new query value would be within the bounds of .096 and .502. Although this bound is relatively loose, it can be obtained without the computational overhead associated with constructing a sensitivity function.

16.2.3 Robustness of MPEs

In this section, we consider the robustness of MPE instantiations with respect to parameter changes. That is, given some evidence $\mathbf{e}$ and a corresponding set of MPE instantiations

---

[1] Note also that $\partial \Pr(\alpha)/\partial \theta_{x|\mathbf{u}} = \Pr^0(\alpha, x, \mathbf{u})/\theta_{x|\mathbf{u}}^0$ when $\theta_{x|\mathbf{u}}^0 \neq 0$.

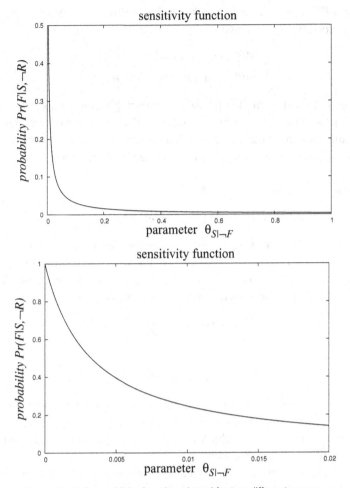

Figure 16.4: A sensitivity function plotted for two different ranges.

$\mathbf{x}_1, \ldots, \mathbf{x}_n$, our goal in this section is to identify parameter changes that are guaranteed to preserve these MPE instantiations. Note that a parameter change may increase or decrease the probability of these instantiations without necessarily changing their identity (i.e., adding or removing instantiations to the set).

Consider a parameter $\theta_{x|\mathbf{u}}$ that we plan to change and assume for now that variable X is binary. Our first observation is that the MPE probability can be decomposed as[2]

$$\text{MPE}_P(\mathbf{e}) = \max(\text{MPE}_P(x\mathbf{u}, \mathbf{e}), \text{MPE}_P(\bar{x}\mathbf{u}, \mathbf{e}), \text{MPE}_P(\neg\mathbf{u}, \mathbf{e})).$$

That is, we can partition network instantiations that are compatible with evidence $\mathbf{e}$ into three groups depending on whether they are compatible with $x\mathbf{u}$, $\bar{x}\mathbf{u}$, or $\neg\mathbf{u}$. We can then compute the MPE probability for each category and take the maximum of all three probabilities. This decomposition is useful as it reveals the following. When changing the value of parameter $\theta_{x|\mathbf{u}}$, and correspondingly $\theta_{\bar{x}|\mathbf{u}}$, only $\text{MPE}_P(x\mathbf{u}, \mathbf{e})$ and $\text{MPE}_P(\bar{x}\mathbf{u}, \mathbf{e})$

---

[2] Let $\mathbf{u}_1, \ldots, \mathbf{u}_n$ be the instantiations of variables $\mathbf{U}$ that are distinct from $\mathbf{u}$. The notation $\neg\mathbf{u}$ is then a shorthand for $(\mathbf{U}=\mathbf{u}_1) \vee \ldots \vee (\mathbf{U}=\mathbf{u}_n)$.

change while $\text{MPE}_P(\neg\mathbf{u}, \mathbf{e})$ remains unchanged as it does not depend on parameters $\theta_{x|\mathbf{u}}$ and $\theta_{\bar{x}|\mathbf{u}}$. More specifically, we have

$$\text{MPE}_P(x\mathbf{u}, \mathbf{e}) = r(x\mathbf{u}, \mathbf{e}) \cdot \theta_{x|\mathbf{u}}$$
$$\text{MPE}_P(\bar{x}\mathbf{u}, \mathbf{e}) = r(\bar{x}\mathbf{u}, \mathbf{e}) \cdot \theta_{\bar{x}|\mathbf{u}}, \qquad (16.7)$$

where $r(x\mathbf{u}, \mathbf{e})$ and $r(\bar{x}\mathbf{u}, \mathbf{e})$ are the partial derivatives given in Chapter 12 (see (12.10)), which are independent of parameters $\theta_{x|\mathbf{u}}$ and $\theta_{\bar{x}|\mathbf{u}}$. Therefore, if we have these derivatives we can immediately predict the amount of change that $\text{MPE}_P(x\mathbf{u}, \mathbf{e})$ undergoes as a result of changing $\theta_{x|\mathbf{u}}$. Similarly we can predict the change in $\text{MPE}_P(\bar{x}\mathbf{u}, \mathbf{e})$ as a result of changing $\theta_{\bar{x}|\mathbf{u}}$.

Suppose now that we have

$$\text{MPE}_P(x\mathbf{u}, \mathbf{e}) = \text{MPE}_P(\bar{x}\mathbf{u}, \mathbf{e}) = \text{MPE}_P(\neg\mathbf{u}, \mathbf{e}).$$

This implies that some MPE instantiations are compatible with $x\mathbf{u}$, some are compatible with $\bar{x}\mathbf{u}$, and some with $\neg\mathbf{u}$. If we now increase the value of parameter $\theta_{x|\mathbf{u}}$, the value of parameter $\theta_{\bar{x}|\mathbf{u}}$ will decrease. This means that $\text{MPE}_P(x\mathbf{u}, \mathbf{e})$ will increase, $\text{MPE}_P(\bar{x}\mathbf{u}, \mathbf{e})$ will decrease, and $\text{MPE}_P(\neg\mathbf{u}, \mathbf{e})$ will stay the same, leading to

$$\text{MPE}_P(x\mathbf{u}, \mathbf{e}) > \text{MPE}_P(\bar{x}\mathbf{u}, \mathbf{e})$$

and

$$\text{MPE}_P(x\mathbf{u}, \mathbf{e}) > \text{MPE}_P(\neg\mathbf{u}, \mathbf{e}).$$

Given these changes, only MPE instantiations that are compatible with $x\mathbf{u}$ will survive: their identity stays the same even though their probability increases. On the other hand, MPE instantiations that are compatible with either $\bar{x}\mathbf{u}$ or $\neg\mathbf{u}$ disappear as their probability is dominated by those compatible with $x\mathbf{u}$.

Together with (16.7), these observations lead to the following conditions which are necessary and sufficient for preserving MPE instantiations when changing parameters $\theta_{x|\mathbf{u}}$ and $\theta_{\bar{x}|\mathbf{u}}$:

- If an MPE instantiation is compatible with $x\mathbf{u}$, it is preserved as long as the following inequalities hold:

$$r(\mathbf{e}, x\mathbf{u}) \cdot \theta_{x|\mathbf{u}} \geq r(\mathbf{e}, \bar{x}\mathbf{u}) \cdot \theta_{\bar{x}|\mathbf{u}}$$
$$r(\mathbf{e}, x\mathbf{u}) \cdot \theta_{x|\mathbf{u}} \geq \text{MPE}_P(\mathbf{e}, \neg\mathbf{u}).$$

- If an MPE instantiation is compatible with $\bar{x}\mathbf{u}$, it is preserved as long as the following inequalities hold:

$$r(\mathbf{e}, \bar{x}\mathbf{u}) \cdot \theta_{\bar{x}|\mathbf{u}} \geq r(\mathbf{e}, x\mathbf{u}) \cdot \theta_{x|\mathbf{u}}$$
$$r(\mathbf{e}, \bar{x}\mathbf{u}) \cdot \theta_{\bar{x}|\mathbf{u}} \geq \text{MPE}_P(\mathbf{e}, \neg\mathbf{u}).$$

- If an MPE instantiation is compatible with $\neg\mathbf{u}$, it is preserved as long as the following inequalities hold:

$$\text{MPE}_P(\mathbf{e}, \neg\mathbf{u}) \geq r(\mathbf{e}, x\mathbf{u}) \cdot \theta_{x|\mathbf{u}}$$
$$\text{MPE}_P(\mathbf{e}, \neg\mathbf{u}) \geq r(\mathbf{e}, \bar{x}\mathbf{u}) \cdot \theta_{\bar{x}|\mathbf{u}}.$$

We note here that we can easily decide whether an MPE instantiation is compatible with either $x\mathbf{u}$, $\bar{x}\mathbf{u}$, or $\neg\mathbf{u}$ since an MPE instantiation is a complete variable instantiation.

Moreover, the constants $r(x\mathbf{u}, \mathbf{e})$ and $r(\bar{x}\mathbf{u}, \mathbf{e})$ can be computed as given in Chapter 12 (see (12.10)), while $\mathrm{MPE}_P(\mathbf{e}, \neg\mathbf{u})$ can be computed as

$$
\begin{aligned}
\mathrm{MPE}_P(\mathbf{e}, \neg\mathbf{u}) &= \max_{\mathbf{u}^\star \neq \mathbf{u}} \mathrm{MPE}_P(\mathbf{u}^\star, \mathbf{e}) \\
&= \max_{x, \mathbf{u}^\star \neq \mathbf{u}} \mathrm{MPE}_P(x\mathbf{u}^\star, \mathbf{e}) \\
&= \max_{x, \mathbf{u}^\star \neq \mathbf{u}} r(x\mathbf{u}^\star, \mathbf{e}) \cdot \theta_{x|\mathbf{u}^\star}.
\end{aligned}
\tag{16.8}
$$

For a simple example, consider the Bayesian network $A \to B$ with the following CPTs:

A	Θ_A
a	.5
$\bar{a}$	.5

A	B	$\Theta_{B|A}$
a	b	.2
a	$\bar{b}$	.8
$\bar{a}$	b	.6
$\bar{a}$	$\bar{b}$	.4

Assuming we have no evidence, $\mathbf{e} = \mathrm{true}$, there is one MPE instantiation in this case, $a\bar{b}$, which has probability $\mathrm{MPE}_P(\mathbf{e}) = .4$. Suppose now that we plan to change parameters $\theta_{b|a}$ and $\theta_{\bar{b}|a}$ and want to compute the amount of change guaranteed to preserve the MPE instantiation. We have $r(ba, \mathbf{e}) = r(\bar{b}a, \mathbf{e}) = r(b\bar{a}, \mathbf{e}) = r(\bar{b}\bar{a}, \mathbf{e}) = .5$.[3] Moreover, using (16.8), we have $\mathrm{MPE}_P(\bar{a}, \mathbf{e}) = .3$ and $\mathrm{MPE}_P(a, \mathbf{e}) = .4$. We can now easily compute the amount of parameter change that is guaranteed to preserve the MPE instantiation. The conditions we must satisfy are

$$
\begin{aligned}
r(\bar{b}a, \mathbf{e}) \cdot \theta_{\bar{b}|a} &\geq r(ba, \mathbf{e}) \cdot \theta_{b|a} \\
r(\bar{b}a, \mathbf{e}) \cdot \theta_{\bar{b}|a} &\geq \mathrm{MPE}_P(\bar{a}, \mathbf{e}).
\end{aligned}
$$

This leads to $\theta_{\bar{b}|a} \geq \theta_{b|a}$ and $\theta_{\bar{b}|a} \geq .6$. Therefore, the current MPE instantiation is preserved as long as $\theta_{\bar{b}|a} \geq .6$, which has a current value of .8.

We finally point out that these robustness equations can be extended to multivalued variables as follows. If variable X has values $x_1, \ldots, x_m$, where $m \geq 2$, then each of the conditions showed previously consists of m inequalities instead of just two. For example, if an MPE is compatible with $x_i\mathbf{u}$, it is preserved as long as the following inequalities hold:

$$
\begin{aligned}
r(x_i\mathbf{u}, \mathbf{e}) \cdot \theta_{x_i|\mathbf{u}} &\geq r(x_j\mathbf{u}, \mathbf{e}) \cdot \theta_{x_j|\mathbf{u}} \quad \text{for all } j \neq i \\
r(x_i\mathbf{u}, \mathbf{e}) \cdot \theta_{x_i|\mathbf{u}} &\geq \mathrm{MPE}_P(\neg\mathbf{u}, \mathbf{e}).
\end{aligned}
$$

16.3 Query control

We addressed the problem of query robustness in the previous section, where we discussed two types of solutions that vary in their accuracy and computational complexity. We address the inverse problem in this section: identifying parameter changes that are necessary and sufficient to induce a particular query change. For example, we may compute the probability of some event α given evidence β and find it to be .5 even though we believe it should be no less than .9. Our goal would then be to identify necessary and sufficient parameter changes that induce the desirable change in query value. When addressing this

---

[3] These constants can be obtained using (16.7): $r(x\mathbf{u}, \mathbf{e}) = \mathrm{MPE}_P(x\mathbf{u}, \mathbf{e})/\theta_{x|\mathbf{u}}$. This method is generally not as efficient as the method given in Chapter 12. It is also not applicable if $\theta_{x|\mathbf{u}} = 0$.

problem, we can constrain the number of parameters that we are able to change in the process.

We consider two cases in the remainder of this section. In the first case, we assume that only one parameter can be changed. In the second case, we assume that multiple parameters can be changed but they all must belong to the same CPT. Changing multiple parameters that occur in multiple CPTs is also possible based on the techniques we present but the associated computational difficulties make it less interesting practically.

16.3.1 Single parameter changes

We start with some of the more common query constraints that we may want to establish through a parameter change:

$$\Pr(y|\mathbf{e}) \geq \kappa \tag{16.9}$$

$$\Pr(y|\mathbf{e}) \leq \kappa \tag{16.10}$$

$$\Pr(y|\mathbf{e}) - \Pr(z|\mathbf{e}) \geq \kappa \tag{16.11}$$

$$\frac{\Pr(y|\mathbf{e})}{\Pr(z|\mathbf{e})} \geq \kappa. \tag{16.12}$$

Here κ is a constant, evidence $\mathbf{e}$ is an instantiation of variables $\mathbf{E}$, and events y and z are values of the variables Y and Z, respectively, with $Y, Z \notin \mathbf{E}$. For example, if we want to make event y more likely than event z given evidence $\mathbf{e}$, we specify the constraint $\Pr(y|\mathbf{e}) - \Pr(z|\mathbf{e}) \geq 0$. We can also make event y at least twice as likely as event z, given evidence $\mathbf{e}$, by specifying the constraint $\Pr(y|\mathbf{e})/\Pr(z|\mathbf{e}) \geq 2$.

We will start by considering the constraint given by (16.9) and then show how the solution technique can be easily applied to other types of constraints. The key observation here is based on Theorem 16.4, which says that the probability of some event, $\Pr(\alpha)$, is a linear function of any particular parameter $\theta_{x|\mathbf{u}}$:

$$\Pr(\alpha) = \mu_{x|\mathbf{u}}^{\alpha} \cdot \theta_{x|\mathbf{u}} + \nu_{x|\mathbf{u}}^{\alpha}.$$

One major implication of linearity is this: Suppose we apply a change of $\delta_{x|\mathbf{u}}$ to the given parameter. We can then express the new query value as

$$\Pr(\alpha) = \Pr^0(\alpha) + \mu_{x|\mathbf{u}}^{\alpha} \cdot \delta_{x|\mathbf{u}}.$$

Recall that $\Pr^0(\alpha)$ is the probability of α before we apply the parameter change. Now to enforce (16.9), it suffices to ensure that $\Pr(y, \mathbf{e}) \geq \kappa \cdot \Pr(\mathbf{e})$ or, equivalently,

$$\Pr^0(y, \mathbf{e}) + \mu_{x|\mathbf{u}}^{y,\mathbf{e}} \cdot \delta_{x|\mathbf{u}} \geq \kappa \left(\Pr^0(\mathbf{e}) + \mu_{x|\mathbf{u}}^{\mathbf{e}} \cdot \delta_{x|\mathbf{u}} \right).$$

Rearranging the terms, we get the following result.

Corollary 9. *Let* $\mathbf{N}^0$ *and* $\mathbf{N}$ *be two Bayesian networks where* $\mathbf{N}$ *is obtained from* $\mathbf{N}^0$ *by changing a single parameter value* $\theta_{x|\mathbf{u}}^0$ *to the new value* $\theta_{x|\mathbf{u}}$. *Let* $\Pr^0$ *and* $\Pr$ *be the two distributions induced by these networks. To ensure that* $\Pr(y|\mathbf{e}) \geq \kappa$ *holds, the amount of parameter change* $\delta_{x|\mathbf{u}} = \theta_{x|\mathbf{u}} - \theta_{x|\mathbf{u}}^0$ *must be such that*

$$\Pr^0(y, \mathbf{e}) - \kappa \cdot \Pr^0(\mathbf{e}) \geq \delta_{x|\mathbf{u}} \left(-\mu_{x|\mathbf{u}}^{y,\mathbf{e}} + \kappa \cdot \mu_{x|\mathbf{u}}^{\mathbf{e}} \right). \tag{16.13}$$

■

Note that the solution of $\delta_{x|\mathbf{u}}$ in Corollary 9 always has one of the following two forms:

- $\delta_{x|\mathbf{u}} \leq \epsilon$ for some computed $\epsilon < 0$, in which case the new value of $\theta_{x|\mathbf{u}}$ must be in the interval $[0, \theta^0_{x|\mathbf{u}} + \epsilon]$. This case corresponds to a decrease in the current parameter value.
- $\delta_{x|\mathbf{u}} \geq \epsilon$ for some computed $\epsilon > 0$, in which case the new value of $\theta_{x|\mathbf{u}}$ must be in the interval $[\theta^0_{x|\mathbf{u}} + \epsilon, 1]$. This case corresponds to an increase in the current parameter value.

Therefore, ϵ is the minimum amount of change in $\theta_{x|\mathbf{u}}$ that can enforce the query constraint. For some parameters, it is possible to find no legitimate solutions for (16.13), meaning there is no way we can change these parameters to enforce the desired query constraint.

Note that all quantities that appear in (16.13) can be obtained by performing inference on the original network $\mathcal{N}^0$. In fact, if we have an algorithm that can compute in $O(f)$ time the probability of $\mathbf{i}, x, \mathbf{u}$, for a given variable instantiation $\mathbf{i}$ and all parameters $\theta_{x|\mathbf{u}}$ in a Bayesian network, then we can also compute in $O(f)$ time the quantities needed by (16.13), for some query $y|\mathbf{e}$ and all network parameters $\theta_{x|\mathbf{u}}$. Suppose for example, that we are using the jointree algorithm for this computation and we have a jointree of width w and size n (number of clusters). The algorithm can then be used to compute the probability of $\mathbf{i}, x, \mathbf{u}$ in $O(n \exp(w))$ time for any given variable instantiation $\mathbf{i}$ and all parameters $\theta_{x|\mathbf{u}}$. We can therefore use the algorithm to obtain instances of (16.13) for some query $y|\mathbf{e}$ and all network parameters $\theta_{x|\mathbf{u}}$ in $O(n \exp(w))$ time as well. We can do this by running the algorithm twice, once with evidence $\mathbf{e}$ and again with extended evidence $y, \mathbf{e}$. We can verify that we can recover all needed quantities from the marginals computed by the two runs of the jointree algorithm in this case.

Let us now consider an example with respect to the network in Figure 16.3. Given evidence $\mathbf{e} = S, \neg R$, that is, smoke is observed but no report of people evacuating the building, the probability of fire is .246. Suppose however that we believe the probability of fire should be no less than .5 and, hence, decide to identify parameter changes that enforce the constraint $\Pr(F|\mathbf{e}) \geq .5$. Using Corollary 9 and considering every possible parameter in the network, we identify the following parameter changes:

- Increase θ_F from .01 to $\geq .029977$
- Decrease $\theta_{S|\neg F}$ from .01 to $\leq .003269$
- Increase θ_T from .02 to $\geq .801449$
- Increase $\theta_{L|\neg A}$ from .001 to $\geq .923136$
- Increase $\theta_{R|\neg L}$ from .01 to $\geq .776456$

The last three parameter changes can be ruled out based on commonsense considerations. The other parameter changes are either to increase the prior probability of a fire or to decrease the probability of observing smoke without having a fire. Note that the network contains many other parameters that do not yield solutions to (16.13), which means that we cannot satisfy the given query constraint by changing those parameters.

Using similar derivations to those given here, Corollary 9 can be extended to enforce additional types of query constraints as follows:

- To satisfy $\Pr(y|\mathbf{e}) \leq \kappa$, we need a parameter change $\delta_{x|\mathbf{u}}$ such that

$$\Pr^0(y, \mathbf{e}) - \kappa \cdot \Pr^0(\mathbf{e}) \leq \delta_{x|\mathbf{u}} \left(-\mu^{y,\mathbf{e}}_{x|\mathbf{u}} + \kappa \cdot \mu^{\mathbf{e}}_{x|\mathbf{u}}\right). \tag{16.14}$$

- To satisfy $\Pr(y|\mathbf{e}) - \Pr(z|\mathbf{e}) \geq \kappa$, we need a change $\delta_{x|\mathbf{u}}$ such that

$$\Pr^0(y, \mathbf{e}) - \Pr^0(z, \mathbf{e}) - \kappa \cdot \Pr^0(\mathbf{e}) \geq \delta_{x|\mathbf{u}} \left(-\mu_{x|\mathbf{u}}^{y,\mathbf{e}} + \mu_{x|\mathbf{u}}^{z,\mathbf{e}} + \kappa \cdot \mu_{x|\mathbf{u}}^{\mathbf{e}} \right). \tag{16.15}$$

- To satisfy $\Pr(y|\mathbf{e})/\Pr(z|\mathbf{e}) \geq \kappa$, we need a change $\delta_{x|\mathbf{u}}$ such that

$$\Pr^0(y, \mathbf{e}) - \kappa \cdot \Pr^0(z, \mathbf{e}) \geq \delta_{x|\mathbf{u}} \left(-\mu_{x|\mathbf{u}}^{y,\mathbf{e}} + \kappa \cdot \mu_{x|\mathbf{u}}^{z,\mathbf{e}} \right). \tag{16.16}$$

The computational complexity remarks made earlier about (16.16) also apply to these inequalities. For example, using the jointree algorithm we can obtain instances of (16.15) for some queries $y|\mathbf{e}$ and $z|\mathbf{e}$ and all network parameters $\theta_{x|\mathbf{u}}$ by running the algorithm three times, first with evidence $\mathbf{e}$ then with evidence $y, \mathbf{e}$ and finally with evidence $z, \mathbf{e}$. Again, we can verify that all needed quantities can be recovered from the marginals computed by the jointree algorithm in this case.

16.3.2 Multiple parameter changes

We now turn to the problem of satisfying query constraints while allowing more than one parameter to change. However, as mentioned earlier we restrict the changing parameters to one CPT. The main reason for this restriction is computational as it allows us to handle multiple parameters within the same computational complexity required for single parameters.

We first give a concrete example of multiple parameter changes within the same CPT by considering the following CPTs for the multivalued variable X:

Z	Y	X	$\Theta^0_{X|Y,Z}$	$\Theta_{X|Y,Z}$
true	true	x_1	.1	.1
true	true	x_2	.5	.5
true	true	x_3	.4	.4
true	false	x_1	(.8)	.7
true	false	x_2	.1	.15
true	false	x_3	.1	.15
false	true	x_1	(.5)	.7
false	true	x_2	.2	.08
false	true	x_3	.3	.12
false	false	x_1	.3	.4
false	false	x_2	(.7)	.8
false	false	x_3	0	0

Here we have a CPT $\Theta_{X|Y,Z}$ that results from changing three parameter values in the CPT $\Theta^0_{X|Y,Z}$— the ones enclosed in parentheses. Note how each of these changes induces a corresponding change in co-varying parameters. For example, the change in parameter value $\theta^0_{x_1|\bar{y},z}$ (.8 to .7) leads to a corresponding change in co-varying parameters $\theta^0_{x_2|\bar{y},z}$ (.1 to .15) and $\theta^0_{x_3|\bar{y},z}$ (.1 to .15). In general, when applying multiple parameter changes to a particular CPT we are allowed to change only one parameter value $\theta^0_{x|\mathbf{u}}$ for a given parent instantiation $\mathbf{u}$, as all other parameter values $\theta^0_{x^\star|\mathbf{u}}$, $x^\star \neq x$, are co-varying and cannot be changed independently.

The following is the key result underlying the techniques associated with changing multiple parameters.

Theorem 16.5. *Let* $\mathbf{N}^0$ *and* $\mathbf{N}$ *be two Bayesian networks where* $\mathbf{N}$ *is obtained from* $\mathbf{N}^0$ *by changing one parameter value* $\theta^0_{x|\mathbf{u}}$ *for each parent instantiation* $\mathbf{u}$ *in the CPT for variable* X.[4] *Let* Pr^0 *and* Pr *be the two distributions induced by these networks. The value of a query* $\mathrm{Pr}(\alpha)$ *can be expressed in terms of the original network* $\mathbf{N}^0$ *and the new parameter values* $\theta_{x|\mathbf{u}}$ *as*

$$\mathrm{Pr}(\alpha) = \sum_{\mathbf{u}} \mu^{\alpha}_{x|\mathbf{u}} \cdot \theta_{x|\mathbf{u}} + \nu'^{\alpha}_{x|\mathbf{u}},$$

where $\mu^{\alpha}_{x|\mathbf{u}}$ *is given by (16.5), and*

$$\nu'^{\alpha}_{x|\mathbf{u}} = \sum_{x^{\star} \neq x} \rho(x, x^{\star}, \mathbf{u}) \frac{\partial \mathrm{Pr}(\alpha)}{\partial \theta_{x^{\star}|\mathbf{u}}}. \qquad \blacksquare$$

Hence, the new probability $\mathrm{Pr}(\alpha)$ is a linear function of each of the new parameter values $\theta_{x|\mathbf{u}}$ (note that each parent instantiation $\mathbf{u}$ determines a unique value x of X for which we are changing the parameter $\theta^0_{x|\mathbf{u}}$ to $\theta_{x|\mathbf{u}}$). Given this linear relationship, if we apply a change of $\delta_{x|\mathbf{u}}$ to each parameter we can express the new probability $\mathrm{Pr}(\alpha)$ as

$$\mathrm{Pr}(\alpha) = \mathrm{Pr}^0(\alpha) + \sum_{\mathbf{u}} \mu^{\alpha}_{x|\mathbf{u}} \cdot \delta_{x|\mathbf{u}}.$$

To enforce (16.9), it suffices to ensure that $\mathrm{Pr}(y, \mathbf{e}) \geq \kappa \cdot \mathrm{Pr}(\mathbf{e})$ or, equivalently,

$$\mathrm{Pr}^0(y, \mathbf{e}) + \sum_{\mathbf{u}} \mu^{y,\mathbf{e}}_{x|\mathbf{u}} \cdot \delta_{x|\mathbf{u}} \geq \kappa \left(\mathrm{Pr}^0(\mathbf{e}) + \sum_{\mathbf{u}} \mu^{\mathbf{e}}_{x|\mathbf{u}} \cdot \delta_{x|\mathbf{u}} \right).$$

Rearranging the terms, we get the following result.

Corollary 10. *Let* $\mathbf{N}^0$ *and* $\mathbf{N}$ *be two Bayesian networks where* $\mathbf{N}$ *is obtained from* $\mathbf{N}^0$ *by changing one parameter value* $\theta^0_{x|\mathbf{u}}$ *for each parent instantiation* $\mathbf{u}$ *in the CPT for variable* X. *Let* Pr^0 *and* Pr *be the two distributions induced by these networks. To ensure that* $\mathrm{Pr}(y|\mathbf{e}) \geq \kappa$ *holds, the amount of parameter changes* $\delta_{x|\mathbf{u}} = \theta_{x|\mathbf{u}} - \theta^0_{x|\mathbf{u}}$ *must be such that*

$$\mathrm{Pr}^0(y, \mathbf{e}) - \kappa \cdot \mathrm{Pr}^0(\mathbf{e}) \geq \sum_{\mathbf{u}} \delta_{x|\mathbf{u}} \left(-\mu^{y,\mathbf{e}}_{x|\mathbf{u}} + \kappa \cdot \mu^{\mathbf{e}}_{x|\mathbf{u}} \right), \qquad (16.17)$$

where $\mu^{y,\mathbf{e}}_{x|\mathbf{u}}$ *and* $\mu^{\mathbf{e}}_{x|\mathbf{u}}$ *are given by (16.5).* $\qquad \blacksquare$

Parameter changes that ensure the query constraint can be found by first solving for the equality condition in (16.17). This defines a hyperplane that splits the parameter change space into two regions, one of which satisfies the inequality. We also note that the computational complexity of the quantities needed by (16.17) is no worse than those needed by (16.13).

Consider again the Bayesian network in Figure 16.3. Suppose the evidence $\mathbf{e}$ is $R, \neg S$, that is, there is a report of people evacuating the building but no smoke is observed. The probability of alarm tampering is .5 given this evidence but suppose we wish to make it no less than .65 by changing the CPT for variable R. That is, we currently have $\mathrm{Pr}^0(T|\mathbf{e}) = .5$

---

[4] The amount of change can be zero: $\theta^0_{x|\mathbf{u}} = \theta_{x|\mathbf{u}}$.

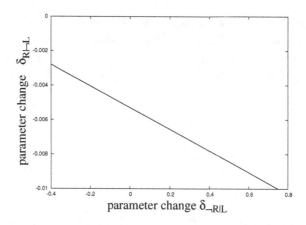

Figure 16.5: The solution space of multiple parameter changes.

but wish to enforce the constraint $\Pr(T\,|\,\mathbf{e}) \geq .65$ by changing multiple parameters in the CPT $\Theta_{R|L}^0$. Assume further that the parameters we wish to change are:

- $\theta_{\neg R|L}^0 = .25$: the probability of not receiving an evacuation report when there is an evacuation (false negative)
- $\theta_{R|\neg L}^0 = .01$, the probability of receiving an evacuation report when there is no evacuation (false positive).

Let $\delta_{\neg R|L}$ and $\delta_{R|\neg L}$ be the changes we wish to apply to these parameters, respectively. Corollary 10 gives us the following characterization of required parameter changes:

$$-.003294 \geq .003901 \cdot \delta_{\neg R|L} + .621925 \cdot \delta_{R|\neg L}.$$

The solution space is plotted in Figure 16.5. The line indicates the set of points where the equality condition $\Pr(T\,|\,\mathbf{e}) = .65$ holds, and the solution space is defined by the region at or below the line. Therefore, we can ensure $\Pr(T\,|\,\mathbf{e}) \geq .65$ by applying any parameter change in this region.

Even though changing single or multiple parameters in the same CPT requires the same computational complexity, the solution space of multiple parameter changes can be more difficult to visualize when the number of parameters is large enough. Yet changing multiple parameters is often necessary in practical applications. For example, if a variable corresponds to some sensor readings, then the parameters appearing in its CPT correspond to false positive and false negative rates of the sensor. In the case of single parameter changes, we are looking for solutions that allow us to only change one of these rates but not the other. With multiple parameter changes, we can in principle change both rates.

Note also that for some variables, there may exist multiple parameter changes that satisfy a particular constraint yet no single parameter change may be sufficient for this purpose. For example, consider again the Bayesian network in Figure 16.3. Suppose we are given evidence $\mathbf{e} = S, R$, that is, smoke is observed and there is a report of people evacuating the building. The probability of alarm tampering is .0284 under this evidence. Suppose now that we pose the question: What parameter changes can we apply to decrease this probability to at most .01? As it turns out, if we restrict ourselves to single parameter changes, then only one parameter change is possible: decrease the prior probability of tampering from its initial value of .02 to at most .007. For example, no single parameter change in the CPT of Alarm would ensure the given constraint, and we may be inclined to believe that the parameters in this CPT are irrelevant to the query. However, if we allow multiple parameter changes in a single CPT, it is possible to satisfy the constraint by changing the CPT for Alarm. One such change is given in the following:

Fire (F)	Tampering (T)	Alarm (A)	$\Theta_{A\mid F,T}$
true	true	true	.088
true	false	true	.999
false	true	true	.354
false	false	true	.001

We finally note that Corollary 10 can be extended to enforce additional types of query constraints as follows:

- To satisfy $\Pr(y\mid e) \leq \kappa$, we need parameter changes $\delta_{x\mid u}$ such that

$$\Pr^0(y, \mathbf{e}) - \kappa \cdot \Pr^0(\mathbf{e}) \leq \sum_{\mathbf{u}} \delta_{x\mid \mathbf{u}} \left(-\mu_{x\mid \mathbf{u}}^{y, \mathbf{e}} + \kappa \cdot \mu_{x\mid \mathbf{u}}^{\mathbf{e}}\right). \tag{16.18}$$

- To satisfy $\Pr(y\mid e) - \Pr(z\mid e) \geq \kappa$, we need parameter changes $\delta_{x\mid u}$ such that

$$\Pr^0(y, \mathbf{e}) - \Pr^0(z, \mathbf{e}) - \kappa \cdot \Pr^0(\mathbf{e}) \geq \sum_{\mathbf{u}} \delta_{x\mid \mathbf{u}} \left(-\mu_{x\mid \mathbf{u}}^{y, \mathbf{e}} + \mu_{x\mid \mathbf{u}}^{z, \mathbf{e}} + \kappa \cdot \mu_{x\mid \mathbf{u}}^{\mathbf{e}}\right). \tag{16.19}$$

- To satisfy $\Pr(y\mid e)/\Pr(z\mid e) \geq \kappa$, we need parameter changes $\delta_{x\mid u}$ such that

$$\Pr^0(y, \mathbf{e}) - \kappa \cdot \Pr^0(z, \mathbf{e}) \geq \sum_{\mathbf{u}} \delta_{x\mid \mathbf{u}} \left(-\mu_{x\mid \mathbf{u}}^{y, \mathbf{e}} + \kappa \cdot \mu_{x\mid \mathbf{u}}^{z, \mathbf{e}}\right). \tag{16.20}$$

Again, the computational complexity of quantities appearing in these inequalities is no worse than the complexity of quantities corresponding to single parameter changes. Hence, we can still characterize multiple parameter changes efficiently for these constraints as long as the changes are restricted to the same CPT.

Bibliographic remarks

The early studies of sensitivity analysis in Bayesian networks have been mostly empirical (e.g., [Laskey, 1995; Pradhan et al., 1996]). The first analytical result relating to current studies is due to Russell et al. [1995], who observed that the probability of evidence is a linear function in each network parameter. This observation was made in the context of learning network parameters using gradient ascent approaches, which called for computing the gradient of the likelihood function with respect to network parameters (see Section 17.3.2). A more general result was then shown in Castillo et al. [1996; 1997], where the probability of evidence was expressed as a polynomial of network parameters in which each parameter has degree 1. Computing the coefficients of this polynomial efficiently using jointrees was discussed in Jensen [1999] and Kjaerulff and van der Gaag [2000], and using circuit propagation in Darwiche [2003].

The CD distance measure is due to Chan and Darwiche [2005a]. The precursors of this measure were initially reported in Chan and Darwiche [2002], where the first results on network-independent sensitivity analysis were presented. The techniques discussed for network-specific sensitivity analysis are due to Coupé and van der Gaag [2002] – see also van der Gaag et al. [2007] for a recent survey. The techniques discussed for sensitivity analysis with multiple parameters are due to Chan and Darwiche [2004] and the ones for MPE robustness are due to Chan and Darwiche [2006].

16.4 Exercises

16.1. Let us say that two probability distributions $\text{Pr}^0(\mathbf{X})$ and $\text{Pr}(\mathbf{X})$ have the same support if for every instantiation $\mathbf{x}$, $\text{Pr}^0(\mathbf{x}) = 0$ iff $\text{Pr}(\mathbf{x}) = 0$. Show that the CD distance satisfies the following property: $D(\text{Pr}^0, \text{Pr}) = \infty$ iff the distributions Pr^0 and Pr do not have the same support.

16.2. Show that the CD distance satisfies the properties of positiveness, symmetry, and triangle inequality.

16.3. Consider a distribution $\text{Pr}(\mathbf{X})$, event α, and show that

$$\frac{\text{Pr}(\alpha)}{\text{Pr}^0(\alpha)} \leq \max_{\mathbf{x} \models \alpha} \frac{\text{Pr}(\mathbf{x})}{\text{Pr}^0(\mathbf{x})}$$

and

$$\frac{\text{Pr}(\alpha)}{\text{Pr}^0(\alpha)} \geq \min_{\mathbf{x} \models \alpha} \frac{\text{Pr}(\mathbf{x})}{\text{Pr}^0(\mathbf{x})}.$$

16.4. Show that the bounds given by Theorem 16.1 are tight in the sense that for every pair of distributions Pr^0 and Pr, there are events α and β such that

$$\frac{O(\alpha \mid \beta)}{O^0(\alpha \mid \beta)} = e^{D(\text{Pr}^0, \text{Pr})}$$

$$\frac{O(\neg\alpha \mid \beta)}{O^0(\neg\alpha \mid \beta)} = e^{-D(\text{Pr}^0, \text{Pr})}.$$

16.5. Show that Inequality 16.2 is implied by Theorem 16.1.

16.6. Consider two Bayesian networks $\mathcal{N}^0$ and $\mathcal{N}$, where network $\mathcal{N}$ is obtained from $\mathcal{N}^0$ by changing a single parameter value θ_x^0 in the CPT of root node X. Show the following for any evidence $\mathbf{e}$,

$$\frac{O(x|\mathbf{e})}{O^0(x|\mathbf{e})} = \frac{O(x)}{O^0(x)}.$$

16.7. Show that $D(\Theta_{X|\mathbf{U}}^0, \Theta_{X|\mathbf{U}}) \geq \max_{\mathbf{u}} D(\Theta_{X|\mathbf{u}}^0, \Theta_{X|\mathbf{u}})$.

16.8. Prove Inequalities 16.14, 16.15, and 16.16.

16.9. Consider the solution space characterized by Inequality 16.17. Call a solution optimal if it minimizes the CD distance between the original and new networks. Show that optimal solutions must satisfy the equality constraint corresponding to Inequality 16.17.

16.10. Suppose that Pr is a distribution obtained from Pr^0 by incorporating soft evidence on events $(\beta_1, \ldots, \beta_n)$ using Jeffrey's rule (see Chapter 3). Show that

$$D(\text{Pr}^0, \text{Pr}) = \ln \max_{i=1}^{n} \frac{\text{Pr}(\beta_i)}{\text{Pr}^0(\beta_i)} - \ln \min_{i=1}^{n} \frac{\text{Pr}(\beta_i)}{\text{Pr}^0(\beta_i)}.$$

16.11. Consider a simplified version of the pregnancy network in Figure 16.1 where we can only administer the scanning test to detect pregnancy. The current probability of pregnancy given a positive scanning test is 0.9983 and the current probability of no pregnancy given a negative scanning test is 0.5967. We wish to apply changes in both the false-positive and false-negative rates of the scanning test by amounts of δ_1 and δ_2, respectively, such that the corresponding probabilities are at least 0.999 and 0.7 (instead of 0.9983 and 0.5967, respectively). Plot the solution spaces of δ_1 and δ_2 such that they satisfy the two constraints and find the unique solution such that the minimum confidence levels are exactly realized by the parameter changes.

16.12. Consider a simplified version of the fire network in Figure 16.3 where we are only interested in the variables Fire, Tampering, and Alarm. Compute the sensitivity function for query $\text{Pr}(F \mid A)$ in terms of parameter $\theta_{A|F,T}$ then again for the same query in terms of parameter $\theta_{A|\neg F, \neg T}$ and plot the functions. From the plots, what would the effects on the query value be if we apply a small absolute change in each of the two parameters? Also, compute the sensitivity functions for the query $\Pr(A \mid F)$ in terms of these two parameters. What is the difference between these two sensitivity functions and the previous two?

16.13. Assume that instead of using the proportional scheme of Definition 16.2, we distribute the parameter change equally among co-varying parameters. In this case, what is the new value of $\theta_{x^*|\mathbf{u}}$? What problem may this scheme face when distributing the parameter change?

16.14. Prove that the proportional scheme of Definition 16.2 is the optimal scheme of distributing parameter changes among co-varying parameters in the sense that it minimizes the CD distance $D(\Pr^0, \Pr)$ among all possible schemes.

16.15. Consider the network in Figure 16.3. The probability of having a fire given that the alarm has triggered is .3667. We now wish to install a smoke detector that responds only to whether smoke is present such that when both the alarm and the smoke detectors trigger, the probability of fire is at least .8. How can we use sensitivity analysis to find the required reliability of the smoke detector? Specify the three elements of the sensitivity analysis process: the Bayesian network that models this scenario, the query constraint you wish to satisfy, and the parameters you are allowed to change. Hint: You may recall how sensors are modeled as soft evidence in Chapter 3.

16.16. Let $\mathcal{N}^0$ and $\mathcal{N}$ be Bayesian networks where network $\mathcal{N}$ is obtained from $\mathcal{N}^0$ by changing the CPTs of variables X and Y from $\Theta^0_{X|\mathbf{U}_X}$ to $\Theta_{X|\mathbf{U}_X}$ and from $\Theta^0_{Y|\mathbf{U}_Y}$ to $\Theta_{Y|\mathbf{U}_Y}$, respectively – that is, changing parameter value $\theta^0_{x|\mathbf{u}_X}$ to some new value $\theta_{x|\mathbf{u}_X}$ for every x and $\mathbf{u}_X$, and $\theta^0_{y|\mathbf{u}_Y}$ to some new value $\theta_{y|\mathbf{u}_Y}$ for every y and $\mathbf{u}_Y$. Let $\Pr^0$ and $\Pr$ be the distributions induced by networks $\mathcal{N}^0$ and $\mathcal{N}$, respectively, and also assume that $\Pr^0(\mathbf{u}_X) > 0$ and $\Pr^0(\mathbf{u}_Y) > 0$ for every $\mathbf{u}_X$ and $\mathbf{u}_Y$. Prove that if the two families $X, \mathbf{U}_X$ and $Y, \mathbf{U}_Y$ are disjoint, that is, they do not share any variables, then

$$D(\Pr^0, \Pr) = D(\Theta^0_{X|\mathbf{U}_X}, \Theta_{X|\mathbf{U}_X}) + D(\Theta^0_{Y|\mathbf{U}_Y}, \Theta_{Y|\mathbf{U}_Y}).$$

Also prove that if the two families are not disjoint, then the sum of the distances between the CPTs is an upper bound on $D(\Pr^0, \Pr)$.

16.17. Let $\mathcal{N}^0$ and $\mathcal{N}$ be Bayesian networks where network $\mathcal{N}$ is obtained from $\mathcal{N}^0$ by changing the CPTs of variables $X_1, \ldots, X_m$ from $\Theta^0_{X_i|\mathbf{U}_{X_i}}$ to $\Theta_{X_i|\mathbf{U}_{X_i}}$ (i.e., changing parameter value $\theta^0_{x_i|\mathbf{u}_{X_i}}$ to some new value $\theta_{x_i|\mathbf{u}_{X_i}}$ for every x_i and $\mathbf{u}_{X_i}$). Let $\Pr^0$ and $\Pr$ be the distributions induced by networks $\mathcal{N}^0$ and $\mathcal{N}$, respectively, and also assume that $\Pr^0(\mathbf{u}_{X_i}) > 0$ for every $\mathbf{u}_{X_i}$. Devise a procedure that computes $D(\Pr^0, \Pr)$. Hint: This procedure can be similar to the one used for computing the MPE probability.

16.5 Proofs

PROOF OF THEOREM 16.1. If distributions $\Pr^0$ and $\Pr$ do not have the same support, we have $D(\Pr^0, \Pr) = \infty$ and thus $-\infty = e^{-D(\Pr^0, \Pr)} \leq O(\alpha|\beta)/O^0(\alpha|\beta) \leq e^{D(\Pr^0, \Pr)} = \infty$. Otherwise, the odds ratio $O(\alpha|\beta)/O^0(\alpha|\beta)$ can be expressed as

$$\frac{O(\alpha|\beta)}{O^0(\alpha|\beta)} = \frac{\Pr(\alpha|\beta)}{\Pr(\neg\alpha|\beta)} \bigg/ \frac{\Pr^0(\alpha|\beta)}{\Pr^0(\neg\alpha|\beta)}$$

$$= \frac{\Pr(\alpha, \beta)}{\Pr(\neg\alpha, \beta)} \bigg/ \frac{\Pr^0(\alpha, \beta)}{\Pr^0(\neg\alpha, \beta)}$$

$$= \frac{\sum_{\mathbf{x}\models\alpha,\beta} \Pr(\mathbf{x})}{\sum_{\mathbf{x}\models\neg\alpha,\beta} \Pr(\mathbf{x})} \bigg/ \frac{\sum_{\mathbf{x}\models\alpha,\beta} \Pr^0(\mathbf{x})}{\sum_{\mathbf{x}\models\neg\alpha,\beta} \Pr^0(\mathbf{x})}$$

$$= \frac{\sum_{\mathbf{x}\models\alpha,\beta} \Pr(\mathbf{x})}{\sum_{\mathbf{x}\models\alpha,\beta} \Pr^0(\mathbf{x})} \bigg/ \frac{\sum_{\mathbf{x}\models\neg\alpha,\beta} \Pr(\mathbf{x})}{\sum_{\mathbf{x}\models\neg\alpha,\beta} \Pr^0(\mathbf{x})}.$$

Using Exercise 16.3, we can now obtain the upper bound on the odds ratio:

$$\frac{O(\alpha|\beta)}{O^0(\alpha|\beta)} \leq \left(\max_{\mathbf{x} \models \alpha, \beta} \frac{Pr(\mathbf{x})}{Pr^0(\mathbf{x})} \right) \bigg/ \left(\min_{\mathbf{x} \models \neg\alpha, \beta} \frac{Pr(\mathbf{x})}{Pr^0(\mathbf{x})} \right)$$

$$\leq \left(\max_{\mathbf{x}} \frac{Pr(\mathbf{x})}{Pr^0(\mathbf{x})} \right) \bigg/ \left(\min_{\mathbf{x}} \frac{Pr(\mathbf{x})}{Pr^0(\mathbf{x})} \right)$$

$$= e^{D(Pr^0, Pr)}.$$

Similarly, we can also obtain the lower bound on the odds ratio:

$$\frac{O(\alpha|\beta)}{O^0(\alpha|\beta)} \geq \left(\min_{\mathbf{x} \models \alpha, \beta} \frac{Pr(\mathbf{x})}{Pr^0(\mathbf{x})} \right) \bigg/ \left(\max_{\mathbf{x} \models \neg\alpha, \beta} \frac{Pr(\mathbf{x})}{Pr^0(\mathbf{x})} \right)$$

$$\geq \left(\min_{\mathbf{x}} \frac{Pr(\mathbf{x})}{Pr^0(\mathbf{x})} \right) \bigg/ \left(\max_{\mathbf{x}} \frac{Pr(\mathbf{x})}{Pr^0(\mathbf{x})} \right)$$

$$= e^{-D(Pr^0, Pr)}.$$

Therefore, we have $e^{-D(Pr^0, Pr)} \leq O(\alpha|\beta)/O^0(\alpha|\beta) \leq e^{D(Pr^0, Pr)}$. If both $O(\alpha|\beta)$ and $O^0(\alpha|\beta)$ take on either 0 or ∞, Theorem 16.1 still holds because $0/0 \overset{def}{=} 1$ and $\infty/\infty \overset{def}{=} 1$. Finally, proving the tightness of the bound is left to Exercise 16.4. ∎

PROOF OF THEOREM 16.2. Using Lemma 16.1, we have that $\max_{\mathbf{x}} (Pr(\mathbf{x})/Pr^0(\mathbf{x})) = \max_x (\theta_{x|\mathbf{u}}/\theta^0_{x|\mathbf{u}})$ and $\min_{\mathbf{x}} (Pr(\mathbf{x})/Pr^0(\mathbf{x})) = \min_x (\theta_{x|\mathbf{u}}/\theta^0_{x|\mathbf{u}})$. Therefore, we have $D(Pr^0, Pr) = D(\Theta^0_{X,\mathbf{u}}, \Theta_{X,\mathbf{u}})$. ∎

Lemma 16.1. *Assume that we change parameter $\theta^0_{x|\mathbf{u}}$ to $\theta_{x|\mathbf{u}}$ for every value x and $Pr^0(\mathbf{u}) > 0$. For every x where $\theta_{x|\mathbf{u}} > 0$ or $\theta^0_{x|\mathbf{u}} > 0$, there must exist some $\mathbf{x} \models x, \mathbf{u}$ such that it satisfies the condition $Pr(\mathbf{x})/Pr^0(\mathbf{x}) = \theta_{x|\mathbf{u}}/\theta^0_{x|\mathbf{u}}$. For all other instantiations $\mathbf{x}$ that do not satisfy this condition, we must have $Pr(\mathbf{x}) = Pr^0(\mathbf{x})$ and thus $Pr(\mathbf{x})/Pr^0(\mathbf{x}) = 1$.[5]*

PROOF. We first note that $Pr(\mathbf{u}) = Pr^0(\mathbf{u}) > 0$. For any instantiation $\mathbf{x}$, either $\mathbf{x} \models \bar{\mathbf{u}}$ or $\mathbf{x} \models x, \mathbf{u}$ for some x. We now consider the different cases of $\mathbf{x}$.

Case: If $\mathbf{x} \models \bar{\mathbf{u}}$, we must have $Pr(\mathbf{x}) = Pr^0(\mathbf{x})$ since we are only changing parameters $\theta^0_{x|\mathbf{u}}$.

Case: If $\mathbf{x} \models x, \mathbf{u}$, we consider four cases of x:

- If $\theta_{x|\mathbf{u}} = \theta^0_{x|\mathbf{u}} = 0$, we must have $Pr(x, \mathbf{u}) = Pr^0(x, \mathbf{u}) = 0$. Therefore, for all instantiaions $\mathbf{x} \models x, \mathbf{u}$, $Pr(\mathbf{x}) = Pr^0(\mathbf{x}) = 0$.

- If $\theta_{x|\mathbf{u}} = 0$ and $\theta^0_{x|\mathbf{u}} > 0$, we must have $Pr(x, \mathbf{u}) = 0$ and $Pr^0(x, \mathbf{u}) > 0$. Therefore, for all instantiations $\mathbf{x} \models x, \mathbf{u}$, either $Pr(\mathbf{x}) = Pr^0(\mathbf{x}) = 0$ or $Pr(\mathbf{x}) = 0$ and $Pr^0(\mathbf{x}) > 0$, giving us $Pr(\mathbf{x})/Pr^0(\mathbf{x}) = 0 = \theta_{x|\mathbf{u}}/\theta^0_{x|\mathbf{u}}$. Moreover, because $Pr^0(x, \mathbf{u}) > 0$ there must exist some $\mathbf{x} \models x, \mathbf{u}$ such that $Pr^0(\mathbf{x}) > 0$ and thus satisfies the condition $Pr(\mathbf{x})/Pr^0(\mathbf{x}) = \theta_{x|\mathbf{u}}/\theta^0_{x|\mathbf{u}}$.

- If $\theta_{x|\mathbf{u}} > 0$ and $\theta^0_{x|\mathbf{u}} = 0$, we must have $Pr(x, \mathbf{u}) > 0$ and $Pr^0(x, \mathbf{u}) = 0$. Therefore, for all instantiations $\mathbf{x} \models x, \mathbf{u}$ either $Pr(\mathbf{x}) = Pr^0(\mathbf{x}) = 0$ or $Pr(\mathbf{x}) > 0$ and $Pr^0(\mathbf{x}) = 0$, giving us $Pr(\mathbf{x})/Pr^0(\mathbf{x}) = \infty = \theta_{x|\mathbf{u}}/\theta^0_{x|\mathbf{u}}$. Moreover, because $Pr(x, \mathbf{u}) > 0$ there must exist some $\mathbf{x} \models x, \mathbf{u}$ such that $Pr(\mathbf{x}) > 0$ and thus satisfies the condition $Pr(\mathbf{x})/Pr^0(\mathbf{x}) = \theta_{x|\mathbf{u}}/\theta^0_{x|\mathbf{u}}$.

- If $\theta_{x|\mathbf{u}} > 0$ and $\theta^0_{x|\mathbf{u}} > 0$, we must have $Pr(x, \mathbf{u}) > 0$ and $Pr^0(x, \mathbf{u}) > 0$. Therefore, for all instantiations $\mathbf{x} \models x, \mathbf{u}$, either $Pr(\mathbf{x}) = Pr^0(\mathbf{x}) = 0$ or $Pr(\mathbf{x}) > 0$ and $Pr^0(\mathbf{x}) > 0$, giving us

---

[5] Either $Pr(\mathbf{x}) = Pr^0(\mathbf{x}) > 0$, and thus $Pr(\mathbf{x})/Pr^0(\mathbf{x}) = 1$, or $Pr(\mathbf{x}) = Pr^0(\mathbf{x}) = 0$, and thus $Pr(\mathbf{x})/Pr^0(\mathbf{x}) \overset{def}{=} 1$.

$\Pr(\mathbf{x})/\Pr^0(\mathbf{x}) = \theta_{x|\mathbf{u}}/\theta^0_{x|\mathbf{u}}$. Moreover, because $\Pr(x, \mathbf{u}) > 0$ and $\Pr^0(x, \mathbf{u}) > 0$ there must exist some $\mathbf{x} \models x, \mathbf{u}$ such that $\Pr(\mathbf{x}) > 0$ and $\Pr^0(\mathbf{x}) > 0$ and thus satisfies the condition $\Pr(\mathbf{x})/\Pr^0(\mathbf{x}) = \theta_{x|\mathbf{u}}/\theta^0_{x|\mathbf{u}}$. ∎

PROOF OF THEOREM 16.3. If $\theta_{x|\mathbf{u}} = \theta^0_{x|\mathbf{u}}$, then both sides of the equation are equal to zero. Suppose now that $\theta_{x|\mathbf{u}} \neq \theta^0_{x|\mathbf{u}}$. If $\theta^0_{x|\mathbf{u}} = 0$ or $\theta^0_{x|\mathbf{u}} = 1$, then both sides of the equation are equal to ∞ (see Exercise 16.1). Suppose now that $\theta^0_{x|\mathbf{u}} \neq 0$ and $\theta^0_{x|\mathbf{u}} \neq 1$. From Definition 16.2, we have

$$
\begin{aligned}
\frac{\theta_{x^\star|\mathbf{u}}}{\theta^0_{x^\star|\mathbf{u}}} &= \frac{\rho(x, x^\star, \mathbf{u})(1 - \theta_{x|\mathbf{u}})}{\theta^0_{x^\star|\mathbf{u}}} \\
&= \frac{\frac{\theta^0_{x^\star|\mathbf{u}}}{1-\theta^0_{x|\mathbf{u}}}(1 - \theta_{x|\mathbf{u}})}{\theta^0_{x^\star|\mathbf{u}}} \\
&= \frac{1 - \theta_{x|\mathbf{u}}}{1 - \theta^0_{x|\mathbf{u}}}.
\end{aligned}
$$

Assume that $\theta_{x|\mathbf{u}} > \theta^0_{x|\mathbf{u}}$. From Theorem 16.2, we have

$$
\begin{aligned}
D(\Pr^0, \Pr) &= \ln \max_x \frac{\theta_{x|\mathbf{u}}}{\theta^0_{x|\mathbf{u}}} - \ln \min_x \frac{\theta_{x|\mathbf{u}}}{\theta^0_{x|\mathbf{u}}} \\
&= \ln \frac{\theta_{x|\mathbf{u}}}{\theta^0_{x|\mathbf{u}}} - \ln \frac{1 - \theta_{x|\mathbf{u}}}{1 - \theta^0_{x|\mathbf{u}}} \\
&= \ln \frac{\theta_{x|\mathbf{u}}}{1 - \theta_{x|\mathbf{u}}} - \ln \frac{\theta^0_{x|\mathbf{u}}}{1 - \theta^0_{x|\mathbf{u}}} \\
&= \ln O(x|\mathbf{u}) - \ln O^0(x|\mathbf{u}) \\
&= \left| \ln O(x|\mathbf{u}) - \ln O^0(x|\mathbf{u}) \right|.
\end{aligned}
$$

We can prove the similar case when $\theta_{x|\mathbf{u}} < \theta^0_{x|\mathbf{u}}$:

$$
\begin{aligned}
D(\Pr^0, \Pr) &= \ln \max_x \frac{\theta_{x|\mathbf{u}}}{\theta^0_{x|\mathbf{u}}} - \ln \min_x \frac{\theta_{x|\mathbf{u}}}{\theta^0_{x|\mathbf{u}}} \\
&= \ln \frac{1 - \theta_{x|\mathbf{u}}}{1 - \theta^0_{x|\mathbf{u}}} - \ln \frac{\theta_{x|\mathbf{u}}}{\theta^0_{x|\mathbf{u}}} \\
&= \ln \frac{1 - \theta_{x|\mathbf{u}}}{\theta_{x|\mathbf{u}}} - \ln \frac{1 - \theta^0_{x|\mathbf{u}}}{\theta^0_{x|\mathbf{u}}} \\
&= -\ln O(x|\mathbf{u}) + \ln O^0(x|\mathbf{u}) \\
&= \left| \ln O(x|\mathbf{u}) - \ln O^0(x|\mathbf{u}) \right|,
\end{aligned}
$$

since $\ln O^0(x|\mathbf{u}) > \ln O(x|\mathbf{u})$. ∎

PROOF OF THEOREM 16.4. We can express $\Pr(\alpha)$ as

$$
\Pr(\alpha) = \frac{\partial \Pr(\alpha)}{\partial \theta_{x|\mathbf{u}}} \theta_{x|\mathbf{u}} + \sum_{x^\star \neq x} \frac{\partial \Pr(\alpha)}{\partial \theta_{x^\star|\mathbf{u}}} \theta^\star_{x^\star|\mathbf{u}} + \sum_{\mathbf{u}^\star \neq \mathbf{u}} \Pr(\mathbf{u}^\star, \alpha).
$$

Since $\text{Pr}(\mathbf{u}^\star, \alpha)$ for all $\mathbf{u}^\star \neq \mathbf{u}$ remains constant under changes of $\theta_{x|\mathbf{u}}$ and $\theta_{x^\star|\mathbf{u}}$, we have $\text{Pr}(\mathbf{u}^\star, \alpha) = \text{Pr}^0(\mathbf{u}^\star, \alpha)$. From Definition 16.2, we have

$$\text{Pr}(\alpha) = \frac{\partial \text{Pr}(\alpha)}{\partial \theta_{x|\mathbf{u}}} \theta_{x|\mathbf{u}} + \sum_{x^\star \neq x} \frac{\partial \text{Pr}(\alpha)}{\partial \theta_{x^\star|\mathbf{u}}} \rho(x, x^\star, \mathbf{u})(1 - \theta_{x|\mathbf{u}}) + \sum_{\mathbf{u}^\star \neq \mathbf{u}} \text{Pr}^0(\mathbf{u}^\star, \alpha).$$

Expanding the expression, we get the values of $\mu_{x|\mathbf{u}}^\alpha$ and $v_{x|\mathbf{u}}^\alpha$ from (16.5) and (16.6), respectively. ∎

PROOF OF THEOREM 16.5. We can express $\text{Pr}(\alpha)$ as

$$\text{Pr}(\alpha) = \sum_{\mathbf{u}} \left(\frac{\partial \text{Pr}(\alpha)}{\partial \theta_{x|\mathbf{u}}} \theta_{x|\mathbf{u}} + \sum_{x^\star \neq x} \frac{\partial \text{Pr}(\alpha)}{\partial \theta_{x^\star|\mathbf{u}}} \theta_{x|\mathbf{u}}^\star \right).$$

From Definition 16.2, we have

$$\text{Pr}(\alpha) = \sum_{\mathbf{u}} \left(\frac{\partial \text{Pr}(\alpha)}{\partial \theta_{x|\mathbf{u}}} \theta_{x|\mathbf{u}} + \sum_{x^\star \neq x} \frac{\partial \text{Pr}(\alpha)}{\partial \theta_{x^\star|\mathbf{u}}} \rho(x, x^\star, \mathbf{u})(1 - \theta_{x|\mathbf{u}}) \right).$$

Expanding the expression, we get the values of $\mu_{x|\mathbf{u}}^\alpha$ and $v_{x|\mathbf{u}}^{\prime\alpha}$ from (16.5) and (16.5), respectively. ∎

17

Learning: The Maximum Likelihood Approach

We discuss in this chapter the process of learning Bayesian networks from data. The learning process is studied under different conditions, which relate to the nature of available data and the amount of prior knowledge we have on the Bayesian network.

17.1 Introduction

Consider Figure 17.1, which depicts a Bayesian network structure from the domain of medical diagnosis (we treated this network in Chapter 5). Consider also the data set depicted in this figure. Each row in this data set is called a *case* and represents a medical record for a particular patient.[1] Note that some of the cases are incomplete, where "?" indicates the unavailability of corresponding data for that patient. The data set is therefore said to be *incomplete* due to these missing values; otherwise, it is called a *complete* data set.

A key objective of this chapter is to provide techniques for estimating the parameters of a network structure given both complete and incomplete data sets. The techniques we provide therefore complement those given in Chapter 5 for constructing Bayesian networks. In particular we can now construct the network structure from either design information or by working with domain experts, as discussed in Chapter 5, and then use the techniques discussed in this chapter to estimate the CPTs of these structures from data. We also discuss techniques for learning the network structure itself, although our focus here is on complete data sets for reasons that we state later.

The simplest problem we treat in this chapter is that of estimating parameters for a given network structure when the data set is complete. This problem is addressed in Section 17.2 and has already been addressed to some extent in Chapter 15 since a complete data set corresponds to a *sample* as defined in that chapter. However, in Chapter 15 a sample was simulated from a given Bayesian network with the goal of estimating certain probabilities by operating on the sample. In this chapter, the sample (i.e., data set) is typically collected from a real-world situation, which provides little control over the sample size. Moreover, the goal now is to estimate all probabilities of the form $\Pr(x|\mathbf{u}) = \theta_{x|\mathbf{u}}$, where $\theta_{x|\mathbf{u}}$ is a network parameter. We indeed adopt the same solution to this problem that we adopted in Chapter 15 while presenting more of its properties from a learning perspective.

The second problem we address in this chapter concerns the estimation of network parameters from an incomplete data set. This is treated in Section 17.3. As we shall see, this problem is computationally much more demanding and the resulting solutions have weaker properties than those obtained for complete data sets.

---

[1] A *case* is also referred to as an *instance, unit, observation, record,* and *subject* in the literature.

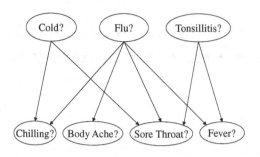

Case	Cold?	Flu?	Tonsillitis?	Chilling?	Bodyache?	Sorethroat?	Fever?
1	true	false	?	true	false	false	false
2	false	true	false	true	true	false	true
3	?	?	true	false	?	true	false
⋮	⋮	⋮	⋮	⋮	⋮	⋮	⋮

Figure 17.1: A Bayesian network structure and a corresponding data set.

The last problem we address concerns the learning of network structures from complete data sets. The treatment of this problem is divided into two orthogonal dimensions. The first dimension, addressed in Section 17.4, deals with the scoring function that we must use when learning network structure (i.e., which network structures should we prefer). The second dimension, addressed in Section 17.5, deals with the computational demands that arise when searching for a network structure that optimizes a certain scoring function.

We can distinguish between three general approaches to the learning problem that adopt different criteria for what parameters and structure we should seek. The first approach is based on the *likelihood principle*, which favors those estimates that have a maximal likelihood, that is, ones that maximize the probability of observing the given data set. This approach is therefore known as the *maximum likelihood approach* to learning and is the one we treat in this chapter.

The second approach requires more input to the learning process as it demands us to define a *meta-distribution* over network structures and parameters. It then reduces the problem of learning to a problem of classical inference in which the data set is viewed as evidence. In particular, it first conditions the meta distribution on the given data set and then uses the posterior meta-distribution as a criterion for defining estimates. This approach is known as the *Bayesian approach* to learning and is treated in Chapter 18.

A third approach for learning Bayesian networks is known as the *constraint-based approach* and applies mostly to learning network structures. According to this approach, we seek structures that respect the conditional independencies exhibited by the given data set. We do not treat this approach in this book but provide some references in the bibliographic remarks section.

All of the previous approaches are meant to induce Bayesian networks that are meaningful independent of the tasks for which they are intended. Consider for example a network that models a set of diseases and a corresponding set of symptoms. This network may be used to perform diagnostic tasks by inferring the most likely disease given a set of observed symptoms. It may also be used for prediction tasks where we infer the most likely symptom given some diseases. If we concern ourselves with only one of these

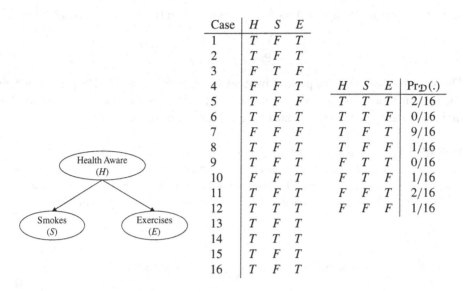

Case	H	S	E
1	T	F	T
2	T	F	T
3	F	T	F
4	F	F	T
5	T	F	F
6	T	F	T
7	F	F	F
8	T	F	T
9	T	F	T
10	F	F	T
11	T	F	T
12	T	T	T
13	T	F	T
14	T	T	T
15	T	F	T
16	T	F	T

H	S	E	$\Pr_{\mathcal{D}}(.)$
T	T	T	2/16
T	T	F	0/16
T	F	T	9/16
T	F	F	1/16
F	T	T	0/16
F	T	F	1/16
F	F	T	2/16
F	F	F	1/16

(a) Network structure   (b) Complete data   (c) Empirical distribution

Figure 17.2: Estimating network parameters from a complete data set.

tasks, say, diagnostics, we can use a more specialized learning principle that optimizes the diagnostic performance of the learned network. In machine-learning jargon, we say that we are learning a *discriminative model* in this case as it is often used to discriminate among patients according to a predefined set of classes (e.g., has cancer or not). This is to be contrasted with learning a *generative model,* which is to be evaluated based on its ability to generate the given data set regardless of how it performs on any particular task. We do not cover discriminative approaches to learning in this book but provide some references in the bibliographic remarks section.

17.2 Estimating parameters from complete data

Consider the simple network structure in Figure 17.2(a) and suppose that our goal is to estimate its parameters from the data set $\mathcal{D}$ given in Figure 17.2(b).

Our estimation approach is based on the assumption that this data set was simulated from the true Bayesian network as given in Section 15.2, that is, the cases are generated independently and according to their true probabilities. Under these assumptions, we can define an *empirical distribution* $\Pr_{\mathcal{D}}(.)$ that summarizes the data set as given in Figure 17.2(c). According to this distribution, the empirical probability of instantiation h, s, e is simply its frequency of occurrence in the data set,

$$\Pr_{\mathcal{D}}(h, s, e) = \frac{\mathcal{D}\#(h, s, e)}{N},$$

where $\mathcal{D}\#(h, s, e)$ is the number of cases in the data set $\mathcal{D}$ that satisfy instantiation $h, s, e,$ and N is the data set size.

We can now estimate parameters based on the empirical distribution. Consider the parameter $\theta_{s|h}$ for example, that corresponds to the probability that a person will smoke given that they are health-aware, $\Pr(s|h)$. Our estimate for this parameter is now given by

$$\Pr_{\mathcal{D}}(s|h) = \frac{\Pr_{\mathcal{D}}(s,h)}{\Pr_{\mathcal{D}}(h)} = \frac{2/16}{12/16} = 1/6.$$

This corresponds to the simplest estimation technique discussed in Chapter 15, where we also provided a key result on the variance of its produced estimates.[2] We restate this result next but after formalizing some of the concepts used here.

Definition 17.1. A *data set* $\mathcal{D}$ for variables $\mathbf{X}$ is a vector $\mathbf{d}_1, \ldots, \mathbf{d}_N$ where each $\mathbf{d}_i$ is called a *case* and represents a partial instantiation of variables $\mathbf{X}$. The data set is *complete* if each case is a complete instantiation of variables $\mathbf{X}$; otherwise, the data set is *incomplete*. The *empirical distribution* for a complete data set $\mathcal{D}$ is defined as

$$\Pr_{\mathcal{D}}(\alpha) \stackrel{def}{=} \frac{\mathcal{D}\#(\alpha)}{N},$$

where $\mathcal{D}\#(\alpha)$ is the number of cases $\mathbf{d}_i$ in the data set $\mathcal{D}$ that satisfy event α, that is, $\mathbf{d}_i \models \alpha$.[3]   ∎

Figure 17.2(b) depicts a complete data set $\mathcal{D}$ for variables H, S, and E, leading to the following:

- $\mathcal{D}\#(\alpha) = 9$ when α is $(H\!=\!T) \wedge (S\!=\!F) \wedge (E\!=\!T)$
- $\mathcal{D}\#(\alpha) = 12$ when α is $(H\!=\!T)$
- $\mathcal{D}\#(\alpha) = 14$, when α is $(H\!=\!T) \vee (E\!=\!T)$.

Figure 17.2(c) depicts the empirical distribution induced by the complete data set in Figure 17.2(b).

Given Definition 17.1, we are then suggesting that we estimate the parameter $\theta_{x|\mathbf{u}}$ by the empirical probability

$$\theta_{x|\mathbf{u}}^{ml} \stackrel{def}{=} \Pr_{\mathcal{D}}(x|\mathbf{u}) = \frac{\mathcal{D}\#(x,\mathbf{u})}{\mathcal{D}\#(\mathbf{u})}. \tag{17.1}$$

The count $\mathcal{D}\#(x,\mathbf{u})$ is called a *sufficient statistic* in this case. More generally, any function of the data is called a *statistic*. Moreover, a sufficient statistic is a statistic that contains all of the information in the data set that is needed for a particular estimation task.

Considering the network structure and corresponding data set in Figure 17.2, we then have the following parameter estimates:

H	S	$\theta_{S|H}^{ml}$
h	s	1/6
h	$\bar{s}$	5/6
$\bar{h}$	s	1/4
$\bar{h}$	$\bar{s}$	3/4

H	E	$\theta_{E|H}^{ml}$
h	e	11/12
h	$\bar{e}$	1/12
$\bar{h}$	e	1/2
$\bar{h}$	$\bar{e}$	1/2

H	θ_H^{ml}
h	3/4
$\bar{h}$	1/4

Note that the estimate $\theta_{x|\mathbf{u}}^{ml}$ will have different values depending on the given data set. However, we expect that the variance of this estimate will decrease as the data set increases

---

[2] In particular, this estimation technique corresponds to the method of *direct sampling* discussed in Section 15.4.

[3] Note that $\mathcal{D}\#(\alpha) = N$ when α is a valid event as it will be satisfied by every case $\mathbf{d}_i$.

in size. In fact, if we assume that the data set $\mathcal{D}$ is a sample of size N simulated from a distribution Pr, then Theorem 15.10 of Chapter 15 tells us that the distribution of estimate $\theta_{x|\mathbf{u}}^{ml}$ is asymptotically Normal and can be approximated by a Normal distribution with mean $\Pr(x|\mathbf{u})$ and variance

$$\frac{\Pr(x|\mathbf{u})(1 - \Pr(x|\mathbf{u}))}{N \cdot \Pr(\mathbf{u})}.$$

Note how the variance depends on the size of data set, N, the probability of parent instantiation, $\Pr(\mathbf{u})$, and the true value of the estimated parameter, $\Pr(x|\mathbf{u})$. In particular, note how sensitive this variance is to $\Pr(\mathbf{u})$, which makes it difficult to estimate the parameter when this probability is quite small. In fact, if this probability is too small and the data set is not large enough, it is not uncommon for the empirical probability $\Pr_{\mathcal{D}}(\mathbf{u})$ to be zero. Under these conditions, the estimate $\Pr_{\mathcal{D}}(x|\mathbf{u})$ is not well defined, leading to what is known as the problem of *zero counts*.[4] We provide a technique for dealing with this problem in Chapter 18, which is based on incorporating prior knowledge into the estimation process.

For the next property of the estimates we have defined, let θ be the set of all parameter estimates for a given network structure G and let $\Pr_\theta(.)$ be the probability distribution induced by structure G and estimates θ. Let us now define the *likelihood* of these estimates as

$$L(\theta|\mathcal{D}) \overset{def}{=} \prod_{i=1}^{N} \Pr_\theta(\mathbf{d}_i). \qquad (17.2)$$

That is, the likelihood of estimates θ is the probability of observing the data set $\mathcal{D}$ under these estimates. We now have the following result.

Theorem 17.1. *Let $\mathcal{D}$ be a complete data set. The parameter estimates defined by (17.1) are the only estimates that maximize the likelihood function[5]*

$$\theta^\star = \underset{\theta}{\operatorname{argmax}} \, L(\theta|\mathcal{D}) \text{ iff } \theta_{x|\mathbf{u}}^\star = \Pr_{\mathcal{D}}(x|\mathbf{u}). \qquad \blacksquare$$

It is for this reason that these estimates are called *maximum likelihood (ML) estimates* and are denoted by θ^{ml}:

$$\theta^{ml} = \underset{\theta}{\operatorname{argmax}} \, L(\theta|\mathcal{D}).$$

We defined these estimates based on the empirical distribution and then showed that they maximize the *likelihood function*. Yet it is quite common to start with the goal of maximizing the likelihood function and then derive these estimates accordingly. This alternative approach is justified by some strong, desirable properties satisfied by estimates that maximize the likelihood function. We indeed follow this approach when dealing with incomplete data in the next section.

Another property of our ML estimates is that they minimize the KL divergence (see Appendix B) between the learned Bayesian network and the empirical distribution.

---

[4] That is, we get a zero if we count the number of cases that satisfy instantiation $\mathbf{u}$.

[5] We assume here that all parameter estimates are well defined; that is, $\Pr_{\mathcal{D}}(\mathbf{u}) > 0$ for every instantiation $\mathbf{u}$ of every parent set $\mathbf{U}$ (see Exercises 17.2 and 17.3).

Theorem 17.2. *Let $\mathcal{D}$ be a complete data set over variables* **X**. *Then*

$$\underset{\theta}{\operatorname{argmax}} L(\theta|\mathcal{D}) = \underset{\theta}{\operatorname{argmin}} KL(\Pr_{\mathcal{D}}(\mathbf{X}), \Pr_{\theta}(\mathbf{X})). \qquad \blacksquare$$

Since ML estimates are unique for a given structure G and complete data set $\mathcal{D}$, the likelihood of these parameters is then a function of the structure G and data set $\mathcal{D}$. We therefore define the *likelihood of structure G* given data set $\mathcal{D}$ as

$$L(G|\mathcal{D}) \overset{def}{=} L(\theta^{ml}|\mathcal{D}),$$

where θ^{ml} are the ML estimates for structure G and data set $\mathcal{D}$. The likelihood function plays a major role in many of the developments in this chapter. However, it turns out to be more convenient to work with the logarithm of the likelihood function, defined as

$$LL(\theta|\mathcal{D}) \overset{def}{=} \log L(\theta|\mathcal{D}) = \sum_{i=1}^{N} \log \Pr_{\theta}(\mathbf{d}_i).$$

The log-likelihood of structure G is defined similarly:

$$LL(G|\mathcal{D}) \overset{def}{=} \log L(G|\mathcal{D}).$$

The likelihood function is ≥ 0, while the log-likelihood function is ≤ 0. However, maximizing the likelihood function is equivalent to maximizing the log-likelihood function. We use $\log_2$ for the log-likelihood function but suppress the base 2 from now forward.

We close this section by pointing out a key property of the log-likelihood function for network structures: it decomposes into a number of components, one for each family in the Bayesian network structure.

Theorem 17.3. *Let G be a network structure and $\mathcal{D}$ be a complete data set of size N. If $X\mathbf{U}$ ranges over the families of structure G, then*

$$LL(G|\mathcal{D}) = -N \sum_{X\mathbf{U}} ENT_{\mathcal{D}}(X|\mathbf{U}), \qquad (17.3)$$

where $ENT_{\mathcal{D}}(X|\mathbf{U})$ is the conditional entropy, defined as

$$ENT_{\mathcal{D}}(X|\mathbf{U}) = -\sum_{x\mathbf{u}} \Pr_{\mathcal{D}}(x\mathbf{u}) \log_2 \Pr_{\mathcal{D}}(x|\mathbf{u}). \qquad \blacksquare$$

This decomposition is critical to the algorithms for learning network structure, discussed in Section 17.4. See also Appendix B for a review of entropy and related concepts from information theory.

17.3 Estimating parameters from incomplete data

The parameter estimates considered in the previous section have a number of interesting properties: they are unique, asymptotically Normal, and maximize the probability of data. Most importantly these estimates are easily computable by performing a single pass on the data set. We proved some of these properties independently yet some of them follow from the others under more general conditions than those we considered here. For example, maximum likelihood estimates are known to be asymptotically Normal for a large class of models that include but are not limited to Bayesian networks. It is therefore common to seek maximum likelihood estimates for incomplete data sets.

The properties of these estimates, however, will depend on the nature of incompleteness we have. Consider for example a network structure $C \to T$ where C represents a medical condition and T represents a test for detecting this condition. Suppose further that the true parameters of this network are

C	θ_c
yes	.25
no	.75

C	T	$\theta_{t|c}$
yes	+ve	.80
yes	−ve	.20
no	+ve	.40
no	−ve	.60

(17.4)

Hence, we have $\Pr(T=+\text{ve}) = \Pr(T=-\text{ve}) = .5$. Consider now the following data sets, all of which are incomplete:

$\mathcal{D}^1$	C	T
1	?	+ve
2	?	+ve
3	?	−ve
4	?	−ve
5	?	−ve
6	?	+ve
7	?	+ve
8	?	−ve

$\mathcal{D}^2$	C	T
1	yes	+ve
2	yes	+ve
3	yes	−ve
4	no	?
5	yes	−ve
6	yes	+ve
7	no	?
8	no	−ve

$\mathcal{D}^3$	C	T
1	yes	+ve
2	yes	+ve
3	?	−ve
4	no	?
5	yes	−ve
6	?	+ve
7	no	?
8	no	−ve

Each of these data sets exhibits a different pattern of data incompleteness. For example, the values of variable C are missing in all cases of the first data set, perhaps because we can never determine this condition directly. We say in this situation that variable C is *hidden* or *latent*. The situation is different in the second data set, where variable C is always observed and variable T has some missing values but is not hidden. The third data set exhibits yet a different pattern of data incompleteness where both variables have some missing values but neither is hidden.

Let us now consider the first data set, $\mathcal{D}^1$, and observe that the cases are split equally between the +ve and −ve values of T. In fact, we expect this to be true in the limit given the distribution generating this data. As shown in Exercise 17.12, the ML estimates are not unique for a class of data sets that includes this one. For example, the exercise shows that the ML estimates for data set $\mathcal{D}^1$ are characterized by the following equation:

$$\theta_{T=+\text{ve}|C=\text{yes}} \cdot \theta_{C=\text{yes}} + \theta_{T=+\text{ve}|C=\text{no}} \cdot \theta_{C=\text{no}} = \frac{1}{2}.$$

Note that the true parameter values in (17.4) satisfy this equation. But the following estimates do as well:

$$\theta_{C=\text{yes}} = 1, \quad \theta_{T=+\text{ve}|C=\text{yes}} = 1/2,$$

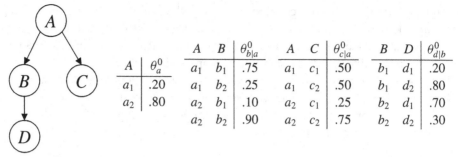

Figure 17.3: A Bayesian network inducing a probability distribution $\Pr_{\theta^0}(.)$.

with $\theta_{T=+ve|C=no}$ taking any value. Hence, the ML estimates are not unique for the given data set. However, this should not be surprising since this data set does not contain enough information to pin down the true parameters. The nonuniqueness of ML estimates is therefore a desirable property in this case, not a limitation.

Let us now consider the second data set, $\mathcal{D}^2$, to illustrate another important point relating to why the data may be missing. Following are two scenarios:

- People who do not suffer from the condition tend not to take the test. That is, the data is missing because the test is not performed.

- People who test negative tend not to report the result. That is, the test is performed but its value is not recorded.

These two scenarios are different in a fundamental way. For example, in the second scenario the fact that a value is missing does provide some evidence that this value must be negative. This issue is discussed in Section 17.3.3 where we show that the ML approach gives the intended results when applied under the first scenario but gives unintended results under the second scenario as it does not integrate all of the information we have about this scenario. However, we show that the ML approach can still be applied under the second scenario but that requires some explication of the mechanism that causes the data to be missing.

We next present two methods that search for ML estimates under incomplete data. Both methods are based on local search, which start with some initial estimates and then iteratively improve on them until some stopping condition is met. Both methods are generally more expensive than the method for complete data yet neither is generally guaranteed to find ML estimates.

17.3.1 Expectation maximization

Consider the structure in Figure 17.3 and suppose that our goal is to find ML estimates for the following data set:

$\mathcal{D}$	A	B	C	D
d_1	?	b_1	c_2	?
d_2	?	b_1	?	d_2
d_3	?	b_2	c_1	d_1
d_4	?	b_2	c_1	d_1
d_5	?	b_1	?	d_2

(17.5)

Suppose further that we are starting with the initial estimates θ^0 given in Figure 17.3, which have the following likelihood:

$$
\begin{aligned}
L(\theta^0|\mathcal{D}) &= \prod_{i=1}^{5} \Pr_{\theta^0}(\mathbf{d}_i) \\
&= \Pr_{\theta^0}(b_1, c_2)\Pr_{\theta^0}(b_1, d_2)\Pr_{\theta^0}(b_2, c_1, d_1)\Pr_{\theta^0}(b_2, c_1, d_1)\Pr_{\theta^0}(b_1, d_2) \\
&= (.135)(.184)(.144)(.144)(.184) \\
&= 9.5 \times 10^{-5}.
\end{aligned}
$$

Note that contrary to the case of complete data, evaluating the terms in this product generally requires inference on the Bayesian network.[6]

Our first local search method, called *expectation maximization* (EM), is based on the method of complete data discussed in the previous section. That is, this method first completes the data set, inducing an empirical distribution, and then uses it to estimate parameters as in the previous section. The new set of parameters are guaranteed to have no less likelihood than the initial parameters, so this process can be repeated until some convergence condition is met.

To illustrate the process of completing a data set, consider again the data set in (17.5). The first case in this data set has two variables with missing values, A and D. Hence, there are four possible completions for this case. Although we do not know which one of these completions is the correct one, we can compute the probability of each completion based on the initial set of parameters we have. This is shown in Figure 17.4, which lists for each case $\mathbf{d}_i$ the probability of each of its completions, $\Pr_{\theta^0}(\mathbf{c}_i|\mathbf{d}_i)$, where $\mathbf{C}_i$ are the variables with missing values in case $\mathbf{d}_i$.

Note that the completed data set defines an (expected) empirical distribution, shown in Figure 17.4(b). According to this distribution, the probability of an instantiation, say, a_1, b_1, c_2, d_2 is computed by considering all its occurrences in the completed data set. However, instead of simply counting the number of such occurrences, we add up the probabilities of seeing them in the completed data set. There are three occurrences of the instantiation a_1, b_1, c_2, d_2 in the completed data set, which result from completing the cases $\mathbf{d}_1, \mathbf{d}_2$, and $\mathbf{d}_5$. Moreover, the probability of seeing these completions is given by

$$
\begin{aligned}
\Pr_{\mathcal{D},\theta^0}(a_1, b_1, c_2, d_2) &= \frac{\Pr_{\theta^0}(a_1, d_2|\mathbf{d}_1) + \Pr_{\theta^0}(a_1, c_2|\mathbf{d}_2) + \Pr_{\theta^0}(a_1, c_2|\mathbf{d}_5)}{N} \\
&= \frac{.444 + .326 + .326}{5} \\
&= .219
\end{aligned}
$$

Note that we are using $\Pr_{\mathcal{D},\theta^0}(.)$ to denote the expected empirical distribution based on parameters θ^0. More generally, we have the following definition.

Definition 17.2. The *expected empirical distribution* of data set $\mathcal{D}$ under parameters θ^k is defined as

$$
\Pr_{\mathcal{D},\theta^k}(\alpha) \stackrel{def}{=} \frac{1}{N} \sum_{\mathbf{d}_i, \mathbf{c}_i \models \alpha} \Pr_{\theta^k}(\mathbf{c}_i|\mathbf{d}_i),
$$

where α is an event and $\mathbf{C}_i$ are the variables with missing values in case $\mathbf{d}_i$.   ∎

---

[6] When the data is complete, each term in the product can be evaluated using the chain rule for Bayesian networks.

$\mathcal{D}$	A	B	C	D	$\mathrm{Pr}_{\theta^0}(\mathbf{C}_i\vert\mathbf{d}_i)$
$\mathbf{d}_1$	?	b_1	c_2	?	
	a_1	b_1	c_2	d_1	$.111 = \mathrm{Pr}_{\theta^0}(a_1, d_1\vert b_1, c_2)$
	a_1	b_1	c_2	d_2	.444
	a_2	b_1	c_2	d_1	.089
	a_2	b_1	c_2	d_2	.356
$\mathbf{d}_2$	?	b_1	?	d_2	
	a_1	b_1	c_1	d_2	$.326 = \mathrm{Pr}_{\theta^0}(a_1, c_1\vert b_1, d_2)$
	a_1	b_1	c_2	d_2	.326
	a_2	b_1	c_1	d_2	.087
	a_2	b_1	c_2	d_2	.261
$\mathbf{d}_3$	?	b_2	c_1	d_1	
	a_1	b_2	c_1	d_1	$.122 = \mathrm{Pr}_{\theta^0}(a_1\vert b_2, c_1, d_1)$
	a_2	b_2	c_1	d_1	.878
$\mathbf{d}_4$	?	b_2	c_1	d_1	
	a_1	b_2	c_1	d_1	$.122 = \mathrm{Pr}_{\theta^0}(a_1\vert b_2, c_1, d_1)$
	a_2	b_2	c_1	d_1	.878
$\mathbf{d}_5$	?	b_1	?	d_2	
	a_1	b_1	c_1	d_2	$.326 = \mathrm{Pr}_{\theta^0}(a_1, c_1\vert b_1, d_2)$
	a_1	b_1	c_2	d_2	.326
	a_2	b_1	c_1	d_2	.087
	a_2	b_1	c_2	d_2	.261

A	B	C	D	$\mathrm{Pr}_{\mathcal{D},\theta^0}(.)$
a_1	b_1	c_1	d_1	0
a_1	b_1	c_1	d_2	.130
a_1	b_1	c_2	d_1	.022
a_1	b_1	c_2	d_2	.219
a_1	b_2	c_1	d_1	.049
a_1	b_2	c_1	d_2	0
a_1	b_2	c_2	d_1	0
a_1	b_2	c_2	d_2	0
a_2	b_1	c_1	d_1	0
a_2	b_1	c_1	d_2	.035
a_2	b_1	c_2	d_1	.018
a_2	b_1	c_2	d_2	.176
a_2	b_2	c_1	d_1	.351
a_2	b_2	c_1	d_2	0
a_2	b_2	c_2	d_1	0
a_2	b_2	c_2	d_2	0

(a) Completed data set with expected values of completed cases

(b) Expected empirical distribution

Figure 17.4: Completing a data set using the probability distribution $\mathrm{Pr}_{\theta^0}(.)$ defined by the Bayesian network in Figure 17.3.

Recall that $\mathbf{d}_i, \mathbf{c}_i \models \alpha$ means that event α is satisfied by complete case $\mathbf{d}_i, \mathbf{c}_i$. Hence, we are summing $\mathrm{Pr}_{\theta^k}(\mathbf{c}_i\vert\mathbf{d}_i)$ for all cases $\mathbf{d}_i$ and their completions $\mathbf{c}_i$ that satisfy event α.

When the data set is complete, $\mathrm{Pr}_{\mathcal{D},\theta^k}(.)$ reduces to the empirical distribution $\mathrm{Pr}_{\mathcal{D}}(.)$, which is independent of parameters θ^k. Moreover, $N \cdot \mathrm{Pr}_{\mathcal{D},\theta^k}(\mathbf{x})$ is called the *expected count* of instantiation $\mathbf{x}$ in data set $\mathcal{D}$, just as $N \cdot \mathrm{Pr}_{\mathcal{D}}(\mathbf{x})$ represents the count of instantiation $\mathbf{x}$ in a complete data set $\mathcal{D}$.

We can now use this expected empirical distribution to estimate parameters, just as we did for complete data. For example, we have the following estimate for parameter $\theta_{c_1\vert a_2}$:

$$\theta^1_{c_1\vert a_2} = \mathrm{Pr}_{\mathcal{D},\theta^0}(c_1\vert a_2) = \frac{\mathrm{Pr}_{\mathcal{D},\theta^0}(c_1, a_2)}{\mathrm{Pr}_{\mathcal{D},\theta^0}(a_2)} = .666$$

Figure 17.5 depicts all parameter estimates based on the expected empirical distribution $\mathrm{Pr}_{\mathcal{D},\theta^0}(.)$, leading to the new estimates θ^1 with likelihood

$$L(\theta^1\vert\mathcal{D}) = \prod_{i=1}^{5} \mathrm{Pr}_{\theta^1}(\mathbf{d}_i)$$
$$= (.290)(.560)(.255)(.255)(.560)$$
$$= 5.9 \times 10^{-3}$$
$$> L(\theta^0\vert\mathcal{D}).$$

Hence, the new estimates have a higher likelihood than the initial ones we started with. This holds more generally as we show next.

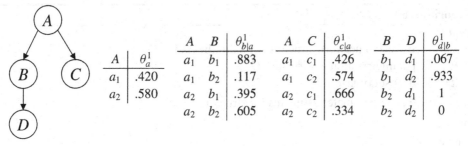

Figure 17.5: A Bayesian network inducing a probability distribution $\Pr_{\theta^1}(.)$.

Definition 17.3. The *EM estimates* for data set $\mathcal{D}$ and parameters θ^k are defined as

$$\theta^{k+1}_{x|\mathbf{u}} \stackrel{def}{=} \Pr_{\mathcal{D},\theta^k}(x|\mathbf{u}). \qquad (17.6)$$

∎

That is, EM estimates are based on the expected empirical distribution, just as our estimates for complete data are based on the empirical distribution. We now have the following key result.

Corollary 11. *EM estimates satisfy the following property:*

$$LL(\theta^{k+1}|\mathcal{D}) \geq LL(\theta^k|\mathcal{D}).$$

∎

This is a corollary of Theorems 17.5 and 17.6 (to be discussed later), which characterize the EM algorithm and also explain its name. However, before we discuss these theorems we show that EM estimates can be computed without constructing the expected empirical distribution. This will form the basis of the EM algorithm to be presented later.

Theorem 17.4. *The expected empirical distribution of data set $\mathcal{D}$ given parameters θ^k can be computed as*

$$\Pr_{\mathcal{D},\theta^k}(\alpha) = \frac{1}{N}\sum_{i=1}^{N}\Pr_{\theta^k}(\alpha|\mathbf{d}_i).$$

∎

That is, we simply iterate over the data set cases while computing the probability of α given each case (i.e., no need to explicitly consider the completion of each case). The EM estimates for data set $\mathcal{D}$ and parameters θ^k can now be computed as

$$\theta^{k+1}_{x|\mathbf{u}} = \frac{\sum_{i=1}^{N}\Pr_{\theta^k}(x\mathbf{u}|\mathbf{d}_i)}{\sum_{i=1}^{N}\Pr_{\theta^k}(\mathbf{u}|\mathbf{d}_i)}. \qquad (17.7)$$

Note that contrary to (17.6), (17.7) does not reference the expected empirical distribution. Instead, this equation computes EM estimates by performing inference on a Bayesian network parameterized by the previous parameter estimates θ^k. For example,

$$\theta^1_{c_1|a_2} = \frac{\sum_{i=1}^{5}\Pr_{\theta^0}(c_1,a_2|\mathbf{d}_i)}{\sum_{i=1}^{5}\Pr_{\theta^0}(a_2|\mathbf{d}_i)} = \frac{0 + .087 + .878 + .878 + .087}{.444 + .348 + .878 + .878 + .348} = .666$$

Note here that the quantities $\Pr_{\theta^0}(c_1,a_2|\mathbf{d}_i)$ and $\Pr_{\theta^0}(a_2|\mathbf{d}_i)$ are obtained by performing inference on the Bayesian network in Figure 17.3, which is parameterized by θ^0. This leads to estimates θ^1 depicted in Figure 17.5. The Bayesian network in this figure can then be used to obtain estimates θ^2 as suggested by (17.7). The process can be repeated until some convergence criterion is met.

Algorithm 50 ML_EM($G, \theta^0, \mathcal{D}$)

---

input:

   G: Bayesian network structure with families $X\mathbf{U}$

   θ^0:   parametrization of structure G

   $\mathcal{D}$:   data set of size N

output: ML/EM parameter estimates for structure G

main:

  1: $k \leftarrow 0$

  2: **while** $\theta^k \neq \theta^{k-1}$ **do** {this test is different in practice}

  3:     $c_{x\mathbf{u}} \leftarrow 0$ for each family instantiation $x\mathbf{u}$

  4:     **for** $i = 1$ to N **do**

  5:        **for** each family instantiation $x\mathbf{u}$ **do**

  6:           $c_{x\mathbf{u}} \leftarrow c_{x\mathbf{u}} + \Pr_{\theta^k}(x\mathbf{u}|\mathbf{d}_i)$ {requires inference on network (G, θ^k)}

  7:        **end for**

  8:     **end for**

  9:     compute parameter estimates θ^{k+1} using $\theta^{k+1}_{x|\mathbf{u}} = c_{x\mathbf{u}} / \sum_{x^\star} c_{x^\star \mathbf{u}}$

10:    $k \leftarrow k + 1$

11: **end while**

12: **return** θ^k

Algorithm 50, ML_EM, provides the pseudocode for the EM algorithm. The convergence test on Line 2 of this algorithm is usually not used in practice. Instead, we terminate the algorithm when the difference between θ^k and θ^{k-1} is small enough or when the change in the log-likelihood is small enough.

There are a number of important observations about the behavior of EM. First, the algorithm may converge to different parameters with different likelihoods depending on the initial estimates θ^0 with which it starts. It is therefore not uncommon to run the algorithm multiple times, starting with different estimates in each iteration (perhaps chosen randomly) and then returning the best estimates found across all iterations. Second, each iteration of the EM algorithm will have to perform inference on a Bayesian network. In particular, in each iteration the algorithm computes the probability of each instantiation $x\mathbf{u}$ given each case $\mathbf{d}_i$ as evidence. Note here that all these computations correspond to posterior marginals over network families. Hence, we want to use an algorithm that can compute family marginals efficiently such as the jointree algorithms, which can implement the inner loop on Line 5 in one jointree propagation. Moreover, it should be noted here that since a data set typically contains many duplicate cases, we do not need to iterate over all cases as suggested on Line 4. Instead, it suffices to iterate over distinct cases as long as the contributions of duplicate cases are accounted for correctly.

We next provide a central result on EM, that immediately implies some of its properties and also explains its name. First, recall the log-likelihood function,

$$LL(\theta|\mathcal{D}) = \sum_{i=1}^{N} \log \Pr_\theta(\mathbf{d}_i).$$

We saw previously how we can maximize this function for a complete data set by choosing parameter estimates based on the empirical distribution

$$\theta_{x|\mathbf{u}} = \Pr_{\mathcal{D}}(x|\mathbf{u}).$$

Consider now the following new function of parameters called the *expected log-likelihood* that computes the log-likelihood of parameters but with respect to a completed data set:

$$\text{ELL}(\theta | \mathcal{D}, \theta^k) \overset{def}{=} \sum_{i=1}^{N} \sum_{\mathbf{c}_i} \left[\log \text{Pr}_\theta(\mathbf{c}_i, \mathbf{d}_i) \right] \text{Pr}_{\theta^k}(\mathbf{c}_i | \mathbf{d}_i).$$

As previously, $\mathbf{C}_i$ are the variables with missing values in case $\mathbf{d}_i$. Recall again the EM estimates based on the expected empirical distribution:

$$\theta_{x|\mathbf{u}}^{k+1} = \text{Pr}_{\mathcal{D}, \theta^k}(x | \mathbf{u}).$$

We now have the following result, which draws a parallel between the two cases of log-likelihood and expected log-likelihood.

Theorem 17.5. *EM parameter estimates are the only estimates that maximize the expected log-likelihood function:*[7]

$$\theta^{k+1} = \underset{\theta}{\text{argmax}} \, \text{ELL}(\theta | \mathcal{D}, \theta^k) \; iff \, \theta_{x|\mathbf{u}}^{k+1} = \text{Pr}_{\mathcal{D}, \theta^k}(x | \mathbf{u}). \qquad \blacksquare$$

Hence, EM is indeed searching for estimates that maximize the expected log-likelihood function, which also explains its name.

Theorem 17.6 shows why the EM algorithm works.

Theorem 17.6. *Parameters that maximize the expected log-likelihood function cannot decrease the log-likelihood function:*

$$\text{If } \theta^{k+1} = \underset{\theta}{\text{argmax}} \, \text{ELL}(\theta | \mathcal{D}, \theta^k), \text{ then } \text{LL}(\theta^{k+1} | \mathcal{D}) \geq \text{LL}(\theta^k | \mathcal{D}). \qquad \blacksquare$$

Theorem 17.6 provides the basis for EM, showing that the estimates it returns can never have a smaller log-likelihood than the estimates with which it starts. However, we should stress that the quality of estimates returned by EM will very much depend on the estimates with which it starts (see Exercise 17.14).

We close this section with the following classical result on EM, showing that it is capable of converging to every local maxima of the log-likelihood function.

Theorem 17.7. *The fixed points of EM are precisely the stationary points of the log-likelihood function.* $\qquad \blacksquare$

The EM algorithm is known to converge very slowly if the fraction of missing data is quite large. It is sometimes sped up using the gradient ascent approach, to be described next. This is done by first running the EM algorithm for a number of iterations to obtain some estimates and then using these estimates as a starting point of the gradient ascent algorithm.

17.3.2 Gradient ascent

Another approach for maximizing the log-likelihood function is to view the problem as one of optimizing a continuous nonlinear function. This is a widely studied problem where most of the solutions are based on local search, which starts by assuming some initial value $\theta_{x|\mathbf{u}}^0$ for each parameter $\theta_{x|\mathbf{u}}$, and then moves through the parameter space in steps of the form $\theta_{x|\mathbf{u}}^{k+1} = \theta_{x|\mathbf{u}}^k + \delta_{x|\mathbf{u}}^k$. Different algorithms use different values for the increment $\delta_{x|\mathbf{u}}^k$

---

[7] We assume here that all parameter estimates are well-defined; that is, $\text{Pr}_{\mathcal{D}, \theta^k}(\mathbf{u}) > 0$ for every instantiation $\mathbf{u}$ of every parent set $\mathbf{U}$.

yet most use gradient information for determining this increment. Recall that for a function $f(v_1, \ldots, v_n)$, the gradient is the vector of partial derivatives $\partial f/\partial v_1, \ldots, \partial f/\partial v_n$. When evaluated at a particular point $(v_1, \ldots, v_n)$, the gradient gives the direction of the greatest increase in the value of f. Hence, a direct use of the gradient, called *gradient ascent*, suggests that we move in the direction of the gradient by incrementing each variable v_i with $\eta \frac{\partial f}{\partial v_i}(v_1, \ldots, v_n)$, where η is a constant known as the *learning rate*. The learning rate decides the size of the step we take in the direction of the gradient and must be chosen carefully, possibly changing its value with different steps. There is a large body of literature on gradient ascent methods that can be brought to bear on this problem. The literature contains a number of variants on gradient ascent such as conjugate gradient ascent, which are known to be more efficient in general.

We note here that we are dealing with a constrained optimization problem as we must maximize the log-likelihood function $\mathrm{LL}(\theta|\mathcal{D})$ based on the gradient $\partial \mathrm{LL}(\theta|\mathcal{D})/\partial \theta_{x|\mathbf{u}}$ while maintaining the constraints $\theta_{x|\mathbf{u}} \in [0, 1]$ and $\sum_x \theta_{x|\mathbf{u}} = 1$. A classic technique for addressing this issue is to search in an alternative parameter space known as the *soft-max* space. That is, we introduce a new variable $\tau_{x|\mathbf{u}}$ with values in $(-\infty, \infty)$ for each parameter $\theta_{x|\mathbf{u}}$. We then define

$$\theta_{x|\mathbf{u}} \stackrel{def}{=} \frac{e^{\tau_{x|\mathbf{u}}}}{\sum_{x^\star} e^{\tau_{x^\star|\mathbf{u}}}}.$$

Any values of the new variables $\tau_{x|\mathbf{u}}$ then induce values for parameters $\theta_{x|\mathbf{u}}$ that satisfy the given constraints. Note, however, that we must now use the following gradient:

$$\frac{\partial \mathrm{LL}(\theta|\mathcal{D})}{\partial \tau_{x|\mathbf{u}}} = \frac{\partial \mathrm{LL}(\theta|\mathcal{D})}{\partial \theta_{x|\mathbf{u}}} \frac{\partial \theta_{x|\mathbf{u}}}{\partial \tau_{x|\mathbf{u}}}. \tag{17.8}$$

Note also that we must be careful in navigating the soft-max parameter space since adding a constant value to each of the new variables $\tau_{x|\mathbf{u}}$ will not change the value of parameter $\theta_{x|\mathbf{u}}$.

Applying gradient ascent methods relies on the ability to compute the gradient. The following result shows how this can be done for the log-likelihood function (see also Exercise 17.10).

Theorem 17.8. *We have*

$$\frac{\partial \mathrm{LL}(\theta|\mathcal{D})}{\partial \theta_{x|\mathbf{u}}} = \sum_{i=1}^{N} \left(\frac{1}{\mathrm{Pr}_\theta(\mathbf{d}_i)} \right) \frac{\partial \mathrm{Pr}_\theta(\mathbf{d}_i)}{\partial \theta_{x|\mathbf{u}}} \tag{17.9}$$

$$= \sum_{i=1}^{N} \frac{\mathrm{Pr}_\theta(x\mathbf{u}|\mathbf{d}_i)}{\theta_{x|\mathbf{u}}}, \quad when \ \theta_{x|\mathbf{u}} \neq 0. \tag{17.10}$$

∎

Equation 17.9 allows us to use arithmetic circuits (as discussed in Chapter 12) to compute the gradient, while (17.10) allows us to compute the gradient using other types of algorithms such as the jointree algorithm, which do not compute derivatives. We finally note that the complexity of computing the gradient is similar to the complexity of performing an iteration of the EM algorithm. In both cases, we need to compute all family marginals with respect to each distinct case in the data set. The number of iterations performed by each algorithm may be different, with the learning rate having a key effect in gradient ascent algorithms.

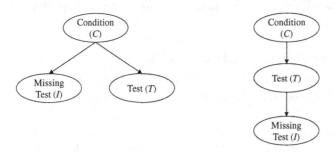

(a) Ignorable mechanism   (b) Nonignorable mechanism

Figure 17.6: Missing-data mechanisms.

17.3.3 The missing-data mechanism

Consider the network structure $C \rightarrow T$ discussed previously, where C represents a medical condition and T represents a test for detecting this condition. Figure 17.6 depicts two extended network structures for this problem, each including an additional variable I that indicates whether the test result is missing in the data set. In Figure 17.6(a), the missing data depends on the condition (e.g., people who do not suffer from the condition tend not to take the test), while in Figure 17.6(b) the missing data depends on the test result (e.g., individuals who test negative tend not to report the result). Hence, these extended structures explicate different dependencies between data missingness and the values of variables in the data set. We say in this case that the structures explicate different *missing-data mechanisms*.

Our goal in this section is to discuss ML estimates that we would obtain with respect to structures that explicate missing-data mechanisms and compare these estimates with those obtained when ignoring such mechanisms (e.g., using the simpler structure $C \rightarrow T$ as we did previously). We start with the following definition.

Definition 17.4. Let G be a network structure, let $\mathcal{D}$ be a corresponding data set, and let **M** be the variables of G that have missing values in the data set. Let **I** be a set of variables called *missing-data indicators* that are in one-to-one correspondence with variables **M**. A network structure that results from adding variables **I** as leaf nodes to G is said to explicate the *missing-data mechanism* and is denoted by $G_\mathbf{I}$. ∎

In Figure 17.6, I is a missing-data indicator and corresponds to variable T. Note that I is always observed, as its value is determined by whether the value of T is missing. We generally use $\mathcal{D}_\mathbf{I}$ to denote an extension of the data set $\mathcal{D}$ that includes missing-data indicators. For example, we have

$\mathcal{D}$	C	T
1	yes	+ve
2	yes	+ve
3	yes	−ve
4	no	?
5	yes	−ve
6	yes	+ve
7	no	?
8	no	−ve

$\mathcal{D}_I$	C	T	I
1	yes	+ve	no
2	yes	+ve	no
3	yes	−ve	no
4	no	?	yes
5	yes	−ve	no
6	yes	+ve	no
7	no	?	yes
8	no	−ve	no

Now that we have two different missing-data mechanisms, we can apply the ML approach in three different ways:

- To the original structure $C \to T$ and the data set $\mathcal{D}$
- To the extended structure G_I in Figure 17.6(a) and the data set $\mathcal{D}_I$
- To the extended structure G_I in Figure 17.6(b) and the data set $\mathcal{D}_I$

That is, we are ignoring the missing-data mechanism in this first case and accounting for it in the second and third cases. Moreover, all three approaches yield estimates for variables C and T as they are shared among all three structures. The question we now face is whether ignoring the missing-data mechanism will change the ML estimates for these variables.

As it turns out, the first and second approaches indeed yield identical estimates that are different from the ones obtained by the third approach. This suggests that the missing-data mechanism can be ignored if it corresponds to the one in Figure 17.6(a) but cannot be ignored if it corresponds to the one in Figure 17.6(b). The following definition provides a general condition for when we can ignore the missing-data mechanism.

> **Definition 17.5.** Let G_I be a network structure that explicates the missing-data mechanism of structure G and data set $\mathcal{D}$. Let $\mathbf{O}$ be variables that are always observed in the data set $\mathcal{D}$ and let $\mathbf{M}$ be the variables that have missing values in the data set. We say that G_I satisfies the *missing at random* (MAR) assumption if $\mathbf{I}$ and $\mathbf{M}$ are d-separated by $\mathbf{O}$ in structure G_I. ∎

Intuitively, G_I satisfies the MAR assumption if once we know the values of variables $\mathbf{O}$, the specific values of variables $\mathbf{M}$ become irrelevant to whether these values are missing in the data set. Figure 17.6(a) satisfies the MAR assumption: once we know the condition of a person, the outcome of their test is irrelevant to whether the test result is missing. Figure 17.6(b) does not satisfy the MAR assumption: even if we know the condition of a person, the test result may still be relevant to whether it will be missing.

If the MAR assumption holds, the missing-data mechanism can be ignored as shown by the following theorem.

> **Theorem 17.9.** *Let G_I and $\mathcal{D}_I$ be a structure and a data set that explicate the missing-data mechanism of G and $\mathcal{D}$. Let θ be the parameters of structure G and θ_I be the parameters of indicator variables $\mathbf{I}$ in structure G_I. If G_I satisfies the MAR assumption, then*
>
> $$\operatorname*{argmax}_{\theta} \mathrm{LL}(\theta|\mathcal{D}) = \operatorname*{argmax}_{\theta} \max_{\theta_I} \mathrm{LL}(\theta, \theta_I|\mathcal{D}_I).$$ ∎

Hence, under the MAR assumption we obtain the same ML estimates θ whether we include or ignore the missing-data mechanism.

Consider now the structure in Figure 17.6(b) and let us present an example of how ignoring this missing-data mechanism can change the ML estimates. To simplify the example, consider a data set with a single case:

$$C = \mathsf{no}, \quad T = ?.$$

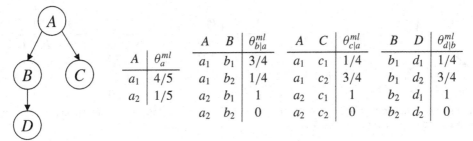

A	θ_a^{ml}
a_1	4/5
a_2	1/5

A	B	$\theta_{b|a}^{ml}$
a_1	b_1	3/4
a_1	b_2	1/4
a_2	b_1	1
a_2	b_2	0

A	C	$\theta_{c|a}^{ml}$
a_1	c_1	1/4
a_1	c_2	3/4
a_2	c_1	1
a_2	c_2	0

B	D	$\theta_{d|b}^{ml}$
b_1	d_1	1/4
b_1	d_2	3/4
b_2	d_1	1
b_2	d_2	0

Figure 17.7: A network structure with its maximum likelihood parameters for the data set in (17.11). The log-likelihood of this structure is -13.3.

If we ignore the missing-data mechanism, that is, compute ML estimates with respect to structure $C \rightarrow T$, we get the following:

- No one has the condition C: $\theta_{C=\text{no}}$ is 1.
- Nothing is learned about the reliability of test T (its parameters are unconstrained).

If we now compute ML estimates with respect to the single case

$$C = \text{no}, \quad T = ?, \quad I = \text{yes},$$

and the missing-data mechanism in Figure 17.6(b), we also get that $\theta_{C=\text{no}}$ is 1 but we also get the following additional constraint (see Exercise 17.18): If the missing-data mechanism is not trivial – that is, if it is not the case that $\theta_{I=\text{yes}|T=-\text{ve}} = \theta_{I=\text{yes}|T=+\text{ve}} = 1$ – then we must have one of the following:

- The test has a true negative rate of 100% and negative test results are always missing, that is, $\theta_{T=-\text{ve}|C=\text{no}} = 1$ and $\theta_{I=\text{yes}|T=-\text{ve}} = 1$.
- The test has a false positive rate of 100% and positive test results are always missing, that is, $\theta_{T=+\text{ve}|C=\text{no}} = 1$ and $\theta_{I=\text{yes}|T=+\text{ve}} = 1$.

These constraints on network parameters are not implied by the ML approach if we ignore the missing-data mechanism. Again, this should not be surprising as the missing-data mechanism in Figure 17.6(b) is not ignorable in this case.

17.4 Learning network structure

We have thus far assumed that we know the structure of a Bayesian network and concerned ourself mostly with estimating the values of its parameters. Our main approach for this estimation has been to search for ML estimates, that is, ones that maximize the probability of observing the given data set. We now assume that the structure itself is unknown and suggest methods for learning it from the given data set. It is natural here to adopt the same approach we adopted for parameter estimation, that is, search for network structures that maximize the probability of observing the given data set. We indeed start with this approach first and then show that it needs some further refinements, leading to a general class of scoring functions for network structures. Our focus here is on learning structures from complete data. Dealing with incomplete data is similar as far as scoring functions are concerned but is much more demanding computationally, as becomes apparent in Section 17.5.

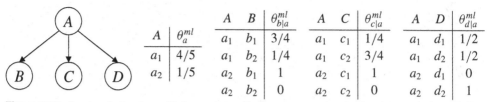

A	θ_a^{ml}
a_1	4/5
a_2	1/5

A	B	$\theta_{b\|a}^{ml}$
a_1	b_1	3/4
a_1	b_2	1/4
a_2	b_1	1
a_2	b_2	0

A	C	$\theta_{c\|a}^{ml}$
a_1	c_1	1/4
a_1	c_2	3/4
a_2	c_1	1
a_2	c_2	0

A	D	$\theta_{d\|a}^{ml}$
a_1	d_1	1/2
a_1	d_2	1/2
a_2	d_1	0
a_2	d_2	1

Figure 17.8: A network structure with its maximum likelihood parameters for the data set in (17.11). The log-likelihood of this structure is -14.1.

Let us now consider Figure 17.7, which depicts a network structure G together with its ML estimates for the following data set:

$\mathcal{D}$	A	B	C	D
$\mathbf{d}_1$	a_1	b_1	c_2	d_1
$\mathbf{d}_2$	a_1	b_1	c_2	d_2
$\mathbf{d}_3$	a_1	b_2	c_1	d_1
$\mathbf{d}_4$	a_2	b_1	c_1	d_2
$\mathbf{d}_5$	a_1	b_1	c_2	d_2

$$(17.11)$$

The log-likelihood of this network structure is given by

$$LL(G|\mathcal{D}) = -13.3$$

Consider now the alternate network structure $G^\star$ depicted in Figure 17.8, together with its ML estimates. This structure has the following likelihood:

$$LL(G^\star|\mathcal{D}) = -14.1,$$

which is smaller than the likelihood for structure G. Hence, we prefer structure G to $G^\star$ if our goal is to search for a maximum likelihood structure.

We next present an algorithm for finding ML tree structures in time and space that are quadratic in the number of nodes in the structure.

17.4.1 Learning tree structures

The algorithm we present in this section is based on a particular scoring measure for tree structures that is expressed in terms of mutual information (see Appendix B). Recall that the mutual information between two variables X and U is a measure of the dependence between these variables in some distribution. Our scoring measure is based on mutual information in the empirical distribution:

$$MI_{\mathcal{D}}(X, U) \overset{def}{=} \sum_{x,u} Pr_{\mathcal{D}}(x, u) \log \frac{Pr_{\mathcal{D}}(x, u)}{Pr_{\mathcal{D}}(x)Pr_{\mathcal{D}}(u)}.$$

In particular, given a tree structure G with edges $U \to X$, our scoring measure is given by

$$tScore(G|\mathcal{D}) \overset{def}{=} \sum_{U \to X} MI_{\mathcal{D}}(X, U).$$

That is, the score is based on adding up the mutual information between every variable and its single parent in the tree structure. Theorem 17.10 states that trees having a maximal likelihood are precisely those trees that maximize the previous score.

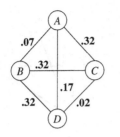

(a) Mutual information graph

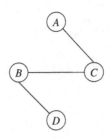

(b) Maximum spanning tree

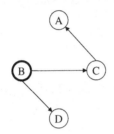

(c) Maximum likelihood tree

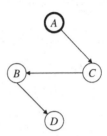

(d) Maximum likelihood tree

Figure 17.9: Searching for ML trees using the data set in (17.11).

Theorem 17.10. *If G is a tree structure, and $\mathcal{D}$ is a complete data set, then*

$$\underset{G}{\operatorname{argmax}}\ \text{tScore}(G|\mathcal{D}) = \underset{G}{\operatorname{argmax}}\ \text{LL}(G|\mathcal{D}).$$
∎

According to Theorem 17.10, we can find a maximum likelihood tree using an algorithm for computing maximum spanning trees. We now illustrate this algorithm by constructing ML trees over variables A, B, C, and D, using the data set in (17.11).

The first step of the algorithm is constructing a complete, undirected graph over all variables as shown in Figure 17.9(a). We include a cost with each edge in the resulting graph representing the mutual information between the two nodes connected by the edge. We then compute a spanning tree with a maximal cost where the cost of a tree is just the sum of costs associated with its edges; see Figure 17.9(b). This method generates an undirected spanning tree that coincides with a number of directed trees. We can then choose any of these directed trees by first selecting a node as a root and then directing edges away from that root. Figures 17.9(c,d) depict two possible directed trees that coincide with the maximum spanning tree in Figure 17.9(b). The resulting tree structures are guaranteed to have a maximal likelihood among all tree structures. For example, each of the trees in Figures 17.9(c,d) has a log-likelihood of -12.1, which is guaranteed to be the largest log-likelihood attained by any tree structure over variables A, B, C, and D.

We can obtain this log-likelihood by computing the probability of each case in the data set using any of these tree structures (and its corresponding ML estimates). We can also use Theorem 17.3, which shows that the log-likelihood corresponds to a sum of terms, one term for each family in the network. For example, if we consider the tree structure G

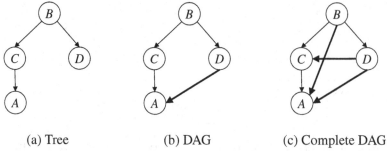

(a) Tree   (b) DAG   (c) Complete DAG

Figure 17.10: Improving the likelihood of a network structure by adding edges.

in Figure 17.9(c), this theorem gives

$$LL(G|\mathcal{D})$$
$$= -N \times (ENT_{\mathcal{D}}(A|C) + ENT_{\mathcal{D}}(B) + ENT_{\mathcal{D}}(C|B) + ENT_{\mathcal{D}}(D|B))$$
$$= -5 \times (.400 + .722 + .649 + .649)$$
$$= -12.1. \tag{17.12}$$

Note how the terms correspond to the families of given tree structure: AC, B, CB, and DB.

17.4.2 Learning DAG structures

Suppose now that our goal is to find a maximum likelihood structure but without restricting ourselves to tree structures. Also consider the DAG structure in Figure 17.10(b), which is obtained by adding an edge $D \rightarrow A$ to the tree structure in Figure 17.10(a); this is the same ML tree in Figure 17.9(c). Using Theorem 17.3, the log-likelihood of this DAG is given by

$$LL(G|\mathcal{D})$$
$$= -N \times (ENT_{\mathcal{D}}(A|C, D) + ENT_{\mathcal{D}}(B) + ENT_{\mathcal{D}}(C|B) + ENT_{\mathcal{D}}(D|B))$$
$$= -5 \times (0 + .722 + .649 + .649)$$
$$= -10.1,$$

which is larger than the log-likelihood of the tree in Figure 17.10(a). Note also that the only difference between the two likelihoods is the entropy term for variable A since this is the only variable with different families in the two structures. In particular, the family of A is AC in the tree and is ACD in the DAG. Moreover,

$$ENT_{\mathcal{D}}(A|C, D) < ENT_{\mathcal{D}}(A|C),$$

and, hence,

$$-ENT_{\mathcal{D}}(A|C, D) > -ENT_{\mathcal{D}}(A|C),$$

which is why the DAG has a larger log-likelihood than the tree. However, this is not completely accidental as shown by Theorem 17.11 .

Theorem 17.11. *If* $U \subseteq U^\star$, *then* $ENT(X|U) \geq ENT(X|U^\star)$.   ∎

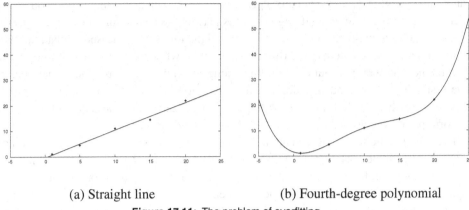

(a) Straight line   (b) Fourth-degree polynomial

Figure 17.11: The problem of overfitting.

That is, by adding more parents to a variable, we never increase its entropy term and, hence, never decrease the log-likelihood of resulting structure.

Corollary 12. *If DAG $G^\star$ is the result of adding edges to DAG G, then*

$$\mathrm{LL}(G^\star|\mathcal{D}) \geq \mathrm{LL}(G|\mathcal{D}).$$ ∎

According to this corollary, which follows immediately from Theorems 17.3 and 17.11, if we simply search for a network structure with maximal likelihood, we end up choosing a complete network structure, that is, a DAG to which no more edges can be added (without introducing directed cycles).[8]

Complete DAGs are undesirable for a number of reasons. First, they make no assertions of conditional independence and, hence, their topology does not reveal any properties of the distribution they induce. Second, a complete DAG over n variables has a treewidth of $n - 1$ and is therefore impossible to work with practically. Third and most importantly, complete DAGs suffer from the problem of *overfitting,* which refers to the use of a model that has too many parameters compared to the available data.

The classical example for illustrating the problem of overfitting is that of finding a polynomial that fits a given set of data points $(x_1, y_1), \ldots, (x_n, y_n)$. Consider the following data points for an example:

x	y
1	1.10
5	4.5
10	11
15	14.5
20	22

Looking at this data set, we expect the relationship between x and y to be linear, suggesting a model of the form $y = ax + b$; see Figure 17.11(a). Yet the linear function does not provide a perfect fit for the data as the relationship is not precisely linear. However, if we insist on a perfect fit we can use a fourth-degree polynomial that is guaranteed to fit the data perfectly (we have five data points and a fourth-degree polynomial has five free

---

[8] Recall that there are $n!$ complete DAGs over n variables. Each of these DAGs corresponds to a total variable ordering $X_1, \ldots, X_n$ in which variable X_i has $X_1, \ldots, X_{i-1}$ as its parents.

parameters). Figure 17.11(b) depicts a perfect fit for the data using such a polynomial. As is clear from this figure, even though the fit is perfect the polynomial does not appear to provide a good generalization of the data beyond the range of the observed data points.

In summary, the problem of overfitting materializes when we focus on learning a model that fits the data well without constraining enough the number of free model parameters. The result is that we end up adopting models that are more complex than necessary. Moreover, such models tend to provide poor generalizations of the data and, therefore, perform poorly on cases that are not part of the given data set.

Even though there is no agreed upon solution to the problem of overfitting, all available solutions tend to be based on a common principle known as *Occam's Razor*, which says that we should prefer simpler models over more complex models, others things being equal. To realize this principle, we need a measure of model complexity and a method for balancing the complexity of a model with its data fit. For Bayesian networks (and many other modeling frameworks), model complexity is measured using the number of independent parameters in the model.

Definition 17.6. Let G be a DAG over variables $X_1, \ldots, X_n$ with corresponding parents $\mathbf{U}_1, \ldots, \mathbf{U}_n$ and let $\mathbf{Y}^{\#}$ denote the number of instantiations for variables $\mathbf{Y}$. The *dimension* of DAG G is defined as

$$\|G\| \;\overset{def}{=}\; \sum_{i=1}^{n} \|X_i \mathbf{U}_i\|$$

$$\|X_i \mathbf{U}_i\| \;\overset{def}{=}\; (X_i^{\#} - 1)\mathbf{U}_i^{\#}. \qquad \blacksquare$$

The dimension of a DAG is therefore equal to the number of independent parameters in its CPTs. Note that for a given parent instantiation $\mathbf{u}_i$, all but one of the parameters $\theta_{x_i|\mathbf{u}_i}$ are independent. For example, considering Figure 17.10 and assuming that variables are all binary, we have the following dimensions for the depicted network structures (from left to right): 7, 9, and 15.

Using this notion of model complexity, we can define the following common class of scoring measures for a network structure G and data set $\mathcal{D}$ of size N:

$$\text{Score}(G|\mathcal{D}) \;\overset{def}{=}\; \text{LL}(G|\mathcal{D}) - \psi(N) \cdot \|G\|. \qquad (17.13)$$

The first component of this score, $\text{LL}(G|\mathcal{D})$, is the log-likelihood function we considered previously. The second component, $\psi(N) \cdot \|G\|$, is a penalty term that favors simpler models, that is, ones with a smaller number of independent parameters. Note that this penalty term has a weight, $\psi(N) \geq 0$, which is a function of the data set size N.

When the penalty weight $\psi(N)$ is a constant that is independent of N, we obtain a score in which model complexity is a secondary issue. To see this, note that the log-likelihood function $\text{LL}(G|\mathcal{D})$ grows linearly in the data set size N (see (17.3)), and will quickly dominate the penalty term. In this case, the model complexity will only be used to distinguish between models that have relatively equal log-likelihood terms. This scoring measure is known as the *Akaike information criterion* (AIC).

Another yet more common choice of the penalty weight is $\psi(N) = \frac{\log_2 N}{2}$, which leads to a more influential penalty term. Note, however, that this term grows logarithmically in N, while the log-likelihood term grows linearly in N. Hence, the influence of model complexity decreases as N grows, allowing the log-likelihood term to eventually dominate the score. This penalty weight gives rise to the *minimum description length* (MDL) score:

$$\text{MDL}(G|\mathcal{D}) \stackrel{def}{=} \text{LL}(G|\mathcal{D}) - \left(\frac{\log_2 N}{2}\right) ||G||. \tag{17.14}$$

For example, the structure in Figure 17.10(a) has the following MDL score:

$$= -12.1 - \left(\frac{\log_2 5}{2}\right)(7)$$
$$= -12.1 - 8.1$$
$$= -20.2,$$

while the one in Figure 17.10(b) has the following score:

$$= -10.1 - \left(\frac{\log_2 5}{2}\right)(9)$$
$$= -10.1 - 10.4$$
$$= -20.5$$

Therefore, the MDL score prefers the first structure even though it has a smaller log-likelihood.

The MDL score is also known as the *Bayesian information criterion* (BIC). It is sometimes expressed as the negative of the score in (17.14), where the goal is to minimize the score instead of maximizing it. Note, however, that both the scores in (17.13) and (17.14) are ≤ 0.

17.5 Searching for network structure

Searching for a network structure that optimizes a particular score can be quite expensive due to the very large number of structures one may need to consider. As a result, greedy algorithms tend to be of more practical use when learning network structures. Systematic search algorithms can also be practical but only under some conditions. However, both classes of algorithms rely for their efficient implementation on a property that most scoring functions have. This property is known as *decomposability* or *modularity* as it allows us to decompose the score into an aggregate of local scores, one for each network family.

Consider for example, the score given in (17.13) and let $X\mathbf{U}$ range over the families of DAG G. This score can be decomposed as

$$\text{Score}(G|\mathcal{D}) = \sum_{X\mathbf{U}} \text{Score}(X, \mathbf{U}|\mathcal{D}), \tag{17.15}$$

where

$$\text{Score}(X, \mathbf{U}|\mathcal{D}) \stackrel{def}{=} -N \cdot \text{ENT}_{\mathcal{D}}(X|\mathbf{U}) - \psi(N) \cdot ||X\mathbf{U}||.$$

Note how the score is a sum of local scores, each contributed by some family $X\mathbf{U}$. Note also how the contribution of each family is split into two parts: one resulting from a decomposition of the log-likelihood component of the score (see (17.3)) and the other resulting from a decomposition of the penalty component (see Definition 17.6).

The previous decomposition enables a number of heuristic and optimal search algorithms to be implemented more efficiently. We discuss some of these methods next.

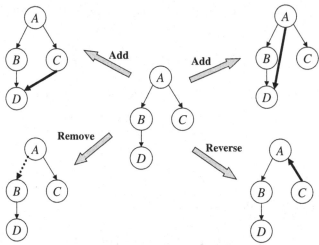

Figure 17.12: Local search for a network structure.

17.5.1 Local search

One can search for a network structure by starting with some initial structure and then modifying it locally to increase its score. The initial structure can be chosen randomly, based on some prior knowledge, or can be a tree structure constructed optimally from data using the quadratic algorithm discussed previously. The local modifications to the structure are then constrained to adding an edge, removing an edge, or reversing an edge while ensuring that the structure remains a DAG (see Figure 17.12). These local changes to the network structure also change the score, possibly increasing or decreasing it. However, the goal is to commit to the change that increases the score the most. If none of the local changes can increase the score, the algorithm terminates and returns the current structure.

A number of observations are in order about this local search algorithm. First, it is not guaranteed to return an optimal network structure, that is, one that has the largest score. The only guarantee provided by the algorithm is that the structure it returns is locally optimal in that no local change can improve its score. This suboptimal behavior of local search can usually be improved by techniques such as *random restarts*. According to this technique, we would repeat the local search multiple times, each time starting with a different initial network, and then return the network with the best score across all repetitions.

The second observation about the previous local search algorithms relates to updating the score after applying local changes. Consider again Figure 17.12 and let G be the network structure in the center and $G^\star$ be the network structure that results from deleting edge $A \to B$. Since this change affects only the family of node B and given the decomposition of (17.15), we have

$$\text{Score}(G^\star|\mathcal{D}) = \text{Score}(G|\mathcal{D}) - \text{Score}(B, A|\mathcal{D}) + \text{Score}(B|\mathcal{D}).$$

That is, to compute the new score, we subtract the contribution of B's old family, $\text{Score}(B, A|\mathcal{D})$, and then add the contribution of B's new family, $\text{Score}(B|\mathcal{D})$. More generally, adding or removing an edge changes only one family, while reversing an edge changes only two families. Hence, the score can always be updated locally as a result of the local network change induced by adding, removing, or reversing an edge.

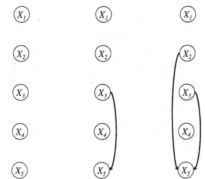

Figure 17.13: Greedy search for a parent set for variable X_5.

17.5.2 Constraining the search space

A common technique for reducing the search space size is to assume a total ordering on network variables and then search only among network structures that are consistent with the chosen order. Suppose for example that we use the variable order $X_1, \ldots, X_n$. The search process can now by viewed as trying to find for each variable X_i a set of parents $\mathbf{U}_i \subseteq X_1, \ldots, X_{i-1}$.

Not only does this technique reduce the size of search space, it also allows us to decompose the search problem into n independent problems, each concerned with finding a set of parents for some network variable. That is, the search problem now reduces to considering each variable X_i independently and then finding a set of parents $\mathbf{U}_i \subseteq X_1, \ldots, X_{i-1}$ that maximize the corresponding local score $\text{Score}(X_i, \mathbf{U}_i|\mathcal{D})$. We next discuss both greedy and optimal methods for maximizing these local scores.

Greedy search

One of the more effective heuristic algorithms for optimizing a family score is known as K3.[9] This algorithm starts with an empty set of parents, successively adding variables to the set one at a time until such additions no longer increase the score. Consider Figure 17.13 for an example, where the goal is to find a set of parents for X_5 from the set of variables $X_1, \ldots, X_4$. The K3 algorithm will start by setting $\mathbf{U}_5$ to the empty set and then finds a variable X_i (if any), $i = 1, \ldots, 4$, that maximizes

$$\text{Score}(X_5, X_i|\mathcal{D}) \geq \text{Score}(X_5|\mathcal{D}).$$

Suppose that X_3 happens to be such a variable. The algorithm then sets $\mathbf{U}_5 = \{X_3\}$ and searches for another variable X_i in X_1, X_2, X_4 that maximizes

$$\text{Score}(X_5, X_3 X_i|\mathcal{D}) \geq \text{Score}(X_5, X_3|\mathcal{D}).$$

Suppose again that X_2 happens to be such a variable, leading to the new set of parents $\mathbf{U}_5 = \{X_2, X_3\}$. It may happen that adding X_1 to this set does not increase the score and neither will adding X_4. In this case, K3 terminates, returning $\mathbf{U}_5 = \{X_2, X_3\}$ as the parent set for X_5.

---

[9] The name K3 refers to the version of this algorithm that optimizes the MDL score, although it also applies to other scores as well. Another version of this heuristic algorithm, called K2, works similarly but uses a different score to be discussed in Chapter 18.

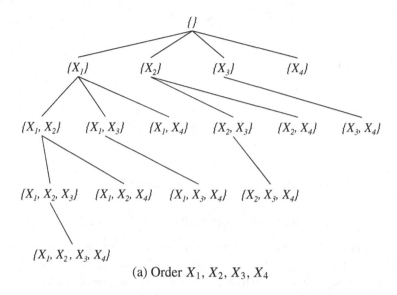

(a) Order X_1, X_2, X_3, X_4

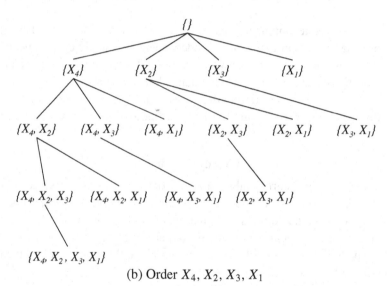

(b) Order X_4, X_2, X_3, X_1

Figure 17.14: A search tree for identifying an optimal parent set for variable X_5, expanded according to two different variable orders.

K3 is a greedy algorithm that is not guaranteed to identify the optimal set of parents $\mathbf{U}_i$, that is, the one that maximizes $\text{Score}(X_i, \mathbf{U}_i | \mathcal{D})$. Therefore, it is not uncommon to use the structure obtained by this algorithm as a starting point for other algorithms, such as the local search algorithm discussed previously or the optimal search algorithm we discuss next.

Optimal search

We next discuss an optimal search algorithm for network structures that is based on branch-and-bound depth-first search. Similar to K3, the algorithm assumes a total order of network variables $X_1, \ldots, X_n$ and searches only among network structures that are consistent with this order. As mentioned previously, this allows us to decompose the search process into n independent search problems.

Figure 17.14(a) depicts a search tree for finding a set of parents $\mathbf{U}_5$ for variable X_5 assuming a total order $X_1, \ldots, X_n$. The first level of this tree has a single node corresponding to an empty set of parents, $\mathbf{U}_5 = \{\}$, and each additional level is obtained by adding a single variable to each parent set at the previous level while avoiding the generation of duplicate sets. Tree nodes are then in one-to-one correspondence with the possible parent sets for X_5. Hence, a search tree for variable X_i has a total of 2^{i-1} nodes, corresponding to the number of subsets we can choose from variables $X_1, \ldots, X_{i-1}$.

We can search the tree in Figure 17.14(a) using depth-first search while maintaining the score s of the best parent set visited thus far. When visiting a node $\mathbf{U}_i$, we need to evaluate $\mathrm{Score}(X_i, \mathbf{U}_i | \mathcal{D})$ and check whether it is better than the score s obtained thus far. Depth-first search guarantees that every parent set is visited, leading us to identify an optimal parent set at the end of the search. However, this optimality comes at the expense of exponential complexity as we have to consider 2^{i-1} parent sets for variable X_i.

The complexity of this algorithm can be improved on average if we can compute for each search node $\mathbf{U}_i$ an upper bound on $\mathrm{Score}(X_i, \mathbf{U}_i^\star | \mathcal{D})$, where $\mathbf{U}_i \subseteq \mathbf{U}_i^\star$. If the computed upper bound at node $\mathbf{U}_i$ is not better than the best score s obtained thus far, then we can prune $\mathbf{U}_i$ and all nodes below it in the search tree since none of these parent sets can be better than the us found thus far. This pruning allows us to escape the exponential complexity in some cases. Clearly, the extent of pruning depends on the quality of upper bound used. Theorem 17.12 provides an upper bound for the MDL score.

Theorem 17.12. *Let $\mathbf{U}_i$ be a parent set and let $\mathbf{U}_i^+$ be the largest parent set appearing below $\mathbf{U}_i$ in the search tree. If $\mathbf{U}_i^\star$ is a parent set in the tree rooted at $\mathbf{U}_i$, then*

$$\mathrm{MDL}(X_i, \mathbf{U}_i^\star | \mathcal{D}) \leq -N \cdot \mathrm{ENT}_{\mathcal{D}}(X_i | \mathbf{U}_i^+) - \psi(N) \cdot ||X_i \mathbf{U}_i||. \qquad \blacksquare$$

This bound needs to be computed at each node $\mathbf{U}_i$ in the search tree. Moreover, unless the bound is greater than the best score obtained thus far, we can prune all nodes $\mathbf{U}_i^\star$. Consider Figure 17.14(a) for an example. At the search node $\mathbf{U}_5 = \{X_2\}$, we get $\mathbf{U}_5^+ = \{X_2, X_3, X_4\}$. Moreover, $\mathbf{U}_5^\star$ ranges over parent sets $\{X_2\}$, $\{X_2, X_3\}$, $\{X_2, X_4\}$, and $\{X_2, X_3, X_4\}$.

Consider now the search tree in Figure 17.14(b) compared to the one in Figure 17.14(a). Both trees enumerate the sixteen parent sets for variable X_5 yet the order of enumeration is different. Consider for example the first branch in each tree. Variable X_1 appears more frequently in the first branch of Figure 17.14(a), while variable X_4 appears more frequently in the first branch of Figure 17.14(b). Suppose now that variable X_4 tends to reduce the entropy of variable X_5 more than does X_1. We then expect the search in Figure 17.14(b) to visit parent sets with higher scores first. For example, the third node visited in Figure 17.14(a) is $\{X_1, X_2\}$, while the third node visited in Figure 17.14(b) is $\{X_4, X_2\}$. Visiting parent sets with higher scores earlier leads to more aggressive pruning, which is why the search tree in Figure 17.14(b) is preferred in this case. That is, we prefer a tree that is expanded according to a variable order $X_{k_1}, \ldots, X_{k_{i-1}}$, where $\mathrm{ENT}(X_i | X_{k_1}) \leq \cdots \leq \mathrm{ENT}(X_i | X_{k_{i-1}})$. It is for this reason that this order of expansion is sometimes adopted by optimal search algorithms.

We close this section by pointing out that our discussion on the search for network structures has been restricted to complete data sets. The main reason for this is computational. For example, the likelihood of a network structure does not admit a closed form when the data set is incomplete. Moreover, it does not decompose into components as given by Theorem 17.3. Hence, algorithms for learning structures with incomplete data typically involve two searches: an outer search in the space of network structures and an inner search in the space of network parameters. We provide some references in the bibliographic remarks section on some techniques for implementing these double searches.

Bibliographic remarks

The EM algorithm was introduced in Dempster et al. [1977] and adopted to Bayesian networks in Lauritzen [1995]. The gradient ascent algorithm was proposed in Russell et al. [1995], which presented the gradient form of Theorem 17.8 (see also Thiesson [1995]). The foundations for handling missing data, including the introduction of the MAR assumption, is given in Rubin [1976]. A more comprehensive treatment of the subject is available in Little and Rubin [2002].

The quadratic algorithm for learning ML tree structures was proposed by Chow and Liu [1968]. The MDL principle was introduced in Rissanen [1978] and then adopted into a score for Bayesian network structures in Bouckaert [1993], Lam and Bacchus [1994], and Suzuki [1993]. The BIC score, which is the same as the MDL score, was introduced in Schwarz [1978] as an approximation of the marginal likelihood function, discussed in Chapter 18. The AIC score was introduced in Akaike [1974].

The K2 algorithm was proposed by Cooper and Herskovits [1991; 1992]. The branch-and-bound algorithm with a fixed variable ordering is due to Suzuki [1993]. The version discussed in this chapter is due to Tian [2000], which proposed the MDL bound of Theorem 17.12.

The complexity of learning network structures is shown to be NP-hard in Chickering [1996]. Methods for learning network structures in the case of incomplete data are presented in Friedman [1998], Meilua and Jordan [1998], Singh [1997], and Thiesson et al. [1999], while methods for learning Bayesian networks with local structure in the CPTs are discussed in Buntine [1991], Díez [1993], Chickering et al. [1997], Friedman and Goldszmidt [1996], and Meek and Heckerman [1997].

A comprehensive coverage of information theory concepts is given in Cover and Thomas [1991], including a thorough discussion of entropy, mutual information, and the KL divergence. A tutorial on learning Bayesian networks is provided in Heckerman [1998], which surveys most of the foundational work on the subject and provides many references for more advanced topics than covered in this chapter. Related surveys of the literature can also be found in Buntine [1996] and Jordan [1998]. The subject of learning Bayesian networks is also discussed in Cowell et al. [1999] and Neapolitan [2004], which provide more details on some of the subjects discussed here and cover additional topics such as networks with continuous variables.

Another approach for learning Bayesian network structures, known as the *constraint-based approach*, follows more closely the definition of Bayesian networks as encoders of conditional independence relationships. According to this approach, we make some judgments about the (conditional) dependencies and independencies that follow from the data and then use them as constraints to reconstruct the network structure. For example, if we determine from the data that variable X is independent of Y given Z, then we can infer that there is no edge between X and Y in the network structure. Two representative algorithms of constraint-based learning are the *IC algorithm* [Pearl, 2000] and the *PC algorithm* Spirtes et al. [2001]. An orthogonal perspective on learning network structures, based on causality is discussed in Heckerman [1995], Glymour and Cooper [1999], and Pearl [2000].

One of the main reasons for learning Bayesian networks is to use them as classifiers, and one of the more common Bayesian network classifiers is the naive Bayes classifier [Duda and Hart, 1973], which is described in Exercise 17.15. Quite a bit of attention has been given to this class of classifiers and its extensions, such as the *tree-augmented naive Bayes* (TAN) classifier [Friedman et al., 1997; Cerquides and de Mantaras, 2005] and its variants [Eamonn J. Keogh, 2002; Webb et al., 2005; Jing et al., 2005]. When learning Bayesian network classifiers discriminatively, one typically maximizes the conditional log-likelihood function defined in Exercise 17.16 as this will typically lead to networks that give better classification performance; see also [Ng and Jordan, 2001]. Note, however, that network parameters that optimize the conditional log-likelihood function may not be meaningful probabilistically. Hence, an estimated parameter value, say, $\theta_{a|\bar{b}} = .8$ should not be interpreted as an estimate .8 of the probability $\Pr(a|\bar{b})$ (contrast this to Theorem 17.1). Moreover, optimizing the conditional log-likelihood function can be computationally more demanding than optimizing the log-likelihood function since the decomposition of Theorem 17.3 no longer holds. Approaches have been proposed for learning arbitrary network structures that optimize the conditional log-likelihood function (e.g., [Guo and Greiner, 2005; Grossman and Domingos, 2004]) and for estimating the parameters of these network structures (e.g., [Greiner et al., 2005; Roos et al., 2005]).

17.6 Exercises

17.1. Consider a Bayesian network structure with the following edges $A \to B$, $A \to C$, and $A \to D$. Compute the ML parameter estimates for this structure given the following data set:

Case	A	B	C	D
1	T	F	F	F
2	T	F	F	T
3	F	F	T	F
4	T	T	F	T
5	F	F	T	T
6	F	T	T	F
7	F	T	T	T
8	T	F	F	T
9	F	F	T	F
10	T	T	T	T

17.2. Consider a Bayesian network structure with edges $A \to B$ and $B \to C$. Compute the ML parameter estimates for this structure given the following data set:

Case	A	B	C
1	T	F	F
2	T	F	F
3	F	F	T
4	T	F	F

Are the ML estimates unique for this data set? If not, how many ML estimates do we have in this case?

17.3. Let G be a network structure with families $X\mathbf{U}$, let $\mathcal{D}$ be a complete data set, and suppose that $\Pr_\mathcal{D}(\mathbf{u}) = 0$ for some instantiation $\mathbf{u}$ of parent set $\mathbf{U}$. Show that the likelihood function $LL(\theta|\mathcal{D})$ is independent of parameters $\theta_{x|\mathbf{u}}$ for all x.

17.4. Let G be a network structure with families $X\mathbf{U}$ and let $\mathcal{D}$ be a complete data set. Prove the following form for the likelihood of structure G:

$$L(G|\mathcal{D}) = \prod_{X\mathbf{U}} \prod_{x\mathbf{u}} \left[\theta^{ml}_{x|\mathbf{u}}\right]^{\mathcal{D}\#(x\mathbf{u})},$$

where $\theta^{ml}_{x|\mathbf{u}}$ is the ML estimate for parameter $\theta_{x|\mathbf{u}}$.

17.5. Consider a Bayesian network with edges $A \to B$, $A \to C$, and the parameters θ:

A	θ_a
T	.3
F	.7

A	B	$\theta_{b|a}$
T	T	.5
T	F	.5
F	T	.8
F	F	.2

A	C	$\theta_{c|a}$
T	T	.1
T	F	.9
F	T	.5
F	F	.5

Consider the following data set $\mathcal{D}$:

Case	A	B	C
1	F	?	T
2	F	T	T
3	?	F	T
4	?	T	F
5	T	F	?

What is the expected empirical distribution for data set $\mathcal{D}$ given parameters θ, $\Pr_{\mathcal{D},\theta}(.)$?

17.6. Consider Exercise 17.5 and assume that the given CPTs are the initial CPTs used by EM. Compute the EM parameter estimates after one iteration of the algorithm.

17.7. Consider Exercise 17.5 and assume that the given CPTs are those used by the gradient ascent approach for estimating parameters. Decide whether this approach increases or decreases the values of parameters $\theta_{\bar{a}}$, $\theta_{b|a}$, and $\theta_{\bar{c}|a}$ in its first iteration. Use the soft-max search space to impose parameter constraints.

17.8. Consider a complete data set $\mathcal{D}$ and let G_1 and G_2 be two complete DAGs. Prove or disprove $LL(G_1|\mathcal{D}) = LL(G_2|\mathcal{D})$. If the equality does not hold, provide a counterexample.

17.9. What happens if we apply the EM algorithm to a complete data set? That is, what estimates does it return as a function of the initial estimates with which it starts?

17.10. Compute the derivative $\dfrac{\partial \theta_{x|\mathbf{u}}}{\partial \tau_{x|\mathbf{u}}}$ given in Equation 17.8.

17.11. Compute an ML tree structure for the data set in Exercise 17.1. What is the total number of ML tree structures for this data set?

17.12. Consider a Bayesian network structure $X \to Y$ and a data set $\mathcal{D}$ of size N, where X is hidden and Y is observed in every case of $\mathcal{D}$. Show that ML estimates are characterized by

$$\sum_x \theta_x \theta_{y|x} = \frac{\mathcal{D}\#(y)}{N}$$

for all values y, that is, ML estimates are those that ensure $\Pr(y) = \mathcal{D}\#(y)/N$ for all y.

17.13. Consider a Bayesian network structure $X \to Y$ and $Y \to Z$ and a data set $\mathcal{D}$ of size N in which Y is hidden yet X and Z are observed in every case of $\mathcal{D}$. Provide a characterization of the ML estimates for this problem, together with some concrete parameter estimates that satisfy the characterization.

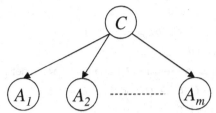

Figure 17.15: A naive Bayes network structure.

17.14. Consider the naive Bayes network structure in Figure 17.15 and suppose that $\mathcal{D}$ is a data set in which variable C is hidden and variables $A_1, \ldots, A_m$ are observed in all cases. Show that if EM is applied to this problem with parameters having uniform initial values, then it will converge in one step, returning the following estimates:

$$\theta_c = \frac{1}{|C|}$$

$$\theta_{a_i|c} = \frac{\mathcal{D}\#(a_i)}{N}.$$

Here $|C|$ is the cardinality of variable C, N is the size of given data set, and $\mathcal{D}\#(a_i)$ is the number of cases in the data set that contain instantiation a_i of variable A_i.

17.15. Consider the naive Bayes network structure in Figure 17.15 and let $\mathrm{Pr}_\theta(.)$ be the distribution induced by this structure and parametrization θ. Let us refer to variable C as the class variable, variables $A_1, \ldots, A_m$ as the attributes, and each instantiation $a_1, \ldots, a_m$ as an instance. Suppose that we now use this network as a classifier where we assign to each instance $a_1, \ldots, a_m$ the class c that maximizes $\mathrm{Pr}_\theta(c|a_1, \ldots, a_m)$. Show that when variable C is binary, the class of instance $a_1, \ldots, a_m$ is c if

$$\log \theta_c + \sum_{i=1}^{m} \log \theta_{a_i|c} \;>\; \log \theta_{\bar{c}} + \sum_{i=1}^{m} \log \theta_{a_i|\bar{c}}.$$

Note: This is known as a *naive Bayes classifier*.

17.16. Consider Exercise 17.15, let $\mathcal{D}$ be a complete data set that contains the cases $c^i, a_1^i, \ldots, a_m^i$ for $i = 1, \ldots, N$, and let $\mathrm{Pr}_{\mathcal{D}}(.)$ be the empirical distribution induced by data set $\mathcal{D}$. Define the *conditional log-likelihood* function as

$$\mathrm{CLL}(\mathcal{D}|\theta) \stackrel{def}{=} \sum_{i=1}^{N} \log \mathrm{Pr}_\theta(c^i|a_1^i, \ldots, a_m^i).$$

Define also the *conditional KL divergence* as

$$\sum_{a_1, \ldots, a_m} \mathrm{Pr}_{\mathcal{D}}(a_1, \ldots, a_m) \cdot \mathrm{KL}(\mathrm{Pr}_{\mathcal{D}}(C|a_1, \ldots, a_m), \mathrm{Pr}_\theta(C|a_1, \ldots, a_m)).$$

Show that a parametrization θ maximizes the conditional log-likelihood function iff it minimizes the conditional KL divergence.

17.17. Consider Exercise 17.16 and let $\mathcal{D}'$ be an incomplete data set that is obtained from data set $\mathcal{D}$ by removing the values of class variable C, that is, $\mathcal{D}'$ contains the cases $a_1^i, \ldots, a_m^i$ for $i = 1, \ldots, N$. Show that

$$\mathrm{LL}(\mathcal{D}|\theta) = \mathrm{CLL}(\mathcal{D}|\theta) + \mathrm{LL}(\mathcal{D}'|\theta).$$

17.18. Consider the structure in Figure 17.6(b) and a data set with a single case:

$$C = no, \quad T = ?, \quad I = yes.$$

Show that the ML estimates are characterized as follows:

- $\theta_{C=no}$ is 1.

- One of the following must be true for the parameters of test T and missing-data indicator I:

- $\theta_{T=-ve|C=no} = 1$ and $\theta_{I=yes|T=-ve} = 1$
- $\theta_{T=+ve|C=no} = 1$ and $\theta_{I=yes|T=+ve} = 1$
- $\theta_{I=yes|T=-ve} = \theta_{I=yes|T=+ve} = 1$.

17.19. Consider the data set $\mathcal{D}$ in Exercise 17.1 and the following network structures:

- G_1: $A \to B$, $B \to C$, $C \to D$, and $A \to D$
- G_2: $A \to B$, $B \to C$, $C \to D$, and $B \to D$.

Which structure has a higher likelihood given $\mathcal{D}$? What is the exact value for $\mathrm{LL}(G_1|\mathcal{D}) - \mathrm{LL}(G_2|\mathcal{D})$?

17.20. Compute the MDL score for the network structure in Figure 17.10(c) given the data set in (17.11).

17.7 Proofs

Lemma 17.1. *Consider a fixed distribution $\mathrm{Pr}_\star(\mathbf{X})$ and a variable distribution $\mathrm{Pr}(\mathbf{X})$. Then*

$$\mathrm{Pr}_\star = \underset{\mathrm{Pr}}{\mathrm{argmax}} \sum_{\mathbf{x}} \mathrm{Pr}_\star(\mathbf{x}) \log \mathrm{Pr}(\mathbf{x}),$$

and $\mathrm{Pr}_\star$ is the only distribution that satisfies this property, that is, $\mathrm{Pr}_\star$ is the only distribution that maximizes this quantity.

PROOF. First, note the following key property of the KL divergence:

$$\mathrm{KL}(\mathrm{Pr}_\star(\mathbf{X}), \mathrm{Pr}(\mathbf{X})) = \sum_{\mathbf{x}} \mathrm{Pr}_\star(\mathbf{x}) \log \frac{\mathrm{Pr}_\star(\mathbf{x})}{\mathrm{Pr}(\mathbf{x})} \geq 0,$$

where $\mathrm{KL}(\mathrm{Pr}_\star, \mathrm{Pr}) = 0$ if and only if $\mathrm{Pr}_\star = \mathrm{Pr}$ [Cover and Thomas, 1991]. It then immediately follows that

$$\sum_{\mathbf{x}} \mathrm{Pr}_\star(\mathbf{x}) \log \mathrm{Pr}_\star(\mathbf{x}) \geq \sum_{\mathbf{x}} \mathrm{Pr}_\star(\mathbf{x}) \log \mathrm{Pr}(\mathbf{x}),$$

with the equality holding if and only if $\mathrm{Pr}_\star = \mathrm{Pr}$. Hence, $\mathrm{Pr}_\star$ is the only distribution that maximizes the given quantity. ∎

PROOF OF THEOREM 17.1. As given in the proof of Theorem 17.3, we have

$$\mathrm{LL}(\theta|\mathcal{D}) = N \sum_{XU} \sum_{x\mathbf{u}} \mathrm{Pr}_{\mathcal{D}}(x\mathbf{u}) \log \mathrm{Pr}_\theta(x|\mathbf{u})$$

$$= N \sum_{XU} \sum_{\mathbf{u}} \mathrm{Pr}_{\mathcal{D}}(\mathbf{u}) \sum_{x} \mathrm{Pr}_{\mathcal{D}}(x|\mathbf{u}) \log \mathrm{Pr}_\theta(x|\mathbf{u}).$$

Therefore, the log-likelihood function decomposes into independent components that correspond to parent instantiations $\mathbf{u}$:

$$\sum_{x} \mathrm{Pr}_{\mathcal{D}}(x|\mathbf{u}) \log \mathrm{Pr}_\theta(x|\mathbf{u}).$$

Each of these components can be maximized independently using Lemma 17.1, which says that the distribution $\mathrm{Pr}_\theta(x|\mathbf{u})$ that maximizes this quantity is unique and is equal to $\mathrm{Pr}_{\mathcal{D}}(x|\mathbf{u})$. ∎

PROOF OF THEOREM 17.2.

$$\mathrm{KL}(\mathrm{Pr}_{\mathcal{D}}(\mathbf{X}), \mathrm{Pr}_{\theta}(\mathbf{X})) = \sum_{\mathbf{x}} \mathrm{Pr}_{\mathcal{D}}(\mathbf{x}) \log \frac{\mathrm{Pr}_{\mathcal{D}}(\mathbf{x})}{\mathrm{Pr}_{\theta}(\mathbf{x})}$$

$$= \sum_{\mathbf{x}} \mathrm{Pr}_{\mathcal{D}}(\mathbf{x}) \log \mathrm{Pr}_{\mathcal{D}}(\mathbf{x}) - \sum_{\mathbf{x}} \mathrm{Pr}_{\mathcal{D}}(\mathbf{x}) \log \mathrm{Pr}_{\theta}(\mathbf{x}).$$

Since the term $\sum_{\mathbf{x}} \mathrm{Pr}_{\mathcal{D}}(\mathbf{x}) \log \mathrm{Pr}_{\mathcal{D}}(\mathbf{x})$ does not depend on the choice of parameters θ, minimizing the KL divergence $\mathrm{KL}(\mathrm{Pr}_{\mathcal{D}}(\mathbf{X}), \mathrm{Pr}_{\theta}(\mathbf{X}))$ corresponds to maximizing $\sum_{\mathbf{x}} \mathrm{Pr}_{\mathcal{D}}(\mathbf{x}) \log \mathrm{Pr}_{\theta}(\mathbf{x})$. We also have

$$\sum_{\mathbf{x}} \mathrm{Pr}_{\mathcal{D}}(\mathbf{x}) \log \mathrm{Pr}_{\theta}(\mathbf{x}) = \sum_{\mathbf{x}} \frac{\mathcal{D}\#(\mathbf{x})}{N} \log \mathrm{Pr}_{\theta}(\mathbf{x})$$

$$= \frac{1}{N} \sum_{\mathbf{x}} \mathcal{D}\#(\mathbf{x}) \log \mathrm{Pr}_{\theta}(\mathbf{x})$$

$$= \frac{1}{N} \sum_{\mathbf{x}} \sum_{\mathbf{d}_i = \mathbf{x}} \log \mathrm{Pr}_{\theta}(\mathbf{d}_i)$$

$$= \frac{1}{N} \sum_{i=1}^{N} \log \mathrm{Pr}_{\theta}(\mathbf{d}_i)$$

$$= \frac{1}{N} \log \prod_{i=1}^{N} \mathrm{Pr}_{\theta}(\mathbf{d}_i)$$

$$= \frac{\log \mathrm{L}(\theta | \mathcal{D})}{N}.$$

Hence, minimizing the KL divergence $\mathrm{KL}(\mathrm{Pr}_{\mathcal{D}}(\mathbf{X}), \mathrm{Pr}_{\theta}(\mathbf{X}))$ is equivalent to maximizing $\log \mathrm{L}(\theta | \mathcal{D})$, which is equivalent to maximizing $\mathrm{L}(\theta | \mathcal{D})$. ∎

PROOF OF THEOREM 17.3. We first consider the decomposition of the log-likelihood function $\mathrm{LL}(\theta | \mathcal{D})$ for an arbitrary set of parameter estimates θ:

$$\mathrm{LL}(\theta | \mathcal{D}) = \sum_{i=1}^{N} \log \mathrm{Pr}_{\theta}(\mathbf{d}_i)$$

$$= \sum_{i=1}^{N} \log \prod_{\mathbf{d}_i \models x\mathbf{u}} \mathrm{Pr}_{\theta}(x | \mathbf{u}) \quad \text{by the chain rule of Bayesian networks}$$

$$= \sum_{i=1}^{N} \sum_{\mathbf{d}_i \models x\mathbf{u}} \log \mathrm{Pr}_{\theta}(x | \mathbf{u})$$

$$= \sum_{XU} \sum_{x\mathbf{u}} \sum_{\mathbf{d}_i \models x\mathbf{u}} \log \mathrm{Pr}_{\theta}(x | \mathbf{u})$$

$$= \sum_{XU} \sum_{x\mathbf{u}} \mathcal{D}\#(x\mathbf{u}) \log \mathrm{Pr}_{\theta}(x | \mathbf{u})$$

$$= N \sum_{XU} \sum_{x\mathbf{u}} \mathrm{Pr}_{\mathcal{D}}(x\mathbf{u}) \log \mathrm{Pr}_{\theta}(x | \mathbf{u}).$$

Let us now consider ML estimates θ^{ml}:

$$\begin{aligned}
LL(\theta^{ml}|\mathcal{D}) &= N \sum_{XU} \sum_{xu} Pr_{\mathcal{D}}(x\mathbf{u}) \log Pr_{\theta^{ml}}(x|\mathbf{u}) \\
&= N \sum_{XU} \sum_{xu} Pr_{\mathcal{D}}(x\mathbf{u}) \log Pr_{\mathcal{D}}(x|\mathbf{u}) \\
&= -N \sum_{XU} ENT_{\mathcal{D}}(X|\mathbf{U}).
\end{aligned}$$

This proves the theorem since $LL(G|\mathcal{D}) = LL(\theta^{ml}|\mathcal{D})$. ∎

PROOF OF THEOREM 17.4. By Definition 17.2, we have

$$\begin{aligned}
Pr_{\mathcal{D},\theta^k}(\alpha) &= \frac{1}{N} \sum_{\mathbf{d}_i \mathbf{c}_i \models \alpha} Pr_{\theta^k}(\mathbf{c}_i|\mathbf{d}_i) \\
&= \frac{1}{N} \sum_{\mathbf{d}_i \mathbf{c}_i \models \alpha} Pr_{\theta^k}(\mathbf{c}_i, \mathbf{d}_i|\mathbf{d}_i) \text{ by definition of conditioning} \\
&= \frac{1}{N} \sum_{\mathbf{d}_i \mathbf{c}_i} Pr_{\theta^k}(\mathbf{c}_i, \mathbf{d}_i, \alpha|\mathbf{d}_i) \\
&= \frac{1}{N} \sum_{\mathbf{d}_i \mathbf{c}_i} Pr_{\theta^k}(\mathbf{c}_i, \alpha|\mathbf{d}_i) \text{ by definition of conditioning} \\
&= \frac{1}{N} \sum_{\mathbf{d}_i} Pr_{\theta^k}(\alpha|\mathbf{d}_i) \text{ by case analysis} \\
&= \frac{1}{N} \sum_{i=1}^{N} Pr_{\theta^k}(\alpha|\mathbf{d}_i).
\end{aligned}$$

The third step follows since $\mathbf{c}_i, \mathbf{d}_i, \alpha$ is inconsistent if $\mathbf{d}_i \mathbf{c}_i \not\models \alpha$ and $\mathbf{c}_i, \mathbf{d}_i, \alpha$ is equivalent to $\mathbf{c}_i, \mathbf{d}_i$ if $\mathbf{d}_i \mathbf{c}_i \models \alpha$. ∎

PROOF OF THEOREM 17.5. We have

$$\begin{aligned}
ELL(\theta|\mathcal{D}, \theta^k) &= \sum_{i=1}^{N} \sum_{\mathbf{c}_i} Pr_{\theta^k}(\mathbf{c}_i|\mathbf{d}_i) \log Pr_{\theta}(\mathbf{c}_i, \mathbf{d}_i) \\
&= \sum_{i=1}^{N} \sum_{\mathbf{c}_i} Pr_{\theta^k}(\mathbf{c}_i|\mathbf{d}_i) \log \prod_{\mathbf{c}_i \mathbf{d}_i \models x\mathbf{u}} Pr_{\theta}(x|\mathbf{u}) \\
&= \sum_{i=1}^{N} \sum_{\mathbf{c}_i} Pr_{\theta^k}(\mathbf{c}_i|\mathbf{d}_i) \sum_{\mathbf{c}_i \mathbf{d}_i \models x\mathbf{u}} \log Pr_{\theta}(x|\mathbf{u}) \\
&= \sum_{XU} \sum_{xu} \sum_{\mathbf{c}_i \mathbf{d}_i \models x\mathbf{u}} Pr_{\theta^k}(\mathbf{c}_i|\mathbf{d}_i) \log Pr_{\theta}(x|\mathbf{u}) \\
&= \sum_{XU} \sum_{xu} \left(\sum_{\mathbf{c}_i \mathbf{d}_i \models x\mathbf{u}} Pr_{\theta^k}(\mathbf{c}_i|\mathbf{d}_i) \right) \log Pr_{\theta}(x|\mathbf{u}) \\
&= \sum_{XU} \sum_{xu} (N Pr_{\mathcal{D},\theta^k}(x\mathbf{u})) \log Pr_{\theta}(x|\mathbf{u}) \text{ by Definition 17.2} \\
&= N \sum_{XU} \sum_{\mathbf{u}} Pr_{\mathcal{D},\theta^k}(\mathbf{u}) \sum_{x} Pr_{\mathcal{D},\theta^k}(x|\mathbf{u}) \log Pr_{\theta}(x|\mathbf{u}).
\end{aligned}$$

We now have a set of independent components, each corresponding to a parent instantiation $\mathbf{u}$:

$$\sum_x \Pr_{\mathcal{D}, \theta^k}(x|\mathbf{u}) \log \Pr_\theta(x|\mathbf{u}).$$

These components can be maximized independently using Lemma 17.1, which says that the only distribution $\Pr_\theta(.)$ that maximizes this quantity is $\Pr_{\mathcal{D}, \theta^k}(.)$. Hence, the parameter estimates given by (17.6) are the only estimates that maximize the log-likelihood function. ∎

PROOF OF THEOREM 17.6. Maximizing the expected log-likelihood function is equivalent to maximizing

$$\sum_{i=1}^N \sum_{\mathbf{c}_i} \Pr_{\theta^k}(\mathbf{c}_i|\mathbf{d}_i) \log \frac{\Pr_\theta(\mathbf{c}_i, \mathbf{d}_i)}{\Pr_{\theta^k}(\mathbf{c}_i, \mathbf{d}_i)}. \tag{17.16}$$

This expression is obtained by subtracting the term

$$\Pr_{\theta^k}(\mathbf{c}_i|\mathbf{d}_i) \log \Pr_{\theta^k}(\mathbf{c}_i, \mathbf{d}_i)$$

from the expected log-likelihood function. This term does not depend on the sought parameters θ and, hence, does not change the optimization problem. We now have

$$
\begin{aligned}
&\sum_{i=1}^N \sum_{\mathbf{c}_i} \Pr_{\theta^k}(\mathbf{c}_i|\mathbf{d}_i) \log \frac{\Pr_\theta(\mathbf{c}_i, \mathbf{d}_i)}{\Pr_{\theta^k}(\mathbf{c}_i, \mathbf{d}_i)} \\
&= \sum_{i=1}^N \sum_{\mathbf{c}_i} \Pr_{\theta^k}(\mathbf{c}_i|\mathbf{d}_i) \log \left(\frac{\Pr_\theta(\mathbf{c}_i|\mathbf{d}_i)}{\Pr_{\theta^k}(\mathbf{c}_i|\mathbf{d}_i)} \frac{\Pr_\theta(\mathbf{d}_i)}{\Pr_{\theta^k}(\mathbf{d}_i)} \right) \\
&= \sum_{i=1}^N \left(\sum_{\mathbf{c}_i} \Pr_{\theta^k}(\mathbf{c}_i|\mathbf{d}_i) \log \frac{\Pr_\theta(\mathbf{d}_i)}{\Pr_{\theta^k}(\mathbf{d}_i)} + \sum_{\mathbf{c}_i} \Pr_{\theta^k}(\mathbf{c}_i|\mathbf{d}_i) \log \frac{\Pr_\theta(\mathbf{c}_i|\mathbf{d}_i)}{\Pr_{\theta^k}(\mathbf{c}_i|\mathbf{d}_i)} \right) \\
&= \sum_{i=1}^N \left(\log \frac{\Pr_\theta(\mathbf{d}_i)}{\Pr_{\theta^k}(\mathbf{d}_i)} + \sum_{\mathbf{c}_i} \Pr_{\theta^k}(\mathbf{c}_i|\mathbf{d}_i) \log \frac{\Pr_\theta(\mathbf{c}_i|\mathbf{d}_i)}{\Pr_{\theta^k}(\mathbf{c}_i|\mathbf{d}_i)} \right) \\
&= \sum_{i=1}^N \left(\log \frac{\Pr_\theta(\mathbf{d}_i)}{\Pr_{\theta^k}(\mathbf{d}_i)} - \mathrm{KL}(\Pr_{\theta^k}(\mathbf{C}_i|\mathbf{d}_i), \Pr_\theta(\mathbf{C}_i|\mathbf{d}_i)) \right).
\end{aligned}
$$

Suppose now that

$$\theta^{k+1} = \underset{\theta}{\operatorname{argmax}} \sum_{i=1}^N \left(\log \frac{\Pr_\theta(\mathbf{d}_i)}{\Pr_{\theta^k}(\mathbf{d}_i)} - \mathrm{KL}(\Pr_{\theta^k}(\mathbf{C}_i|\mathbf{d}_i), \Pr_\theta(\mathbf{C}_i|\mathbf{d}_i)) \right).$$

The quantity maximized above must be ≥ 0 since choosing $\theta^{k+1} = \theta^k$ leads to a zero value. Replacing θ by the optimal parameters θ^{k+1} then gives

$$\sum_{i=1}^N \left(\log \frac{\Pr_{\theta^{k+1}}(\mathbf{d}_i)}{\Pr_{\theta^k}(\mathbf{d}_i)} - \mathrm{KL}(\Pr_{\theta^k}(\mathbf{C}_i|\mathbf{d}_i), \Pr_{\theta^{k+1}}(\mathbf{C}_i|\mathbf{d}_i)) \right) \geq 0.$$

Since the KL divergence is ≥ 0, we now have

$$\sum_{i=1}^N \log \frac{\Pr_{\theta^{k+1}}(\mathbf{d}_i)}{\Pr_{\theta^k}(\mathbf{d}_i)} \geq 0$$

and also

$$\log \prod_{i=1}^{N} \frac{\Pr_{\theta^{k+1}}(\mathbf{d}_i)}{\Pr_{\theta^k}(\mathbf{d}_i)} \geq 0.$$

From the definition of the likelihood function, we then have

$$\log \frac{L(\theta^{k+1}|\mathcal{D})}{L(\theta^k|\mathcal{D})} \geq 0$$

and

$$\log L(\theta^{k+1}|\mathcal{D}) - \log L(\theta^k|\mathcal{D}) \geq 0,$$

which implies that $LL(\theta^{k+1}|\mathcal{D}) \geq LL(\theta^k|\mathcal{D})$. ∎

PROOF OF THEOREM 17.7. We need to consider the gradient of the log-likelihood function under the normalization constraints $\sum_x \theta_{x|\mathbf{u}} = 1$. For this, we construct the Lagrangian

$$f(\theta, \lambda) = LL(\theta|\mathcal{D}) + \sum_X \sum_{\mathbf{u}} \lambda_{X|\mathbf{u}} \left(1 - \sum_x \theta_{x|\mathbf{u}}\right)$$

and set the gradient to zero. The equations $\partial f / \partial \lambda_{X|\mathbf{u}} = 0$ give us our normalization constraints. The equations $\partial f / \partial \theta_{x|\mathbf{u}} = 0$ give us (see Theorem 17.8)

$$\frac{\partial f}{\partial \theta_{x|\mathbf{u}}} = \frac{\partial LL(\theta|\mathcal{D})}{\partial \theta_{x|\mathbf{u}}} - \lambda_{X|\mathbf{u}} = \sum_{i=1}^{N} \frac{1}{\Pr_\theta(\mathbf{d}_i)} \frac{\partial \Pr_\theta(\mathbf{d}_i)}{\partial \theta_{x|\mathbf{u}}} - \lambda_{X|\mathbf{u}} = 0.$$

Rearranging, we get

$$\lambda_{X|\mathbf{u}} = \sum_{i=1}^{N} \frac{1}{\Pr_\theta(\mathbf{d}_i)} \frac{\partial \Pr_\theta(\mathbf{d}_i)}{\partial \theta_{x|\mathbf{u}}}.$$

Multiplying both sides by $\theta_{x|\mathbf{u}}$, we get (see Theorem 12.2 and (12.6) of Chapter 12)

$$\lambda_{X|\mathbf{u}} \theta_{x|\mathbf{u}} = \sum_{i=1}^{N} \frac{1}{\Pr_\theta(\mathbf{d}_i)} \frac{\partial \Pr_\theta(\mathbf{d}_i)}{\partial \theta_{x|\mathbf{u}}} \theta_{x|\mathbf{u}} = \sum_{i=1}^{N} \Pr_\theta(x\mathbf{u}|\mathbf{d}_i). \tag{17.17}$$

Summing all equations for state $\mathbf{u}$, we have

$$\lambda_{X|\mathbf{u}} \sum_x \theta_{x|\mathbf{u}} = \sum_{i=1}^{N} \sum_x \Pr_\theta(x\mathbf{u}|\mathbf{d}_i),$$

and thus,

$$\lambda_{X|\mathbf{u}} = \sum_{i=1}^{N} \Pr_\theta(\mathbf{u}|\mathbf{d}_i).$$

Dividing (17.17) by $\lambda_{X|\mathbf{u}}$ and substituting the previous, we find that a stationary point of the log-likelihood must be a fixed point for EM:

$$\theta_{x|\mathbf{u}} = \frac{\sum_{i=1}^{N} \Pr_\theta(x\mathbf{u}|\mathbf{d}_i)}{\sum_{i=1}^{N} \Pr_\theta(\mathbf{u}|\mathbf{d}_i)}.$$

Reversing the proof, we can also show that a fixed point for EM is a zero-gradient for the log-likelihood. ∎

PROOF OF THEOREM 17.8. We have

$$\frac{\partial LL(\theta|\mathcal{D})}{\partial \theta_{x|\mathbf{u}}} = \frac{\partial \sum_{i=1}^{N} \log \Pr_\theta(\mathbf{d}_i)}{\partial \theta_{x|\mathbf{u}}}$$

$$= \sum_{i=1}^{N} \frac{\partial \log \Pr_\theta(\mathbf{d}_i)}{\partial \theta_{x|\mathbf{u}}}$$

$$= \sum_{i=1}^{N} \left(\frac{1}{\Pr_\theta(\mathbf{d}_i)}\right) \frac{\partial \Pr_\theta(\mathbf{d}_i)}{\partial \theta_{x|\mathbf{u}}}.$$

The second part of this theorem is shown in Theorem 12.2 and (12.6) of Chapter 12. ∎

PROOF OF THEOREM 17.9. The likelihood function for the parameters of structure $G_\mathbf{I}$ has the form

$$L(\theta, \theta_\mathbf{I}|\mathcal{D}_\mathbf{I}) = \prod_k \Pr_{\theta,\theta_\mathbf{I}}(\mathbf{o}^k, \alpha^k, \mathbf{i}^k),$$

where k ranges over the cases of data set $\mathcal{D}_\mathbf{I}$, $\mathbf{o}^k$ are the values of variables $\mathbf{O}$, $\mathbf{i}^k$ are the values of variables $\mathbf{I}$, and α^k are the available values of variables $\mathbf{M}$ (all in case k). Given the MAR assumption, we have

$$\Pr_{\theta,\theta_\mathbf{I}}(\mathbf{o}^k, \alpha^k, \mathbf{i}^k) = \Pr_{\theta,\theta_\mathbf{I}}(\mathbf{i}^k|\mathbf{o}^k)\Pr_{\theta,\theta_\mathbf{I}}(\mathbf{o}^k, \alpha^k).$$

Hence, the likelihood function can be decomposed as

$$L(\theta, \theta_\mathbf{I}|\mathcal{D}_\mathbf{I}) = \left(\prod_k \Pr_{\theta,\theta_\mathbf{I}}(\mathbf{i}^k|\mathbf{o}^k)\right)\left(\prod_k \Pr_{\theta,\theta_\mathbf{I}}(\mathbf{o}^k, \alpha^k)\right).$$

Note that the first component depends only on parameters $\theta_\mathbf{I}$ and the second component depends only on parameters θ. Moreover, if $\Pr_\theta(.)$ is the distribution induced by structure G and parameters θ, then

$$\prod_k \Pr_{\theta,\theta_\mathbf{I}}(\mathbf{o}^k, \alpha^k) = \prod_k \Pr_\theta(\mathbf{o}^k, \alpha^k)$$

$$= L(\theta|\mathcal{D}).$$

We then have

$$L(\theta, \theta_\mathbf{I}|\mathcal{D}_\mathbf{I}) = \left(\prod_k \Pr_{\theta,\theta_\mathbf{I}}(\mathbf{i}^k|\mathbf{o}^k)\right) L(\theta|\mathcal{D}).$$

Since the first component depends only on parameters $\theta_\mathbf{I}$, we have

$$\underset{\theta}{\operatorname{argmax}} L(\theta|\mathcal{D}) = \underset{\theta}{\operatorname{argmax}} \underset{\theta_\mathbf{I}}{\max} L(\theta, \theta_\mathbf{I}|\mathcal{D}_\mathbf{I}). \qquad \blacksquare$$

PROOF OF THEOREM 17.10. First, note the definitions of entropy, conditional entropy, and mutual information:

$$\mathrm{ENT}_\mathcal{D}(X) = -\sum_x \Pr_\mathcal{D}(x) \log \Pr_\mathcal{D}(x)$$

$$\mathrm{ENT}_\mathcal{D}(X|U) = -\sum_{x,u} \Pr_\mathcal{D}(x, u) \log \Pr_\mathcal{D}(x|u)$$

$$\mathrm{MI}_\mathcal{D}(X, U) = \sum_{x,u} \Pr_\mathcal{D}(x, u) \log \frac{\Pr_\mathcal{D}(x, u)}{\Pr_\mathcal{D}(x)\Pr_\mathcal{D}(u)}.$$

Expanding the definition of mutual information and substituting the definitions of entropy and conditional entropy leads to

$$\text{MI}_{\mathcal{D}}(X, U) = \text{ENT}_{\mathcal{D}}(X) - \text{ENT}_{\mathcal{D}}(X|U).$$

Suppose now that X ranges over the nodes of a tree structure G and U is the parent of X. By Theorem 17.3, we have

$$\text{LL}(G|\mathcal{D}) = -N \sum_{XU} \text{ENT}_{\mathcal{D}}(X|U).$$

Hence, we also have

$$\text{LL}(G|\mathcal{D}) = -N \sum_{XU} (\text{ENT}_{\mathcal{D}}(X) - \text{MI}_{\mathcal{D}}(X, U))$$

$$= -N \sum_{XU} \text{ENT}_{\mathcal{D}}(X) + N \sum_{XU} \text{MI}_{\mathcal{D}}(X, U).$$

Note that neither N nor the term $-N \sum_{XU} \text{ENT}_{\mathcal{D}}(X)$ depend on the tree structure G. Hence,

$$\underset{G}{\text{argmax}} \, \text{LL}(G|\mathcal{D}) = \underset{G}{\text{argmax}} \sum_{XU} \text{MI}_{\mathcal{D}}(X, U) = \underset{G}{\text{argmax}} \, \text{tScore}(G|\mathcal{D}),$$

which proves the theorem. ∎

PROOF OF THEOREM 17.11. Let $\mathbf{U}^{\star} = \mathbf{U} \cup \mathbf{U}'$ where $\mathbf{U} \cap \mathbf{U}' = \emptyset$. The mutual information between X and $\mathbf{U}'$ given $\mathbf{U}$ is defined as [Cover and Thomas, 1991]

$$\text{MI}_{\mathcal{D}}(X, \mathbf{U}'|\mathbf{U}) \overset{def}{=} \text{ENT}_{\mathcal{D}}(X|\mathbf{U}) - \text{ENT}_{\mathcal{D}}(X|\mathbf{U}, \mathbf{U}').$$

It is also known that [Cover and Thomas, 1991]

$$\text{MI}_{\mathcal{D}}(X, \mathbf{U}'|\mathbf{U}) \geq 0.$$

We then have

$$\text{ENT}_{\mathcal{D}}(X|\mathbf{U}) - \text{ENT}_{\mathcal{D}}(X|\mathbf{U}, \mathbf{U}') \geq 0$$

and

$$\text{ENT}_{\mathcal{D}}(X|\mathbf{U}) \geq \text{ENT}_{\mathcal{D}}(X|\mathbf{U}^{\star}).$$ ∎

PROOF OF THEOREM 17.12. Consider first the MDL score:

$$\text{MDL}(X_i \mathbf{U}_i^{\star}|\mathcal{D}) = -N \cdot \text{ENT}_{\mathcal{D}}(X_i|\mathbf{U}_i^{\star}) - \psi(N) \cdot ||X_i \mathbf{U}_i^{\star}||.$$

Note also that $\mathbf{U}_i \subseteq \mathbf{U}_i^{\star} \subseteq \mathbf{U}_i^{+}$. By Theorem 17.11, we have $\text{ENT}_{\mathcal{D}}(X_i|\mathbf{U}_i^{+}) \leq \text{ENT}_{\mathcal{D}}(X_i|\mathbf{U}_i^{\star})$ and, hence,

$$-N \cdot \text{ENT}_{\mathcal{D}}(X_i|\mathbf{U}_i^{+}) \geq -N \cdot \text{ENT}_{\mathcal{D}}(X_i|\mathbf{U}_i^{\star}).$$

By Definition 17.6, we have $||X_i \mathbf{U}_i|| \leq ||X_i \mathbf{U}_i^{\star}||$ and, hence,

$$-\psi(N) \cdot ||X_i \mathbf{U}_i|| \geq -\psi(N) \cdot ||X_i \mathbf{U}_i^{\star}||.$$

This immediately leads to

$$\text{MDL}(X_i \mathbf{U}_i^{\star}|\mathcal{D}) \leq -N \cdot \text{ENT}_{\mathcal{D}}(X_i|\mathbf{U}_i^{+}) - \psi(N) \cdot ||X_i \mathbf{U}_i||.$$ ∎

18

Learning: The Bayesian Approach

We discuss in this chapter a particular approach to learning Bayesian networks from data, known as the Bayesian approach, which is marked by its ability to integrate prior knowledge into the learning process and to reduce learning to a problem of inference.

18.1 Introduction

Consider the network structure in Figure 18.1 and suppose that our goal is to estimate network parameters based on the data set shown in the figure. We discussed this problem in Chapter 17 where we introduced the maximum likelihood principle for learning. Our goal in this chapter is to present another principle for learning that allows us to reduce the learning process to a problem of inference. This method, known as *Bayesian learning*, is marked by its ability to integrate prior knowledge into the learning process and subsumes the maximum likelihood approach under certain conditions.

To illustrate the Bayesian approach to learning, consider again the structure in Figure 18.1, which has five parameter sets: $\theta_H = (\theta_h, \theta_{\bar{h}})$, $\theta_{S|h} = (\theta_{s|h}, \theta_{\bar{s}|h})$, $\theta_{S|\bar{h}} = (\theta_{s|\bar{h}}, \theta_{\bar{s}|\bar{h}})$, $\theta_{E|h} = (\theta_{e|h}, \theta_{\bar{e}|h})$, and $\theta_{E|\bar{h}} = (\theta_{e|\bar{h}}, \theta_{\bar{e}|\bar{h}})$. Suppose that we know the values of two of these parameter sets as

$$\theta_{S|h} = (.1, .9)$$

$$\theta_{E|h} = (.8, .2).$$

Suppose further that we have prior knowledge to the effect that

$$\theta_H \in \{(.75, .25), (.90, .10)\}$$

$$\theta_{S|\bar{h}} \in \{(.25, .75), (.50, .50)\}$$

$$\theta_{E|\bar{h}} \in \{(.50, .50), (.75, .25)\},$$

where each of the two values are considered equally likely. The Bayesian approach to learning can integrate this information into the learning process by constructing the *meta-network* shown in Figure 18.2. Here variables θ_H, $\theta_{S|\bar{h}}$, $\theta_{E|\bar{h}}$ represent the possible values of unknown network parameters, where the CPTs of these variables encode our prior knowledge about these parameters. Moreover, variables H_i, S_i, and E_i represent the values that variables H, S, and E take in case i of the data set, allowing us to assert the data set as evidence on the given network.

By explicitly encoding prior knowledge about network parameters and by treating data as evidence, the Bayesian approach can now reduce the process of learning to a process of computing posterior distributions:

$$\mathbb{P}(\theta_H, \theta_{S|\bar{h}}, \theta_{E|\bar{h}} | \mathcal{D}),$$

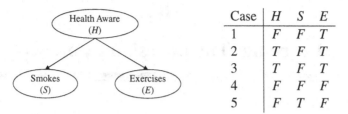

Case	H	S	E
1	F	F	T
2	T	F	T
3	T	F	T
4	F	F	F
5	F	T	F

Figure 18.1: A network structure with a complete data set.

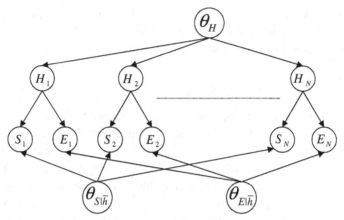

Figure 18.2: Bayesian learning as inference on a meta-Bayesian network.

where $\mathbb{P}$ is the distribution induced by the meta-network and $\mathcal{D}$ is the evidence entailed by the data set. As we have two possible values for each of the unknown parameter sets, we have eight possible parameterizations for the base network in Figure 18.1. Hence, the previous posterior distribution can be viewed as providing a ranking over these possible parameterizations.

The Bayesian approach can extract various quantities from this posterior distribution. For example, we can identify parameter estimates that have the highest probability:

$$\underset{\theta_H, \theta_{S|\bar{h}}\theta_{E|\bar{h}}}{\operatorname{argmax}} \mathbb{P}(\theta_H, \theta_{S|\bar{h}}\theta_{E|\bar{h}}|\mathcal{D}).$$

These are known as *MAP estimates*, for maximum a posteriori estimates, and are closely related to maximum likelihood estimates, as we see later.

The Bayesian approach does not commit to a single value of network parameters θ as it can work with a distribution over the possible values of these parameters, $\mathbb{P}(\theta|\mathcal{D})$. As a result, the Bayesian approach can compute the expected value of a given query with respect to the distribution over network parameters. For example, the expected probability of observing a person that both smokes and exercises can be computed as

$$\sum_{\theta} \operatorname{Pr}_{\theta}(s, e)\mathbb{P}(\theta|\mathcal{D}),$$

where $\operatorname{Pr}_{\theta}(.)$ is the distribution induced by the base network in Figure 18.1 and parametrization θ. That is, we are computing eight different probabilities for s, e, one for each parametrization θ, and then taking their average weighted by the posterior parameter distribution $\mathbb{P}(\theta|\mathcal{D})$. We see later that when the data set is complete, the Bayesian approach can be realized by working with a single parametrization, making it quite similar to the maximum likelihood approach.

We will start in Section 18.2 by defining the notion of a meta-network formally and then describe a particular class of meta-networks that is commonly assumed in Bayesian learning. We then consider parameter estimation in Section 18.3 while assuming that each parameter has a finite number of possible values. We then treat the continuous case in Section 18.4 and finally discuss the learning of network structures in Section 18.5.

18.2 Meta-networks

In this section, we characterize a class of meta-networks that is commonly assumed in Bayesian learning. We start with the notion of a *parameter set*, which is a set of co-varying network parameters.

Definition 18.1. Let X be a variable with values $x_1, \ldots, x_k$ and let $\mathbf{U}$ be its parents. A *parameter set* for variable X and parent instantiation $\mathbf{u}$, denoted by $\theta_{X|\mathbf{u}}$, is the set of network parameters $(\theta_{x_1|\mathbf{u}}, \ldots, \theta_{x_k|\mathbf{u}})$. A parameter set that admits a finite number of values is said to be *discrete*; otherwise, it is said to be *continuous*. ∎

The parameter set $\theta_{S|\bar{h}}$ in Figure 18.2 was assumed to admit the following two values:

$$\theta_{S|\bar{h}} \in \{(.25, .75), (.50, .50)\}.$$

This parameter set is therefore discrete and each of its values corresponds to an assignment of probabilities to the set of co-varying parameters $(\theta_{s|\bar{h}}, \theta_{\bar{s}|\bar{h}})$. Hence, if $\theta_{S|\bar{h}} = (.25, .75)$, then $\theta_{s|\bar{h}} = .25$ and $\theta_{\bar{s}|\bar{h}} = .75$.

To further spell out our notational conventions for parameter sets, consider the following expression:

$$\sum_{\theta_{S|\bar{h}}} \theta_{s|\bar{h}} \theta_{\bar{s}|\bar{h}}.$$

That is, we are summing over all possible values of the parameter set $\theta_{S|\bar{h}}$ and then multiplying the values of parameters corresponding to each element of the summand. This expression therefore evaluates to

$$(.25)(.75) + (.50)(.50).$$

We write a number of expressions later that resemble the form given here.

We are now ready to define meta-networks formally.

Definition 18.2. Let G be a network structure. A *meta-network* of size N for structure G is constructed using N instances of structure G with variable X in G appearing as X_i in the ith instance of G. Moreover, for every variable X in G and its parent instantiation $\mathbf{u}$, the meta-network contains the parameter set $\theta_{X|\mathbf{u}}$ and corresponding edges $\theta_{X|\mathbf{u}} \to X_1, \ldots, \theta_{X|\mathbf{u}} \to X_N$. ∎

Figure 18.2 contains a meta-network for the structure $S \leftarrow H \rightarrow E$. Note, however, that this meta-network does not contain parameter sets $\theta_{S|h}$ and $\theta_{E|h}$ as the values of these variables are fixed in this example. A full meta-network that includes all parameter sets is shown in Figure 18.3(a).

In the rest of this chapter, we distinguish between the *base network*, which is a classical Bayesian network, and the *meta-network* as given by Definition 18.2. We also use θ

to denote the set of all parameters for the base network and call it a *parametrization*. Equivalently, θ represents the collection of parameter sets in the meta-network. The distribution induced by a base network and parametrization θ is denoted by $\mathrm{Pr}_\theta(.)$ and called a *base distribution*. The distribution induced by a meta-network is denoted by $\mathbb{P}(.)$ and called a *meta-distribution*.

18.2.1 Prior knowledge

In the Bayesian approach to learning, prior knowledge on network parameters is encoded in the meta-network using the CPTs of parameter sets. For example, we assumed in Figure 18.2 that the two values of parameter set $\theta_{S|\bar{h}}$ are equally likely. Hence, the CPT of this parameter set is

$\theta_{S|\bar{h}} = (\theta_{s|\bar{h}}, \theta_{\bar{s}|\bar{h}})$	$\mathbb{P}(\theta_{S|\bar{h}})$
$(.25, .75)$	50%
$(.50, .50)$	50%

These CPTs are then given as input to the learning process and lead to a major distinction with the maximum likelihood approach to learning, which does not factor such information into the learning process.

The CPTs of other variables in a meta-network (i.e., those that do not correspond to parameter sets) are determined by the intended semantics of such networks. In particular, consider a variable X in the base network having parents $\mathbf{U}$ and let $X_1, \ldots, X_n$ be the instances of X and $\mathbf{U}_1, \ldots, \mathbf{U}_n$ be the instances of $\mathbf{U}$ in the meta-network. All instances of X have the same CPT in the meta-network:

$$\mathbb{P}(X_i | \mathbf{u}_i, \theta_{X|\mathbf{u}^1}, \ldots, \theta_{X|\mathbf{u}^m}) = \theta_{X|\mathbf{u}^j}, \text{ where } \mathbf{u}^j = \mathbf{u}_i. \tag{18.1}$$

That is, given that parents $\mathbf{U}_i$ take on the value $\mathbf{u}_i$, the probability of X_i will be determined only by the corresponding parameter set, $\theta_{X|\mathbf{u}_i}$. Consider the meta-network in Figure 18.3(a) and instances S_i. We then have

$$\mathbb{P}(S_i | H_i = h, \theta_{S|h}, \theta_{S|\bar{h}}) = \theta_{S|h}$$
$$\mathbb{P}(S_i | H_i = \bar{h}, \theta_{S|h}, \theta_{S|\bar{h}}) = \theta_{S|\bar{h}}.$$

18.2.2 Data as evidence

In addition to representing prior knowledge about network parameters, the Bayesian approach allows us to treat data as evidence. Consider for example the following complete data set:

Case	H	S	E
1	h	$\bar{s}$	e
2	h	$\bar{s}$	$\bar{e}$
3	$\bar{h}$	s	$\bar{e}$

We can interpret each case i as providing evidence on variables H_i, S_i, and E_i in the meta-network. Hence, the data set can be viewed as the following variable instantiation:

$$\mathcal{D} = (H_1 = h) \wedge (S_1 = \bar{s}) \wedge (E_1 = e) \wedge \ldots \wedge (H_3 = \bar{h}) \wedge (S_3 = s) \wedge (E_3 = \bar{e}).$$

We can assert this data set as evidence on the meta-network and then compute the corresponding posterior distribution on network parameters.

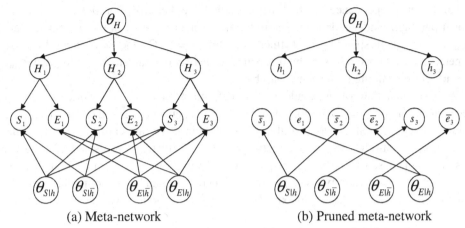

(a) Meta-network   (b) Pruned meta-network

Figure 18.3: Pruning edges of a meta-network based on a complete data set.

For the meta-network in Figure 18.3(a), we initially have the following distribution on parameter sets:

$$\mathbb{P}(\theta_H, \theta_{S|h}, \theta_{S|\bar{h}}, \theta_{E|h}, \theta_{E|\bar{h}}) = \mathbb{P}(\theta_H)\mathbb{P}(\theta_{S|h})\mathbb{P}(\theta_{S|\bar{h}})\mathbb{P}(\theta_{E|h})\mathbb{P}(\theta_{E|\bar{h}}).$$

Note how the prior distribution could be decomposed in this case, which is possible for any meta-network given by Definition 18.2 (since parameter sets are root nodes and are therefore d-separated). In fact, we next show that this decomposition holds for the posterior distribution as well, given that the data set is complete:

$$\mathbb{P}(\theta_H, \theta_{S|h}, \theta_{S|\bar{h}}, \theta_{E|h}, \theta_{E|\bar{h}}|\mathcal{D}) = \mathbb{P}(\theta_H|\mathcal{D})\mathbb{P}(\theta_{S|h}|\mathcal{D})\mathbb{P}(\theta_{S|\bar{h}}|\mathcal{D})\mathbb{P}(\theta_{E|h}|\mathcal{D})\mathbb{P}(\theta_{E|\bar{h}}|\mathcal{D}).$$

Figure 18.3(b) provides the key insight behind this decomposition. Here variables are instantiated according to their values in the data set, allowing us to prune edges that are either outgoing from observed variables (see Section 6.9.2) or representing superfluous dependencies (see (18.1)). All edges outgoing from variables H_1, H_2, and H_3 fall into the first category. All other pruned edges fall into the second category. For example, the edge $\theta_{S|\bar{h}} \rightarrow S_1$ is now superfluous given that H_1 is instantiated to h, that is, S_1 no longer depends on the parameter set $\theta_{S|\bar{h}}$ in this case. These two types of edge pruning are guaranteed to lead to a meta-network in which every parameter set is disconnected from all other parameter sets.

18.2.3 Parameter independence

We can now easily prove the following key result.

Theorem 18.1. *Consider a meta-network as given by Definition 18.2 and let Σ_1 and Σ_2 each contain a collection of parameter sets, $\Sigma_1 \cap \Sigma_2 = \emptyset$. The following conditions, known as parameter independence, are then guaranteed to hold:*

- *Σ_1 and Σ_2 are independent, $\mathbb{P}(\Sigma_1, \Sigma_2) = \mathbb{P}(\Sigma_1)\mathbb{P}(\Sigma_2)$.*
- *Σ_1 and Σ_2 are independent given any complete data set $\mathcal{D}$, $\mathbb{P}(\Sigma_1, \Sigma_2|\mathcal{D}) = \mathbb{P}(\Sigma_1|\mathcal{D})\mathbb{P}(\Sigma_2|\mathcal{D})$.* ∎

Parameter independence is sometimes classified as either *global* or *local*. In particular, global parameter independence refers to the independence between two parameter sets, $\theta_{X|u}$ and $\theta_{Y|v}$, corresponding to distinct variables $X \neq Y$. On the other hand, local parameter independence refers to the independence between parameter sets, $\theta_{X|u}$ and $\theta_{X|u^\star}$, $u \neq u^\star$, corresponding to the same variable X.

We point out that we may adopt other definitions of a meta-network that do not necessarily embody the condition of parameter independence (see Exercise 18.3). Yet parameter independence is almost always assumed in Bayesian learning as it simplifies the complexity of inference on meta-networks. This is critical for Bayesian learning since this method is based on reducing the problem of learning to a problem of inference. We also point out that certain types of parameter dependence can be accommodated without affecting the computational complexity of approaches we discuss next (see Exercise 18.4).

18.3 Learning with discrete parameter sets

Now that we have settled the basic formalities needed by the Bayesian approach, we discuss Bayesian learning in this section for both complete and incomplete data while confining ourselves to discrete parameter sets. This allows us to introduce the main concepts underlying Bayesian learning without introducing additional machinery for handling continuous variables. Continuous parameter sets are then treated in Section 18.4.

Consider again the network structure and corresponding data set $\mathcal{D}$ in Figure 18.1. Recall that two of the parameter sets have known values in this example:

$$\theta_{S|h} = (.1, .9)$$
$$\theta_{E|h} = (.8, .2).$$

Moreover, the remaining parameter sets have the following possible values:

$$\theta_H \in \{(.75, .25), (.90, .10)\},$$
$$\theta_{S|\bar{h}} \in \{(.25, .75), (.50, .50)\},$$
$$\theta_{E|\bar{h}} \in \{(.50, .50), (.75, .25)\},$$

leading to eight possible parameterizations.

Suppose now that our goal is to compute the probability of observing a smoker who exercises regularly, that is, s, e. According to the maximum likelihood approach, we must first find the maximum likelihood estimates θ^{ml} based on the given data and then use them to compute this probability. Among the eight possible parameterizations in this case, the one with maximum likelihood (i.e., the one that maximizes the probability of data) is

$$\theta^{ml} : \quad \theta_H = (.75, .25), \ \theta_{S|\bar{h}} = (.25, .75), \ \theta_{E|\bar{h}} = (.50, .50).$$

If we plug in these parameter values in the base network of Figure 18.1, we obtain the following probability of observing a smoker who exercises regularly:

$$\Pr_{\theta^{ml}}(s, e) \approx 9.13\%.$$

However, the Bayesian approach treats this problem differently. In particular, it views the data set $\mathcal{D}$ as evidence on variables $H_1, S_1, E_1, \ldots, H_5, S_5, E_5$ in the meta-network of Figure 18.2. It then computes the posterior on variables S_6 and E_6 by performing inference on this meta-network, leading to

$$\mathbb{P}(S_6 = s, E_6 = e | \mathcal{D}) \approx 11.06\%.$$

The Bayesian approach is therefore not estimating any parameters as is done in the maximum likelihood approach. Theorem 18.2 provides an interpretation of what the Bayesian approach is really doing.

Theorem 18.2. *Given discrete parameter sets and a data set $\mathcal{D}$ of size N, we have*

$$\mathbb{P}(\alpha_{N+1}|\mathcal{D}) = \sum_{\theta} \text{Pr}_{\theta}(\alpha)\mathbb{P}(\theta|\mathcal{D}). \qquad (18.2)$$

Here event α_{N+1} is obtained from α by replacing every occurrence of variable X by its instance X_{N+1}. ∎

For example, if α is $S=s$, $E=e$, then α_6 is $S_6=s$, $E_6=e$. In the previous example, we then have

$$\mathbb{P}(S_6=s, E_6=e|\mathcal{D}) = \sum_{\theta} \text{Pr}_{\theta}(S=s, E=e)\mathbb{P}(\theta|\mathcal{D}).$$

The Bayesian approach is therefore considering every possible parametrization θ, computing the probability $\text{Pr}_{\theta}(S=s, E=e)$ using the base network, and then taking a weighted average of the computed probabilities. In other words, the Bayesian approach is computing the expected value of $\text{Pr}_{\theta}(S=s, E=e)$.

Theorem 18.2 holds for any data set, whether complete or not. However, if the data set is complete, then we can compute the expectation of Theorem 18.2 by performing inference on the base network as long as it is parameterized using the following estimates.

Definition 18.3. Let $\theta_{X|\mathbf{u}}$ be a discrete parameter set. The *Bayesian estimate* for parameter $\theta_{x|\mathbf{u}}$ given data set $\mathcal{D}$ is defined as

$$\theta_{x|\mathbf{u}}^{be} \overset{def}{=} \sum_{\theta_{X|\mathbf{u}}} \theta_{x|\mathbf{u}} \cdot \mathbb{P}(\theta_{X|\mathbf{u}}|\mathcal{D}).$$ ∎

That is, the Bayesian estimate is the expectation of $\theta_{x|\mathbf{u}}$ according to the posterior distribution of parameter set $\theta_{X|\mathbf{u}}$. The set of all Bayesian estimates $\theta_{x|\mathbf{u}}^{be}$ is denoted by θ^{be}. We now have the following key result.

Theorem 18.3. *Given discrete parameter sets and a complete data set $\mathcal{D}$ of size N, we have*

$$\mathbb{P}(\alpha_{N+1}|\mathcal{D}) = \text{Pr}_{\theta^{be}}(\alpha), \qquad (18.3)$$

where θ^{be} are the Bayesian estimates given data set $\mathcal{D}$. ∎

Recall again that the probability $\mathbb{P}(\alpha_{N+1}|\mathcal{D})$ is an expectation of the probability $\text{Pr}_{\theta}(\alpha)$. Hence, Theorem 18.3 says that we can compute this expectation by performing inference on a base network that is parameterized by the Bayesian estimates. It is for this reason that computing the Bayesian estimates is a focus of attention for Bayesian learning under complete data.

18.3.1 Computing Bayesian estimates

Bayesian learning is relatively well-behaved computationally when the data set is complete (and given the assumption of parameter independence). We saw this already in the previous section where computations with respect to the meta-network could be reduced to ones on the base network. However, this reduction is based on our ability to compute Bayesian estimates, as those estimates are needed to parameterize the base network. As it turns out, these estimates are also easy to compute given Theorem 18.4.

Theorem 18.4. *Let $\theta_{X|\mathbf{u}}$ be a discrete parameter set and let $\mathcal{D}$ be a complete data set. We then have*

$$\mathbb{P}(\theta_{X|\mathbf{u}}|\mathcal{D}) = \eta \, \mathbb{P}(\theta_{X|\mathbf{u}}) \prod_{x} \left[\theta_{x|\mathbf{u}}\right]^{\mathcal{D}\#(x\mathbf{u})}, \tag{18.4}$$

where η is a normalizing constant. ∎

Consider now the parameter set $\theta_{E|\bar{h}}$ with values $\{(.50, .50), (.75, .25)\}$ and a uniform prior. Also consider the following data set $\mathcal{D}$ from Figure 18.1:

Case	H	S	E
1	F	F	T
2	T	F	T
3	T	F	T
4	F	F	F
5	F	T	F

We then have the following posterior:

$$\mathbb{P}(\theta_{E|\bar{h}} = (.50, .50)|\mathcal{D}) = \eta \times .50 \times \left[.50\right]^1 \left[.50\right]^2$$

$$\mathbb{P}(\theta_{E|\bar{h}} = (.75, .25)|\mathcal{D}) = \eta \times .50 \times \left[.75\right]^1 \left[.25\right]^2.$$

Normalizing, we get

$$\mathbb{P}(\theta_{E|\bar{h}} = (.50, .50)|\mathcal{D}) \approx 72.73\%$$

$$\mathbb{P}(\theta_{E|\bar{h}} = (.75, .25)|\mathcal{D}) \approx 27.27\%.$$

We can now immediately compute the Bayesian estimate for every parameter by taking its expectation according to this posterior:

$$\theta_{e|\bar{h}}^{be} = .50 \times 72.73\% + .75 \times 27.27\% \approx .57$$

$$\theta_{\bar{e}|\bar{h}}^{be} = .50 \times 72.73\% + .25 \times 27.27\% \approx .43$$

The Bayesian estimate for parameter set $\theta_{E|\bar{h}} = (\theta_{e|\bar{h}}, \theta_{\bar{e}|\bar{h}})$ is then $(.57, .43)$ in this case.

18.3.2 Closed forms for complete data

We now summarize the computations that are known to have closed forms under complete data. We assume here a base network with families $X\mathbf{U}$ and a complete data set $\mathcal{D}$ of size N:

- The prior probability of network parameters (see Theorem 18.1):

$$\mathbb{P}(\theta) = \prod_{X\mathbf{U}} \prod_{\mathbf{u}} \mathbb{P}(\theta_{X|\mathbf{u}}) \tag{18.5}$$

- The posterior probability of network parameters (see Theorem 18.1):

$$\mathbb{P}(\theta|\mathcal{D}) = \prod_{X\mathbf{U}} \prod_{\mathbf{u}} \mathbb{P}(\theta_{X|\mathbf{u}}|\mathcal{D}) \tag{18.6}$$

- The likelihood of network parameters (see Exercise 18.5):

$$\mathbb{P}(\mathcal{D}|\theta) = \prod_{i=1}^{N} \mathbb{P}(\mathbf{d}_i|\theta) = \prod_{i=1}^{N} \mathrm{Pr}_\theta(\mathbf{d}_i) \qquad (18.7)$$

- The marginal likelihood (see Theorem 18.3):[1]

$$\mathbb{P}(\mathcal{D}) = \prod_{i=1}^{N} \mathbb{P}(\mathbf{d}_i|\mathbf{d}_1,\ldots,\mathbf{d}_{i-1}) = \prod_{i=1}^{N} \mathrm{Pr}_{\theta_i^{be}}(\mathbf{d}_i) \qquad (18.8)$$

where θ_i^{be} are the Bayesian estimates for data set $\mathbf{d}_1,\ldots,\mathbf{d}_{i-1}$.

In addition to the Bayesian estimates, we can easily compute MAP estimates under complete data. Recall that MAP estimates are those that have a maximal posterior probability:

$$\theta^{ma} = \underset{\theta}{\operatorname{argmax}}\, \mathbb{P}(\theta|\mathcal{D}).$$

Given (18.6), we then have

$$\theta_{X|\mathbf{u}}^{ma} = \underset{\theta_{X|\mathbf{u}}}{\operatorname{argmax}}\, \mathbb{P}(\theta_{X|\mathbf{u}}|\mathcal{D}).$$

It is worth mentioning here the relationship between MAP and maximum likelihood parameters. Since,

$$\mathbb{P}(\theta|\mathcal{D}) = \frac{\mathbb{P}(\mathcal{D}|\theta)\mathbb{P}(\theta)}{\mathbb{P}(\mathcal{D})} \propto \mathbb{P}(\mathcal{D}|\theta)\mathbb{P}(\theta),$$

the only difference between MAP and maximum likelihood parameters is in the prior $\mathbb{P}(\theta)$. Hence, if all network parameterizations are equally likely, that is, $\mathbb{P}(\theta)$ is a uniform distribution, then MAP and maximum likelihood parameters will coincide:

$$\underset{\theta}{\operatorname{argmax}}\, \mathbb{P}(\theta|\mathcal{D}) = \underset{\theta}{\operatorname{argmax}}\, \mathbb{P}(\mathcal{D}|\theta).$$

18.3.3 Dealing with incomplete data

Consider again the network structure in Figure 18.1 and the incomplete data set $\mathcal{D}$:

Case	H	S	E
1	?	F	T
2	?	F	T
3	?	F	T
4	?	F	F
5	?	T	F

Suppose now that our goal is to compute the probability of observing a smoker who exercises regularly. As with the case of complete data, the Bayesian approach asserts the previous data set as evidence on the network in Figure 18.2 and then poses the following query:

$$\mathbb{P}(S_6 = s, E_6 = e|\mathcal{D}) \approx 10.77\%.$$

---

[1] Since $\mathbb{P}(\mathcal{D}|\theta)$ is called the likelihood of parameters θ, the quantity $\mathbb{P}(\mathcal{D})$ is called the *marginal likelihood* since it equals $\sum_\theta \mathbb{P}(\mathcal{D}|\theta)\mathbb{P}(\theta)$.

Case	H	S	E		Case	H	S	E		Case	H	S	E
1	?	F	T		1	T	?	?		1	T	?	?
2	F	?	T		2	?	T	?		2	?	F	?
3	?	F	T		3	T	?	?		3	F	?	?

(a) Incomplete data set $\mathcal{D}$ (b) Completion $\mathcal{D}^c$ (c) Completion $\mathcal{D}^c$

Figure 18.4: A data set and two of its completions (out of eight possible completions). Note that $\mathcal{D}, \mathcal{D}^c$ is a complete data set.

Note, however, that we can no longer obtain the answer to this query by performing inference on a base network as suggested by Theorem 18.3 since this theorem depends on data completeness.

When the data set is incomplete, evaluating $\mathbb{P}(\alpha_{N+1}|\mathcal{D})$ is generally hard. Therefore, it is not uncommon to appeal to approximate inference techniques in this case. We discuss two of these techniques next.

Approximating the marginal likelihood

The first set of techniques focuses on approximating the *marginal likelihood*, $\mathbb{P}(\mathcal{D})$, as this provides a handle on computing $\mathbb{P}(\alpha_{N+1}|\mathcal{D})$:

$$\mathbb{P}(\alpha_{N+1}|\mathcal{D}) = \frac{\mathbb{P}(\alpha_{N+1}, \mathcal{D})}{\mathbb{P}(\mathcal{D})}.$$

Note here that $\alpha_{N+1}, \mathcal{D}$ is a data set of size $N+1$, just as $\mathcal{D}$ is a data set of size N – assuming that α_{N+1} is a variable instantiation and can therefore be treated as a case.

The marginal likelihood $\mathbb{P}(\mathcal{D})$ can be approximated using stochastic sampling techniques discussed in Chapter 15. A common application of these techniques is in the context of the *candidate method*, which requires us to approximate $\mathbb{P}(\theta|\mathcal{D})$ for some parametrization θ and then use this approximation to compute the marginal likelihood as

$$\mathbb{P}(\mathcal{D}) = \frac{\mathbb{P}(\mathcal{D}|\theta)\mathbb{P}(\theta)}{\mathbb{P}(\theta|\mathcal{D})}.$$

Note here that the likelihood $\mathbb{P}(\mathcal{D}|\theta)$ can be computed exactly by performing inference on the base network as given by (18.7). The prior $\mathbb{P}(\theta)$ can also be computed exactly as given by (18.5).

To approximate $\mathbb{P}(\theta|\mathcal{D})$, we observe the following:

$$\mathbb{P}(\theta|\mathcal{D}) = \sum_{\mathcal{D}^c} \mathbb{P}(\theta|\mathcal{D}, \mathcal{D}^c)\mathbb{P}(\mathcal{D}^c|\mathcal{D}),$$

where $\mathcal{D}^c$ is a *completion* of the data set $\mathcal{D}$, assigning values to exactly those variables that have missing values in $\mathcal{D}$ (see Figure 18.4). Hence, $\mathbb{P}(\theta|\mathcal{D})$ is an expectation of $\mathbb{P}(\theta|\mathcal{D}, \mathcal{D}^c)$ with respect to the distribution $\mathbb{P}(\mathcal{D}^c|\mathcal{D})$. We can then use the techniques discussed in Chapter 15 for estimating expectations. For example, we can use Gibbs sampling for this purpose, as suggested by Exercise 18.15.

Using MAP estimates

Another technique for dealing with incomplete data is based on the following approximation:

$$\mathbb{P}(\alpha_{N+1}|\mathcal{D}) = \sum_{\theta} \mathrm{Pr}_{\theta}(\alpha)\mathbb{P}(\theta|\mathcal{D}) \approx \mathrm{Pr}_{\theta^{ma}}(\alpha),$$

where θ^{ma} are the MAP parameter estimates defined as

$$\theta^{ma} \stackrel{def}{=} \underset{\theta}{\mathrm{argmax}}\ \mathbb{P}(\theta|\mathcal{D}).$$

That is, instead of summing over all parameter estimates θ, we restrict ourselves to MAP estimates θ^{ma}. Note that this approximation can be computed by performing inference on a base network that is parameterized by these MAP estimates, just as we did with the Bayesian estimates.

The approximation here is usually justified for large data sets where the posterior $\mathbb{P}(\theta|\mathcal{D})$ becomes sharper while peaking at the MAP estimates. Note, however, that computing MAP estimates is also hard, so we typically appeal to local search methods. We next describe an EM algorithm that searches for MAP estimates and has similar properties to the EM algorithm discussed in Chapter 17 for finding maximum likelihood estimates.

Our goal here is to find a parametrization θ that maximizes $\mathbb{P}(\theta|\mathcal{D})$. As mentioned previously, $\mathbb{P}(\theta|\mathcal{D})$ can be expressed as

$$\mathbb{P}(\theta|\mathcal{D}) = \sum_{\mathcal{D}^c} \mathbb{P}(\theta|\mathcal{D}, \mathcal{D}^c)\mathbb{P}(\mathcal{D}^c|\mathcal{D}),$$

where $\mathcal{D}^c$ is a completion of data set $\mathcal{D}$, assigning values to exactly those variables that have missing values in $\mathcal{D}$ (see Figure 18.4). We can therefore think of $\mathbb{P}(\theta|\mathcal{D})$ as an expectation of $\mathbb{P}(\theta|\mathcal{D}, \mathcal{D}^c)$ computed with respect to the distribution $\mathbb{P}(\mathcal{D}^c|\mathcal{D})$. Our goal is then to find a parametrization θ that maximizes this expectation.

Suppose instead that we maximize the following expectation:

$$e(\theta|\mathcal{D}, \theta^k) \stackrel{def}{=} \sum_{\mathcal{D}^c} \Big[\log \mathbb{P}(\theta|\mathcal{D}, \mathcal{D}^c) \Big] \mathbb{P}(\mathcal{D}^c|\mathcal{D}, \theta^k).$$

That is, we are now computing the expectation of $\log \mathbb{P}(\theta|\mathcal{D}, \mathcal{D}^c)$ instead of $\mathbb{P}(\theta|\mathcal{D}, \mathcal{D}^c)$. Moreover, we are computing this expectation with respect to the distribution $\mathbb{P}(\mathcal{D}^c|\mathcal{D}, \theta^k)$ instead of $\mathbb{P}(\mathcal{D}^c|\mathcal{D})$ where θ^k is some arbitrary parametrization.

The resulting expectation is clearly not equal to the original expectation in which we are interested. As such, it cannot yield the MAP estimates we are after. As it turns out, maximizing this new expectation is guaranteed to at least improve on the parametrization θ^k.

Theorem 18.5. *If* $\theta^{k+1} = \mathrm{argmax}_\theta\ e(\theta|\mathcal{D}, \theta^k)$, *then* $\mathbb{P}(\theta^{k+1}|\mathcal{D}) \geq \mathbb{P}(\theta^k|\mathcal{D})$. $\qquad\blacksquare$

We can therefore use this observation as a basis for developing a local search algorithm for MAP estimates. That is, we start with some initial estimates θ^0, typically chosen randomly, and generate a sequence of estimates $\theta^0, \theta^1, \theta^2, \ldots$ until some convergence criterion is met. If estimate θ^{k+1} is obtained from estimate θ^k as given by Theorem 18.5, we are then guaranteed that the probability of these estimates will be nondecreasing.

To complete the description of the algorithm, all we need to show is how to optimize the expectation $e(\theta|\mathcal{D}, \theta^k)$. This is actually straightforward once we obtain the following *expected counts*.

Definition 18.4. Given a data set $\mathcal{D}$, the *expected count* of event α given parameter estimates θ^k is defined as

$$\mathcal{D}\#(\alpha|\theta^k) \stackrel{def}{=} \sum_{\mathcal{D}^c} \Big([\mathcal{D}\mathcal{D}^c]\#(\alpha) \Big) \mathbb{P}(\mathcal{D}^c|\mathcal{D}, \theta^k). \qquad\blacksquare$$

Algorithm 51 MAP_EM_D($G, \theta^0, \mathcal{D}$)

---

input:

 G: Bayesian network structure with families $X\mathbf{U}$

 θ^0: parametrization of structure G

 $\mathcal{D}$: data set of size N

output: MAP/EM parameter estimates for structure G

main:

 1: $k \leftarrow 0$

 2: **while** $\theta^k \neq \theta^{k-1}$ **do** {this test is different in practice}

 3:   $c_{x\mathbf{u}} \leftarrow 0$ for each family instantiation $x\mathbf{u}$

 4:   **for** $i = 1$ to N **do**

 5:    **for** each family instantiation $x\mathbf{u}$ **do**

 6:     $c_{x\mathbf{u}} \leftarrow c_{x\mathbf{u}} + \Pr_{\theta^k}(x\mathbf{u}|\mathbf{d}_i)$ {requires inference on network (G, θ^k)}

 7:    **end for**

 8:   **end for**

 9:   compute parameters θ^{k+1} using $\theta^{k+1}_{X|\mathbf{u}} = \operatorname{argmax}_{\theta_{X|\mathbf{u}}} \mathbb{P}(\theta_{X|\mathbf{u}}) \prod_x \left[\theta_{x|\mathbf{u}}\right]^{c_{x\mathbf{u}}}$

 10: $k \leftarrow k + 1$

 11: **end while**

 12: **return** θ^k

That is, we consider every completion $\mathcal{D}^c$ of data set $\mathcal{D}$, compute the count of α with respect to the complete data set $\mathcal{D}\mathcal{D}^c$ (see Definition 17.1), and finally take the average of these counts weighted by the distribution $\mathbb{P}(\mathcal{D}^c|\mathcal{D}, \theta^k)$. Interestingly enough, we can obtain this expected count without enumerating all possible completions $\mathcal{D}^c$. In particular, Exercise 18.10 asks for a proof to the following closed form:

$$\mathcal{D}\#(\alpha|\theta^k) = \sum_{i=1}^{N} \Pr_{\theta^k}(\alpha|\mathbf{d}_i). \tag{18.9}$$

According to (18.9), we can obtain an expected count by performing inference on the base network that is parameterized by θ^k. Once we have these expected counts, we can optimize the expectation $e(\theta|\mathcal{D}, \theta^k)$ as shown by Theorem 18.6.

Theorem 18.6. $\theta^{k+1} = \operatorname{argmax}_\theta e(\theta|\mathcal{D}, \theta^k)$ *iff*

$$\theta^{k+1}_{X|\mathbf{u}} = \operatorname*{argmax}_{\theta_{X|\mathbf{u}}} \mathbb{P}(\theta_{X|\mathbf{u}}) \prod_x \left[\theta_{x|\mathbf{u}}\right]^{\mathcal{D}\#(x\mathbf{u}|\theta^k)}. \qquad \blacksquare$$

Recall now Theorem 18.4, which provides a closed form for the posterior of a parameter set given complete data. Theorem 18.6 is then showing that to optimize $e(\theta|\mathcal{D}, \theta^k)$, all we need is to compute the posterior for each parameter set $\theta_{X|\mathbf{u}}$ while treating the expected counts as coming from a complete data set. We can then optimize the expectation $e(\theta|\mathcal{D}, \theta^k)$ by simply finding the MAP estimate $\theta^{k+1}_{X|\mathbf{u}}$ for each of the computed posteriors. Algorithm 51 provides the pseudocode for computing MAP estimates using the described EM algorithm.

We effectively reduced an incomplete-data MAP problem to a sequence of complete-data MAP problems. The only computational demand here is that of computing the expected counts, which are needed to compute the posteriors of each complete-data problem.

18.4 Learning with continuous parameter sets

We have thus far worked only with discrete parameter sets. For example, we assumed in Figure 18.3 that the parameter set $\theta_{S|\bar{h}}$ has only two values $(.25, .75)$ and $(.50, .50)$ since our prior knowledge precluded all other values for network parameters $(\theta_{s|\bar{h}}, \theta_{\bar{s}|\bar{h}})$. On the other hand, if we allow all possible values for these parameters, the parameter set $\theta_{S|\bar{h}}$ will then be continuous (i.e., having an infinite number of values).

To apply Bayesian learning in this context, we need a method for capturing prior knowledge on continuous parameter sets (CPTs are only appropriate for discrete parameter sets). We also need to discuss the semantics of meta-networks that contain continuous variables. We have not defined the semantics of such networks in this text as our treatment is restricted to networks with discrete variables (except for the treatment of continuous sensor readings in Section 3.7). We address both of these issues in the next two sections.

18.4.1 Dirichlet priors

Consider the parameter set $\theta_H = (\theta_h, \theta_{\bar{h}})$ in Figure 18.3 and suppose that we expect it has the value $(.75, .25)$ yet we do not rule out other values, such as $(.90, .10)$ and $(.40, .60)$. Suppose further that our belief in other values decreases as they deviate more from the expected value $(.75, .25)$. One way to specify this knowledge is using a Dirichlet distribution, which requires two numbers ψ_h and $\psi_{\bar{h}}$, called *exponents*, where

$$\frac{\psi_h}{\psi_h + \psi_{\bar{h}}}$$

is the expected value of parameter θ_h and

$$\frac{\psi_{\bar{h}}}{\psi_h + \psi_{\bar{h}}}$$

is the expected value of parameter $\theta_{\bar{h}}$. For example, we can use the exponents $\psi_h = 7.5$ and $\psi_{\bar{h}} = 2.5$ to obtain the expectation $(\frac{7.5}{7.5+2.5}, \frac{2.5}{7.5+2.5}) = (.75, .25)$. We can also use the exponents $\psi_h = 75$ and $\psi_{\bar{h}} = 25$ to obtain the same expectation $(\frac{75}{75+25}, \frac{25}{75+25})$. As is clear from this example, there is an infinite number of exponents that we can use, all of which lead to the same expected value of network parameters.

According to the semantics of a Dirichlet distribution, which we provide formally next, these different values of the exponents are not all the same. In particular, the sum of these exponents, $\psi_h + \psi_{\bar{h}}$, is interpreted as a measure of confidence in the expectations they lead to. This sum is called the *equivalent sample size* of the Dirichlet distribution, where a larger equivalent sample size is interpreted as providing more confidence in the corresponding expectations.

To provide more intuition into the Dirichlet distribution, think of the exponent ψ_h as the number of health-aware individuals observed before encountering the current data set, and similarly for the exponent $\psi_{\bar{h}}$. According to this interpretation, the exponents $(\psi_h = 7.5, \psi_{\bar{h}} = 2.5)$ and $(\psi_h = 75, \psi_{\bar{h}} = 25)$ can both be used to encode the belief that 75% of the individuals are health-aware yet the second set of exponents imply a stronger belief as they are based on a larger sample.

Consider now variable E in Figure 18.3 and suppose that it takes three values:

- e_1: the individual does not exercise at all
- e_2: the individual exercises but not regularly
- e_3: the individual exercises regularly.

Suppose now that we wish to encode our prior knowledge about the parameter set $\theta_{E|h} = (\theta_{e_1|h}, \theta_{e_2|h}, \theta_{e_3|h})$. If we expect this set to have the value $(.10, .60, .30)$, we can then use the exponents

$$\psi_{e_1|h} = 10, \quad \psi_{e_2|h} = 60, \quad \psi_{e_3|h} = 30,$$

which lead to the expectations

$$\frac{10}{10 + 60 + 30}, \quad \frac{60}{10 + 60 + 30}, \quad \frac{30}{10 + 60 + 30}.$$

We are now ready to present the formal definition of the Dirichlet distribution.

Definition 18.5. A *Dirichlet distribution* for a continuous parameter set $\theta_{X|\mathbf{u}}$ is specified by a set of *exponents*, $\psi_{x|\mathbf{u}} \geq 1$.[2] The *equivalent sample size* of the distribution is defined as

$$\psi_{X|\mathbf{u}} \overset{def}{=} \sum_x \psi_{x|\mathbf{u}}.$$

The Dirichlet distribution has the following density:

$$\rho(\theta_{X|\mathbf{u}}) \overset{def}{=} \eta \prod_x \left[\theta_{x|\mathbf{u}}\right]^{\psi_{x|\mathbf{u}}-1},$$

where η is a normalizing constant

$$\eta \overset{def}{=} \frac{\Gamma(\psi_{X|\mathbf{u}})}{\prod_x \Gamma(\psi_{x|\mathbf{u}})}.$$

Here $\Gamma(.)$ is the Gamma function, which is an extension of the factorial function to real numbers.[3]   ■

The Dirichlet density function may appear somewhat involved yet we only use it in proving Theorem 18.9. Aside from this theorem, we only need the following well-known properties of the Dirichlet distribution, which we provide without proof. First, the expected value of network parameter $\theta_{x|\mathbf{u}}$ is given by

$$\text{Ex}(\theta_{x|\mathbf{u}}) = \frac{\psi_{x|\mathbf{u}}}{\psi_{X|\mathbf{u}}}. \tag{18.10}$$

Next, the variance of this parameter is given by

$$\text{Va}\left(\theta_{x|\mathbf{u}}\right) = \frac{\text{Ex}(\theta_{x|\mathbf{u}})(1 - \text{Ex}(\theta_{x|\mathbf{u}}))}{\psi_{X|\mathbf{u}} + 1}. \tag{18.11}$$

Note that the larger the equivalent sample size, $\psi_{X|\mathbf{u}}$, the smaller the variance and, hence, the more confidence we have in the expected values of network parameters. The final

---

[2] The Dirichlet distribution can be defined for exponents $0 < \psi_{x|\mathbf{u}} < 1$ but its behavior for these exponents leads to mathematical complications that we try to avoid here. For example (18.12) does not hold in this case.

[3] The Gamma function is generally defined as $\Gamma(a) = \int_0^\infty x^{a-1}e^{-x}dx$. We have $\Gamma(1) = 1$ and $\Gamma(a+1) = a\Gamma(a)$, which means that $\Gamma(a) = (a-1)!$ when a is an integer ≥ 1.

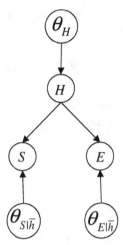

Figure 18.5: A meta-network with continuous parameter sets.

property we use of the Dirichlet distribution concerns the mode of a parameter set, which is the value having the largest density. This is given by

$$\mathrm{Md}\left(\theta_{x|\mathbf{u}}\right) = \frac{\psi_{x|\mathbf{u}} - 1}{\psi_{X|\mathbf{u}} - |X|}, \tag{18.12}$$

where $|X|$ is the number of values for variable X. We close this section by noting that a Dirichlet distribution with two exponents is also known as the *beta distribution.*

18.4.2 The semantics of continuous parameter sets

A meta-network with discrete parameter sets induces a probability distribution but a meta-network with continuous parameter sets induces a density function. Consider for example the meta-network in Figure 18.5 and suppose that all parameter sets are continuous. The density function specified by this meta-network is given by

$$\rho(\theta_H, \theta_{S|\bar{h}}, \theta_{E|\bar{h}}, H, S, E) = \rho(\theta_H)\rho(\theta_{S|\bar{h}})\rho(\theta_{E|\bar{h}})\mathbb{P}(H|\theta_H)\mathbb{P}(S|H, \theta_{S|\bar{h}})\mathbb{P}(E|H, \theta_{E|\bar{h}}).$$

Hence, similar to Bayesian networks with discrete variables, the semantics of a network with continuous variables is defined by the chain rule, except that we now have a product of densities (for continuous variables) and probabilities (for discrete variables). The other difference we have is when computing marginals. For example, the marginal over parameter sets is a density given by

$$\rho(\theta_H, \theta_{S|\bar{h}}, \theta_{E|\bar{h}}) = \sum_{h,s,e} \rho(\theta_H, \theta_{S|\bar{h}}, \theta_{E|\bar{h}}, H = h, S = s, E = e),$$

while the marginal over discrete variables is a distribution given by[4]

$$\mathbb{P}(H, S, E) = \int \int \int \rho(\theta_H, \theta_{S|\bar{h}}, \theta_{E|\bar{h}}, H, S, E) d\theta_H d\theta_{S|\bar{h}} d\theta_{E|\bar{h}}.$$

The more general rule is this: Discrete variables are summed out while continuous variables are integrated over. The result is a probability only if all continuous variables are

---

[4] Suppose that $\theta_{X|\mathbf{u}} = (\theta_{x_1|\mathbf{u}}, \dots, \theta_{x_k|\mathbf{u}})$. Integrating over a parameter set $\theta_{X|\mathbf{u}}$ is a shorthand notation for successively integrating over parameters $\theta_{x_1|\mathbf{u}}, \dots, \theta_{x_{k-1}|\mathbf{u}}$ while fixing the value of $\theta_{x_k|\mathbf{u}}$ to $1 - \sum_{i=1}^{k-1} \theta_{x_i|\mathbf{u}}$.

integrated over; otherwise, the result is a density. For example, the marginal over parameter set $\theta_{S|\bar{h}}$ is a density given by

$$\rho(\theta_{S|\bar{h}}) = \int \int \left[\sum_{h,s,e} \rho(\theta_H, \theta_{S|\bar{h}}, \theta_{E|\bar{h}}, H=h, S=s, E=e) \right] d\theta_H d\theta_{E|\bar{h}}.$$

Density behaves like probability as far as independence is concerned. For example, since the meta-network satisfies parameter independence, we have

$$\rho(\theta_H, \theta_{S|\bar{h}}, \theta_{E|\bar{h}}) = \rho(\theta_H)\rho(\theta_{S|\bar{h}})\rho(\theta_{E|\bar{h}})$$

and

$$\rho(\theta_H, \theta_{S|\bar{h}}, \theta_{E|\bar{h}}|\mathcal{D}) = \rho(\theta_H|\mathcal{D})\rho(\theta_{S|\bar{h}}|\mathcal{D})\rho(\theta_{E|\bar{h}}|\mathcal{D})$$

when the data set $\mathcal{D}$ is complete. Density also behaves like probability as far as conditioning is concerned. For example,

$$\rho(H|\theta_H) = \frac{\rho(\theta_H, H)}{\rho(\theta_H)}$$

and

$$\rho(\theta_H|H) = \frac{\rho(\theta_H, H)}{\mathbb{P}(H)}.$$

18.4.3 Bayesian learning

We can now state the main theorems for Bayesian learning with continuous parameter sets, which parallel the ones for discrete sets. We start with the following parallel to Theorem 18.2.

Theorem 18.7. *Given continuous parameter sets and a data set $\mathcal{D}$ of size N, we have*[5]

$$\mathbb{P}(\alpha_{N+1}|\mathcal{D}) = \int \text{Pr}_\theta(\alpha)\rho(\theta|\mathcal{D})d\theta. \tag{18.13}$$

∎

That is, the quantity $\mathbb{P}(\alpha_{N+1}|\mathcal{D})$ is an expectation of the probability $\text{Pr}_\theta(\alpha)$, which is defined with respect to the base network.

Now the parallel to Definition 18.3:

Definition 18.6. *Let $\theta_{X|\mathbf{u}}$ be a continuous parameter set. The Bayesian estimate for network parameter $\theta_{x|\mathbf{u}}$ given data set $\mathcal{D}$ is defined as*

$$\theta_{x|\mathbf{u}}^{be} \overset{\text{def}}{=} \int \theta_{x|\mathbf{u}} \cdot \rho(\theta_{X|\mathbf{u}}|\mathcal{D})d\theta_{X|\mathbf{u}}.$$

∎

As in the discrete case, we can sometimes reduce inference on a meta-network to inference on a base network using the Bayesian estimates θ^{be}. This is given by the following parallel to Theorem 18.3.

---

[5] Integrating over a parametrization θ is a shorthand notation for successively integrating over each of its parameter sets.

Theorem 18.8. *Given continuous parameter sets and a complete data set $\mathcal{D}$ of size N, we have*

$$\mathbb{P}(\alpha_{N+1}|\mathcal{D}) = \text{Pr}_{\theta^{be}}(\alpha),\qquad(18.14)$$

where θ^{be} are the Bayesian estimates given data set $\mathcal{D}$. ∎

18.4.4 Computing Bayesian estimates

The Bayesian estimates are at the heart of the Bayesian approach to learning when the data set is complete. This is due to Theorem 18.8, which allows us to reduce Bayesian learning to inference on a base network that is parameterized by the Bayesian estimates. However, the computation of these estimates hinges on an ability to compute posterior marginals over parameter sets, which is needed in Definition 18.6. The following parallel to Theorem 18.4 provides a closed form for these posteriors.

Theorem 18.9. *Consider a meta-network where each parameter set $\theta_{X|\mathbf{u}}$ has a prior Dirichlet density $\rho(\theta_{X|\mathbf{u}})$ specified by exponents $\psi_{x|\mathbf{u}}$. Let $\mathcal{D}$ be a complete data set. The posterior density $\rho(\theta_{X|\mathbf{u}}|\mathcal{D})$ is then a Dirichlet density, specified by the following exponents:*

$$\psi'_{x|\mathbf{u}} = \psi_{x|\mathbf{u}} + \mathcal{D}\#(x\mathbf{u}).\qquad(18.15)$$

∎

Consider now the parameter set $\theta_{S|h} = (\theta_{s|h}, \theta_{\bar{s}|h})$ with a prior density $\rho(\theta_{S|h})$ specified by the exponents

$$\psi_{s|h} = 1 \quad \text{and} \quad \psi_{\bar{s}|h} = 9.$$

The prior expectation of parameter $\theta_{s|h}$ is then .1. Consider now the data set

Case	H	S	E
1	F	F	T
2	T	F	T
3	T	F	T
4	F	F	F
5	F	T	F

The posterior density $\rho(\theta_{S|h}|\mathcal{D})$ is also Dirichlet, specified by the exponents

$$\psi'_{s|h} = 1 + 0 = 1 \quad \text{and} \quad \psi'_{\bar{s}|h} = 9 + 2 = 11.$$

The posterior expectation of parameter $\theta_{s|h}$ is now $1/12$.

More generally, the posterior expectation of parameter $\theta_{x|\mathbf{u}}$ given complete data is given by

$$\theta^{be}_{x|\mathbf{u}} = \frac{\psi_{x|\mathbf{u}} + \mathcal{D}\#(x\mathbf{u})}{\psi_{X|\mathbf{u}} + \mathcal{D}\#(\mathbf{u})},\qquad(18.16)$$

where $\psi_{x|\mathbf{u}}$ are the exponents of the prior Dirichlet distribution and $\psi_{X|\mathbf{u}}$ is its equivalent sample size. This is the Bayesian estimate in the context of Dirichlet distributions. Moreover, given (18.12) the MAP estimate given complete data is

$$\theta^{ma}_{x|\mathbf{u}} = \frac{\psi_{x|\mathbf{u}} + \mathcal{D}\#(x\mathbf{u}) - 1}{\psi_{X|\mathbf{u}} + \mathcal{D}\#(\mathbf{u}) - |X|}.\qquad(18.17)$$

In this example, the MAP estimate for parameter $\theta_{s|h}$ is 0.

Let us now compare these estimates with the maximum likelihood estimate given by (17.1):

$$\theta_{x|\mathbf{u}}^{ml} = \frac{\mathcal{D}\#(x\mathbf{u})}{\mathcal{D}\#(\mathbf{u})}.$$

Note that contrary to maximum likelihood estimates, the Bayesian (and sometimes MAP) estimates do not suffer from the problem of zero counts. That is, these estimates are well-defined even when $\mathcal{D}\#(\mathbf{u}) = 0$. Note also that the Bayesian and MAP estimates converge to the maximum likelihood estimates as the data set size tends to infinity, assuming the data set is generated by a strictly positive distribution.

Consider now the prior Dirichlet distribution, called a *noninformative* prior, in which all exponents are equal to one: $\psi_{x|\mathbf{u}} = 1$. The expectation of parameter $\theta_{x|\mathbf{u}}$ is $1/|X|$ under this prior, leading to a uniform distribution for variable X given any parent instantiation $\mathbf{u}$. Under this prior, the Bayesian estimate given a complete data is

$$\theta_{x|\mathbf{u}}^{be} = \frac{1 + \mathcal{D}\#(x\mathbf{u})}{|X| + \mathcal{D}\#(\mathbf{u})}.$$

Moreover, the MAP estimate is

$$\theta_{x|\mathbf{u}}^{ma} = \frac{\mathcal{D}\#(x\mathbf{u})}{\mathcal{D}\#(\mathbf{u})},$$

which coincides with the maximum likelihood estimate.[6]

18.4.5 Closed forms for complete data

We now summarize the computations for continuous parameter sets that are known to have closed forms under complete data. We assume here a base network with families $X\mathbf{U}$ and a complete data set $\mathcal{D}$ of size N:

- The prior density of network parameters:

$$\rho(\theta) = \prod_{X\mathbf{U}} \prod_{\mathbf{u}} \rho(\theta_{X|\mathbf{u}}) \tag{18.18}$$

- The posterior density of network parameters:

$$\rho(\theta|\mathcal{D}) = \prod_{X\mathbf{U}} \prod_{\mathbf{u}} \rho(\theta_{X|\mathbf{u}}|\mathcal{D}) \tag{18.19}$$

- The likelihood of network parameters (same as 18.7):

$$\mathbb{P}(\mathcal{D}|\theta) = \prod_{i=1}^{N} \mathrm{Pr}_{\theta}(\mathbf{d}_i) \tag{18.20}$$

- The marginal likelihood:

$$\mathbb{P}(\mathcal{D}) = \prod_{X\mathbf{U}} \prod_{\mathbf{u}} \frac{\Gamma(\psi_{X|\mathbf{u}})}{\Gamma(\psi_{X|\mathbf{u}} + \mathcal{D}\#(\mathbf{u}))} \prod_{x} \frac{\Gamma(\psi_{x|\mathbf{u}} + \mathcal{D}\#(x\mathbf{u}))}{\Gamma(\psi_{x|\mathbf{u}})}. \tag{18.21}$$

---

[6] Note, however, that this equality is not implied by the fact that parameters $\theta_{x|\mathbf{u}}$ have equal expectations. For example, if all exponents are equal to 10, then all parameters have equal expectations yet the MAP and maximum likelihood estimates do not coincide.

The last equation is stated and proved in Theorem 18.12 on Page 514. The proof provides an alternative form that does not use the Gamma function but the form here, which may seem surprising at first, is more commonly cited in the literature.

18.4.6 Dealing with incomplete data

The techniques for dealing with incomplete data are similar to those for discrete parameter sets: approximating the marginal likelihood using stochastic sampling and using MAP estimates as computed by EM. We briefly discuss these techniques next in the context of continuous parameter sets. We also discuss large-sample approximations of the marginal likelihood, which can be more efficient computationally than stochastic sampling approaches.

Using MAP estimates

We previously provided an EM algorithm that searches for MAP estimates of discrete parameter sets. The algorithm has a parallel for continuous parameter sets, which we describe next.

Our goal here is to find parameter estimates that maximize the density $\rho(\theta|\mathcal{D})$, which can be expressed in terms of the following expectation:

$$\rho(\theta|\mathcal{D}) = \sum_{\mathcal{D}^c} \rho(\theta|\mathcal{D}, \mathcal{D}^c)\mathbb{P}(\mathcal{D}^c|\mathcal{D}).$$

Recall that $\mathcal{D}^c$ is a completion of the data set $\mathcal{D}$.

Instead of optimizing this quantity, we optimize the following expectation:

$$e(\theta|\mathcal{D}, \theta^k) \stackrel{def}{=} \sum_{\mathcal{D}^c} \Big[\log \rho(\theta|\mathcal{D}, \mathcal{D}^c) \Big] \mathbb{P}(\mathcal{D}^c|\mathcal{D}, \theta^k),$$

where θ^k are some initial estimates. The resulting estimates from this new optimization problem are then guaranteed to improve on the initial estimates, as shown by Theorem 18.10.

Theorem 18.10. *If $\theta^{k+1} = \text{argmax}_\theta \, e(\theta|\mathcal{D}, \theta^k)$, then $\rho(\theta^{k+1}|\mathcal{D}) \geq \rho(\theta^k|\mathcal{D})$.* ∎

The description of the new EM algorithm is completed by Theorem 18.11, which shows how we can maximize the new expectation.

Theorem 18.11. $\theta^{k+1} = \text{argmax}_\theta \, e(\theta|\mathcal{D}, \theta^k)$ *iff*

$$\theta^{k+1}_{x|\mathbf{u}} = \frac{\mathcal{D}\#(x\mathbf{u}|\theta^k) + \psi_{x|\mathbf{u}} - 1}{\mathcal{D}\#(\mathbf{u}|\theta^k) + \psi_{X|\mathbf{u}} - |X|}.$$ ∎

Hence, all we need is to compute the expected counts $\mathcal{D}\#(.|\theta^k)$ using (18.9), which requires inference on the base network.

Let us now recall Theorem 18.9, which provides a closed form for the posterior Dirichlet density under complete data, and (18.12), which provides a closed form for the modes of a Dirichlet distribution (i.e., the values of parameters that have a maximal density). Theorem 18.11 then suggests that we compute a posterior Dirichlet distribution for each parameter set while treating the expected counts as coming from a complete data set. It then suggests that we take the modes of these computed posteriors as our parameter estimates. Hence, once again we reduced a MAP problem for incomplete data to a

---

Algorithm 52 MAP_EM_C(G, θ^0, $\mathcal{D}$, $\psi_{x|\mathbf{u}}/\psi_{X|\mathbf{u}}$)

---

input:

G:	Bayesian network structure with families $X\mathbf{U}$
θ^0:	parametrization of structure G
$\mathcal{D}$:	data set of size N
$\psi_{x|\mathbf{u}}/\psi_{X|\mathbf{u}}$:	Dirichlet prior for each parameter set $\theta_{X|\mathbf{u}}$ of structure G

output: MAP/EM parameter estimates for structure G

main:

1:   $k \leftarrow 0$
2:   **while** $\theta^k \neq \theta^{k-1}$ **do** {this test is different in practice}
3:     $c_{x\mathbf{u}} \leftarrow 0$ and $c_{\mathbf{u}} \leftarrow 0$ for each family instantiation $x\mathbf{u}$
4:     **for** $i = 1$ to N **do**
5:       **for** each family instantiation $x\mathbf{u}$ **do**
6:         $c_{x\mathbf{u}} \leftarrow c_{x\mathbf{u}} + \text{Pr}_{\theta^k}(x\mathbf{u}|\mathbf{d}_i)$ {requires inference on network (G, θ^k)}
7:         $c_{\mathbf{u}} \leftarrow c_{\mathbf{u}} + \text{Pr}_{\theta^k}(\mathbf{u}|\mathbf{d}_i)$
8:       **end for**
9:     **end for**
10:    compute parameters θ^{k+1} using $\theta_{x|\mathbf{u}}^{k+1} = (c_{x\mathbf{u}} + \psi_{x|\mathbf{u}} - 1)/(c_{\mathbf{u}} + \psi_{X|\mathbf{u}} - |X|)$
11:    $k \leftarrow k + 1$
12: **end while**
13: **return** θ^k

---

sequence of MAP problems for complete data. Moreover, the only computational demand here is in computing the expected counts, which are needed to define the posteriors for each complete-data problem. Algorithm 52 provides the pseudocode for computing MAP estimates using the described EM algorithm.

The marginal likelihood: Stochastic sampling approximations

The marginal likelihood can also be approximated using the candidate method discussed previously for discrete parameter sets. That is, for some parametrization θ, we can compute the marginal likelihood using the following identity:

$$\mathbb{P}(\mathcal{D}) = \frac{\mathbb{P}(\mathcal{D}|\theta)\rho(\theta)}{\rho(\theta|\mathcal{D})}.$$

As with discrete parameter sets, the likelihood $\mathbb{P}(\mathcal{D}|\theta)$ can be computed exactly by performing inference on the base network as given by (18.20). The prior density $\rho(\theta)$ can also be computed exactly as given by (18.18). Finally, the density $\rho(\theta|\mathcal{D})$ can be approximated using Gibbs sampling (see Exercise 18.15).

The marginal likelihood: Large-sample approximations

We now discuss a class of approximations for the marginal likelihood that is motivated by some properties that hold for large data sets. Consider the simple network $A \rightarrow B$, where variables A and B are binary. This network has six parameters yet only three of them are independent. Suppose now that we choose the following independent parameters,

$$\theta = (\theta_{a_1}, \theta_{b_1|a_1}, \theta_{b_1|a_2}),$$

leaving out dependent parameters θ_{a_2}, $\theta_{b_2|a_1}$, and $\theta_{b_2|a_2}$. The density $\rho(\mathcal{D}, \theta)$ can now be viewed as a function $f(\theta_{a_1}, \theta_{b_1|a_1}, \theta_{b_1|a_2})$ of these independent parameters where the marginal likelihood is the result of integrating over all independent parameters:

$$\mathbb{P}(\mathcal{D}) = \int \int \int f(\theta_{a_1}, \theta_{b_1|a_1}, \theta_{b_1|a_2}) d\theta_{a_1} d\theta_{b_1|a_1} d\theta_{b_1|a_2}.$$

The main observation underlying large-sample approximations concerns the behavior of the function f as the data set size tends to infinity. In particular, under certain conditions this function becomes peaked at MAP parameter estimates, allowing it to be approximated by a multivariate Gaussian $g(\theta_{a_1}, \theta_{b_1|a_1}, \theta_{b_1|a_2})$ whose mean are the MAP estimates. By integrating over the independent parameters of this Gaussian, we obtain the following approximation of the marginal likelihood, which is known as the *Laplace approximation*:

$$\log \mathbb{P}(\mathcal{D}) \approx \log \mathbb{P}(\mathcal{D}|\theta^{ma}) + \log \rho(\theta^{ma}) + \frac{d}{2} \log(2\pi) - \frac{1}{2} \log |\Sigma|. \tag{18.22}$$

Here d is the number of independent parameters, θ^{ma} are the MAP estimates, and Σ is the Hessian of $-\log \rho(\mathcal{D}, \theta)$ evaluated at the MAP estimates. That is, Σ is the matrix of second partial derivatives:

$$\Sigma = \begin{bmatrix} -\dfrac{\partial^2 \log \rho(\mathcal{D}, \theta)}{\partial \theta_{a_1} \partial \theta_{a_1}}(\theta^{ma}) & -\dfrac{\partial^2 \log \rho(\mathcal{D}, \theta)}{\partial \theta_{a_1} \partial \theta_{b_1|a_1}}(\theta^{ma}) & -\dfrac{\partial^2 \log \rho(\mathcal{D}, \theta)}{\partial \theta_{a_1} \partial \theta_{b_1|a_2}}(\theta^{ma}) \\[2em] -\dfrac{\partial^2 \log \rho(\mathcal{D}, \theta)}{\partial \theta_{a_1} \partial \theta_{b_1|a_1}}(\theta^{ma}) & -\dfrac{\partial^2 \log \rho(\mathcal{D}, \theta)}{\partial \theta_{b_1|a_1} \partial \theta_{b_1|a_1}}(\theta^{ma}) & -\dfrac{\partial^2 \log \rho(\mathcal{D}, \theta)}{\partial \theta_{b_1|a_1} \partial \theta_{b_1|a_2}}(\theta^{ma}) \\[2em] -\dfrac{\partial^2 \log \rho(\mathcal{D}, \theta)}{\partial \theta_{a_1} \partial \theta_{b_1|a_2}}(\theta^{ma}) & -\dfrac{\partial^2 \log \rho(\mathcal{D}, \theta)}{\partial \theta_{b_1|a_1} \partial \theta_{b_1|a_2}}(\theta^{ma}) & -\dfrac{\partial^2 \log \rho(\mathcal{D}, \theta)}{\partial \theta_{b_1|a_2} \partial \theta_{b_1|a_2}}(\theta^{ma}) \end{bmatrix}$$

Computing the Laplace approximation requires a number of auxiliary quantities, some of which are straightforward to obtain, while others can be computationally demanding. In particular, we must first compute the MAP estimates θ^{ma} as discussed in the previous section. We must also compute the prior density of MAP estimates $\rho(\theta^{ma})$ and their likelihood $\mathbb{P}(\mathcal{D}|\theta^{ma})$. Both of these quantities can be computed as given by (18.18) and (18.20), respectively. We must finally compute the Hessian Σ and its determinant $|\Sigma|$. Computing the Hessian requires the computation of second partial derivatives, as discussed in Exercise 18.20. The determinant of matrix Σ can be computed in $O(d^3)$.

The Laplace approximation can be quite accurate. For example, it is known to have a relative error that is $O(1/N)$ under certain conditions, which include the existence of unique MAP estimates. However, the main computational problem with the Laplace approximation is in computing the Hessian and its determinant. This can be especially problematic when the number of independent parameters d is large. To deal with this difficulty, it is not uncommon to simplify the Hessian by assuming

$$\frac{\partial^2 \log \rho(\mathcal{D}, \theta)}{\partial \theta_{x|\mathbf{u}} \partial \theta_{y|\mathbf{v}}}(\theta^{ma}) = 0$$

for $X \neq Y$.

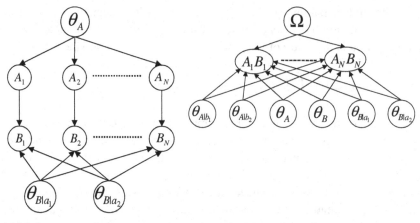

    (a) Meta-network (parameters)   (b) Meta-network (structure)

Figure 18.6: Bayesian learning with unknown network structure.

Another simplification of the Laplace approximation involves retaining only those terms that increase with the data set size N and replacing the MAP estimates by maximum likelihood estimates. Since the likelihood term $\log \mathbb{P}(\mathcal{D}|\theta^{ma})$ increases linearly in N and the determinant term $\log |\Sigma|$ is known to increase as $d \log N$, we get

$$\log \mathbb{P}(\mathcal{D}) \approx \log \mathbb{P}(\mathcal{D}|\theta^{ml}) - \frac{d}{2} \log N.$$

This approximation is known as the *Bayesian information criteria* (BIC). It also corresponds to the MDL score discussed in Chapter 17. This should not be surprising, as the main difference between the maximum likelihood and Bayesian approaches is in the prior on network parameters, and the effect of these priors is known to diminish as the sample size tends to infinity.

18.5 Learning network structure

Our discussion of the Bayesian learning approach has thus far assumed that we know the network structure yet are uncertain about network parameters. We now consider the more general case where both network structure and parameters are unknown. To handle this case, we consider a *structural meta-network* that not only includes parameter sets but also an additional variable to capture all possible network structures. Figure 18.6(b) depicts such a network for a problem that includes two variables A and B.

There are a number of differences between this structural meta-network and the one in Figure 18.6(a), which assumes a fixed network structure. First, we have now lumped variables A and B into a single variable AB that has four values $a_1 b_1$, $a_1 b_2$, $a_2 b_1$, and $a_2 b_2$. Second, we have included an additional variable Ω that has three values, corresponding to the three possible structures over two variables:

Ω	Network structure	Parameter sets
G_1	A, B	θ_A, θ_B
G_2	$A \to B$	$\theta_A, \theta_{B|a_1}, \theta_{B|a_2}$
G_3	$B \to A$	$\theta_B, \theta_{A|b_1}, \theta_{A|b_2}$

The third difference is that the structural meta-network has six parameter sets instead of three, as shown in the previous table, to account for network structures G_1 and G_3. The meta-network in Figure 18.6(b) is then saying that the distribution over variables A, B is determined by the network structure Ω and the values of parameter sets θ_A, θ_B, $\theta_{B|a_1}$, $\theta_{B|a_2}$, $\theta_{A|b_1}$, and $\theta_{A|b_2}$.

In principle, the Bayesian approach is the same whether we have a fixed network structure or not. However, the main difference is that:

- We need more information to specify a structural meta-network.
- Inference on a structural meta-network is more difficult.

Regarding the first point, note that we now need a prior distribution over network structures (the CPT for variable Ω). We also need to specify priors over many more parameter sets to cover every possible network structure. As to the increased complexity of inference, note for example that

$$\mathbb{P}(\alpha_{N+1}|\mathcal{D}) = \sum_G \mathbb{P}(\alpha_{N+1}|\mathcal{D}, G)\mathbb{P}(G|\mathcal{D}),$$

where $\mathbb{P}(\alpha_{N+1}|\mathcal{D}, G)$ is the computational problem we treated earlier in Sections 18.3 and 18.4 (structure G was kept implicit in those sections).

However, this computation is not feasible in practice as it requires summing over all possible network structures G. Two simplification techniques are typically brought to bear on this difficulty. According to the first technique, called *selective model averaging*, we restrict the learning process to a subset of network structures to reduce the size of summation. According to the second and more common technique, known as *model selection*, we search for a network structure that has the highest posterior probability and then use this structure for answering further queries. In particular, we search for a network structure that satisfies

$$G^\star = \underset{G}{\text{argmax}} \, \mathbb{P}(G|\mathcal{D}).$$

This is the same as searching for a structure that satisfies

$$G^\star = \underset{G}{\text{argmax}} \, \frac{\mathbb{P}(\mathcal{D}|G)\mathbb{P}(G)}{\mathbb{P}(\mathcal{D})} = \underset{G}{\text{argmax}} \, \mathbb{P}(\mathcal{D}|G)\mathbb{P}(G)$$

since the marginal likelihood $\mathbb{P}(\mathcal{D})$ does not depend on the network structure G. We can also write this as

$$G^\star = \underset{G}{\text{argmax}} \, \log \mathbb{P}(\mathcal{D}|G) + \log \mathbb{P}(G).$$

This score is now very similar to those discussed in Section 17.4. This is known as a *Bayesian scoring measure*, where its two components can be interpreted similarly to the two components of the general measure given by (17.13). In particular, the component $\log \mathbb{P}(G)$ can be viewed as a penalty term, typically assigning lower probabilities to more complex network structures. Moreover, the component $\log \mathbb{P}(\mathcal{D}|G)$ can be viewed as a measure of fit for the structure G to data set $\mathcal{D}$. In fact, we next define some specific Bayesian scoring measures and show that they can be decomposed similar to the measure in (17.13), allowing us to use techniques from Section 17.5 when searching for a network structure.

18.5.1 The BD score

The Bayesian score is actually a class of scores. We next discuss one of the more common subclasses of Bayesian scores known as *Bayesian Dirichlet (BD)*, which is based on some assumptions we considered earlier:

- Parameter independence
- Dirichlet priors
- Complete data sets.

Under these assumptions, the marginal likelihood given a network structure G, $\mathbb{P}(\mathcal{D}|G)$, is provided by (18.21) (the structure G is implicit in that equation). The BD score of a Bayesian network structure G with families $X\mathbf{U}$ is then given by

$$
\begin{aligned}
\mathrm{BD}(G|\mathcal{D}) &\overset{def}{=} \mathbb{P}(\mathcal{D}|G)\mathbb{P}(G) \\
&= \mathbb{P}(G) \prod_{X\mathbf{U}} \prod_{\mathbf{u}} \frac{\Gamma(\psi_{X|\mathbf{u}})}{\Gamma(\psi_{X|\mathbf{u}} + \mathcal{D}\#(\mathbf{u}))} \prod_{x} \frac{\Gamma(\psi_{x|\mathbf{u}} + \mathcal{D}\#(x\mathbf{u}))}{\Gamma(\psi_{x|\mathbf{u}})}.
\end{aligned}
\qquad (18.23)
$$

This is still a family of scores as one must also define the probability of every structure G and provide a Dirichlet prior for each parameter set $\theta_{X|\mathbf{u}}$ of structure G. Specifying these elements of a BD score is rather formidable in practice, so different assumptions are typically used to simplify this specification process.

Suppose for example that we have a total ordering $X_1, \ldots, X_n$ on network variables where variable X_j can be a parent of variable X_i only if $j < i$. Suppose further that p_{ji} is the probability of X_j being a parent of X_i ($p_{ji} = 0$ if $j \geq i$). If $X_i\mathbf{U}_i$ are the families of structure G and if the presence of edges in a particular structure are assumed to be mutually independent, the probability of structure G is then given by

$$
\mathbb{P}(G) = \prod_{X_i\mathbf{U}_i} \left[\prod_{X_j \in \mathbf{U}_i} p_{ji} \right] \left[\prod_{X_j \notin \mathbf{U}_i} (1 - p_{ji}) \right].
\qquad (18.24)
$$

Note how the prior distribution decomposes into a product of terms, one for each family in the given structure. Note also that we only need $n(n-1)/2$ probability assessments, p_{ji}, to fully specify the prior distribution on all network structures. These assessments can be reduced significantly if we are certain about the presence of certain edges, $p_{ji} = 1$, or absence of these edges, $p_{ji} = 0$.[7]

Assumptions have also been made to simplify the specification of the Dirichlet priors, including the use of noninformative priors where all exponents $\psi_{x|\mathbf{u}}$ are set to 1 (this is known as the K2 score). We next provide a more realistic set of assumptions that leads to a more sophisticated score.

---

[7] We can adopt a similar prior distribution without having to impose a total ordering on the variables but this slightly complicates the score description.

18.5.2 The BDe score

The BDe score (for BD likelihood equivalence) is a common instance of the BD family, which is based on some additional assumptions. The most important of these assumptions are:

- Parameter modularity
- Likelihood equivalence.

Parameter modularity says that the Dirichlet prior for parameter set $\theta_{X|\mathbf{u}}$ is the same in every network structure that contains this parameter set. Consider for example the two network structures $G_1 : A \to B, B \to C$ and $G_2 : A \to B, A \to C$. Variable B has the same set of parents, A, in both structures. Hence, the parameter set $\theta_{B|a}$ with its prior distribution is shared between structures G_1 and G_2 according to parameter modularity.

The structural meta-network in Figure 18.6 embeds this assumption of parameter modularity, leading to only six Dirichlet priors:

Ω	Network structure	Parameter sets
G_1	A, B	$\theta_A, \ \theta_B$
G_2	$A \to B$	$\theta_A, \ \theta_{B|a_1}, \ \theta_{B|a_2}$
G_3	$B \to A$	$\theta_B, \ \theta_{A|b_1}, \ \theta_{A|b_2}$

If we did not have parameter modularity, we would need eight priors instead, corresponding to eight distinct parameter sets:

Ω	Network structure	Parameter sets
G_1	A, B	$\theta_A^{G_1}, \ \theta_B^{G_1}$
G_2	$A \to B$	$\theta_A^{G_2}, \ \theta_{B|a_1}^{G_2}, \ \theta_{B|a_2}^{G_2}$
G_3	$B \to A$	$\theta_B^{G_3}, \ \theta_{A|b_1}^{G_3}, \ \theta_{A|b_2}^{G_3}$

Hence, the Dirichlet prior for parameter set $\theta_A^{G_1}$ could be different from the one for $\theta_A^{G_2}$.

The characteristic assumption of the BDe score is that of *likelihood equivalence*, which says that a data set should never discriminate among network structures that encode the same set of conditional independencies.[8] That is, if structures G_1 and G_2 represent the same set of conditional independencies, then $\mathbb{P}(\mathcal{D}|G_1) = \mathbb{P}(\mathcal{D}|G_2)$. An example of this happens when the two structures are complete, as neither structure encodes any conditional independencies.

As it turns out, these assumptions in addition to some other weaker assumptions[9] imply that the exponent $\psi_{x|\mathbf{u}}$ of any parameter set $\theta_{X|\mathbf{u}}$ has the following form:

$$\psi_{x|\mathbf{u}} = \psi \cdot \Pr(x, \mathbf{u}), \tag{18.25}$$

---

[8] The assumptions of *prior equivalence* and *score equivalence* have also been discussed. Prior equivalence says that the prior probabilities of two network structures are the same if they represent the same set of conditional independencies. Score equivalence holds when we have both prior equivalence and likelihood equivalence.

[9] These include the assumption that every complete structure has a nonzero probability and the assumption that all parameter densities are positive.

where

- $\psi > 0$ is called the *equivalent sample size*.
- Pr is called the *prior distribution* and is defined over the base network.

The prior distribution is typically specified using a Bayesian network called the *prior network*. Together with an equivalent sample size, the prior network is all we need to specify the Dirichlet prior for every parameter set. Note, however, that obtaining the value of an exponent using (18.25) requires inference on the prior network.

To shed more light on the semantics of a prior network and equivalent sample size, consider the Dirichlet distribution they define for a given parameter set $\theta_{X|\mathbf{u}}$. First, note that the equivalent sample size for this Dirichlet is

$$\psi_{X|\mathbf{u}} = \sum_x \psi \cdot \Pr(x, \mathbf{u}) = \psi \Pr(\mathbf{u}).$$

Moreover, given the properties of a Dirichlet distribution see (18.10) and (18.11), we have the following expectation and variance for parameter $\theta_{x|\mathbf{u}}$:

$$Ex(\theta_{x|\mathbf{u}}) = \Pr(x|\mathbf{u})$$
$$Va\left(\theta_{x|\mathbf{u}}\right) = \frac{\Pr(x|\mathbf{u})(1 - \Pr(x|\mathbf{u}))}{\psi \cdot \Pr(\mathbf{u}) + 1}.$$

Hence, the prior network provides expectations for the parameters of any network structure. Moreover, the equivalent sample size ψ has a direct impact on our confidence in these expectations: a larger ψ implies a larger confidence. The confidence in these expected values also increases as the probability $\Pr(\mathbf{u})$ increases.

Since the BDe score is based on the assumption of likelihood equivalence, it leads to the same marginal likelihood for network structures that encode the same set of conditional independencies. Moreover, it is known that decreasing the equivalent sample size ψ diminishes the impact that the prior network has on the BDe score. We also mention that adopting a prior network with no edges is not an uncommon choice when using the BDe score. Another choice for the prior network is one that includes uniform CPTs, leading to exponents $\psi_{x|\mathbf{u}} = \psi/X^{\#}\mathbf{U}^{\#}$ where $X^{\#}\mathbf{U}^{\#}$ is the number of instantiations for the family $X\mathbf{U}$. This instance of the BDe score is known as BDeu (for BDe uniform).

For an example of specifying Dirichlet exponents in the BDe score, consider a domain with two binary variables A and B. Let the equivalent sample size be $\psi = 12$ and the prior distribution be

A	B	Pr(.)
a_1	b_1	1/4
a_1	b_2	1/6
a_2	b_1	1/4
a_2	b_2	1/3

Equation 18.25 then gives the following Dirichlet exponents:

ψ_{a_1}	ψ_{a_2}	ψ_{b_1}	ψ_{b_2}	$\psi_{b_1\|a_1}$ $= \psi_{a_1\|b_1}$	$\psi_{b_2\|a_1}$ $= \psi_{a_2\|b_1}$	$\psi_{b_1\|a_2}$ $= \psi_{a_1\|b_2}$	$\psi_{b_2\|a_2}$ $= \psi_{a_2\|b_2}$
5	7	6	6	3	2	3	4

Consider now the data set $\mathbf{d}_1 = a_1 b_1$, $\mathbf{d}_2 = a_1 b_2$, the structure $G : A \to B$, and let us use the closed form in (18.21) to compute the likelihood of structure G:

$$\mathbb{P}(\mathbf{d}_1, \mathbf{d}_2 | G)$$
$$= \left[\frac{\Gamma(\psi_A)}{\Gamma(\psi_A + \mathcal{D}\#(\top))} \frac{\Gamma(\psi_{a_1} + \mathcal{D}\#(a_1))}{\Gamma(\psi_{a_1})} \frac{\Gamma(\psi_{a_2} + \mathcal{D}\#(a_2))}{\Gamma(\psi_{a_2})} \right]$$
$$\left[\frac{\Gamma(\psi_{B|a_1})}{\Gamma(\psi_{B|a_1} + \mathcal{D}\#(a_1))} \frac{\Gamma(\psi_{b_1|a_1} + \mathcal{D}\#(b_1 a_1))}{\Gamma(\psi_{b_1|a_1})} \frac{\Gamma(\psi_{b_2|a_1} + \mathcal{D}\#(b_2 a_1))}{\Gamma(\psi_{b_2|a_1})} \right]$$
$$\left[\frac{\Gamma(\psi_{B|a_2})}{\Gamma(\psi_{B|a_2} + \mathcal{D}\#(a_2))} \frac{\Gamma(\psi_{b_1|a_2} + \mathcal{D}\#(b_1 a_2))}{\Gamma(\psi_{b_1|a_2})} \frac{\Gamma(\psi_{b_2|a_2} + \mathcal{D}\#(b_2 a_2))}{\Gamma(\psi_{b_2|a_2})} \right].$$

Recall that $\top$ is the trivial variable instantiation and, hence, $\mathcal{D}\#(\top)$ is the size of data set, which is 2 in this case. Substituting the values of exponents and data counts, we get

$$\mathbb{P}(\mathbf{d}_1, \mathbf{d}_2 | G) = \left[\frac{\Gamma(12)}{\Gamma(12+2)} \frac{\Gamma(5+2)}{\Gamma(5)} \frac{\Gamma(7+0)}{\Gamma(7)} \right]$$
$$\left[\frac{\Gamma(5)}{\Gamma(5+2)} \frac{\Gamma(3+1)}{\Gamma(3)} \frac{\Gamma(2+1)}{\Gamma(2)} \right]$$
$$\left[\frac{\Gamma(7)}{\Gamma(7+0)} \frac{\Gamma(3+0)}{\Gamma(3)} \frac{\Gamma(4+0)}{\Gamma(4)} \right]$$
$$= \frac{1}{26}.$$

We can verify that the likelihood of structure $G : B \to A$ is also $1/26$, which is to be expected as both structures encode the same set of conditional independencies.

18.5.3 Searching for a network structure

Consider now the logarithm of the BD score given in (18.23):

$$\log \mathrm{BD}(G | \mathcal{D}) = \log \mathbb{P}(G)$$
$$+ \sum_{X\mathbf{U}} \log \prod_{\mathbf{u}} \frac{\Gamma(\psi_{X|\mathbf{u}})}{\Gamma(\psi_{X|\mathbf{u}} + \mathcal{D}\#(\mathbf{u}))} \prod_x \frac{\Gamma(\psi_{x|\mathbf{u}} + \mathcal{D}\#(x\mathbf{u}))}{\Gamma(\psi_{x|\mathbf{u}})}. \qquad (18.26)$$

If the distribution over network structures, $\mathbb{P}(G)$, decomposes into a product over families, as in (18.24), the whole BD score is then a sum of scores, one for each family:

$$\log \mathrm{BD}(G | \mathcal{D}) = \sum_{X\mathbf{U}} \log \mathrm{BD}(X, \mathbf{U} | \mathcal{D}).$$

This BD score has the same structure as the one given in (17.15). Therefore, the heuristic and optimal search algorithms discussed in Section 17.5 can now be exploited to search for a network structure that maximizes the BD score and its variants, such as the BDe and BDeu scores.

We close this section by pointing out that our discussion on the search for network structures is restricted to complete data sets for the same computational reasons we encountered in Chapter 17. That is, the posterior $\mathbb{P}(G|\mathcal{D}) \propto \mathbb{P}(\mathcal{D}|G)\mathbb{P}(G)$ does not admit a closed form, and neither does it decompose into family components, when the data set is incomplete. Hence, algorithms for learning structures under incomplete data may have to use approximations such as the Laplace approximation to compute $\mathbb{P}(\mathcal{D}|G)$.[10] Even then, evaluating the score of a network structure continues to be demanding, making the search for a network structure quite expensive in general.

Bibliographic remarks

The material discussed in this chapter has its roots in the seminal work of Cooper and Herskovits [1991; 1992], who provided some of the first results on learning Bayesian networks, including the BD score, the K2 score, and the derivation of (18.21) and (18.14). The BD score was refined in Buntine [1991], who proposed the BDeu score and the prior distribution on network structures given by (18.24). The BD score was further refined in Heckerman et al. [1995], who introduced the general form of the likelihood equivalence assumption, leading to the BDe score. Interestingly, the BDe score was derived from a set of assumptions that includes parameter modularity and independence but not the assumption of Dirichlet priors (parameter modularity was first made explicit in Heckerman et al. [1995]). Yet these assumptions were shown to imply such priors; see also Geiger and Heckerman [1995]. Related work on Bayesian learning was also reported in Dawid and Lauritzen [1993] and Spiegelhalter et al. [1993]. A real medical example is discussed with some detail in Spiegelhalter et al. [1993], which also provides links to mainstream statistical methods such as model comparison. A particular emphasis on learning undirected structures can be found in Dawid and Lauritzen [1993].

The terms of global and local (parameter) independence were introduced in Spiegelhalter and Lauritzen [1990]. Relaxing these assumptions to situations that include parameter equality is addressed computationally in Thiesson [1997].

The complexity of learning network structures was addressed in Chickering [1996] and Chickering et al. [1995; 2004]. For example, it was shown in Chickering [1996] that for a general class of Bayesian scores, learning a network that maximizes the score is NP-hard even when the data set is small, and each node has at most two parents. Heuristic search algorithms are discussed and evaluated in Heckerman et al. [1995]. Methods for learning network structures in the case of incomplete data are presented in Friedman [1998], Meilua and Jordan [1998], Singh [1997], and Thiesson et al. [1999], while methods for learning Bayesian networks with local structure in the CPTs are discussed in Buntine [1991], Díez [1993], Chickering et al. [1997], Friedman and Goldszmidt [1996], and Meek and Heckerman [1997].

The candidate method for approximating the marginal likelihood is discussed in Chib [1995]. A number of approximation techniques for the marginal likelihood are surveyed and discussed in Chickering and Heckerman [1997]. This includes a detailed discussion of the Laplace approximation with references to its origins, in addition to a number of alternative approximations such as Cheeseman and Stutz [1995]. The study contains an empirical evaluation and corresponding discussion of some practical issues that arise when implementing these approximation approaches.

---

[10] In the Laplace approximation given by (18.22), the structure G is left implicit.

A comprehensive tutorial on learning Bayesian networks is provided in Heckerman [1998], who surveys most of the foundational work on the subject and provides many references for more advanced topics than covered in this chapter. Related surveys of the literature can also be found in Buntine [1996] and Jordan [1998]. The subject of learning Bayesian networks is also discussed in Cowell et al. [1999] and Neapolitan [2004], who provide more details on some of the subjects discussed here and cover additional topics such as networks with continuous variables.

18.6 Exercises

18.1. Consider the meta-network in Figure 18.2 and the corresponding data set $\mathcal{D}$:

Case	H	S	E
1	F	F	T
2	T	F	T
3	T	F	T
4	F	F	F
5	F	T	F

Assume the following fixed values of parameter sets:

$$\theta_{S|h} = (.1, .9),$$

$$\theta_{E|h} = (.8, .2).$$

For the remaining sets, suppose that we have the following prior distributions:

$\theta_H = (\theta_h, \theta_{\bar{h}})$	$\mathbb{P}(\theta_H)$	$\theta_{S|\bar{h}} = (\theta_{s|\bar{h}}, \theta_{\bar{s}|\bar{h}})$	$\mathbb{P}(\theta_{S|\bar{h}})$	$\theta_{E|\bar{h}} = (\theta_{e|\bar{h}}, \theta_{\bar{e}|\bar{h}})$	$\mathbb{P}(\theta_{E|\bar{h}})$
(.75, .25)	80%	(.25, .75)	10%	(.50, .50)	35%
(.90, .10)	20%	(.50, .50)	90%	(.75, .25)	65%

Compute the following given the data set $\mathcal{D}$:

(a) The maximum likelihood parameter estimates.

(b) The MAP parameter estimates.

(c) The Bayesian parameter estimates.

Compute the probability of observing an individual who is a smoker and exercises regularly given each of the above parameter estimates. Compute also $\mathbb{P}(S_6 = s, E_6 = e|\mathcal{D})$ with respect to the meta-network.

18.2. Consider a network structure $A \rightarrow B$ where variables A and B are binary. Suppose that we have the following priors on parameter sets:

$\theta_A = (\theta_{a_1}, \theta_{a_2})$	$\mathbb{P}(\theta_A)$
(.80, .20)	70%
(.20, .80)	30%

$\theta_{B|a_1} = (\theta_{b_1|a_1}, \theta_{b_2|a_1})$	$\mathbb{P}(\theta_{B|a_1})$
(.90, .10)	50%
(.10, .90)	50%

$\theta_{B|a_2} = (\theta_{b_1|a_2}, \theta_{b_2|a_2})$	$\mathbb{P}(\theta_{B|a_2})$
(.95, .05)	60%
(.05, .95)	40%

Compute the posterior distributions of parameter sets given the data set

$\mathcal{D}$	A	B
$\mathbf{d}_1$	a_1	b_2
$\mathbf{d}_2$	a_1	b_2
$\mathbf{d}_3$	a_1	b_1
$\mathbf{d}_4$	a_2	b_2

Compute also the expected parameter values given this data set. Finally, evaluate the query $\mathbb{P}(A_5 = a_1 | B_5 = b_2, \mathcal{D})$.

18.3. Consider Exercise 18.2. Describe a meta-network that captures the following constraint $\theta_{B|a_1} = (.90, .10)$ iff $\theta_{B|a_2} = (.05, .95)$.

18.4. Consider a Bayesian network structure with three binary variables $A, B,$ and C and two edges $A \rightarrow B$ and $A \rightarrow C$. Suppose that the CPTs for variables B and C are equal and these CPTs are independent of the one for variable A. Draw the structure of a meta-network for this situation. Develop a closed form for computing the posterior distribution on parameter set $\theta_{B|a_1}$ given a complete data set $\mathcal{D}$. Assume first that parameter sets are discrete, deriving a closed form that resembles Equation 18.4. Then generalize the form to continuous parameter sets with Dirichlet distributions.

18.5. Consider a meta-network as given by Definition 18.2. Let Σ contain X_N for every variable X in structure G and let Γ contain $X_1, \ldots, X_{N-1}$ for every variable X in structure G. Show that Σ is d-separated from Γ by the nodes representing parameter sets.

18.6. Consider Theorem 18.2 and show that $\Pr_\theta(\alpha) = \mathbb{P}(\alpha_i | \theta)$, where α_i results from replacing every variable X in α by its instance X_i.

18.7. Consider Theorem 18.3 and show that

$$\mathbb{P}(\alpha_{N+1} | \beta_{N+1}, \mathcal{D}) = \Pr_{\theta^{be}}(\alpha | \beta).$$

18.8. Consider Theorem 18.2 and show that

$$\mathbb{P}(\alpha_{N+1} | \beta_{N+1}, \mathcal{D}) = \sum_\theta \Pr_\theta(\alpha | \beta) \mathbb{P}(\theta | \beta_{N+1}, \mathcal{D}).$$

18.9. Consider Theorem 18.4. Show that

$$\mathbb{P}(\mathcal{D} | \theta_{X|\mathbf{u}}) \propto \prod_x \left[\theta_{x|\mathbf{u}} \right]^{\mathcal{D}\#(x\mathbf{u})}.$$

18.10. Prove Equation 18.9.

18.11. Prove Equation 18.27 which appears on Page 514.

18.12. Let $\mathcal{D}$ be an incomplete data set and let $\mathcal{D}^c$ denote a completion of $\mathcal{D}$. Show that the expected value of a network parameter $\theta_{x|\mathbf{u}}$ given data set $\mathcal{D}$ is

$$\text{Ex}(\theta_{x|\mathbf{u}}) = \sum_{\mathcal{D}^c} f(\mathcal{D}\mathcal{D}^c) \mathbb{P}(\mathcal{D}^c | \mathcal{D}),$$

where $f(\mathcal{D}\mathcal{D}^c)$ is the value of the Bayesian estimate $\theta_{x|\mathbf{u}}^{be}$ given the complete data set $\mathcal{D}\mathcal{D}^c$.

18.13. Consider a network structure $A \rightarrow B$ where variables A and B are binary and the Dirichlet priors are given by the following exponents:

ψ_{a_1}	ψ_{a_2}	$\psi_{b_1|a_1}$	$\psi_{b_2|a_1}$	$\psi_{b_1|a_2}$	$\psi_{b_2|a_2}$
10	30	2	2	10	40

Suppose that we are given the following data set $\mathcal{D}$:

	A	B
$\mathbf{d}_1$	a_1	b_2
$\mathbf{d}_2$	a_1	b_1
$\mathbf{d}_3$	a_2	b_1

Compute:

(a) The Bayesian parameter estimates $\theta_{a_1}^{be}, \theta_{b_1|a_1}^{be},$ and $\theta_{b_1|a_2}^{be}$.

(b) The marginal likelihood $\mathbb{P}(\mathcal{D})$.

18.14. Consider the network structure $A \to B$ and the Dirichlet priors from Exercise 18.13. Compute the expected values of parameters θ_{a_1}, $\theta_{b_1|a_1}$, and $\theta_{b_1|a_2}$ given the following data set:

	A	B
d_1	a_1	b_2
d_2	?	b_1
d_3	a_2	?

Hint: Perform case analysis on the missing values in the data set.

18.15. Consider a meta-network that induces a meta-distribution $\mathbb{P}$, let $\mathcal{D}$ be an incomplete data set, and let θ be a parametrization. Describe a Gibbs sampler that can be used for estimating the expectation of $\mathbb{P}(\theta|\mathcal{D}, \mathcal{D}^c)$ with respect to the distribution $\mathbb{P}(\mathcal{D}^c|\mathcal{D})$ where $\mathcal{D}^c$ is a completion of the data set $\mathcal{D}$. That is, describe a Gibbs-Markov chain for the distribution $\mathbb{P}(\mathbf{C}|\mathcal{D})$, where $\mathbf{C}$ are the variables with missing values in $\mathcal{D}$, and then show how we can simulate this chain. Solve this problem for both discrete and continuous parameter sets.

18.16. Identify the relationship between the expected counts of Definition 18.4 and the expected empirical distribution of Definition 17.2.

18.17. Show that Algorithm 50, ML_EM, is a special case of Algorithm 52, MAP_EM_C, in the case where all parameter sets $\theta_{X|\mathbf{u}}$ have noninformative priors (i.e., all Dirichlet exponents are equal to 1). Note: In this case, the fixed points of Algorithm 52 are also stationary points of the log-likelihood function.

18.18. The Hessian matrix of the Laplace approximation is specified in terms of three types of second partial derivatives, with respect to:

- A single parameter $\theta_{x|\mathbf{u}}$
- Parameters $\theta_{x|\mathbf{u}}$ and $\theta_{x^\star|\mathbf{u}}$ of the same parameter set $\theta_{X|\mathbf{u}}$, where $x \neq x^\star$
- Parameters $\theta_{x|\mathbf{u}}$ and $\theta_{y|\mathbf{v}}$ of two different parameter sets $\theta_{X|\mathbf{u}}$ and $\theta_{Y|\mathbf{v}}$.

(a) Show that the partial derivative of the Dirichlet density of parameter set $\theta_{X|\mathbf{u}}$ with respect to parameter $\theta_{x|\mathbf{u}}$ is

$$\frac{\partial \rho(\theta_{X|\mathbf{u}})}{\partial \theta_{x|\mathbf{u}}} = \frac{\psi_{x|\mathbf{u}} - 1}{\theta_{x|\mathbf{u}}} \cdot \rho(\theta_{X|\mathbf{u}}).$$

(b) Given (a), show that the partial derivative of the prior density of network parameters $\rho(\theta)$ is

$$\frac{\partial \rho(\theta)}{\partial \theta_{x|\mathbf{u}}} = \frac{\psi_{x|\mathbf{u}} - 1}{\theta_{x|\mathbf{u}}} \cdot \rho(\theta).$$

(c) Given (a) and (b), show how to compute the second partial derivatives

$$\frac{\partial^2 \rho(\theta)}{\partial \theta_{x|\mathbf{u}} \partial \theta_{x|\mathbf{u}}}, \qquad \frac{\partial^2 \rho(\theta)}{\partial \theta_{x|\mathbf{u}} \partial \theta_{x^\star|\mathbf{u}}}, \qquad \frac{\partial^2 \rho(\theta)}{\partial \theta_{x|\mathbf{u}} \partial \theta_{y|\mathbf{v}}}.$$

18.19. Analogously to Exercise 18.18, consider partial derivatives of the likelihood of network parameters $\mathbb{P}(\mathcal{D}|\theta)$.

(a) Show that the partial derivative of the likelihood $\mathbb{P}(\mathcal{D}|\theta)$ with respect to parameter $\theta_{x|\mathbf{u}}$ is

$$\frac{\partial \mathbb{P}(\mathcal{D}|\theta)}{\partial \theta_{x|\mathbf{u}}} = \mathbb{P}(\mathcal{D}|\theta) \cdot \frac{\mathcal{D}\#(x\mathbf{u}|\theta)}{\theta_{x|\mathbf{u}}}.$$

(b) Given (a), show how to compute the second partial derivatives

$$\frac{\partial^2 \mathbb{P}(\mathcal{D}|\theta)}{\partial \theta_{x|\mathbf{u}} \partial \theta_{x|\mathbf{u}}}, \qquad \frac{\partial^2 \mathbb{P}(\mathcal{D}|\theta)}{\partial \theta_{x|\mathbf{u}} \partial \theta_{x^\star|\mathbf{u}}}, \qquad \frac{\partial^2 \mathbb{P}(\mathcal{D}|\theta)}{\partial \theta_{x|\mathbf{u}} \partial \theta_{y|\mathbf{v}}}.$$

18.20. Consider the second partial derivative

$$\frac{\partial^2 \log \rho(\mathcal{D}, \theta)}{\partial \theta_{x|\mathbf{u}} \partial \theta_{y|\mathbf{v}}}(\theta^{ma})$$

used in the Laplace approximation. Show how this derivative can be computed by performing inference on a Bayesian network with parametrization θ^{ma}. What is the complexity of computing all the second partial derivatives (i.e., computing the Hessian)? Hint: Use the fact that $\rho(\mathcal{D}, \theta) = \mathbb{P}(\mathcal{D}|\theta)\rho(\theta)$ and consider Exercises 18.18 and 18.19.

18.21. Extend the structural meta-network in Figure 18.6 to allow for reasoning about incomplete data sets. That is, the meta-network needs to have additional nodes to allow us to assert an incomplete data set as evidence.

18.22. Consider a BDe score that is specified by a prior distribution Pr. Let G be a complete network structure and $\mathbf{d}$ be a complete case. Show that $\text{Pr}(\mathbf{d}) = \mathbb{P}(\mathbf{d}|G)$ where $\mathbb{P}$ is the corresponding meta-distribution. Note: This exercise provides additional semantics for the prior distribution of a BDe score.

18.23. Consider the BDe score, a sample size of $\psi = 12$, and the prior distribution

A	B	Pr(.)
a_1	b_1	1/4
a_1	b_2	1/6
a_2	b_1	1/4
a_2	b_2	1/3

Consider also the data set $\mathbf{d}_1 = a_1 b_1$, $\mathbf{d}_2 = a_1 b_2$ and the structures $G_1 : A \to B$ and $G_2 : A, B$. Compute the likelihood of each structure using Equation 18.21.

18.24. Consider the BDe score, a sample size of $\psi = 12$, and the prior distribution

A	B	Pr(.)
a_1	b_1	1/4
a_1	b_2	1/6
a_2	b_1	1/4
a_2	b_2	1/3

Consider also the data set $\mathbf{d}_1 = a_1 b_1$, $\mathbf{d}_2 = a_1 b_2$ and the structure $G : A \to B$. Compute the probabilities $\mathbb{P}(\mathbf{d}_1|G)$, $\mathbb{P}(\mathbf{d}_2|\mathbf{d}_1, G)$ and $\mathbb{P}(\mathbf{d}_1, \mathbf{d}_2|G)$. Compute the same quantities for the structure $G : B \to A$ as well.

18.7 Proofs

PROOF OF THEOREM 18.1. Let Γ contain all variables that are not parameter sets (i.e., variables instantiated by a complete data set). We need to show the following: If Σ_1 and Σ_2 contain a collection of parameter sets each, $\Sigma_1 \cap \Sigma_2 = \emptyset$, then Σ_1 and Σ_2 are independent and they remain independent given Γ.

Independence holds initially since parameter sets are root nodes in a meta-network and since root nodes are d-separated from each other in a Bayesian network. Hence, Σ_1 and Σ_2 are d-separated in the meta-network.

To show that parameter independence continues to hold given a complete data set $\mathcal{D}$ (i.e., given Γ), we point out the two types of edge pruning discussed in Section 18.2.2. Pruning these edges makes each pair of parameter sets disconnected from each other; hence, Σ_1 and Σ_2 are d-separated by Γ in the pruned meta-network. Moreover, the joint distribution $\mathbb{P}'(., \mathcal{D})$ induced by the pruned meta-network agrees with the joint distribution $\mathbb{P}(., \mathcal{D})$ induced by the original meta-network. Hence, the two meta-networks agree on the independence of Σ_1 and Σ_2 given $\mathcal{D}$. ∎

PROOF OF THEOREM 18.2. We have

$$\mathbb{P}(\alpha_{N+1}|\mathcal{D}) = \sum_\theta \mathbb{P}(\alpha_{N+1}|\mathcal{D}, \theta)\mathbb{P}(\theta|\mathcal{D})$$

$$= \sum_\theta \mathbb{P}(\alpha_{N+1}|\theta)\mathbb{P}(\theta|\mathcal{D})$$

$$= \sum_\theta \mathrm{Pr}_\theta(\alpha)\mathbb{P}(\theta|\mathcal{D}).$$

The second step is left to Exercise 18.5 and the third step is left to Exercise 18.6. ∎

PROOF OF THEOREM 18.3. According to Theorem 18.2, we have

$$\mathbb{P}(\alpha_{N+1}|\mathcal{D}) = \sum_\theta \mathrm{Pr}_\theta(\alpha)\mathbb{P}(\theta|\mathcal{D}).$$

Hence, all we need to show is that

$$\mathrm{Pr}_{\theta^{be}}(\alpha) = \sum_\theta \mathrm{Pr}_\theta(\alpha)\mathbb{P}(\theta|\mathcal{D}).$$

In fact, it suffices to show this result for complete instantiations **d** of the base network G since:

$$\mathrm{Pr}_{\theta^{be}}(\alpha) = \sum_{\mathbf{d}\models\alpha} \mathrm{Pr}_{\theta^{be}}(\mathbf{d})$$

$$= \sum_{\mathbf{d}\models\alpha}\sum_\theta \mathrm{Pr}_\theta(\mathbf{d})\mathbb{P}(\theta|\mathcal{D})$$

$$= \sum_\theta \left(\sum_{\mathbf{d}\models\alpha} \mathrm{Pr}_\theta(\mathbf{d})\right)\mathbb{P}(\theta|\mathcal{D})$$

$$= \sum_\theta \mathrm{Pr}_\theta(\alpha)\mathbb{P}(\theta|\mathcal{D}).$$

Recall here that $\mathbf{d} \models \alpha$ reads: instantiation **d** satisfies event α.

Suppose now that $X_1\mathbf{U}_1, \ldots, X_n\mathbf{U}_n$ are the families of base network G and let $\mathbf{u}_1, \ldots, \mathbf{u}_n$ be the instantiations of parents $\mathbf{U}_1, \ldots, \mathbf{U}_n$ in network instantiation **d**. Let us also decompose a particular parametrization θ into two components: $\theta_{\mathbf{d}}$, which contains values of parameter sets $\theta_{X_1|\mathbf{u}_1}, \ldots, \theta_{X_n|\mathbf{u}_n}$ that are relevant to the probability of **d**, and $\theta_{\bar{\mathbf{d}}}$, which contains the values of remaining parameter sets (irrelevant to **d**). Note that the probability of network instantiation **d**, $\mathrm{Pr}_\theta(\mathbf{d})$, depends only on the $\theta_{\mathbf{d}}$ component of parametrization θ. We then have

$$\sum_{\theta=\theta_{\mathbf{d}},\theta_{\bar{\mathbf{d}}}} \mathrm{Pr}_\theta(\mathbf{d})\mathbb{P}(\theta|\mathcal{D}) = \sum_{\theta_{\mathbf{d}},\theta_{\bar{\mathbf{d}}}} \mathrm{Pr}_{\theta_{\mathbf{d}},\theta_{\bar{\mathbf{d}}}}(\mathbf{d})\mathbb{P}(\theta_{\mathbf{d}}|\mathcal{D})\mathbb{P}(\theta_{\bar{\mathbf{d}}}|\mathcal{D})$$

$$= \sum_{\theta_{\bar{\mathbf{d}}},\theta_{X_1|\mathbf{u}_1},\ldots,\theta_{X_n|\mathbf{u}_n}} \mathrm{Pr}_{\theta_{\mathbf{d}},\theta_{\bar{\mathbf{d}}}}(\mathbf{d})\mathbb{P}(\theta_{X_1|\mathbf{u}_1}, \ldots, \theta_{X_n|\mathbf{u}_n}|\mathcal{D})\mathbb{P}(\theta_{\bar{\mathbf{d}}}|\mathcal{D})$$

$$= \sum_{\theta_{\bar{\mathbf{d}}},\theta_{X_1|\mathbf{u}_1},\ldots,\theta_{X_n|\mathbf{u}_n}} \mathrm{Pr}_{\theta_{\mathbf{d}},\theta_{\bar{\mathbf{d}}}}(\mathbf{d})\left(\prod_{i=1}^n \mathbb{P}(\theta_{X_i|\mathbf{u}_i}|\mathcal{D})\right)\mathbb{P}(\theta_{\bar{\mathbf{d}}}|\mathcal{D})$$

$$= \sum_{\theta_{\bar{\mathbf{a}}}, \theta_{X_1|\mathbf{u}_1}, \ldots, \theta_{X_n|\mathbf{u}_n}} \left(\prod_{x_i \sim \mathbf{d}} \theta_{x_i|\mathbf{u}_i} \right) \left(\prod_{i=1}^{n} \mathbb{P}(\theta_{X_i|\mathbf{u}_i}|\mathcal{D}) \right) \mathbb{P}(\theta_{\bar{\mathbf{a}}}|\mathcal{D})$$

$$= \sum_{\theta_{\bar{\mathbf{a}}}, \theta_{X_1|\mathbf{u}_1}, \ldots, \theta_{X_n|\mathbf{u}_n}} \left(\prod_{x_i \sim \mathbf{d}} \theta_{x_i|\mathbf{u}_i} \cdot \mathbb{P}(\theta_{X_i|\mathbf{u}_i}|\mathcal{D}) \right) \mathbb{P}(\theta_{\bar{\mathbf{a}}}|\mathcal{D})$$

$$= \sum_{\theta_{X_1|\mathbf{u}_1}, \ldots, \theta_{X_n|\mathbf{u}_n}} \left(\prod_{x_i \sim \mathbf{d}} \theta_{x_i|\mathbf{u}_i} \cdot \mathbb{P}(\theta_{X_i|\mathbf{u}_i}|\mathcal{D}) \right) \sum_{\theta_{\bar{\mathbf{a}}}} \mathbb{P}(\theta_{\bar{\mathbf{a}}}|\mathcal{D}).$$

Observing that $\sum_{\theta_{\bar{\mathbf{a}}}} \mathbb{P}(\theta_{\bar{\mathbf{a}}}|\mathcal{D}) = 1$, we now have

$$\sum_{\theta} \mathrm{Pr}_{\theta}(\mathbf{d})\mathbb{P}(\theta|\mathcal{D}) = \sum_{\theta_{X_1|\mathbf{u}_1}, \ldots, \theta_{X_n|\mathbf{u}_n}} \prod_{x_i \sim \mathbf{d}} \theta_{x_i|\mathbf{u}_i} \cdot \mathbb{P}(\theta_{X_i|\mathbf{u}_i}|\mathcal{D})$$

$$= \prod_{x_i \sim \mathbf{d}} \sum_{\theta_{X_i|\mathbf{u}_i}} \theta_{x_i|\mathbf{u}_i} \cdot \mathbb{P}(\theta_{X_i|\mathbf{u}_i}|\mathcal{D})$$

$$= \prod_{x_i \sim \mathbf{d}} \theta_{x_i|\mathbf{u}_i}^{be}$$

$$= \mathrm{Pr}_{\theta^{be}}(\mathbf{d}). \qquad \blacksquare$$

PROOF OF THEOREM 18.4. Consider the meta-network after we have pruned all edges given the complete data set $\mathcal{D}$, as given in Section 18.2.2. Each parameter set $\theta_{X|\mathbf{u}}$ becomes part of an isolated network structure that satisfies the following properties:

- It is a naive Bayes structure with $\theta_{X|\mathbf{u}}$ as its root and some instances X_i of X as its children. For example, in Figure 18.3(b) $\theta_{E|h}$ is the root of a naive Bayes network with variables E_1 and E_2 as its children. Similarly, θ_H is the root of a naive Bayes network with variables H_1, H_2, and H_3 as its children.

- Instance X_i is connected to $\theta_{X|\mathbf{u}}$ only if its parents are instantiated to $\mathbf{u}$ in the data set $\mathcal{D}$. If not, the edge $\theta_{X|\mathbf{u}} \to X_i$ is superfluous and then pruned.

- The number of instances X_i connected to $\theta_{X|\mathbf{u}}$ is therefore $\mathcal{D}\#(\mathbf{u})$.

- The number of instances X_i connected to $\theta_{X|\mathbf{u}}$ and having value x is $\mathcal{D}\#(x\mathbf{u})$.

Let us now decompose the data set $\mathcal{D}$ into two parts, $\mathcal{D}^1$ and $\mathcal{D}^2$, where $\mathcal{D}^1$ is the instantiation of variables that remain connected to parameter set $\theta_{X|\mathbf{u}}$ after pruning. We then have

$$\mathbb{P}(\theta_{X|\mathbf{u}}|\mathcal{D}) = \mathbb{P}(\theta_{X|\mathbf{u}}|\mathcal{D}^1)$$

$$= \frac{\mathbb{P}(\mathcal{D}^1|\theta_{X|\mathbf{u}})\mathbb{P}(\theta_{X|\mathbf{u}})}{\mathbb{P}(\mathcal{D}^1)}.$$

Let X_i, $i \in I$, be the instances of X that remain connected to parameter set $\theta_{X|\mathbf{u}}$ and let x_i be their instantiated values. We then have

$$\mathbb{P}(\mathcal{D}^1|\theta_{X|\mathbf{u}}) = \prod_{i \in I} \mathbb{P}(X_i = x_i|\theta_{X|\mathbf{u}})$$

$$= \prod_{i \in I} \theta_{x_i|\mathbf{u}}$$

$$= \prod_{x} \left[\theta_{x|\mathbf{u}} \right]^{\mathcal{D}\#(x\mathbf{u})}.$$

Hence,

$$\mathbb{P}(\theta_{X|\mathbf{u}}|\mathcal{D}) = \eta \, \mathbb{P}(\theta_{X|\mathbf{u}}) \prod_x \left[\theta_{x|\mathbf{u}}\right]^{\mathcal{D}\#(x\mathbf{u})},$$

where the normalizing constant η is $1/\mathbb{P}(\mathcal{D}^1)$. ∎

PROOF OF THEOREM 18.5. Suppose that $\theta^{k+1} = \operatorname{argmax}_\theta e(\theta|\mathcal{D}, \theta^k)$. It then follows that

$$e(\theta^{k+1}|\mathcal{D}, \theta^k) - e(\theta^k|\mathcal{D}, \theta^k) \geq 0$$

and

$$\sum_{\mathcal{D}^c} \mathbb{P}(\mathcal{D}^c|\mathcal{D}, \theta^k) \log \mathbb{P}(\theta^{k+1}|\mathcal{D}, \mathcal{D}^c) - \sum_{\mathcal{D}^c} \mathbb{P}(\mathcal{D}^c|\mathcal{D}, \theta^k) \log \mathbb{P}(\theta^k|\mathcal{D}, \mathcal{D}^c) \geq 0.$$

Moreover,

$$\sum_{\mathcal{D}^c} \mathbb{P}(\mathcal{D}^c|\mathcal{D}, \theta^k) \log \frac{\mathbb{P}(\theta^{k+1}|\mathcal{D}, \mathcal{D}^c)}{\mathbb{P}(\theta^k|\mathcal{D}, \mathcal{D}^c)} \geq 0$$

$$\sum_{\mathcal{D}^c} \mathbb{P}(\mathcal{D}^c|\mathcal{D}, \theta^k) \log \left(\frac{\mathbb{P}(\mathcal{D}^c|\mathcal{D}, \theta^{k+1})}{\mathbb{P}(\mathcal{D}^c|\mathcal{D}, \theta^k)} \frac{\mathbb{P}(\mathcal{D}, \theta^{k+1})}{\mathbb{P}(\mathcal{D}, \theta^k)}\right) \geq 0$$

$$\sum_{\mathcal{D}^c} \mathbb{P}(\mathcal{D}^c|\mathcal{D}, \theta^k) \log \frac{\mathbb{P}(\mathcal{D}^c|\mathcal{D}, \theta^{k+1})}{\mathbb{P}(\mathcal{D}^c|\mathcal{D}, \theta^k)} + \sum_{\mathcal{D}^c} \mathbb{P}(\mathcal{D}^c|\mathcal{D}, \theta^k) \log \frac{\mathbb{P}(\mathcal{D}, \theta^{k+1})}{\mathbb{P}(\mathcal{D}, \theta^k)} \geq 0.$$

Moving the first term to the right-hand side, we get

$$\sum_{\mathcal{D}^c} \mathbb{P}(\mathcal{D}^c|\mathcal{D}, \theta^k) \log \frac{\mathbb{P}(\mathcal{D}, \theta^{k+1})}{\mathbb{P}(\mathcal{D}, \theta^k)} \geq \sum_{\mathcal{D}^c} \mathbb{P}(\mathcal{D}^c|\mathcal{D}, \theta^k) \log \frac{\mathbb{P}(\mathcal{D}^c|\mathcal{D}, \theta^k)}{\mathbb{P}(\mathcal{D}^c|\mathcal{D}, \theta^{k+1})}.$$

The right-hand side is now a KL divergence, which is ≥ 0. We therefore have

$$\sum_{\mathcal{D}^c} \mathbb{P}(\mathcal{D}^c|\mathcal{D}, \theta^k) \log \frac{\mathbb{P}(\mathcal{D}, \theta^{k+1})}{\mathbb{P}(\mathcal{D}, \theta^k)} \geq 0$$

$$\log \frac{\mathbb{P}(\mathcal{D}, \theta^{k+1})}{\mathbb{P}(\mathcal{D}, \theta^k)} \sum_{\mathcal{D}^c} \mathbb{P}(\mathcal{D}^c|\mathcal{D}, \theta^k) \geq 0$$

$$\log \frac{\mathbb{P}(\mathcal{D}, \theta^{k+1})}{\mathbb{P}(\mathcal{D}, \theta^k)} \geq 0.$$

It then follows that

$$\mathbb{P}(\mathcal{D}, \theta^{k+1}) \geq \mathbb{P}(\mathcal{D}, \theta^k) \text{ and } \mathbb{P}(\theta^{k+1}|\mathcal{D}) \geq \mathbb{P}(\theta^k|\mathcal{D}). ∎$$

PROOF OF THEOREM 18.6. In the following proof, $X\mathbf{u}$ ranges over the indices of parameter sets, that is, X is a variable in the base network and $\mathbf{u}$ is an instantiation of its parents. We have

$$e(\theta|\mathcal{D}, \theta^k) = \sum_{\mathcal{D}^c} \mathbb{P}(\mathcal{D}^c|\mathcal{D}, \theta^k) \log \mathbb{P}(\theta|\mathcal{D}, \mathcal{D}^c)$$

$$= \sum_{\mathcal{D}^c} \mathbb{P}(\mathcal{D}^c|\mathcal{D}, \theta^k) \log \prod_{X\mathbf{u}} \mathbb{P}(\theta_{X|\mathbf{u}}|\mathcal{D}, \mathcal{D}^c)$$

$$= \sum_{\mathcal{D}^c} \mathbb{P}(\mathcal{D}^c|\mathcal{D}, \theta^k) \sum_{X\mathbf{u}} \log \mathbb{P}(\theta_{X|\mathbf{u}}|\mathcal{D}, \mathcal{D}^c)$$

$$= \sum_{X\mathbf{u}} \sum_{\mathcal{D}^c} \mathbb{P}(\mathcal{D}^c|\mathcal{D}, \theta^k) \log \mathbb{P}(\theta_{X|\mathbf{u}}|\mathcal{D}, \mathcal{D}^c).$$

To maximize $e(\theta|\mathcal{D}, \theta^k)$, we therefore need to maximize a number of independent problems. That is, we need to choose parameter sets $\theta_{X|\mathbf{u}}$ independently to maximize

$$\sum_{\mathcal{D}^c} \mathbb{P}(\mathcal{D}^c|\mathcal{D}, \theta^k) \log \mathbb{P}(\theta_{X|\mathbf{u}}|\mathcal{D}, \mathcal{D}^c),$$

which is the same as maximizing (see Theorem 18.4):

$$\sum_{\mathcal{D}^c} \mathbb{P}(\mathcal{D}^c|\mathcal{D}, \theta^k) \log \mathbb{P}(\theta_{X|\mathbf{u}}) \prod_x \left[\theta_{x|\mathbf{u}} \right]^{[\mathcal{D}\mathcal{D}^c]\#(x\mathbf{u})}$$

$$= \sum_{\mathcal{D}^c} \mathbb{P}(\mathcal{D}^c|\mathcal{D}, \theta^k) \log \mathbb{P}(\theta_{X|\mathbf{u}}) + \sum_{\mathcal{D}^c} \sum_x \mathbb{P}(\mathcal{D}^c|\mathcal{D}, \theta^k) \log \left[\theta_{x|\mathbf{u}} \right]^{[\mathcal{D}\mathcal{D}^c]\#(x\mathbf{u})}$$

$$= \log \mathbb{P}(\theta_{X|\mathbf{u}}) + \sum_x \sum_{\mathcal{D}^c} \mathbb{P}(\mathcal{D}^c|\mathcal{D}, \theta^k) \left[[\mathcal{D}\mathcal{D}^c]\#(x\mathbf{u}) \right] \log \theta_{x|\mathbf{u}}$$

$$= \log \mathbb{P}(\theta_{X|\mathbf{u}}) + \sum_x \log \theta_{x|\mathbf{u}} \sum_{\mathcal{D}^c} \mathbb{P}(\mathcal{D}^c|\mathcal{D}, \theta^k) \left[[\mathcal{D}\mathcal{D}^c]\#(x\mathbf{u}) \right]$$

$$= \log \mathbb{P}(\theta_{X|\mathbf{u}}) + \sum_x \left[\log \theta_{x|\mathbf{u}} \right] \mathcal{D}\#(x\mathbf{u}|\theta^k) \text{ by Definition 18.4}$$

$$= \log \left[\mathbb{P}(\theta_{X|\mathbf{u}}) \prod_x \left[\theta_{x|\mathbf{u}} \right]^{\mathcal{D}\#(x\mathbf{u}|\theta^k)} \right].$$

Finally, maximizing this expression is the same as maximizing

$$\mathbb{P}(\theta_{X|\mathbf{u}}) \prod_x \left[\theta_{x|\mathbf{u}} \right]^{\mathcal{D}\#(x\mathbf{u}|\theta^k)}. \qquad \blacksquare$$

PROOF OF THEOREM 18.7. The proof is similar to that for Theorem 18.2 except that we integrate instead of summing over parameterizations. $\blacksquare$

PROOF OF THEOREM 18.8. The proof is similar to that for Theorems 18.3 except that we integrate instead of summing over parameterizations. $\blacksquare$

PROOF OF THEOREM 18.9. This proof is based on that for Theorem 18.4. In particular, if we define $\mathcal{D}^1$ as defined in that proof, we have

$$
\begin{aligned}
\rho(\theta_{X|\mathbf{u}}|\mathcal{D}) &= \rho(\theta_{X|\mathbf{u}}|\mathcal{D}^1) \\
&= \frac{\mathbb{P}(\mathcal{D}^1|\theta_{X|\mathbf{u}})\rho(\theta_{X|\mathbf{u}})}{\mathbb{P}(\mathcal{D}^1)} \\
&= \frac{\mathbb{P}(\mathcal{D}^1|\theta_{X|\mathbf{u}}) \cdot \eta \prod_x \left[\theta_{x|\mathbf{u}}\right]^{\psi_{x|\mathbf{u}}-1}}{\mathbb{P}(\mathcal{D}^1)},
\end{aligned}
$$

where η is the normalizing constant for the Dirichlet density $\rho(\theta_{X|\mathbf{u}})$. Moreover, as shown in the proof of Theorem 18.4, we have

$$
\mathbb{P}(\mathcal{D}^1|\theta_{X|\mathbf{u}}) = \prod_x \left[\theta_{x|\mathbf{u}}\right]^{\mathcal{D}\#(x\mathbf{u})}.
$$

Hence, we have

$$
\begin{aligned}
\rho(\theta_{X|\mathbf{u}}|\mathcal{D}) &= \frac{\left(\prod_x \left[\theta_{x|\mathbf{u}}\right]^{\mathcal{D}\#(x\mathbf{u})}\right) \cdot \eta \prod_x \left[\theta_{x|\mathbf{u}}\right]^{\psi_{x|\mathbf{u}}-1}}{\mathbb{P}(\mathcal{D}^1)} \\
&= \frac{\eta \prod_x \left[\theta_{x|\mathbf{u}}\right]^{\psi_{x|\mathbf{u}}+\mathcal{D}\#(x\mathbf{u})-1}}{\mathbb{P}(\mathcal{D}^1)}.
\end{aligned}
$$

This is a Dirichlet density with exponents $\psi_{x|\mathbf{u}} + \mathcal{D}\#(x\mathbf{u})$ and normalizing constant $\eta / \mathbb{P}(\mathcal{D}')$. ∎

PROOF OF THEOREM 18.10. The proof for this theorem resembles that for Theorem 18.5. ∎

PROOF OF THEOREM 18.11. In the following proof, $X\mathbf{u}$ ranges over the indices of parameter sets, that is, X is a variable in the base network and $\mathbf{u}$ is an instantiation of its parents. We have

$$
\begin{aligned}
e(\theta|\mathcal{D}, \theta^k) &= \sum_{\mathcal{D}^c} \mathbb{P}(\mathcal{D}^c|\mathcal{D}, \theta^k) \log \rho(\theta|\mathcal{D}, \mathcal{D}^c) \\
&= \sum_{\mathcal{D}^c} \mathbb{P}(\mathcal{D}^c|\mathcal{D}, \theta^k) \log \prod_{X\mathbf{u}} \rho(\theta_{X|\mathbf{u}}|\mathcal{D}, \mathcal{D}^c) \\
&= \sum_{\mathcal{D}^c} \mathbb{P}(\mathcal{D}^c|\mathcal{D}, \theta^k) \sum_{X\mathbf{u}} \log \rho(\theta_{X|\mathbf{u}}|\mathcal{D}, \mathcal{D}^c) \\
&= \sum_{X\mathbf{u}} \sum_{\mathcal{D}^c} \mathbb{P}(\mathcal{D}^c|\mathcal{D}, \theta^k) \log \rho(\theta_{X|\mathbf{u}}|\mathcal{D}, \mathcal{D}^c).
\end{aligned}
$$

Maximizing $e(\theta|\mathcal{D}, \theta^k)$ is then equivalent to choosing each parameter set $\theta_{X|\mathbf{u}}$ independently to maximize

$$
\sum_{\mathcal{D}^c} \mathbb{P}(\mathcal{D}^c|\mathcal{D}, \theta^k) \log \rho(\theta_{X|\mathbf{u}}|\mathcal{D}, \mathcal{D}^c).
$$

Substituting the value of the posterior density $\rho(\theta_{X|\mathbf{u}}|\mathcal{D}, \mathcal{D}^c)$ as given by Theorem 18.9 and using simplifications similar to those used in the proof of Theorem 18.6, we can show that maximizing this expression is the same as maximizing the following:

$$\prod_x \left[\theta_{x|\mathbf{u}}\right]^{\psi_{x|\mathbf{u}} + \mathcal{D}\#(x\mathbf{u}|\theta_k) - 1},$$

which is an un-normalized Dirichlet distribution. Using (18.12), the mode of this Dirichlet is given by

$$\theta_{x|\mathbf{u}} = \frac{\mathcal{D}\#(x\mathbf{u}|\theta_k) + \psi_{x|\mathbf{u}} - 1}{\mathcal{D}\#(\mathbf{u}|\theta_k) + \psi_{X|\mathbf{u}} - |X|}. \qquad \blacksquare$$

Theorem 18.12. *Given a network structure with families $X\mathbf{U}$ and a complete data set $\mathcal{D}$, we have*

$$\mathbb{P}(\mathcal{D}) = \prod_{X\mathbf{U}} \prod_{\mathbf{u}} \frac{\Gamma(\psi_{X|\mathbf{u}})}{\Gamma(\psi_{X|\mathbf{u}} + \mathcal{D}\#(\mathbf{u}))} \prod_x \frac{\Gamma(\psi_{x|\mathbf{u}} + \mathcal{D}\#(x\mathbf{u}))}{\Gamma(\psi_{x|\mathbf{u}})}. \qquad \blacksquare$$

PROOF. Given a complete data set $\mathcal{D} = \mathbf{d}_1, \dots, \mathbf{d}_N$, define $\mathcal{D}_i = \mathbf{d}_1, \dots, \mathbf{d}_i$. Equations 18.14 and 18.16, with the chain rule of Bayesian networks, give

$$\mathbb{P}(\mathbf{d}_i | \mathcal{D}_{i-1}) = \prod_{x\mathbf{u} \sim \mathbf{d}_i} \frac{\psi_{x|\mathbf{u}} + \mathcal{D}_{i-1}\#(x\mathbf{u})}{\psi_{X|\mathbf{u}} + \mathcal{D}_{i-1}\#(\mathbf{u})}.$$

Using this equation and the chain rule of probability calculus, we get

$$\mathbb{P}(\mathcal{D}) = \prod_{i=1}^{N} \mathbb{P}(\mathbf{d}_i | \mathcal{D}_{i-1}) = \prod_{i=1}^{N} \prod_{x\mathbf{u} \sim \mathbf{d}_i} \frac{\psi_{x|\mathbf{u}} + \mathcal{D}_{i-1}\#(x\mathbf{u})}{\psi_{X|\mathbf{u}} + \mathcal{D}_{i-1}\#(\mathbf{u})}.$$

Rearranging the terms in this expression, we get (see Exercise 18.11)

$$\mathbb{P}(\mathcal{D}) = \prod_{X\mathbf{U}} \prod_{\mathbf{u}} \frac{\prod_x (\psi_{x|\mathbf{u}})(\psi_{x|\mathbf{u}} + 1) \dots (\psi_{x|\mathbf{u}} + \mathcal{D}\#(x\mathbf{u}) - 1)}{(\psi_{X|\mathbf{u}})(\psi_{X|\mathbf{u}} + 1) \dots (\psi_{X|\mathbf{u}} + \mathcal{D}\#(\mathbf{u}) - 1)}. \qquad (18.27)$$

This closed form is commonly expressed using the Gamma function, $\Gamma(.)$, which is known to satisfy the following property:

$$\frac{\Gamma(a+k)}{\Gamma(a)} = a(a+1) \dots (a+k-1),$$

where $a > 0$ and k is a non-negative integer. Given this property, we have

$$\mathbb{P}(\mathcal{D}) = \prod_{X\mathbf{U}} \prod_{\mathbf{u}} \frac{\Gamma(\psi_{X|\mathbf{u}})}{\Gamma(\psi_{X|\mathbf{u}} + \mathcal{D}\#(\mathbf{u}))} \prod_x \frac{\Gamma(\psi_{x|\mathbf{u}} + \mathcal{D}\#(x\mathbf{u}))}{\Gamma(\psi_{x|\mathbf{u}})}. \qquad \blacksquare$$

Appendix A

Notation

Variables and Instantiations (see Page 20)

A	variable (upper case)
a	value of variable A (lower case)
$\mathbf{A}$	set of variables (upper case)
	instantiation of variables $\mathbf{A}$ (lower case)
$\top$	trivial instantiation (i.e., instantiation of an empty set of variables)
$x_1, \ldots, x_n$	event $(X_1 = x_1) \wedge \ldots \wedge (X_n = x_n)$
A, a	event $A = \text{true}$ (assuming A is a binary variable)
$\neg A, \bar{a}$	event $A = \text{false}$ (assuming A is a binary variable)
$\mathbf{x} - Y$	the result of erasing the value of variable Y from instantiation $\mathbf{x}$
$\mathbf{x} - \mathbf{Y}$	the result of erasing the values of variables $\mathbf{Y}$ from instantiation $\mathbf{x}$
$\mathbf{x} \sim \mathbf{y}$	instantiations $\mathbf{x}$ and $\mathbf{y}$ are compatible (agree on the values of common variables)
$\mathbf{X}^{\#}$	number of instantiations for variables $\mathbf{X}$
$\|X\|$	number of values for variable X

Logic

$\wedge$	conjunction connective
$\vee$	disjunction connective
$\neg$	negation connective
$\Longrightarrow$	implication connective
$\Longleftrightarrow$	equivalence connective
α, β, γ	events (propositional sentences)
true	a valid sentence or
	the value of propositional variable
false	an inconsistent sentence or
	the value of propositional variable
ω	world (truth assignment, complete variable instantiation): maps each variable to a value
$\omega \models \alpha$	world ω satisfies sentence α / sentence α is true at world ω
$Mods(\alpha)$	the models of sentence α / worlds at which sentence α is true
$\beta \models \alpha$	sentence β implies sentence α
$\models \alpha$	sentence α is valid

Probability

$\Pr(\alpha)$	probability of event α
$\Pr(\alpha\|\beta)$	probability of α given β
$O(\alpha)$	odds of event α
$O(\alpha\|\beta)$	odds of α given β
$\Pr(\mathbf{X})$	probability distribution over variables $\mathbf{X}$ (a factor)
$\Pr(\mathbf{x})$	probability of instantiation $\mathbf{x}$ (a number)
$\Pr_\theta(.)$	probability distribution induced by a Bayesian network with parameters θ
$\Pr_{\mathcal{D}}(.)$	probability distribution induced by a complete data set $\mathcal{D}$
$I_{\Pr}(\mathbf{X}, \mathbf{Z}, \mathbf{Y})$	$\mathbf{X}$ independent of $\mathbf{Y}$ given $\mathbf{Z}$ in distribution $\Pr$
$\text{ENT}(X)$	entropy of variable X
$\text{ENT}(X\|Y)$	conditional entropy of variable X given variable Y
$\text{MI}(X; Y)$	mutual information between variables X and Y
$\text{KL}(\Pr, \Pr')$	KL divergence between two distributions

Networks and Parameters

(G, Θ)	Bayesian network with DAG G and CPTs Θ
$X\mathbf{U}$	network family: a node X and its parents $\mathbf{U}$
$\Theta_{X\|\mathbf{U}}$	CPT for node X and its parents $\mathbf{U}$
$\theta_{x\|\mathbf{u}}$	network parameter: probability of x given $\mathbf{u}$
$\theta_{x\|\mathbf{U}}$	parameters for value x of variable X given its parents $\mathbf{U}$: if $\mathbf{U}$ has instantiations $\mathbf{u}_1, \ldots, \mathbf{u}_n$, then $\theta_{x\|\mathbf{U}} = (\theta_{x\|\mathbf{u}_1}, \ldots, \theta_{x\|\mathbf{u}_n})$
$\theta_{X\|\mathbf{u}}$	parameter set for variable X given parent instantiation $\mathbf{u}$: if X has values $x_1, \ldots, x_n$, then $\theta_{X\|\mathbf{u}} = (\theta_{x_1\|\mathbf{u}}, \ldots, \theta_{x_n\|\mathbf{u}})$
$\theta_{x\|\mathbf{u}}^{ml}$	maximum likelihood (ML) estimate for parameter $\theta_{x\|\mathbf{u}}$
$\theta_{x\|\mathbf{u}}^{ma}$	MAP estimate for parameter $\theta_{x\|\mathbf{u}}$
$\theta_{x\|\mathbf{u}}^{be}$	Bayesian estimate for parameter $\theta_{x\|\mathbf{u}}$
$\theta_{x\|\mathbf{u}} \sim \mathbf{z}$	parameter $\theta_{x\|\mathbf{u}}$ is compatible with instantiation $\mathbf{z}$ (i.e., instantiations $x\mathbf{u}$ and $\mathbf{z}$ must be compatible)

Factors

$f(\mathbf{X})$	factor f over variables $\mathbf{X}$
$\text{vars}(f)$	variables of factor f
$f(\mathbf{x})$	number assigned by factor f to instantiation $\mathbf{x}$
$f[\mathbf{x}]$	instantiation assigned by extended factor f to $\mathbf{x}$
$\sum_X f$	result of summing out variable X from factor f
$\max_X f$	result of maximizing out variable X from factor f
$f_1 f_2$	result of multiplying factors f_1 and f_2
f_1/f_2	result of dividing factor f_1 by f_2
$f^{\mathbf{e}}$	result of reducing factor f given evidence $\mathbf{e}$

Appendix B

Concepts from Information Theory

Consider the *entropy* of variable X,

$$\text{ENT}(X) \overset{def}{=} \sum_x \Pr(x) \log_2 \frac{1}{\Pr(x)} = -\sum_x \Pr(x) \log_2 \Pr(x),$$

and assume that $0 \log_2 0 = 0$ by convention.

Intuitively, the entropy can be thought of as measuring the *uncertainty* we have about the value of variable X. For example, suppose X is a boolean variable where $\Pr(X = \text{true}) = p$ and $\Pr(X = \text{false}) = 1 - p$. Figure B.1 plots the entropy of X for varying values of p. Entropy is non-negative, so when $p = 0$ or 1, the entropy of X is zero and at a minimum: there is no uncertainty about the value of X. When $p = .5$, the distribution $\Pr(X)$ is uniform and the entropy is at a maximum: we have no information about the value of X.

We can also define the *conditional entropy* of X given another variable Y,

$$
\begin{aligned}
\text{ENT}(X|Y) \overset{def}{=} & \sum_{x,y} \Pr(x, y) \log_2 \frac{1}{\Pr(x|y)} \\
= & \sum_y \Pr(y) \sum_x \Pr(x|y) \log_2 \frac{1}{\Pr(x|y)} \\
= & \sum_y \Pr(y)\text{ENT}(X|y),
\end{aligned}
$$

which measures the average uncertainty about the value of X after learning the value of Y. It is possible to show that the entropy never increases after conditioning,

$$\text{ENT}(X|Y) \leq \text{ENT}(X).$$

That is, on average learning the value of Y reduces our uncertainty about X. However, for a particular instance y, we may have $\text{ENT}(X|y) > \text{ENT}(X)$.

We can also define the *mutual information* between variables X and Y,

$$\text{MI}(X; Y) \overset{def}{=} \sum_{x,y} \Pr(x, y) \log_2 \frac{\Pr(x, y)}{\Pr(x)\Pr(y)},$$

which measures the amount of information variables X and Y have about each other. Mutual information is non-negative and equal to zero if and only if X and Y are independent. On the other hand, it is easy to see that $\text{MI}(X; X) = \text{ENT}(X)$. We can also think of mutual information as the degree to which knowledge of one variable reduces the uncertainty in the other:

$$
\begin{aligned}
\text{MI}(X; Y) & = \text{ENT}(X) - \text{ENT}(X|Y) \\
& = \text{ENT}(Y) - \text{ENT}(Y|X).
\end{aligned}
$$

517

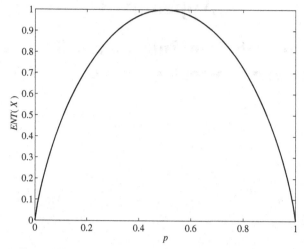

Figure B.1: $\mathrm{ENT}(X) = -p \log_2 p - (1-p) \log_2 (1-p)$.

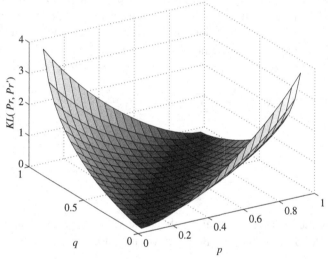

Figure B.2: $\mathrm{KL}(X, Y) = p \log_2 \frac{p}{q} + (1-p) \log_2 \frac{1-p}{1-q}$.

Mutual information then measures the uncertainty reduced or, alternatively, information gained about one variable due to observing the other.

Extending these notions to sets of variables is straightforward. For example, the *joint entropy* of a joint distribution over variables **X**,

$$\mathrm{ENT}(\mathbf{X}) = -\sum_{\mathbf{x}} \Pr(\mathbf{x}) \log_2 \Pr(\mathbf{x}),$$

measures the uncertainty we have in the joint state of variables **X**.

Finally, consider the *Kullback-Leibler divergence*, which is often abbreviated as the KL divergence and sometimes referred to as the *relative entropy:*

$$\mathrm{KL}(\Pr, \Pr') \stackrel{def}{=} \sum_{\mathbf{x}} \Pr(\mathbf{x}) \log_2 \frac{\Pr(\mathbf{x})}{\Pr'(\mathbf{x})}.$$

The KL divergence is non-negative and equal to zero if and only if distributions Pr and Pr′ are equivalent. By convention, we assume that $0 \log_2 \frac{0}{p} = 0$. Note that the KL divergence is not a true distance measure as it does not obey the triangle inequality and is not symmetric, that is, $KL(Pr, Pr') \neq KL(Pr', Pr)$ in general.

For example, suppose that X is a boolean variable where $\Pr(X=\text{true}) = p$ and $\Pr'(X=\text{true}) = q$. Figure B.2 plots the KL divergence between $\Pr(X)$ and $\Pr'(X)$ for varying values of p and q. When $p = q$, the distributions are equivalent and the divergence is zero. As p approaches one and q approaches zero (and vice versa), the divergence goes to infinity.

Appendix C

Fixed Point Iterative Methods

Given a function f, a *fixed point* for f is a value $x^\star$ such that

$$x^\star = f(x^\star).$$

We can identify such values using *fixed point iteration*. We start with some initial value upon which we repeatedly apply our function f. That is, we compute new values x_t using the preceding value x_{t-1}:

$$x_t = f(x_{t-1}).$$

For example, if we start with an initial value x_0, we compute in the first few iterations:

$$x_1 = f(x_0)$$
$$x_2 = f(x_1) = f(f(x_0))$$
$$x_3 = f(x_2) = f(f(x_1)) = f(f(f(x_0))).$$

For suitable functions f, this iterative process tends to converge to a fixed point $x^\star$.

Many problems can be formulated as fixed point problems, which we can try to solve using this iterative procedure. For example, suppose we want to solve the following equation:

$$g(x) = 2x^2 - x - \frac{3}{8} = 0.$$

We can formulate this problem as a fixed point problem. After rearranging, we find that one solution is equivalent to

$$x = \sqrt{\frac{1}{2}\left(x + \frac{3}{8}\right)}.$$

We can then search for a fixed point of the following function,

$$f(x) = \sqrt{\frac{1}{2}\left(x + \frac{3}{8}\right)},$$

where the value $x^\star = f(x^\star)$ gives us a zero of the function $g(x)$. If we start with initial value $x_0 = .1$, we find that $x_1 = f(x_0) \approx .4873$ and $x_2 = f(x_1) \approx .6566$.

Figure C.1 illustrates the dynamics of this search for the first few iterations. In this example, the fixed point iterations are converging toward the fixed point of $f(x)$, which exists at the intersection of $f(x)$ and the line $h(x) = x$. This value $x^\star = .75$ yields a zero for the original function $g(x)$, as desired.

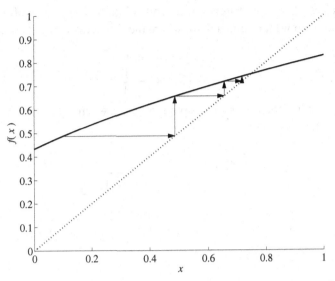

Figure C.1: A convergent search for a fixed point of $f(x)$ (solid line). Also plotted is $h(x) = x$ (dotted line).

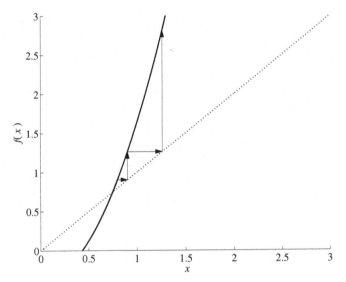

Figure C.2: A divergent search for a fixed point of $f(x)$ (solid line). Also plotted is $h(x) = x$ (dotted line).

Even for the same problem, different fixed point formulations can converge quickly, converge slowly, or may not converge at all. For example, we could have searched instead for a fixed point of the following function:

$$f(x) = 2x^2 - \frac{3}{8}.$$

This function has two fixed points: $x^\star = -.25$ and $x^\star = .75$, both zeros of the original function $g(x)$. If we started with an initial value of $x_0 = .8$, iterations yield increasingly larger values, away from any fixed point (see Figure C.2).

We can also use fixed point iteration to find solutions to systems of equations. For example, suppose we want to find a point where the following two circles intersect:

$$x^2 + y^2 = 1$$
$$(x - 1)^2 + y^2 = \frac{1}{4}.$$

We can formulate this problem as a fixed point problem where we search for a fixed point of the following function:

$$f\left(\begin{bmatrix} x \\ y \end{bmatrix} \right) = \begin{bmatrix} \sqrt{1 - y^2} \\ \sqrt{\frac{1}{4} - (x - 1)^2} \end{bmatrix},$$

where the vector $\begin{bmatrix} x^* \\ y^* \end{bmatrix} = f(\begin{bmatrix} x^* \\ y^* \end{bmatrix})$ gives us a point of intersection. If we start with an initial vector $\begin{bmatrix} x_0 \\ y_0 \end{bmatrix} = \begin{bmatrix} .5 \\ .5 \end{bmatrix}$, we find that $\begin{bmatrix} x_1 \\ y_1 \end{bmatrix} \approx \begin{bmatrix} .8660 \\ .4817 \end{bmatrix}$ and $\begin{bmatrix} x_2 \\ y_2 \end{bmatrix} \approx \begin{bmatrix} .8763 \\ .4845 \end{bmatrix}$. Continued iterations converge to the fixed point $\begin{bmatrix} x^* \\ y^* \end{bmatrix} = \begin{bmatrix} \frac{7}{8} \\ \frac{\sqrt{15}}{8} \end{bmatrix}$.

Appendix D

Constrained Optimization

Consider a constrained optimization problem of the following form:

$$
\begin{aligned}
&\text{minimize} \quad f(x) \\
&\text{subject to} \quad g_j(x) = 0, \quad j = 1, \ldots, m,
\end{aligned}
\tag{D.1}
$$

where we search for a vector $x = (x_1, \ldots, x_n)$ that minimizes an objective function $f : \mathbb{R}^n \to \mathbb{R}$ subject to equality constraints specified by functions $g_j : \mathbb{R}^n \to \mathbb{R}$. Our goal here is to review Lagrange's method for approaching this class of problems, which formulates the constrained optimization task as an unconstrained one.

Consider first an unconstrained optimization problem that asks for points x that

$$
\text{minimize} \quad f(x).
\tag{D.2}
$$

Recall also that a multivariate function f has a *local minimum* at a point x if $f(x) \leq f(y)$ for all points y near x. That is, x is a local minimum if there exists a ball with center x (equivalently, a disk in two dimensions) where f is at least as small at x as it is at all other points inside the ball. Similarly, a function f has a *local maximum* at a point x if $f(x) \geq f(y)$ for all points y near x. A function f has a *global minimum* at x if $f(x) \leq f(y)$ for all y in the domain of f. Similarly, f has a *global maximum* at x if $f(x) \geq f(y)$ for all y in the domain of f. Minima and maxima are referred to collectively as *extreme points*, which may also be local or global.

We consider an extreme point an *optimal point* if it is a solution to our optimization problem (D.2). Again, a point x is locally optimal if it is a solution for (D.2) over points near x and globally optimal if it is a solution for all points in the domain of f. All extreme points, and hence all optimal points that solve our optimization problem, are also *stationary points*. A point x is a stationary point if the partial derivative of f with respect to all variables x_i is zero at the point x. That is, the gradient vector of f is zero at x, or simply $\nabla f(x) = (\frac{\partial f}{\partial x_1}(x), \ldots, \frac{\partial f}{\partial x_n}(x)) = 0$. Since all optimal points are stationary points, we can first search for stationary points and then determine if they are optimal or not once we find them. Unfortunately, stationary points may be neither minima nor maxima: they may be *saddle* points, or points of *inflection*. Second derivative tests can be used to determine whether a stationary point is a minima, maxima, or saddle point.

Using the method of *Lagrange multipliers*, we can convert the constrained optimization problem in (D.1) to the unconstrained problem in (D.2). In particular, when we are given an objective function f and constraints $g_j(x) = 0$, we search for stationary points of the *Lagrangian L*:

$$
L(x, \lambda) = f(x) + \sum_j \lambda_j g_j(x).
$$

That is, we want the point x and the point $\lambda = (\lambda_1, \ldots, \lambda_m)$ where $\nabla L(x, \lambda) = 0$. Here $\lambda = (\lambda_1, \ldots, \lambda_m)$ are newly introduced variables called Lagrange multipliers that help enforce these constraints.

If we set the gradient to zero, $\nabla L(x, \lambda) = 0$, we have a system of $n + m$ equations we now want to solve in terms of each of our n variables x_i and each of our m multipliers λ_j. When we set to zero the partial derivative of L with respect to variables x_i, we have

$$\frac{\partial L}{\partial x_i} = \frac{\partial f}{\partial x_i} + \sum_j \lambda_j \frac{\partial g_j}{\partial x_i} = 0.$$

When we set to zero the partial derivatives with respect to multipliers λ_j, we have

$$\frac{\partial L}{\partial \lambda_j} = g_j = 0,$$

recovering our equality constraints.

To see how stationary points of the Lagrangian yield solutions to our constrained optimization problem, consider the following simple example. Suppose we want to identify the point (x, y) on the unit circle centered at the origin, closest to the point $(\frac{1}{2}, \frac{1}{2})$. That is, we want to minimize the (square of the) distance between (x, y) and $(\frac{1}{2}, \frac{1}{2})$:

$$f(x, y) = \left(x - \frac{1}{2}\right)^2 + \left(y - \frac{1}{2}\right)^2,$$

subject to the constraint that the point (x, y) lies on the unit circle,

$$g(x, y) = x^2 + y^2 - 1 = 0.$$

We first construct the Lagrangian,

$$L(x, y, \lambda) = f(x, y) + \lambda g(x, y)$$
$$= \left(x - \frac{1}{2}\right)^2 + \left(y - \frac{1}{2}\right)^2 + \lambda(x^2 + y^2 - 1),$$

where we introduce the multiplier λ for our single constraint. Setting to zero the partial derivatives of $L(x, y, \lambda)$ with respect to x, y, and λ, we get the following system of equations:

$$2x - 1 + 2\lambda x = 0$$
$$2y - 1 + 2\lambda y = 0$$
$$x^2 + y^2 - 1 = 0.$$

Rearranging, we get

$$x = \frac{1}{2} \frac{1}{1 + \lambda}$$
$$y = \frac{1}{2} \frac{1}{1 + \lambda}$$
$$x^2 + y^2 = 1.$$

Substituting the first and second equation into the third and again rearranging, we find that

$$\frac{1}{1 + \lambda} = \pm\sqrt{2}.$$

Substituting back into the first two equations, we find that

$$(x, y) = \pm \left(\frac{\sqrt{2}}{2}, \frac{\sqrt{2}}{2} \right)$$

are stationary points of our objective function. By evaluating $f(x, y)$ at each point, we can see that

$$f \left(\frac{\sqrt{2}}{2}, \frac{\sqrt{2}}{2} \right) = \frac{3 - 2\sqrt{2}}{2}$$

is a global minimum and

$$f \left(-\frac{\sqrt{2}}{2}, -\frac{\sqrt{2}}{2} \right) = \frac{3 + 2\sqrt{2}}{2}$$

is a global maximum.

Bibliography

S. M. Aji and R. McEliece. The generalized distributive law and free energy minimization. In *Proceedings of the 39th Allerton Conference on Communication, Control and Computing*, pages 672–681, 2001.

H. Akaike. A new look at the statistical model identification. *IEEE Transactions on Automatic Control*, 19:716–723, 1974.

D. Allen and A. Darwiche. New advances in inference by recursive conditioning. In *Proceedings of the Conference on Uncertainty in Artificial Intelligence*, pages 2–10. Morgan Kaufmann, San Francisco, CA, 2003.

D. Allen and A. Darwiche. Optimal Time–Space Tradeoff in Probabilistic Inference. In *Advances in Bayesian Network*, volume 146, pages 39–55. Studies in Fuzziness and Soft Computing. Springer-Verlag, New York, 2004.

D. Allen and A. Darwiche. RC-Link: genetic linkage analysis using bayesian networks. *International Journal of Approximate Reasoning*, 48(2):499–525, 2008.

D. Allen, A. Darwiche, and J. Park. A greedy algorithm for time-space tradeoff in probabilistic inference. In *Proceedings of the Second European Workshop on Probabilistic Graphical Models*, pages 1–8, 2004.

S. Andreassen, F. V. Jensen, S. K. Andersen, B. Falck, U. Kjærulff, M. Woldbye, A. R. Sorensen, A. Rosenfalck, and F. Jensen. MUNIN – an expert EMG assistant. In J. E. Desmedt, editor, *Computer-Aided Electromyography and Expert Systems*, chapter 21. Elsevier Science Publishers, Amsterdam, 1989.

S. Andreassen, M. Suojanen, B. Falck, and K. G. Olesen. Improving the diagnostic performance of MUNIN by remodelling of the diseases. In *Proceedings of the 8th Conference on AI in Medicine in Europe*, pages 167–176. Springer-Verlag, Berlin, 2001.

S. Andreassen, M. Woldbye, B. Falck, and S. K. Andersen. MUNIN – a causal probabilistic network for interpretation of electromyographic findings. In J. McDermott, editor, *Proceedings of the 10th International Joint Conference on Artificial Intelligence*, pages 366–372. Morgan Kaufmann, San Francisco, CA, 1987.

S. Arnborg, D. G. Corneil, and A. Proskurowski. Complexity of finding embeddings in a *k*-tree. *SIAM Journal on Algebraic and Discrete Methods*, 8:277–284, 1987.

S. Arnborg and A. Proskurowski. Characterization and recognition of partial 3-trees. *SIAM Journal on Algebraic and Discrete Methods*, 7:305–314, 1986.

F. Bacchus, S. Dalmao, and T. Pitassi. Value elimination: Bayesian inference via backtracking search. In *Proceedings of the 19th Annual Conference on Uncertainty in Artificial Intelligence*, pages 20–28. Morgan Kaufmann, San Francisco, CA, 2003.

R. I. Bahar, E. A. Frohm, C. M. Gaona, G. D. Hachtel, E. Macii, A. Pardo, and F. Somenzi. Algebraic decision diagrams and their applications. In *IEEE/ACM International Conference on CAD*, pages 188–191. IEEE Computer Society Press, Santa Clara, CA, 1993.

T. Bayes. An essay towards solving a problem in the doctrine of chances. *Philosophical Transactions of the Royal Society*, 3:370–418, 1963.

A. Becker, R. Bar-Yehuda, and D. Geiger. Random algorithms for the loop cutset problem. In *Proceedings of the 15th Conference on Uncertainty in Artificial Intelligence*, pages 49–56. Morgan Kaufmann, San Francisco, CA, 1999.

A. Becker and D. Geiger. Approximation algorithms for the loop cutset problem. In *Proceedings of the Tenth Conference on Uncertainty in Artificial Intelligence*, pages 60–68, 1994.

U. Bertele and F. Brioschi. *Nonserial Dynamic Programming*. Academic Press, New York, 1972.

D. P. Bertsekas and J. N. Tsitsiklis. *Introduction to Probability*. Athena Scientific, Nashua, NH, 2002.

B. Bidyuk and R. Dechter. Cutset sampling with likelihood weighting. In *Proceedings of the 22nd Annual Conference on Uncertainty in Artificial Intelligence*. AUAI Press, Arlington, VA, 2006.

H. L. Bodlaender. A partial k-arboretum of graphs with bounded treewidth. *Theoretical Computer Science*, 209:1–45, 1998.

H. L. Bodlaender. Discovering treewidth. In *Proceedings of the 31st Conference on Current Trends in Theory and Practice of Computer Science*, volume 3381, pages 1–16. Lecture Notes in Computer Science. Springer, New York, January 2005.

H. L. Bodlaender. Treewidth: characterizations, applications, and computations. In F. V. Fomin, editor, *Proceedings of the 32nd International Workshop on Graph-Theoretic Concepts in Computer Science*, volume 4271, pages 1–14. Lecture Notes in Computer Science. Springer, New York, 2006.

H. L. Bodlaender. Treewidth: structure and algorithms. In G. Prencipe and S. Zaks, editors, *Proceedings of the 14th International Colloquium on Structural Information and Communication Complexity*, volume 4474, pages 11–25. Lecture Notes in Computer Science. Springer, New York, 2007.

H. L. Bodlaender, A. Grigoriev, and A. M. C. A. Koster. Treewidth lower bounds with brambles. In *Proceedings of the 13th Annual European Symposium on Algorithms*, volume 3669, pages 391–402. Lecture Notes in Computer Science. Springer-Verlag, New York, 2005.

H. L. Bodlaender, A. M. C. A. Koster, and T. Wolle. Contraction and treewidth lower bounds. In *Proceedings of the 12th Annual European Symposium on Algorithms*, volume 3221, pages 628–689. Lecture Notes in Computer Science. Springer, New York, January 2004.

H. L. Bodlaender, A. M. C. A. Koster, and F. van den Eijkhof. Pre-processing rules for triangulation of probabilistic networks. *Computational Intelligence*, 21(3):286–305, 2005.

H. L. Bodlaender, A. M. C. A. Koster, and T. Wolle. Contraction and treewidth lower bounds. *Journal of Graph Algorithms and Applications*, 10(1):5–49, 2006.

R. R. Bouckaert. Probabilistic network construction using the minimum description length principle. In *Lecture Notes in Computer Science*, volume 747, pages 41–48. Springer, New York, 1993.

C. Boutilier, N. Friedman, M. Goldszmidt, and D. Koller. Context-specific independence in Bayesian networks. In *Proceedings of the 12th Conference on Uncertainty in Artificial Intelligence*, pages 115–123. Morgan Kaufmann, San Francisco, CA, 1996.

W. Buntine. Theory refinement on Bayesian networks. In *Proceedings of the Seventh Conference on Uncertainty in Artificial Intelligence*, pages 52–60. Morgan Kaufmann, Los Angeles, CA, July 1991.

W. Buntine. A guide to the literature on learning graphical models. *IEEE Transactions on Knowledge and Data Engineering*, 8:195–210, 1996.

E. Castillo, J. M. Gutiérrez, and A. S. Hadi. Goal oriented symbolic propagation in Bayesian networks. In *Proceedings of the AAAI National Conference*, pages 1263–1268. AAAI Press, Menlo Park, CA, 1996.

E. Castillo, J. M. Gutiérrez, and A. S. Hadi. Sensitivity analysis in discrete Bayesian networks. *IEEE Transactions on Systems, Man, and Cybernetics*, 27:412–423, 1997.

J. Cerquides and R. Lopez de Mantaras. TAN classifiers based on decomposable distributions. *Machine Learning*, 59(3):323–354, 2005.

H. Chan and A. Darwiche. When do numbers really matter? *Journal of Artificial Intelligence Research*, 17:265–287, 2002.

H. Chan and A. Darwiche. Sensitivity analysis in Bayesian networks: from single to multiple parameters. In *Proceedings of the Twentieth Conference on Uncertainty in Artificial Intelligence*, pages 67–75. AUAI Press, Arlington, VA, 2004.

H. Chan and A. Darwiche. A distance measure for bounding probabilistic belief change. *International Journal of Approximate Reasoning*, 38:149–174, 2005a.

H. Chan and A. Darwiche. On the revision of probabilistic beliefs using uncertain evidence. *Artificial Intelligence*, 163:67–90, 2005b.

H. Chan and A. Darwiche. On the robustness of most probable explanations. In *Proceedings of the 22nd Conference on Uncertainty in Artificial Intelligence*, pages 63–71. AUAI Press, Arlington, VA, 2006.

E. Charniak. Bayesian networks without tears. *AI Magazine*, 12(4):50–63, 1991.

M. Chavira, D. Allen, and A. Darwiche. Exploiting evidence in probabilistic inference. In *Proceedings of the 21st Conference on Uncertainty in Artificial Intelligence*, pages 112–119. AUAI Press, Arlington, VA, 2005.

M. Chavira and A. Darwiche. Compiling Bayesian networks with local structure. In *Proceedings of the 19th International Joint Conference on Artificial Intelligence*, pages 1306–1312. Professional Book Center, Denver, CO, 2005.

M. Chavira and A. Darwiche. Encoding CNFS to empower component analysis. In *Proceedings of the Ninth International Conference on Theory and Applications of Satisfiability Testing*, pages 61–74. Springer, New York, 2006.

M. Chavira and A. Darwiche. Compiling Bayesian networks using variable elimination. In *Proceedings of the 20th International Joint Conference on Artificial Intelligence*, pages 2443–2449. AAAI Press, Menlo Park, CA, 2007.

M. Chavira and A. Darwiche. On probabilistic inference by weighted model counting. *Artificial Intelligence Journal*, 172(6–7):772–799, 2008.

M. Chavira, A. Darwiche, and M. Jaeger. Compiling relational Bayesian networks for exact inference. *International Journal of Approximate Reasoning*, 42(1–2):4–20, 2006.

P. Cheeseman and J. Stutz. Bayesian classification (AutoClass): theory and results. In U. Fayyad, G. Piatesky-Shapiro, P. Smyth, and R. Uthurusamy, editors, *Advances in Knowledge Discovery and Data Mining*, pages 153–180. AAAI Press, Menlo Park, CA, 1995.

J. Cheng and M. J. Druzdzel. BN-AIS: an adaptive importance sampling algorithm for evidential reasoning in large Bayesian networks. *Journal of Artificial Intelligence Research*, 13:155–188, 2000.

S. Chib. Marginal likelihood from the Gibbs output. *Journal of the American Statistical Association*, 90:1313–1321, 1995.

D. Chickering. Learning Bayesian networks is NP-complete. In D. Fisher and H. Lenz, editors, *Learning from Data*, pages 121–130. Springer-Verlag, New York, 1996.

D. Chickering, D. Geiger, and D. Heckerman. Learning Bayesian networks: search methods and experimental results. In *Proceedings of the Fifth Conference on Artificial Intelligence and Statistics*, pages 112–128. Society for Artificial Intelligence in Statistics, Ft. Lauderbale, FL, 1995.

D. Chickering and D. Heckerman. Efficient approximations for the marginal likelihood of Bayesian networks with hidden variables. *Machine Learning*, 29:181–212, 1997.

D. Chickering, D. Heckerman, and C. Meek. A Bayesian approach to learning Bayesian networks with local structure. In D. Geiger and P. Shenoy, editors, *Proceedings of the Thirteenth Conference on Uncertainty in Artificial Intelligence*, pages 80–89. Morgan Kaufmann, Providence, RI, 1997.

D. Chickering, D. Heckerman, and C. Meek. Large-sample learning of Bayesian networks is NP-hard. *Journal of Machine Learning Research*, 5:1287–1330, 2004.

A. Choi, M. Chavira, and A. Darwiche. Node splitting: a scheme for generating upper bounds in bayesian networks. In *Proceedings of the 23rd Conference on Uncertainty in Artificial Intelligence*, pages 57–66. AUAI Press, Arlington, VA, 2007.

A. Choi and A. Darwiche. An edge deletion semantics for belief propagation and its practical impact on approximation quality. In *Proceedings of the National Conference on Artificial Intelligence*. AAAI Press, Menlo Park, CA, 2006.

A. Choi and A. Darwiche. Approximating the partition function by deleting and then correcting for model edges. In *Proceedings of the 24th Conference on Uncertainty in Artificial Intelligence*. AUAI Press, Arlington, VA, 2008.

C. Chow and C. Liu. Approximating discrete probability distributions with dependence trees. *IEEE Transactions on Information Theory*, 14:462–467, 1968.

G. Cooper. Bayesian belief–network inference using recursive decomposition. Technical Report KSL-90-05. Knowledge Systems Laboratory, Stanford, CA, 94305, 1990a.

G. Cooper. The computational complexity of probabilistic inference using Bayesian belief networks. *Artificial Intelligence*, 42(2–3): 393–405, 1990b.

G. Cooper and E. Herskovits. A Bayesian method for constructing Bayesian belief networks from databases. In *Proceedings of the Seventh Conference on Uncertainty in*

Artificial Intelligence, pages 86–94. Morgan Kaufmann, Los Angeles, CA, 1991.

G. Cooper and E. Herskovits. A Bayesian method for the induction of probabilistic networks from data. *Machine Learning*, 9:309–347, 1992.

T. H. Cormen, C. E. Leiserson, and R. L. Rivest. *Introduction to Algorithms*. MIT press, Cambridge, MA, 1990.

V. M. H. Coupé and L. C. van der Gaag. Properties of sensitivity analysis of bayesian belief networks. *Annals of Mathematics and Artificial Intelligence*, 36:323–356, 2002.

T. M. Cover and J. A. Thomas. *Elements of Information Theory*. Wiley, New York, 1991.

R. Cowell, A. Dawid, S. Lauritzen, and D. Spiegelhalter. *Probabilistic Networks and Expert Systems*. Springer, New York, 1999.

P. Dagum and M. Luby. Approximating probabilistic inference in Bayesian belief networks is NP-hard. *Artificial Intelligence*, 60(1):141–153, 1993.

A. Darwiche. Conditioning algorithms for exact and approximate inference in causal networks. In *Proceedings of the 11th Conference on Uncertainty in Artificial Intelligence*, pages 99–107. Morgan Kaufmann, San Francisco, CA, 1995.

A. Darwiche. A differential approach to inference in Bayesian networks. In *Proceedings of the 16th Conference on Uncertainty in Artificial Intelligence*, pages 123–132, 2000.

A. Darwiche. Recursive conditioning. *Artificial Intelligence*, 126(1–2):5–41, 2001.

A. Darwiche. A logical approach to factoring belief networks. In *Proceedings of the Eighth International Conference on Principles of Knowledge Representation and Reasoning*, pages 409–420. Morgan Kaufmann, San Francisco, CA, 2002.

A. Darwiche. A differential approach to inference in Bayesian networks. *Journal of the ACM*, 50(3):280–305, 2003.

A. Darwiche. New advances in compiling CNF to decomposable negation normal form. In *Proceedings of European Conference on Artificial Intelligence*, pages 328–332. IOS Press, Amsterdam, 2004.

A. Darwiche and M. Hopkins. Using recursive decomposition to construct elimination orders, jointrees and dtrees. In *Trends in Artificial Intelligence, Lecture notes in AI, 2143*, pages 180–191. Springer-Verlag, New York, 2001.

A. Darwiche and P. Marquis. A knowledge compilation map. *Journal of Artificial Intelligence Research*, 17:229–264, 2002.

A. Dawid. Conditional independence in statistical theory. *Journal of the Royal Statistical Society, Series B*, 41(1):1–31, 1979.

A. Dawid and S. Lauritzen. Hyper Markov laws in the statistical analysis of decomposable graphical models. *Annals of Statistics*, 21:1272–1317, 1993.

T. Dean and K. Kanazawa. A model for reasoning about persistence and causation. *Computational Intelligence* 5(3):142–150, 1989.

R. Dechter. Bucket elimination: a unifying framework for probabilistic inference. In *Proceedings of the 12th Conference on Uncertainty in Artificial Intelligence*, pages 211–219. Morgan Kaufmann, San Francisco, CA, 1996.

R. Dechter. Bucket elimination: a unifying framework for reasoning. *Artificial Intelligence*, 113:41–85, 1999.

R. Dechter. *Constraint Processing*. Morgan Kaufmann, San Francisco, CA, 2003.

R. Dechter and Y. El Fattah. Topological parameters for time-space tradeoff. *Artificial Intelligence*, 125(1–2):93–118, 2001.

R. Dechter, K. Kask, and R. Mateescu. Iterative join-graph propagation. In *Proceedings of the Conference on Uncertainty in Artificial Intelligence*, pages 128–136. Morgan Kaufmann, San Francisco, CA, 2002.

R. Dechter and D. Larkin. Bayesian inference in the presence of determinism. In C. M. Bishop and B. Frey, editors, *Proceedings of the Ninth International Workshop on Artificial Intelligence and Statistics*, Key West, FL. The Society for Artificial Intelligence and Statistics, NJ, 2003.

R. Dechter and I. Rish. Mini-buckets: a general scheme for bounded inference. *Journal of the ACM*, 50(2):107–153, 2003.

M. H. DeGroot. *Probability and Statistics*. Addison Wesley, Boston, MA, 2002.

A. Dempster, N. Laird, and D. Rubin. Maximum likelihood from incomplete data via the EM algorithm. *Journal of the Royal Statistical Society, Series B*, 39:1–38, 1977.

F. J. Díez. Parameter adjustment in Bayesian networks: the generalized noisy-or gate. In *Proceedings of the Ninth Conference on Uncertainty in Artificial Intelligence*, pages 99–105. Morgan Kaufmann, San Francisco, CA, 1993.

F. J. Díez. Local conditioning in Bayesian networks. *Artificial Intelligence*, 87(1):1–20, 1996.

F. J. Díez and S. F. Galán. An efficient factorization for the noisy MAX. *International Journal of Intelligent Systems*, 18:165–177, 2003.

A. Doucet, N. de Freitas, and N. Gordon. *Sequential Monte Carlo Methods in Practice*. Springer, New York, 2001.

A. Doucet, N. de Freitas, K. P. Murphy, and S. J. Russell. Rao-blackwellised particle filtering for dynamic bayesian networks. In *Proceedings of the 16th Conference on Uncertainty in Artificial Intelligence*, pages 176–183. Morgan Kaufmann, San Francisco, CA, 2000.

P. A. Dow and R. E. Korf. Best-first search for treewidth. In *Proceedings of the 22nd Conference on Artificial Intelligence*. AAAI Press, CA, 2007.

P. A. Dow and R. E. Korf. Best-first search with a maximum edge cost function. In *Proceedings of the Tenth International Symposium on Artificial Intelligence and Mathematics*, Ft. Lauderdale, FL, 2008.

R. Duda and P. Hart, editors. *Pattern Classification and Scene Analysis*. Wiley, New York, 1973.

D. Edwards. *Introduction to Graphical Modelling*, Second edition. Springer, New York, 2000.

G. Elidan, I. McGraw, and D. Koller. Residual belief propagation: Informed scheduling for asynchronous message passing. In *Proceedings of the Conference on Uncertainty in Artificial Intelligence*. AUAI Press, Arlington, VA, 2006.

M. Fishelson and D. Geiger. Exact genetic linkage computations for general pedigrees. *Bioinformatics*, 18(1):189–198, 2002.

M. Fishelson and D. Geiger. Optimizing exact genetic linkage computations. In *Proceedings of the International Conference on Research in Computational Molecular Biology*, pages 114–121. ACM Press, New York, 2003.

B. Frey, editor. *Graphical Models for Machine Learning and Digital Communication*. MIT Press, Cambridge, MA, 1998.

B. Frey and D. MacKay. A revolution: belief propagation in graphs with cycles. In *Proceedings of the Conference on Neural Information Processing Systems*, pages 479–485. MIT Press, Cambridge, MA, 1997.

N. Friedman. The Bayesian structural EM algorithm. In *Proceedings of the Fourteenth Conference on Uncertainty in Artificial Intelligence Learning*, pages 129–138. Morgan Kaufmann, San Mateo, CA, 1998.

N. Friedman, D. Geiger, and M. Goldszmidt. Bayesian network classifiers. *Machine Learning*, 29:131–163, 1997.

N. Friedman and M. Goldszmidt. Learning Bayesian networks with local structure. In *Proceedings of the Twelfth Conference on Uncertainty in Artificial Intelligence*, pages 252–262. Morgan Kaufmann, Portland, OR, 1996.

R. Fung and K. Chang. Weighing and integrating evidence for stochastic simulation in Bayesian networks. In *Proceedings of the Fifth Workshop on Uncertainty in Artificial Intelligence*, Windsor, ON, pages 112–117. 1989. Also in M. Henrion, R. Shachter, L. Kanal, and J. Lemmer, editors, *Uncertainty in Artificial Intelligence*, volume 5, pages 209–219. North-Holland, New York, 1990.

R. Fung and B. del Favero. Backward simulation in Bayesian networks. In *Proceedings of the Tenth Annual Conference on Uncertainty in Artificial Intelligence*, pages 227–234. Morgan Kaufmann, San Mateo, CA, 1994.

P. Gärdenfors. *Knowledge in Flux: Modeling the Dynamics of Epistemic States*. MIT Press, Cambridge, MA, 1988.

F. Gavril. The intersection graphs of subtrees in trees are exactly the chordal graphs. *Journal of Combinatorial Theory Series B*, 16:47–56, 1974.

D. Geiger and D. Heckerman. A characterization of the Dirichlet distribution with application to learning Bayesian networks. In *Proceedings of the Eleventh Conference on Uncertainty in Artificial Intelligence,* Montreal, Quebec, pages 196–207. Morgan Kaufmann, CA, 1995. See also Technical Report TR-95-16. Microsoft Research, Redmond, WA, February 1995.

D. Geiger and J. Pearl. Logical and algorithmic properties of conditional independence. Technical Report 870056 (R-97). Computer Science Department, UCLA, February 1988a.

D. Geiger and J. Pearl. On the logic of causal models. In *Proceedings of the 4th Workshop on Uncertainty in Artificial Intelligence*, pages 136–147, St. Paul, MN, 1988b. Also in R. Shachter, T. Levitt, L. Kanal, and J. Lemmer, editors, *Uncertainty in Artificial Intelligence*, volume 4, pages 3–14. Amsterdam, 1990.

M. R. Genesereth and N. J. Nilsson. *Logical Foundations of Artificial Intelligence*. Morgan Kaufmann, San Mateo, CA, 1987.

W. Gibbs. *Elementary Principles of Statistical Mechanics*. Yale University Press, 1902.

W. Gilks, S. Richardson, and D. Spiegelhalter. *Markov Chain Monte Carlo in Practice*. Chapman and Hall, London, England, 1996.

C. Glymour and G. Cooper, editors. *Computation, Causation, and Discovery*. MIT Press, Cambridge, MA, 1999.

V. Gogate and R. Dechter. A complete anytime algorithm for treewidth. In *Proceedings of the 20th Annual Conference on Uncertainty in Artificial Intelligence*, pages 201–220. AUAI Press, Arlington, VA, 2004.

V. Gogate and R. Dechter. Approximate inference algorithms for hybrid bayesian networks with discrete constraints. In *Proceedings of the Conference on Uncertainty in Artificial Intelligence*, pages 209–216. AUAI Press, Arlington, VA, 2005.

M. Goldszmidt and J. Pearl. Qualitative probabilities for default reasoning, belief revision, and causal modeling. *Artificial Intelligence*, 84(1–2):57–112, July 1996.

M. C. Golumbic. *Algorithmic Graph Theory and Perfect Graphs*. Academic Press, New York, 1980.

I. J. Good. *Probability and the Weighing of Evidence*. Charles Griffin, London, 1950.

I. J. Good. *Good Thinking: The Foundations of Probability and Its Applications*. University of Minnesota Press, Minneapolis, MN, 1983.

R. Greiner, X. Su, B. Shen, and W. Zhou. Structural extension to logistic regression: discriminative parameter learning of belief net classifiers. *Machine Learning*, 59(3):297–322, 2005.

D. Grossman and P. Domingos. Learning Bayesian network classifiers by maximizing conditional likelihood. In *Proceedings of the 21st International Conference on Machine Learning*, pages 361–368. ACM Press, New York, 2004.

Y. Guo and R. Greiner. Discriminative model selection for belief net structures. In *Twentieth National Conference on Artificial Intelligence*, Pittsburgh, PA, pages 770–776. AAAI Press, Menlo Park, CA, 2005.

D. Heckerman. A tractable inference algorithm for diagnosing multiple diseases. In *Proceedings of the Fifth Conference on Uncertainty in Artificial Intelligence*, pages 174–181. Elsevier, New York, 1989.

D. Heckerman. A bayesian approach to learning causal networks. In *Proceedings of the Eleventh Conference on Uncertainty in Artificial Intelligence*, Montreal, Quebec, pages 285–295. Morgan Kaufmann, San Francisco, CA, 1995.

D. Heckerman. A tutorial on learning with Bayesian networks. In *Learning in graphical models*, pages 301–354. Kluwer, The Netherlands, 1998.

D. Heckerman, D. Geiger, and D. Chickering. Learning Bayesian networks: the combination of knowledge and statistical data. *Machine Learning*, 20:197–243, 1995.

M. Henrion. Propagating uncertainty in Bayesian networks by probalistic logic sampling. In *Uncertainty in Artificial Intelligence 2*, pages 149–163. Elsevier Science Publishing, New York, 1988.

M. Henrion. Some practical issues in constructing belief networks. In L. N. Kanal, T. S. Levitt, and J. F. Lemmer, editors, *Uncertainty in Artificial Intelligence* volume 3, pages 161–173. Elsevier Science Publishers B.V., North Holland, 1989.

L. D. Hernandez, S. Moral, and A. Salmeron. A Monte Carlo algorithm for probabilistic propagation in belief networks based on importance sampling and stratified simulation techniques. *International Journal of Approximate Reasoning*, 18:53–91, 1998.

J. Hoey, R. St-Aubin, A. Hu, and G. Boutilier. SPUDD: stochastic planning using decision diagrams. In *Proceedings of the 15th Conference on Uncertainty in Artificial Intelligence*, pages 279–288. Morgan Kaufmann, San Francisco, CA, 1999.

M. Hopkins and A. Darwiche. A practical relaxation of constant-factor treewidth approximation algorithms. In *Proceedings of the First European Workshop on Probabilistic Graphical Models*, pages 71–80, 2002.

E. J. Horvitz, H. J. Suermondt, and G. Cooper. Bounded conditioning: flexible inference for decisions under scarce resources. In *Proceedings of the Conference on Uncertainty in Artificial Intelligence, Windsor, ON*, pages 182–193. Association for Uncertainty in Artificial Intelligence, Mountain View, CA, August 1989.

R. A. Howard. From influence to relevance to knowledge. In R. M. Oliver and J. Q. Smith, editors, *Influence Diagrams, Belief Nets, and Decision Analysis*, pages 3–23. Wiley, New York, 1990.

R. A. Howard and J. E. Matheson. Influence diagrams. In *Principles and Applications of Decision Analysis*, volume 2, pages 719–762. Strategic Decision Group, Menlo Park, CA, 1984.

J. Hrastad. Tensor rank is NP-complete. *Journal of Algorithms*, 11:644–654, 1990.

C. Huang and A. Darwiche. Inference in belief networks: a procedural guide. *International Journal of Approximate Reasoning*, 15(3):225–263, 1996.

J. Huang, M. Chavira, and A. Darwiche. Solving MAP exactly by searching on compiled arithmetic circuits. In *Proceedings of the 21st National Conference on Artificial Intelligence*, pages 143–148. AAAI Press, Menlo Park, CA, 2006.

F. Hutter, H. H. Hoos, and T. Stützle. Efficient stochastic local search for MPE solving. In *Proceedings of the International Joint Conference on Artificial Intelligence*, pages 169–174. Professional Book Center, Denver, CO, 2005.

T. Jaakkola. Tutorial on variational approximation methods. In D. Saad and M. Opper, editors, *Advanced Mean Field Methods: Theory and Practice*, chapter 10, pages 129–159. MIT Press, Cambridge, MA, 2001.

E. T. Jaynes. *Probability Theory: The Logic of Science*. Cambridge University Press, Cambridge, England, 2003.

R. Jeffrey. *The Logic of Decision*. McGraw-Hill, New York, 1965.

F. V. Jensen. *An Introduction to Bayesian Networks*. Springer-Verlag, New York, 1996.

F. V. Jensen. Gradient descent training of Bayesian networks. In *Proceedings of the Fifth European Conference on Symbolic and Quantitative Approaches to Reasoning with Uncertainty*, pages 5–9. Springer, New York, 1999.

F. V. Jensen. *Bayesian Networks and Decision Graphs*. Springer-Verlag, New York, 2001.

F. Jensen and S. K. Andersen. Approximations in Bayesian belief universes for knowledge based systems. In *Proceedings of the Sixth Conference on Uncertainty in Artificial Intelligence*, Cambridge, MA, pages 162–169. Elsevier, New York, July 1990.

F. V. Jensen and F. Jensen. Optimal Junction Trees. In *Proceedings of the Tenth Conference on Uncertainty in Artificial Intelligence*, Seattle, WA, pages 360–366. Morgan Kaufmann, San Francisco, CA, 1994.

F. V. Jensen, S. Lauritzen, and K. G. Olesen. Bayesian updating in recursive graphical models by local computation. *Computational Statistics Quarterly*, 4:269–282, 1990.

F. V. Jensen and T. D. Nielsen. *Bayesian Networks and Decision Graphs*. Springer, New York, 2007.

Y. Jing, V. Pavlovic, and J. Rehg. Efficient discriminative learning of Bayesian network classifiers via boosted augmented naive Bayes. In *Proceedings of the International Conference on Machine Learning*. ACM Press, New York, 2005.

M. Jordan, editor. *Learning in Graphical Models*. Kluwer, The Netherlands, 1998.

M. Jordan, Z. Ghahramani, T. Jaakkola, and L. K. Saul. An introduction to variational methods for graphical models. *Machine Learning*, 37(2):183–233, 1999.

K. Kask and R. Dechter. Stochastic local search for bayesian networks. In *Workshop on AI and Statistics*, pages 113–122. Morgan Kaufmann, San Francisco, CA, 1999.

K. Kask and R. Dechter. A general scheme for automatic generation of search heuristics from specification dependencies. *Artificial Intelligence*, 129:91–131, 2001.

J. H. Kim and J. Pearl. A computational model for combined causal and diagnostic reasoning in inference systems. In *Proceedings of the International Joint Conference on Artificial Intelligence*, pages 190–193. Karlsruhe, Germany, 1983.

U. Kjaerulff. Triangulation of graphs – algorithms giving small total state space. Technical Report R-90-09. Department of Mathematics and Computer Science, University of Aalborg, Denmark, 1990.

U. Kjaerulff and L. C. van der Gaag. Making sensitivity analysis computationally efficient. In *Proceedings of the 16th Conference on Uncertainty in Artificial Intelligence*. Morgan Kaufmann, San Francisco, CA, 2000.

V. Kolmogorov and M. J. Wainwright. On the optimality of tree-reweighted max-product message passing. In *Proceedings of the Conference on Uncertainty in Artificial Intelligence*, pages 316–323. AUAI Press, Arlington, VA, 2005.

A. M. C. A. Koster, T. Wolle, and H. L. Bodlaender. Degree-based treewidth lower bounds. In *Proceedings of the 4th International Workshop on Experimental and Efficient Algorithms*, volume 3503, pages 101–112. Lecture

Notes in Computer Science. Springer, New York, 2005.

W. Lam and F. Bacchus. Learning Bayesian belief networks: an approach based on the MDL principle. *User Modeling and User-Adapted Interaction*, 10:269–293, 1994.

K. B. Laskey. Sensitivity analysis for probability assessments in Bayesian networks. *IEEE Transactions on Systems, Man, and Cybernetics*, 25:901–909, 1995.

S. Lauritzen. The EM algorithm for graphical association models with missing data. *Computational Statistics and Data Analysis*, 19:191–201, 1995.

S. Lauritzen. *Graphical Models*. Oxford Science Publications, Oxford, England, 1996.

S. Lauritzen and D. J. Spiegelhalter. Local computations with probabilities on graphical structures and their application to expert systems. *Journal of Royal Statistics Society, Series B*, 50(2):157–224, 1988.

V. Lepar and P. Shenoy. A comparison of Lauritzen-Spiegelhalter, HUGIN, and Shenoy-Shafer architectures for computing marginals of probability distributions. In *Proceedings of the Fourteenth Annual Conference on Uncertainty in Artificial Intelligence*, pages 328–337. Morgan Kaufmann, San Francisco, CA, 1998.

D. R. Lick and A. T. White. k-degenerate graphs. *SIAM Journal of Discrete Mathematics*, 22:1082–1096, 1970.

Y. Lin and M. Druzdzel. Computational advantages of relevance reasoning in Bayesian belief networks. In *Proceedings of the 13th Annual Conference on Uncertainty in Artificial Intelligence*, pages 342–350. Morgan Kaufmann, San Francisco, CA, 1997.

R. J. A. Little and D. B. Rubin. *Statistical Analysis with Missing Data*. Wiley, NJ, 2002.

R. Marinescu and R. Dechter. AND/OR branch-and-bound for graphical models. In *Proceedings of the International Joint Conference on Artificial Intelligence*, pages 224–229. Professional Book Center, Denver, CO, 2005.

R. Marinescu and R. Dechter. Memory intensive branch-and-bound search for graphical models. In *National Conference on Artificial Intelligence*. AAAI Press, Menlo Park, CA, 2006.

R. Marinescu, K. Kask, and R. Dechter. Systematic vs. non-systematic algorithms for solving the MPE task. In *Proceedings of the Conference on Uncertainty in Artificial Intelli-*

gence, pages 394–402. Morgan Kaufmann, San Francisco, CA, 2003.

R. Mateescu and R. Dechter. AND/OR cutset conditioning. In *International Joint Conference on Artificial Intelligence*, pages 230–235. Professional Book Center, Denver, CO, 2005.

R. Mateescu and R. Dechter. Compiling constraint networks into AND/OR multi-valued decision diagrams. In *Constraint Porgramming*. Springer, New York, 2006.

J. McCarthy. Programs with common sense. In *Proceedings of the Teddington Conference on the Mechanization of Thought Processes*, 1959. http://www-formal.stanford.edu/jmc/mcc59.html.

J. McCarthy. Epistemological problems of artificial intelligence. In *Proceedings of the Fifth International Joint Conference on Artificial Intelligence*, 1977. Invited talk: http://www-formal.stanford.edu/jmc/epistemological.pdf.

J. McCarthy. Circumscription – a form of non-monotonic reasoning. *Artificial Intelligence*, 13:27–39, 1980.

D. McDermott and J. Doyle. Nonmonotonic logic I. *Artificial Intelligence*, 13:41–72, 1980.

R. McEliece, D. MacKay, and J. Cheng. Trubo decoding as an instance of Pearl's belief propagation algorithm. *IEEE Journal on Selected Areas in Communication*, 16:140–152, 1998.

R. McEliece, D. MacKay, and J.-F. Cheng. Turbo decoding as an instance of Pearl's belief propagation algorithm. *IEEE Journal on Selected Areas in Communications*, 16(2):140–152, 1998.

C. Meek and D. Heckerman. Structure and parameter learning for causal independence and causal interaction models. In *Proceedings of the Thirteenth Conference on Uncertainty in Artificial Intelligence*, Morgan Kaufmann, Providence, RI, August 1997.

M. Meilua and M. Jordan. Estimating dependency structure as a hidden variable. In *Advances in Neural Information Processing Systems 10*, volume 10. Morgan Kaufmann, San Mateo, CA, 1998.

R. A. Miller, F. E. Fasarie, and J. D. Myers. Quick medical reference (QMR) for diagnostic assistance. *Medical Computing*, 3:34–48, 1986.

T. P. Minka. *A Family of Algorithms for Approximate Bayesian Inference*. PhD thesis. MIT Cambridge, MA, 2001.

S. Moral and A. Salmeron. Dynamic importance sampling computation in Bayesian networks. In *Proceedings of Seventh European Conference on Symbolic and Quantitative Approaches to Reasoning with Uncertainty*, pages 137–148. Springer, New York, 2003.

R. Neal. Probabilistic inference using Markov chain Monte Carlo methods. Technical Report CRG-TR-93-1. Department of Computer Science, University of Toronto, September 1993.

R. Neal. Improving asymptotic variance of MCMC estimators: non-reversible chains are better. Technical Report 0406. Department of Statistics, University of Toronto, 2004.

R. Neapolitan. *Learning Bayesian Networks*. Prentice Hall, NJ, 2004.

A. Y. Ng and M. I. Jordan. On discriminative versus generative classifiers: a comparison of logistic regression and naive Bayes. In *Advances in Neural Information Processing Systems 14*, pages 841–848. MIT Press, Cambridge, MA, 2001.

T. Nielsen, P. Wuillemin, F. Jensen, and U. Kjaerulff. Using ROBDDs for inference in Bayesian networks with troubleshooting as an example. In *Proceedings of the 16th Conference on Uncertainty in Artificial Intelligence*, pages 426–435. Morgan Kaufmann, San Francisco, CA, 2000.

L. Ortiz and L. Kaelbling. Adaptive importance sampling for estimation in structured domains. In *Proceedings of the 16th Annual Conference on Uncertainty in Artificial Intelligence*, pages 446–454. Morgan Kaufmann, San Francisco, CA, 2000.

J. Park. Using weighted MAXSAT engines to solve MPE. In *Proceedings of the Eighteenth National Conference on Artificial Intelligence*, pages 682–687. AAAI Press, Menlo Park, CA, 2002.

J. Park and A. Darwiche. Approximating MAP using stochastic local search. In *Proceedings of the 17th Conference on Uncertainty in Artificial Intelligence*, pages 403–410. Morgan Kaufmann, San Francisco, CA, 2001.

J. Park and A. Darwiche. Solving MAP exactly using systematic search. In *Proceedings of the 19th Conference on Uncertainty in Artificial Intelligence*, pages 459–468. Morgan Kaufmann, San Francisco, CA, 2003a.

J. Park and A. Darwiche. A differential semantics for jointree algorithms. In *Advances in Neural Information Processing Systems 15*, volume 1, pages 299–307. MIT Press, Cambridge, MA, 2003b.

J. Park and A. Darwiche. Morphing the HUGIN and Shenoy-Shafer architectures. In *Trends in Artificial Intelligence, Lecture Notes in AI, 2711*, pages 149–160. Springer-Verlag, New York, 2003c.

J. Park and A. Darwiche. Complexity results and approximation strategies for MAP explanations. *Journal of Artificial Intelligence Research*, 21:101–133, 2004a.

J. Park and A. Darwiche. A differential semantics for jointree algorithms. *Artificial Intelligence*, 156:197–216, 2004b.

R. C. Parker and R. A. Miller. Using causal knowledge to create simulated patient cases: the CPCS project as an extension of Internist-1. In *Proceedings of the Eleventh Annual Symposium on Computer Applications in Medical Care*, pages 473–480. IEEE Computer Society Press, 1987.

M. J. Pazzani and E. J. Keogh. Learning augmented Bayesian classifiers: a comparison of distribution-based and classification-based approaches. *International Journal on Artificial Intelligence Tools*, 11:587–601, 2002.

J. Pearl. Reverend Bayes on inference engines: a distributed hierarchical approach. In *Proceedings of the National Conference on Artificial Intelligence*, Pittsburgh, PA, pages 133–136. AAAI Press, Menlo Park, CA, 1982.

J. Pearl. Bayesian networks: a model of self-activated memory for evidential reasoning. In *Proceedings, Cognitive Science Society*, Irvine, CA, pages 329–334. Lawrence Erlbaum, Philadelphia, PA, 1985.

J. Pearl. A constraint-propagation approach to probabilistic reasoning. In L. N. Kanal and J. F. Lemmer, editors, *Uncertainty in Artificial Intelligence*, pages 357–369. North-Holland, Amsterdam, 1986a.

J. Pearl. Fusion, propagation, and structuring in belief networks. *Artificial Intelligence*, 29:241–288, 1986b.

J. Pearl. Evidential reasoning using stochastic simulation of causal models. *Artificial Intelligence*, 32:245–257, 1987.

J. Pearl. *Probabilistic Reasoning in Intelligent Systems: Networks of Plausible Inference*. Morgan Kaufmann, San Mateo, CA, 1988.

J. Pearl. *Causality: Models, Reasoning, and Inference*. Cambridge University Press, New York, 2000.

J. Pearl and A. Paz. Graphoids: graph-based logic for reasoning about relevance relations. Technical Report 850038 (R-53). Computer Science Department, UCLA, 1986.

J. Pearl and A. Paz. Graphoids: a graph-based logic for reasoning about relevance relations. In B. Duboulay, D. Hogg and L. Steels, editors, *Advances in Artificial Intelligence-II*, pages 357–363. North-Holland, Amsterdam, 1987.

A. Peot and R. Shachter. Fusion and propagation with multiple observations in belief networks. *Artificial Intelligence*, 48(3):299–318, 1991.

A. G. Percus, G. Istrate, and C. Moore, editors, Introduction: where statistical physics meets computation. In *Computational Complexity and Statistical Physics*, chapter 1, pages 3–24. Oxford University Press, Oxford, England, 2006.

D. Poole and N. L. Zhang. Exploiting contextual independence in probabilistic inference. *Journal of Artificial Intelligence*, 18:263–313, 2003.

M. Pradhan, M. Henrion, G. Provan, B. Del Favero, and K. Huang. The sensitivity of belief networks to imprecise probabilities: an experimental investigation. *Artificial Intelligence*, 85:363–397, 1996.

M. Pradhan, G. Provan, B. Middleton, and M. Henrion. Knowledge engineering for large belief networks. In *Uncertainty in Artificial Intelligence: Proceedings of the Tenth Conference*, pages 484–490. Morgan Kaufmann, San Francisco, CA, 1994.

L. R. Rabiner. A tutorial on hidden Markov models and selected applications in speech recognition. *Proceedings of the IEEE*, 77(2):257–286, 1989.

R. Reiter. A logic for default reasoning. *Artificial Intelligence*, 13:81–132, 1980.

J. Rissanen. Modeling by shortest data description. *Automatica*, 14(1):465–471, 1978.

C. P. Robert and G. Casella. *Monte Carlo Statistical Methods*. Springer, New York, 2004.

N. Robertson and P. D. Seymour. Graph minors. II. Algorithmic aspects of tree-width. *Journal of Algorithms*, 7:309–322, 1986.

N. Robertson and P. D. Seymour. Graph minors. X. Obstructions to tree-decomposition. *Journal of Combinatorial Theory Series B*, 52:153–190, 1991.

N. Robertson and P. D. Seymour. Graph minors. XIII. The disjoint paths problem. *Journal of Combinatorial Theory Series B*, 63:65–110, 1995.

T. Roos, H. Wettig, P. Grünwald, P. Myllymäki, and H. Tirri. On discriminative Bayesian network classifiers and logistic regression. *Machine Learning*, 59(3), 2005.

D. J. Rose. Triangulated graphs and the elimination process. *Journal of Mathematical Analysis and Applications*, 32:597–609, 1970.

D. Roth. On the hardness of approximate reasoning. *Artificial Intelligence*, 82(1–2):273–302, April 1996.

D. Rubin. Inference and missing data. *Biometrika*, 3:581–592, 1976.

R. Y. Rubinstein. *Simulation and the Monte Carlo Method*. Wiley, New York, 1981.

D. E. Rumelhart. Toward an interactive model of reading. Technical Report CHIP-56. University of California, La Jolla, CA, 1976.

S. Russell, J. Binder, D. Koller, and K. Kanazawa. Local learning in probabilistic networks with hidden variables. In *Proceedings of the Fourteenth International Joint Conference on Artificial Intelligence,* Montreal, Quebec, pages 1146–1152. Morgan Kaufmann, San Mateo, CA, 1995.

S. Russell and P. Norvig. *Artificial Intelligence: A Modern Approach*. Prentice Hall, NJ, 2003.

A. Salmeron, A. Cano, and S. Moral. Importance sampling in Bayesian networks using probability trees. *Computational Statistics and Data Analysis*, 34:387–413, 2000.

T. Sang, P. Beame, and H. Kautz. Solving Bayesian networks by weighted model counting. In *Proceedings of the Twentieth National Conference on Artificial Intelligence*, volume 1, pages 475–482. AAAI Press, Menlo Park, CA, 2005.

S. Sanner and D. A. McAllester. Affine algebraic decision diagrams (AADDS) and their application to structured probabilistic inference. In *Proceedings of the International Joint Conference on Artificial Intelligence*, pages 1384–1390. Professional Book Center, Denver, CO, 2005.

P. Savicky and J. Vomlel. Tensor rank-one decomposition of probability tables. In *Proceedings of the Eleventh Conference on Information Processing and Management of Uncertainty in Knowledge-based Systems*, pages 2292–2299. Springer, New York, 2006.

G. Schwarz. Estimating the dimension of a model. *Annals of Statistics*, 6:461–464, 1978.

R. Shachter. Evaluating influence diagrams. *Operations Research*, 34(6):871–882, 1986.

R. Shachter. Evidence absorption and propagation through evidence reversals. *Uncertainty in Artificial Intelligence*, 5:173–189, 1990.

R. Shachter, B. D. D'Ambrosio, and B. del Favero. Symbolic probabilistic inference in belief networks. In *Proceedings of the Conference on Uncertainty in Artificial Intelligence*, pages 126–131. Elsevier, New York, 1990.

R. Shachter, S. K. Andersen, and P. Szolovits. Global conditioning for probabilistic inference in belief networks. In *Proceedings of the Conference on Uncertainty in Artificial Intelligence*, Seattle, WA, pages 514–522, Morgan Kaufmann, San Francisco, CA, 1994.

R. Shachter and M. Peot. Simulation approaches to general probabilistic inference on belief networks. In M. Henrion, R. Shachter, L. N. Kanal, and J. F. Lemmer, editors, *Uncertainty in Artificial Intelligence 5*, pages 221–231. Elsevier Science Publishing, New York, 1989.

G. Shafer. Propagating belief functions in qualitative markov trees. *International Journal of Approximate Reasoning*, 4(1):349–400, 1987.

P. Shenoy. Binary join trees. In *Proceedings of the 12th Conference on Uncertainty in Artificial Intelligence*, pages 492–49. Morgan Kaufmann, San Francisco, CA, 1996.

P. Shenoy and G. Shafer. Axioms for probability and belief–function propagation. *Uncertainty in Artificial Intelligence*, 4, pages 169–198. Elsevier, New York, 1990.

Y. Shibata. On the tree representation of chordal graphs. *Journal of Graph Theory*, 12(3):421–428, 1988.

S. E. Shimony. Finding MAPs for belief networks is NP-hard. *Artificial Intelligence*, 68:399–410, 1994.

M. Shwe, B. Middleton, D. Heckerman, M. Henrion, E. Horvitz, H. Lehmann, and G. Cooper. Probabilistic diagnosis using a reformulation of the INTERNIST-1/QMR knowledge base I. The probabilistic model and inference algorithms. *Methods of Information in Medicine*, 30:241–255, 1991.

M. Singh. Learning Bayesian networks from incomplete data. In *Proceedings of the Fourteenth National Conference on Artificial Intelligence*, pages 534–539, Providence, RI. AAAI Press, Menlo Park, CA, 1997.

D. Spiegelhalter, A. Dawid, S. Lauritzen, and R. Cowell. Bayesian analysis in expert systems. *Statistical Science*, 8:219–282, 1993.

D. Spiegelhalter and S. Lauritzen. Sequential updating of conditional probabilities on directed graphical structures. *Networks*, 20:579–605, 1990.

P. Spirtes, C. Glymour, and R. Scheines. *Causation, Prediction, and Search*, second edition. MIT Press, Cambridge, MA, 2001.

W. Spohn. Stochastic independence, causal independence, and shieldability. *Journal of Philosophical Logic*, 9:73–99, 1980.

S. Srinivas. A generalization of the noisy-or model. In *Proceedings of the Conference on Uncertainty in Artificial Intelligence*, pages 208–218. Morgan Kaufmann, San Francisco, CA, 1993.

M. Studeny. Conditional independence relations have no finite complete characterization. In *Proceedings of the 11th Prague Conference on Information Theory, Statistical Decision Foundation and Random Processes*, pages 27–31. Springer, New York, 1990.

H. J. Suermondt. *Explanation in Bayesian Belief Networks*. PhD thesis. Stanford, CA, 1992.

H. J. Suermondt, G. Cooper, and D. E. Heckerman. A combination of cutset conditioning with clique–tree propagation in the pathfinder system. In *Proceedings of the Sixth Conference on Uncertainty in Artificial Intelligence*, pages 245–253. Morgan Kaufmann, San Francisco, CA, 1991.

X. Sun, M. J. Druzdzel, and C. Yuan. Dynamic weighting A* search-based MAP algorithm for Bayesian networks. In *Proceedings of the Twentieth International Joint Conference on Artificial Intelligence*, pages 2385–2390. AAAI Press, Menlo Park, CA, 2007.

J. Suzuki. A construction of Bayesian networks from databases based on an MDL principle. In D. Heckerman and A. Mamdani, editors, *Proceedings of the Ninth Conference on Uncertainty in Artificial Intelligence*, pages 266–273, Washington, DC. Morgan Kaufmann, CA, 1993.

G. Szekeres and H. S. Wilf. An inequality for the chromatic number of a graph. *Journal of Combinatorial Theory*, 4:1–3, 1968.

M. F. Tappen and W. Freeman. Comparison of graph cuts with belief propagation for stereo, using identical MRF parameters. In *Proceedings of the International Conference on Computer Vision*, pages 900–907, 2003.

B. Thiesson. Accelerated quantification of Bayesian networks with incomplete data. In *Proceedings of the First International Conference on Knowledge Discovery and Data Mining*, pages 306–311, Montreal, Quebec. Morgan Kaufmann, CA, August 1995.

B. Thiesson. Score and information for recursive exponential models with incomplete data. In *Proceedings of the Thirteenth Conference on Uncertainty in Artificial Intelligence,* Providence, RI. Morgan Kaufmann, CA, 1997.

B. Thiesson, C. Meek, D. Chickering, and D. Heckerman. Computationally efficient methods for selecting among mixtures of graphical models, with discussion. In *Bayesian Statistics 6: Proceedings of the Sixth Valencia International Meeting*, pages 631–656. Clarendon Press, Oxford, 1999.

J. Tian. A branch-and-bound algorithm for MDL learning Bayesian networks. In C. Boutilier and M. Goldszmidt, editors, *Proceedings of the Sixteenth Conference on Uncertainty in Artificial Intelligence*, pages 580–588, Stanford, CA, 2000.

L. C. van der Gaag, S. Renooij, and V. M. H. Coupé. Sensitivity analysis of probabilistic networks. In *Advances in Probabilistic Graphical Models, Studies in Fuzziness and Soft Computing*, volume 213, pages 103–124. Springer, Berlin, 2007.

R. A. van Engelen. Approximating Bayesian belief networks by arc removal. *IEEE Transactions on Pattern Analysis and Machine Intelligence*, 19(8):916–920, 1997.

T. Verma. Causal networks: semantic and expressiveness. Technical Report R-65. Cognetive Systems Laboratory, UCLA, 1986.

T. Verma and J. Pearl. Causal networks: semantics and expressiveness. In R. Shachter, T. S. Lewitt, L. N. Kanal and J. F. Lemmer, editors, *Uncertainty in Artificial Intelligence*, volume 4, pages 69–76. Elsevier Science Publishers, Amsterdam, 1990a.

T. Verma and J. Pearl. Equivalence and synthesis of causal models. In *Proceedings of the Sixth Conference on Uncertainty in Artificial Intelligence*, pages 220–227, Cambridge, MA, 1990b. Also in P. Bonissone, M. Henrion, L. N. Kanal, and J. F. Lemmer, editors, *Uncertainty in Artificial Intelligence 6*, pages 225–268. Elsevier Science Publishers, B.V., Amsterdam, 1991.

A. Viterbi. Error bounds for convolutional codes and an asymptotically optimum decoding algorithm. *IEEE Transactions on Information Theory*, 13(2):260–269, 1967.

J. Vomlel. Exploiting functional dependence in Bayesian network inference. In *Proceedings of the Eighteenth Conference on Uncertainty in Artificial Intelligence*, pages 528–535. Morgan Kaufmann, CA, 2002.

M. J. Wainwright, T. Jaakkola, and A. S. Willsky. Tree-based reparameterization for approximate inference on loopy graphs. In *Proceedings of the Annual Conference on Neural Information Processing Systems*, pages 1001–1008. MIT Press, Cambridge, MA, 2001.

M. J. Wainwright, T. Jaakkola, and A. S. Willsky. MAP estimation via agreement on trees: message-passing and linear programming. *IEEE Transactions on Information Theory*, 51(11):3697–3717, 2005.

L. Wasserman. *All of Statistics*. Springer, New York, 2004.

G. I. Webb, J. R. Boughton, and Z. Wang. Not so naive Bayes: aggregating one-dependence estimators. *Machine Learning* 58(1):5–24, 2005.

J. Whittaker. *Graphical Models in Applied Multivariate Statistics*. Wiley, Chichester, England, 1990.

S. Wright. Correlation and causation. *Journal of Agricultural Research*, 20:557–585, 1921.

J. Yedidia. An idiosyncratic journey beyond mean field theory. In D. Saad and M. Opper, editors, *Advanced Mean Field Methods: Theory and Practice*, chapter 3, pages 21–35. MIT Press, Cambridge, MA, 2001.

J. Yedidia, W. Freeman, and Y. Weiss. Generalized belief propagation. In *Proceedings of the Conference on Neural Information Processing Systems*, pages 689–695. MIT Press, Cambridge, MA, 2000.

J. Yedidia, W. Freeman, and Y. Weiss. Constructing free-energy approximations and generalized belief propagation algorithms. *IEEE Transactions on Information Theory*, 51(7):2282–2312, 2005.

J. York. Use of the Gibbs sampler in expert systems. *Artificial Intelligence*, 56:111–130, 1992.

C. Yuan and M. J. Druzdzel. An importance sampling algorithm based on evidence prepropagation. In *Proceedings of the 19th Conference on Uncertainty in Artificial Intelligence*, pages 624–631. Morgan Kaufmann, San Francisco, CA, 2003.

C. Yuan and M. J. Druzdzel. Importance sampling algorithms for Bayesian networks: principles and performance. *Mathematical and Computer Modelling*, 43:1189–1207, 2006.

C. Yuan, T.-C. Lu, and M. J. Druzdzel. Annealed MAP. In *Proceedings of the Conference on Uncertainty in Artificial Intelligence*, pages 628–635. AUAI Press, Arlington, VA, 2004.

N. L. Zhang and D. Poole. A simple approach to Bayesian network computations. In *Proceedings of the Tenth Conference on Uncertainty in Artificial Intelligence*, pages 171–178. Morgan Kaufmann, San Francisco, CA, 1994.

N. L. Zhang and D. Poole. Exploiting causal independence in Bayesian network inference. *Journal of Artificial Intelligence Research*, 5:301–328, 1996.

Index